The Changing Shape of Metropolitan America: Commuting Patterns, Urban Fields, and Decentralization Processes, 1960–1970

The Changing Shape of Metropolitan America

Commuting Patterns, Urban Fields, and Decentralization Processes, 1960–1970

Brian J.L. Berry and Quentin Gillard

Ballinger Publishing Company • Cambridge, Massachusetts
A Subsidiary of J.B. Lippincott Company

International Standard Book Number: 0-88410-424-9

Printed in the United States of America

Contents

Note: Index to maps appearing on pages 130–697 will be
found in Table 3.1, pp. 41–43.

Chapter 1

Prologue: "The American Way"

A turning point has been reached in the American urban experience. Counter-urbanization has replaced urbanization as the domi-
nant force shaping the nation's settlement patterns. A similar
tendency has been noted in other western nations. This study lays
out the facts of the changes that have taken place in the shape of
American metropolitan regions, and speculates about the nature of
the process.

To those who wrote about nineteenth and early twentieth-cen-
tury industrial urbanization, the essence was size, density, and
heterogeneity. "Urbanization is a process of population concentration," wrote Hope Tisdale in 1942. "It implies a movement from
a state of less concentration to a state of more concentration."
But since 1970 American metropolitan regions have grown less rapidly
than the nation, actually losing population to nonmetropolitan territory by net out-migration --1.8 million persons between March,
1970 and March, 1974 according to the estimates of the U.S. Bureau

of the Census. Because the migrants come from particular social
and economic groups, very specific subgroups have been left behind,
decreasing the heterogeneity of the older urban cores.

The process of counter-urbanization therefore has as its
essence decreasing size, decreasing density, and decreasing heterogeneity. To mimic Tisdale: counter-urbanization is a process of
population deconcentration; it implies a movement from a state of
more concentration to a state of less concentration.

Many of the demographic facts of the recent changes have been
spelled out in excellent research reports issued by the Bureau of
the Census, authored by Richard L. Forstall. Table 1.1 is derived
from these materials and reveals, among other things, the following
salient characteristics:

1. Since 1970, the nation's SMSAs have grown more slowly
   than the nation as a whole, and substantially less
   rapidly than non-SMSA America, a development that stands
   in contrast with all preceding decades back to the early
   nineteenth century.

2. On a net basis, the SMSAs are now losing migrants to
   non-SMSA territory, although they still show slight
   total immigration because of recent immigrants from
   abroad.

3. The decline in SMSA growth is largely accounted for
   by the largest metropolitan areas, particularly those
   located in the Northeast and North Central regions.
   The eight metropolitan areas exceeding three million
   population have lost two-thirds of a million net migrants since 1970, and their central counties have
   declined in population absolutely by more than a
   quarter of a million. Altogether the central cities
   of the nation's SMSAs grew at an average annual rate
   of 0.6 percent between 1960 and 1970, but declined
   at an average annual rate of -0.4 percent after 1970
   (annexations excluded). Much of the decline is attri-
   butable to a post-1970 decline of central city white
   populations at a rate of 1 percent per annum (1960-
   1970 the white population remained stable in the aggregate). Meanwhile Black and other minority populations
   have continued to decline in nonmetropolitan America
   since 1970, and the farm population has stabilized
   at approximately 9.5 million persons.

Table 1.1

POPULATION, CHANGE, AND COMPONENTS OF CHANGE FOR VARIOUS GROUPS OF METROPOLITAN AND NONMETROPOLITAN COUNTIES:
1960 to 1970 and 1970 to 1973

(Numbers in thousands. Minus sign (-) denotes decrease)

Residence Category	Population			Population change				Natural increase				Net migration			
	July 1, 1973 (provisional)	April 1, 1970 (census)1/	April 1, 1960 (census)	1970-1973		1960-1970		1970-1973		1960-1970		1970-1973		1960-1970	
				Number	Percent	Number	Percent	Number	Percent	Number	Percent	Number	Percent	Number	Percent
UNITED STATES	209,851	203,300	179,323	6,551	3.2	23,977	13.4	4,917	2.4	20,841	11.6	1,634	0.8	3,135	1.7
Inside SMSA's 1/	153,350	149,093	127,348	4,258	2.9	21,744	17.1	3,768	2.5	15,637	12.3	489	0.3	6,107	4.8
Outside SMSA's	56,501	54,207	51,975	2,293	4.2	2,232	4.3	1,149	2.1	5,204	10.0	1,144	2.1	-2,972	-5.7
Metropolitan Areas over 3,000,000 2/	56,189	55,635	47,763	554	1.0	7,872	16.5	1,218	2.2	5,464	11.4	-664	-1.2	2,408	5.0
New York Area	16,657	16,701	15,126	-45	-0.3	1,576	10.4					-305	-1.8	218	1.4
Los Angeles Area	10,131	9,983	7,752	147	1.5	2,231	28.8					-119	-1.2	1,164	15.0
Chicago Area	7,689	7,611	6,794	78	1.0	817	12.0					-124	-1.6	-17	-0.2
Philadelphia Area	5,653	5,628	5,024	25	0.4	604	12.0					-75	-1.3	91	1.8
Detroit Area	4,691	4,669	4,122	22	0.5	547	13.3					-114	-2.4	9	0.2
San Francisco Area	4,544	4,423	3,492	121	2.7	932	26.7					23	0.5	485	13.9
Boston Area	3,783	3,710	3,358	73	2.0	352	10.5					15	0.4	32	0.9
Washington SMSA	3,042	2,910	2,097	132	4.5	813	38.8					34	1.2	426	20.3
Metropolitan Areas of 1 - 3,000,000 by Region	35,705	34,448	28,497	1,257	3.6	5,951	20.9	861	2.5	3,510	12.3	396	1.1	2,441	8.6
Northeast	3,720	3,751	3,712	-30	-0.8	38	1.0	42	1.1	289	7.8	-73	-1.9	-251	-6.8
Pittsburgh SMSA	2,367	2,401	2,405	-35	-1.4	-4	-0.2					-56	-2.3	-167	-6.9
Buffalo SMSA	1,353	1,349	1,307	4	0.3	42	3.2					-16	-1.2	-84	-6.4
North Central	12,427	12,381	10,868	46	0.4	1,513	13.9	318	2.6	1,369	12.6	-272	-2.2	144	1.3
St. Louis SMSA	2,388	2,411	2,144	-23	-0.9	266	12.4					-78	-3.2	21	1.0
Cleveland SMSA	1,997	2,064	1,909	-67	-3.2	154	8.1					-109	-5.3	-45	-2.4
Minneapolis-St. Paul	1,994	1,965	1,598	28	1.4	368	23.0					-30	-1.5	119	7.4
Milwaukee SMSA	1,432	1,404	1,279	28	2.0	125	9.8					-4	-0.3	-38	-3.0
Cincinnati SMSA	1,126	1,134	1,039	-8	-0.7	95	9.2					-36	-3.2	-31	-3.0
Kansas City SMSA	1,295	1,274	1,109	21	1.6	165	14.9					-14	-1.1	30	2.7
Indianapolis SMSA	1,139	1,111	944	28	2.5	167	17.7					-8	-0.7	37	3.9
Columbus SMSA	1,057	1,018	845	39	3.8	173	20.4					+6	0.6	52	6.1

Table 1.1 Continued.

Residence Category	Population July 1, 1973 (provisional)	Population April 1, 1970 (census)[1]	Population April 1, 1960 (census)	Pop. change 1970-1973 Number	Percent	Pop. change 1960-1970 Number	Percent	Natural increase 1970-1973 Number	Percent	Natural increase 1960-1970 Number	Percent	Net migration 1970-1973 Number	Percent	Net migration 1960-1970 Number	Percent
Metropolitan Areas of 1 - 3,000,000 by Region Continued															
Florida	3,376	2,976	2,078	400	13.4	898	43.2	21	0.7	135	6.5	379	12.7	764	36.7
Miami Area[2]	2,106	1,888	1,269	218	11.5	619	48.8					196	10.4	511	40.2
Tampa-St. Petersburg	1,271	1,089	809	182	16.7	279	34.5					182	16.7	253	31.3
Other South Atlantic	3,845	3,667	2,973	178	4.9	694	23.3	102	2.8	411	13.8	76	2.1	282	9.5
Baltimore SMSA	2,117	2,117	2,071	45	2.2	267	14.8					5	0.3	53	2.9
Atlanta SMSA	1,728	1,596	1,169	133	8.3	426	36.5					71	4.4	230	19.7
South Central[3]	5,930	5,675	4,305	255	4.5	1,370	31.8	213	3.8	693	16.1	42	0.7	677	15.7
Dallas-Fort Worth	2,442	2,378	1,738	63	2.7	640	36.8					-24	-1.0	362	20.8
Houston SMSA	2,138	1,999	1,430	139	7.0	569	39.8					52	2.6	311	21.8
Cincinnati SMSA	257	251	229	6	2.4	22	9.4					(Z)	0.1	-5	-2.1
New Orleans SMSA	1,093	1,046	907	47	4.4	139	15.4					14	1.4	8	0.9
West	6,406	5,998	4,561	408	6.8	1,438	31.5	163	2.7	613	13.4	244	4.1	825	18.1
San Diego SMSA	1,470	1,358	1,033	112	8.2	325	31.4					72	5.3	169	16.4
Seattle SMSA	1,385	1,425	1,107	-40	-2.8	317	28.7					-68	-4.8	187	16.9
Denver SMSA	1,366	1,239	935	127	10.2	305	32.6					86	7.0	163	17.4
Phoenix SMSA	1,119	969	664	150	15.5	306	46.1					114	11.7	190	28.6
Portland SMSA	1,066	1,007	822	59	5.9	185	22.5					40	4.0	117	14.2
Other SMSA Territory by Region	61,456	59,009	51,088	2,447	4.1	7,921	15.5	1,690	2.9	6,662	13.0	757	1.3	1,259	2.5
Northeast	13,517	13,225	11,828	292	2.2	1,397	11.8					60	0.5	312	2.6
North Central	14,761	14,447	12,820	313	2.2	1,627	12.7					-88	-0.6	6	(Z)
Florida	3,072	2,735	2,015	338	12.3	720	35.7					271	9.9	443	22.0
Other South Atlantic	7,556	7,317	6,285	238	3.3	1,032	16.4					6	0.1	126	2.0
South Central[3]	14,458	13,753	12,178	705	5.1	1,575	12.9					218	1.6	-248	-2.0
West	8,093	7,532	5,962	561	7.4	1,570	26.3					290	3.8	620	10.4
Counties with 20 percent or more commuters to SMSA's	4,099	3,848	3,474	251	6.5	373	10.7	74	1.9	315	9.1	177	4.6	58	1.7
Northeast (20 counties)	1,047	970	794	77	8.0	176	22.2					63	6.4	111	14.0
North Central (51 counties)	1,212	1,154	1,077	58	5.0	78	7.2					37	3.2	-5	-0.5
Florida (6 counties)	78	67	48	11	16.7	19	39.6					11	16.7	17	34.9
Other South Atlantic (41 counties)	730	697	659	33	4.7	38	5.8					17	2.4	-37	-5.6
South Central[3] (57 counties)	963	898	848	65	7.2	50	5.9					45	5.0	-36	-4.2
West (5 counties)	68	61	49	6	10.6	12	25.4					5	7.8	8	16.5

Table 1.1 Continued.

Residence Category	Population			Population change				Natural increase				Net migration			
	July 1, 1973 (provisional)	April 1, 1970 (census)[4]	April 1, 1960 (census)	1970-1973 Number	Percent	1960-1970 Number	Percent	1970-1973 Number	Percent	1960-1970 Number	Percent	1970-1973 Number	Percent	1960-1970 Number	Percent
Counties with 10-19 percent commuters to SMSA's	9,683	9,269	8,636	414	4.5	633	7.3	182	2.0	792	9.2	232	2.5	-159	-1.8
Northeast (27 counties)	1,933	1,843	1,703	90	4.9	140	8.2					64	3.5	23	1.3
North Central (107 counties)	3,327	3,228	3,019	99	3.1	209	6.9					38	1.2	-51	-1.7
Florida (8 counties)	283	246	193	37	15.2	53	27.3					35	14.3	37	19.2
Other South Atlantic (61 counties)	1,569	1,511	1,468	58	3.8	43	2.9					20	1.3	-124	-8.4
South Central[3] (96 counties)	2,174	2,083	1,952	91	4.4	131	6.7					46	2.2	-67	-3.4
West (16 counties)	396	357	300	39	10.8	57	19.0					30	8.3	22	7.4
Peripheral Counties by Region	42,719	41,091	39,865	1,628	4.0	1,226	3.1	893	2.2	4,097	10.3	735	1.8	-2,871	-7.2
Northeast	3,823	3,673	3,490	150	4.1	183	5.2					84	2.3	-119	-3.4
North Central	13,493	13,101	12,919	392	3.0	182	1.4					201	1.5	-823	-6.4
Florida	868	767	617	100	13.1	150	24.4					80	10.5	67	10.9
Other South Atlantic	7,585	7,347	7,183	239	3.2	164	2.3					44	0.6	-694	-9.7
South Central[3]	10,021	9,723	9,718	298	3.1	5	0.1					76	0.8	-1,061	-10.9
West	6,929	6,481	5,938	449	6.9	542	9.1					250	3.9	-243	-4.1

FOOTNOTES

(Z) Less than 500 or 0.05 percent.

1/ SMSA's as defined by OMB as of December 31, 1974, except in New England, where definitions in terms of entire counties have been substituted. Population size groups are as of 1973.

2/ Reflects certain combinations of SMSA's, as specified below.

3/ Comprises East South Central and West South Central Divisions.

4/ Includes corrections in local and national totals determined after 1970 census complete-count tabulations were made.

5/ Boone, Campbell, and Kenton Counties, Ky., are in the South Central Divisions; the remainder of the Cincinnati SMSA is in the North Central Region.

SMSA combinations are as follows: New York Area comprises New York SMSA, Jersey City SMSA, Long Branch-Asbury Park SMSA, Nassau-Suffolk SMSA, New Brunswick-Perth Amboy-Sayreville SMSA, Newark SMSA, and Paterson-Clifton-Passaic SMSA; Philadelphia Area comprises Philadelphia SMSA, Trenton SMSA, and Wilmington SMSA; Boston Area comprises Essex, Middlesex, Norfolk, Plymouth, and Suffolk Counties, Mass.; Chicago Area comprises Chicago and Gary-Hammond-East Chicago SMSA's; Detroit Area comprises Detroit and Ann Arbor SMSA's; Miami Area comprises Miami and Fort Lauderdale-Hollywood SMSA's; Los Angeles Area comprises Los Angeles-Long Beach, Anaheim-Santa Ana-Garden Grove, Oxnard-Simi Valley-Ventura, and Riverside-San Bernadino-Ontario SMSA's; San Francisco Area comprises San Francisco-Oakland, San Jose, and Vallejo-Napa SMSA's.

Table 1.1 Continued.

Source of data: Richard L. Forstall, "Trends in Metropolitan and Nonmetropolitan Population Growth Since 1970" (Washington, D.C.: Population Division, U.S. Bureau of the Census, Rev. May 20, 1975), summarizing the following -- 1960 population and 1960-70 natural increase from U.S. Bureau of the Census, Current Population Reports, Series P-25, No. 461, "Components of Population Change by County: 1960 to 1970"; and 1970 Census of Population and Housing, PHC(2)-1, "General Demographic Trends for Metropolitan Areas, 1960 to 1970." 1970 and 1973 populations and 1970-73 natural increase and net migration from U.S. Bureau of the Census, Current Population Reports, Series P-25, Nos. 527, 530-532, and 535, "Estimates of the Population of [State] Counties and Metropolitan Areas: July 1, 1972 and 1973," for New York, Maryland, Alaska, California, and Texas, respectively; Current Population Reports, Series P-26, Nos. 49-93, "Estimates of the Population of [State] Counties and Metropolitan Areas: July 1, 1972 and 1973," for the other 45 States. The 1970 populations in these reports include corrections in local and national totals determined after 1970 census complete-count tabulations were made. 1960-70 population change computed from 1960 and 1970 populations; 1960-70 net migration computed by subtracting 1960-70 natural increase from 1960-70 population change; these data may differ from those in Series P-25, No. 461 and Series PHC(2), No. 1 as a result of reflecting corrections in 1970 local and national totals.

4. Particularly impressive are the reversals in migration trends in the largest metropolitan areas and
in the furthermost peripheral counties: the metropolitan regions with populations exceeding 3 million
gained migrants between 1960 and 1970 but have lost
since 1970; the nation's peripheral nonmetropolitan
counties lost migrants between 1960 and 1970 but
have gained since 1970.The balance of migration flows
has been reversed.

5. Rapid growth has taken place in smaller metropolitan
areas, particularly in Florida, the South, and the
West; in exurban counties located outside SMSAs as
currently defined, but with substantial daily commuting to metropolitan areas; and in peripheral counties
not tied into metropolitan labor markets.

To some, the census figures summarized in Table 1.1
but a temporary perturbation, an anomaly caused by recent conditions of stagflation that will surely vanish as economic conditions improve. But such an attitude is hardly credible; twenti-
eth-century trends have all pointed towards this ultimate trend
reversal and the creation of what Irving Kristol terms "an urban
civilization without cities." As early as 1902, H.G. Wells
wrote that the "railway-begotten" giant cities he knew were in
all probability destined to such a process of dissection and
diffusion as to amount almost to obliteration within a measurable
further space of years. "The coming cities", he said, "will
present a new and entirely different phase of human distribution.
The city will diffuse itself until it has taken up considerable
areas and many of the characteristics of what is now country.
The country will take itself many of the qualities of the city.
The old antithesis will cease, the boundary lines will altogether disappear." Similarly, Ana Weber suggested in his remark-
able study of nineteenth-century urban growth that "the most
encouraging feature of the whole situation is the tendency
towards the development of suburban towns (which) denotes a
diminution in the intensity of concentration. The rise of the
suburbs it is, which furnishes the solid basis of hope that the

evils of city life, so far as they result from over-crowding, may in large part be removed. If concentration of population seems desired to continue, it will be a modified concentration which offers the advantages of both city and country life." Later Frank Lloyd Wright argued that "Broadacre City" was the most desirable settlement pattern for mankind, and Lewis Mumford called for a new reintegration of men and nature in dispersed urban regions to cite but a few cases.

Throughout the twentieth century all trends have pointed in these directions. Every public opinion survey has indicated that popular preferences are for smaller places and lower densities, with richer environmental amenities. The trend has been one leading unremittingly towards the reversal of the processes of population concentration unleashed by technologies of the industrial revolution, towards the contemporary rural renaissance, and to the changed shape of metropolitan America that is the subject of this work.

Richard L. Morrill has pointed out that many immediate forces appear to have contributed to the migration reversal, among which are (1) industrial decentralization, (2) metropolitan unemployment and general economic depression, (3) metropolitan insecurity and discomfort, (4) the search for amenities, (5) retirement, (6) the welfare system, and (7) the prevalence of urban "amenities" in rural areas - all motivated by a preference for non-metropolitan areas. He notes the following:

> 1. In recent years, two forms of industrial decentralization have been occurring; first, within industrial regions (like New England, Ohio-Indiana-Illinois, etc.) are some shifts back to or development of plants in smaller cities and towns--that is, to areas with fairly good infrastructure, transport, accessibility, but without the high economic and social costs of such metropolises as Cleveland, Boston or Detroit.
>
> Second, there has been a diffusion of relatively more labor-intensive industries to the remaining portions

of the white, rural and small town south or border states, for example, the Ozarks, Tennessee Valley and parts of Appalachia. This is a first wave industrialization into less prosperous non-metropolitan areas. Both these forms of industrial decentralization have the effect of providing local job opportunities, reducing or even reversing the flow of migrants.

2. The last period of rural resurgence was the Great Depression. Thus, some of the return may reflect depression, with many of the unemployed or underemployed preferring to be so in their home towns rather than in the metropolis. Many of these people may even have withdrawn from the labor force, at least temporarily.

3. Metropolitan insecurity and discomfort--crime, perceived threats to self and property, noise and pollution--is no myth in the minds of many metropolitan residents, many of whom may again be returning to the relatively cleaner and safer small-town environments. This motivation appears significant both to the elderly and to families with young children.

4. Evidently many are still moving for amenity values, into regions they like, irrespective of job opportunities. While movement to the traditional amenity areas of Florida and Arizona continues, there has been a dramatic shift away from California, and from metropolitan areas generally, to the Pacific Northwest, the Rocky Mountains, upper New England, and even to the Ozarks, Appalachia, and Upper Michigan.

5. A subset of the above amenity-conscious migrants are retirees, although the latter tend to return to their home environments, again perceived as attractive, or to warmer climate areas, while many amenity-seekers are younger, and newly adopting areas perceived as unspoiled.

6. Just possibly, improvements in the level of welfare, broadly defined, have enabled many people to move (back) to preferred non-metropolitan environments through early retirement, part-time work or even withdrawal from the labor for force. People can manage, at reduced levels of living, through such transfer payments as social security, food stamps, aid-to-dependent children, Medicare and Medicaid, and better unemployment compensation. Presumably, some really are "welfare bums" and are willing to live off those who work; others may be content to live in genteel poverty, and find part-time work preferable to the intensity of the metropolitan "rat-race."

7. Finally, improved transportation, the possibility of very long distance commuting, and the universality of electricity and television have very simply extended the "urban way of life" far out beyond the boundaries of metropolitan areas.

Perhaps the last of these items is the key, the factor that has removed constraints of the home-work relationship and permitted the reassertion of fundamental predispositions of the American culture. These predispositions, because they are antithetical to urban concentration, have resulted in many of the contradictions of recent decades. Yet the resulting conflicts appear to be resolving themselves through the process of counterurbanization, producing a new systhesis, what Marx termed "a new settlement pattern for mankind."

We should go back 200 years, to Hector de Crevecoeur's Letters from an American Farmer. "Who, then, is the American?" he asked, and his answer was a description of basic American culture traits. As J. Wreford Watson notes, foremost among these was a love of newness. Second was the overwhelming desire to be near to nature. Freedom to move was essential if goals were to be realized. Individualism was basic to the self-made man's pursuit of his goals, and violence was the accompaniment if not the condition of success--the competitive urge, the struggle to succeed, the fight to win. Finally, de Crèvecoeur perceived a great melting pot of peoples, and a manifest sense of destiny.

How have these traits played a role in determining the nation's settlement patterns? There has been no more evocative description of the consequences fo the love of newness for American metropolitan structure than Homer Hoyt's discussion of The Structure and Growth of Residential Neighborhoods in American Cities, published in 1939. Hoyt said that the erection of new dwellings on the periphery sets in motion forces tending to draw population from older houses and to cause all groups to move up a step, leaving the oldest and cheapest houses to be occupied by the poorest families or to be vacated. The constant competition of new areas is itself a cause of neighborhood shifts. Every building boom, with its crop of structures equipped with the latest modern devices, pushes all existing structures a notch down in the scale of desirability. The high grade areas tend to preempt the most desirable residential land. Intermediate rental groups tend to occupy the sectors in each city that are adjacent to the high rent area. Occupants of houses in the low rent categories tend to move out in bands from the center of the city by filtering up. There is a constant outward movement of neighborhoods because as neighborhoods become older they tend to be less desirable. As he noted, "a neighborhood composed of new houses in the latest modern style is at its apex. Physical deterioration of structures and the aging of families constantly lessen the vital powers of the neighborhood. The steady process of deterioration is hastened by obsolescence; a new and more modern type of structure relegates all existing structures to lower ranks of desirability." Hoyt's perceptions cut right to the core of much of that which has transpired, for the accompaniment of the process of counter-urbanization is urban decay and the abandonment of the non-achieving social underclass in the oldest high-density neighborhoods.

The love of newness joins with the desire to be near nature to explain the key role that amenities play in settlement transformations. H.G.Wells' 1902 forecasts should be recalled. "Many of our railway-begotten giant cities," he said, "are destined to such a process of dissection and diffusion as to amount almost to obliteration within a measurable further space of years. These coming cities will present a new and entirely different phase of human distribution. The social history of the middle and later thirds of the nineteenth century all over the civilized world has been the history of a giganticrush of population into the magic

radius of -for most people- four miles, to suffer there physical
and moral disaster far more appalling than any famine or pesti-
lence that ever swept the world. But new forces bring with them
the distinct promise of a centrifugal application that may finally
be equal to the complete reduction of all our present congestions.
What will be the forces acting upon the prosperous household?
The passion for nature and that craving for a little private imper-
ium are the chief centrifugal inducements. The city will diffuse
itself until it has taken upon considerable areas and many of the
characteristics of what is now country. We may call these coming
town provinces 'urban regions'." Almost as an echo comes that
sociological essay of the 1950's that proclaimed in its title that
"the suburbs are the frontier."

To occupy this new frontier, close to nature, and to keep
on adjusting to succeeding waves of growth has demanded freedom
to move. Americans are the world's most mobile people. Forty
million Americans change residence each year; the likelihood was
that each American born during the 1960s would change residence
an average of 14 times in his or her lifetime. As Peter Morrison
has remarked "the typical Anerican's life might be characterized
as a prolonged odyssey. Marriage, childbearing, military service,
higher education, changes from one employer to another or shifts
from one plant or office location to another with the same employer,
divorce, retirement -- all may bring a change in residence and
locale, not to speak of upward social mobility which may impel
people to move for other reasons as well." Now as in the past
Americans continue to migrate for reasons that are connected to
the working of national economic and social systems. The quick
exploitation of new resources or knowledge requires the abandonment of old enterprises along with the development of the new.

And migration is also an <u>assortative</u> mechanism, filtering and sifting the population as its members undergo social mobility. Yet again, there is an antiphonal note. Filtering in housing markets, for example, is a process that has positive welfare consequences if new construction exceeds the rate necessary to house normal growth and produces an excess housing supply at the point where the filtering originates; if such new construction exerts a downward pressure on the rents and prices of existing housing, permitting lower income families to obtain better housing bargains relative to their existing housing quarters; if the upward mobility is apart from any changes caused by rising incomes and/or declining rent/income ratios; and if a decline in quality is not necessarily forced by reductions in maintenance and repair to the extent that rents and prices are forced down; and finally if a mechanism exists to remove the worst housing from the market without adversely affecting rents and prices of housing at the lowest level. Part of the reason for the decline of older inner cities is that the last two conditions have not been met: deterioration has accelerated in many older neighborhoods, and abandonment has become contagious, frequently adversely affecting access by low-income residents to the better-quality housing available locally.

Contrary to the views of most hadicals, however, urban expansion and urban decay are not caused by a single-minded conspiracy among large-scale institutions and investors. They result instead from myriad decisions made individually within a tradition of privatism. This tradition has been called by Sam Bass Warner "the most important element of American culture for understanding the development of cities." It has meant that the cities of the United States depended for their wages, employment, and general prosperity on the aggregate successes and failures of thousands of individual enterprises, not upon community action.

It has also meant that the physical forms of American cities, their lots, houses, factories and streets have been the outcome of a real estate market of profit-seeking builders, land specu- lators, and large investors. And it has meant that the local politics of American cities have depended for their actors, and for a good deal of their subject matter, on the changing focus of men's private economic activities. Privatism has prevailed throughout America's history, and a consequence is a preference for governmental fragmentation and for interest-group politics under presumed conditions of democratic pluralism. Antitheti- cally, it has also meant that American city planning has been curative rather than future-oriented, reactive rather than going somewhere.

Achievement in the mainstream has involved an individual fight to succeed. But violence is a pervasive underpinning in other ways too. Acrimonious confrontations mark the fights to control turf within cities --such is the nature of the con- flict on school busing-- while for the underclass abandoned in deteriorating ghettos, crime and violence is a way of life. President Johnson's Commission on Crimes of Violence reported that if present trends continue we can expect further social fragmentation of the urban environment, greater segregation of different racial groups and economic classes, and the polariza- tion of attitudes on a variety of issues. It is logical, the commissioners noted, to expect the establishment of the 'defen- sive city' consisting of an economically declining central busi- ness district in the inner city protected by people shopping or working in building during daylight hours and 'sealed off' by police during night-time hours. "Highrise apartments and resi- dential compounds," they said, "will be fortified cells for

upper-, middle-, and high-income populations living in prime locations, and suburban neighborhoods, geographically removed from the
central city, will be 'safe areas,' protected mainly by racial and
economic homogeneity."

Thus, instead of the melting pot, there is cultural pluralism.
In the expanding frontiers of suburban America, upwardly mobile
individuals from a variety of backgrounds traditionally have been
readily integrated into the achievement-oriented mainstream of
society. When the heterogeneity of American cities was caused
primarily by the influx of successive immigrant waves, the policy
of encouraging such assimilation was taken for granted ideologically.
But even in the suburbs, what poured out of the melting pot has
crystallized into a complex mosaic of sharply-differentiated
achievement-related communities, counterposed against those who
have been unable or unwilling to move out of the cities. For many,
the national ideal of integration remains inaccessible --in particular, to the unassimilatable blacks, browns and reds, for whom
segregation within the central cities remains the rule, and battle
lines are drawn along neighborhood boundaries and at the gates of
the schools. For others, integration is undesirable --perceived
destructive of self-identity by the unassimilated ethnics, and to
be combatted by members of the new communities, not the least
those seeking a return to simpler ways in rural communes.

But this is to run ahead of the evidence to be presented in
this volume, essentially an atlas of the commuting areas of each
of the nation's SMSAs in 1970 and of the changes that took place
in these areas between 1960 and 1970, together with some analysis
of the patterns and changes, and national summaries. The commuting
data are discussed in Chapter 2. Chapter 3 serves as a guide to
the atlas. The patterns of change in commuting are examined in
Chapter 4, and the conclusions are drawn together in Chapter 5.

This is followed by the atlas, consisting of 283 metropolitan map sets. Each set comprises six maps: of the 1970 commuting areas of the central city and of its central business district (CBD); of 1960-1970 changes in the central city's commuting area; and of reverse commuting from the central city in 1960 and 1970, together with changes 1960-1970.

Why commuting? Some history will clarify this point. In the early 1960s Karl E. Fox began to explore the feasibility of developing a national system of regional accounts that would bear an explicit relationship to the national accounts, as an essential ingredient of regional development planning. He encountered many difficulties. Data were available on earnings but not on expenditures. Certain key statistics were recorded by place of residence, others by place of work, and yet others not at all.

What he was seeking was a set of regional units, each of which was relatively "closed" in the short run i.e. a region within which earnings would equal expenditures. Such a regional definition would be satisfied, he argued, by an area so bounded that it would be both a labor market, the area within which in the short run workers will compete for locally-available jobs, and a housing market, the area within which job holders are willing to contemplate a place of residence. A set of closed regions summing to the nation was far preferable for accounting purposes, he argued, to a regional system in which complex set of short-run interregional "leakages" and other transfer payments had to be made. And following from his interest in labor markets and housing markets, commuting appeared to Fox to be the most appropriate definitional variable to derive such a set of regions.

He found that whereas the intention of the Bureau of the Budget's (now Office of Management and Budget) system of Standard Metropolitan Statistical areas was to define areas of daily inter-

dependency, quite rightly using commuting as a criterion, in practice the SMSAs fell short of the mark. The Bureau's interagency
committee given the responsibility for defining SMSAs had to balance a variety of competing interest groups and believed that it
was fundamentally important to separate urban (SMSA) from rural
(non-SMSA) counties. This was accomplished in a variety of ways,
one of which was to exclude from an SMSA any county in which less
than 15 per cent of the workers residing there commuted to work in
the SMSA's central city. To Fox, then, the SMSAs were as useful
for regional accounting as a leaky bathtub for canoeing the Atlantic Ocean.

He began to politic for a reevaluation of statistical
practice, and persuaded two senior members of the Bureau of the
Census, Morris Hansen and Conrad Taeuber, and Paul Webbink of the
Social Science Research Council, that the task would be worthwhile.
An SSRC Committee was established with Bureau of the Census and
Bureau of the Budget support. A research project was begun under
Brian J. L. Berry's direction at the University of Chicago to re-
examine the process of SMSA definition, and to study the nation's
commuting areas using 1960 census data.

This study was completed in 1968, and published as the
Bureau of the Census' Working Paper No. 28, Metropolitan Area
Definition: A Re-evaluation of Concept and Statistical Practice.
Among the recommendations were a significant relaxation of the
ways that counties were excluded from SMSAs and, because of the
considerable inter-metropolitan commuting in certain regions of
the country, the consistent definition of a new national set of
consolidated metropolitan regions.

The findings were initially resisted by the members of
the interagency committee as disturbing the compromise they had
reached between urban and rural interests. However, since 1968

the exclusionary criteria have gradually been relaxed, and in 1975 the Office of Management and Budget did announce a set of 13 Standard Consolidated Statistical Areas containing one-third of the total population of the United States, viz: Chicago-Gary, New York-Newark-Jersey City, Boston-Lawrence-Lowell, Cincinnati-Hamilton, Cleveland-Akron-Lorain, Detroit-Ann Arbor, Houston-Galveston, Los Angeles-Long Beach-Anaheim, Miami-Fort Lauderdale, Milwaukee-Racine, Philadelphia-Wilmington-Trenton, San Francisco-Oakland-San Jose, and Seattle-Tacoma. Each of these new consolidated areas includes an SMSA with a population of at least one million, plus one or more adjoining SMSAs related to it by continuously developed high density population corridors and metropolitan commuting of workers.

The more immediate results of the study were found elsewhere. The map of commuting areas became the key input data used by Henry de Graffe to derive the Office of Business Economics' (now Bureau of Economic Analysis) system of Economic Areas of the United States . These 173 areas, composed of county building blocks, completely disaggregate the U.S. into labor markets that as nearly as possible, are closed in the short run (i.e. they satisfy Fox's requirement). This closure has made possible BEA's Regional Economics Information System, a regular accounting of earnings and employment for each region in the U.S.

Elsewhere, too, the results were used. The commuting maps were used to plan the corridors for the Appalachian development highways, to define the development districts for Appalachia, to derive growth centers for the Upper Great Lakes Regional Commission, and to lay out a national urban-regional growth framework (Brian J. L. Berry, Growth Centers in the American Urban System. Ballinger, 1973).

The working materials from the first study were preserved in Chicago, contemplating the present investigation. As the 1970 census materials became available, funding was sought and obtained from the Ford Foundation to permit the earlier study to be repeated using the newer data, to enable 1960-1970 changes to be codified, and to analyze the reasons for the changes. This volume is the result.

Chapter 2

The Commuting Data

In 1960, for the first time, the Census of Population and Housing included a question to determine the commuting behavior of the population of the United States. Item P28 of the Household Questionnaire read as follows:

P28. What city and county did he work in last week?

a) City or town:_____
b) If city or town, did he work inside the city limits?
   Yes_____   No_____
c) County:_____   State: _____

Some items in the census were requested of every family unit in the country. Others, the journey-to-work question among them, were sampled by assigning the letters A, B, C and D to each successive housing unit visited, with housing unit A designated as the sample unit. In group quarters, such as institutions, every fourth person was selected, to maintain the 25 percent sampling rate.

A two-stage data collection process was used. The information required of every person and housing unit was obtained in the first stage, and sample data were collected at a separate and later stage. An Advance Census Report (ACR) was sent to all occupied housing units throughout the country in the last week of March, 1960, to be completed and held for the census enumerator's visit. When the enumerator collected the ACR he left at every fourth household the Household Questionnaire, to be completed and mailed to the District Office of the Bureau of the Census. In the less densely settled areas of the country enumeration was accomplished in a single stage, however, by enumerators who recorded sample data for every fourth household on their initial visit. The single stage method was used over half the land area of the country, but included only 20 percent of the population.

Once schedules had been assembled in the District Offices of the Bureau of the Census, the information on them was transcribed to special FOSDIC schedules by employees of the Bureau (FOSDIC= Film Optical Sensing Device for Input to Computers). The FOSDIC schedlles were microfilmed, and FOSDIC scanned the microfilms and converted marks on the schedules directly into magnetic impressions on the tapes that were then used for preparation of census reports.

Household question P28 was thus transcribed in the following manner:

P28a.   If he worked last week (yes-in P22) what city
         or town did he work in last week?
         Not in a city   skip to P28c
         This city
         Different city(specify): _____

P28b.   If city or town, did he work inside city
         limits?
         Yes   No

P28c.   What county and state did he work in?

       This county
       Different county (specify): _____
                state: _____

Four-digit codes were used to identify cities and counties as places of work, according to the Bureau of the Census' Universal Area Code (UAC) system of Workplace Locations. Approximately 4,300 workplace alternatives are recognized:

   (a)   central cities of SMSAs;

   (b)   other cities of 50,000 population or more;

   (c)   counties with no towns classified under (a) or (b);

   (d)   county remainders where counties include cities under (a) or (b);

   (e)   minor civil divisions (MCDs) in the New England States.

However, certain restrictions were applied in coding the workplaces for any segment of the country. Individual and household data were assembled into totals for each of the country's 43,000 Standard Location Area (SLAs -- census tracts in tracted areas, MCDs or combinations of MCDs elsewhere). For each county in the country, it was then decided what initially appeared to be the 13 most important UAC workplace locations for residents of each county. These 13 UAC districts, plus "other" and "unknown" categories, were then used as the basis for aggregating the journey-to-work information for each SLA in the county. Theoretically, then, the 1960 journey-to-work data were assembled into a 43,000 SLA by 4,300 UAC matrix of from-to journey-to-work information; however, the SLAs were in fact grouped into some 4,300 submatrices, each of which had only 13 columns and two balance categories.

An example of one of these submatrices, that for Tract NIT-44
(Niles township in DuPage county, Illinois) is presented in Table
2.1 below. Table 2.2 shows the 13 UAC work place locations for
this SLA. For this particular SLA only four UAC workplace locations were of significance, 3301 (Chicago city), 3302-3308 (Cook
County), 3316 (DuPage County itself), and 3312-3313 (Lake County)
with 47.8, 42.5, 0.7, and 1.1 percent of the resident workers in
Niles township commuting to these UAC workplace locations respectively. Note that 4.5 percent of the resident workers worked in
places other than the thirteen listed and 3.4 percent did not
report this workplace location.

For each principal UAC workplace, such as 3301, the City of
Chicago, a reporting booklet was prepared from these data listing
all SLAs sending commuters to it, and for each of the SLAs showing
how many and what proportion of the resident workers traveled to
each of its 13 UAC alternatives or fell in one or the other of the
balance categories. With such information in hand it was possible
to plot a map for each UAC and surrounding territory, showing the
percentage of the workers resident in each SLA commuting to the
UAC. (The commuting rate to any UAC is defined as the number commuting from the SLA to the UAC divided by the total number of
workers resident in the SLA). Because of the regular decline of
the commuting rate with distance, it was also possible to contour
the percentages to depict the commuting field of that workplace.
The outer limit of this field is described by a zero contour
beyond which there is no reported inward commuting; this zero contour delineates both a housing market and a labor market: the area
within which jobs and homes are brought into balance --the area
which serves as a bounded "container" for the journey-to-work.

Table 2.1

SUBMATRIX OF JOURNEY-TO-WORK INFORMATION
FOR NILES TWP, DuPAGE CO, ILLINOIS, 1960

Information Tract 939

Serial Number	Area Code	Name
412109390320	0390	Tract NIT-44 Niles Twp

	Degrees	Minutes	Seconds
Longitude	87	47	53
Latitude	42	3	58

Total Employed	Population	Commuters Out		Mode of Transportation	
766	2259	Total	738	Total	738

Number	Ident		Pct	Mode	Pct
353	3301	3301	47.8	Railroad	19.4
314	3302	3308	42.5	Subway or Elevated	0.
5	3316	3316	0.7	Bus or Streetcar	1.8
0	3309	3311	0.	Other Means	1.1
8	3312	3313	1.1	Private Auto.Pool	67.3
0	3317	3317	0.	Walked	4.9
0	3314	3315	0.	Worked at Home	1.6
0	3201	3203	0.	Not Reported	3.9
0	3204	3204	0.		
0	3205	3204	0.		
0	3538	3538	0.		
0	3537	3537	0.		
0	3560	3561	0.		
33	Elsewhere		4.5		
25	Unreported		3.4		

Table 2.2

UAC WORKPLACE LOCATIONS FOR THE NILES TOWNSHIP SLA.

IDENTIFICATION NO.		NAME
3301	3301	Chicago city
3302	3308	Cook Co.
3316	3316	DuPage Co.
3309	3311	Kane Co.
3312	3313	Lake Co.
3317	3317	McHenry Co.
3314	3315	Will Co.
3201	3203	Gary, Hammond, E.Chicago cities, Ind.
3204	3204	balance of Lake Co, Ind.
3205	3205	Kendall Co.
3538	3538	Kenosha Co, Wisc
3537	3537	Racine Co, Wisc
3560	3561	Winnebago Co.

Note: The identification numbers are inclusive, thus all numbers between 3302 and 3308 refer to workplace locations within Cook Co. but for this SLA have not been identified individually. For other SLAs they might be distinguished depending on their relative importance as workplace locations for that particular SLA.

Commuting fields were mapped in 1960 for every SMSA central city, for urban centers in the 25,000 to 50,000 population range lying outside SMSA's and many small places (at this latter end we were not comprehensive in our coverage). Each field showed a gradual distance-decay; the greater the distance from workplaces, the smaller the proportion of the residents of areas commuting in.

In 1960, place of work was identified only by county and city. In 1970, for the first time in a decennial census, the exact address (number and street name) of the place of work was requested. Persons working at more than one job were asked to report the location of the job at which they worked the greatest number of hours during the census week. Salesmen, deliverymen, and others who work in several places each week were requested to give the address at which they began work each day, if they reported to a central headquarters. For cases in which daily work was not begun at a central place each day, the person was asked to report the exact address of the place where he worked the most hours during the census week. If his employer operated in more than one location (such as a grocery store chain or public school system), the exact address of the location or branch where the respondent worked was requested. When the number of street name could not be given, the name of the building or the name of the company for which he worked was to be entered. The data on place of work were derived from answers to question 29c, viz:

29c.   Where did he work <u>last week</u>?

        If he worked in more than one place, print where he worked most last week.
        If he travels about in his work or if the place does not have a numbered address, see instruction sheet.

        (1) Address (Number and street name) _____
        (2) Name of city, town, village, etc. _____
        (3) Inside the limits of this city, town, village, etc.?
            Yes
            No
        (4) County _____
        (5) State _____ (6) Zip Code_____

The question was asked of all persons 14 years old and over in the 15-percent sample who reported working during the reference week, i.e., the week prior to enumeration. Place of work refers to the geographic location at which civilians at work during the reference week and Armed Forces personnel (except those on leave, sick, etc.) carried out their occupational or job activities.

In addition to the above exact data on the place of work, the 1970 Census added seven additional UAC workplace locations for each SLA, and separated the central business district (CBD) from the central city of many of the larger SMSA's, and a variety of smaller ones, too.

Thus, Tables 2.3 and 2.4 show the submatrices of data for tract 0208 in Weirton, W. Virginia and for Chester Town, Middlesex Co, Connecticut. The record type row below the tract code indicates the racial-cultural breakdown of commuters for each SLA, types 1 through 4, signifying total, white, Black and Spanish-speaking populations, respectively. The relevant UAC workplaces for these two SLA's are shown in Table 2.5. Thus, for instance, 78.91 percent of the resident workers of tract 0208 in Weirton city actually worked within the city limits (data item 03 and 05 combined in Table 2.5). The next most important workplace location for this tract in 1970 was that part of Jefferson Co. in Ohio that did not include Steubenville city, accounting for 7.325 of the resident workers. Similarly, for Chester Town (MCD Code 005) in Middlesex Co, Conn, the most important workplace other than Middlesex Co. itself, was the New London-Groton-Norwich SMSA. (The MCD Code derives from the Geographical Identification Code Scheme, as published by the U.S. Department of Commerce, Social and Economic Statistics Administration, Bureau of the Census, 1972, in the PHC (R)-3 series.)

Table 2.3

SUBMATRIX OF JOURNEY-TO-WORK INFORMATION
FOR TRACT 0208 IN WEIRTON, W. VIRGINIA

029 1970 County Code

Tract Code	0208		0208	0208		0208	0208	0208
Record Type	1		1	2		2	4	4
Count of Persons At Work By:Place of Work	Count	%	Count	%		Count	%	
Place 1	31	3.440	31	3.440				
Place 2	66	7.325	66	7.325				
Place 3	620	68.812	620	68.812		15	68.181	
Place 4								
Place 5	91	10.099	91	10.099				
Place 6	26	2.885	26	2.885		7	31.818	
Place 7	41	4.550	41	4.550				
Place 8	8	.887	8	.887				
Place 9	9	.998	9	.998				
Place 10								
Place 11	9	.998	9	.998				
Place 12								
Place 13								
Place 14								
Place 15								
Place 16								
Place 17								
Place 18								
Place 19								
Place 20								
Total At Work	901			601			22	
Place Not Reported	69	7.113	69	7.113				
Population At Work By Means of Transport.								
Driver of Auto	632	64.621	632	64.621		16	72.727	
Passenger of Auto	134	13.701	134	13.701				
Bus or Streetcar	153	15.644	153	15.644		6	27.272	
Subway or Elevated Railroad								
Taxicab								
Walked Only	37	3.783	37	3.783				
Other Means	15	1.533	15	1.533				
Worked at Home	7	.715	7	.715				
Total	578			578			22	

Table 2.4

SUBMATRIX FOR JOURNEY-TO-WORK INFORMATION
FOR CHESTER TOWN, MIDDLESEX CO, CONNECTICUT.

007 1970 County Code

MCD Code	005	005	005	005	005	005
Record Type	1	1	2	2	3	3
Count of Persons At Work By:Place of Work						
Place 1	17	1.443	17	1.451		
Place 2	24	2.037	24	2.049		
Place 3						
Place 4						
Place 5						
Place 6	20	1.697	20	1.707		
Place 7						
Place 8						
Place 9						
Place 10						
Place 11	8	.679	8	.683		
Place 12						
Place 13	15	1.273	15	1.280		
Place 14						
Place 15	13	1.103	13	1.10		
Place 16	27	2.292	27	2.305		
Place 17	11	.933	11	.939		
Place 18	76	6.451	76	6.490		
Place 19	967	82.088	960	81.981	7	100.000
Place 20						
Total At Work	1178		1171		7	
Place Not Reported	24	1.996	8	.678	16	69.565
Population At Work By Means of Transport.						
Driver of Auto	970	77.662	970	79.119		
Passenger of Auto	184	14.731	184	15.008		
Bus or Streetcar						
Subway or Elevated						
Railroad	9	.720	9	.734		
Taxicab						
Walked Only	55	4.403	32	2.610	23	100.000
Other Means	6	.480	6	.489		
Worked at Home	25	2.001	25	2.039		
Total	1249		1226		23	

Table 2.5

UAC WORKPLACE LOCATIONS FOR HANCOCK COUNTY, W. VA.
AND MIDDLESEX COUNTY, CONN. 1970.

(Hancock County)   Steubenville-Weirton
Ohio-W. Va. SMSA

Data
Item   Places of Work

01 Steubenville city, Ohio
02   Remainder of Jefferson Co., Ohio
03 Weirton city (part)
04   Remainder of Hancock Co.
05 Weirton city (part)
06   Remainder of Brooke Co.
07 Wheeling city
08   Remainder of Ohio Co.
09 Marchall Co.
10 Belmont Co., Ohio
11 Pittsburgh city, Pennsylvania
12   Remainder of Allegheny Co., Pa.
13 Beaver Co., Pennsylvania
14 Washington Co., Pennsylvania
15 Westmoreland Co., Pennsylvania
16 Columbiana Co., Ohio
17 Carroll Co., Ohio
18 Canton, Ohio SMSA
19 Youngstown-Warren, Ohio SMSA
20 Butler Co., Pennsylvania

(Middlesex County)   Nonmetropolitan

01 Hartford city, Hartford Co.
02 Hartford SMSA, Hartford Co.-inner ring
03 Cromwell town
04 Glastonbury and Rocky Hill towns, Hartford Co.
05   Remainder of Hartford SMSA, Hartford Co.
06 New Britain city, Hartford Co.
07 Berlin town, Hartford Co.
08 Plainville and Southington towns, Hartford Co.
09   Remainder of Hartford Co.
10 Meriden city, New Haven Co.
11 Wallingford and Madison towns, New Haven Co.
12 New Haven city, New Haven Co.
13   Remainder of New Haven SMSA
14   Remainder of New Haven Co. (nonmetro)
15 New London and Norwich cities and Groton town,
      New London Co.
16   Remainder of New London-Groton-Norwich SMSA,
      New London Co.
17 New London Co. (nonmetro)
18 Middletown city
19   Remainder of Middlesex Co. (nonmetro)
20 Tolland Co. (nonmetro)

Thus, it was possible to up-date with 1970 data the 1960 commuting fields of all the country's SMSA's, to plot and map the changes in extent and intensity of each commuting field, to plot and contour the number and percentages of resident workers who commuted to the CBD of the larger metropolitan areas (data were only available for tracted areas within the SMSA), and to plot and contour both reverse commuting from each central city in 1960 and in 1970 and the change in reverse commuting from 1960 to 1970.

The plotting and contouring of the commuting to the central city and CBD in 1970 and the reverse commuting maps was relatively straightforward. The same procedures were followed in 1970 as in 1960. However, the change in commuting to the central city and change in reverse commuting maps deserve a more detailed explanation. For both maps, the percentage point change in commuting was obtained by simply superimposing the relevant 1960 and 1970 maps over a triangular-hexagonal grid and noting the percentage point differences on the points of the grid and then contouring this change on a map. The change in reversal commuting maps are straightforward, but the change in commuting to the central city maps were further complicated for some metropolitan areas by a number of characteristics of the 1960 data.

For example, for many of the smallest SMSA's in 1960, the central city was only separately identified as a workplace for tracts and/or minor unit divisions within the central county. Outside the central county the central city was combined with the central county as one workplace, and thus a change map was not plotted since the data outside the central county were not comparable from 1960 to 1970. For still larger SMSA's, the central city was usually identified separately as a work-

place for SLA's at considerable distance from the central city,
but for some sectors of the commuting field, particularly where
a State boundary cut the field, the data were again combined with
that of the central county, or sometimes even with the entire
SMSA. In those cases where these sectors were relatively small,
the data was considered to be representative of the 'true' commuting to the central city field and consequently treated as such
for the purposes of calculating and constructing the change map.

Other problems arose with the case of multiple-named SMSA's,
for example Gary-Hammond-E. Chicago. Separate data for Gary
were available in 1960 from within the SMSA, but Hammond and
E. Chicago were combined with Gary as a single UAC workplace location outside Lake County. Thus there is a separate reverse commuting map for Gary in 1960, but the commuting to the central city
map is for the combined cities of Gary, Hammond, and E. Chicago.
In 1970 however, all three cities were identified separately as
workplaces, so individual reverse commuting maps were prepared
for 1970 along with commuting to the CBD maps for Gary and Hammond
(a CBD was not identified for E. Chicago in 1970). However, in
order to preserve comparability between 1960 and 1970, the 1970
commuting to the central city map combines all three cities and
thus the change map shows the change in commuting to all three
central cities.

Altogether, 283 metropolitan map sets were prepared, including all SMSAs defined at the time of collection of the 1970 Census
except three, Columbia MO, Reading PA, and Santa Rosa CA, in the
contiguous United States, and Honolulu HA. All data and working
maps for Columbia were removed from our research laboratory and
could not be replaced. Serious base map deficiencies and inade-
quacies of the computer file records precluded mapping of the

materials for Reading and Santa Rosa. Honolulu was not mapped
because only the contiguous 48 states were included in the study.
Eight other SMSAs defined on the basis of the 1970 census data
did not have SMSA status at the time that the Bureau of the Census coded the 1970 commuting data, and so they also were excluded from the study. These areas are: Britol CT, Bryan-College
Station TX, La Crosse WI, Nashua NH, Owensboro KY, Petersburg-
Colonial Heights VA, and Sherman-Denison TX.

Chapter 3

A Guide to the Commuting Atlas

The key product of the study is the set of commuting maps
that occupies the bulk of this volume. As noted in Chapter 2, in
both 1960 and 1970, data on the percentages of workers residing in
every census tract or minor civil division sending commuters to any
given workplace area were plotted on maps, and contours were inter-
polated to delineate the commuting field of the workplace area.
Maps for 1960 and 1970 were compared to derive 1960-1970 changes.
Finally, a set of six summary maps was prepared for each metropolitan region (less if the CBD was not defined as a separate workplace
for the metropolitan area, or if 1960 data were unavailable). The
conventions used on each of these maps are described on the next
four pages(Figures 3.1 and 3.2; example: Cedar Rapids, IA).

The example is of a complete set of six maps, drawn directly
from the other portion of the book. The accompanying descriptions
serve as a legend to each of the 283 map sets appearing in that
section.

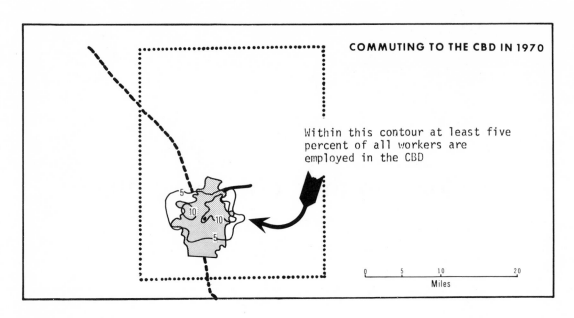

COMMUTING TO THE CBD IN 1970

Within this contour at least five percent of all workers are employed in the CBD

0   5   10   20
Miles

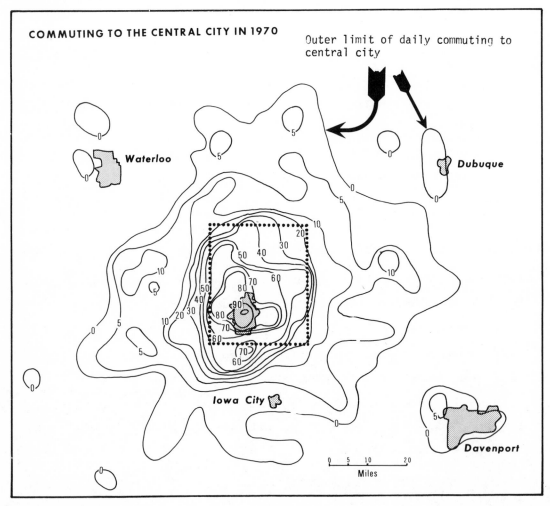

COMMUTING TO THE CENTRAL CITY IN 1970

Outer limit of daily commuting to central city

Waterloo

Dubuque

Iowa City

Davenport

0   5   10   20
Miles

Figure 3.1. Example of the Commuting Maps

The left-hand pair of each metropolitan map set consists of two
commuting fields, one for the CBD as workplace area, and the
second for the entire central city (including the CBD) as a
workplace.

Contour values. The contours indicate the percentage of workers
residing in a census tract, or minor civil division in an untracted area, who are employed in the stated workplace. The maximum extent of the commuting field of the central city is indicated
by the zero commuting line, i.e. the outer limit within which at
least someone was reported as commuting, but beyond which no
commuters were noted. The five percent contour is used as the
outer limit of the CBD commuting area because for many outlying
tracts and MCDs, no separate CBD commuting data were reported
even in areas where CBDs are defined, and so the zero line is
indeterminate.

Shading. In both maps, the central city is shaded, as are other
surrounding central cities.

Dotted lines are used to indicate the boundaries of the SMSA in
both the central city and CBD commuting maps. Note the change
of scale between the two.

Figure 3.2   Example of the Reverse Commuting
              and Commuting Change Maps.

The right hand of each metropolitan map set consists of three
reverse commuting maps, and one commuting change map for the central city.

Contour values. In the 1960 and 1970 reverse commuting maps, the
contours show the percentage of residents in each census tract
who work outside the central city. The contours on the 1960-1970
change in reverse commuting map, and on the 1960-1970 change in
commuting to the central city map, are of percentage differences:
percentage commuting in 1970 minus percentage commuting in 1960.

Shading. On the change in reverse commuting map, those areas in
which reverse commuting increased by ten percentage points or
more are given a dotted shade. On the change in commuting to the
central city map, central cities are indicated by a dotted shade,
areas in which 1970 commuting is five or more percentage points
less than in 1960 are given a shading of dashed lines (minuses),
and areas into which the outer limit of the commuting area extended between 1960 and 1970 are cross-hatched. Areas left white
had either modest commuting change, or within higher values
unshaded contours experienced substantial increases in commuting
to the central city or on the reverse commuting change map,
decreases in reverse commuting (increasing self-containment of
the central city). Thus, reverse commuting increased most markedly
in northern Cedar Rapids (top right-hand map), changing only
moderately elsewhere. Commuting to Cedar Rapids decreased in the
zone midway between Cedar Rapids and Waterloo, but increased substantially elsewhere as the city's employment base grew. The
Cedar Rapids commuting area extended generally in a north-easterly
direction towards Dubuque.

Lines. Interstate highways are indicated by lines, dashed if under
construction in 1970.

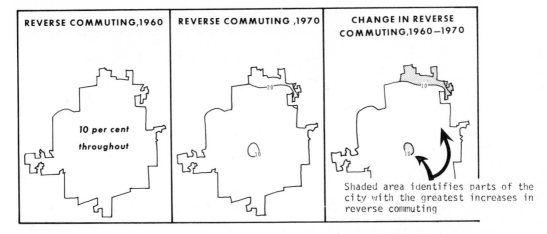

REVERSE COMMUTING, 1960

10 per cent throughout

REVERSE COMMUTING, 1970

CHANGE IN REVERSE COMMUTING, 1960–1970

Shaded area identifies parts of the city with the greatest increases in reverse commuting

CEDAR RAPIDS, IA.

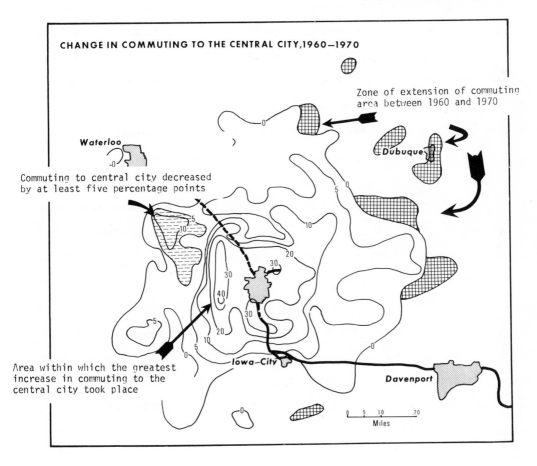

CHANGE IN COMMUTING TO THE CENTRAL CITY, 1960–1970

Zone of extension of commuting area between 1960 and 1970

Waterloo

Commuting to central city decreased by at least five percentage points

Dubuque

Iowa-City

Davenport

Area within which the greatest increase in commuting to the central city took place

0   5   10   20
Miles

Table 3.1 lists the complete sequence of metropolitan map sets, together with their page numbers. As noted earlier, the only omissions from the list of SMSAs defined at the time that the 1970 census was taken are Columbia MO, Reading PA, and Santa Rosa CA. Separate map sets are provided for many cities placed by the Office of Management and Budget into multiple-center SMSAs, e.g. Dallas and Fort Worth TX.

It is recommended at this juncture that the reader take a little time to page through the maps to become familiar with the different patterns that are evidenced, before going on to read Chapter 4. Boston, for example (pages 192-193) presents an example of a commuting area which expanded scarcely at all during the decade, except out on to Cape Cod. Instead, there was a massive decrease in suburban commuting to the central city and, except in one or two limited areas, a decrease in reverse commuting from the central city to the suburbs. These trends point to a progressive detachment of the central city and suburban labor markets. In contrast, Kansas City's commuting area (pages 350-351) expanded outwards in all directions in the decade. Except for a few localized patches, suburban commuting rates to the central city increased. Milwaukee's commuting area extended outwards too (pages 420-421), and while suburban commuting rates to the central city increased in the outer suburbs, there also a significant decrease in dependency upon central city jobs in the inner suburban ring, and throughout most of the city there was a dramatic increase in reverse commuting. The changes in Rochester, NY's commuting area are similar (pages 542-543), but those of San Antonio (pages 570-571) are more like Kansas City: expansion, increasing suburban dependence on central city jobs, and decreasing reverse commuting characterize this Texan case.

It is the reasons for these similarities and differences that are explored in Chapter 4.

Table 3.1

GUIDE TO THE METROPOLITAN MAP SET

Chapter 4

Patterns of Change in Commuting:
The Evidence Codified

The inspection of the atlas of commuting maps recommended at the end of the previous chapter should have revealed the complexity of the patterns involved, and of the types of change that unfolded between 1960 and 1970. It now remains to fit the patterns together, and to isolate some of the reasons for the differential changes. What are the patterns? What are the similarities? What are the differences? These are discussed in turn.

Figures 4.1 and 4.2 lay out the spatial patterns. The first map simply presents the extent and configuration of central city commuting areas in 1970; the second does the same for the commuting areas of those CBDs for which the Bureau of the Census reported data. Much of the country is covered by a complex overlapping network of central city commuting fields, standing in sharp contrast to the limited extent of CBD-oriented space revealed by Figure 4.2, and calling into question the use of uni-centered (= CBD-centered) urban models.

46

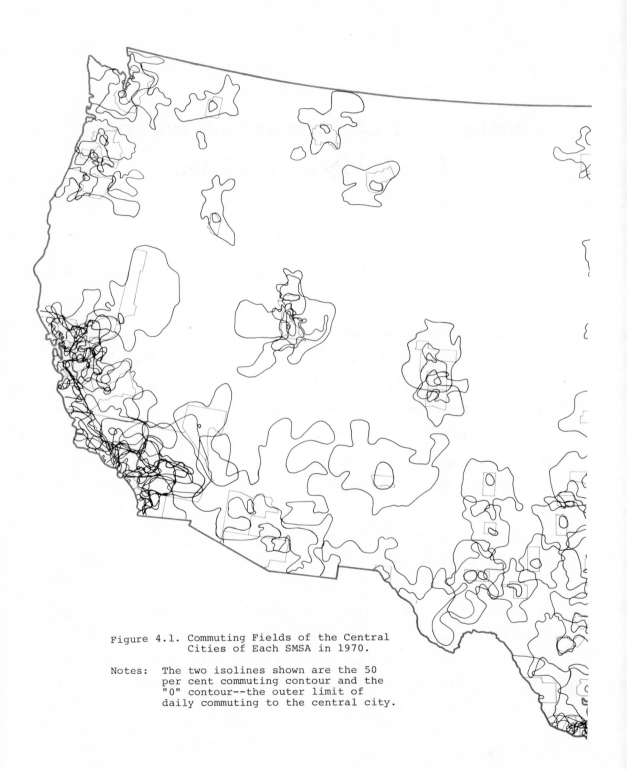

Figure 4.1. Commuting Fields of the Central
Cities of Each SMSA in 1970.

Notes: The two isolines shown are the 50
per cent commuting contour and the
"0" contour--the outer limit of
daily commuting to the central city.

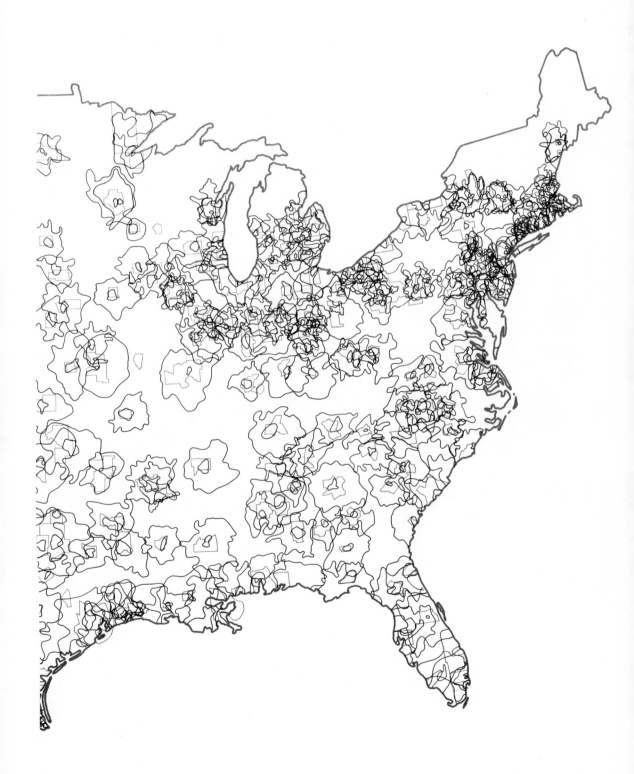

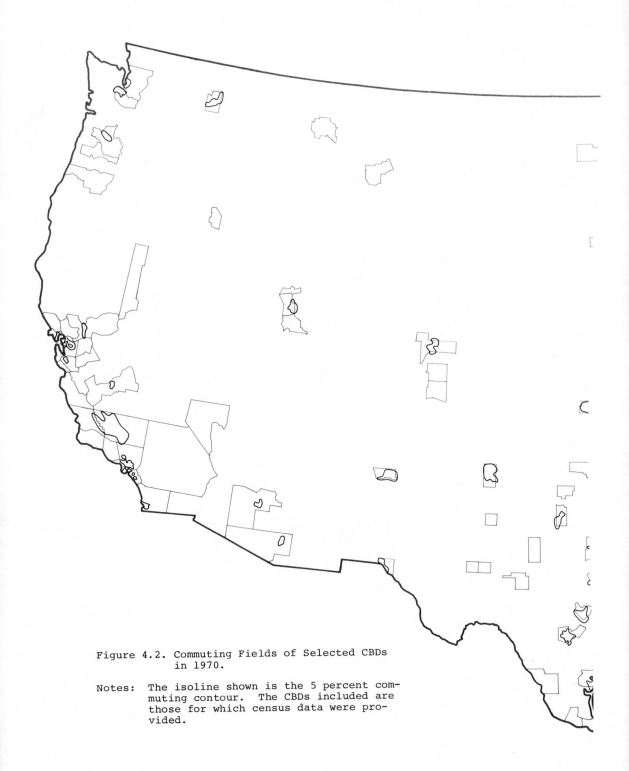

Figure 4.2. Commuting Fields of Selected CBDs
          in 1970.

Notes: The isoline shown is the 5 percent com-
        muting contour. The CBDs included are
        those for which census data were pro-
        vided.

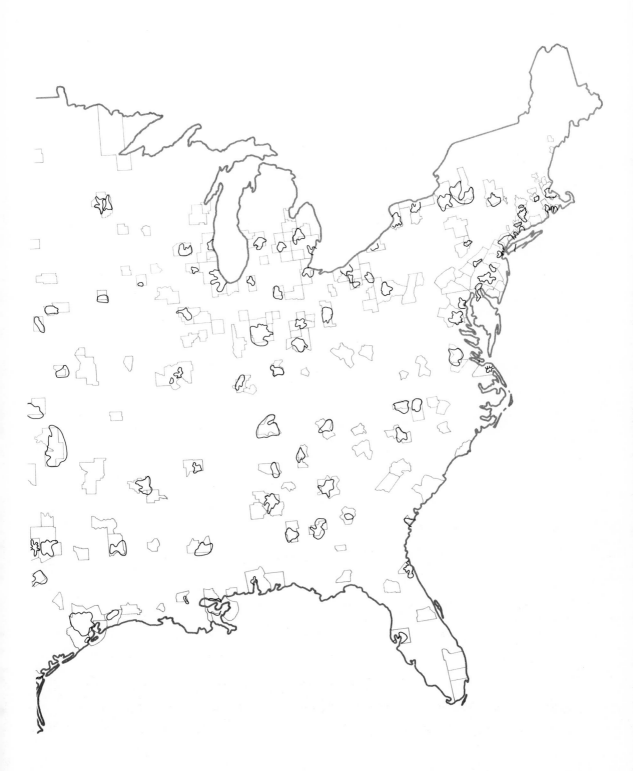

The proportion of workers commuting to a given workplace decreases with distance, but at what rate and in what manner? And what, if any, were the changes in commuting gradients between 1960 and 1970? To answer these questions, a nationwide probability sample was taken of 853 census tracts (and minor civil divisions in untracted areas), stratified by size and region. Commuting rates from each tract were coded: (a) to the nearest central city (CC); (b) to the county within which the central city was located (CTY); and (c) to the Standard Metropolitan Statistical Area defined around the city (SMSA). The percentage commuting was recorded for both 1960 and 1970, and the change in percentage (1970-1960) was calculated. Rand McNally road distance from the tract to the city also was recorded. Cities were classified by the population size of the SMSA in which they were located (I-over 1 million; II-350,000 to 1 million; III-200,000 to 350,000; IV-100,000 to 200,000; V-less than 100,000) and by census region (NE-North East; GL-Great Lakes; GP-Great Plains; SE-South East; SW-South West; RM-Rocky Mountains; FW-Far West).

With these data in hand, linear and negative exponential models were fitted to determine the relationship between the percentage commuting (P) and distance (D) in both 1960 and 1970, where P_0 is the percentage of residents living around the city center who work within the city, viz:

Linear Model: $\quad P = P_0 - bD$

Neg. exponential model: $P = P_0 e^{-bD}$

Separate calculations were made for three successively larger definitions of the workplace area--percent commuting to the central city (PCC), to the central county (PCTY), and to the SMSA (PSMSA). The total sample of 853 observations was used to obtain relationships for the entire country (T), and separate models were fitted for commuting to cities in each of the five size classes (I-V) and

in each of the seven census regions (NE-FW), making a total of 156
equations, in all that were fitted to the data. The results are recorded in Tables 4.1-4.4, and in the accompanying graphs.

Comparison of the tables reveals that the negative exponential
models offered a consistently better fit than the linear ones, with
higher coefficients of determination in all 156 cases. Apparently,
then, the same distance-decay model that has been found to be a good
representation of urban population densities is an equally-good representation of the shape of urban commuting fields.

Urban population density gradients have been shown to vary by
city size and region, and to have fallen dramatically since World
War II. See Figure 4.3. Can the same be said for the negative exponential commuting gradients? The evidence from Tables 4.2 and 4.4
may best be visualized in graphic form. Figures 4.4-4.6 compare the
1960 and 1970 evidence for the three separate definitions of the
workplace--the central city, central county, and SMSA. Distance-
decay gradients that were roughly parallel in 1960, but higher
for the larger workplace areas, became flatter in 1970 as dispersion
took place. The maximum commuting radius of central cities increased
from an average of 58 to 64 miles, of central counties from 64 to 72
miles, and of SMSAs from 66 to 76 miles in the decade.

These are national averages, however, and there are substantial variations by city size and location. Figure 4.7 presents the
central-city graphs for each size class, and Figure 4.8 for each census region. Certain systematic differences begin to emerge. For
example, cities of the largest size class show increasing dispersion
(decreasing density gradient with constant intercept), the outer commuting radius extending from an average of 60 to close to 68 miles
(Figure 4.7a). Northeastern cities saw their maximum commuting radius
increase from 42 to 49 miles, while dependence upon central city jobs
decreased in an inner 12 mile radius· Southeastern cities, on the other
hand, showed increasing central-city dependency throughout, and rapid
expansion.

Table 4.1
COMMUTING-DISTANCE RELATIONSHIPS
FOR CENTRAL CITIES, CENTRAL COUNTIES AND SMSAs, 1960 AND 1970:
LINEAR MODEL FOR METROPOLITAN SIZE GROUPS

Model		Analysis for 1960						Analysis for 1970					
		Inter-cept	Coeff.	Std. Error	F	R^2	N	Inter-cept	Coeff.	Std. Error	F	R^2	N
Linear													
Total	PCC	68.81	-1.32	.037	1272.65	.59	853	69.65	-1.31	.033	1579.96	.65	853
	PCTY	88.99	-1.58	.043	1336.93	.61	853	89.63	-1.54	.040	1474.70	.63	853
	PSMSA	94.22	-1.60	.043	1373.70	.62	853	95.39	-1.56	.040	1544.10	.64	853
I	PCC	75.19	-1.40	.059	558.82	.73	213	69.75	-1.26	.055	521.99	.71	213
	PCTY	92.84	-1.65	.063	684.17	.76	213	91.80	-1.55	.061	657.90	.76	213
	PSMSA	104.31	-1.69	.066	661.69	.76	213	105.37	-1.62	.059	738.69	.78	213
II	PCC	73.55	-1.46	.069	446.03	.67	217	75.47	-1.42	.058	608.13	.74	217
	PCTY	94.91	-1.78	.078	527.44	.71	217	96.32	-1.72	.069	614.89	.74	217
	PSMSA	98.58	-1.79	.076	557.78	.72	217	100.48	-1.73	.065	697.27	.76	217
III	PCC	62.26	-1.04	.095	120.25	.40	181	65.57	-1.21	.085	206.03	.54	181
	PCTY	91.18	-1.32	.109	146.98	.45	181	91.97	-1.30	.101	165.89	.48	181
	PSMSA	94.21	-1.34	.106	159.04	.47	181	95.35	-1.33	.098	138.89	.51	181
IV	PCC	71.51	-1.82	.103	311.25	.69	140	74.93	-1.83	.095	372.73	.73	140
	PCTY	87.45	-1.97	.149	175.05	.56	140	88.56	-1.97	.130	229.10	.62	140
	PSMSA	94.31	-2.08	.137	231.40	.63	140	94.65	-2.06	.120	296.66	.68	140
V	PCC	62.86	-1.15	.104	122.42	.55	102	64.13	-1.14	.097	138.59	.58	102
	PCTY	71.09	-1.24	.112	122.45	.55	102	72.26	-1.24	.106	136.38	.58	102
	PSMSA	71.09	-1.24	.112	122.47	.55	102	72.29	-1.24	.106	136.43	.58	102

Table 4.2
COMMUTING-DISTANCE RELATIONSHIPS
FOR CENTRAL CITIES, CENTRAL COUNTIES AND SMSAs, 1960 AND 1970:
NEGATIVE EXPONENTIAL MODEL FOR SIZE GROUPS

Model	Analysis for 1960						Analysis for 1970					
	Inter-cept	Coeff.	Std. Error	F	R²	N	Inter-cept	Coeff.	Std. Error	F	R²	N
Neg. Exponential												
Total												
Log PCC	4.26	-0.072	.002	2058.06	.71	853	4.36	-0.068	.001	2421.64	.74	853
Log PCTY	4.64	-0.073	.002	1836.98	.68	853	4.68	-0.065	.002	1779.47	.68	853
Log PSMSA	4.76	-0.071	.002	1690.73	.67	853	4.79	-0.063	.002	1581.37	.65	853
I												
Log PCC	4.58	-0.075	.002	1307.71	.86	213	4.48	-0.066	.002	908.73	.81	213
Log PCTY	4.89	-0.076	.002	1085.20	.84	213	4.83	-0.064	.002	698.29	.77	213
Log PSMSA	5.11	-0.072	.003	662.75	.76	213	5.05	-0.060	.003	470.29	.69	213
II												
Log PCC	4.53	-0.079	.003	868.89	.80	217	4.60	-0.068	.002	928.94	.81	217
Log PCTY	4.88	-0.080	.003	828.44	.79	217	4.90	-0.068	.002	783.17	.78	217
Log PSMSA	4.98	-0.080	.003	780.74	.78	217	4.98	-0.067	.002	730.31	.77	217
III												
Log PCC	4.03	- .057	.004	180.04	.50	181	4.22	-0.069	.004	375.66	.68	181
Log PCTY	4.61	- .059	.004	181.72	.50	181	4.66	-0.054	.004	191.96	.52	181
Log PSMSA	4.67	- .058	.004	189.62	.51	181	4.72	-0.055	.004	193.04	.52	181
IV												
Log PCC	4.31	-0.091	.005	405.72	.75	140	4.50	-0.088	.004	551.91	.80	140
Log PCTY	4.54	-0.087	.006	218.31	.61	140	4.67	-0.081	.005	297.81	.68	140
Log PSMSA	4.71	-0.085	.005	254.65	.65	140	4.80	-0.079	.004	347.11	.72	140
V												
Log PCC	3.68	-0.064	.005	176.26	.64	102	3.90	-0.063	.004	204.30	.67	102
Log PCTY	3.99	-0.066	.005	185.22	.65	102	4.11	-0.063	.004	204.71	.67	102
Log PSMSA	3.99	-0.066	.005	185.28	.65	102	4.11	-0.063	.004	204.74	.67	102

COMMUTING-DISTANCE RELATIONSHIPS
FOR CENTRAL CITIES, CENTRAL COUNTIES AND SMSAs, 1960 AND 1970:
LINEAR MODEL FOR REGIONS

Model	Analysis for 1960						Analysis for 1970					
	Inter-cept	Coeff.	Std. Error	F	R^2	N	Inter-cept	Coeff.	Std. Error	F	R^2	N
Linear												
Northeast												
PCC	67.98	-1.74	.131	175.63	.61	112	59.72	-1.47	.116	160.69	.59	112
PCTY	91.83	-2.14	.147	210.68	.66	112	89.08	-1.96	.149	173.53	.61	112
PSMSA	101.76	-2.28	.129	314.66	.74	112	100.07	-2.12	.125	289.04	.72	112
Gt. Lakes												
PCC	72.51	-1.73	.104	275.95	.66	142	71.13	-1.65	.087	358.87	.72	142
PCTY	86.93	-1.99	.114	305.65	.69	142	88.37	-1.97	.095	429.15	.75	142
PSMSA	97.79	-2.09	.115	330.58	.70	142	99.60	-2.09	.098	452.87	.76	142
Gt. Plains												
PCC	76.58	-1.65	.091	330.68	.74	120	80.56	-1.66	.079	442.67	.79	120
PCTY	101.39	-2.06	.092	505.42	.81	120	101.44	-1.98	.085	549.69	.82	120
PSMSA	103.33	-2.02	.096	440.39	.79	120	103.03	-1.93	.089	474.11	.80	120
Southeast												
PCC	79.90	-1.89	.088	458.73	.76	145	81.31	-1.83	.081	518.57	.78	145
PCTY	96.72	-2.13	.110	373.40	.72	145	99.35	-2.10	.095	491.22	.77	145
PSMSA	98.47	-2.11	.114	340.62	.70	145	101.81	-2.07	.102	411.27	.74	145
Southwest												
PCC	75.91	-1.46	.087	280.46	.71	119	83.01	-1.50	.076	395.53	.77	119
PCTY	97.84	-1.78	.089	398.47	.77	119	98.36	-1.70	.083	422.79	.78	119
PSMSA	98.06	-1.78	.090	394.23	.77	119	98.69	-1.70	.083	418.18	.78	119
Rocky Mts.												
PCC	67.58	-1.09	.074	220.57	.68	107	69.02	-1.09	.069	251.48	.71	107
PCTY	88.03	-1.37	.087	250.39	.70	107	89.70	-1.36	.081	283.09	.73	107
PSMSA	88.44	-1.37	.086	255.88	.71	107	90.79	-1.36	.079	295.70	.74	107
Far West												
PCC	58.59	-.082	.097	71.98	.40	108	55.94	-0.89	.077	132.25	.56	108
PCTY	85.19	-1.03	.124	68.48	.39	108	83.57	-0.99	.117	71.57	.40	108
PSMSA	97.97	-1.04	.116	81.04	.43	108	98.09	-1.02	.107	90.65	.46	108

Table 4.4
COMMUTING-DISTANCE RELATIONSHIPS
FOR CENTRAL CITIES, CENTRAL COUNTIES AND SMSAs, 1960 AND 1970:
NEGATIVE EXPONENTIAL MODEL FOR REGIONS

Model	Analysis for 1960						Analysis for 1970					
	Inter-cept	Coeff.	Std. Error	F	R^2	N	Inter-cept	Coeff.	Std. Error	F	R^2	N
Neg. Exponential												
Northeast												
Log PCC	4.46	-0.104	.005	362.11	.77	112	4.24	-0.086	.006	238.69	.68	112
Log PCTY	4.92	-0.104	.006	290.07	.73	112	4.75	-0.084	.006	183.49	.63	112
Log PSMSA	5.11	-0.101	.006	316.15	.74	112	4.96	-0.081	.006	207.64	.65	112
Lakes												
Log PCC	4.44	-0.090	.004	519.69	.79	142	4.57	-0.089	.003	685.69	.83	142
Log PCTY	4.72	-0.091	.004	549.34	.80	142	4.85	-0.088	.003	680.71	.83	142
Log PSMSA	4.95	-0.089	.004	510.17	.78	142	5.05	-0.089	.004	548.32	.80	142
Plains												
Log PCC	4.55	-0.085	.003	661.18	.85	120	4.62	-0.076	.003	612.95	.84	120
Log PCTY	4.94	-0.087	.003	633.32	.84	120	4.92	-0.076	.003	512.66	.81	120
Log PSMSA	4.97	-0.085	.004	482.17	.80	120	4.93	-0.072	.004	368.94	.76	120
Southeast												
Log PCC	4.77	-0.098	.004	665.95	.82	145	4.77	-0.085	.003	589.23	.80	145
Log PCTY	5.03	-0.097	.005	441.49	.76	145	5.02	-0.082	.004	443.49	.76	145
Log PSMSA	5.06	-0.095	.005	376.05	.72	145	5.04	-0.079	.004	349.63	.71	145
Southwest												
Log PCC	4.47	-0.074	.003	577.38	.83	119	4.63	-0.065	.003	414.92	.78	119
Log PCTY	4.86	-0.075	.003	534.30	.82	119	4.83	-0.064	.003	334.75	.74	119
Log PSMSA	4.86	-0.074	.003	525.37	.82	119	4.84	-0.064	.003	334.34	.74	119
Rocky Mts.												
Log PCC	4.16	-0.060	.004	293.34	.74	107	4.30	-0.059	.003	332.10	.76	107
Log PCTY	4.56	-0.063	.004	292.05	.74	107	4.66	-0.058	.003	327.56	.76	107
Log PSMSA	4.58	-0.063	.004	289.30	.73	107	4.69	-0.058	.003	314.76	.75	107
Far West												
Log PCC	3.87	-0.050	.004	124.38	.54	108	3.88	-0.056	.003	279.04	.72	108
Log PCTY	4.46	-0.052	.005	109.77	.51	108	4.50	-0.048	.004	117.66	.53	108
Log PSMSA	4.80	-0.049	.005	97.02	.48	108	4.82	-0.044	.004	99.90	.49	108

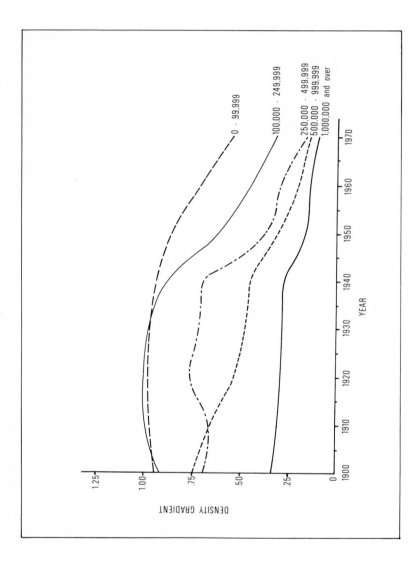

Figure 4.3.   Changes in the Negative Exponential
Urban Population Density Gradient,
1900–1970, by City Size Class.

Source: After Barry Edmonston, Population
Distribution in American Cities.
Lexington Books, 1975, p. 74.

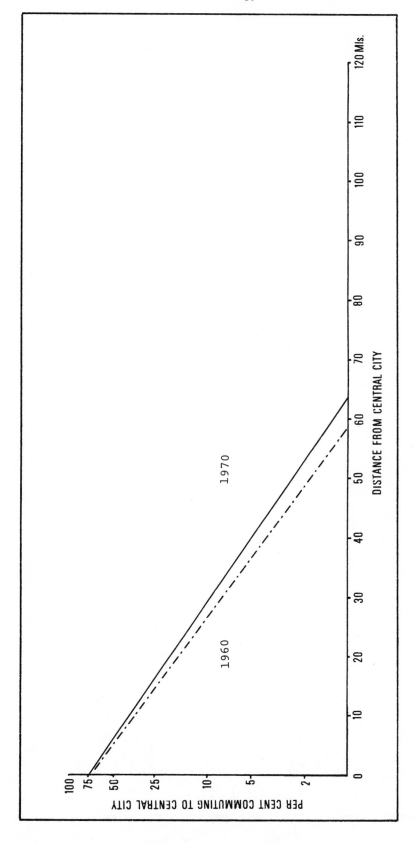

Figure 4.4. Percent Commuting to the Central City, 1960 and 1970.

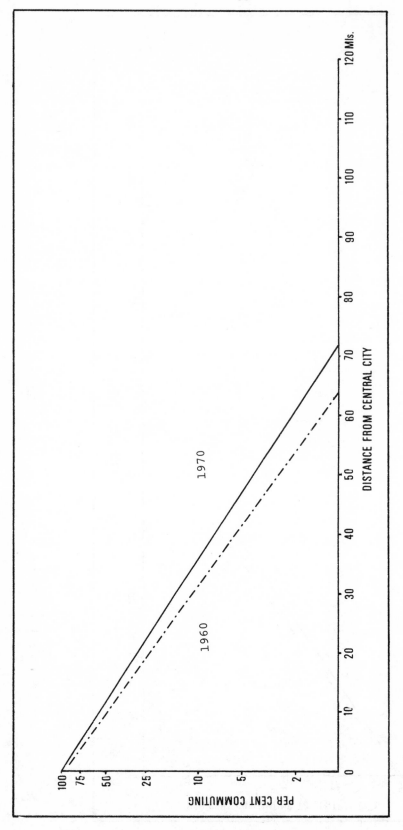

Figure 4.5. Percent Commuting to the Central County, 1960 and 1970.

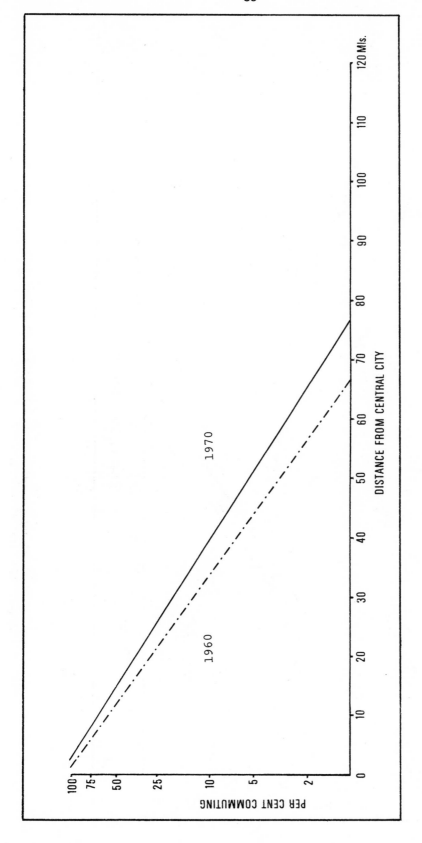

Figure 4.6. Percent Commuting to the SMSA, 1960 and 1970.

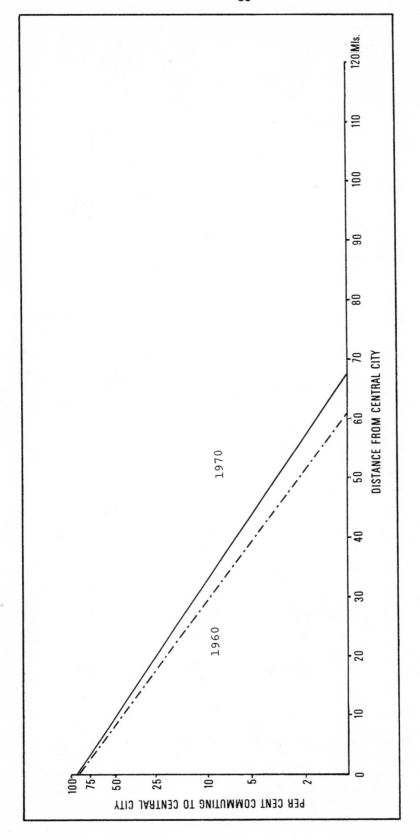

Figure 4.7. Commuting to the Central City in 1960 and 1970, by City Size.
(a) City Size Class I.

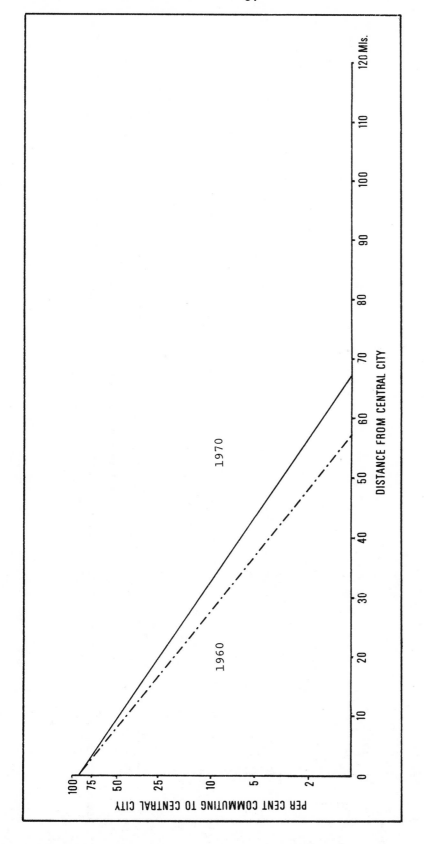

Figure 4.7. Commuting to the Central City in 1960 and 1970, by City Size.
(b) City Size Class II.

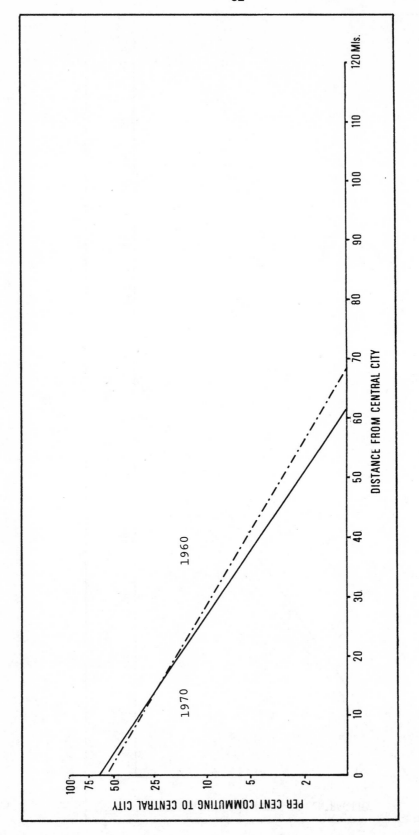

Figure 4.7. Commuting to the Central City in 1960 and 1970, by City Size. (c) City Size Class III.

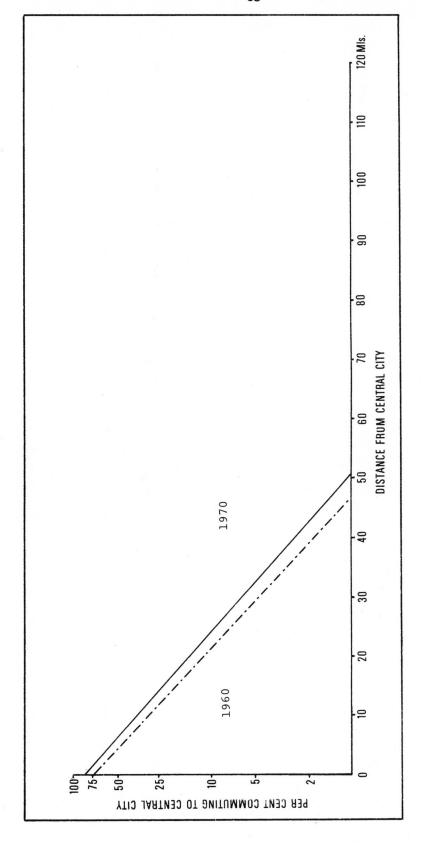

Figure 4.7. Commuting to the Central City in 1960 and 1970, by City Size. (d) City Size Class IV.

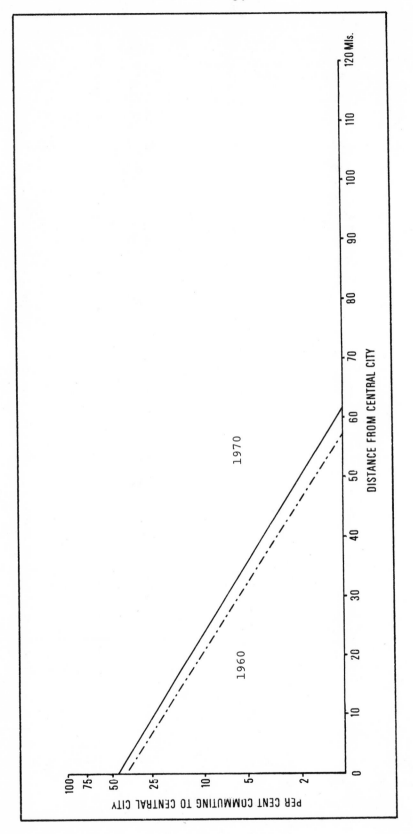

Figure 4.7. Commuting to the Central City in 1960 and 1970, by City Size.
(e) City Size Class V.

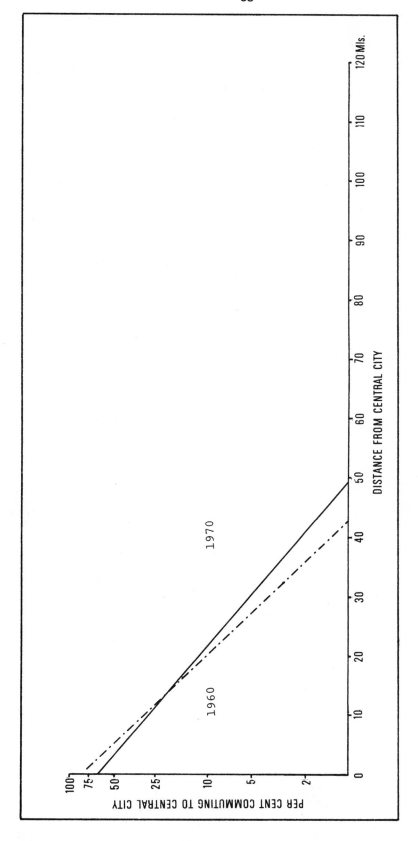

Figure 4.8. Commuting to the Central City in 1960 and 1970, by Region.
(a) Northeast

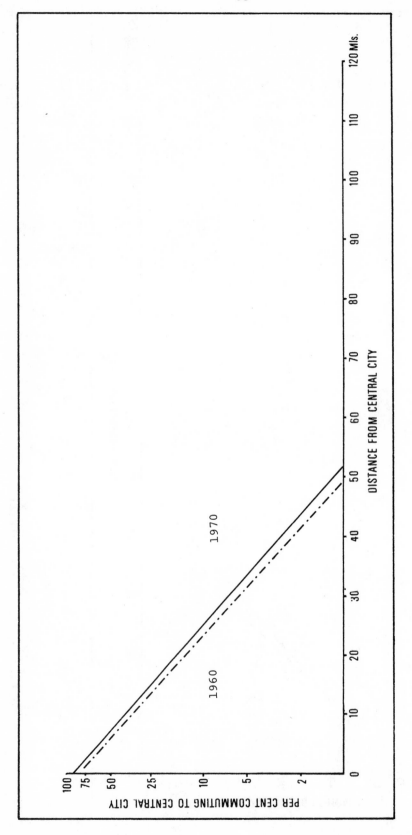

Figure 4.8. Commuting to the Central City in 1960 and 1970, by Region. (b) Great Lakes

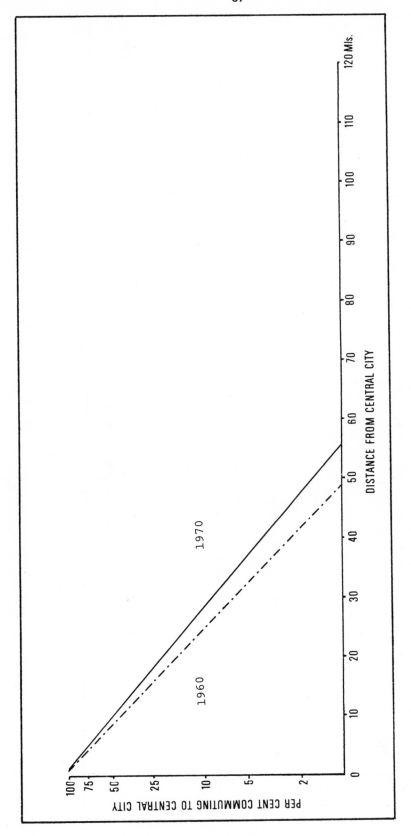

Figure 4.8   Commuting to the Central City in 1960 and 1970, by Region.
(c) Southeast

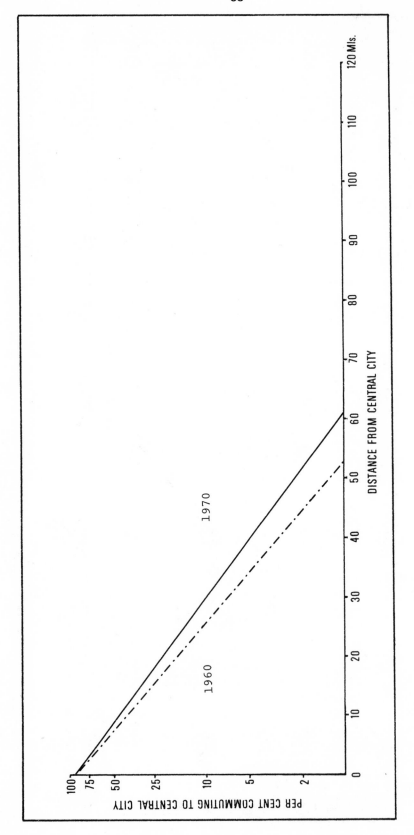

Figure 4.8. Commuting to the Central City in 1960 and 1970, by Region. (d) Great Plains

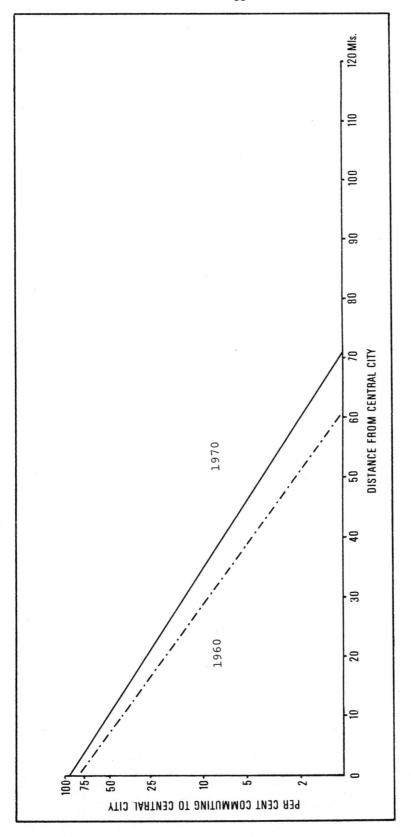

Figure 4.8   Commuting to the Central City in 1960 and 1970, by Region.
(e) Southwest

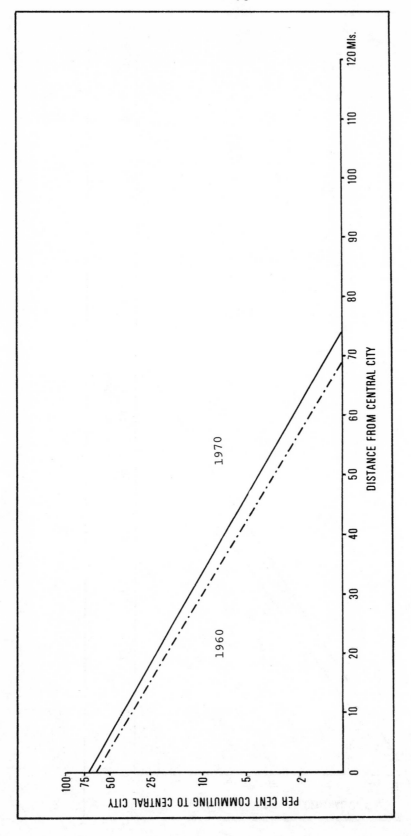

Figure 4.8. Commuting to the Central City in 1960 and 1970, by Region. (f) Rocky Mountains.

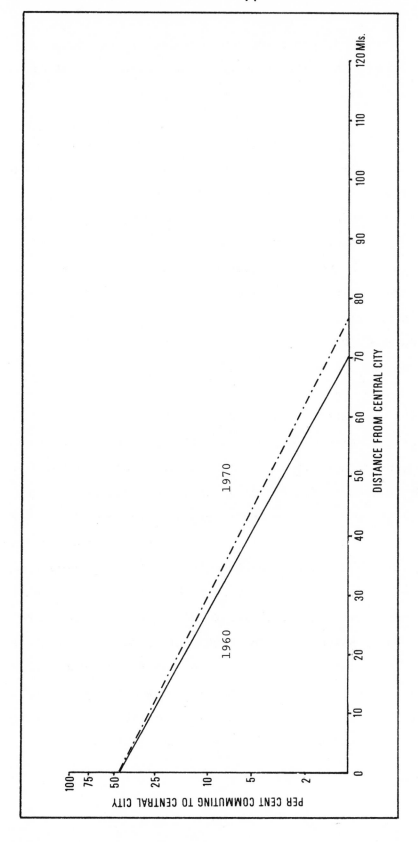

Figure 4.8. Commuting to the Central City in 1960 and 1970, by Region. (g) Far West

Figures 4.9 and 4.10 provide more details of the changes, showing respectively the nationwide pictures of expansion of commuting areas in the decade, and of decreasing central-city job dependency. To capture the nature of these changes, first- second- and third-degree polynomials of the relationship between the change in percentage commuting and distance, from the central city were computed, again for both city-size classes and regions, and for the three different workplace definitions (central city, central county, and SMSA). The dependent variable, change in percentage commuting (CP) is defined as the percentage commuting in 1970 (P_{70}) minus the percentage commuting in 1960 (P_{60}) : $CP = P_{70} - P_{60}$. The polynomial equations are thus:

First degree $\quad CP = a + bD$

Second degree $\quad CP = a + bD = cD^2$

Third degree $\quad CP = a + bD + cD^2 + dD^3$

The results are presented in Tables 4.5 and 4.6, and are graphed in Figures 4.11-4.12. Figures 4.12a, and 4.12b in particular, bring out the commuting change-distance relationships: an inner zone of decreasing dependence on central city jobs, widest in extent for the largest cities and those in the northeast, followed by a zone of increasing commuting to the central city that peaks furthest out for the largest cities, and then by decline again. The wave-motion analogy of the patterns of change, varying by sity size and region, is hard to ignore. The same wavelike regularities are reproduced by the third-degree polynomials for both central counties and SMSAs as workplaces (Figures 4.12 c-d and 4.12 e-f). As expected, the inner zone of decline decreases as the size of workplace region is increased, but it still is most definitely there for central counties of the largest SMSAs and for those in the northeast.

The eye is drawn irrevocably in Figure 4.9 to the vast areas
of California and the Southwest, where long distance automobile
commuting is producing an even more far-flung dispersed urban region,
to the filling of the intermetropolitan peripheries along the Gulf
and Atlantic coasts, and to radial expansion of commuting fields
elsewhere.

Yet equally notable are the zones within SMSAs where significant decreases in central-city job dependency are taking place.
As may be seen in Figure 4.10, these zones form a string within
the Northeastern megalopolis, form several clusters in the old manufacturing belt westwards to Chicago, and are most extensive in
Southern California, wehre multi-centered dispersion continues to
take its toll of such center-city job orientation as remains.

There are differences by city size and by region, as Figures
4.4 and 4.12 reveal. The city size classes can be arrayed by both
increasing width of the inner zone of decline, by distance of the
outer crest of maximum growth of center city commuting, and by the
center radius of commuting expansion. A similar array may be
prepared by regions.

What such arrays reveal is the convergence in form of metropolitan regions. The greatest rates of decline of center-city job
orientation are in those regions which traditionally were the
most highly centralized; there suburban commuting rates to the
central city are declining, and reverse commuting from the central
city is increasing. The greatest rates of peripheral expansion
are in those regions where interurban peripheries remain to be
filled; improved highways have, in these areas, facilitated
the continuing space-filling extension of metropolitan commuting
fields, at the expense of nonmetropolitan America.

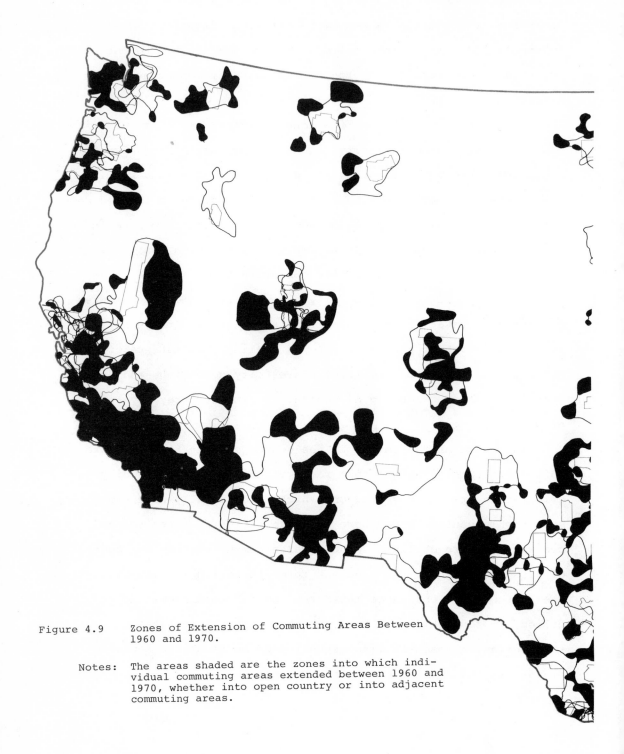

Figure 4.9   Zones of Extension of Commuting Areas Between
              1960 and 1970.

  Notes: The areas shaded are the zones into which indi-
            vidual commuting areas extended between 1960 and
            1970, whether into open country or into adjacent
            commuting areas.

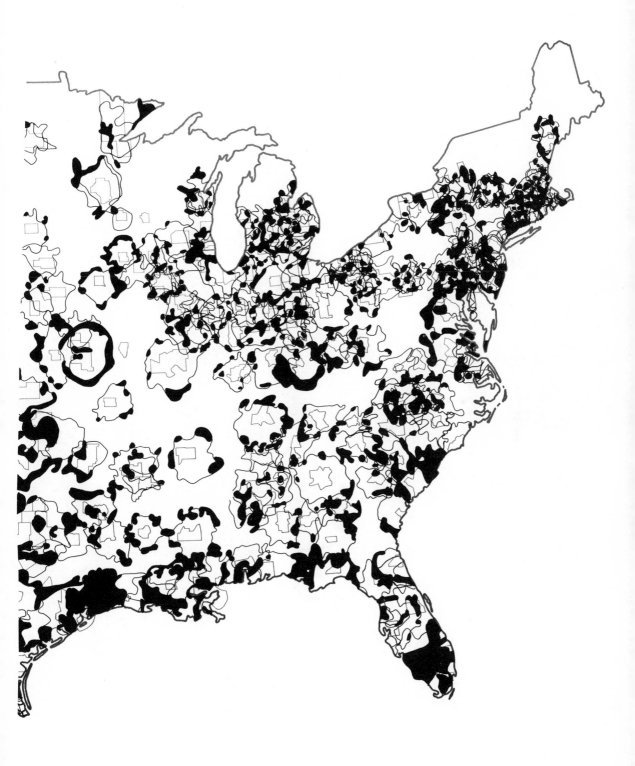

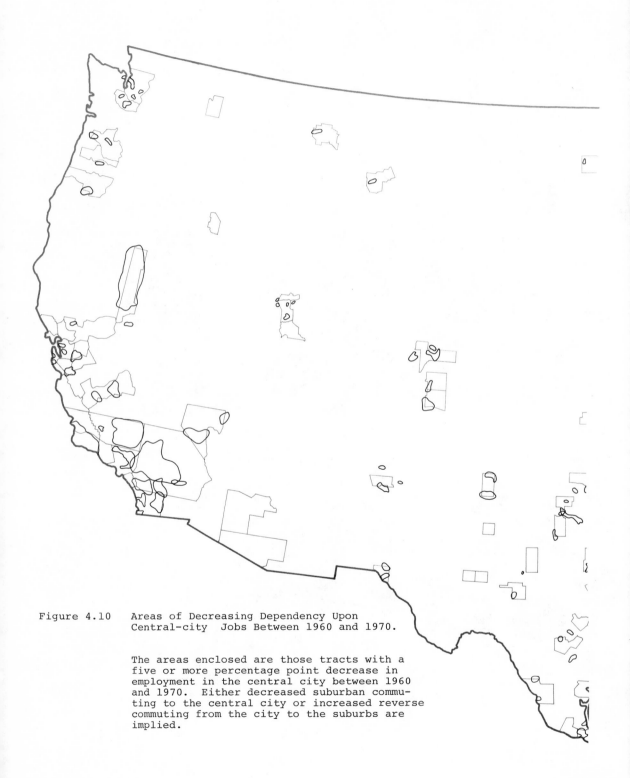

Figure 4.10   Areas of Decreasing Dependency Upon
               Central-city Jobs Between 1960 and 1970.

               The areas enclosed are those tracts with a
               five or more percentage point decrease in
               employment in the central city between 1960
               and 1970. Either decreased suburban commu-
               ting to the central city or increased reverse
               commuting from the city to the suburbs are
               implied.

Table 4.5

CHANGE IN COMMUTING TO CENTRAL CITY, CENTRAL COUNTY, AND SMSA, 1960-1970
FIRST, SECOND AND THIRD DEGREE POLYNOMIAL MODELS FOR METROPOLITAN SIZE GROUPS

Model		Inter-cept	Coeff.	Std. Error	Coeff.	Std. Error	Coeff.	Std. Error	F	R^2	N
Total	CPCC Lin.	.8490	.0072	.0180					.1660	.00019	853
	2nd Deg.	-.5950	.1634	.0409	-.0022	.0005			9.0110	.021	853
	3rd Deg.	-2.7868	.5469	.0775	-.0122	.0018	.00006	.00001	17.3906	.058	853
	CPCTY Lin.	.6365	.0463	.0140					11.6022	.0135	853
	2nd Deg.	-.6294	.1833	.0312	-.0019	.0004			17.7430	.0400	853
	3rd Deg.	-1.9001	.4056	.0596	-.0077	.0014	.00003	.00001	18.4105	.0611	853
	CPSMSA Lin.	1.1780	.0424	.0140					9.1951	.0107	853
	2nd Deg.	-.0788	.1783	.0321	-.0019	.0004			15.6980	.036	853
	3rd Deg.	-1.3353	.3981	.0614	-.0077	.0014	.00003	.00001	16.5135	.055	853
I	CPCC Lin.	-5.4341	.1470	.0210					48.7673	.188	213
	2nd Deg.	-8.2540	.4750	.0662	-.0048	.0009			40.9250	.280	213
	3rd Deg	-9.0530	.6457	.1594	-.0107	.0050	.00005	.00004	27.7959	.285	213
	CPCTY Lin.	-1.0395	.0998	.0240					17.3222	.076	213
	2nd Deg.	-4.0051	.4451	.0763	-.0051	.0011			20.7910	.165	213
	3rd Deg.	-4.7939	.6137	.1841	-.0108	.0058	.00005	.00005	14.1993	.169	213
	CPSMSA Lin.	1.0610	.0724	.0254					8.0921	.037	213
	2nd Deg.	-1.7350	.3980	.0820	-.0048	.0012			13.0374	.110	213
	3rd Deg.	-2.8132	.6285	.1973	-.0126	.0062	.00007	.00005	9.2681	.117	213
II	CPCC Lin.	1.9170	.0350	.0420					.7060	.003	217
	2nd Deg.	-.9270	.3790	.1240	-.0053	.0018			4.6790	.042	217
	3rd Deg.	-3.6217	.9735	.2693	-.0265	.0087	.00019	.00008	5.2431	.069	217
	CPCTY Lin.	1.4106	.0633	.0270					5.6980	.026	217
	2nd Deg.	-1.6480	.4332	.0762	-.0057	.0011			16.4146	.133	217
	3rd Deg.	-2.7060	.6667	.1668	-.0140	.0054	.00007	.00005	11.8419	.143	217
	CPSMSA Lin.	1.8970	.0640	.0280					5.3450	.024	217
	2nd Deg.	-1.3808	.4602	.0790	-.0061	.0012			17.1450	.138	217
	3rd Deg.	-2.6103	.7315	.1727	-.0158	.0056	.00008	.00005	12.5803	.151	217

Model		Inter-cept	Coeff.	Std. Error	Coeff.	Std. Error	Coeff.	Std. Error	F	R^2	N
III	CPCC Lin.	3.3109	−.1720	.0520					11.0630	.058	181
	2nd Deg.	2.6070	−.0960	.1222	−.0009	.0014			5.7510	.061	181
	3rd Deg.	−3.3742	1.0757	.2502	−.0357	.0067	.00023	.00004	13.6289	.188	181
	CPCTY Lin.	.7950	.0211	.0211					1.0060	.006	181
	2nd Deg.	−.0680	.1143	.0492	−.0012	.0006			2.6955	.029	181
	3rd Deg.	−1.1241	.3212	.1069	−.0073		.00004	.00002	3.4071	.055	181
	CPSMSA Lin.	1.1431	.0130	.0220					.3571	.002	181
	2nd Deg.	.5999	.0933	.0510	−.0092	.0006			1.6913	.019	181
	3rd Deg.	−.6212	.2933	.1109	−.0635	.0030	−.00004	.00002	2.5133	.041	181
IV	CPCC Lin.	3.4180	−.0131	.0421					.0970	.0007	140
	2nd Deg.	−.7382	−.4382	.1240	−.0092	.0024			7.4519	.0007	140
	3rd Deg.	−2.4568	1.5695	.2803	−.0635	.0125	−.00064	.00014	12.2051	.2121	140
	CPCTY Lin.	F Level or Tolerance Level Insufficient for Computation									140
	2nd Deg.	−.6561	.2992	.1544	−.0060	.0030			2.0756	.0294	140
	3rd Deg.	−2.7227	1.0309	.3669	−.0412	.0163	−.00041	.00019	3.0236	.0625	140
	CPSMSA Lin.	−.3370	−.0250	.0510					.2342	.0017	140
	2nd Deg.	−1.1263	.2709	.1554	−.0050	.0030			1.5233	.0218	140
	3rd Deg.	−2.0760	.6071	.3745	−.0212	.0166	−.00019	.00019	1.3396	.029	140
V	CPCC Lin.	1.2780	.0075	.0332					.0511	.0005	102
	2nd Deg.	.4740	.0694	.0663	−.0007	.0006			.6066	.0121	102
	3rd Deg.	−1.7623	.4471	.1624	−.0096	.0036	−.00004	.00002	2.5679	.073	102
	CPCTY Lin.	F Level or Tolerance Level Insufficient for Computation									102
	2nd Deg.	.6706	.0344	.0936	−.0004	.0009			.1141	.0023	102
	3rd Deg.	−.6163	.2518	.2355	−.0055	.0052	.00003	.00002	.4134	.0125	102
	CPSMSA Lin.	F Level or Tolerance Level Insufficient for Computation									102
	2nd Deg.	.7185	.0327	.0935	−.0004	.0009			.1098	.0022	102
	3rd Deg.	−.5488	.2468	.2354	−.0055	.0052	−.00002	.00002	.4005	.012	102

Table 4.6

CHANGE IN COMMUTING TO CENTRAL CITY, CENTRAL COUNTY, AND SMSA, 1960-1970
FIRST, SECOND AND THIRD DEGREE POLYNOMIAL MODELS OF REGIONS

Model	Inter-cept	Coeff.	Std. Error	Coeff.	Std. Error	Coeff.	Std. Error	F	R^2	N
NE CPCC Lin.	-8.2629	.2674	.2086	-.0079	.0040			16.5590	.131	112
2nd Deg.	-10.7548	.6562	.2519	-.0079	.0040			10.4147	.160	112
3rd Deg.	-11.0372	-.7315	.4529	-.0113	.0187	.00004	.0002	6.8934	.161	112
CPCTY Lin.	-2.7520	.1736	.0829	-.0039	.0052			4.3840	.038	112
2nd Deg.	-3.9943	.3674	.2671	-.0039	.0052			2.4755	.043	112
3rd Deg.	-2.7989	-.0484	.5787	.0106	.0239	-.00017	.0003	1.7699	.047	112
CPSMSA Lin.	-1.6912	.1624	.0782	-.0035	.0049			4.3152	.038	112
2nd Deg.	-2.7960	.3347	.2519	-.0035	.0049			2.4073	.042	112
3rd Deg.	-1.2287	-.0835	.5450	.0155	.0225	-.0002	.0003	1.8509	.049	112
GL CPCC Lin.	-1.3838	.0848	.0395	-.0106	.0021			4.6159	.032	142
2nd Deg.	-5.1871	.6466	.1178	-.0106	.0021			15.2942	.180	142
3rd Deg.	-8.2360	1.5402	.2389	-.0518	.0099	-.00047	.00011	17.3850	.274	142
CPCTY Lin.	-1.4316	.0312	.0306	-.0087	.0016			1.0401	.007	142
2nd Deg.	-1.6941	.4930	.0904	-.0087	.0016			15.0502	.007	142
3rd Deg.	-3.6136	1.0556	.1873	-.0346	.0078	.0003	.00009	14.6336	.241	142
CPSMSA Lin.	F Level or Tolerance Level Insufficient for Computation									
2nd Deg.	-.1193	.2866	.1142	-.0054	.0020	.0002		3.4585	.047	142
3rd Deg.	-1.4337	.6718	.2434	-.0231	.0101	.0002	.0001	3.4081	.069	142
GP CPCC Lin.	3.9820	-.0120	.0502	-.0051	.0027			.0573	.0005	120
2nd Deg.	2.0762	.2814	.1639	-.0051	.0027			1.7947	.030	120
3rd Deg.	1.5017	1.2221	.3839	-.0419	.0139	.0004	.0001	3.6801	.087	120
CPCTY Lin.	-.0469	.0767	.0263	-.0040	.0014			8.5133	.067	120
2nd Deg.	-1.4514	.3073	.0841	-.0040	.0014			8.6647	.129	120
3 d Deg.	-1.8724	.4180	.2027	-.0084	.0074	.0004	.00007	5.8650	.132	120
CPSMSA Lin.	0.2996	.0899	.0279	-.0034	.0015			10.3517	.081	120
2nd Deg.	-1.5755	.2863	.0905	-.0034	.0015			7.9521	.120	120
3rd Deg.	-1.4878	.2632	.2186	-.0025	.0079	-.00001	.00008	5.2612	.120	120

SE CPCC Lin.	1.4086	.0556	.0383	-.0101	.0022			2.1090	.015	145
2nd Deg.	-2.5169	.5912	.1237	-.0454	.0127	.0004	.0002	11.4412	.139	145
3rd Deg.	-5.4063	1.3639	.2992					10.6577	.185	145
CPTY Lin.	2.6334	.0314	.0517	-.0089	.0032			.3670	.003	145
2nd Deg.	-0.7982	.4996	.1742	-.0361	.0182	.00032	.00021	4.1393	.055	145
3rd Deg.	-3.0762	1.0964	.4296					3.5535	.070	145
CPSMSA Lin.	3.3389	.0401	.0536	-.0107	.0032			.5597	.004	145
2nd Deg.	-0.8253	.6083	.1784	-.0384	.0187	.00032	.00021	5.8383	.076	145
3rd Deg.	-3.1377	1.2141	.4401					4.6814	.091	145
SW CPCC Lin.	7.0998	-.0433	.0476	-.0053	.0023			.8279	.007	119
2nd Deg.	4.5182	.2975	.1588	-.0306	.0126	.00025	.00012	2.9491	.048	119
3rd Deg.	2.2681	.8681	.3545					3.0690	.074	119
CPTY Lin.	.5250	.0787	.0282	-.0047	.0014			7.7726	.062	119
2nd Deg.	-1.7894	.3843	.0916	-.0083	.0070	.00004	.00007	10.3501	.151	119
3rd Deg.	-1.9740	.4307	.1979					5.1731	.119	119
CPSMSA Lin.	.6288	.0754	.0280	-.0047	.0013			7.2302	.058	119
2nd Deg.	-1.6617	.3778	.0910	-.0013	.0072	.00006	.00007	10.0080	.147	119
3rd Deg.	-2.1133	.5449	.2028					6.9069	.153	119
RM CPCC Lin.	1.4466	.0039	.0268	-.0013	.0008			.0210	.0002	107
2nd Deg.	.3229	.1107	.0699	-.0130	.0042	.00007	.00003	1.3767	.026	107
3rd Deg.	-1.4404	.5929	.1744					4.2990	.111	107
CPCTY Lin.	1.6723	.0132	.0212	-.0017	.0006			.3891	.004	107
2nd Deg.	.1865	.1545	.0541	-.0126	.0033	.00006	.00002	4.1918	.075	107
3rd Deg.	-1.8458	.6096	.1348					8.3188	.195	107
CPSMSA Lin.	2.3548	.0104	.0227	-.0021	.0006			.2090	.002	107
2nd Deg.	-.5373	.1831	.0570	-.0127	.0032	.00007	.00002	5.4734	.095	107
3rd Deg.	-1.8463	.6107	.1342					8.3573	.196	107
FW CPCC Lin.	-2.6513	-.0656	.0559	-.0004	.0012			1.3741	.013	108
2nd Deg.	-2.1132	-.1075	.1275	-.0076	.0058	.00004	.00003	.7484	.014	108
3rd Deg.	-4.6791	.2638	.2918					1.1693	.033	108
CPCTY Lin.	-1.6244	.0361	.0239	-.0006	.0005			2.2877	.0211	108
2nd Deg.	-2.3261	.0908	.0541	-.0009	.0025	.00000	.00001	1.7783	.033	108
3rd Deg.	-2.4309	.1059	.1251					1.1805	.033	108
CPSMSA Lin.	.1242	.0190	.0276	-.0005	.0006			.4756	.004	108
2nd Deg.	-.4809	.0661	.0627	-.001	.0029	.00000	.00001	.5876	.011	108
3rd Deg.	-.7660	.1074	.1448					.4218	.012	108

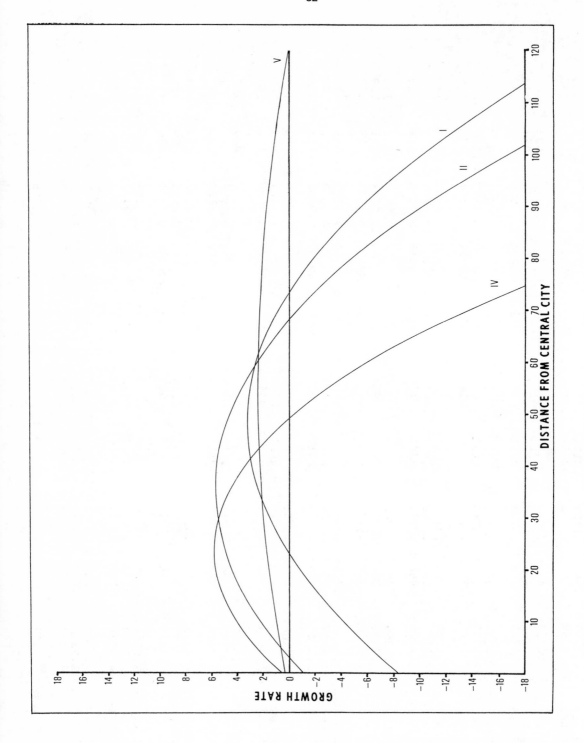

Figure 4.11. Second-degree Commuting Change Patterns- (a) Central Cities by Size Class.

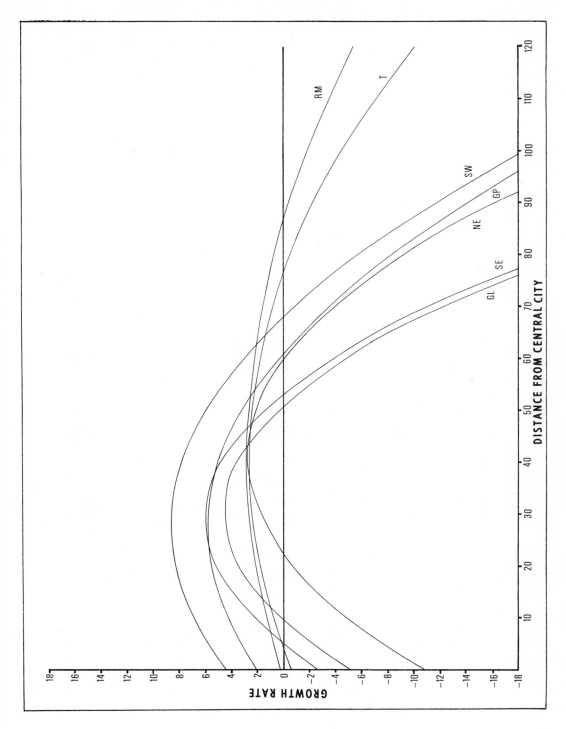

Figure 4.11. Second-degree Commuting Change Patterns- (b) Central Cities by Region.

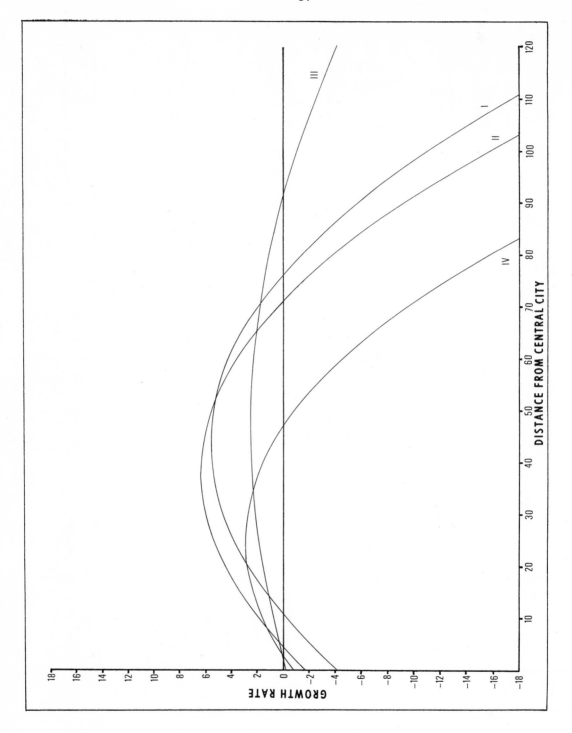

Figure 4.11. Second-degree Commuting Change Patterns- (c) Central Counties by Size Class.

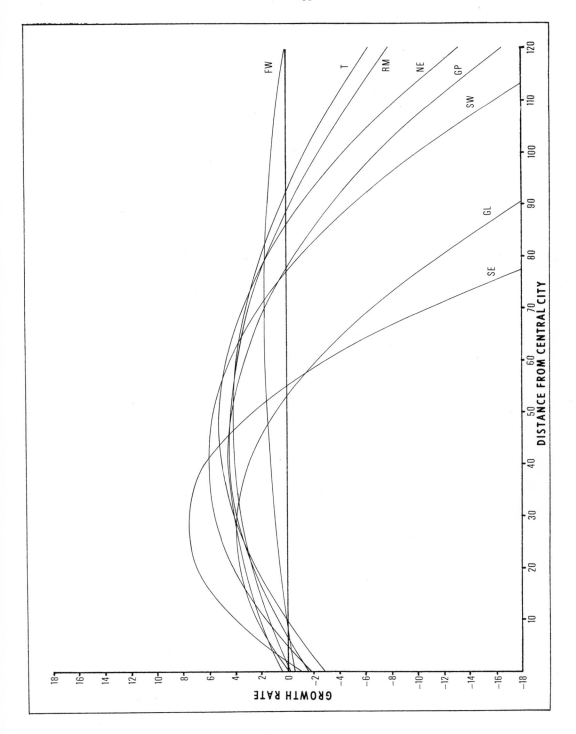

Figure 4.11. Second-degree Commuting Change Patterns- (d) Central Counties by Region.

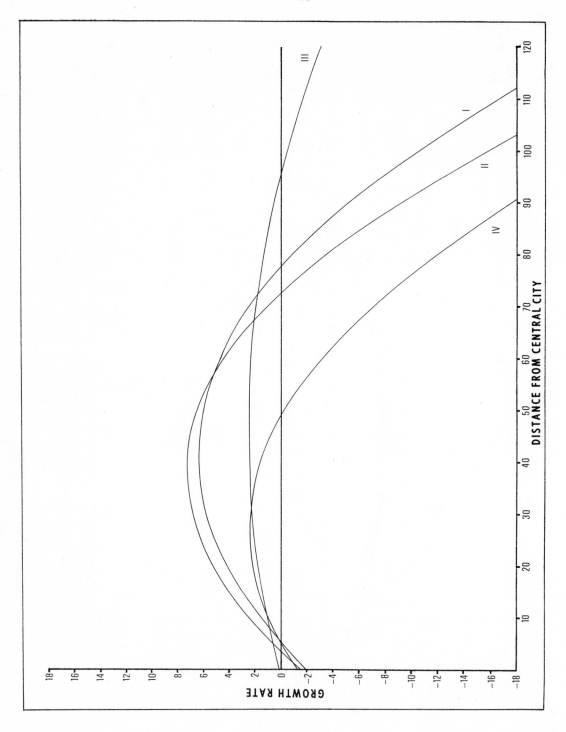

Figure 4.11. Second-degree Commuting Change Patterns- (e) SMSAs by Size Class.

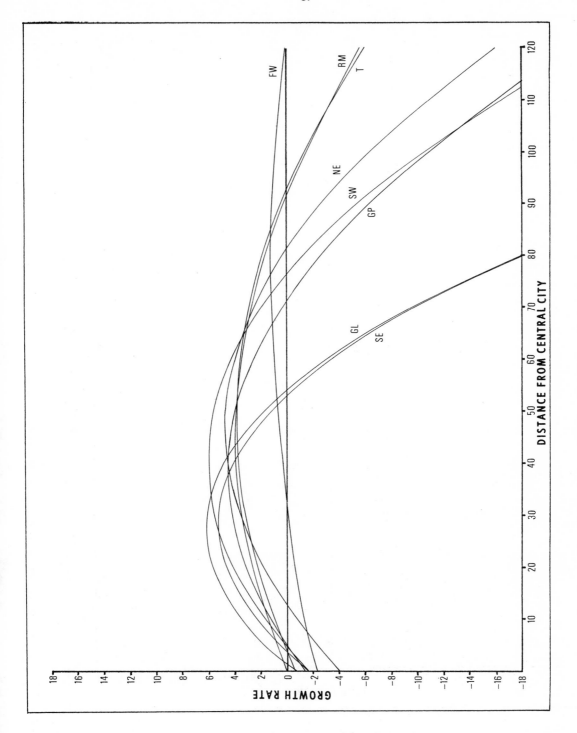

Figure 4.11. Second-degree Commuting Change Patterns— (f) SMSAs by Region.

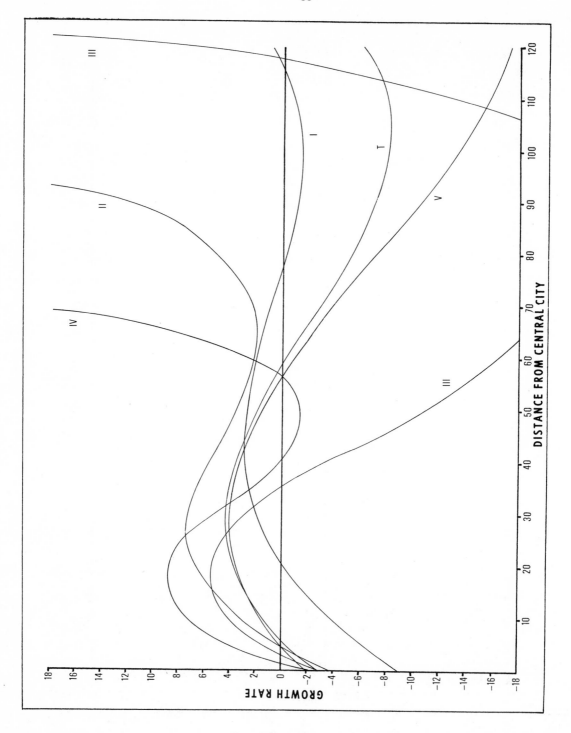

Figure 4.12.   Third-degree Commuting Change Patterns - (a) Central Cities by Size Class.

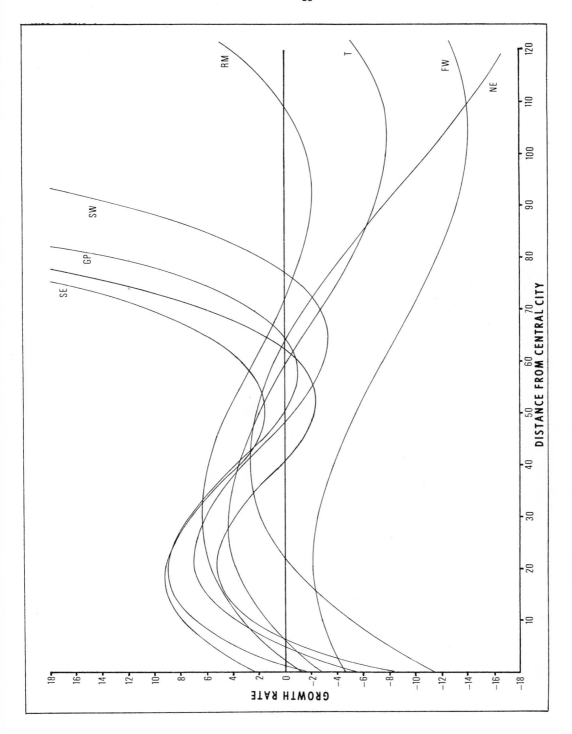

Figure 4.12.   Third-degree Commuting Change Patterns—   (b) Central Cities by Region.

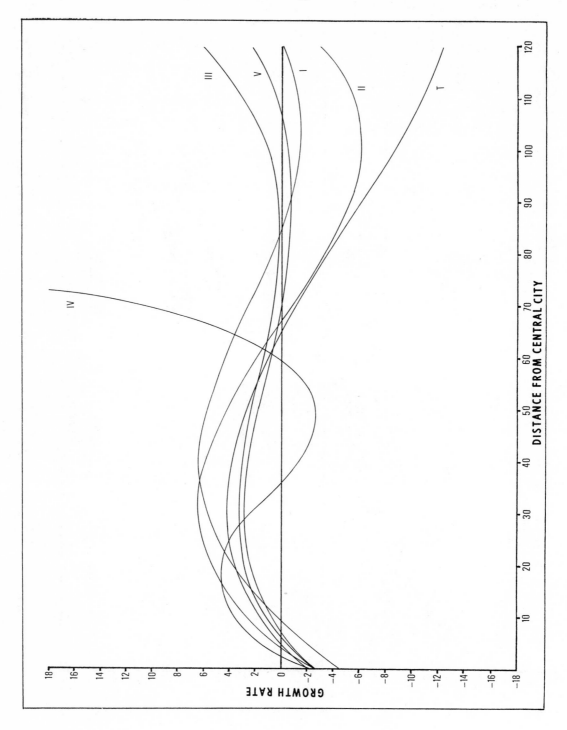

Figure 4.12. Third-degree Commuting Change Patterns— (c) Central Counties by Size Class.

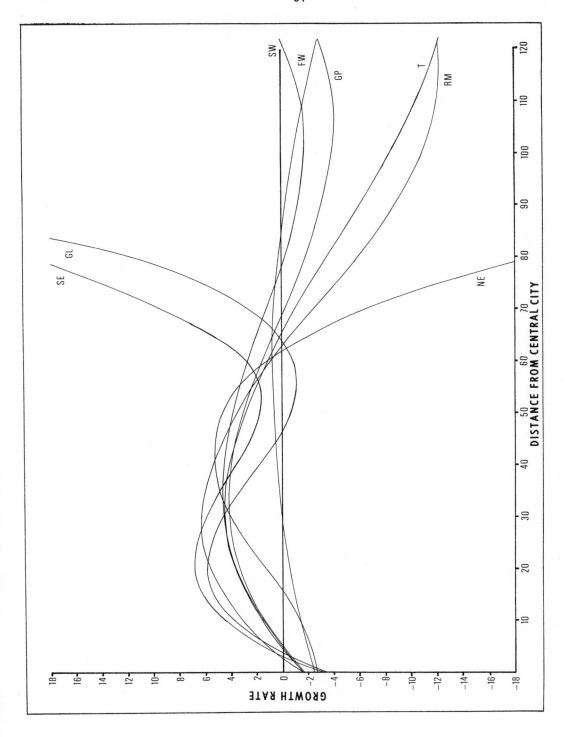

Figure 4.12. Third-degree Commuting Change Patterns- (d) Central Counties by Region.

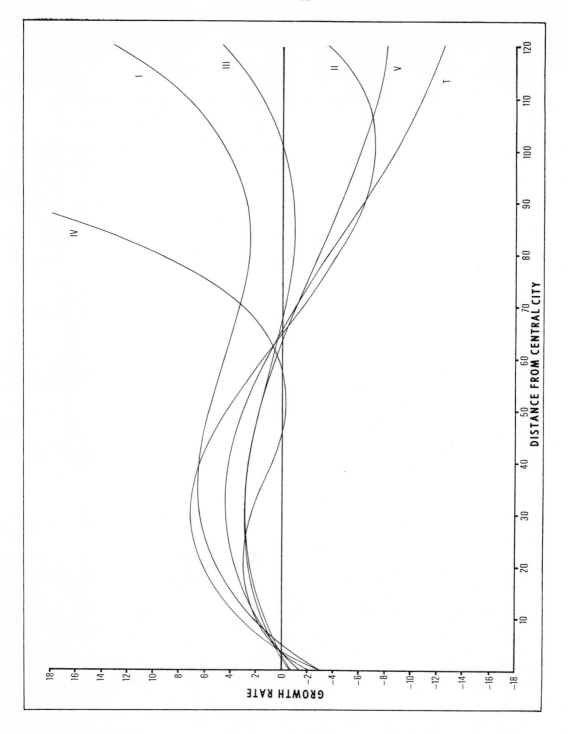

Figure 4.12. Third-degree Commuting Change Patterns— (e) SMSAs by Size Class.

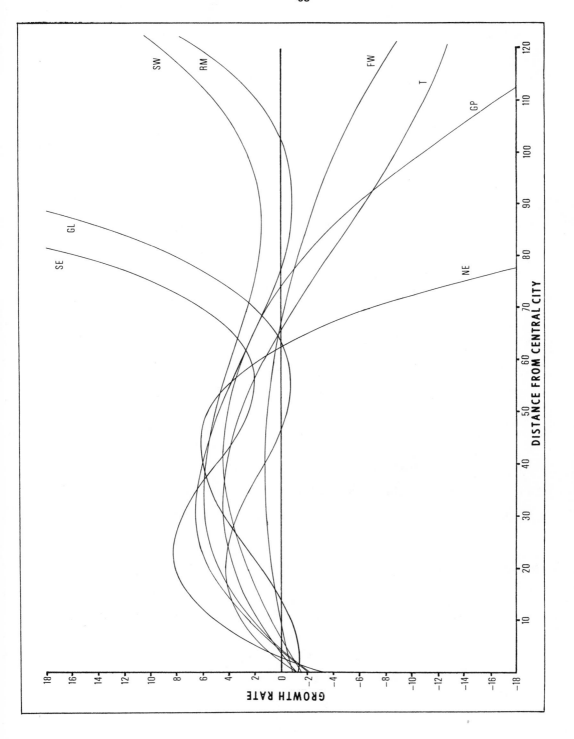

Figure 4.12. Third-degree Commuting Change Patterns— (f) SMSAs by Region.

What factors are correlated with the changes so far documented? To answer this question, 1960-1970 changes in each of the
commuting areas were classified in each of three ways:

(a) Whether the commuting area showed general expansion, as
    in the case of Kansas City, selective expansion along
    particular axes, or evidenced little growth at all, as
    in the case of Boston.

(b) Whether or not commuting rates to the central city
    increased generally in the decade, showed a pattern of
    increase along one axis and decrease along another as
    in the case of Chicago, or decreased generally, as in
    the case of Boston.

(c) Whether reverse commuting from the central city increased
    generally throughout the city, showed selective increases
    or decreases from one neighborhood to another, or decrease
    generally as central city residents became more depen-
    dent upon central city jobs.

These three classifications were compared with such variables

as population size, the SMSA and the central city's population

growth rates in the decade, the growth rate of the central city's

white population, the percentage change in its nonwhite population,

the growth rates of SMSA and central city employment, the city:

SMSA population and employment growth ratios, and the SMSA and

city retail sales growth rates and the city: SMSA retail sales

growth ratio.

The results are tabulated in Table 4.7, and the following

conclusions are evident:

(a) General expansion of commuting areas, increase of commu-
    ting to the central city, and decline of reverse commu-
    ting are most evident in smaller SMSAs with the greatest
    SMSA and city population and employment growth rates,
    the greatest increases in white population and the
    greatest relative decreases in the nonwhite percentage,
    and growing relative shares of the city with respect to
    the SMSA population and economy.

(b) Commuting areas showing little or no expansion, with
    general decreases of commuting to the central city, are
    thos of large declining or slow-growth SMSAs and cities,

with declining white and expanding nonwhite populations, and with central cities losing population
and economy relative to the SMSA.

(c) Decreases in commuting to the central city are
characteristic of the largest urban regions, with
growing employment in the SMSA but lagging employment and rapidly-increasing minority populations
in the central city.

(d) Likewise, the most widespread increases of reverse
commuting are found in the largest urban regions
where the SMSA is growing but the central city is
lagging, and where the nonwhite population increase
in the central city is most rapid.

Table 4.7

CHANGE IN SHAPE OF COMMUTING AREA

VARIABLE	SIZE OF COMMUTING AREA			COMMUTING TO CENTRAL CITY			REVERSE COMMUTING		
	General Expansion	Selective Growth	Little Change	General Increase	Selective Incr/Decr	General Decrease	General Increase	Selective Incr/Decr	General Decrease
SMSA POPULATION									
<100,000	38.0	52.4	9.5	61.9	33.3	4.8	8.0	48.0	44.0
100-200,000	21.3	67.5	11.3	56.3	40.0	3.8	13.5	58.0	28.4
200-350,000	36.5	49.2	14.3	41.3	50.8	8.0	17.5	63.5	19.0
350-1,000,000	36.9	45.6	17.5	43.9	47.4	8.8	12.3	68.4	19.3
>1,000,000	14.8	66.7	18.5	14.8	59.3	25.9	34.6	61.5	3.8
SMSA GROWTH RATE									
<0.0	10.7	67.9	21.4	7.2	35.7	3.6	3.4	62.1	34.5
0.0-0.29	27.8	59.4	12.8	8.0	48.1	3.2	16.1	62.0	21.9
0.3-0.59	50.0	32.1	17.9	14.3	35.7	3.6	22.6	54.8	22.6
0.6-0.89	100.0	0.0	0.0	0.0	75.0	0.0	25.0	75.0	0.0
>0.9	100.0	0.0	0.0	0.0	100.0	0.0	100.0	0.0	0.0
CITY GROWTH RATE									
<0.0	19.3	60.6	20.2	32.1	54.1	12.8	20.4	60.2	19.4
0.0-0.49	36.1	54.1	9.8	56.6	39.3	4.1	10.5	63.7	25.8
0.5-0.99	50.0	40.0	10.0	50.0	40.0	10.0	18.2	54.5	27.3
1.0-1.49	100.0	0.0	0.0	100.0	0.0	0.0	66.7	33.3	0.0
>1.5	100.0	0.0	0.0	50.0	50.0	0.0	0.0	50.0	50.0
GROWTH RATE OF CITY'S WHITE POPULATION									
<0.0	19.5	62.6	17.9	35.8	51.2	13.0	19.2	61.7	19.2
0.0-0.49	37.0	50.9	12.0	55.6	39.8	4.7	11.8	62.7	25.5
0.5-0.99	66.6	33.3	0.0	55.6	44.4	0.0	0.0	54.5	45.5
1.0-1.49	50.0	50.0	0.0	50.0	50.0	0.0	75.0	25.0	25.0
>1.50	100.0	0.0	0.0	50.0	50.0	0.0	0.0	50.0	50.0

CHANGE IN SHAPE OF COMMUTING AREA

VARIABLE	SIZE OF COMMUTING AREA			COMMUTING TO CENTRAL CITY			REVERSE COMMUTING		
	General Expansion	Selective Growth	Little Change	General Increase	Selective Incr/Decr	General Decrease	General Increase	Selective Incr/Decr	General Decrease
PERCENT CHANGE IN CITY'S NONWHITE POP.									
<-10.0	100.0	0.0	0.0	50.0	50.0	0.0	0.0	0.0	100.0
-9.9-0.0	31.6	50.0	18.4	52.6	44.7	2.6	14.3	61.9	23.8
0.0-9.9	31.4	56.6	12.2	47.1	43.9	9.0	15.0	61.5	23.5
10.0-19.9	0.0	69.2	30.8	7.7	76.9	15.4	28.6	64.3	7.1
>20.0	0.0	50.0	50.0	0.0	50.0	50.0	50.0	50.0	0.0
GROWTH RATE SMSA EMPLOYMENT									
<0.0	33.3	50.0	16.7	16.7	50.0	33.3	0.0	50.0	50.0
0.0-0.49	26.5	60.7	12.8	8.0	46.0	46.0	15.7	63.5	20.8
0.5-0.99	50.0	25.0	25.0	15.0	45.0	40.0	16.7	50.0	33.3
>1.0	60.0	40.0	0.0	0.0	40.0	60.0	60.0	0.0	40.0
GROWTH RATE CITY EMPLOYMENT									
<0.0	12.9	64.5	22.6	9.7	64.5	25.8	12.9	80.6	6.5
0.0-0.49	34.5	54.9	10.6	49.6	44.2	6.2	12.1	61.2	26.7
0.5-0.99	60.0	30.0	10.0	0.0	10.0	10.0	9.1	36.4	54.5
>1.0	---	---	---	---	---	---	---	---	---
POPULATION GROWTH RATIO OF CITY TO SMSA									
<-1.0	25.0	53.6	21.4	32.1	46.4	21.4	11.1	63.0	25.9
-1.0-0.0	18.3	61.7	20.0	21.7	66.7	11.7	30.5	52.5	16.9
0.0-0.99	39.2	51.9	8.9	50.6	44.3	5.1	15.4	69.2	15.4
1.00-1.49	30.0	53.3	16.7	60.0	36.7	3.3	6.2	65.6	28.1
>1.50	31.9	52.4	10.6	66.0	23.4	6.4	7.7	55.8	36.5

CHANGE IN SHAPE OF COMMUTING AREA

	SIZE OF COMMUTING AREA			COMMUTING TO CENTRAL CITY			REVERSE COMMUTING		
	General Expansion	Selective Growth	Little Change	General Increase	Selective Incr/Decr	General Decrease	General Increase	Selective Incr/Decr	General Decrease
EMPLOYMENT GROWTH RATIO OF CITY TO SMSA									
<0.0	10.3	69.0	20.7	10.3	62.1	27.5	13.8	82.7	3.4
0.0-0.49	33.3	50.0	16.7	20.8	66.7	12.6	29.2	66.7	4.2
0.5-0.99	42.0	50.0	8.0	54.0	40.0	6.0	7.7	57.7	34.6
1.0-1.49	26.4	55.9	17.6	58.8	41.1	0.0	11.1	61.1	27.8
>1.50	41.2	58.8	0.0	64.7	23.5	11.8	5.9	47.1	47.1
GROWTH RATE SMSA RETAIL SALES									
0.0-0.49	28.6	53.2	18.2	50.6	37.7	11.7	11.4	53.2	35.4
0.5-0.99	28.5	60.1	11.4	44.3	48.7	7.0	17.1	65.8	17.1
1.0-1.49	71.4	14.3	14.3	42.9	42.9	14.3	11.1	55.6	33.3
>1.5	0.0	66.7	33.3	33.3	66.7	0.0	33.3	66.7	0.0
GROWTH RATE CITY RETAIL SALES									
<0.0	0.0	100.0	0.0	0.0	50.0	25.0	---	---	---
0.0-0.49	25.3	57.7	16.9	35.9	52.8	4.9	40.0	60.0	0.0
0.5-0.99	34.5	53.6	11.9	58.3	38.1	0.0	17.8	60.7	21.4
1.0-1.99	70.0	30.0	0.0	70.0	30.0	0.0	11.4	62.0	26.4
>1.99	0.0	0.0	100.0	100.0	0.0	0.0	15.4	53.8	30.8
RETAIL GROWTH RATIO OF CITY TO SMSA									
<0.0	0.0	100.0	0.0	0.0	50.0	50.0	40.0	60.0	0.0
0.0-0.99	28.1	56.2	15.7	40.5	10.2	10.2	17.2	65.8	17.1
1.0-1.24	40.5	51.4	8.1	67.6	0.0	0.0	2.3	44.2	52.5
1.25-1.49	25.0	75.0	0.0	50.0	0.0	0.0	20.0	80.0	0.0
>1.50	37.5	37.5	25.0	75.0	0.0	0.0	25.0	37.5	37.5

Chapter 5

The Changing Shape of Metropolitan America

Metropolitan commuting fields changed dramatically during

the 1960s. Already extensive in 1960, they penetrated much deeper

into nonmetropolitan America during the decade (Figure 5.1). And,

as documented in Chapter 4, not only did more extensive types of

cross-commuting emerge, particularly in the low-slung far-flung

metropolitan regions of the nation's southern and western sunbelt

rimlands, but in the cores of the larger metropolitan regions in

the northeastern industrial-belt heartland, core-orientation

waned and reverse commuting increased, particularly in those cen-

ters with the most rapidly-expanding black and brown minorities.

The changes reflect the restructuring of that nation's set-

tlement patterns that is occurring at metropolitan, regional and

national scales. The distinguished American historian Oscar Handlin

pointed to the shift as early as 1963:

> Some decades ago a significant change appeared.
> The immediate local causes seemed to be the two wars,
> the depression, and new shifts in technology and popu-
> lation. However, these may be but manifestations of some
> large turning point in the history of the society of
> which the modern city is part. The differences between
> city and country have been attenuated almost to the vani-

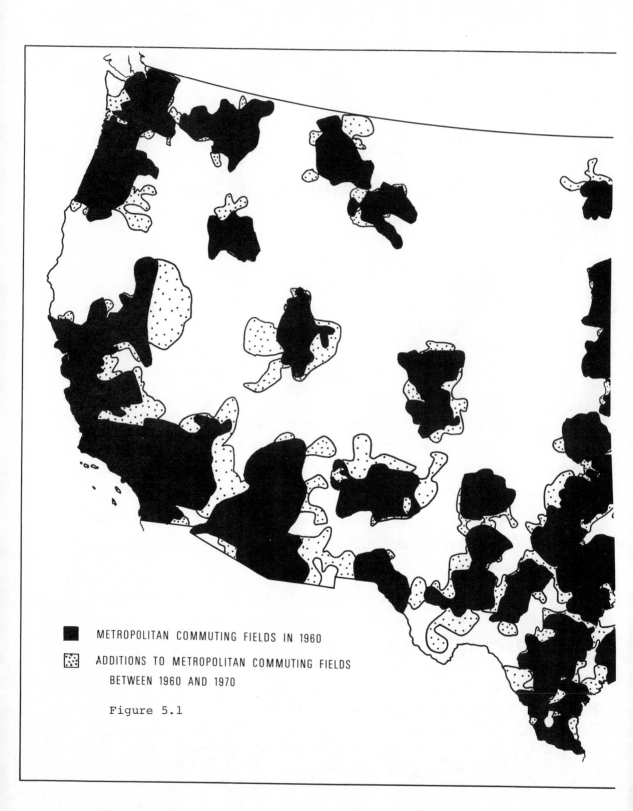

METROPOLITAN COMMUTING FIELDS IN 1960

ADDITIONS TO METROPOLITAN COMMUTING FIELDS
BETWEEN 1960 AND 1970

Figure 5.1

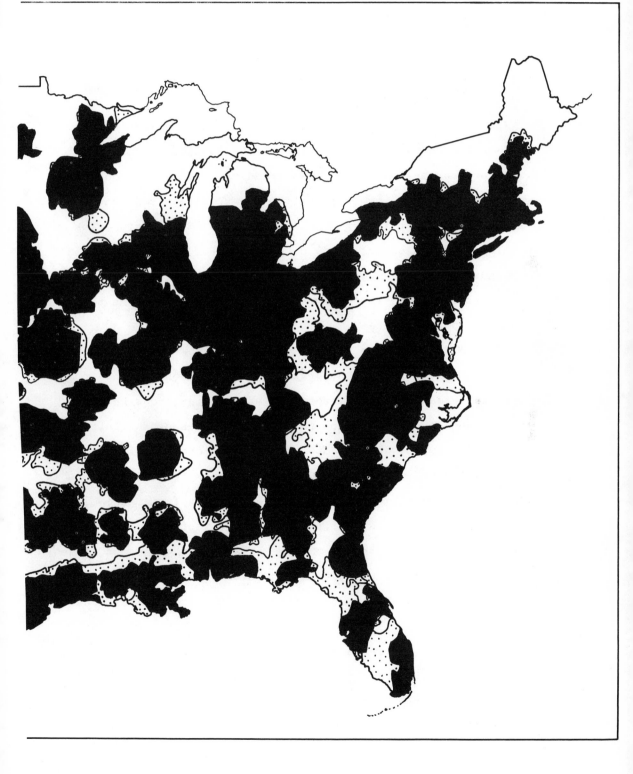

shing point. The movement of people, goods and messages
has become so rapid and has extended over such a long
period as to create a new situation. To put it bluntly,
the urbanization of the whole society may be in process
of destroying the distinctive role of the modern city.
What is new is the effective motivation--the insistence
upon constructing small, coherent communities. Increasingly, the men who now people the metropolis long for the
security of isolation from the life about them. They
strive to locate their families in space, with a minimum
of connections to the hazards of the external world.

The facts of change became unmistakable in the 1960's. As

the Commission on Population Growth and the American Future pointed

out, the population of metropolitan areas grew by 27 millions

between 1960 and 1970, two-thirds from growth within constant

boundaries, and one-third by annexation of expanding peripheries

into which the population is now dispersing. Of the growth inside

1960 boundaries, three quarters was due to natural increase, and of

the one quarter due to immigration, more came from overseas than

from nonmetropolitan areas.

After 1970, even the net migration gain from nonmetropolitan

areas turned around to a net migration loss. Persons moving _from_

metropolitan areas exceeded movers _to_ metropolitan areas between

March 1970 and March 1975. According to estimates of the Current

Population Survey, 6,721,000 persons 5 years old and over moved out

of metropolitan areas and 5,127,000 moved into metropolitan areas

in this period, resulting in a net migration loss from metropolitan

to non-metropolitan areas of 1,594,000. This represented a shift

from the migration patterns of the previous 5-year period of close

to two million persons, because for the 1965-1970 period, data

from the 1970 census show a net inmigration to metropolitan areas

of 352,133 persons 5 years old and over, representing the balance

between 4,809,000 immigrants and 5,457,000 outmigrants. Thus,

five-year metropolitan inmigration declined from 5.8 to 5.1 million

persons, while outmigration increased from 5.4 to 6.7 millions. The

decline is concentrated in the nation's central cities. In the per-

iod 1960-1970, an annual average suburban growth of 875,000 due to
net inmigration exceeded the yearly central city decline due to
net inmigration of 344,900. But between 1970 and 1975, even though
yearly suburban growth increased to 1,084,600, it has been far
outstripped by the yearly central city exodus of 1,403,600 persons--
four times the rate of the preceding decade! In the 5-year period
from March 1970 to March 1975, central cities of metropolitan areas
lost 13,005,000 persons 5 years old and over, mostly to suburban
jurisdictions, and only gained 5,987,000 persons, for a net loss
of 7,018,000; this 2 percent loss in total population is accounted
for entirely by declines in the white population, especially that
of the largest SMSAs.

The result of these migration shifts has been to slow the
rate of metropolitan growth overall, but not to reverse it because
natural increase still exceeds the migration loss, and foreign
immigrants continue to cluster in the larger SMSAs. The equation
does vary from one metropolitan region to another, however, and in
those SMSAs whose net outmigration rate has been high enough and/or
rate of natural increase has been low enough, the SMSA population as
a whole has declined, not simply that of the central city. On the
other hand, the migration shift has contributed to a dramatic reversal in the fortunes of many nonmetropolitan areas. As Table
5.1 reveals, nonmetropolitan growth exceeded that of metropolitan
areas between 1970 and 1975, the first time in this century that
this has been so. Among several factors involved in this development, as noted in Chapter 1, are increases in the number of jobs
in some cities and towns in nonmetropolitan areas; development of
retirement communities in nonmetropolitan areas that attract older
migrants from metropolitan territory; and suburban development
occurring beyond the boundaries of metropolitan areas, especially
those with close and increasing commuting ties to adjacent

Table 5.1. Population and Change for Specified Groups of Metropolitan and Nonmetropolitan Counties: 1960-70 and 1970-74. [Numbers in thousands; SCSA's and SMSA's (in New England, county equivalents of SMSA's) areas defined by the Office of Management and Budget December 31, 1975].

| | POPULATION | | | POPULATION CHANGE | | | |
| | July 1, 1974 (Provisional) | April 1, 1970 (Census) 1/ | April 1, 1960 (Census) | 1970-1974 | | 1960-1970 | |
				Number	Percent	Number	Percent
UNITED STATES	211,390	203,304	179,311	8,087	4.0	23,993	13.4
Counties inside SMSA's	154,934	149,821	127,939	5,113	3.4	21,882	17.1
SCSA's and SMSA's of 3,000,000 or more	56,060	55,775	47,863	285	0.5	7,912	16.5
SCSA's and SMSA's of 1-3,000,000	39,174	37,402	30,969	1,771	4.7	6,433	20.8
Other SMSA's	59,701	56,643	49,107	3,057	5.4	7,537	15.3
Counties outside SMSA's	56,457	53,483	51,372	2,973	5.6	2,111	4.1
178 counties with 20 percent or more commuters to SMSA's	4,372	4,009	3,655	364	9.1	354	9.7
334 counties with 10-19 percent commuters to SMSA's	9,912	9,349	8,705	563	6.0	644	7.4
471 counties with 3-9 percent commuters to SMSA's	14,261	13,497	12,805	763	5.7	692	5.4
1,481 counties with less than 3 percent commuters to SMSA's	27,912	26,628	26,207	1,284	4.8	422	1.6

1/ Includes corrections in local and national totals determined after 1970 census complete-count tabulations were made.

Source: Derived from Current Population Reports, Series P-25 and P-26 (county estimates). Breakdown by commuting based on 1970 census commuting data.

metropolitan regions.

Who are the migrants? Persons engaging in the different forms of residential mobility typically differ from persons who do not move and, as a result, have an impact on areas of origin and destination greater than their numbers would imply. Highest mobility rates are usually found among persons in their twenties, reflecting the establishment of new households by young adults who have just finished school recently married, or newly entered the labor force. Although 41.3 percent of all persons 5 years old and over moved during the 5-year period, the rate for persons 25 to 29 years was 72.0 percent. Persons in their early twenties and early thirties also had high mobility rates (both about 60 percent). Children 5 to 14 years had higher mobility rates (reflecting the younger age of their parents) than persons 15 to 19 years old.

One consequence is that the nation's elderly population shows a pattern of concentration in old neighborhoods in smaller towns and rural areas, except where retirees have migrated to new sunbelt communities.

Migration patterns differ by race as well, with blacks being more likely to change residence than whites (45.7 and 40.7 percent, respectively). But blacks tend to move shorter distances than whites; in the 1970-75 period 35.7 percent of blacks 5 years and over moved within the same county as compared with only 22.7 percent of whites. Whites, however, have higher rates of inter-county and interstate migration than blacks.

Educational attainment also influences the likelihood of migration. College graduates are more likely to move between counties or States than high school graduates who,

in turn, migrate more often than persons with only a grade
school education. Among persons 18 years old and over, 29.5
percent of those with 4 or more year of college moved to a
different county between March 1970 and March 1975, compared
with 16.1 percent of those who have completed only 4 years
of high school and 9.0 percent of those with only 8 years of
education or less.

The presence and ages of own children in a family influ-
ence the likelihood of moving. Among married men who were
25 to 34 years old and living with their wives, those with
no own children under 18 are more residentially mobile than
those with own children under 18. Also, husband-wife families (head 25 to 34 years) whose children are all under six
years old are more residentially mobile than those with children over six years. Thus, the presence of school-age children acts to reduce the geographic mobility of these families.

These factors are reflected in the migration trends. Persons moving to central cities were slightly younger than persons moving from central cities. In the 1970-75 period the
median age of immigrants to central cities was 25.1 years,
compared with a median age of 27.6 years among outmigrants.
Blacks were relatively more numerous in the migration stream
to central cities than in the stream from central cities. In
the 1970-75 period, blacks constituted 12.3 percent of inmi-
grants (5 years old and over) to central cities and 7.5 percent of outmigrants. A continuation of this migration pattern would contribute to raising the percent black in central
cities. Differences in rates of natural increase also contribute to altering the percent black.

There are other aspects of these shifts. The economic problems of cities were compounded between 1970 and 1974 by the fact that not only more families and unrelated individuals left cities than moved to cities during this period, but that the average incomes in 1973 of outmigrants were higher than those for families and unrelated individuals who moved to cities between 1970 and 1974. For example, the mean income in 1973 for families who moved out of cities during this period was about $14,200 compared with about $12,900 for families who moved into cities. The result has been a progressively greater concentration of low income families in the central cities of metropolitan areas. The aggregate income in 1973 of families and unrelated individuals living in central cities in 1970 was about $267.4 billion. The aggregate income in 1973 of families and unrelated individuals who moved out of cities between 1970 and 1974 was about $55.3 billion while that for families and unrelated individuals who moved into cities during this period was about $25 billion. Thus if there had been no migration in and out of cities between 1970 and 1974, there would have been about $29.6 billion more income available to families and unrelated individuals living in cities in 1974 than was actually the case.

Thus, the process of population concentration that was the essence of urbanization in the previous century of national growth appears to have ended. Migration takes place between metropolitan areas on an inter-regional scale, and intra-regionally through an accelerating dispersion of people and jobs outward into the expanding metropolitan periphery, coupled with the abandonment of minorities and poor in the central city. Nearly 40 million Americans change their homes each year. Roughly one in 15 Americans--a total of 13 million people--migrate across a county line. And the outward urge dominates. In the two decades

1950-1970 the average population density of all urbanized areas
in the United States dropped from 5,408 persons per square mile
to 3,376; for central cities the decline was from 7,786 to 4,463.
For a long period of time, of course, the rule has been the newer
the growth, the lower the density. But whatever the density, it
continues to decline, although more rapidly in the central cities
that grew in the wave of industrial urbanization than elsewhere.
Most metropolitan growth is, as a consequence, to be found in
rapidly-dispersing suburban and exurban territory. In short,
there has been a shift in the locus of new growth--residential,
industrial, commercial--to the expanding periphery. Many suburban areas now provide all the essential services formerly concentrated in the city core; new outlying locations provide for
shopping needs, jobs, entertainment, medical care and the like.
The CBD has declined as the city core (Figures 5.2-5.5) and
declining densities combined with the loss of inner city jobs
has meant the collapse of mass transit (Figures 5.6-5.9). Population dispersion has been accompanied by an equally intensive
sorting-out process. Suburban and exurban communities are inter-
nally homogeneous, while highly differentiated from each other
along class, age and ethnic lines, just as the white suburbs are
differentiated in their turn from the central cities in which the
nation's blacks and other racial minorities are increasingly concentrated.

To some, for example political scientist Edward C.
Banfield, what has been happening is readily explainable
within the context of a growth and melting-pot theory of
the core-oriented industrial metropolis:

> Much of what has happened-- as well as of
> what is happening --in the typical city or metro-
> politan area can be understood in terms of three
> imperatives. The first is demographic: if the

population of a city increases, the city must
expand in one direction or another --up, down,
or from the centre outward. The second is technological: if it is feasible to transport large
numbers of people outward (by train, bus, and
automobile) but not upward or downward (by ele-
vator), the city must expand outward. The third
is economic: if the distribution of wealth and
income is such that some can afford new housing
and the time and money to commute considerable
distances to work while others cannot, the expanding periphery of the city must be occupied by
the first group (the "well-off") while the older,
inner parts of the city, where most of the jobs
are, must be occupied by the second group (the
"not well-off"). The word "imperatives" is used
to emphasize the inexorable, constraining charac-
ter of the three factors that together comprise
the logic of metropolitan growth.

Banfield's argument has some validity, but he misses what
is quintessential in the nature of contemporary change --
the emergence of a new urban form , of which the commuting
shifts are dramatic indicators. Throughout the twentieth century
all trends have pointed in the same direction. Every public
opinion survey has indicated that popular preferences are for
smaller places and lower densities, with richer environmental
amenities. The trend has been one leading unremittingly towards
the reversal of the processes of population concentration unleashed
by technologies of the industrial revolution, a reversal finally
achieved after 1970.

Let us trace out the logic of this argument with care.
Social scientists have been taught to believe that the structure of systems operates on behavior through the mediation
of cognition, and that structure is in turn composed of
those bundles and sequences of behavior that we term processes. In the United States, these relationships have a
particular form. The 1972 report of the President's
Domestic Council stated:

Patterns of growth are influenced by count-
less decisions made by individuals, families, and
businesses. These decisions are aimed at achieving

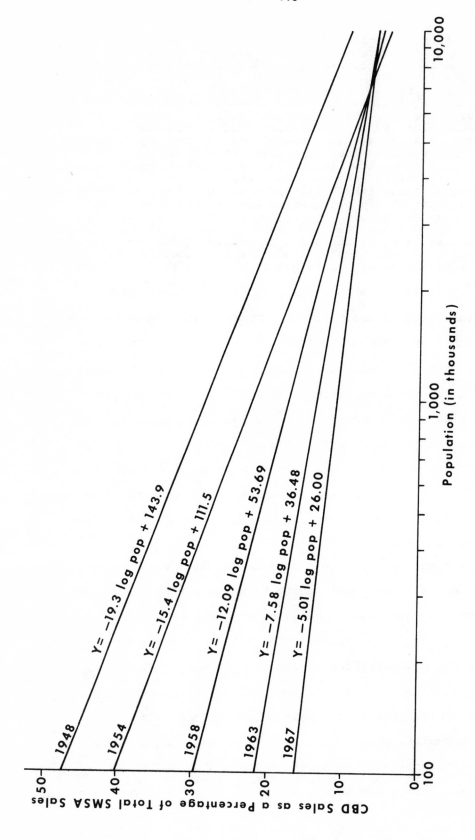

Figure 5.2. Decline of the CBD as a Shopping Nucleus: Nationwide Trends.

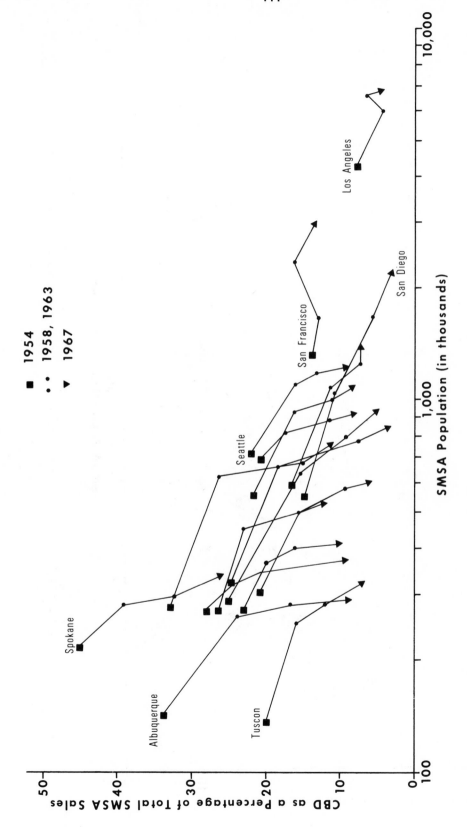

Figure 5.3. Decline of the CBD as a Shopping Nucleus: Western Cases.

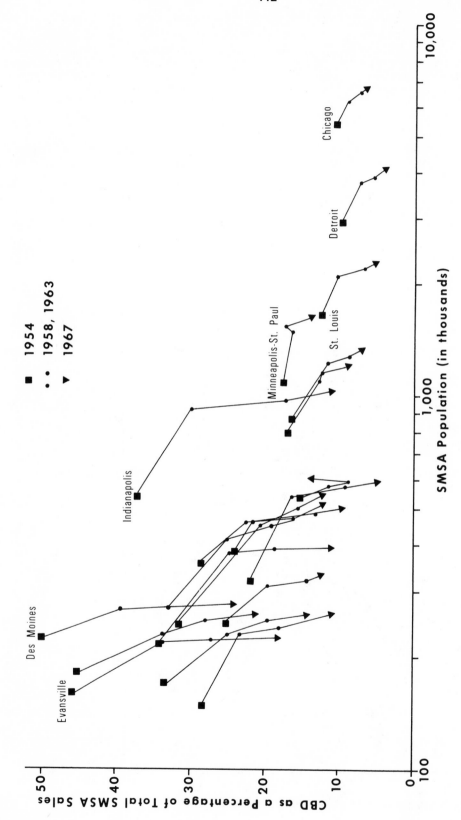

Figure 5.4.   Decline of the CBD as a Shopping Nucleus: Middle Western Cases.

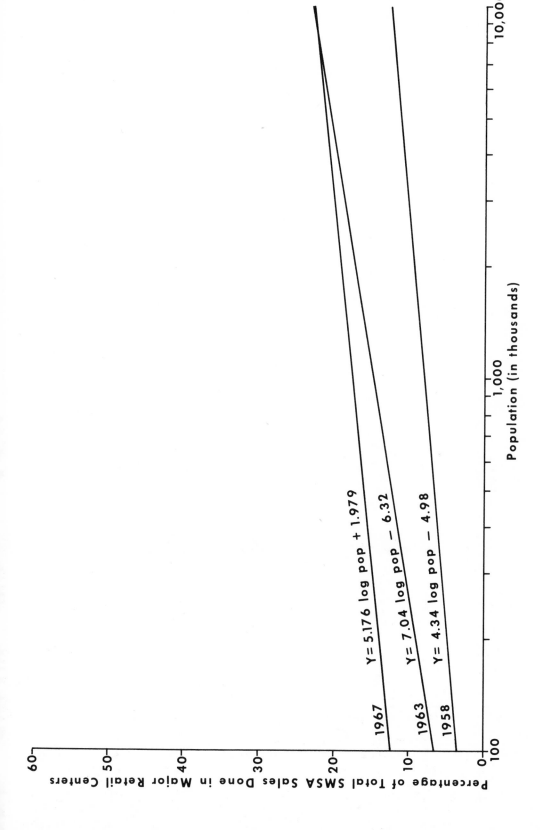

Figure 5.5. Rise of the Planned Shopping Center.

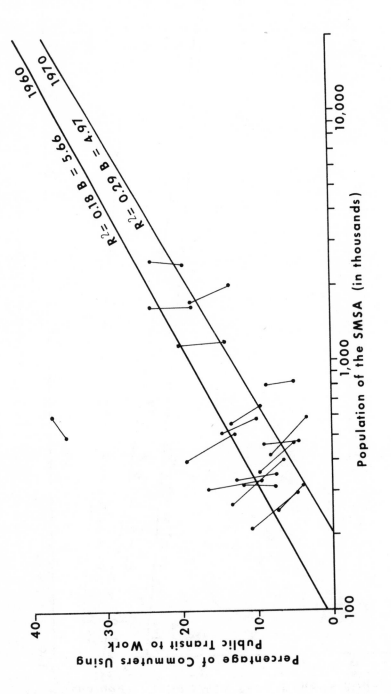

Figure 5.6.   Decline in Public Transit Usage, 1960-1970:
The Eastern Seaboard.

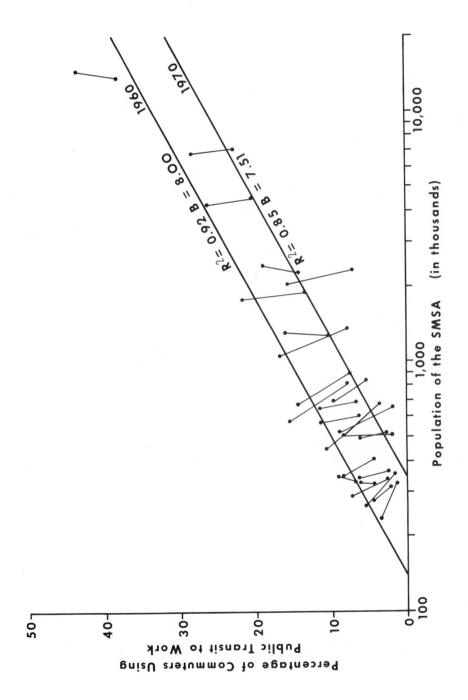

Figure 5.7 Decline in Public Transit Usage, 1960-1970:
The Northeastern Manufacturing Belt.

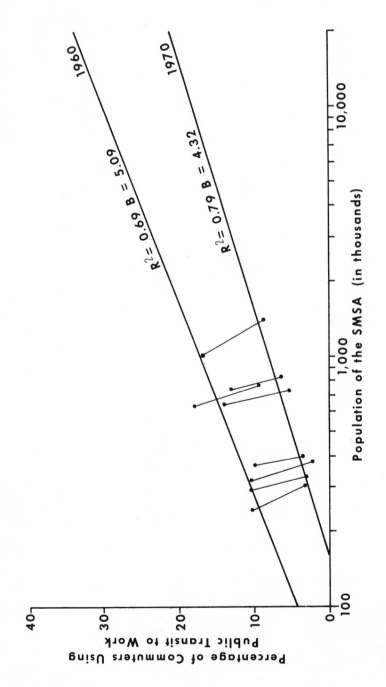

Figure 5.8. Decline in Public Transit Usage, 1960-1970: The South.

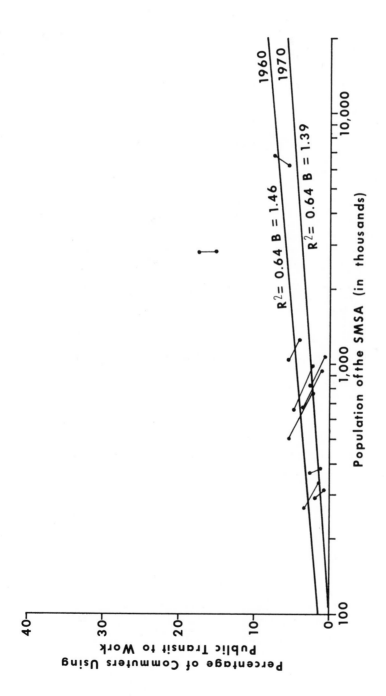

Figure 5.9. Decline in Public Transit Usage, 1960-1970:
California and the South-West.

the personal goals of those who make them, and
reflect healthy free choices in our society. Locational shifts by individuals reflect, in part,
a search for better job opportunities or for a
better climate, while businessmen relocate where
they can operate most efficiently and therefore
make the most profit.
    The factors that influence these decisions
may be susceptible to changes that will alter
the emerging growth patterns, but, in a Nation
that values freedom in the private sector and
democratic choice in the public, the decisions
themselves cannot be dictated.
    In many nations, the central government has
undertaken forceful, comprehensive policies to
control the process of growth. Similar policies
have not been adopted in the United States for
several reasons. Among the most important of
these is the form of government . . . (which)
preserves the ability of citizens to have a
major voice in determining policies that most
directly affect them . . . Another important
reason . . . is the sheer size of the Nation . . .
decisions can best reflect specific community
factors and objectives if they are made at the
local level. Accordingly, it is not feasible
for the highest level of government to design
policies for development that can operate suc-
cessful in all parts of the Nation.

This ideological preference for democratic pluralism

in a federal system has meant that the change has come

about less because of the governmental constraints imposed

upon choice, but because changing technology and communi-

cations media have changed both the structure of the sys-

tem and the role of cognitive mediation in individual

decision making.

What has happened is that four new driving forces have

emerged: the emergence of a nationally integrated society;

the emergence of the post-industrial political economy;

the rising cultural pluralism of the American public; and

the increasing role played by communications rather than

transportation in locational choice. These developments,

American planner Melvin Webber says, seem to be mutually

reinforcing. In concert, they are rapidly eroding tradi-

tional patterns of human interaction and settlement, born
in the industrial revolution.

Let us deal first with the emergence of a national society. What is meant here is Daniel Bell's widely-accepted
view that the United States has moved from merely being a
political entity comprising diverse regions held together
by a common symbolism to a true "national" society in which
changes taking place in one section of the society have an
immediate and repercussive effect in all others. Bell
credits the change to the revolution in communication and
transportation -- the rise of national network television,
coast-to-coast telephone dialing, simultaneous publication
of national news media and jet transport. The result is that
Americans share in common many daily experiences as a national
community, with the same retail chains, the same network
news programs, the same televised sports events, the same
type of large employers, either business or government.
For those many Americans who have become rootless through
frequent job transfers, the experiences of national community may be more frequent and real than experiences of
local community. This coalescence into a national society
has profound political implications. It has led to efforts
toward national, rather than regional and local solutions
to social problems and, by definition, the expansion of
central government into the field of social policy. It has
also led to consistent nationwide trends in decentralization and in racial polarization, whereas previously
regional differences in perception led to regional differences in behavior.

To these changes may be added the idea of a post-
industrial society -- one concerned with high-technology
high value added information processing activities. When
Colin Clark wrote The Conditions of Economic Progress in
1940 he charted changing employment structures alongside
a variety of indices of economic development, showing the
progressive shift in industrial nations from primary occu-
pations to secondary (manufacturing) and to the tertiary
(distributive and administrative) sectors as sources of growth.
More recently, Daniel Bell has popularized the idea of the
emergence of quaternary and quinary sources of growth in a
post-industrial society that has five dimensions: creation of a service economy; the pre-eminence of the profes-
sional and technical class; the centrality of theoretical
knowledge as the source of innovation and policy formula-
tion in society; the possibility of self-sustaining technological growth and transformation; and the creation of a
new intellectual technology centering on information and
information processing. Such ingredients of a post-industrial economy tend to be "footloose" rather than transport-
oriented either to raw materials or markets, and they use
high-grade highly skilled high-priced labor. Amenities --
preferred residential settings -- for this labor loom ever
larger in the locational decisions of the firms, and the
employees form part of a national rather than any local
labor market.

Consider, then, the problem of cultural pluralism.
Race and ethnicity now dominate the public life of most
American cities. Residential patterns, neighborhood

schools, shops, community newspapers, hospitals, old-age
homes, cemeteries, savings and loan associations, charita-
ble, fraternal and cultural organizations attest to the role
of ethnicity. Public decisions affecting home ownership,
schools, public housing, police, shopkeepers, allocation
of state and federal funds and welfare are increasingly
perceived in terms of nationality-group or racial-group
attachments. Ethnicity defines interest groups in the city,
is recognized in the public decision-making process, is
rewarded and encouraged by the politicians and established
institutions.

These patterns, formerly varying substantially from
one region of the country to another, are now nationwide
in their consistency.

What are the underlying social dynamics? David McClellan
in The Achieving Society has pointed out that the drive for
achievement is a variable of key importance within the "mainstream" American culture -- a culture in which status and
self-respect come from what a person does, in the material
world, rather than from his ancestry or his holiness.

Social and spatial mobility are one key, built into and
interrelated within individuals' nervous systems as a result
of the attitudes and pressures of the culture. Children
must "get ahead" and "improve themselves" through education.
Workers must ascend the job hierarchy. Earnings must be
spent on the best possible homes and material possessions in
the best possible neighborhoods. Any increase in job or
financial status must be matched by a move to a better neigh-

borhood. "Downgrading" of the neighborhood through entry
of those perceived to be of lower status must be fought,
and if it cannot be contained one must flee to avoid the
inevitable resulting loss of status.

When a family seeks a home they look for other things
too, of course. The prime decision relates to the home--
its price and type, determined by achieved status, and by the
family's needs at the stage in life cycle that the choice
is made. Since a large number of homes qualify within
these first bounds for all but the poor, neighborhood
considerations then come into play. The scale of urban regions
has brought complexity and the rapidity of urban change
produces uncertainty and insecurity. The whole is too large
for the individual to comprehend. In the search for self-
identity in a mass society, he seeks to minimize disorder
by living in a neighborhood in which life is comprehensible
and social relations predictable. Indeed , he moves out of
"his" neighborhood when he can no longer predict the consequences of a particular pattern of behavior. He seeks an
enclave of relative homogeneity: a territory free from status competition because his neighbors are "just like him";
a turf compatible in outlook because his neighbors are at
similar stages in the life cycle; a safe area, free from
status-challenging ethnic or racial minorities; a haven from
complexity, to be protected and safeguarded by whatever
means: legal, institutional, and frequently illegal violence,
each symptom of defensive territoriality protecting that
which has been achieved.

The resulting homogeneous niches are exquisitely reticulated in geographic space. High-status neighborhoods seek out zones of superior residential amenity near water, trees, and higher ground, free from the risk of floods and away from smoke and factories, and increasingly in the furthest accessible peripheries. Middle-status neighborhoods press as close to the high status as feasible. To the low-status resident, least able to afford costs of commuting, are relinquished the least desirable areas adjacent to industrial zones radiating from the centre of the city along railroads and rivers, the zones of highest pollution and the oldest, most deteriorated homes. In the cores of the ghettos, widespread abandonment of properties marks the extremes of neglect.

What all of this means is that the black resident of the metropolis finds himself in a central-city ghetto abandoned both by whites and, increasingly, by employment. The flight of white city-dwellers into the expanding peripheries of metropolitan regions is an accelerating phenomenon as minorities move towards majority status in the city centers, and all evidence points to industry following population into the suburbs at an accelerating rate. The exurban ringes of many of the nation's urban regions have now pushed one hundred miles and more from the traditional city centers. More important, the core-orientation implied in the use of the terms "central city" and "central county" is fast on the wane. Today's urban systems appear to be multi-nodal multi-connected social systems in action, in which the centralization of the population into metropolitan areas has been counterbalanced by a reverse thrust of decentralization. The situation is very different from the period at the end of the nineteenth century from which we derive the concept of urbanization. Decentralization and an outward urge have replaced centralization and core orientation; differentiation and segregation substitute for the integrative role of the melting pot.

These trends and changes should, of course, be put back into the context of changing transportation and communications technology. Concentrated industrial metropoli only developed because proximity meant lower transportation and communication costs for those interdependent specialists who had to interact with each other frequently or intensively, and could only do so on a face to face basis. But shortened distances also meant higher densities and costs of congestion, high rent, loss of privacy, and the like. What we are seeing today is the provision of the ability to communicate effectively without the need for face-to-face transactions. The question that then arises is whether high-scale societies may develop which are not city-based, in the sense of providing for intense face-to-face interactions? It was the demand for ease of communication that first brought men into cities. Could long-distance communication combine with the space-spanning capacities of the new communications technologies to concoct a solvent that could dissolve the city?

What is being focussed on here is what J. J. Servan-Schreiber has called the essence of "The American Challenge", the compression of time and space in a way that was inconceivable even 10 years ago, with attendant intensification of human experience alongside lessing demands for movement

because of centralized information sources and instantaneous
communication. Servan-Schreiber points out that the time-
lag between invention and manufacture was 112 years for
photography (1727-1839), 56 years for the telephone (1820-
76), 35 years for radio (1867-1902), 15 years for radar (1925-
40), 12 years for television (1922-34), 5 years for the
transistor (1948-53) and 3 years for the integrated cir-
cuit (1958-61). This convergence is the most salient characteristic of American life today.

Virtually all the technological developments of industrial times have had the effect of reducing the constraints
of geographic space. Within the urbanized sectors of the
society, the developments in transportation and communications, especially, have made it possible for each genera-
tion to live farther from raw materials resources, for
information users to rely upon information sources that
are spatially distant.

During this century, the automobile and the telephone
have made possible the suburb and, when combined with the
railroad and the airplane, the development of the western
reaches of the continent. Contemporary developments in communications fit directly, onto this historic trend line
that was traced earlier by the pony express, the telegraph,
and the telephone. By supplying better channels for trans-
mitting information and meaning, they will improve the
capacities of partners in social intercourse to transact
their business at great distances. The prospectus is clear.
Many of the constraints that have limited locators to choices

among metropolitan areas and places within them continue to be relaxed. The consequence can only be still further dispersion, still more widespread commuting fields, and still further changes in the nature of settlement in the United States.

THE METROPOLITAN MAP SET

For index see Table 3.1, pp. 41-43

COMMUTING TO THE CBD IN 1970

NO DATA COLLECTED

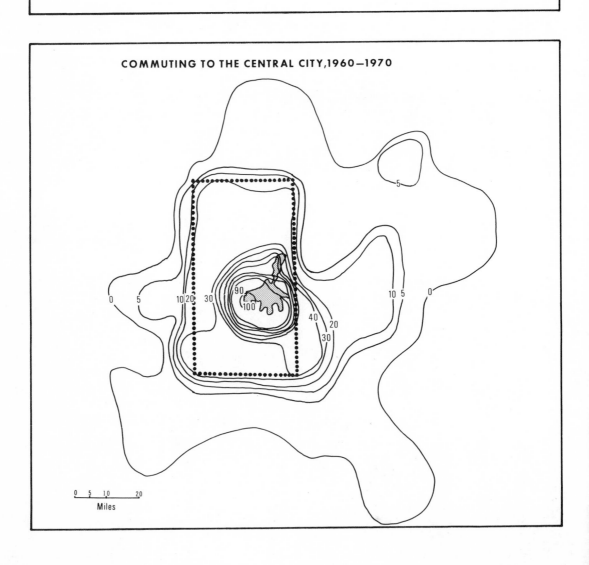

COMMUTING TO THE CENTRAL CITY, 1960—1970

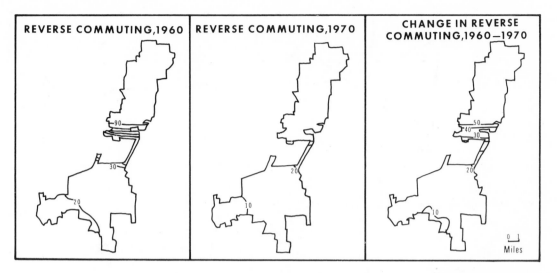

REVERSE COMMUTING, 1960

REVERSE COMMUTING, 1970

CHANGE IN REVERSE COMMUTING, 1960—1970

ABILENE, TX.

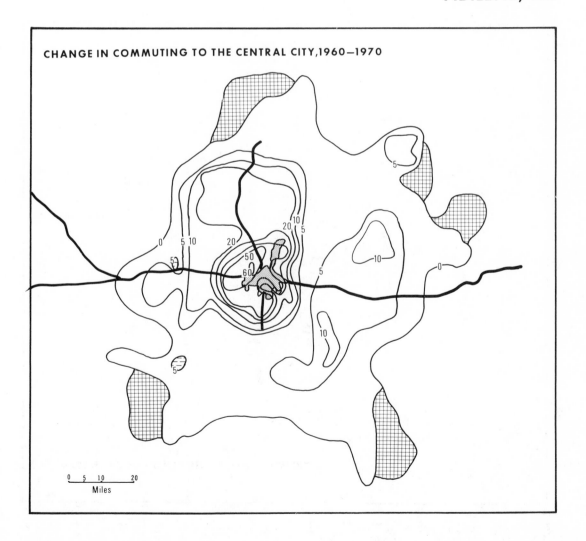

CHANGE IN COMMUTING TO THE CENTRAL CITY, 1960—1970

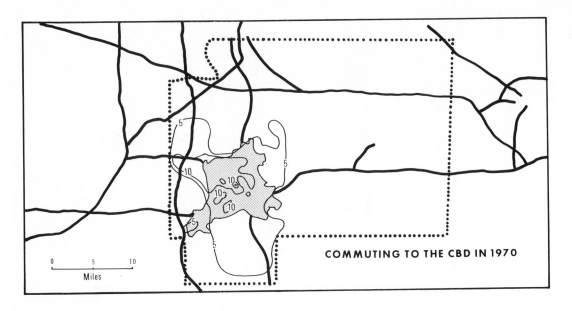

COMMUTING TO THE CBD IN 1970

0   5   10
Miles

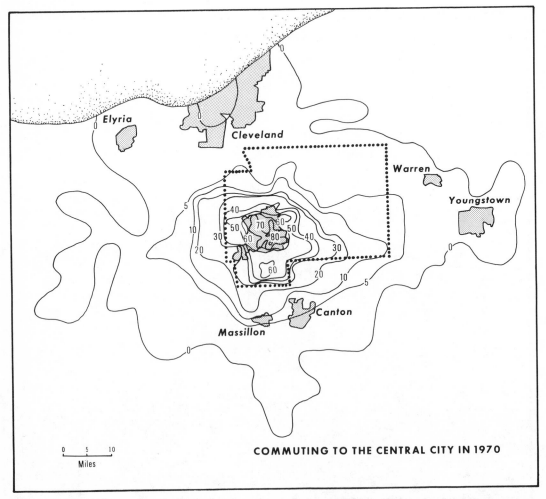

COMMUTING TO THE CENTRAL CITY IN 1970

0   5   10
Miles

133

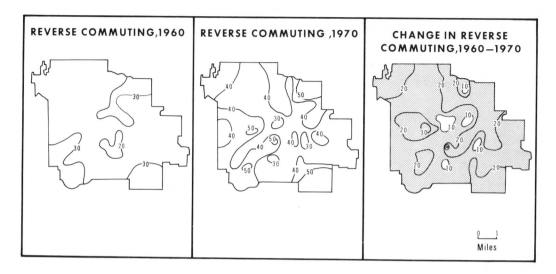

REVERSE COMMUTING, 1960

REVERSE COMMUTING, 1970

CHANGE IN REVERSE
COMMUTING, 1960—1970

0   1
Miles

AKRON, OH.

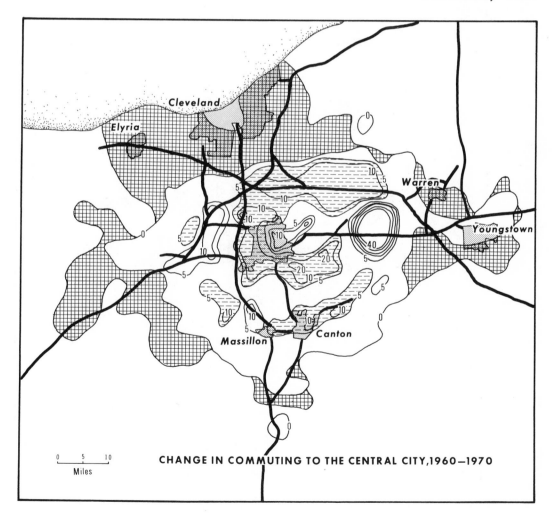

CHANGE IN COMMUTING TO THE CENTRAL CITY, 1960—1970

0   5   10
Miles

COMMUTING TO THE CBD IN 1970

NO DATA COLLECTED

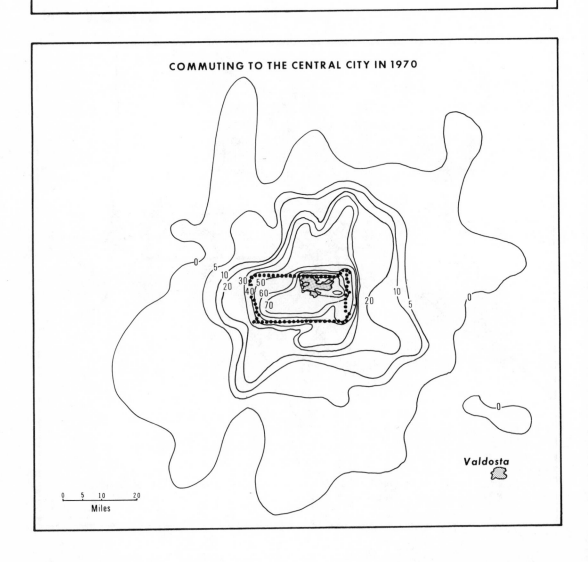

COMMUTING TO THE CENTRAL CITY IN 1970

Valdosta

0   5   10   20
Miles

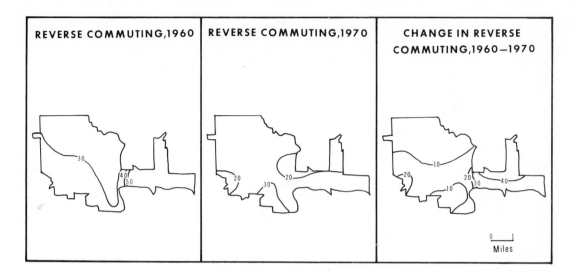

REVERSE COMMUTING, 1960

REVERSE COMMUTING, 1970

CHANGE IN REVERSE COMMUTING, 1960—1970

ALBANY, GA.

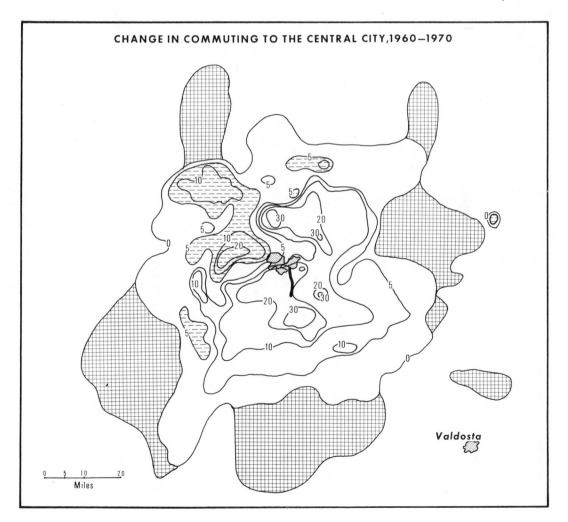

CHANGE IN COMMUTING TO THE CENTRAL CITY, 1960—1970

Valdosta

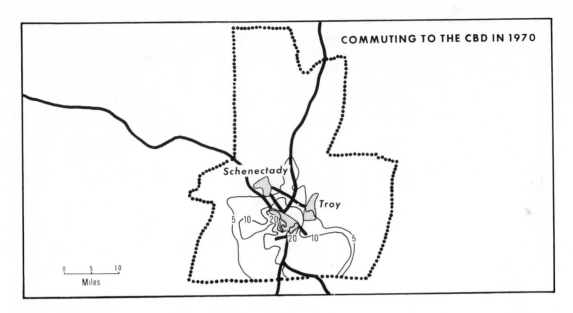

COMMUTING TO THE CBD IN 1970

Schenectady

Troy

Miles

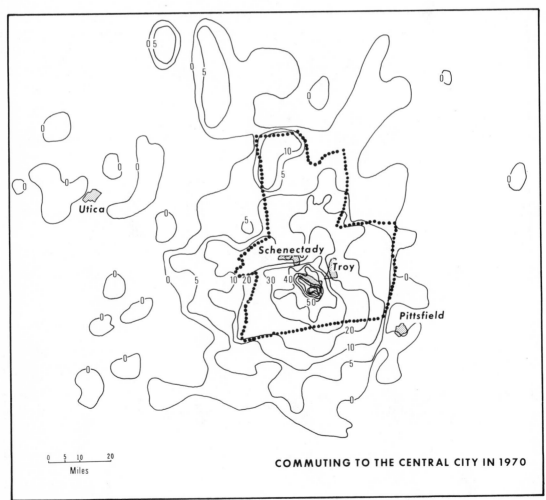

Utica

Schenectady

Troy

Pittsfield

Miles

COMMUTING TO THE CENTRAL CITY IN 1970

137

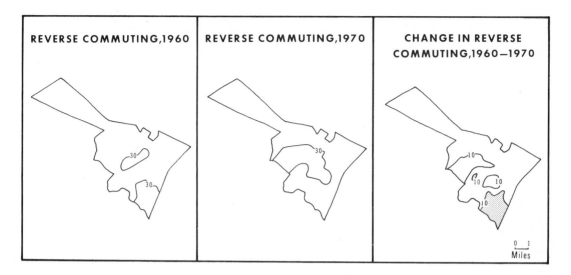

REVERSE COMMUTING, 1960 | REVERSE COMMUTING, 1970 | CHANGE IN REVERSE COMMUTING, 1960–1970

ALBANY, N.Y.

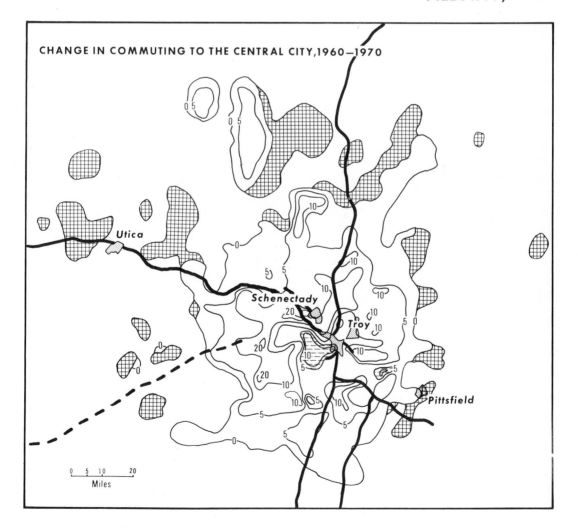

CHANGE IN COMMUTING TO THE CENTRAL CITY, 1960–1970

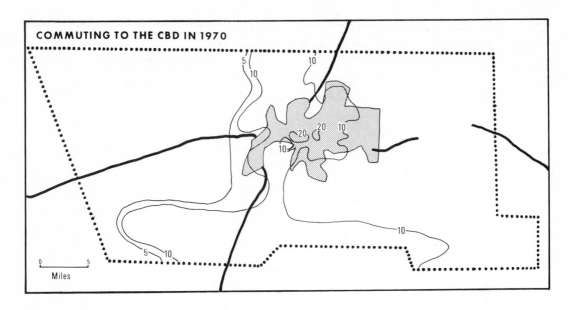

COMMUTING TO THE CBD IN 1970

Miles

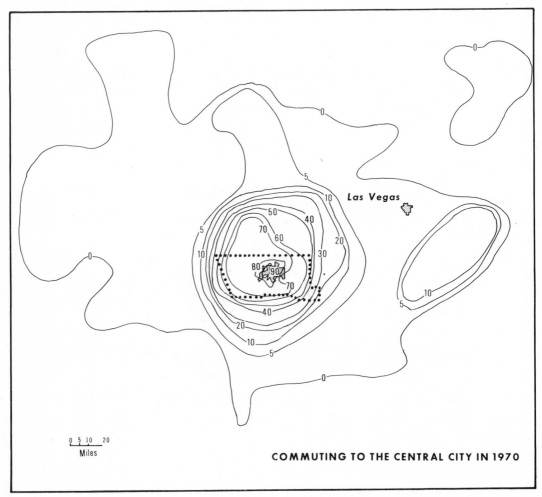

Las Vegas

Miles

COMMUTING TO THE CENTRAL CITY IN 1970

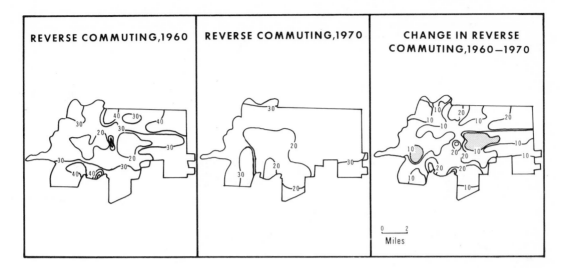

REVERSE COMMUTING, 1960

REVERSE COMMUTING, 1970

CHANGE IN REVERSE COMMUTING, 1960—1970

ALBUQUERQUE, N.M.

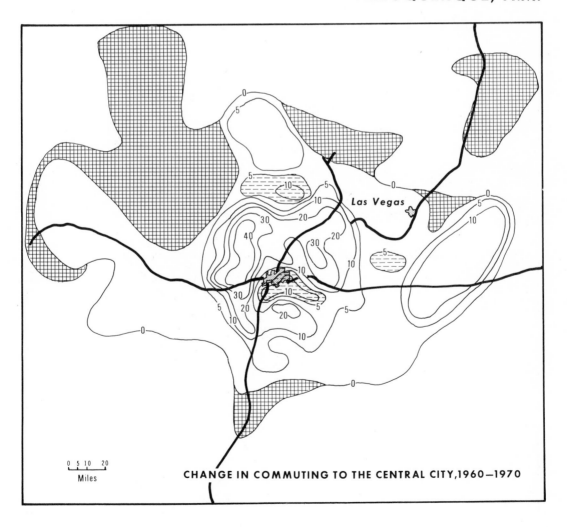

CHANGE IN COMMUTING TO THE CENTRAL CITY, 1960—1970

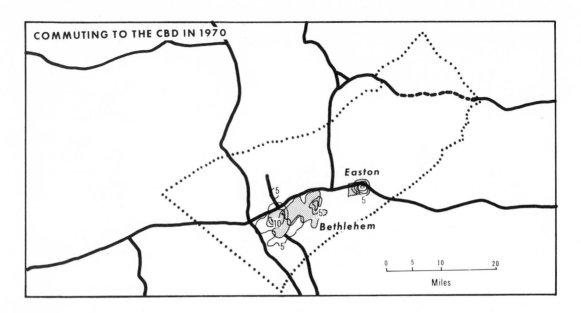

COMMUTING TO THE CBD IN 1970

Easton

Bethlehem

0 5 10 20
Miles

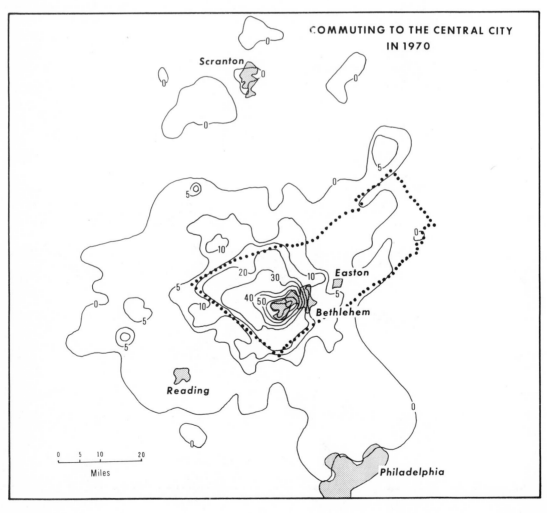

COMMUTING TO THE CENTRAL CITY
IN 1970

Scranton

Easton

Bethlehem

Reading

Philadelphia

0 5 10 20
Miles

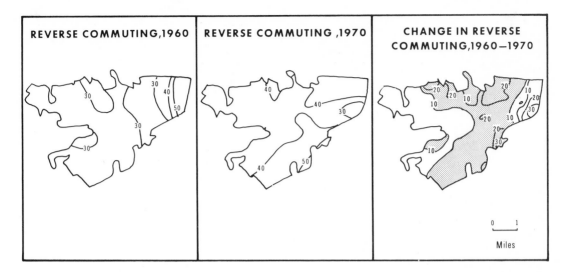

REVERSE COMMUTING, 1960

REVERSE COMMUTING, 1970

CHANGE IN REVERSE COMMUTING, 1960—1970

ALLENTOWN, PA.

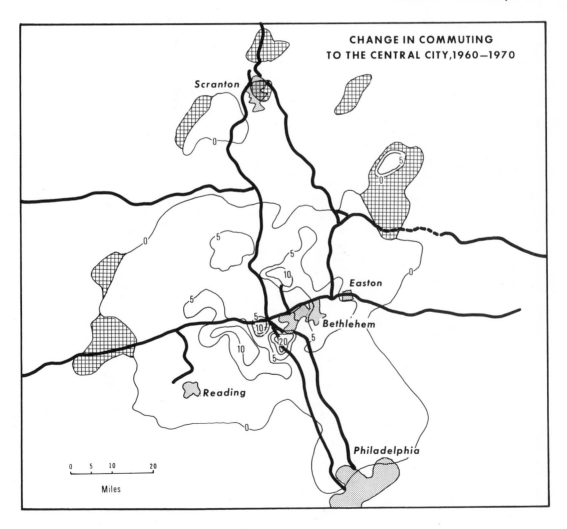

CHANGE IN COMMUTING TO THE CENTRAL CITY, 1960—1970

COMMUTING TO THE CBD IN 1970

NO DATA COLLECTED

COMMUTING TO THE CENTRAL CITY IN 1970

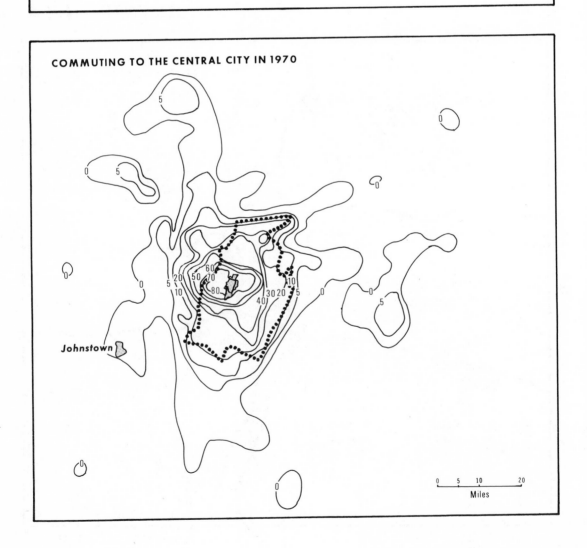

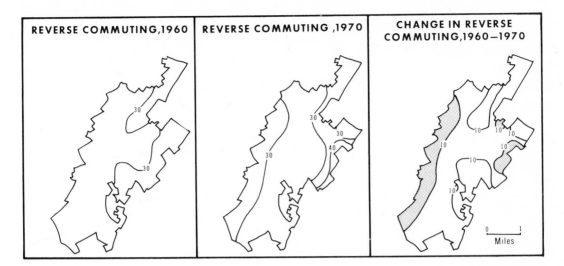

REVERSE COMMUTING,1960   REVERSE COMMUTING ,1970   CHANGE IN REVERSE COMMUTING,1960—1970

ALTOONA, PA.

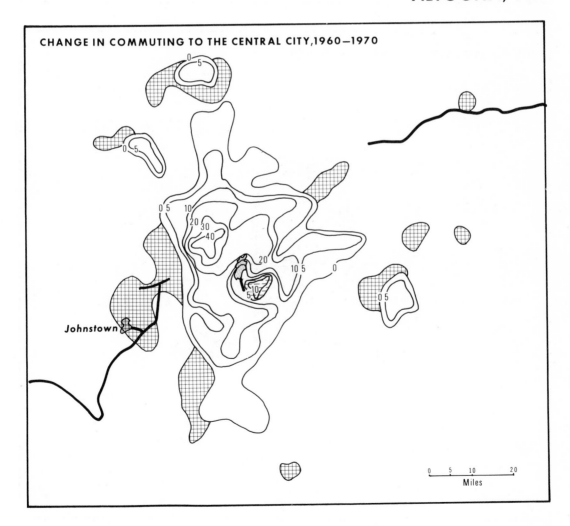

CHANGE IN COMMUTING TO THE CENTRAL CITY,1960—1970

Johnstown

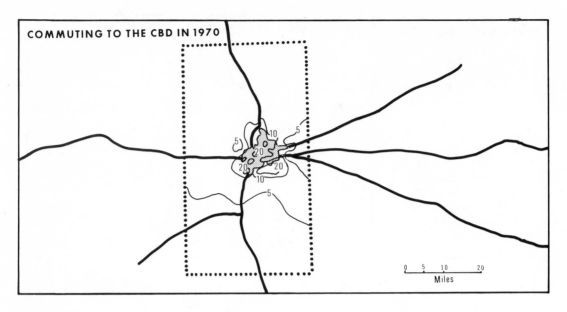

COMMUTING TO THE CBD IN 1970

0 5 10 20
Miles

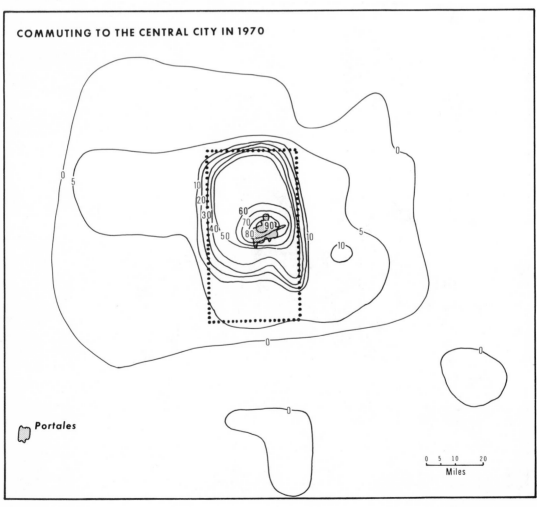

COMMUTING TO THE CENTRAL CITY IN 1970

Portales

0 5 10 20
Miles

145

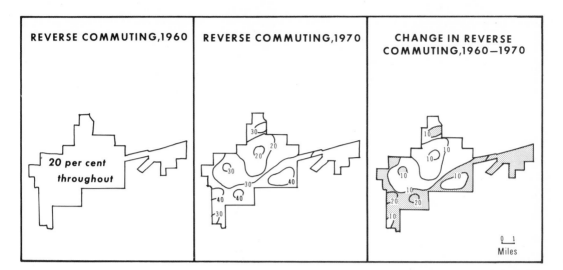

AMARILLO, TX.

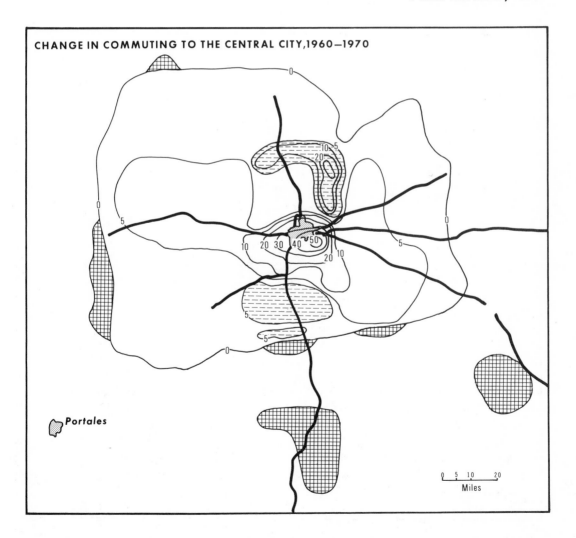

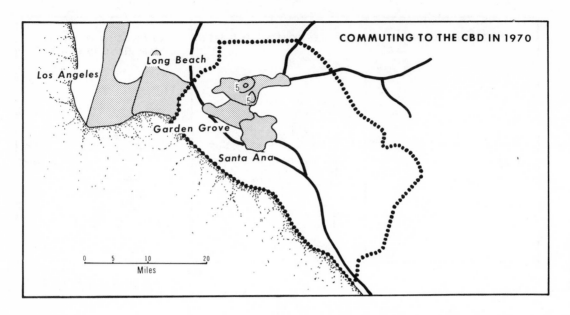

COMMUTING TO THE CBD IN 1970

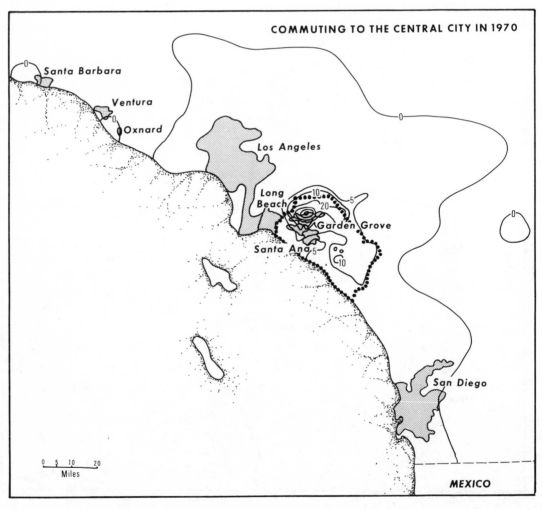

COMMUTING TO THE CENTRAL CITY IN 1970

REVERSE COMMUTING,1960	REVERSE COMMUTING ,1970	CHANGE IN REVERSE COMMUTING,1960—1970
NO DATA COLLECTED		NO DATA COLLECTED

80

60

70

80

80

80

0 1
Miles

ANAHEIM, CA.

CHANGE IN COMMUTING TO THE CENTRAL CITY,1960—1970

NO DATA COLLECTED

COMMUTING TO THE CBD IN 1970

NO DATA COLLECTED

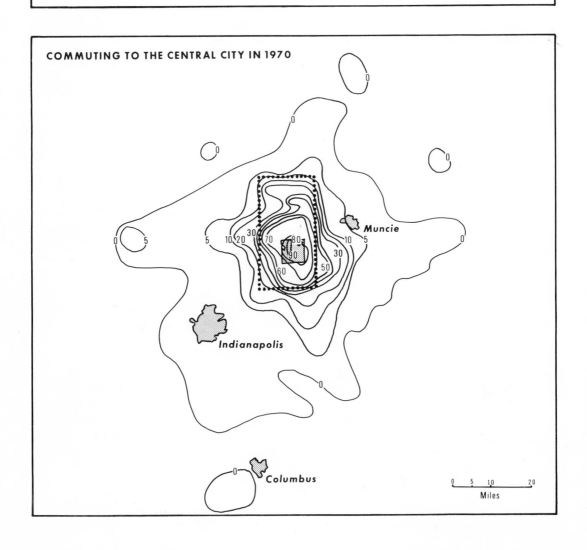

COMMUTING TO THE CENTRAL CITY IN 1970

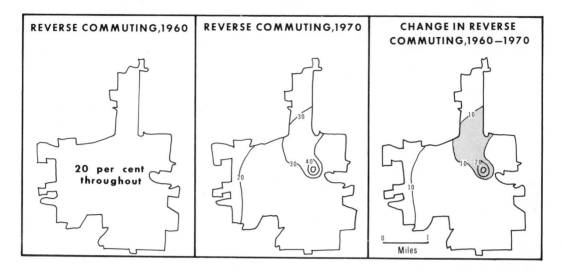

| REVERSE COMMUTING, 1960 | REVERSE COMMUTING, 1970 | CHANGE IN REVERSE COMMUTING, 1960—1970 |

20 per cent throughout

ANDERSON, IN.

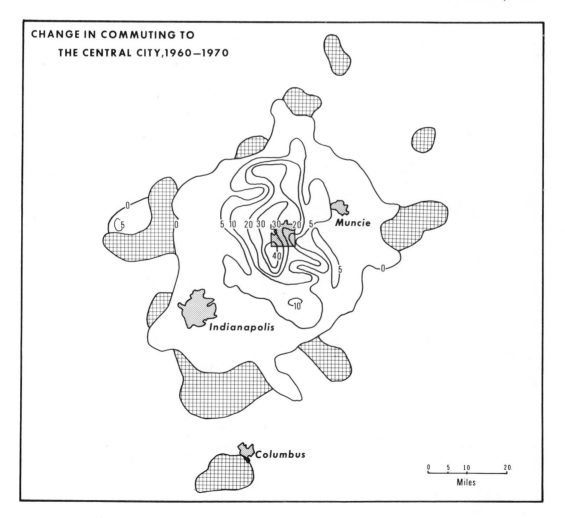

CHANGE IN COMMUTING TO THE CENTRAL CITY, 1960—1970

150

COMMUTING TO THE CBD IN 1970

NO DATA COLLECTED

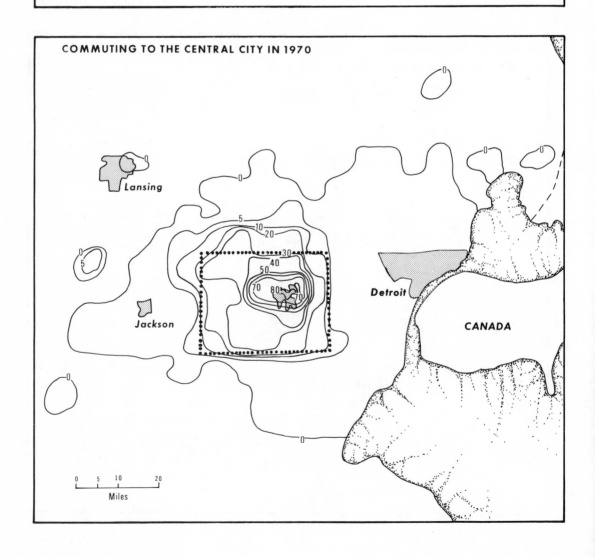

COMMUTING TO THE CENTRAL CITY IN 1970

Lansing

Jackson

Detroit

CANADA

0 5 10 20
Miles

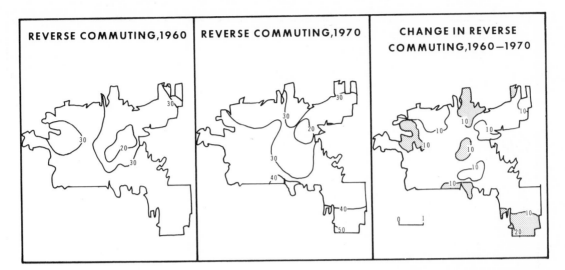

REVERSE COMMUTING, 1960

REVERSE COMMUTING, 1970

CHANGE IN REVERSE COMMUTING, 1960–1970

ANN ARBOR, MI.

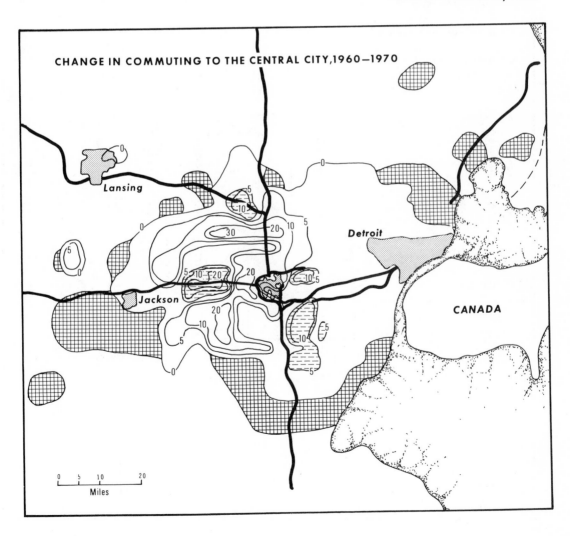

CHANGE IN COMMUTING TO THE CENTRAL CITY, 1960–1970

Lansing

Detroit

Jackson

CANADA

Miles

COMMUTING TO THE CBD IN 1970

NO DATA COLLECTED

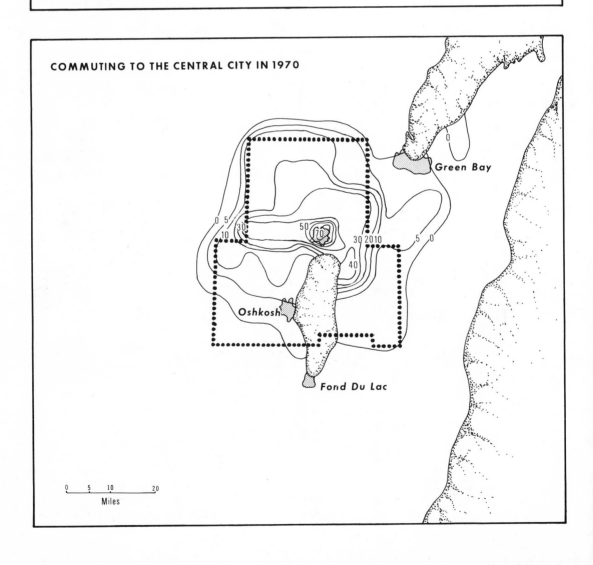

COMMUTING TO THE CENTRAL CITY IN 1970

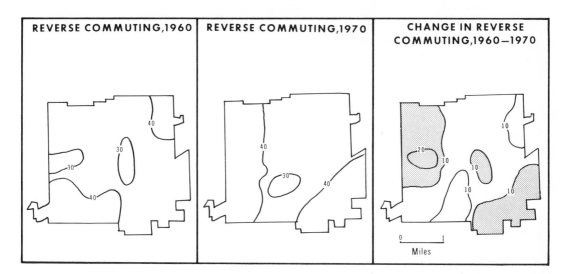

REVERSE COMMUTING, 1960

REVERSE COMMUTING, 1970

CHANGE IN REVERSE COMMUTING, 1960–1970

APPLETON, WI.

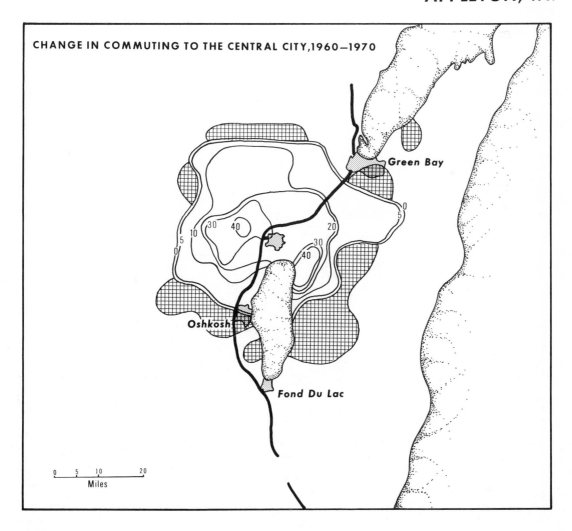

CHANGE IN COMMUTING TO THE CENTRAL CITY, 1960–1970

COMMUTING TO THE CBD IN 1970

NO DATA COLLECTED

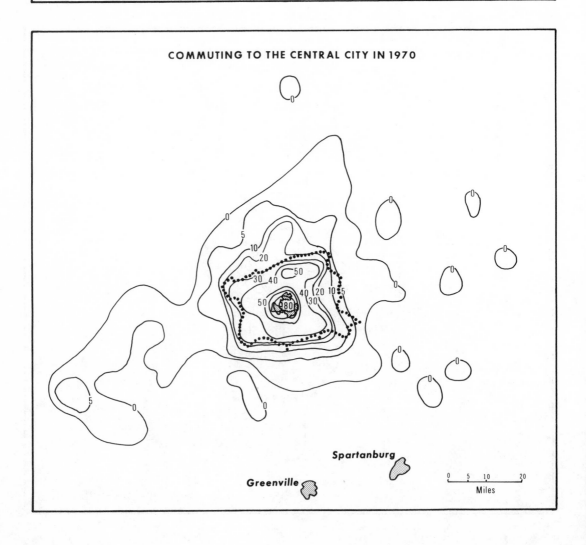

COMMUTING TO THE CENTRAL CITY IN 1970

Spartanburg

Greenville

0   5   10   20
Miles

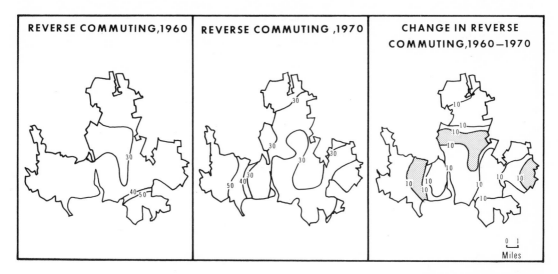

REVERSE COMMUTING,1960

REVERSE COMMUTING ,1970

CHANGE IN REVERSE COMMUTING,1960–1970

ASHEVILLE, N.C.

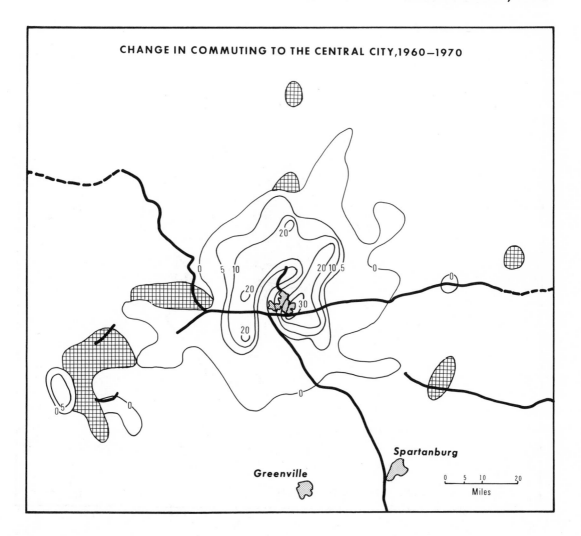

CHANGE IN COMMUTING TO THE CENTRAL CITY,1960–1970

Spartanburg

Greenville

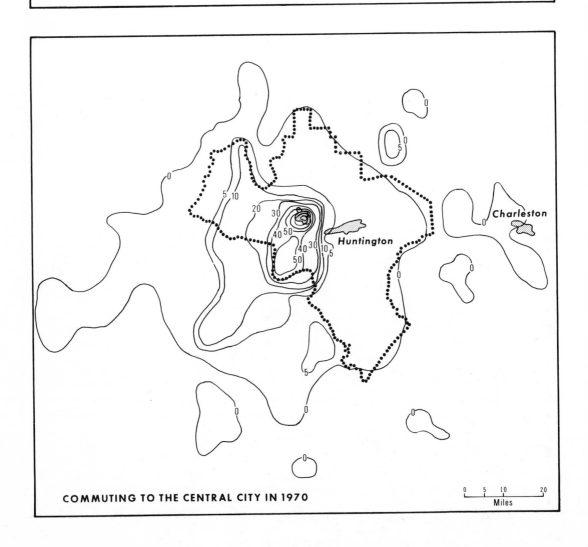

COMMUTING TO THE CBD IN 1970

NO DATA COLLECTED

COMMUTING TO THE CENTRAL CITY IN 1970

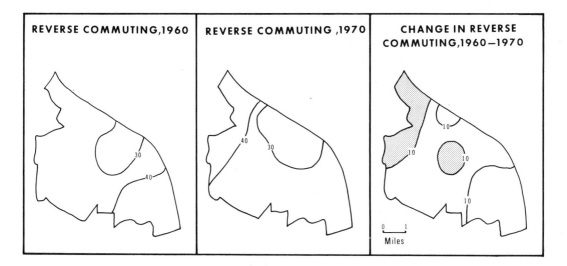

REVERSE COMMUTING, 1960

REVERSE COMMUTING, 1970

CHANGE IN REVERSE COMMUTING, 1960—1970

ASHLAND, KY.

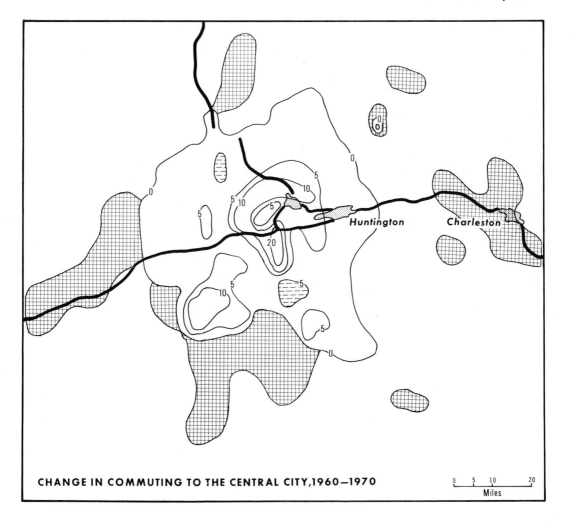

CHANGE IN COMMUTING TO THE CENTRAL CITY, 1960—1970

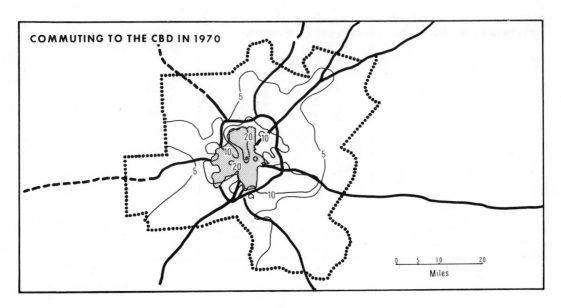

COMMUTING TO THE CBD IN 1970

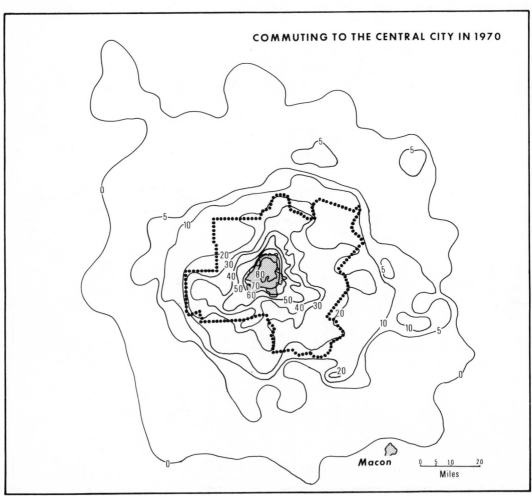

COMMUTING TO THE CENTRAL CITY IN 1970

Macon

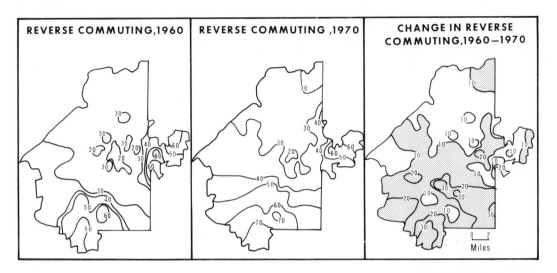

ATLANTA, GA.

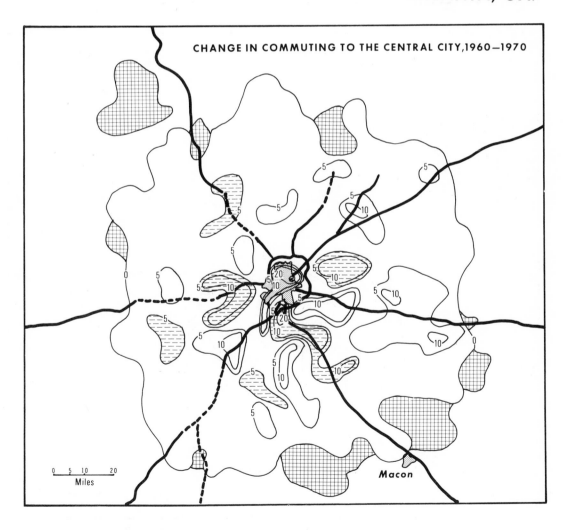

CHANGE IN COMMUTING TO THE CENTRAL CITY,1960—1970

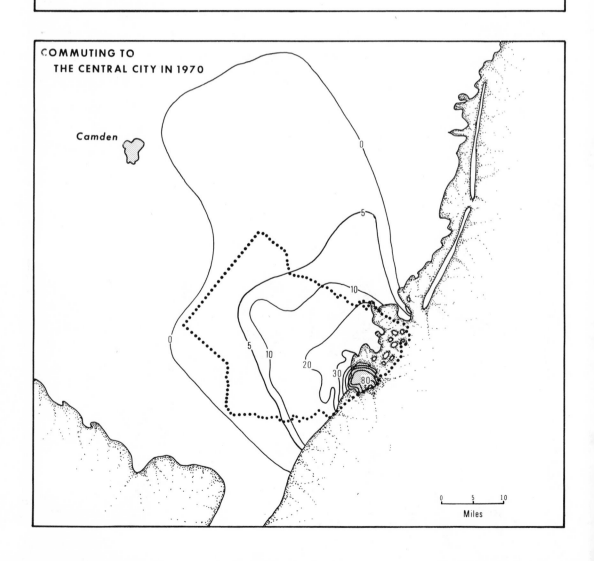

COMMUTING TO THE CBD IN 1970

NO DATA COLLECTED

COMMUTING TO
THE CENTRAL CITY IN 1970

Camden

0
5
10
0
5
10
20
30
80

0   5   10
Miles

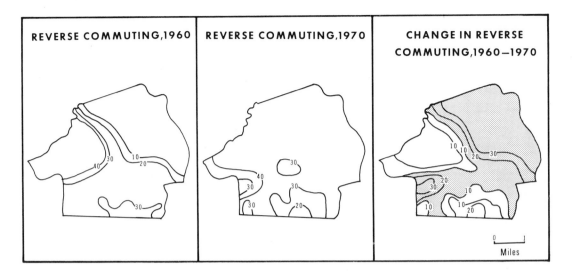

REVERSE COMMUTING,1960 | REVERSE COMMUTING,1970 | CHANGE IN REVERSE COMMUTING,1960–1970

ATLANTIC CITY, N.J.

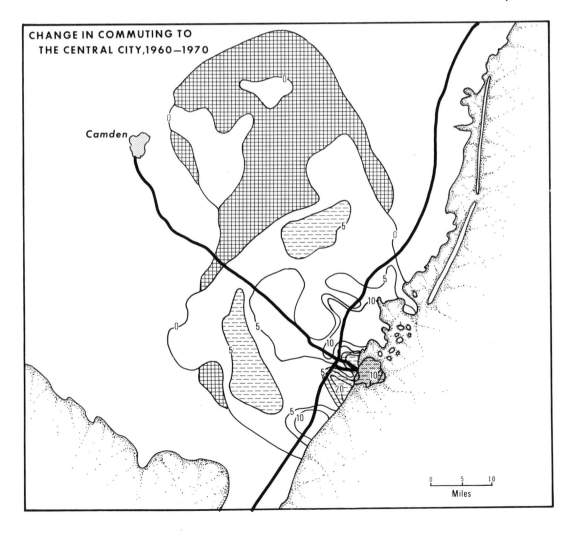

CHANGE IN COMMUTING TO THE CENTRAL CITY,1960–1970

Camden

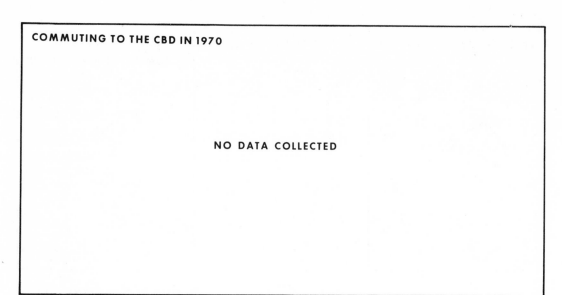

COMMUTING TO THE CBD IN 1970

NO DATA COLLECTED

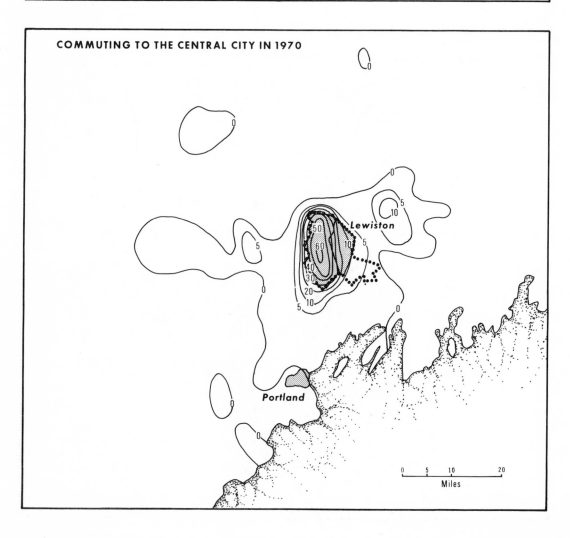

COMMUTING TO THE CENTRAL CITY IN 1970

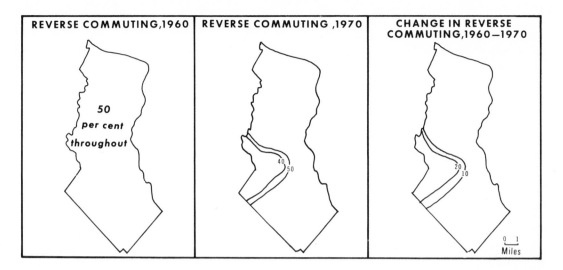

| REVERSE COMMUTING,1960 | REVERSE COMMUTING ,1970 | CHANGE IN REVERSE COMMUTING,1960—1970 |

50 per cent throughout

AUBURN, ME.

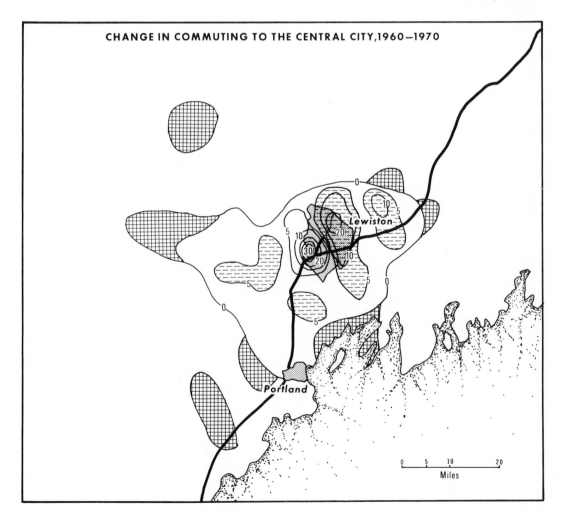

CHANGE IN COMMUTING TO THE CENTRAL CITY,1960—1970

COMMUTING TO THE CBD IN 1970

NO DATA COLLECTED

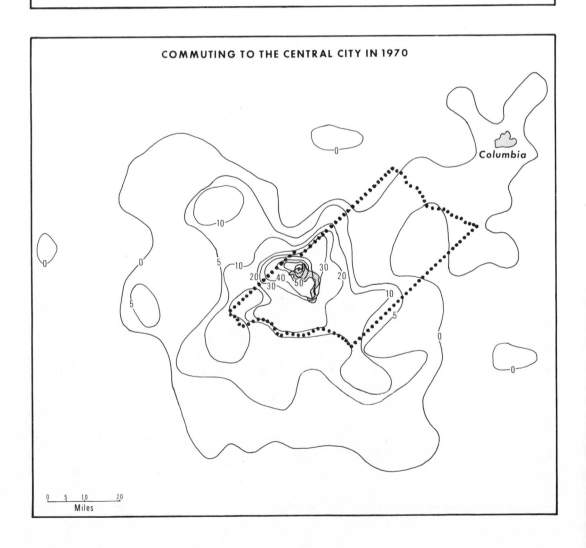

COMMUTING TO THE CENTRAL CITY IN 1970

165

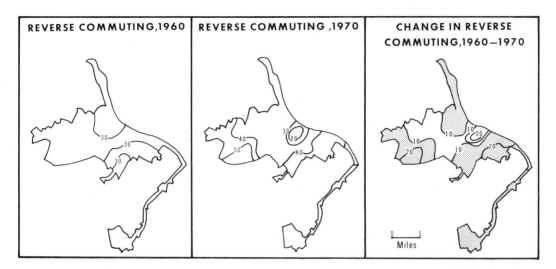

| REVERSE COMMUTING,1960 | REVERSE COMMUTING ,1970 | CHANGE IN REVERSE COMMUTING,1960—1970 |

AUGUSTA, GA.

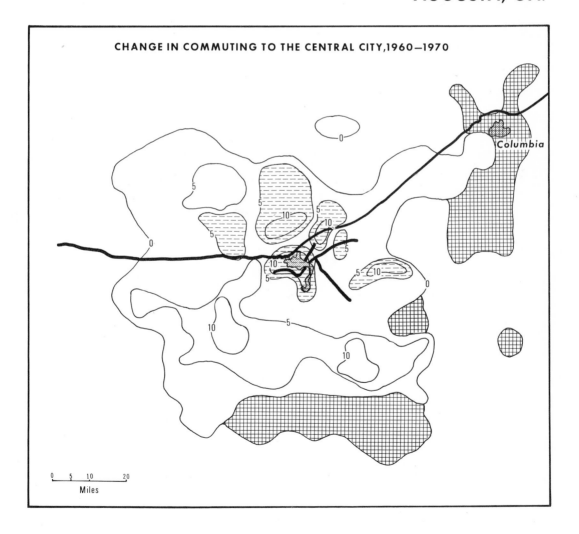

CHANGE IN COMMUTING TO THE CENTRAL CITY,1960—1970

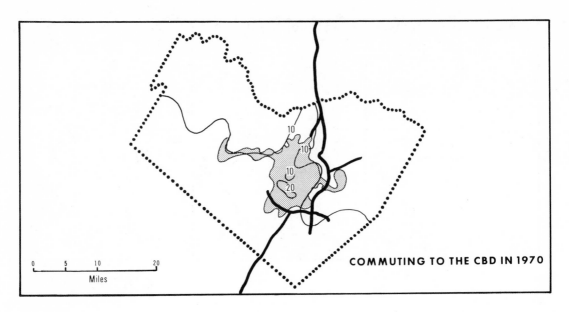

COMMUTING TO THE CBD IN 1970

0   5   10   20
Miles

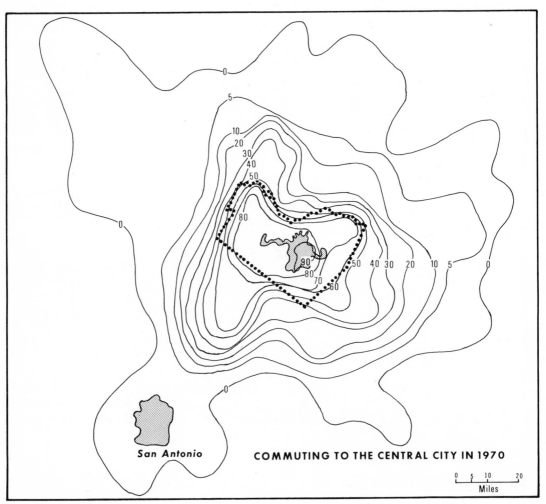

San Antonio

COMMUTING TO THE CENTRAL CITY IN 1970

0   5   10   20
Miles

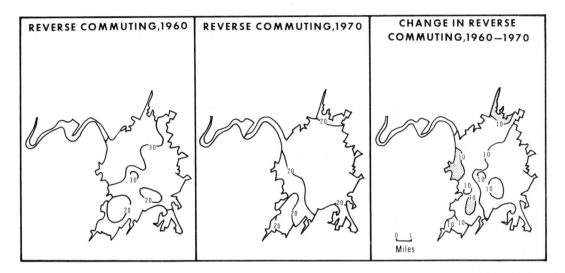

| REVERSE COMMUTING,1960 | REVERSE COMMUTING,1970 | CHANGE IN REVERSE COMMUTING,1960–1970 |

AUSTIN, TX.

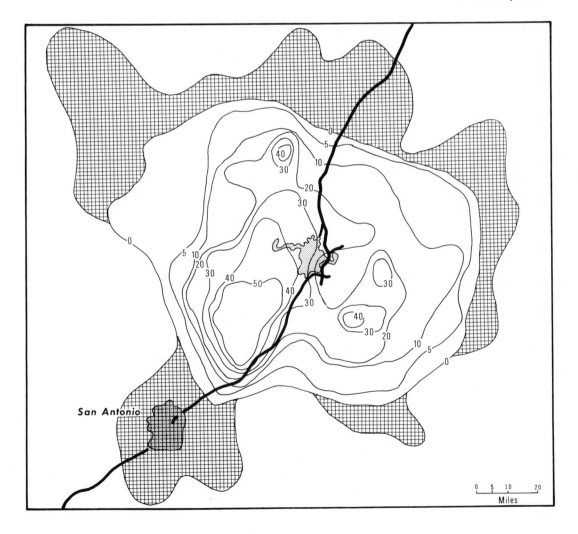

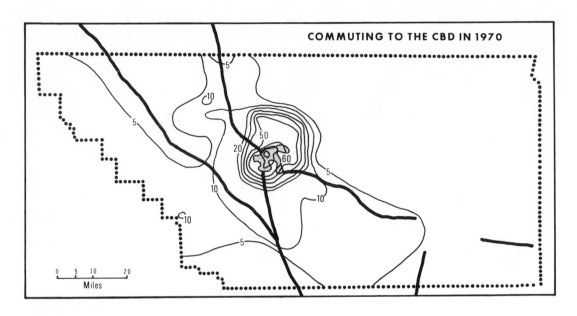

COMMUTING TO THE CBD IN 1970

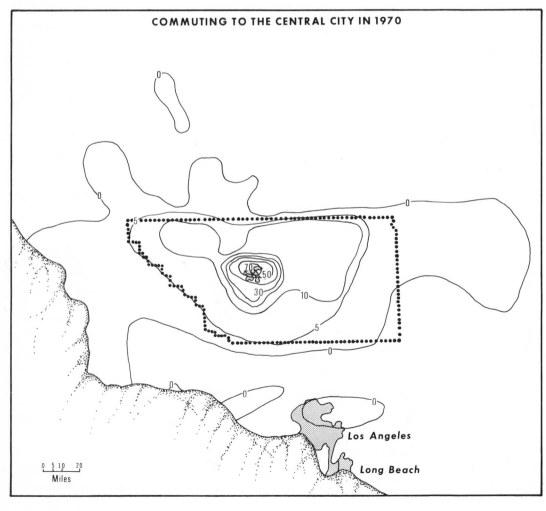

COMMUTING TO THE CENTRAL CITY IN 1970

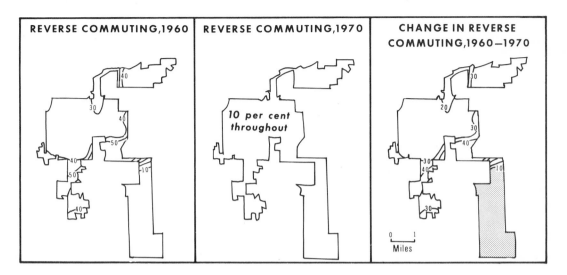

BAKERSFIELD, CA.

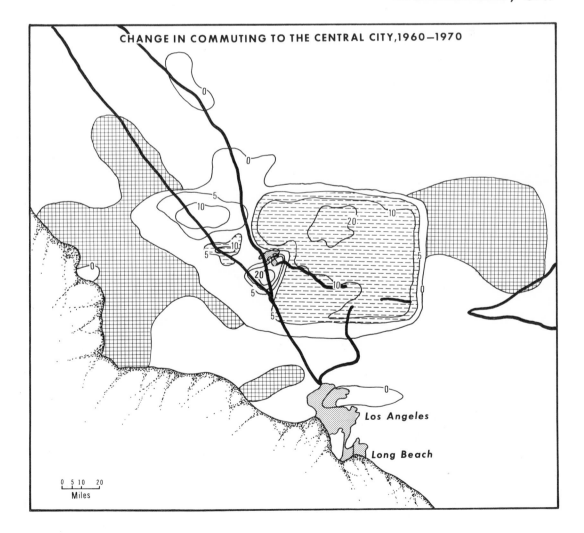

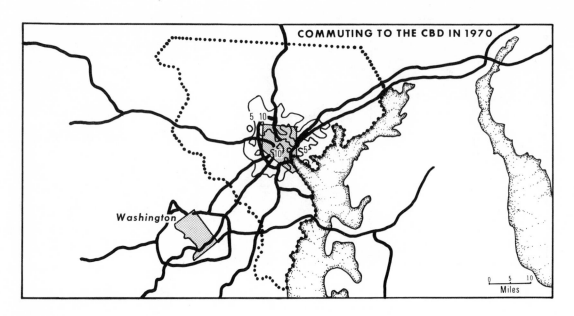

COMMUTING TO THE CBD IN 1970

Washington

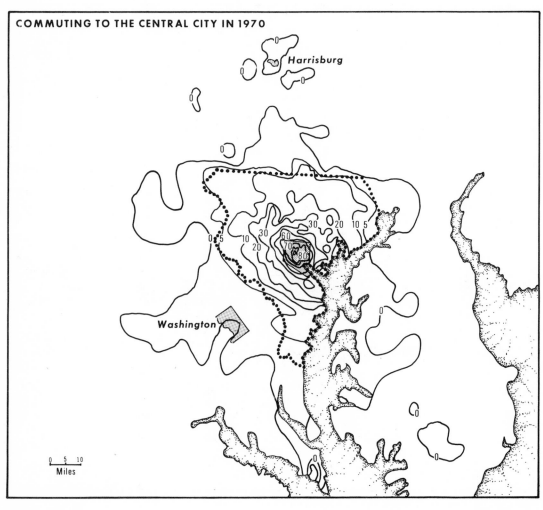

COMMUTING TO THE CENTRAL CITY IN 1970

Harrisburg

Washington

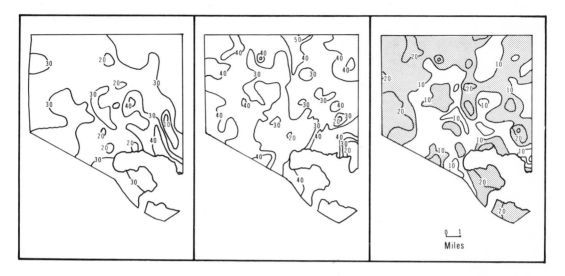

BALTIMORE, MD.

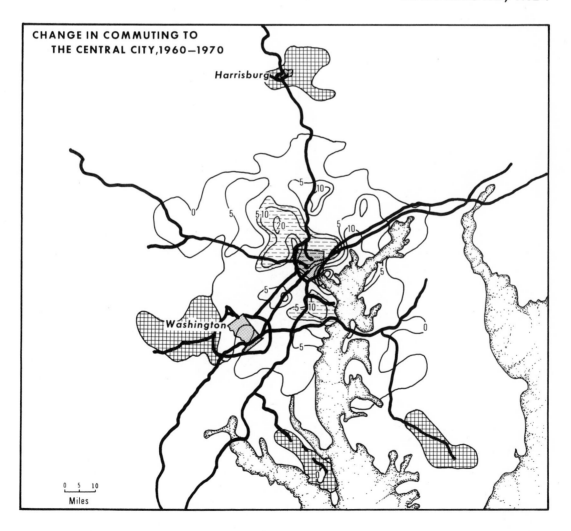

CHANGE IN COMMUTING TO
THE CENTRAL CITY,1960—1970

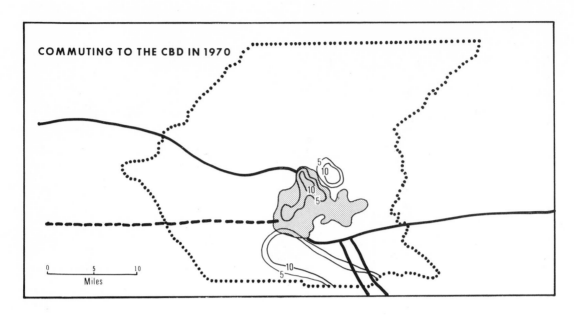

COMMUTING TO THE CBD IN 1970

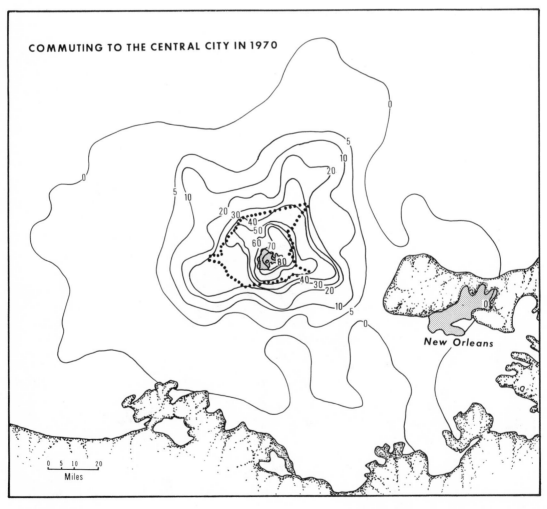

COMMUTING TO THE CENTRAL CITY IN 1970

New Orleans

173

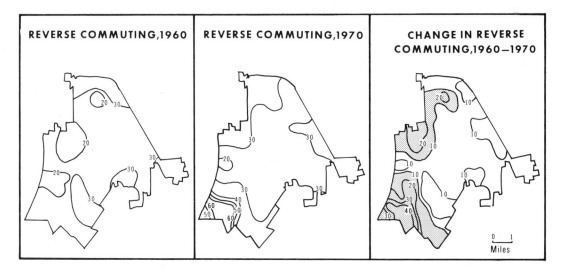

REVERSE COMMUTING,1960

REVERSE COMMUTING,1970

CHANGE IN REVERSE
COMMUTING,1960—1970

BATON ROUGE, LA.

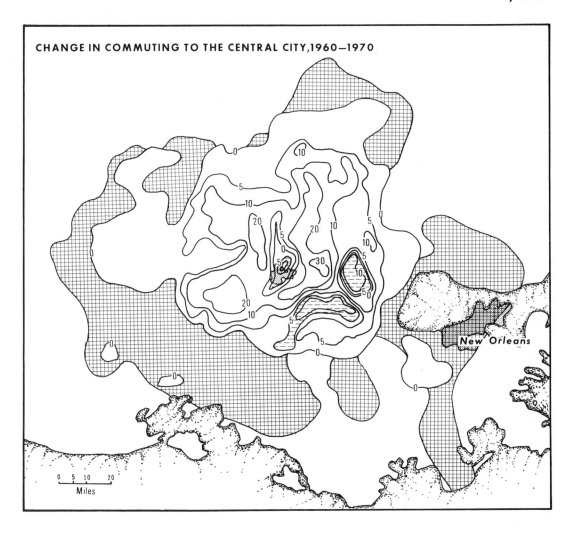

CHANGE IN COMMUTING TO THE CENTRAL CITY,1960—1970

New Orleans

Miles

COMMUTING TO THE CBD IN 1970

NO DATA COLLECTED

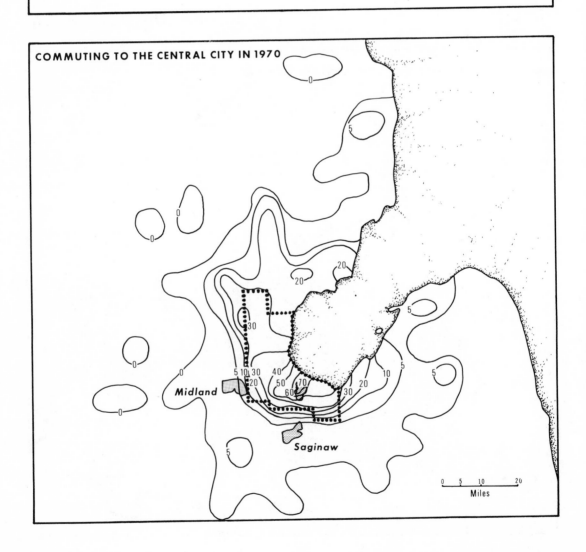

COMMUTING TO THE CENTRAL CITY IN 1970

Midland

Saginaw

0   5   10   20
Miles

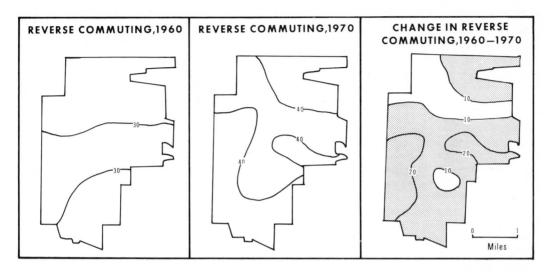

BAY CITY, MI.

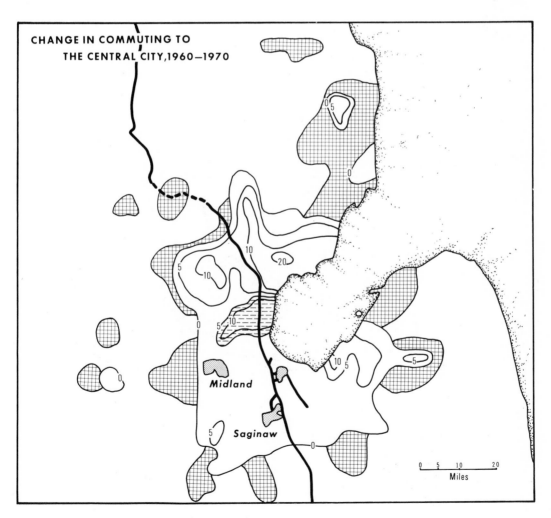

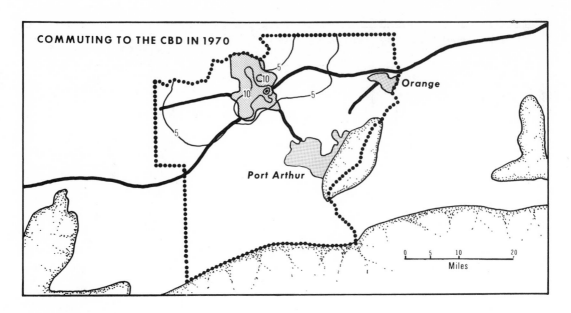

COMMUTING TO THE CBD IN 1970

Orange

Port Arthur

0 5 10 20
Miles

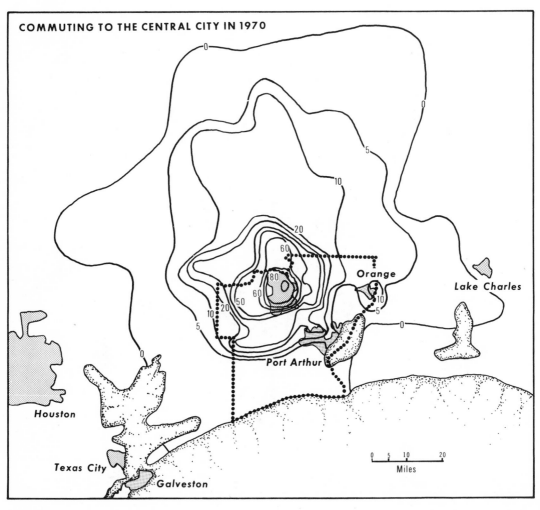

COMMUTING TO THE CENTRAL CITY IN 1970

Orange

Lake Charles

Houston

Port Arthur

Texas City

Galveston

0 5 10 20
Miles

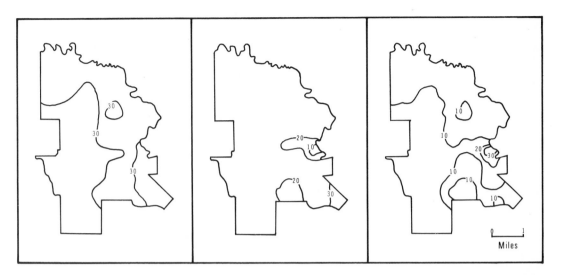

BEAUMONT, TX.

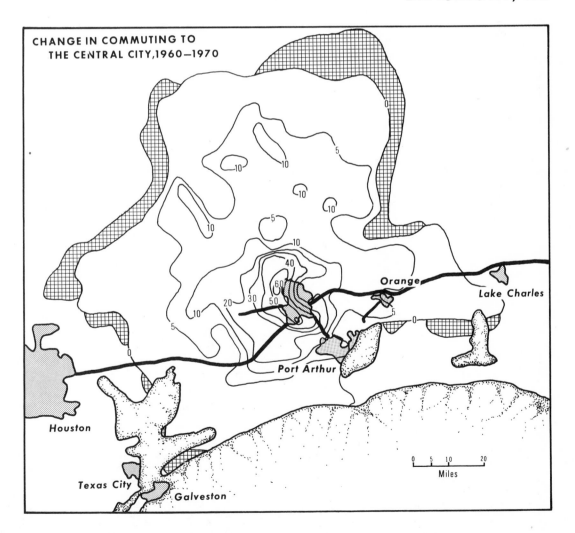

CHANGE IN COMMUTING TO
THE CENTRAL CITY, 1960–1970

COMMUTING TO THE CBD IN 1970

NO DATA COLLECTED

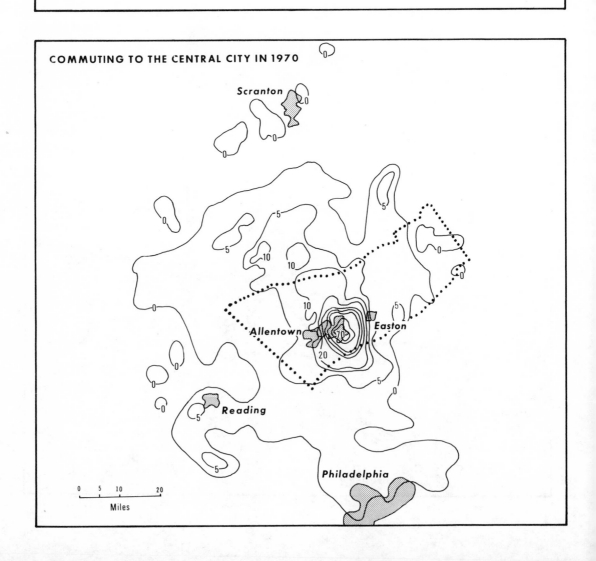

COMMUTING TO THE CENTRAL CITY IN 1970

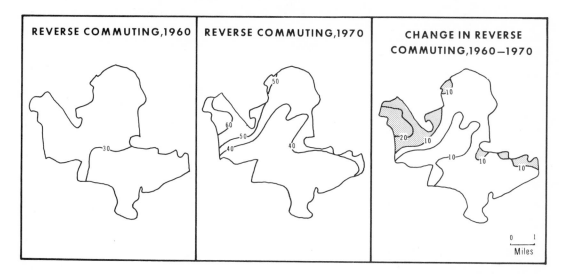

REVERSE COMMUTING,1960 | REVERSE COMMUTING,1970 | CHANGE IN REVERSE COMMUTING,1960—1970

BETHLEHEM, PA.

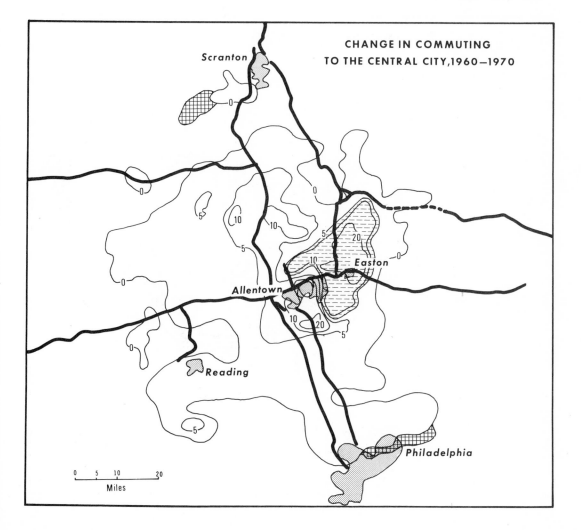

CHANGE IN COMMUTING TO THE CENTRAL CITY,1960—1970

COMMUTING TO THE CBD IN 1970

NO DATA COLLECTED

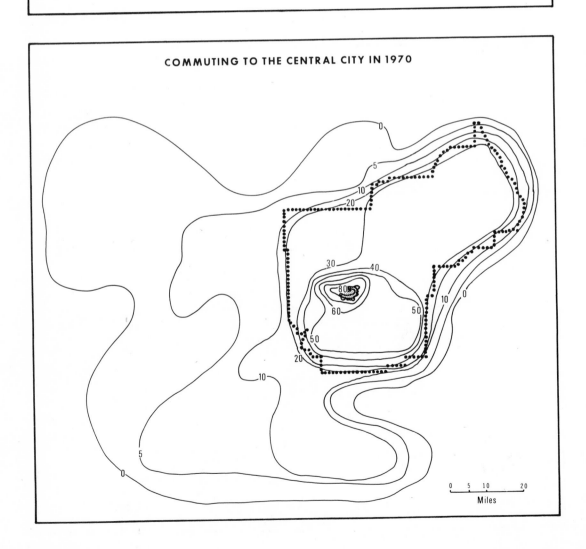

COMMUTING TO THE CENTRAL CITY IN 1970

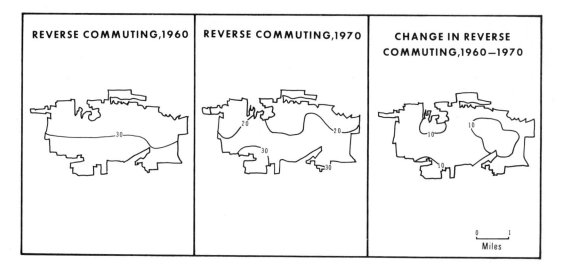

REVERSE COMMUTING, 1960

REVERSE COMMUTING, 1970

CHANGE IN REVERSE
COMMUTING, 1960—1970

BILLINGS, MT.

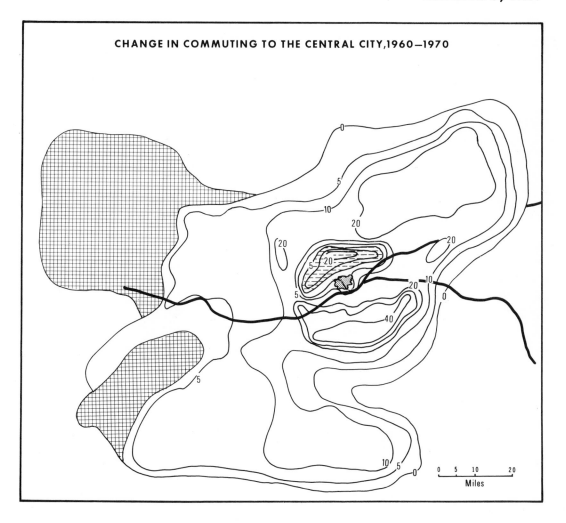

CHANGE IN COMMUTING TO THE CENTRAL CITY, 1960—1970

COMMUTING TO THE CBD IN 1970

NO DATA COLLECTED

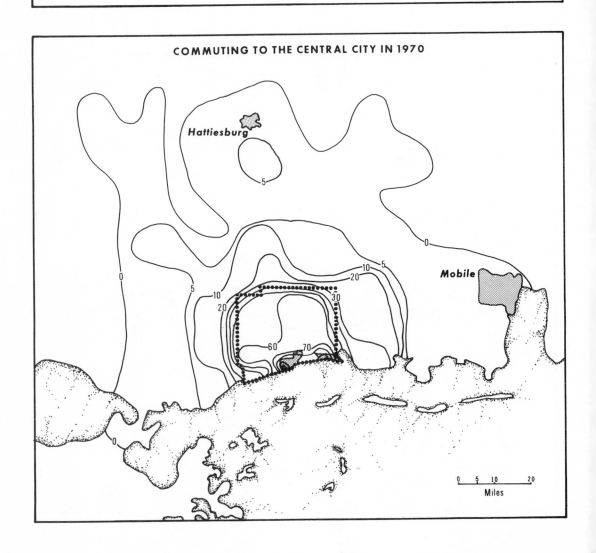

COMMUTING TO THE CENTRAL CITY IN 1970

Hattiesburg

Mobile

Miles

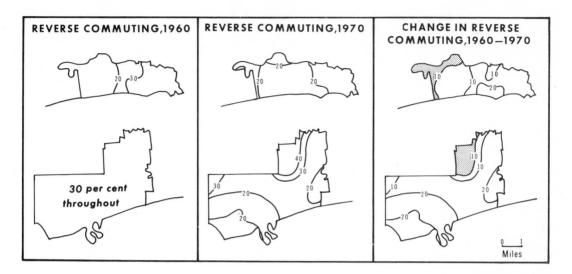

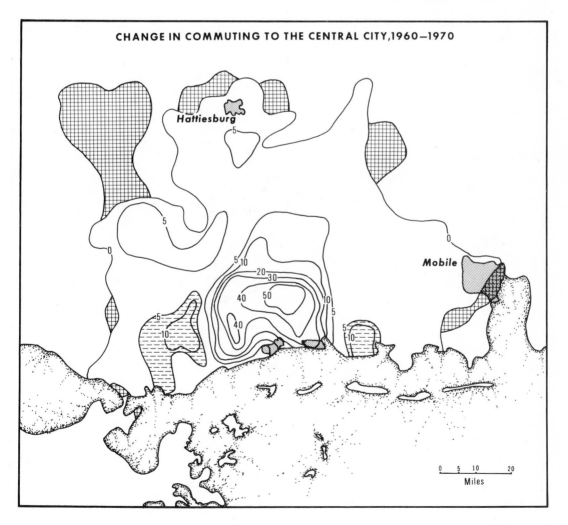

BILOXI - GULFPORT, MS.

CHANGE IN COMMUTING TO THE CENTRAL CITY, 1960–1970

COMMUTING TO THE CBD IN 1970

NO DATA COLLECTED

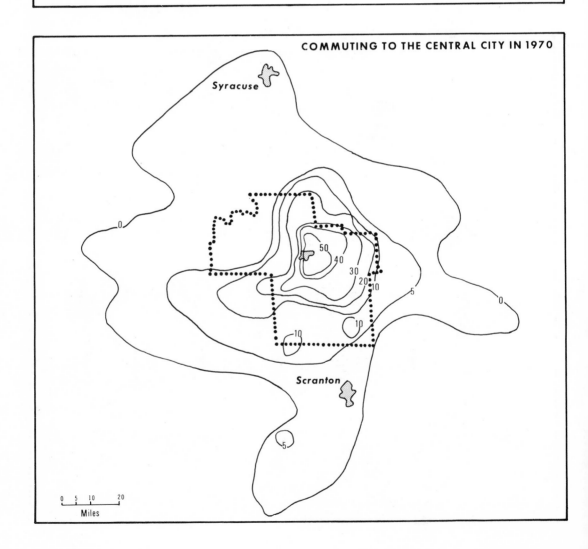

COMMUTING TO THE CENTRAL CITY IN 1970

Syracuse

50
40
30
20
10
10
5
0
0
10
10
5

Scranton

5

0   5   10   20
Miles

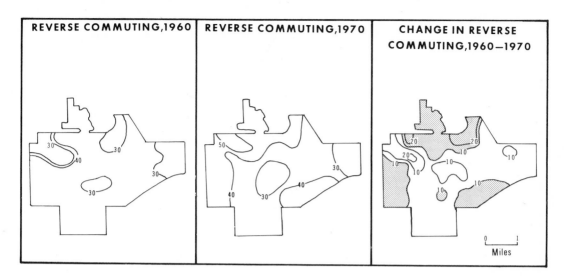

REVERSE COMMUTING, 1960

REVERSE COMMUTING, 1970

CHANGE IN REVERSE COMMUTING, 1960—1970

BINGHAMTON, N.Y.

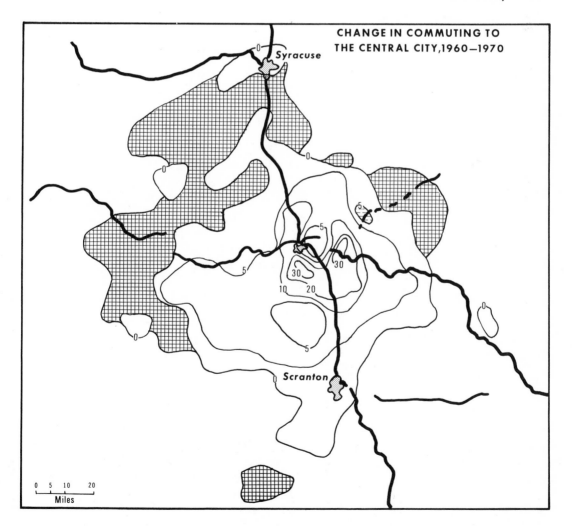

CHANGE IN COMMUTING TO THE CENTRAL CITY, 1960—1970

Syracuse

Scranton

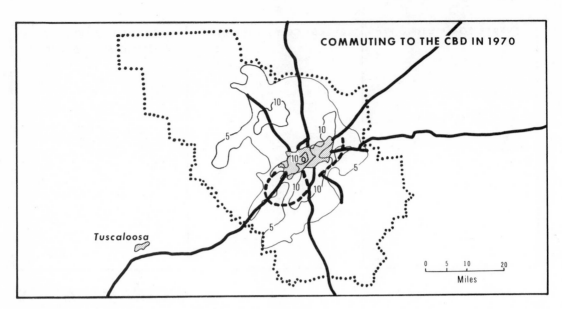

COMMUTING TO THE CBD IN 1970

Tuscaloosa

0 5 10   20
Miles

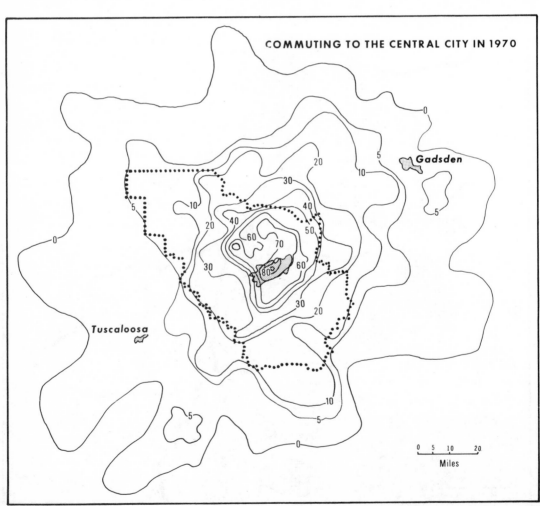

COMMUTING TO THE CENTRAL CITY IN 1970

Gadsden

Tuscaloosa

0 5 10   20
Miles

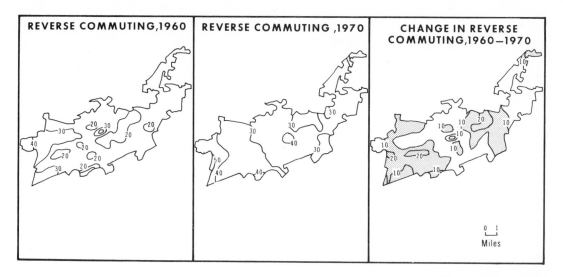

REVERSE COMMUTING, 1960

REVERSE COMMUTING, 1970

CHANGE IN REVERSE
COMMUTING, 1960–1970

0 1
Miles

BIRMINGHAM, AL.

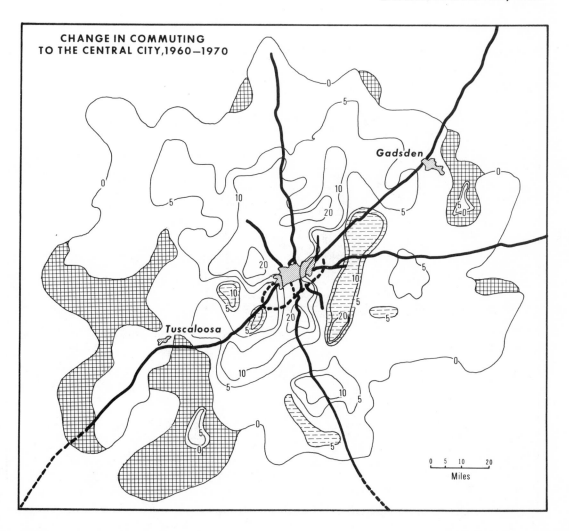

CHANGE IN COMMUTING
TO THE CENTRAL CITY, 1960–1970

Gadsden

Tuscaloosa

0 5 10 20
Miles

COMMUTING TO THE CBD IN 1970

NO DATA COLLECTED

COMMUTING TO THE CENTRAL CITY IN 1970

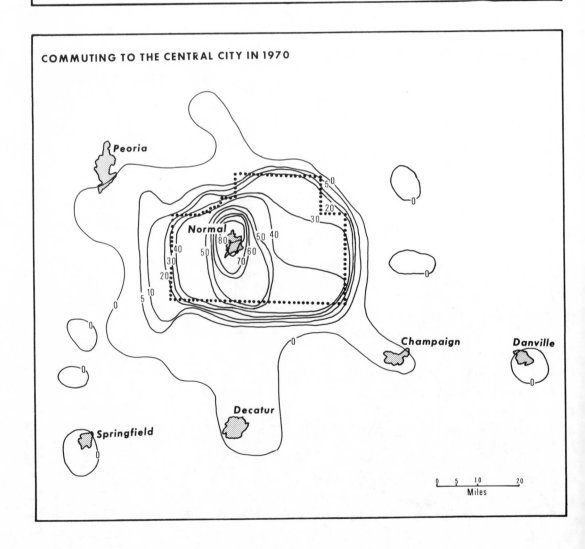

REVERSE COMMUTING,1960	REVERSE COMMUTING ,1970	CHANGE IN REVERSE COMMUTING,1960—1970
NO DATA COLLECTED	20 20	NO DATA COLLECTED
	0 1 Miles	

BLOOMINGTON, IL.

CHANGE IN COMMUTING TO THE CENTRAL CITY,1960—1970

NO DATA COLLECTED

COMMUTING TO THE CBD IN 1970

NO DATA COLLECTED

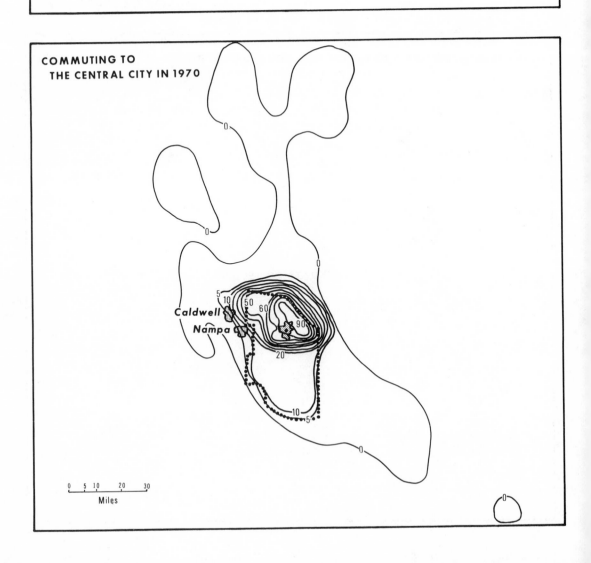

COMMUTING TO
THE CENTRAL CITY IN 1970

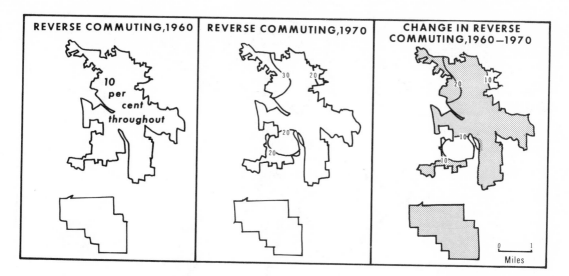

REVERSE COMMUTING, 1960

REVERSE COMMUTING, 1970

CHANGE IN REVERSE COMMUTING, 1960—1970

10 per cent throughout

BOISE, ID.

CHANGE IN COMMUTING TO THE CENTRAL CITY, 1960—1970

NO DATA COLLECTED

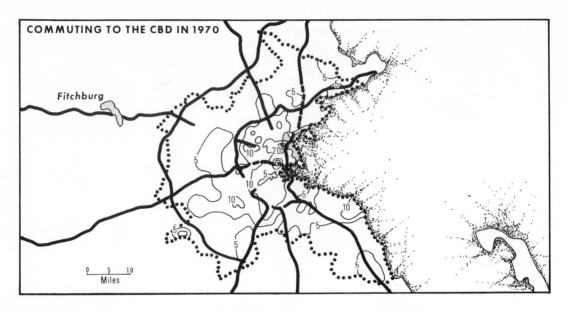

COMMUTING TO THE CBD IN 1970

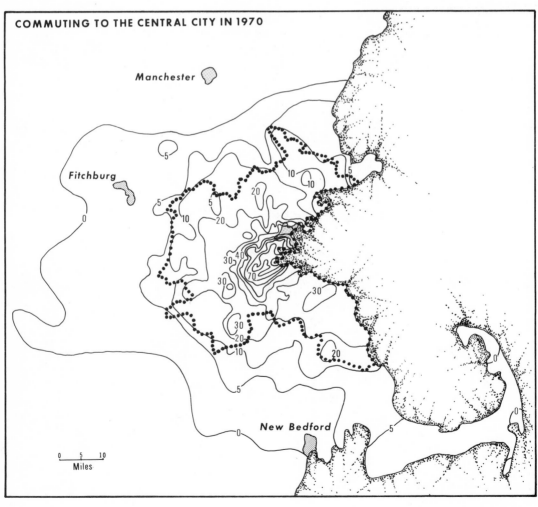

COMMUTING TO THE CENTRAL CITY IN 1970

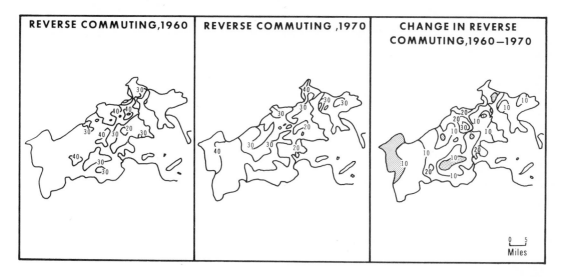

REVERSE COMMUTING,1960 | REVERSE COMMUTING ,1970 | CHANGE IN REVERSE COMMUTING,1960—1970

BOSTON, MA.

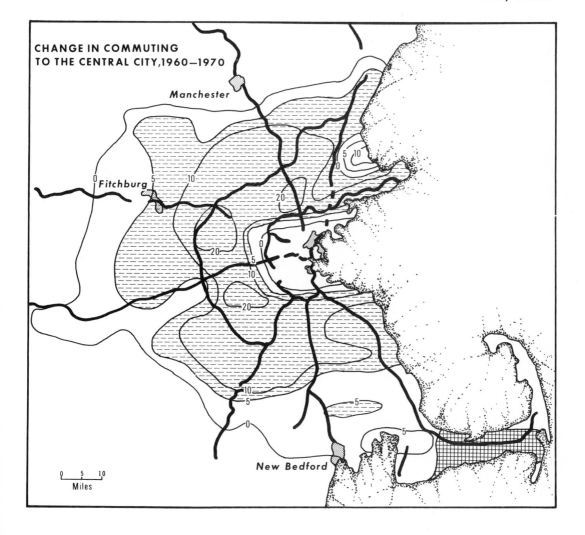

CHANGE IN COMMUTING
TO THE CENTRAL CITY,1960—1970

Manchester

Fitchburg

New Bedford

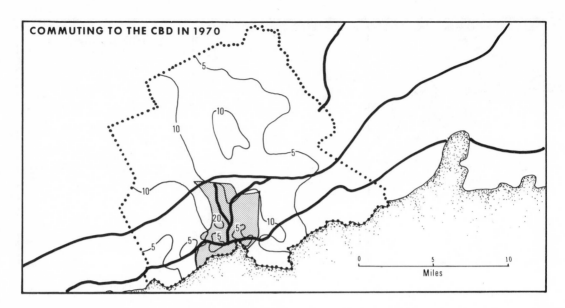

COMMUTING TO THE CBD IN 1970

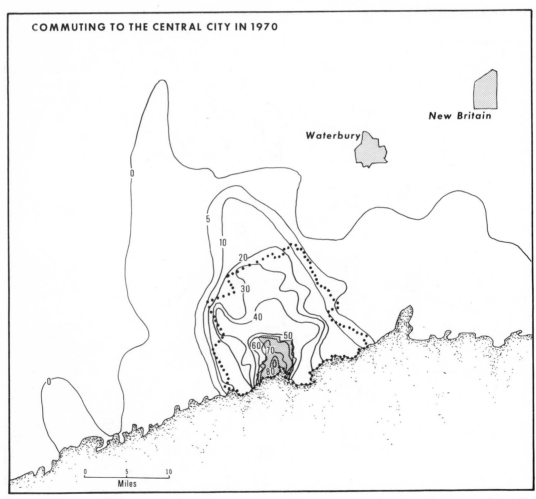

COMMUTING TO THE CENTRAL CITY IN 1970

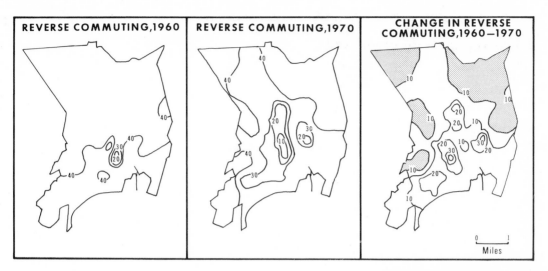

REVERSE COMMUTING, 1960

REVERSE COMMUTING, 1970

CHANGE IN REVERSE COMMUTING, 1960–1970

BRIDGEPORT, CT.

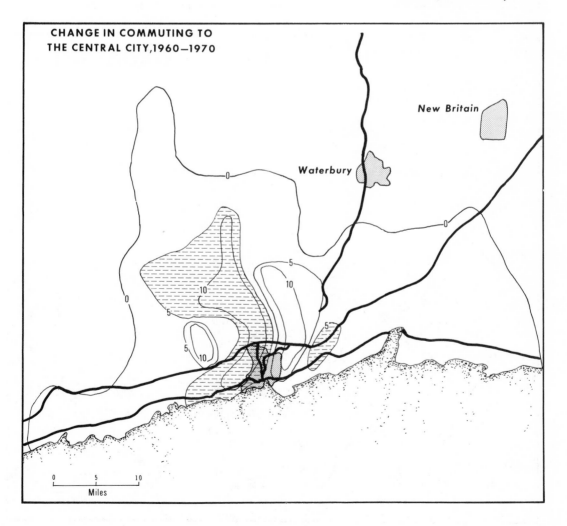

CHANGE IN COMMUTING TO THE CENTRAL CITY, 1960–1970

New Britain

Waterbury

COMMUTING TO THE CBD IN 1970

NO DATA COLLECTED

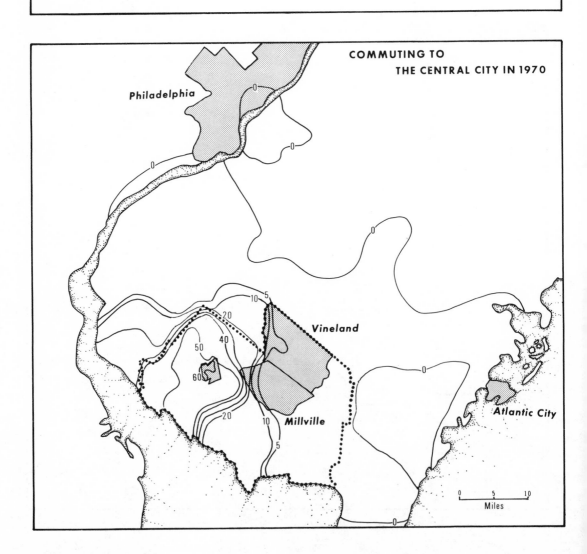

COMMUTING TO
THE CENTRAL CITY IN 1970

Philadelphia

Vineland

Millville

Atlantic City

0   5   10
Miles

REVERSE COMMUTING,1960	REVERSE COMMUTING,1970	CHANGE IN REVERSE COMMUTING,1960—1970
NO DATA COLLECTED	50 · 0 1 Miles	NO DATA COLLECTED

BRIDGETON, N.J.

CHANGE IN COMMUTING TO THE CENTRAL CITY,1960—1970

NO DATA COLLECTED

COMMUTING TO THE CBD IN 1970

NO DATA COLLECTED

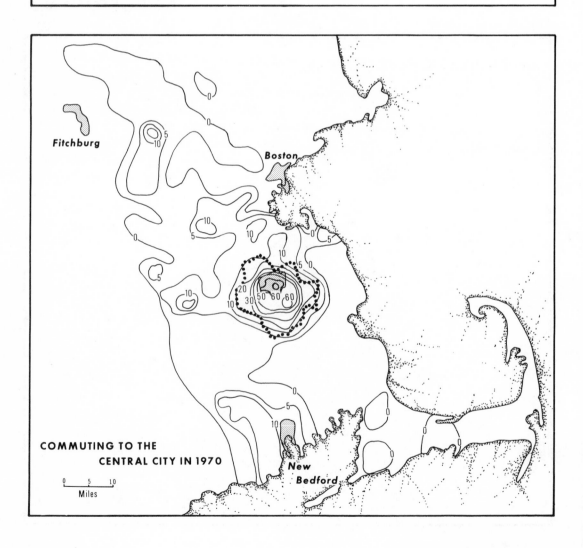

COMMUTING TO THE
CENTRAL CITY IN 1970

0   5   10
Miles

Fitchburg

Boston

New
Bedford

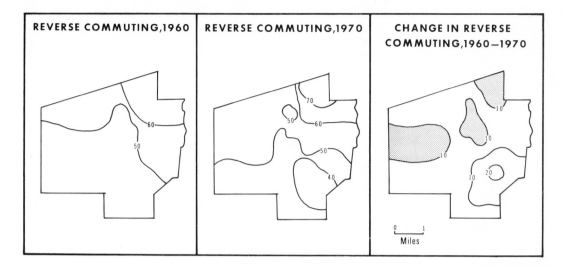

REVERSE COMMUTING, 1960

REVERSE COMMUTING, 1970

CHANGE IN REVERSE COMMUTING, 1960—1970

BROCKTON, MA.

CHANGE IN COMMUTING TO THE CENTRAL CITY, 1960—1970

COMMUTING TO THE CBD IN 1970

NO DATA COLLECTED

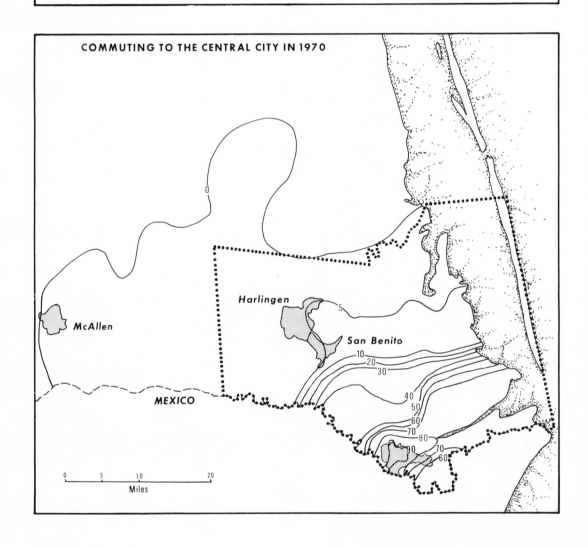

COMMUTING TO THE CENTRAL CITY IN 1970

McAllen

Harlingen

San Benito

MEXICO

0
5
10
20
Miles

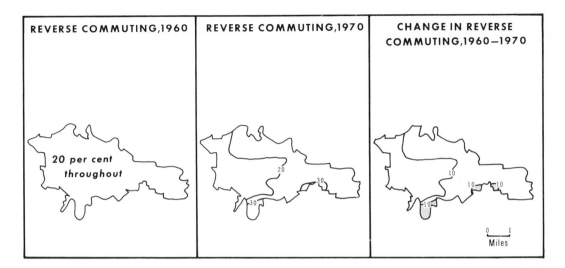

| REVERSE COMMUTING,1960 | REVERSE COMMUTING,1970 | CHANGE IN REVERSE COMMUTING,1960—1970 |

BROWNSVILLE, TX.

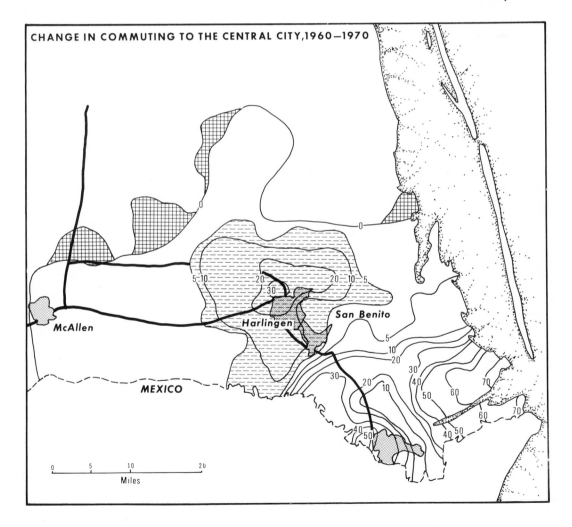

CHANGE IN COMMUTING TO THE CENTRAL CITY,1960—1970

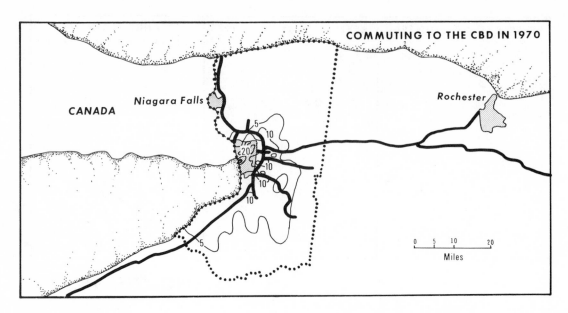

COMMUTING TO THE CBD IN 1970

CANADA

Niagara Falls

Rochester

5
10
20
10
10
10
5
5

0   5   10   20
Miles

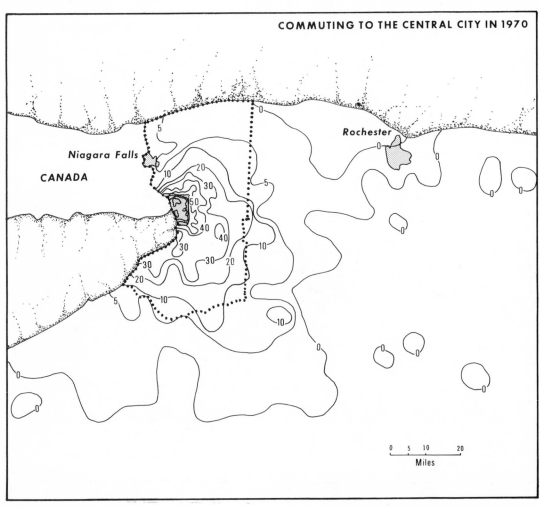

COMMUTING TO THE CENTRAL CITY IN 1970

CANADA

Niagara Falls

Rochester

0
5
10
20
30
50
40
40
30
30
20
10
5
20
10
5
10
0
0
0
0
0
0
0
0
0

0   5   10   20
Miles

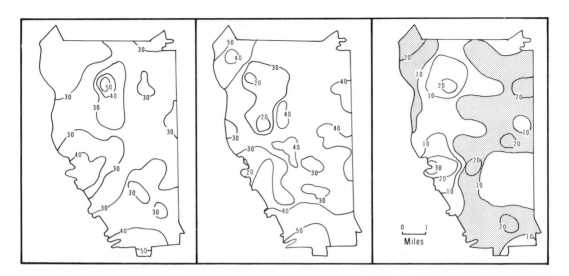

BUFFALO, N.Y.

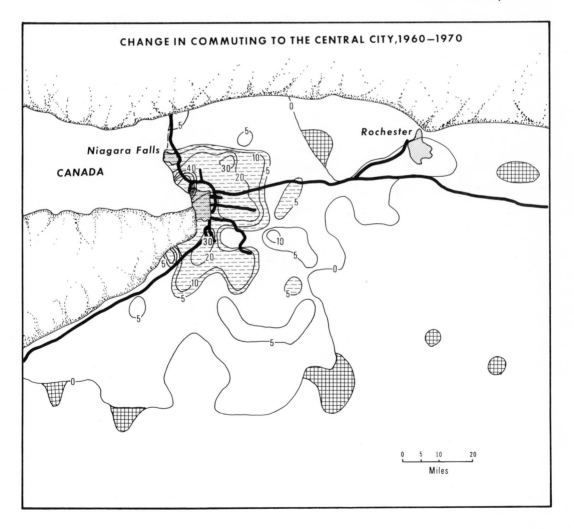

CHANGE IN COMMUTING TO THE CENTRAL CITY, 1960–1970

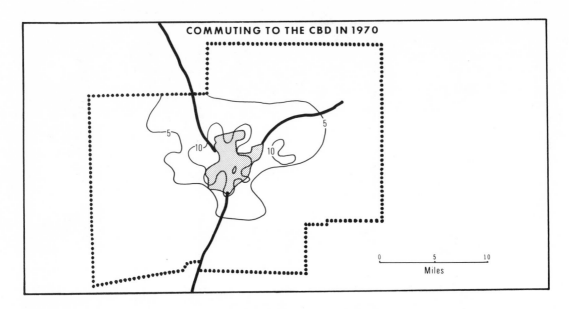

COMMUTING TO THE CBD IN 1970

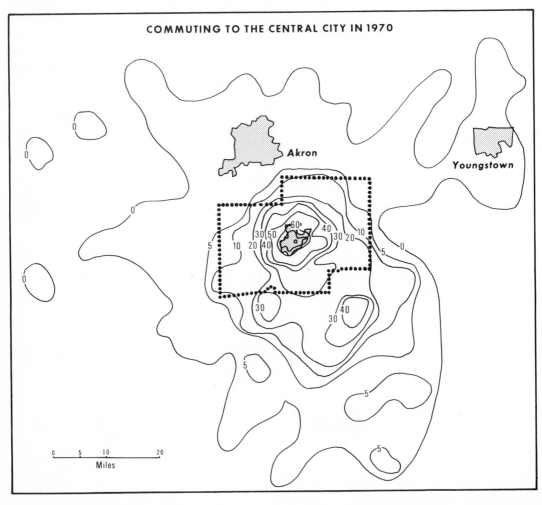

COMMUTING TO THE CENTRAL CITY IN 1970

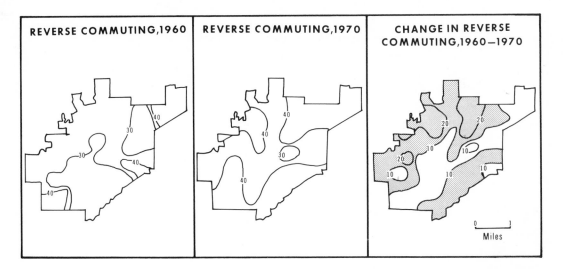

REVERSE COMMUTING, 1960

REVERSE COMMUTING, 1970

CHANGE IN REVERSE COMMUTING, 1960—1970

CANTON, OH.

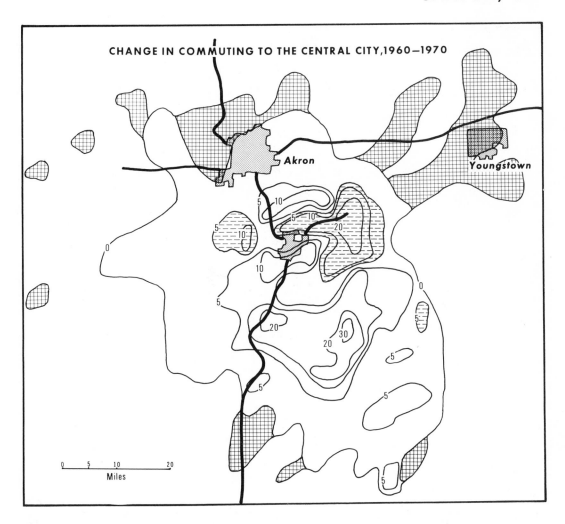

CHANGE IN COMMUTING TO THE CENTRAL CITY, 1960—1970

Akron

Youngstown

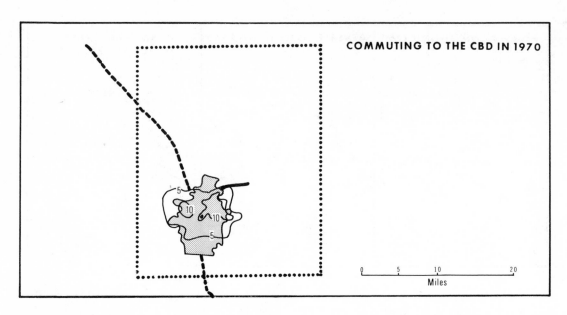

COMMUTING TO THE CBD IN 1970

0   5   10   20
Miles

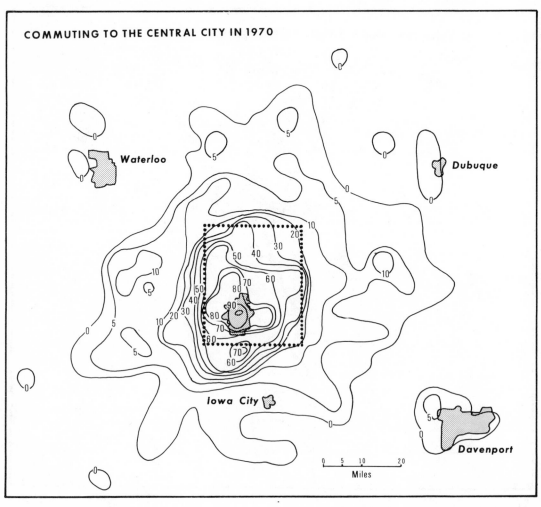

COMMUTING TO THE CENTRAL CITY IN 1970

Waterloo

Dubuque

Iowa City

Davenport

0   5   10   20
Miles

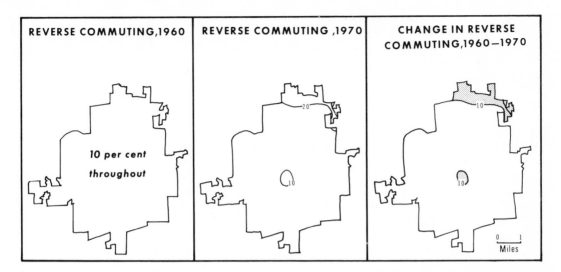

REVERSE COMMUTING,1960

REVERSE COMMUTING ,1970

CHANGE IN REVERSE COMMUTING,1960—1970

10 per cent throughout

CEDAR RAPIDS, IA.

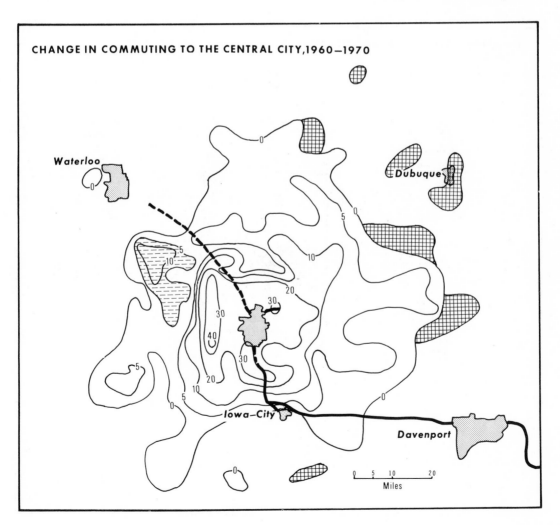

CHANGE IN COMMUTING TO THE CENTRAL CITY,1960—1970

Waterloo

Dubuque

Iowa-City

Davenport

COMMUTING TO THE CBD IN 1970

NO DATA COLLECTED

COMMUTING TO THE CENTRAL CITY IN 1970

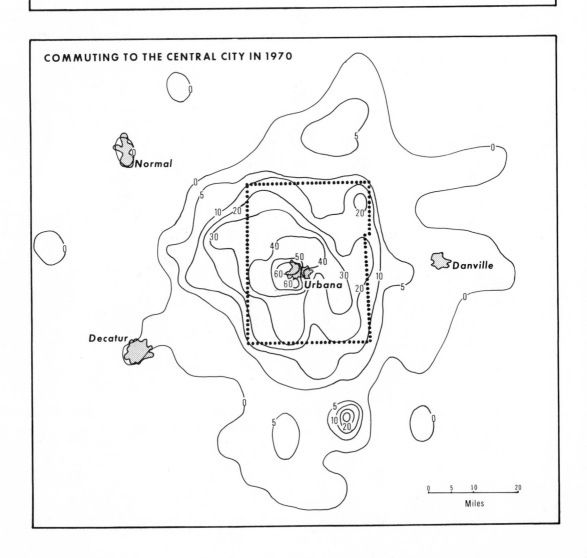

209

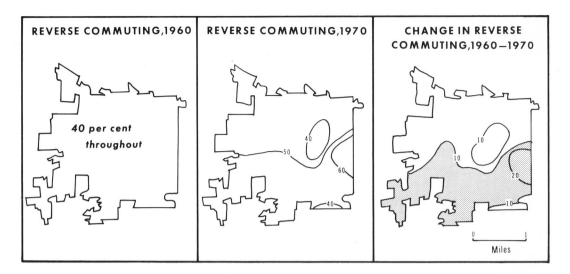

CHAMPAIGN, IL.

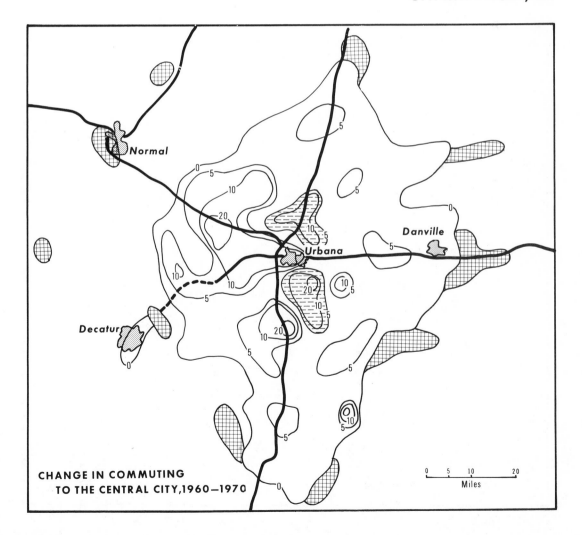

COMMUTING TO THE CBD IN 1970

NO DATA COLLECTED

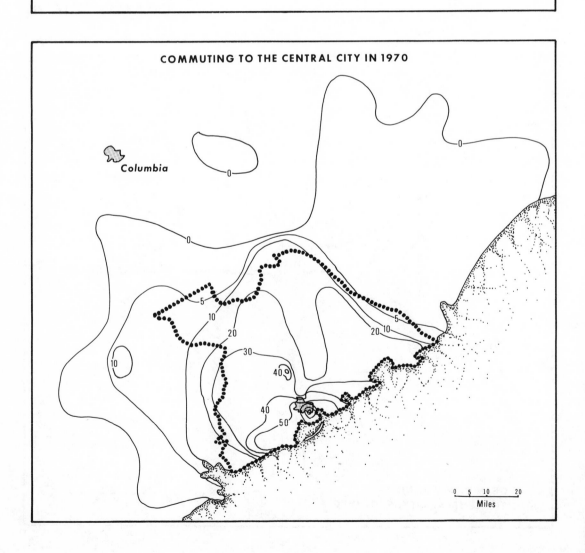

COMMUTING TO THE CENTRAL CITY IN 1970

Columbia

0

0

0

5

10

20

30

40

40

50

10

5

20 10

0 5 10 20
Miles

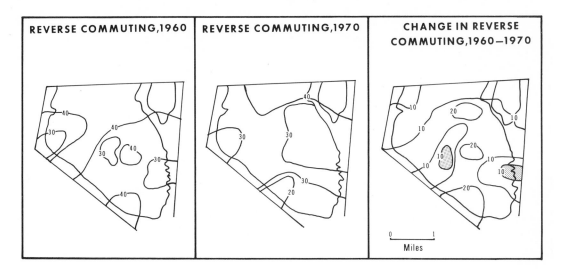

REVERSE COMMUTING,1960   REVERSE COMMUTING,1970   CHANGE IN REVERSE
                                                     COMMUTING,1960—1970

CHARLESTON, S.C.

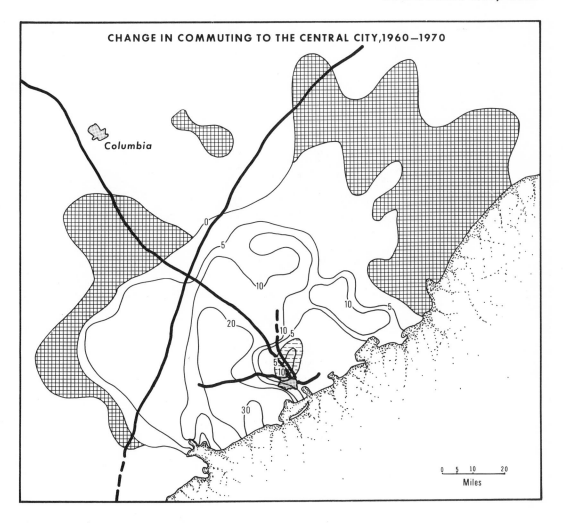

CHANGE IN COMMUTING TO THE CENTRAL CITY,1960—1970

COMMUTING TO THE CBD IN 1970

NO DATA COLLECTED

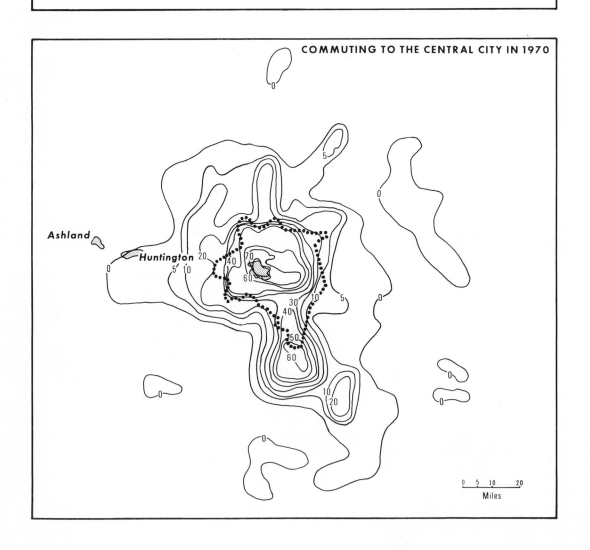

COMMUTING TO THE CENTRAL CITY IN 1970

Ashland

Huntington

0 5 10   20
Miles

213

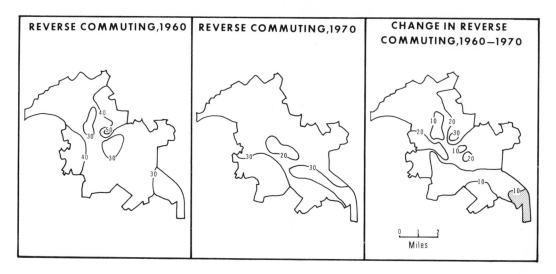

| REVERSE COMMUTING,1960 | REVERSE COMMUTING,1970 | CHANGE IN REVERSE COMMUTING,1960—1970 |

CHARLESTON, W.V.

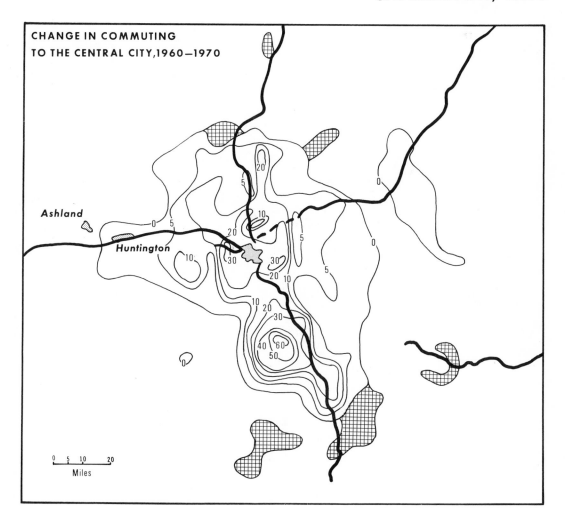

CHANGE IN COMMUTING
TO THE CENTRAL CITY,1960—1970

Ashland

Huntington

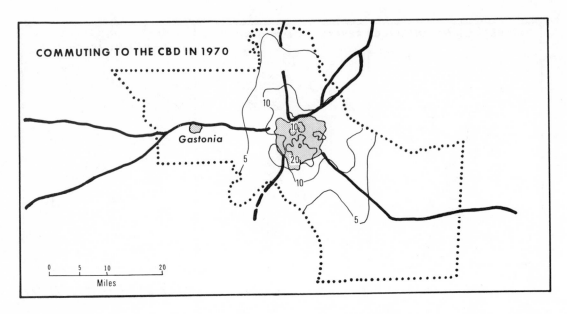

COMMUTING TO THE CBD IN 1970

Gastonia

0   5   10   20
Miles

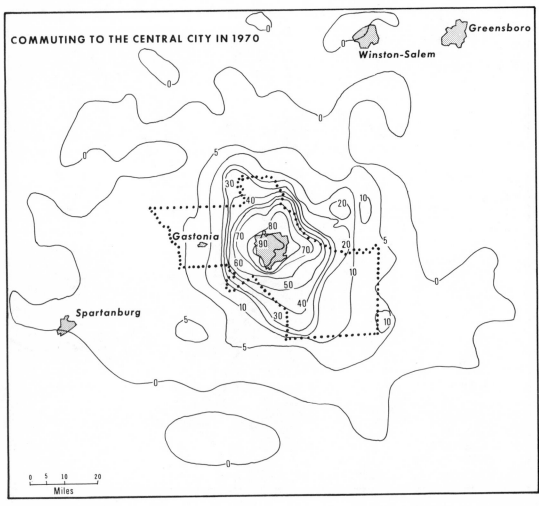

COMMUTING TO THE CENTRAL CITY IN 1970

Winston-Salem

Greensboro

Gastonia

Spartanburg

0 5 10   20
Miles

215

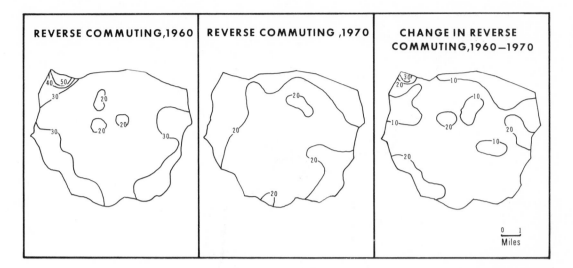

| REVERSE COMMUTING, 1960 | REVERSE COMMUTING, 1970 | CHANGE IN REVERSE COMMUTING, 1960—1970 |

CHARLOTTE, N.C.

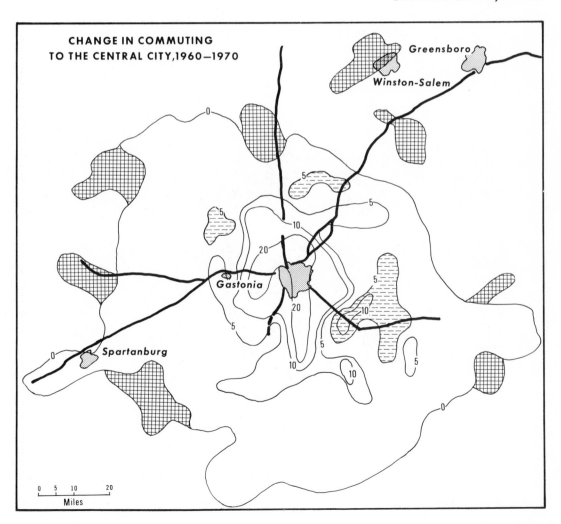

CHANGE IN COMMUTING
TO THE CENTRAL CITY, 1960—1970

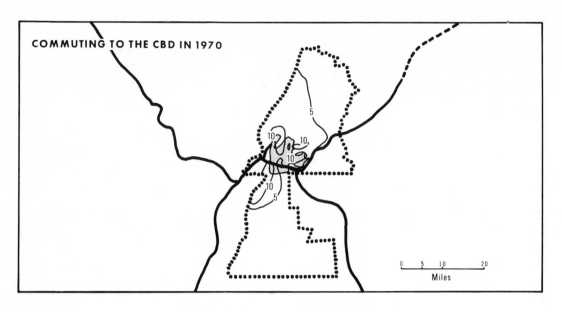

COMMUTING TO THE CBD IN 1970

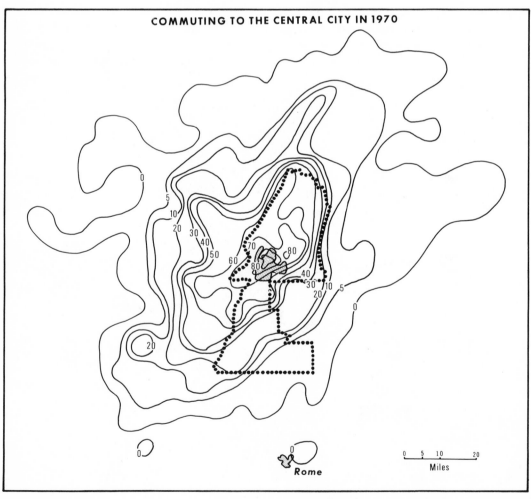

COMMUTING TO THE CENTRAL CITY IN 1970

Rome

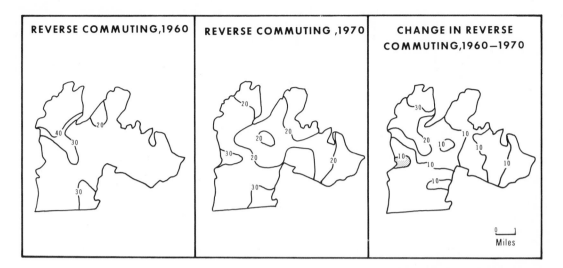

REVERSE COMMUTING,1960   REVERSE COMMUTING ,1970   CHANGE IN REVERSE COMMUTING,1960—1970

CHATTANOOGA, TN.

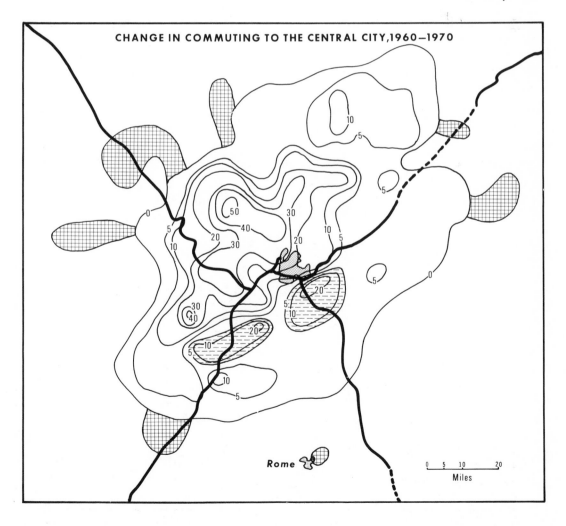

CHANGE IN COMMUTING TO THE CENTRAL CITY,1960—1970

Rome

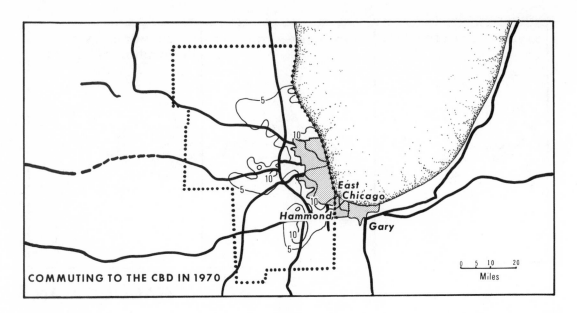

COMMUTING TO THE CBD IN 1970

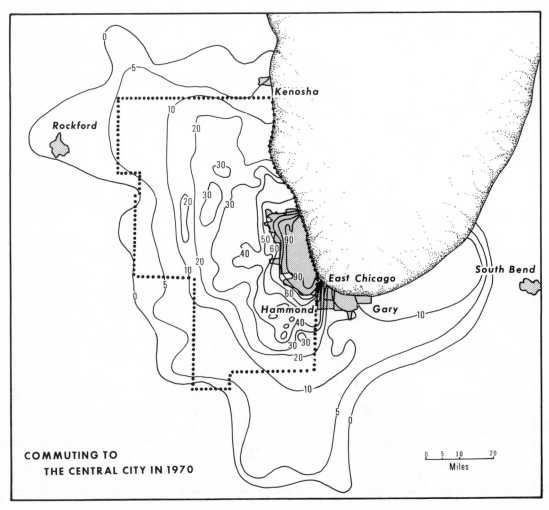

COMMUTING TO
THE CENTRAL CITY IN 1970

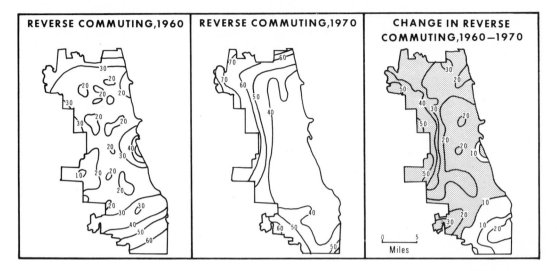

CHICAGO, IL.

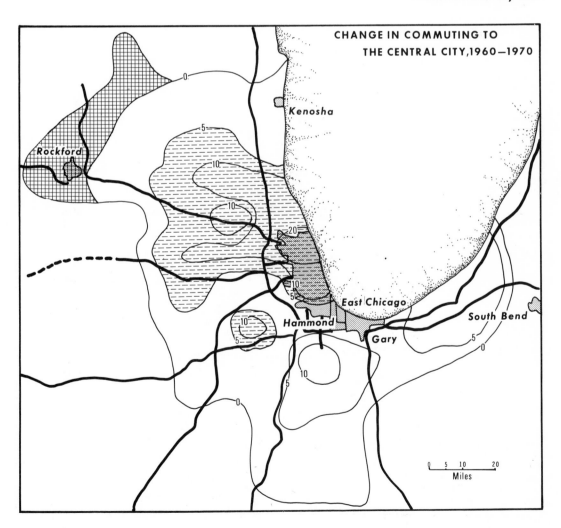

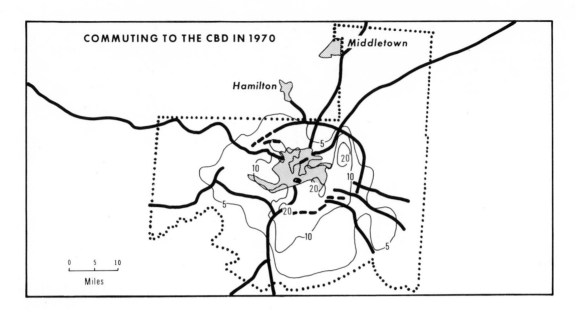

COMMUTING TO THE CBD IN 1970

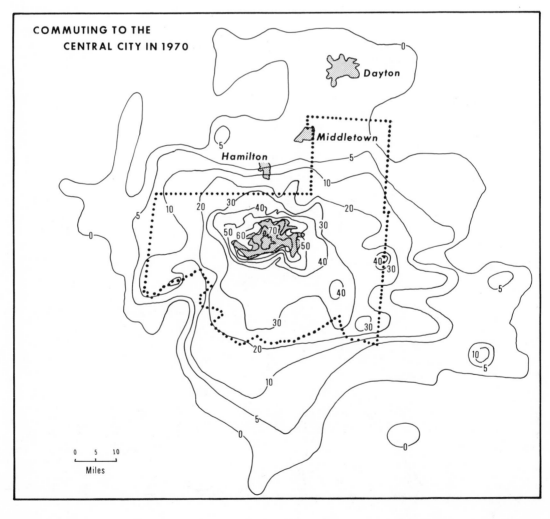

COMMUTING TO THE
CENTRAL CITY IN 1970

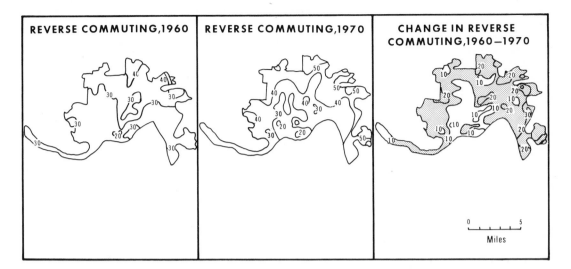

REVERSE COMMUTING, 1960

REVERSE COMMUTING, 1970

CHANGE IN REVERSE COMMUTING, 1960—1970

CINCINNATI, OH.

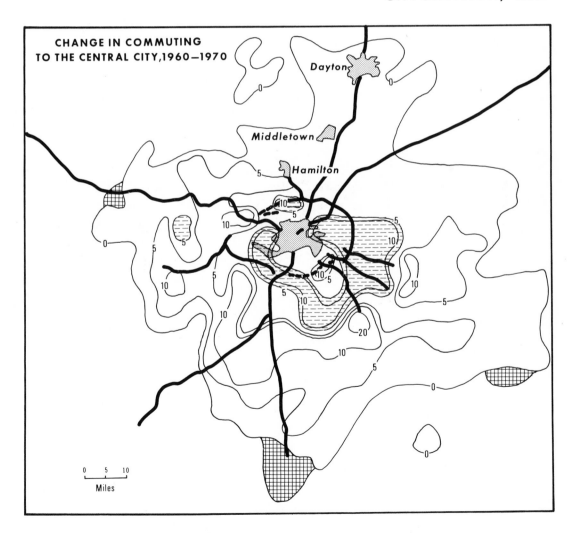

CHANGE IN COMMUTING TO THE CENTRAL CITY, 1960—1970

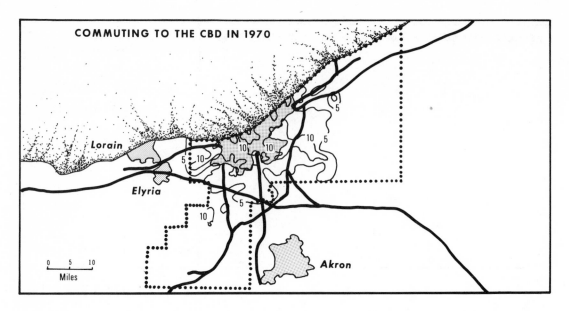

COMMUTING TO THE CBD IN 1970

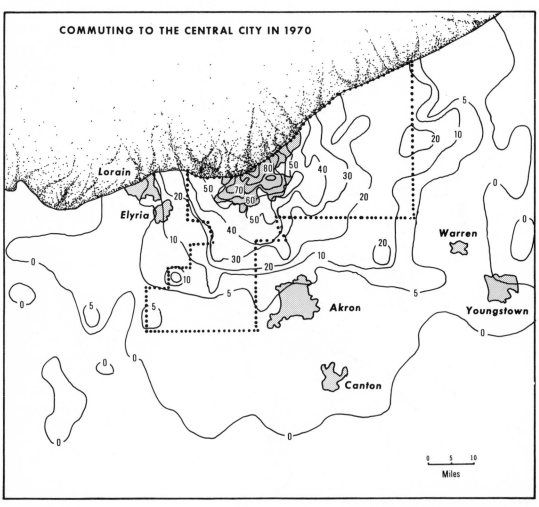

COMMUTING TO THE CENTRAL CITY IN 1970

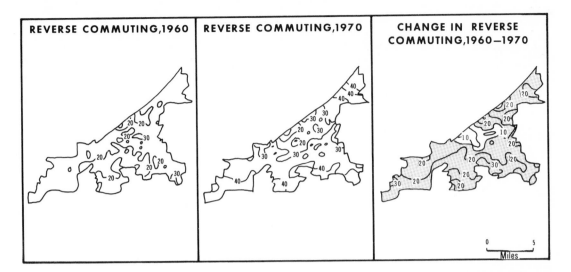

CLEVELAND, OH.

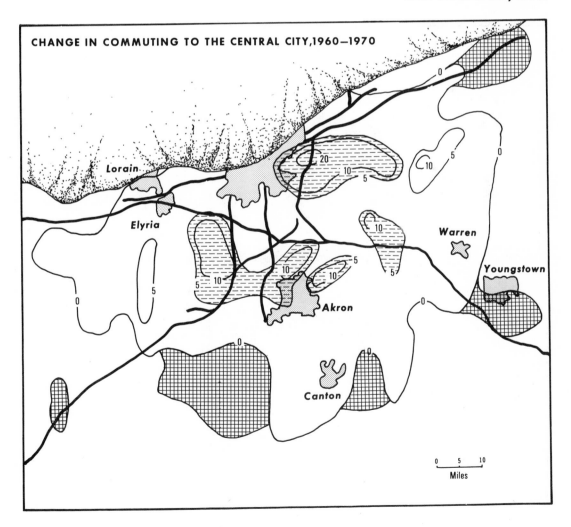

COMMUTING TO THE CBD IN 1970

NO DATA COLLECTED

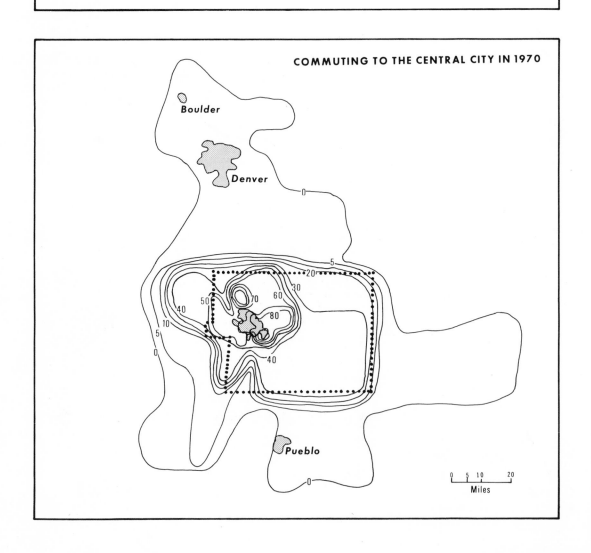

COMMUTING TO THE CENTRAL CITY IN 1970

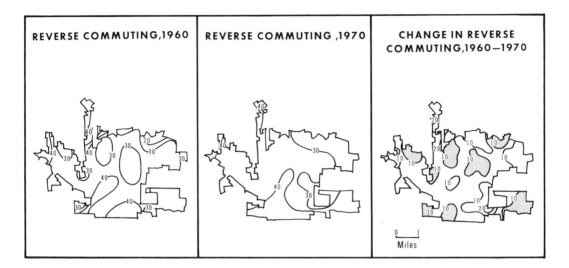

REVERSE COMMUTING, 1960

REVERSE COMMUTING, 1970

CHANGE IN REVERSE COMMUTING, 1960—1970

COLORADO SPRINGS, CO.

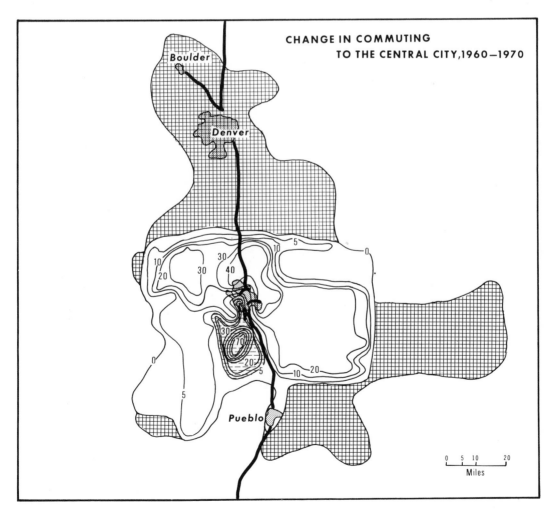

CHANGE IN COMMUTING TO THE CENTRAL CITY, 1960—1970

Boulder

Denver

Pueblo

COMMUTING TO THE CBD IN 1970

NO DATA COLLECTED

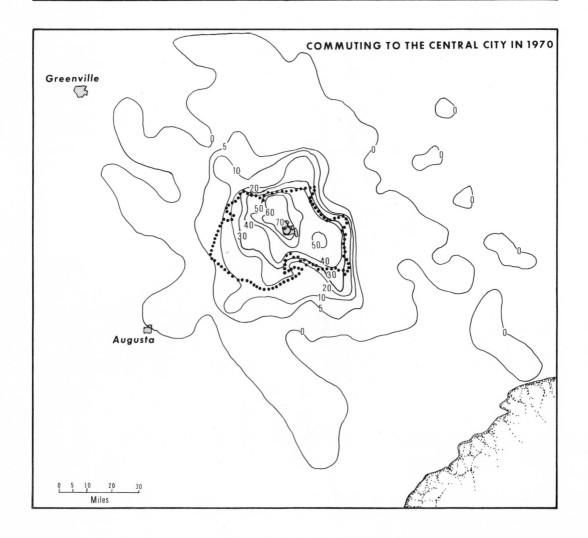

COMMUTING TO THE CENTRAL CITY IN 1970

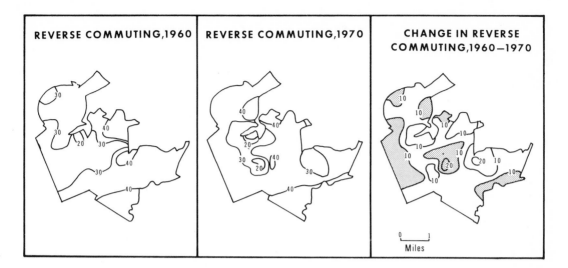

REVERSE COMMUTING,1960   REVERSE COMMUTING,1970   CHANGE IN REVERSE COMMUTING,1960–1970

COLUMBIA, S.C.

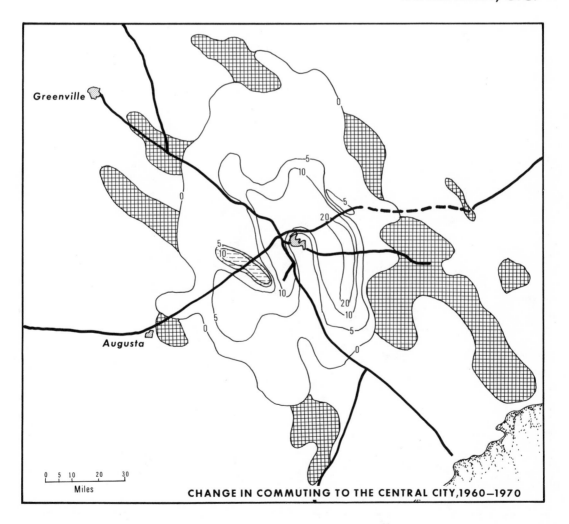

CHANGE IN COMMUTING TO THE CENTRAL CITY,1960–1970

228

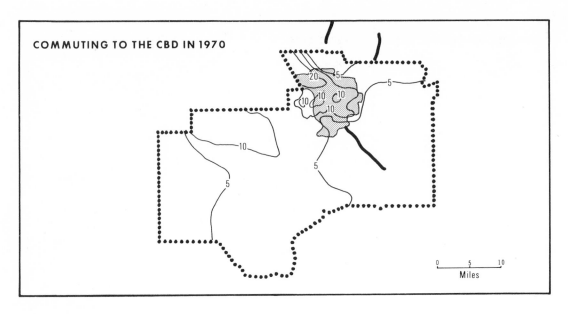

COMMUTING TO THE CBD IN 1970

0   5   10
Miles

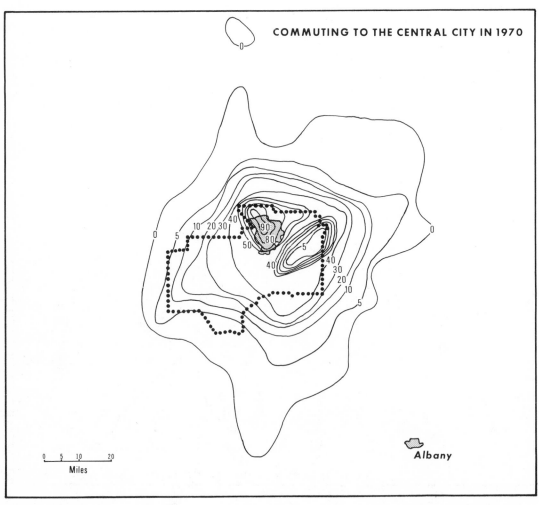

COMMUTING TO THE CENTRAL CITY IN 1970

Albany

0 5 10   20
Miles

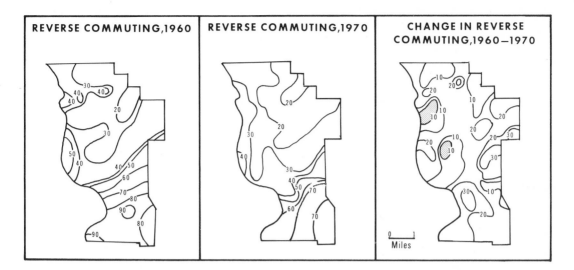

REVERSE COMMUTING,1960

REVERSE COMMUTING,1970

CHANGE IN REVERSE COMMUTING,1960—1970

COLUMBUS, GA.

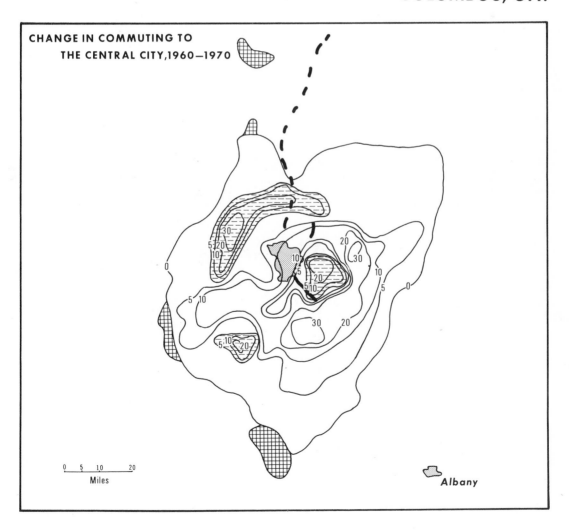

CHANGE IN COMMUTING TO
THE CENTRAL CITY,1960—1970

Albany

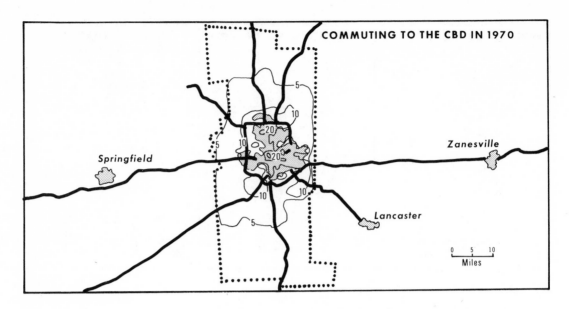

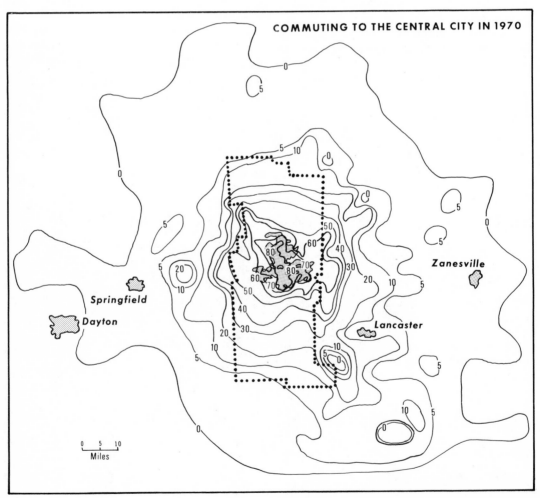

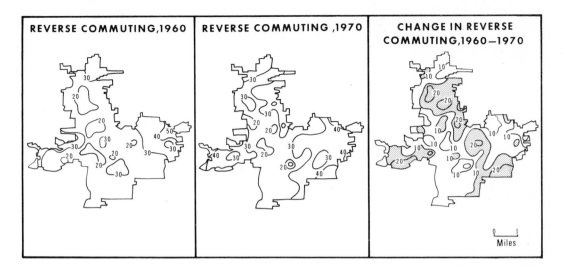

COLUMBUS, OH.

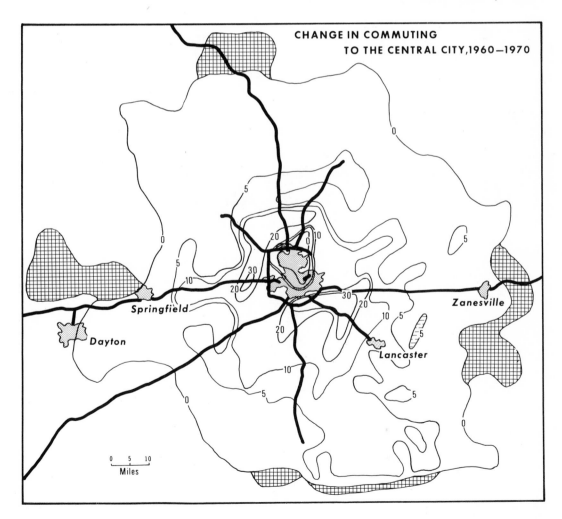

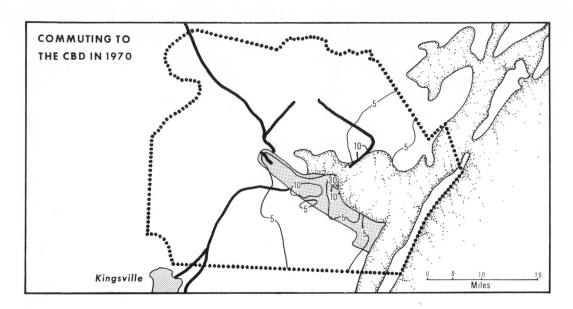

COMMUTING TO
THE CBD IN 1970

Kingsville

Miles

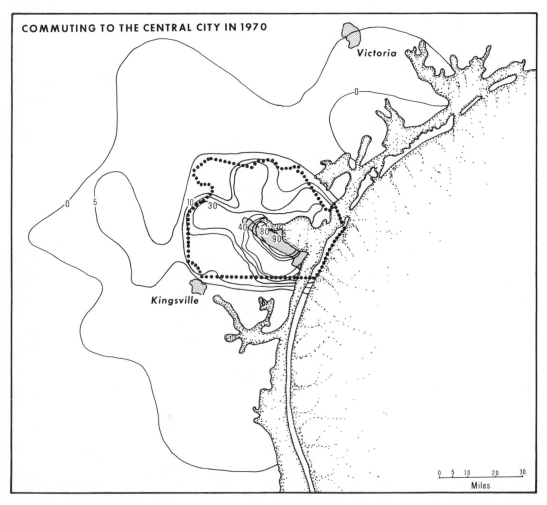

COMMUTING TO THE CENTRAL CITY IN 1970

Victoria

Kingsville

Miles

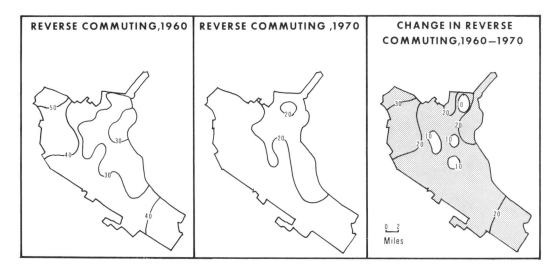

CORPUS CHRISTI, TX.

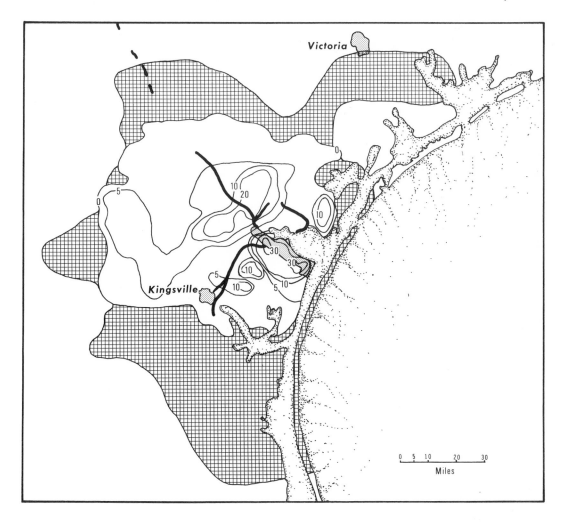

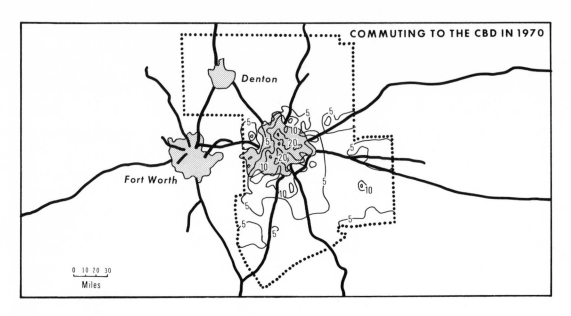

COMMUTING TO THE CBD IN 1970

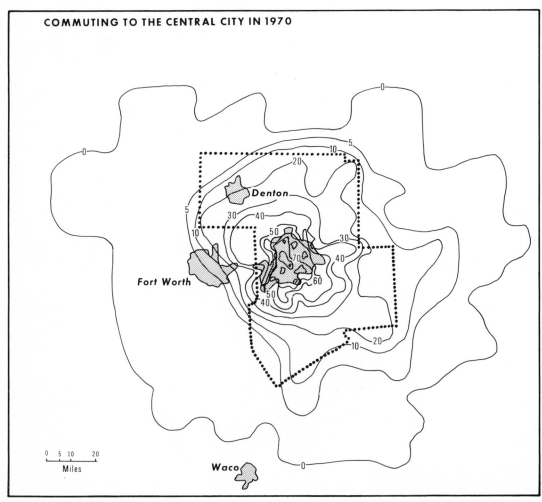

COMMUTING TO THE CENTRAL CITY IN 1970

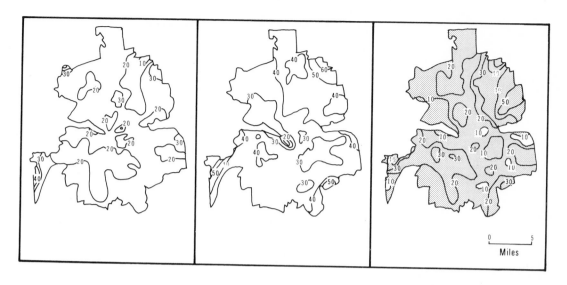

DALLAS, TX.

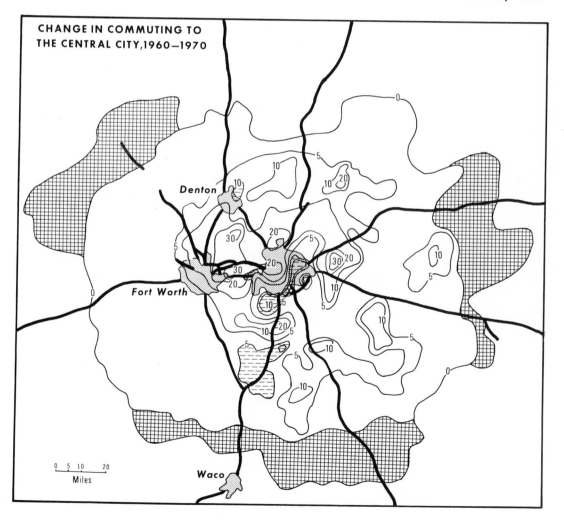

COMMUTING TO THE CBD IN 1970

NO DATA COLLECTED

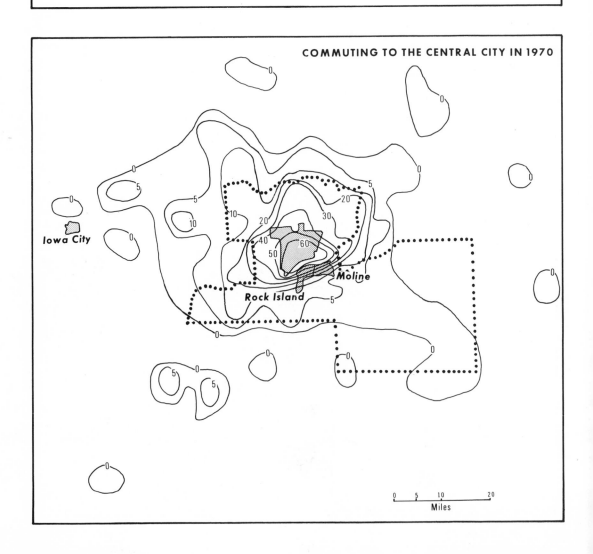

COMMUTING TO THE CENTRAL CITY IN 1970

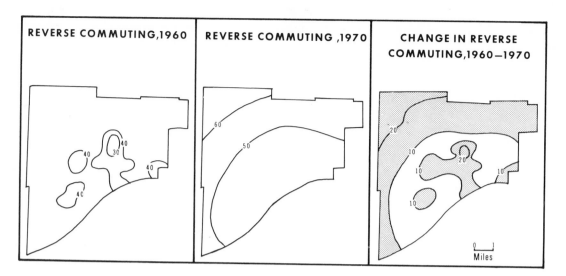

REVERSE COMMUTING, 1960

REVERSE COMMUTING, 1970

CHANGE IN REVERSE COMMUTING, 1960–1970

DAVENPORT, IA.

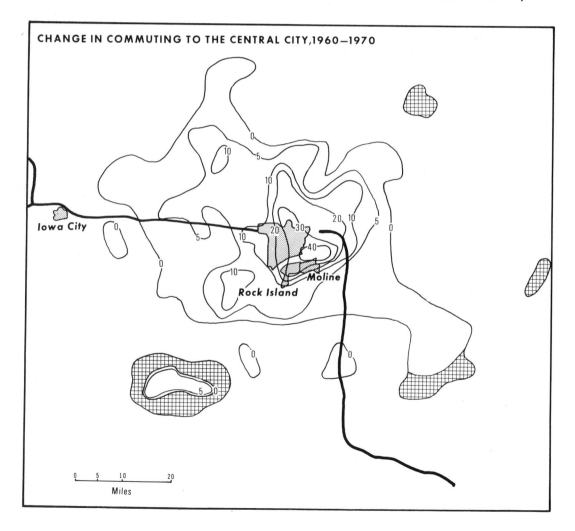

CHANGE IN COMMUTING TO THE CENTRAL CITY, 1960–1970

Iowa City

Rock Island

Moline

0 5 10 20
Miles

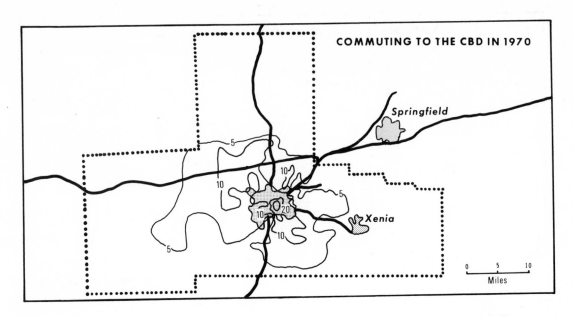

COMMUTING TO THE CBD IN 1970

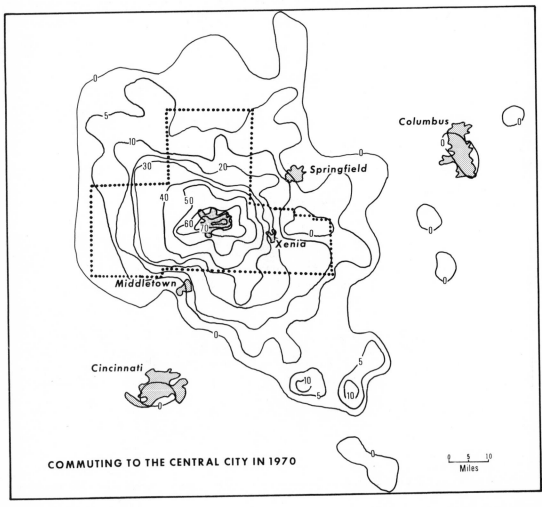

COMMUTING TO THE CENTRAL CITY IN 1970

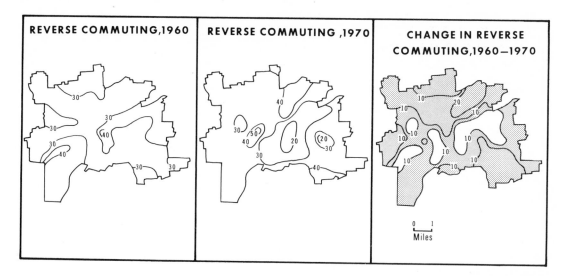

REVERSE COMMUTING, 1960

REVERSE COMMUTING, 1970

CHANGE IN REVERSE
COMMUTING, 1960–1970

DAYTON, OH.

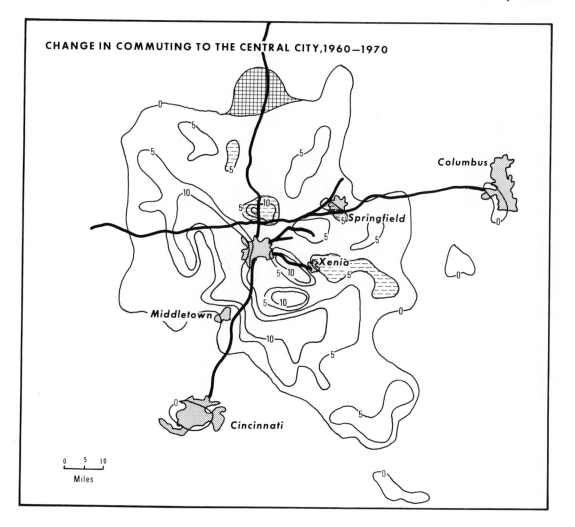

CHANGE IN COMMUTING TO THE CENTRAL CITY, 1960–1970

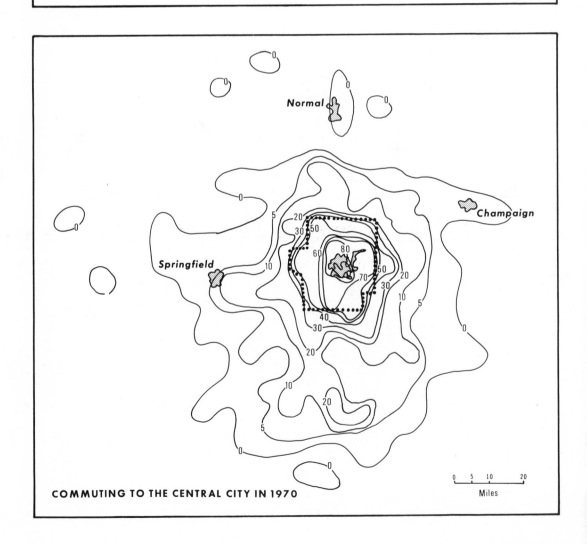

COMMUTING TO THE CBD IN 1970

NO DATA COLLECTED

COMMUTING TO THE CENTRAL CITY IN 1970

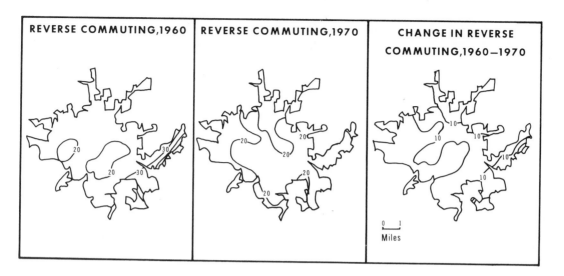

REVERSE COMMUTING, 1960

REVERSE COMMUTING, 1970

CHANGE IN REVERSE COMMUTING, 1960–1970

0 1
Miles

DECATUR, IL.

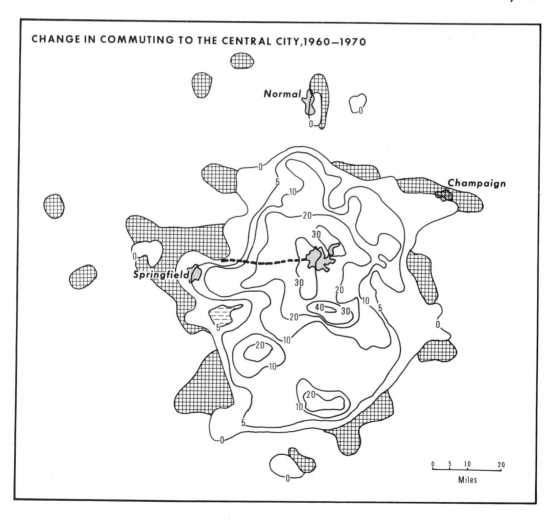

CHANGE IN COMMUTING TO THE CENTRAL CITY, 1960–1970

Normal

Champaign

Springfield

0 5 10 20
Miles

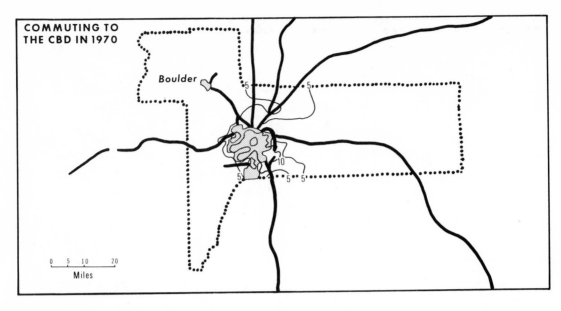

COMMUTING TO
THE CBD IN 1970

Boulder

5   5

10

5   5   5

0   5   10   20
Miles

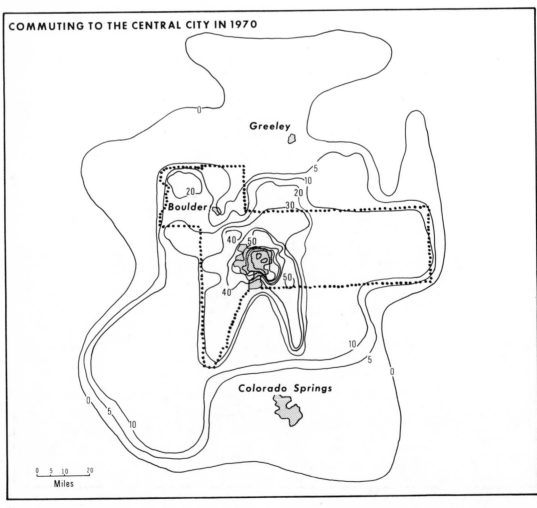

COMMUTING TO THE CENTRAL CITY IN 1970

0

Greeley

5

10

20

20

30

Boulder

40   50

40

50

40

10

5

0

10

5

Colorado Springs

0

5

10

0   5   10   20
Miles

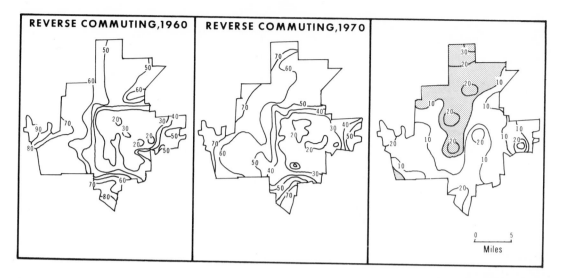

REVERSE COMMUTING, 1960   REVERSE COMMUTING, 1970

DENVER, CO.

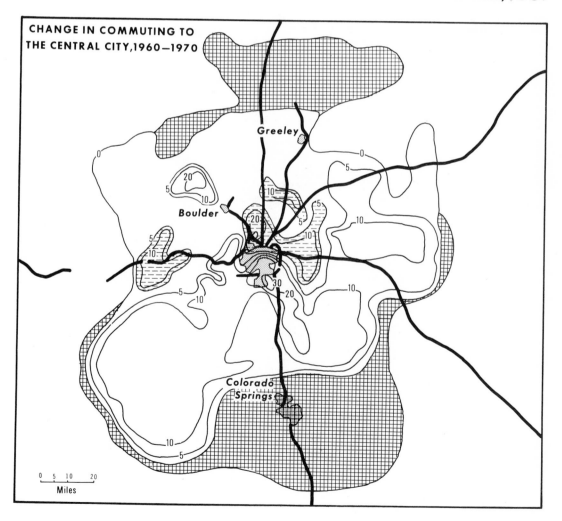

CHANGE IN COMMUTING TO
THE CENTRAL CITY, 1960—1970

Greeley

Boulder

Colorado
Springs

0 5 10   20
Miles

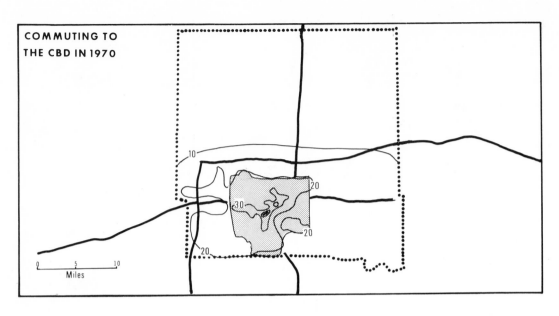

COMMUTING TO
THE CBD IN 1970

0   5   10
Miles

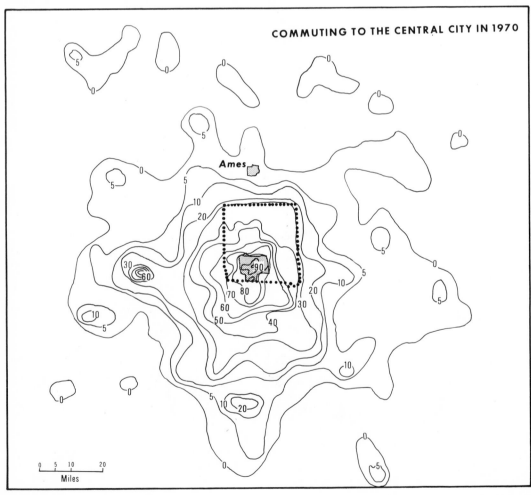

COMMUTING TO THE CENTRAL CITY IN 1970

Ames

0 5 10   20
Miles

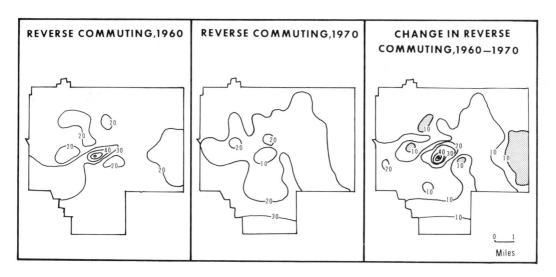

REVERSE COMMUTING,1960

REVERSE COMMUTING,1970

CHANGE IN REVERSE COMMUTING,1960—1970

DES MOINES, IA.

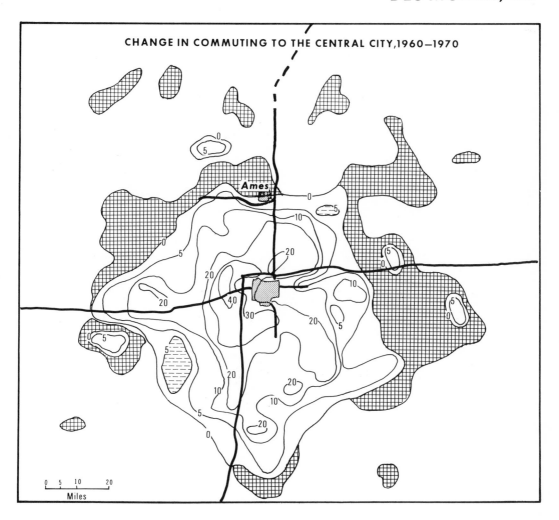

CHANGE IN COMMUTING TO THE CENTRAL CITY,1960—1970

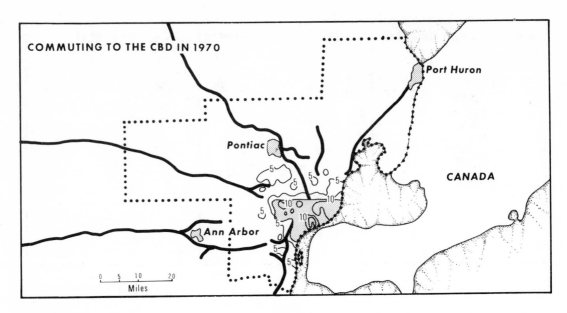

COMMUTING TO THE CBD IN 1970

Pontiac

Ann Arbor

Port Huron

CANADA

0 5 10   20
Miles

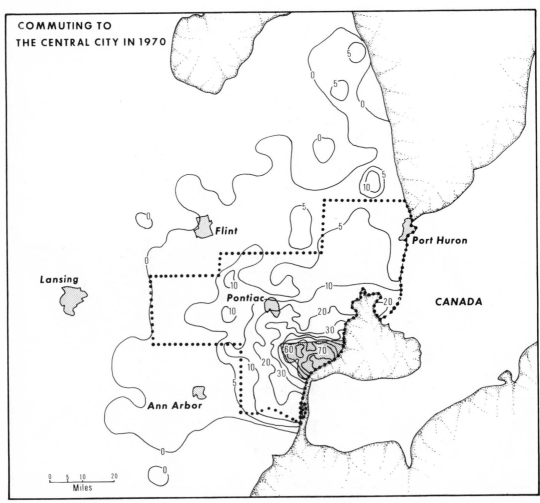

COMMUTING TO
THE CENTRAL CITY IN 1970

Flint

Lansing

Pontiac

Port Huron

CANADA

Ann Arbor

0 5 10   20
Miles

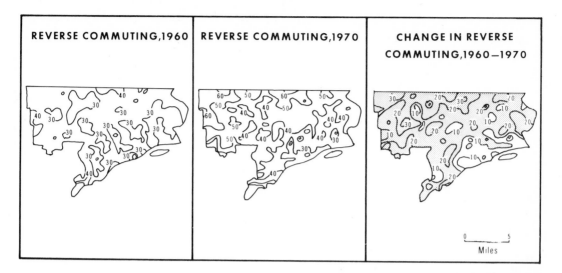

REVERSE COMMUTING,1960

REVERSE COMMUTING,1970

CHANGE IN REVERSE
COMMUTING,1960—1970

DETROIT, MI.

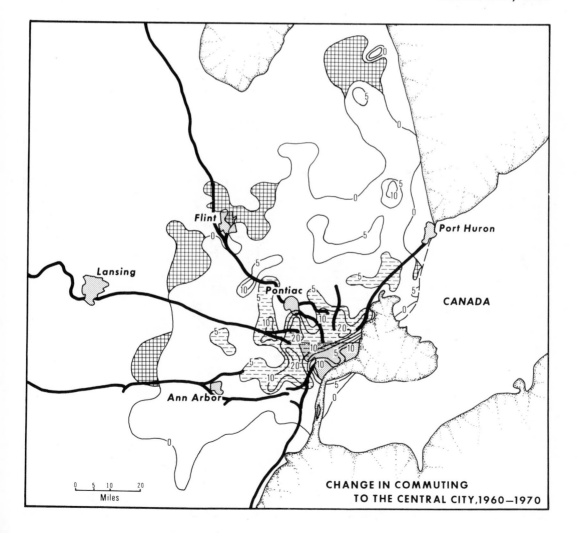

CHANGE IN COMMUTING
TO THE CENTRAL CITY,1960—1970

COMMUTING TO THE CBD IN 1970

NO DATA COLLECTED

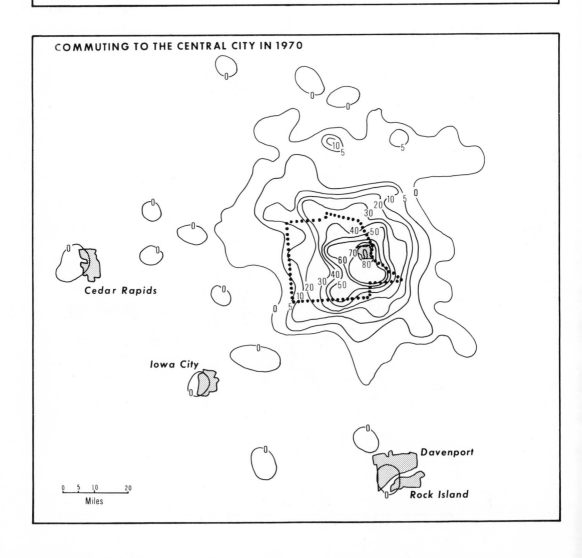

COMMUTING TO THE CENTRAL CITY IN 1970

Cedar Rapids

Iowa City

Davenport

Rock Island

0 5 10   20
Miles

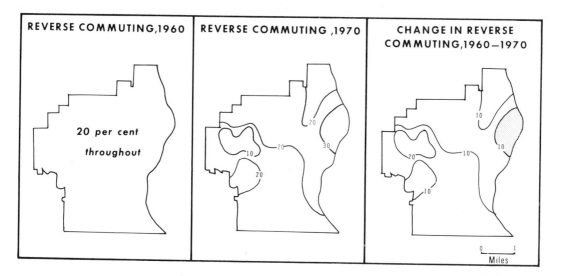

REVERSE COMMUTING, 1960

REVERSE COMMUTING, 1970

CHANGE IN REVERSE COMMUTING, 1960-1970

20 per cent throughout

DUBUQUE, IA.

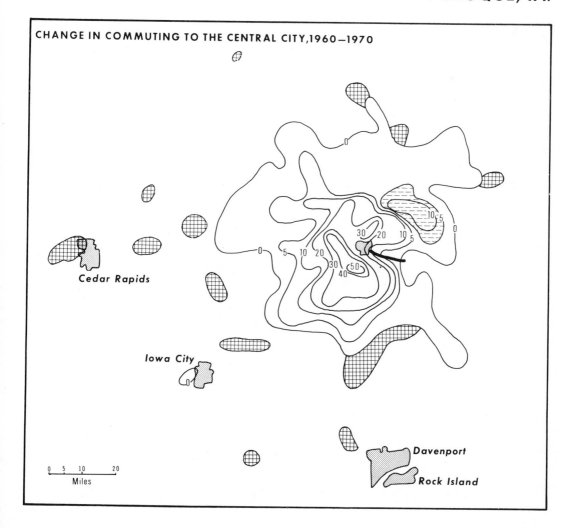

CHANGE IN COMMUTING TO THE CENTRAL CITY, 1960-1970

Cedar Rapids

Iowa City

Davenport

Rock Island

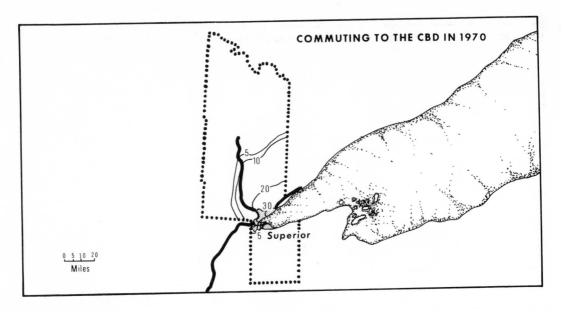

COMMUTING TO THE CBD IN 1970

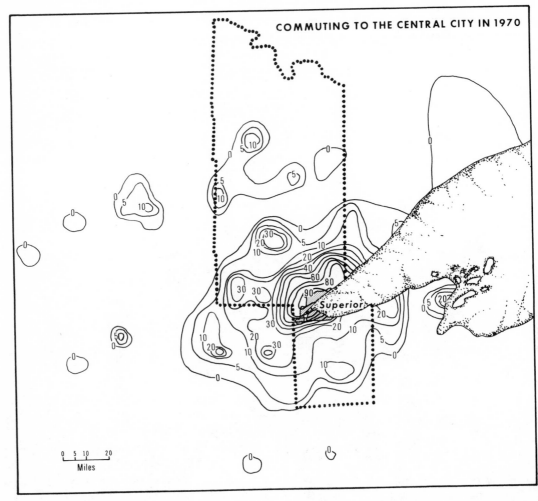

COMMUTING TO THE CENTRAL CITY IN 1970

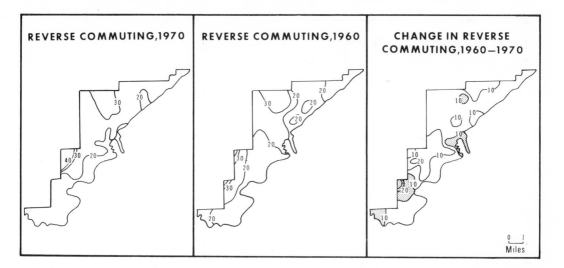

DULUTH, MN.

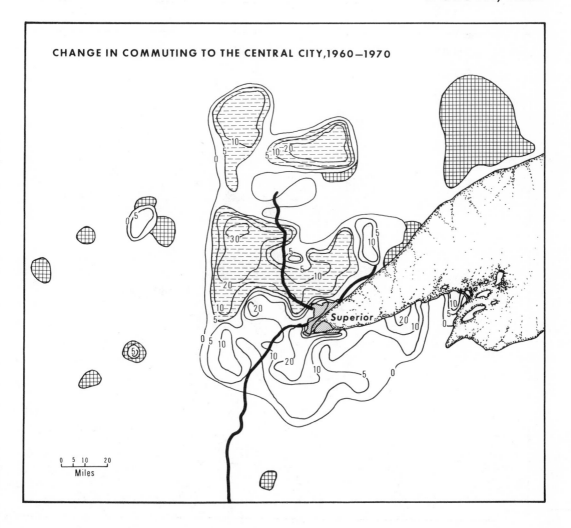

COMMUTING TO THE CBD IN 1970

NO DATA COLLECTED

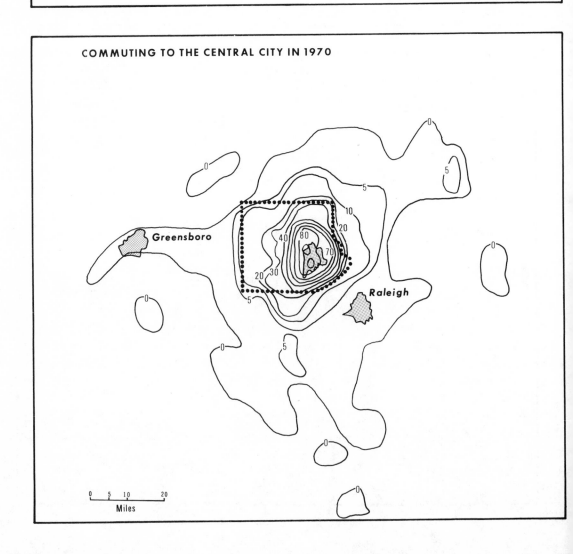

COMMUTING TO THE CENTRAL CITY IN 1970

Greensboro

Raleigh

0   5   10   20
Miles

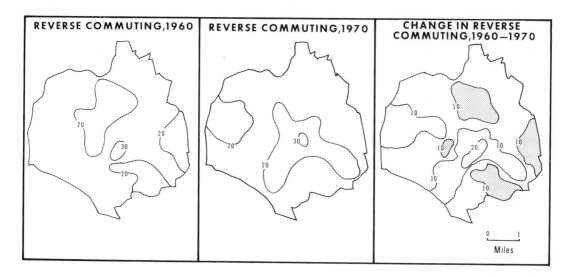

REVERSE COMMUTING, 1960

REVERSE COMMUTING, 1970

CHANGE IN REVERSE COMMUTING, 1960—1970

DURHAM, N.C.

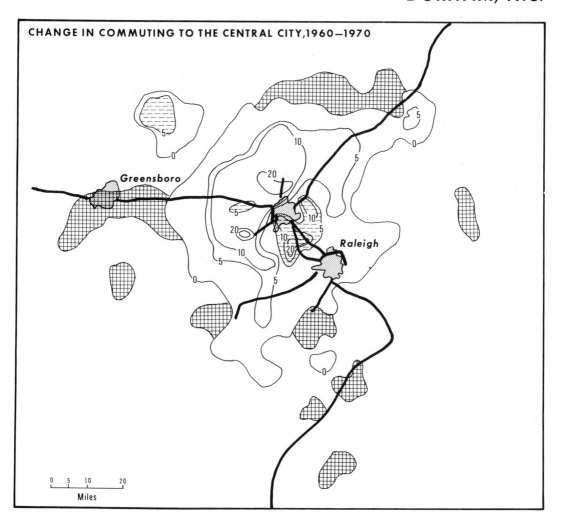

CHANGE IN COMMUTING TO THE CENTRAL CITY, 1960—1970

Greensboro

Raleigh

COMMUTING TO THE CBD IN 1970

NO DATA COLLECTED

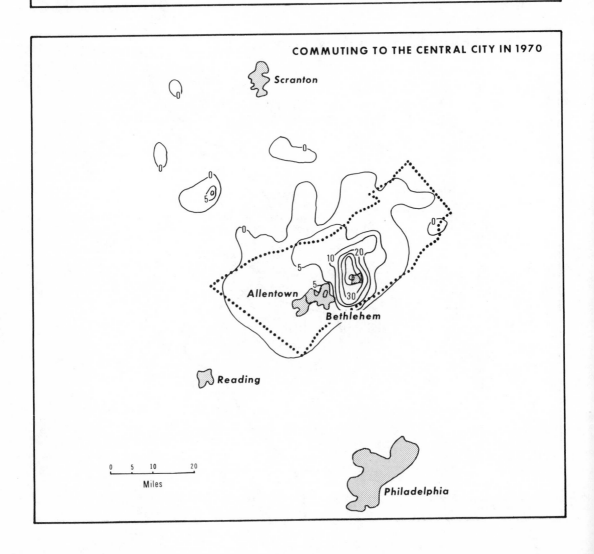

COMMUTING TO THE CENTRAL CITY IN 1970

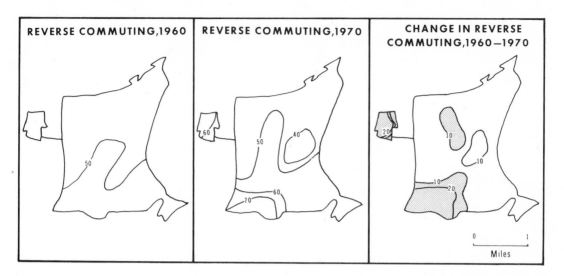

REVERSE COMMUTING, 1960

REVERSE COMMUTING, 1970

CHANGE IN REVERSE COMMUTING, 1960–1970

EASTON, PA.

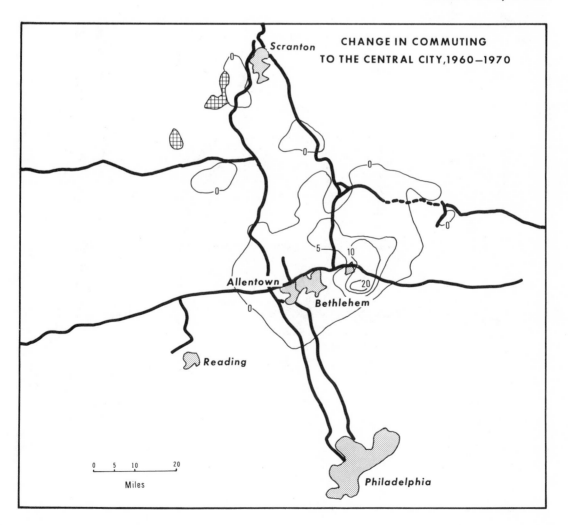

CHANGE IN COMMUTING TO THE CENTRAL CITY, 1960–1970

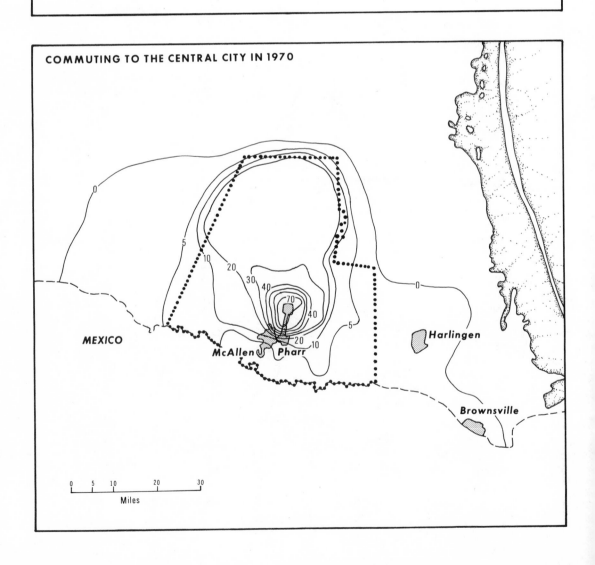

COMMUTING TO THE CBD IN 1970

NO DATA COLLECTED

COMMUTING TO THE CENTRAL CITY IN 1970

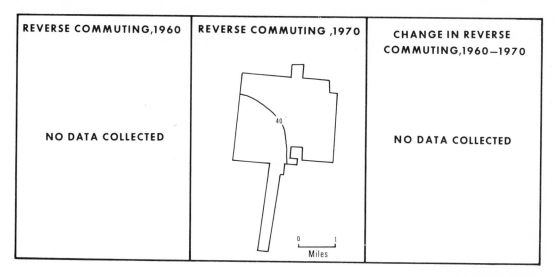

REVERSE COMMUTING,1960	REVERSE COMMUTING ,1970	CHANGE IN REVERSE COMMUTING,1960—1970
NO DATA COLLECTED	40	NO DATA COLLECTED

0   1
Miles

EDINBURG, TX.

CHANGE IN COMMUTING TO THE CENTRAL CITY,1960—1970

NO DATA COLLECTED

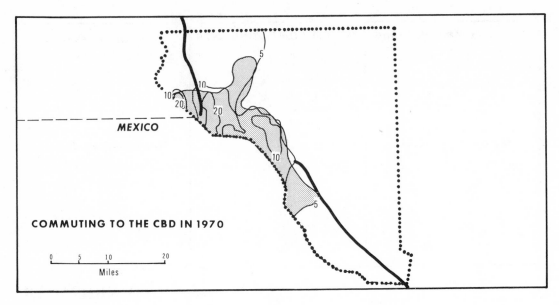

COMMUTING TO THE CBD IN 1970

MEXICO

0 5 10   20
Miles

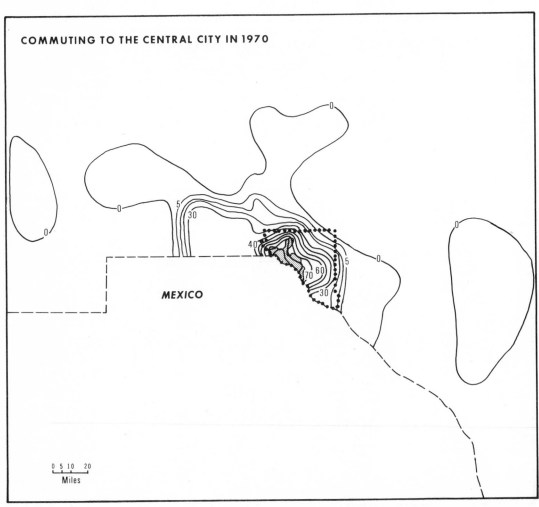

COMMUTING TO THE CENTRAL CITY IN 1970

MEXICO

0 5 10 20
Miles

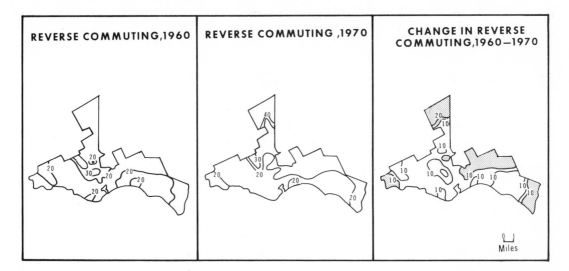

REVERSE COMMUTING, 1960   REVERSE COMMUTING , 1970   CHANGE IN REVERSE COMMUTING, 1960—1970

EL PASO, TX.

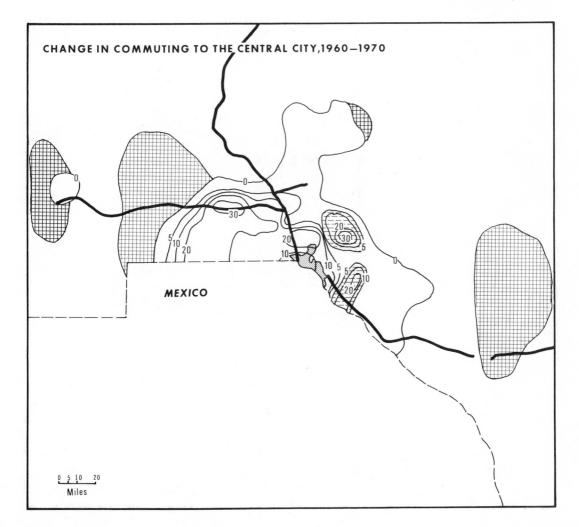

CHANGE IN COMMUTING TO THE CENTRAL CITY, 1960—1970

MEXICO

COMMUTING TO THE CBD IN 1970

NO DATA COLLECTED

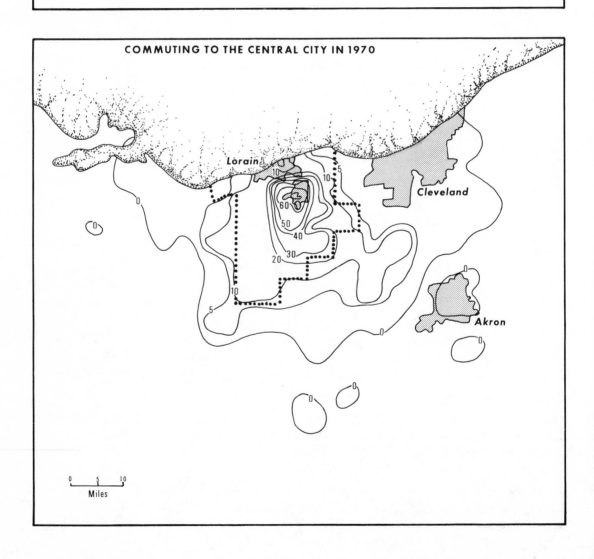

COMMUTING TO THE CENTRAL CITY IN 1970

Lorain

Cleveland

Akron

0   5   10
Miles

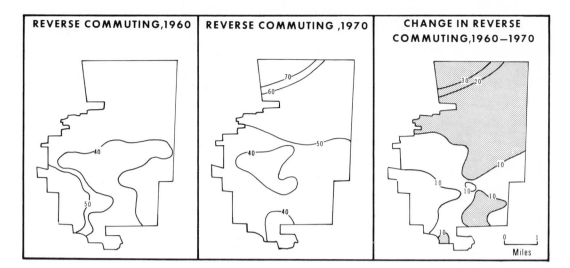

| REVERSE COMMUTING,1960 | REVERSE COMMUTING ,1970 | CHANGE IN REVERSE COMMUTING,1960—1970 |

ELYRIA, OH.

CHANGE IN COMMUTING TO THE CENTRAL CITY,1960—1970

NO DATA COLLECTED

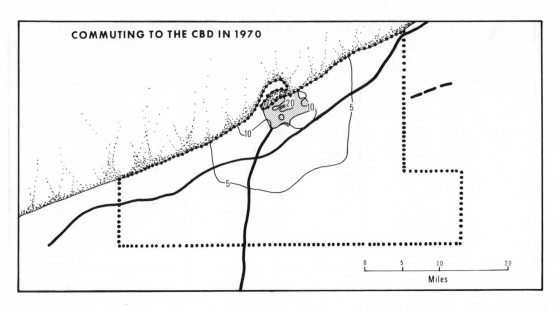

COMMUTING TO THE CBD IN 1970

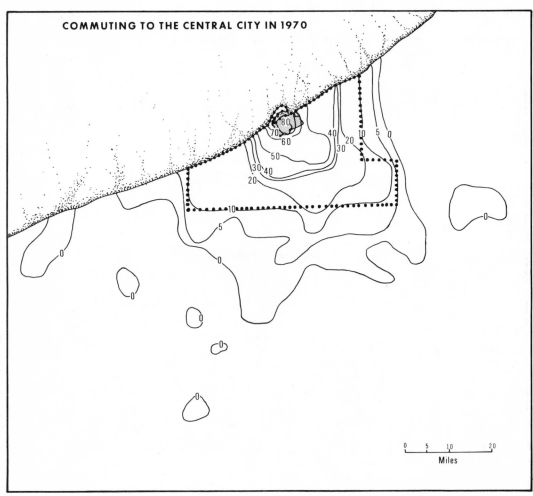

COMMUTING TO THE CENTRAL CITY IN 1970

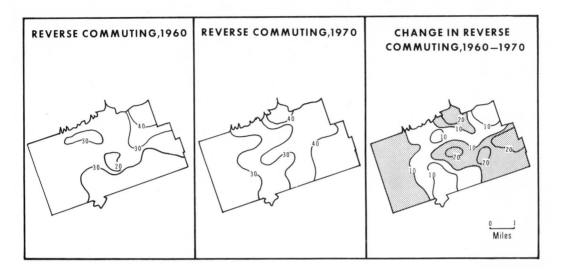

| REVERSE COMMUTING,1960 | REVERSE COMMUTING,1970 | CHANGE IN REVERSE COMMUTING,1960—1970 |

ERIE, PA.

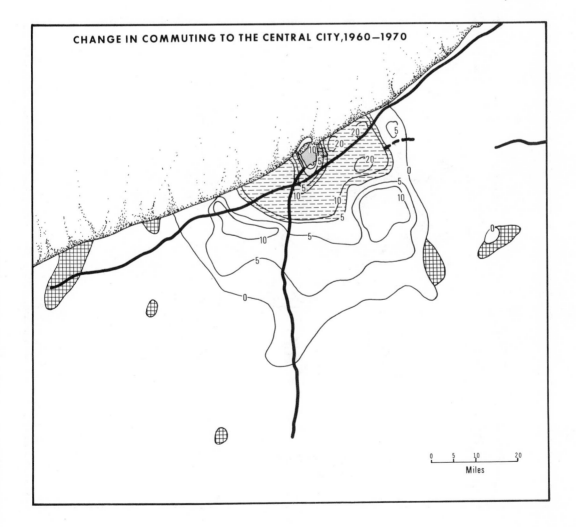

CHANGE IN COMMUTING TO THE CENTRAL CITY,1960—1970

COMMUTING TO THE CBD IN 1970

NO DATA COLLECTED

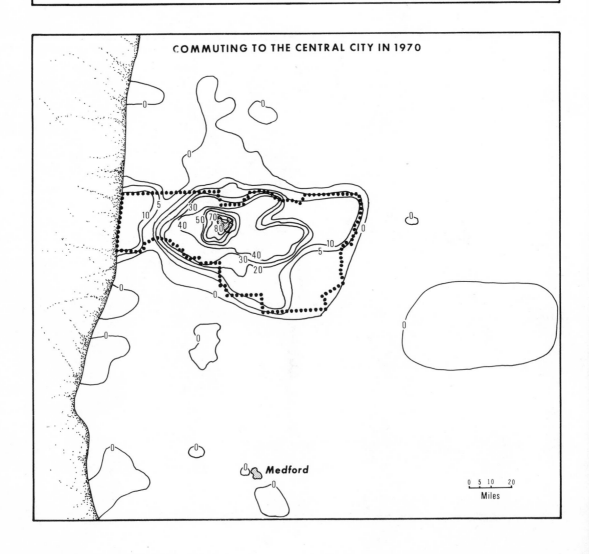

COMMUTING TO THE CENTRAL CITY IN 1970

Medford

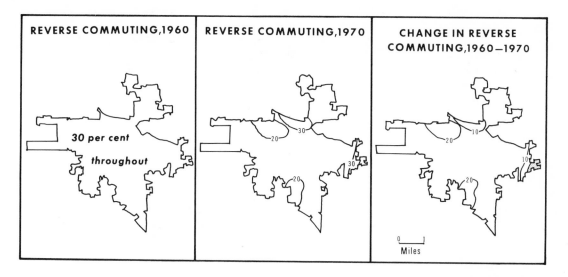

EUGENE, OR.

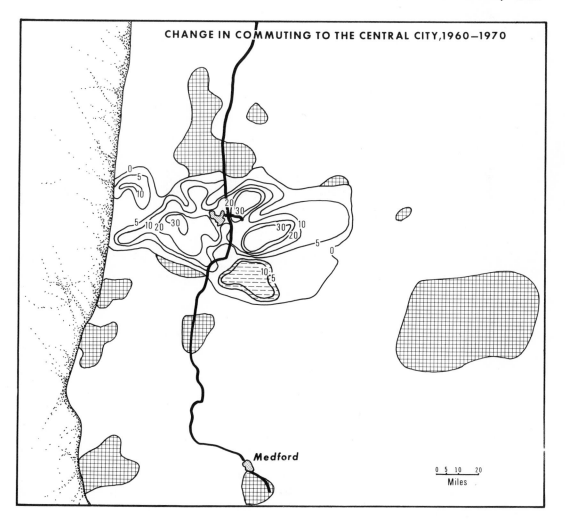

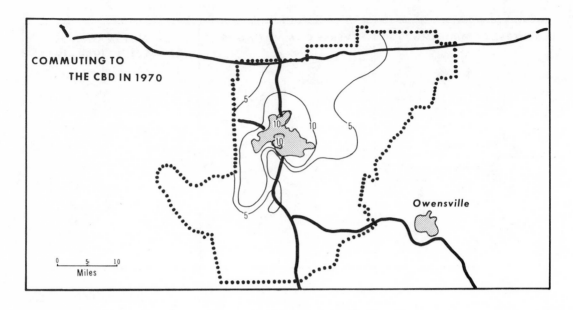

COMMUTING TO
THE CBD IN 1970

Owensville

0   5   10
Miles

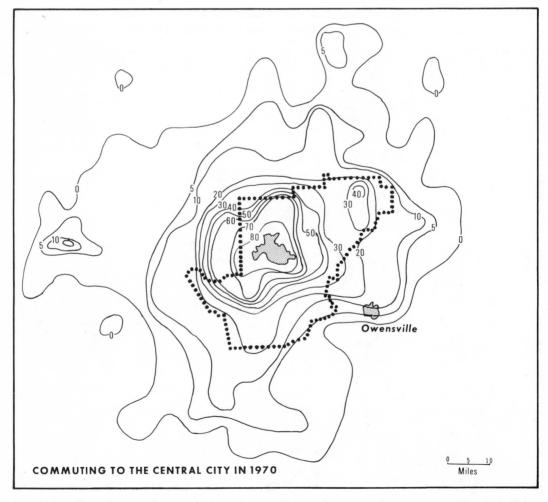

Owensville

0   5   10
Miles

COMMUTING TO THE CENTRAL CITY IN 1970

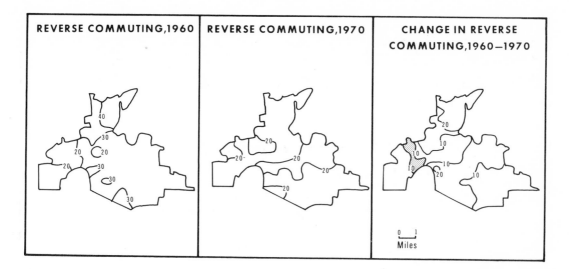

REVERSE COMMUTING, 1960

REVERSE COMMUTING, 1970

CHANGE IN REVERSE
COMMUTING, 1960–1970

0   1
Miles

EVANSVILLE, IN.

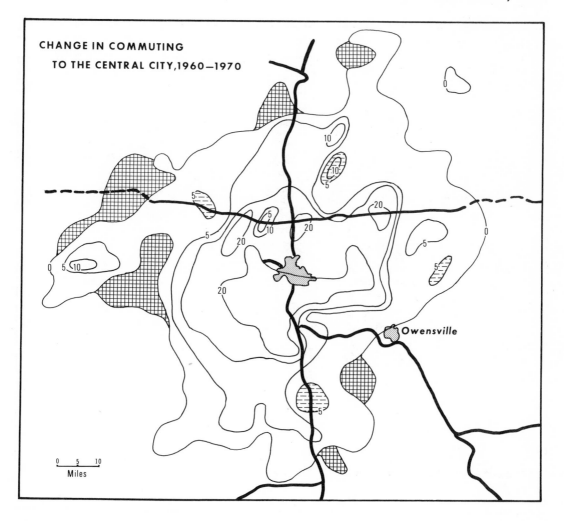

CHANGE IN COMMUTING
TO THE CENTRAL CITY, 1960–1970

Owensville

0   5   10
Miles

COMMUTING TO THE CBD IN 1970

NO DATA COLLECTED

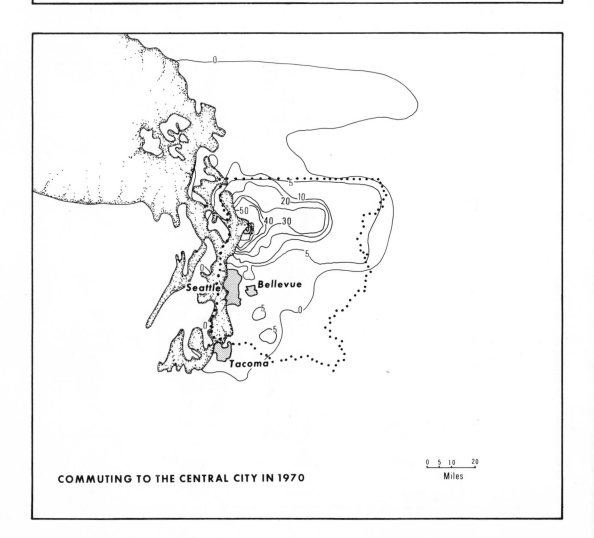

COMMUTING TO THE CENTRAL CITY IN 1970

0 5 10   20
Miles

REVERSE COMMUTING, 1960	REVERSE COMMUTING, 1970	CHANGE IN REVERSE COMMUTING, 1960—1970
NO DATA COLLECTED		NO DATA COLLECTED

REVERSE COMMUTING, 1970

30
-30-
30
30
40
50
-50-
-50-
-60-

0   1
Miles

EVERETT, WA.

CHANGE IN COMMUTING TO THE CENTRAL CITY, 1960—1970

NO DATA COLLECTED

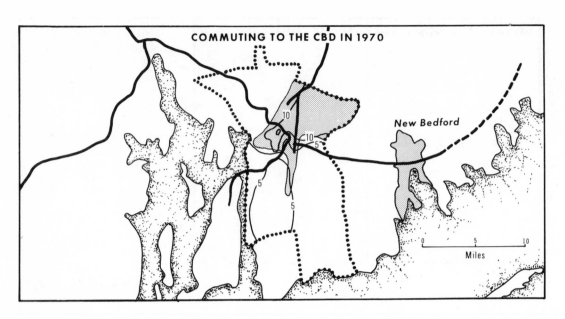

COMMUTING TO THE CBD IN 1970

New Bedford

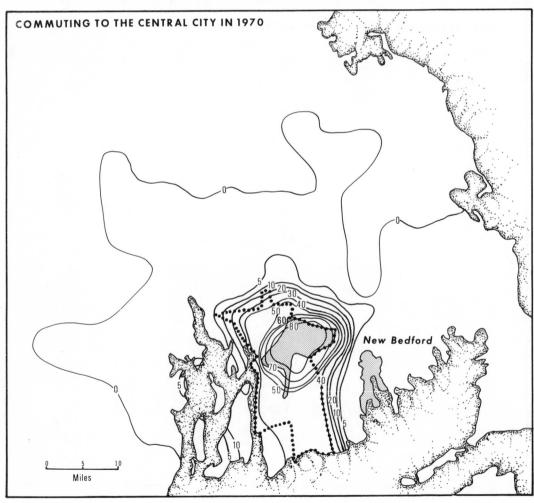

COMMUTING TO THE CENTRAL CITY IN 1970

New Bedford

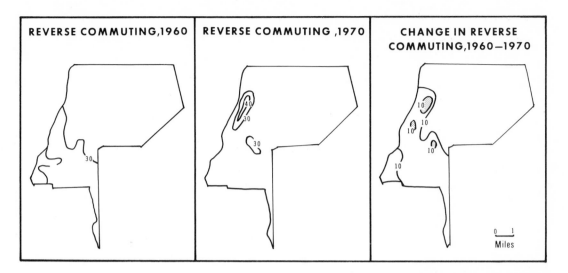

REVERSE COMMUTING, 1960

REVERSE COMMUTING, 1970

CHANGE IN REVERSE COMMUTING, 1960—1970

FALL RIVER, MA.

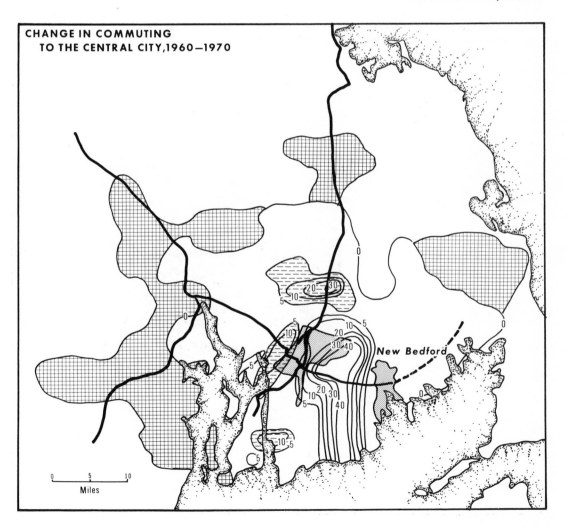

CHANGE IN COMMUTING TO THE CENTRAL CITY, 1960—1970

New Bedford

COMMUTING TO THE CBD IN 1970

NO DATA COLLECTED

COMMUTING TO THE CENTRAL CITY IN 1970

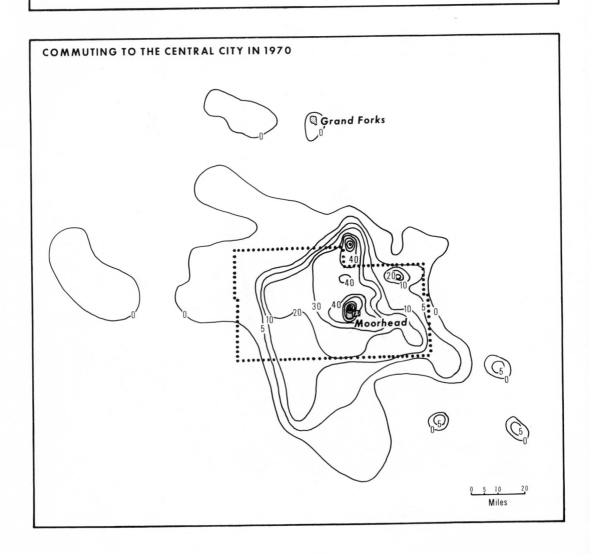

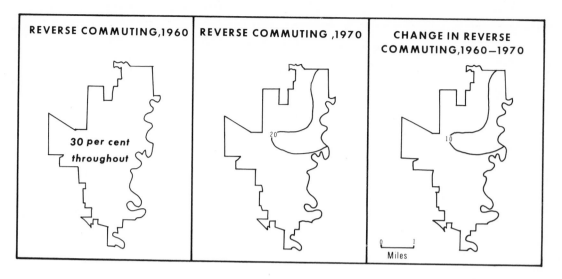

REVERSE COMMUTING,1960

REVERSE COMMUTING,1970

CHANGE IN REVERSE COMMUTING,1960—1970

30 per cent throughout

FARGO, N.D.

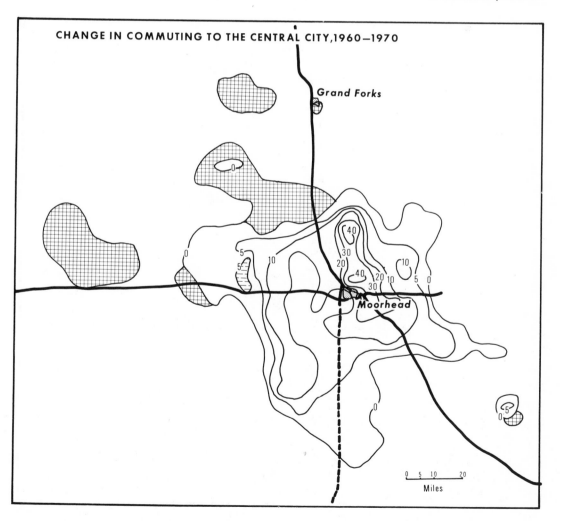

CHANGE IN COMMUTING TO THE CENTRAL CITY,1960—1970

Grand Forks

Moorhead

COMMUTING TO THE CBD IN 1970

NO DATA COLLECTED

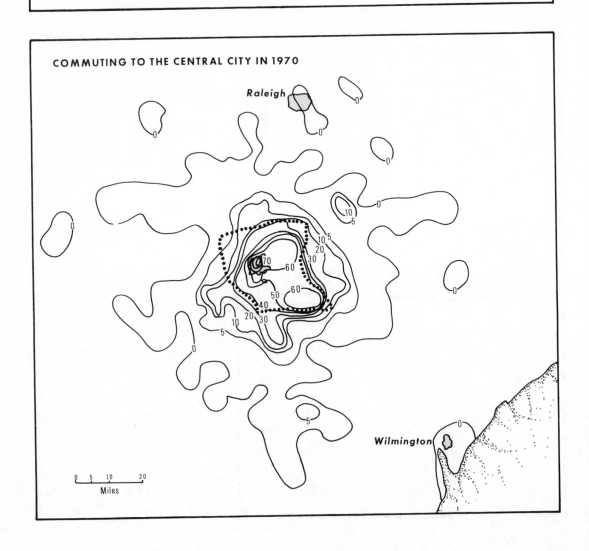

COMMUTING TO THE CENTRAL CITY IN 1970

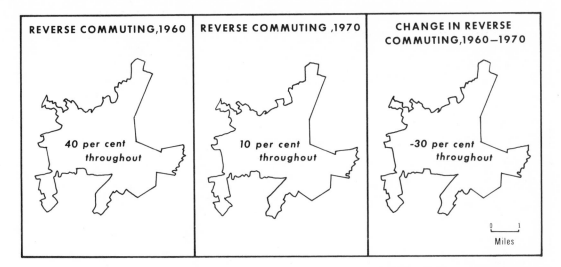

REVERSE COMMUTING,1960

40 per cent throughout

REVERSE COMMUTING ,1970

10 per cent throughout

CHANGE IN REVERSE COMMUTING,1960—1970

-30 per cent throughout

0   1
Miles

FAYETTEVILLE, N.C.

CHANGE IN COMMUTING TO THE CENTRAL CITY,1960—1970

NO DATA COLLECTED

COMMUTING TO THE CBD IN 1970

NO DATA COLLECTED

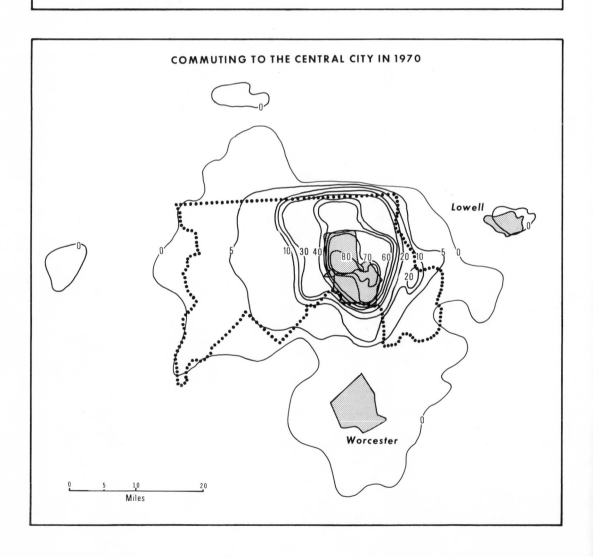

COMMUTING TO THE CENTRAL CITY IN 1970

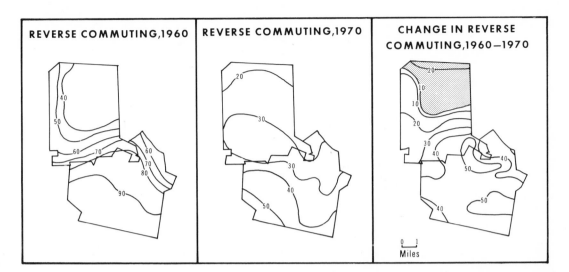

REVERSE COMMUTING,1960   REVERSE COMMUTING,1970   CHANGE IN REVERSE COMMUTING,1960—1970

FITCHBURG - LEOMINSTER, MA.

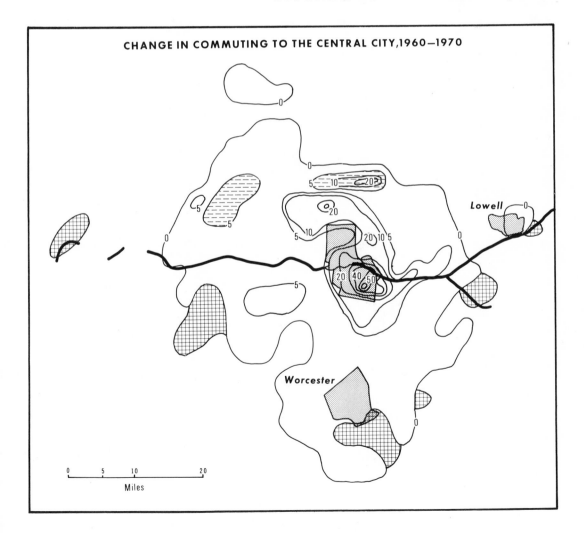

CHANGE IN COMMUTING TO THE CENTRAL CITY,1960—1970

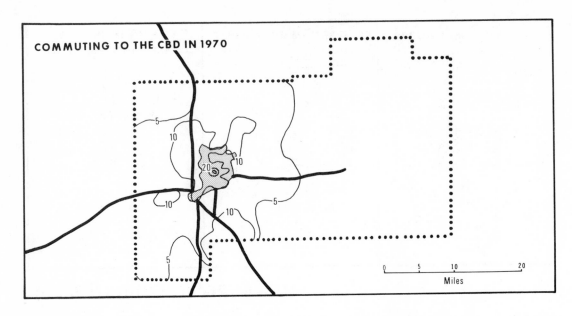

COMMUTING TO THE CBD IN 1970

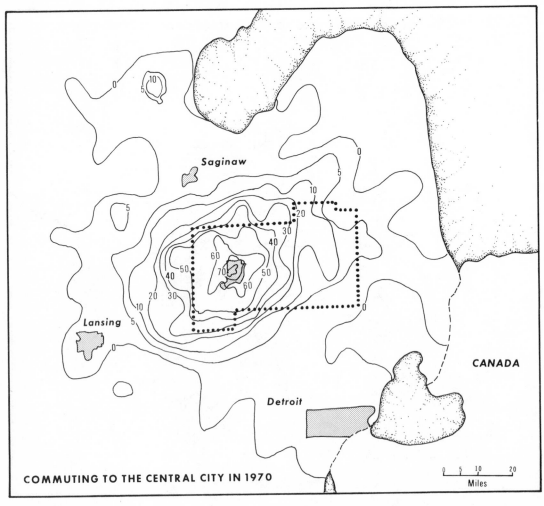

COMMUTING TO THE CENTRAL CITY IN 1970

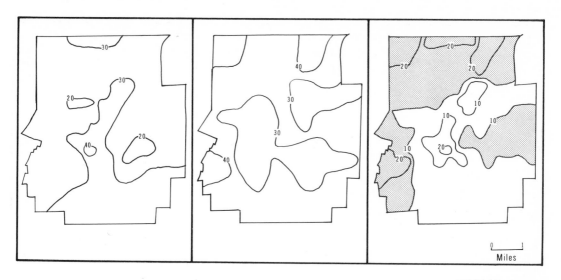

FLINT, MI.

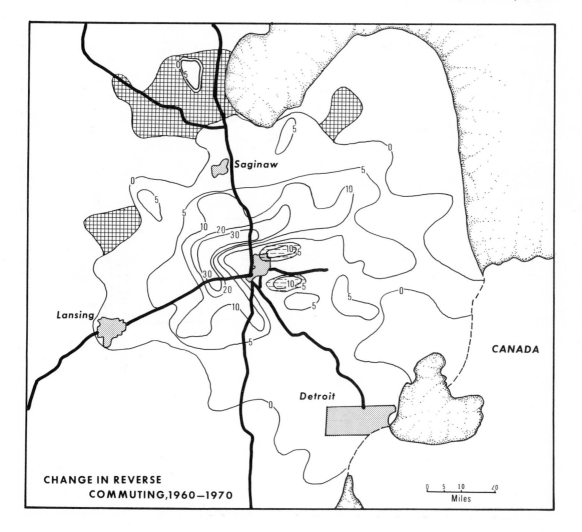

CHANGE IN REVERSE
COMMUTING, 1960–1970

COMMUTING TO THE CBD IN 1970

NO DATA COLLECTED

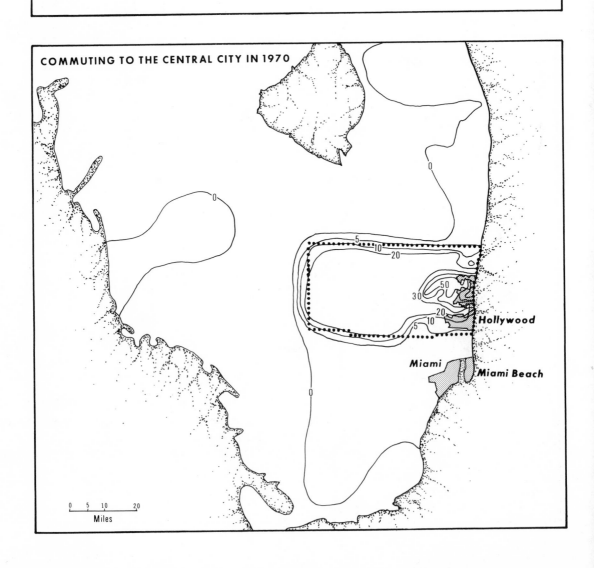

COMMUTING TO THE CENTRAL CITY IN 1970

Hollywood

Miami

Miami Beach

0 5 10 20
Miles

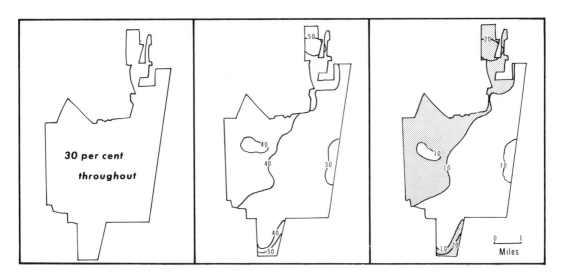

FORT LAUDERDALE, FL.

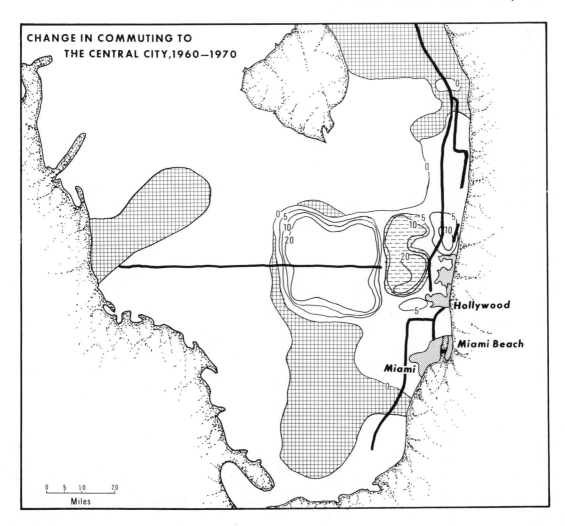

CHANGE IN COMMUTING TO
THE CENTRAL CITY, 1960—1970

COMMUTING TO THE CBD IN 1970

NO DATA COLLECTED

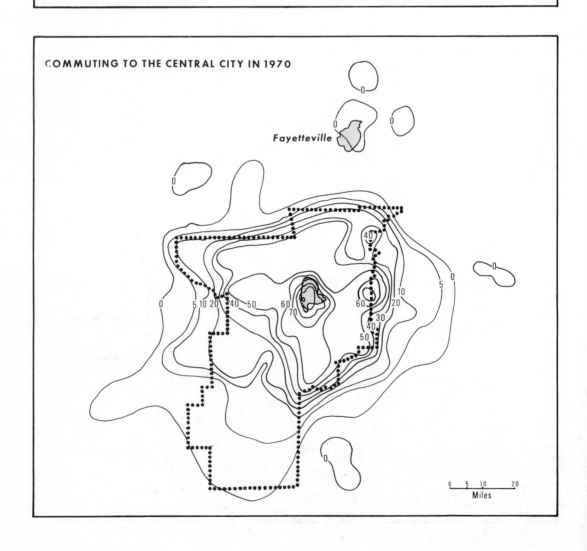

COMMUTING TO THE CENTRAL CITY IN 1970

Fayetteville

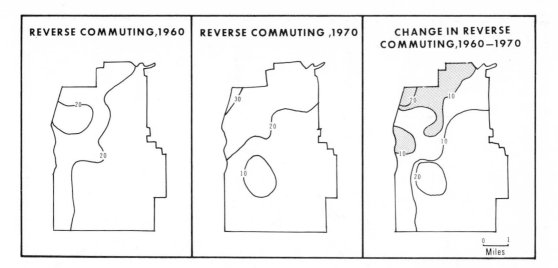

REVERSE COMMUTING,1960 REVERSE COMMUTING ,1970 CHANGE IN REVERSE COMMUTING,1960–1970

FORT SMITH, AR.

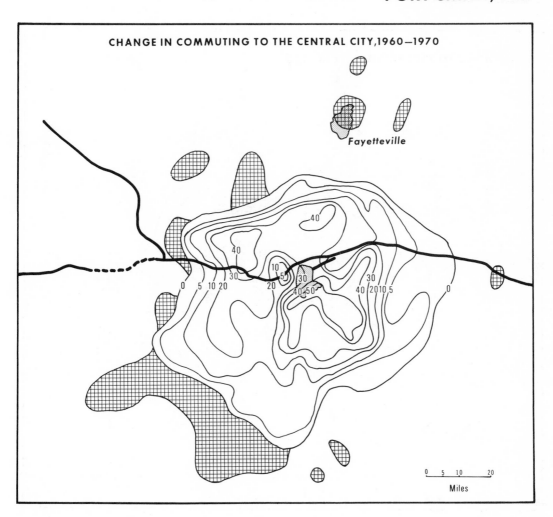

CHANGE IN COMMUTING TO THE CENTRAL CITY,1960–1970

Fayetteville

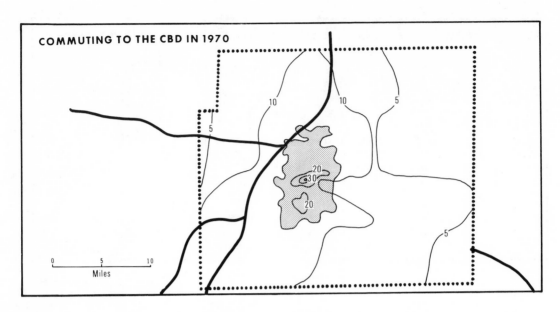

COMMUTING TO THE CBD IN 1970

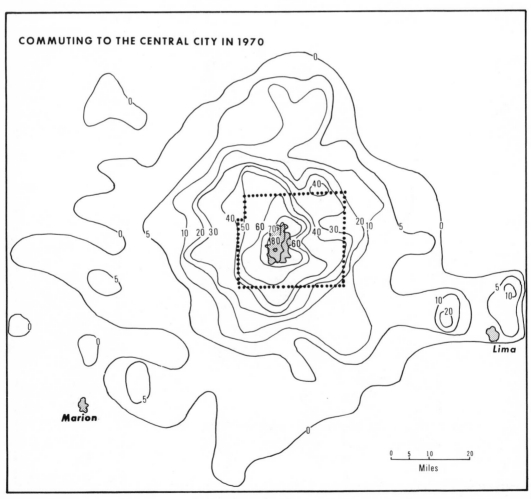

COMMUTING TO THE CENTRAL CITY IN 1970

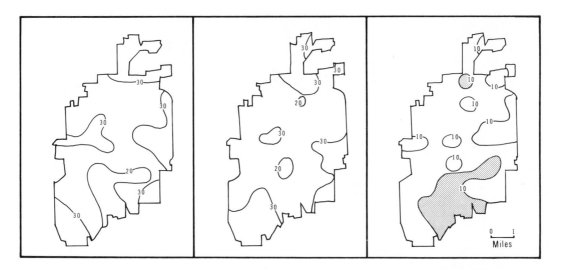

FORT WAYNE, IN.

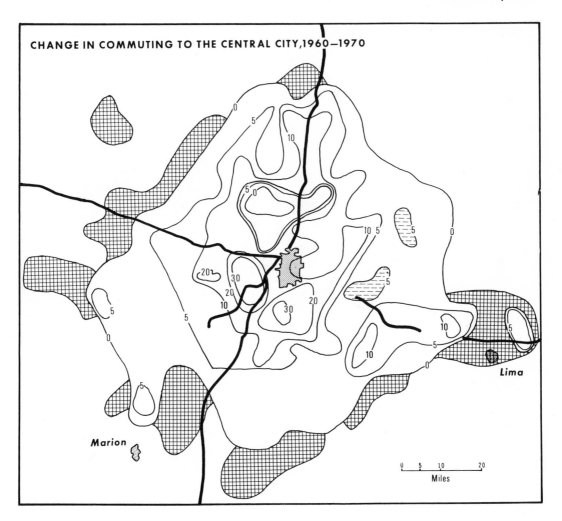

CHANGE IN COMMUTING TO THE CENTRAL CITY, 1960–1970

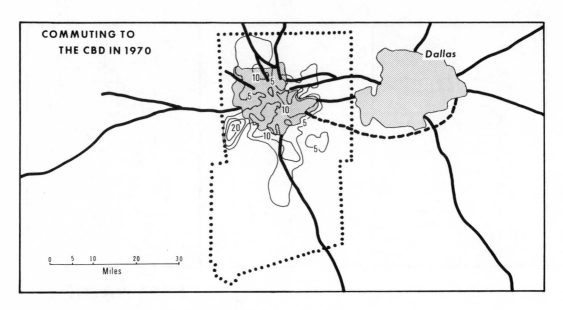

COMMUTING TO
THE CBD IN 1970

Dallas

0   5   10   20   30
Miles

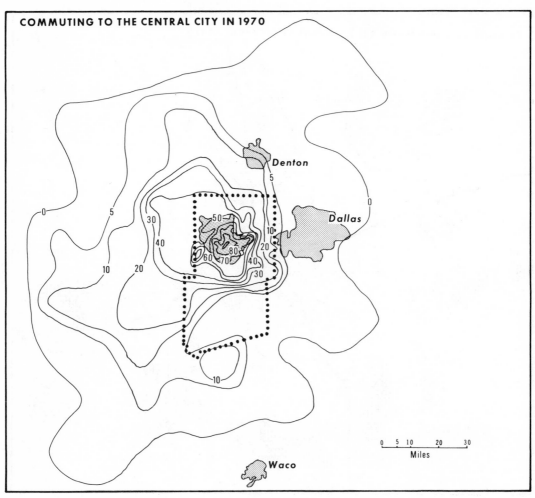

COMMUTING TO THE CENTRAL CITY IN 1970

Denton

Dallas

Waco

0   5 10   20   30
Miles

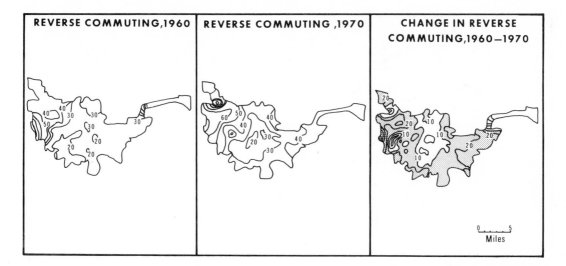

REVERSE COMMUTING, 1960

REVERSE COMMUTING, 1970

CHANGE IN REVERSE COMMUTING, 1960—1970

FORT WORTH, TX.

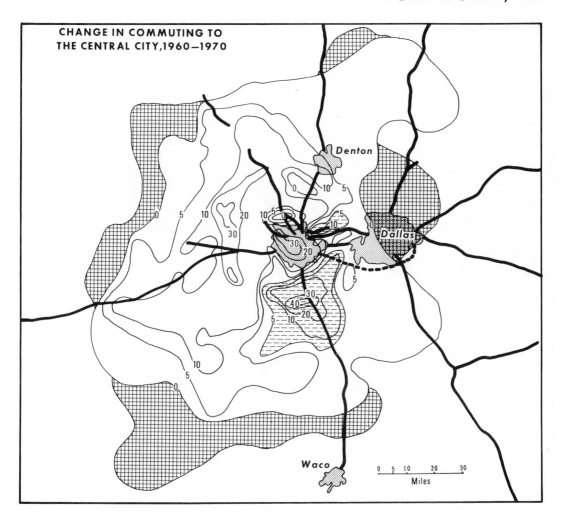

CHANGE IN COMMUTING TO THE CENTRAL CITY, 1960—1970

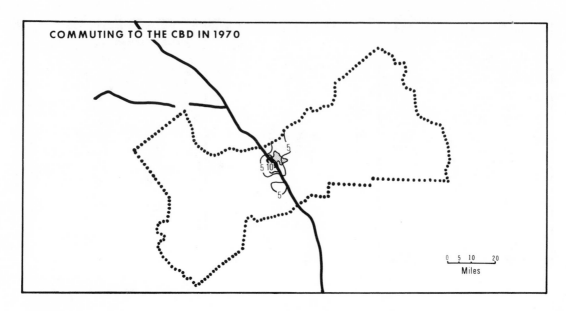

COMMUTING TO THE CBD IN 1970

0 5 10 20
Miles

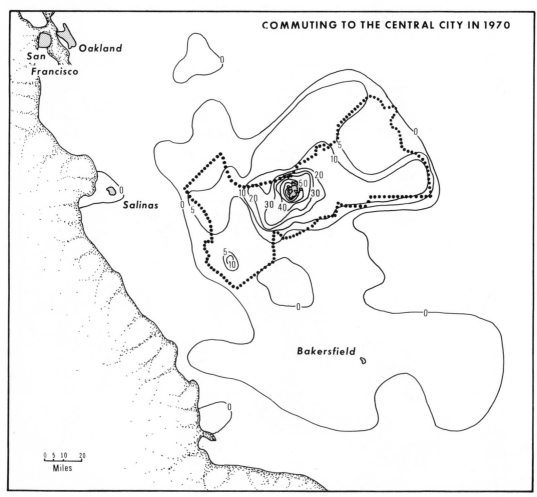

COMMUTING TO THE CENTRAL CITY IN 1970

San Francisco

Oakland

Salinas

Bakersfield

0 5 10 20
Miles

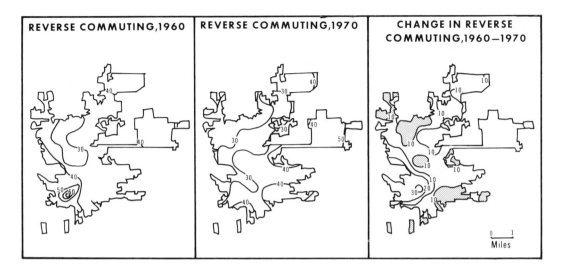

REVERSE COMMUTING, 1960

REVERSE COMMUTING, 1970

CHANGE IN REVERSE COMMUTING, 1960—1970

0   1
Miles

FRESNO, CA.

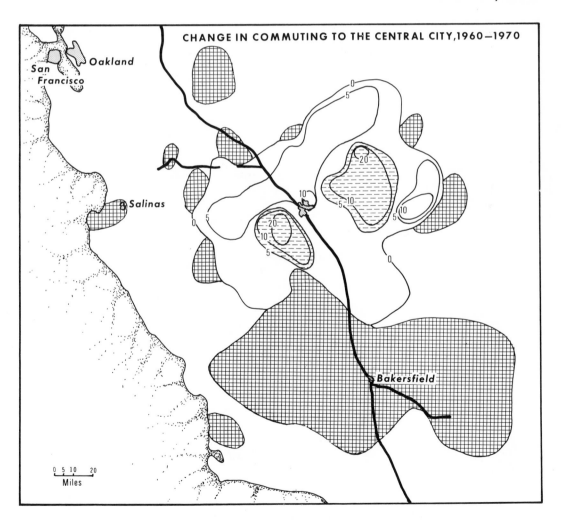

CHANGE IN COMMUTING TO THE CENTRAL CITY, 1960—1970

San Francisco

Oakland

Salinas

Bakersfield

0 5 10   20
Miles

290

COMMUTING TO THE CBD IN 1970

NO DATA COLLECTED

COMMUTING TO THE CENTRAL CITY IN 1970

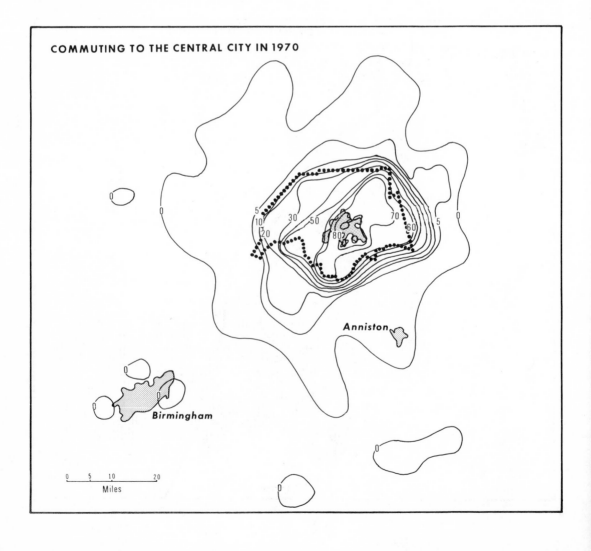

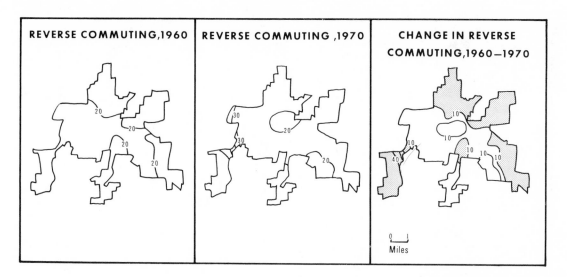

REVERSE COMMUTING,1960

REVERSE COMMUTING ,1970

CHANGE IN REVERSE
COMMUTING,1960—1970

GADSDEN, AL.

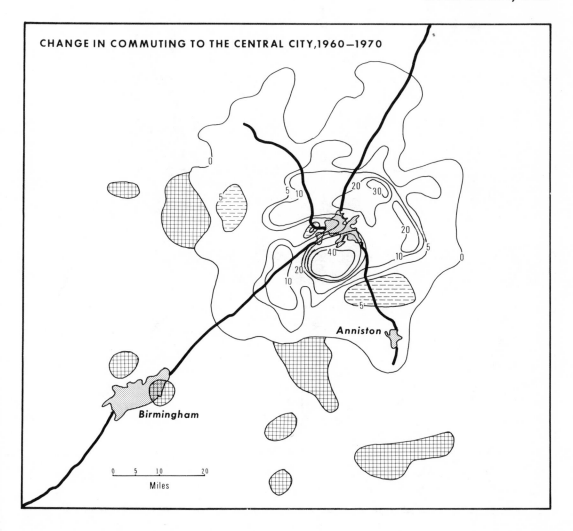

CHANGE IN COMMUTING TO THE CENTRAL CITY,1960—1970

Anniston

Birmingham

COMMUTING TO THE CBD IN 1970

NO DATA COLLECTED

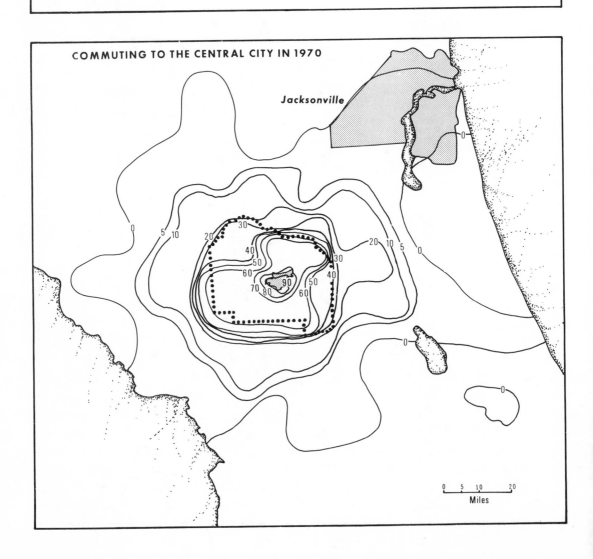

COMMUTING TO THE CENTRAL CITY IN 1970

Jacksonville

293

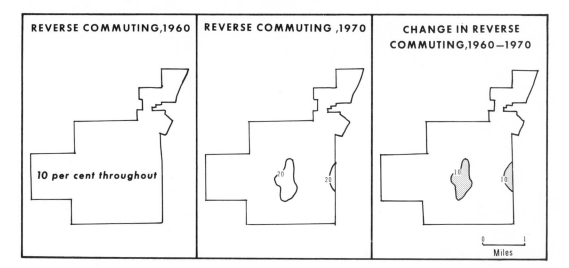

GAINSVILLE, FL.

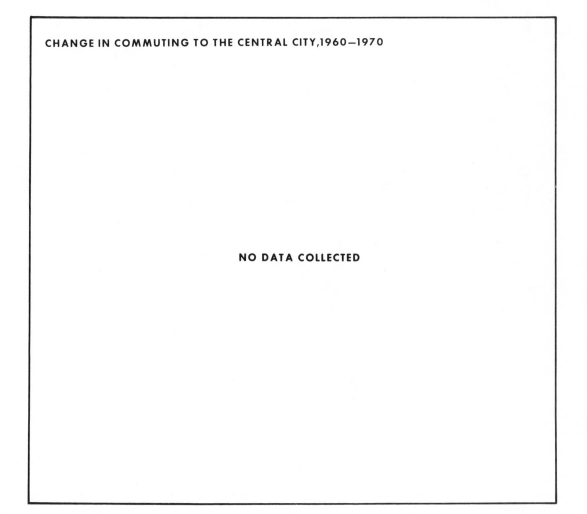

COMMUTING TO THE CBD IN 1970

NO DATA COLLECTED

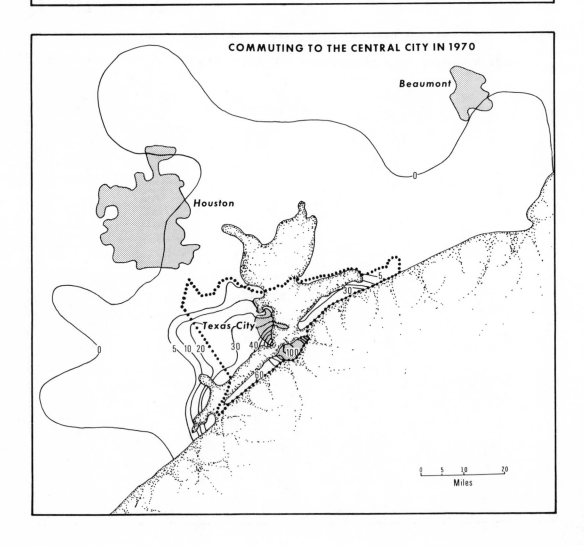

COMMUTING TO THE CENTRAL CITY IN 1970

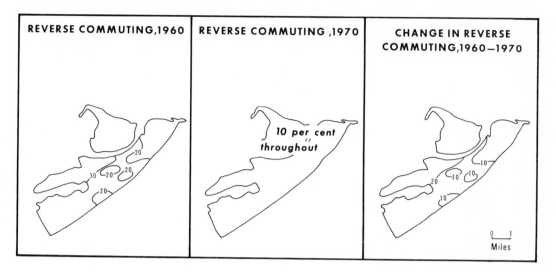

GALVESTON, TX.

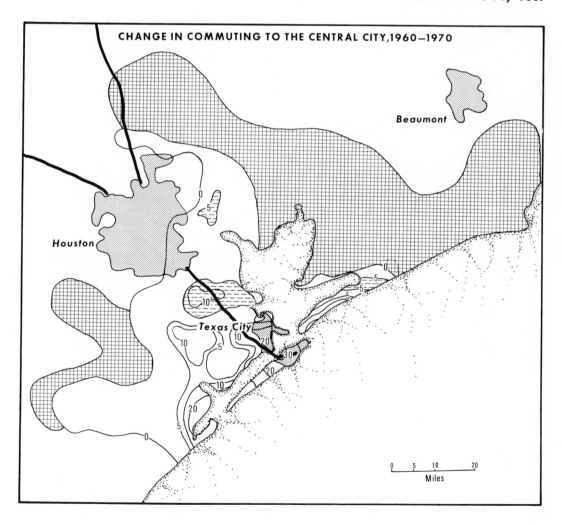

COMMUTING TO THE CBD IN 1970

NO DATA COLLECTED

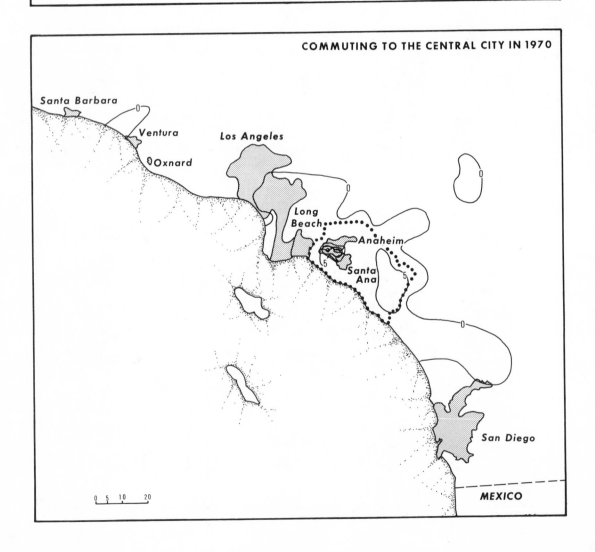

COMMUTING TO THE CENTRAL CITY IN 1970

Santa Barbara

Ventura

Oxnard

Los Angeles

Long Beach

Anaheim

Santa Ana

San Diego

MEXICO

0 5 10 20

REVERSE COMMUTING,1960	REVERSE COMMUTING ,1970	CHANGE IN REVERSE COMMUTING,1960—1970
NO DATA COLLECTED		NO DATA COLLECTED

90

80

90

0   1
Miles

GARDEN GROVE, CA.

CHANGE IN COMMUTING TO THE CENTRAL CITY,1960—1970

NO DATA COLLECTED

COMMUTING TO THE CBD IN 1970

NO DATA COLLECTED

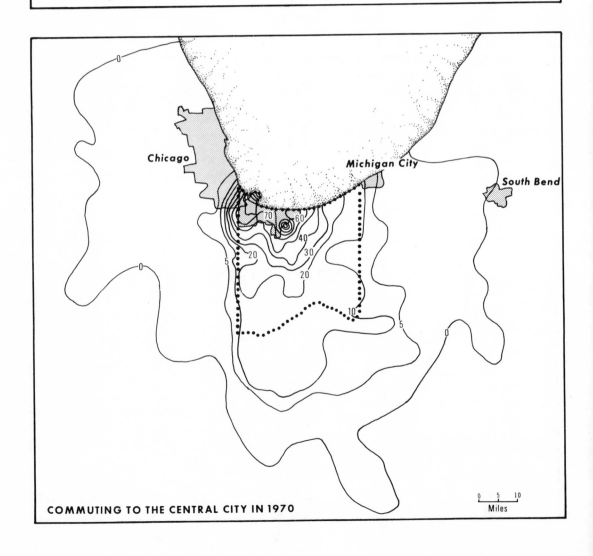

COMMUTING TO THE CENTRAL CITY IN 1970

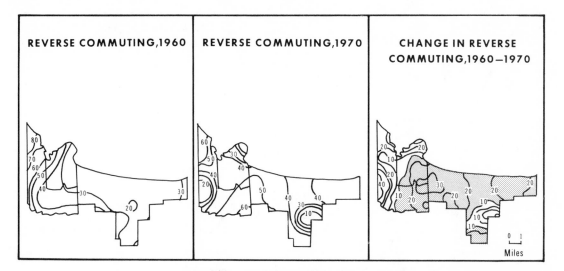

REVERSE COMMUTING, 1960

REVERSE COMMUTING, 1970

CHANGE IN REVERSE
COMMUTING, 1960–1970

GARY - HAMMOND - EAST CHICAGO, IN.

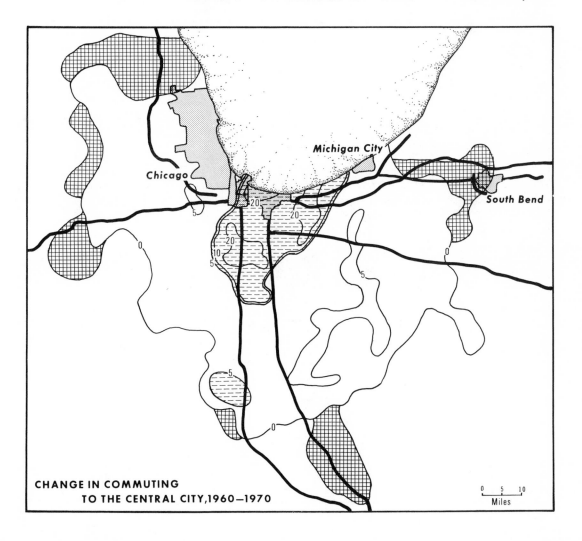

CHANGE IN COMMUTING
TO THE CENTRAL CITY, 1960–1970

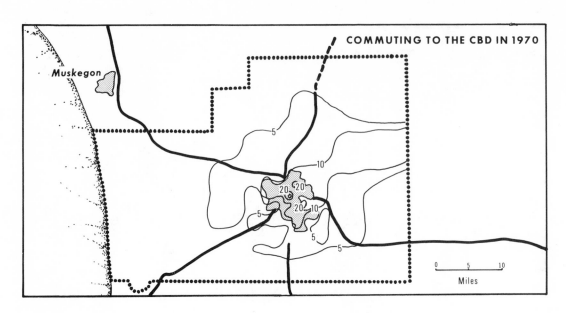

COMMUTING TO THE CBD IN 1970

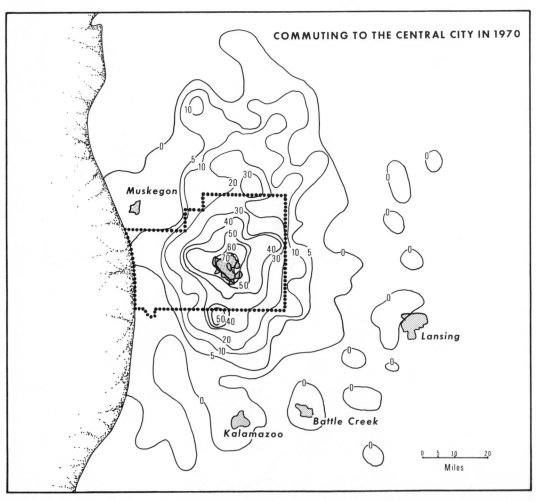

COMMUTING TO THE CENTRAL CITY IN 1970

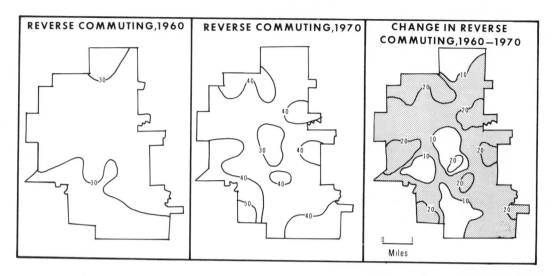

REVERSE COMMUTING,1960

REVERSE COMMUTING,1970

CHANGE IN REVERSE
COMMUTING,1960—1970

GRAND RAPIDS, MI.

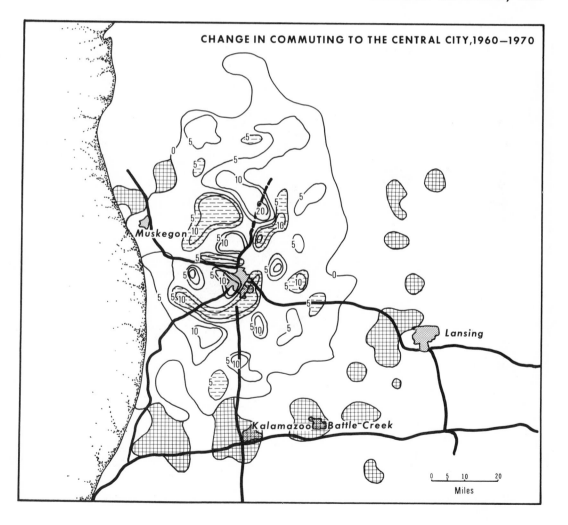

CHANGE IN COMMUTING TO THE CENTRAL CITY,1960—1970

Muskegon

Lansing

Kalamazoo Battle-Creek

COMMUTING TO THE CBD IN 1970

NO DATA COLLECTED

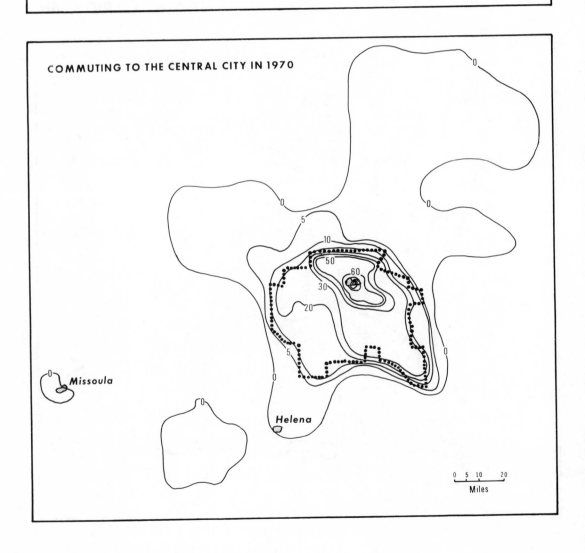

COMMUTING TO THE CENTRAL CITY IN 1970

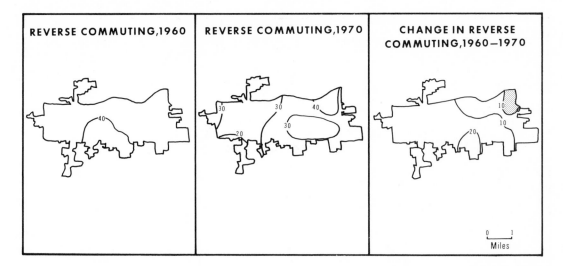

REVERSE COMMUTING, 1960

REVERSE COMMUTING, 1970

CHANGE IN REVERSE COMMUTING, 1960—1970

0   1
Miles

GREAT FALLS, MT.

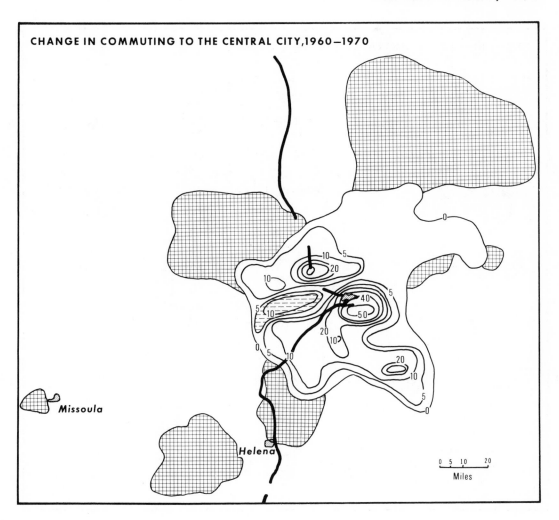

CHANGE IN COMMUTING TO THE CENTRAL CITY, 1960—1970

Missoula

Helena

0 5 10   20
Miles

COMMUTING TO THE CBD IN 1970

NO DATA COLLECTED

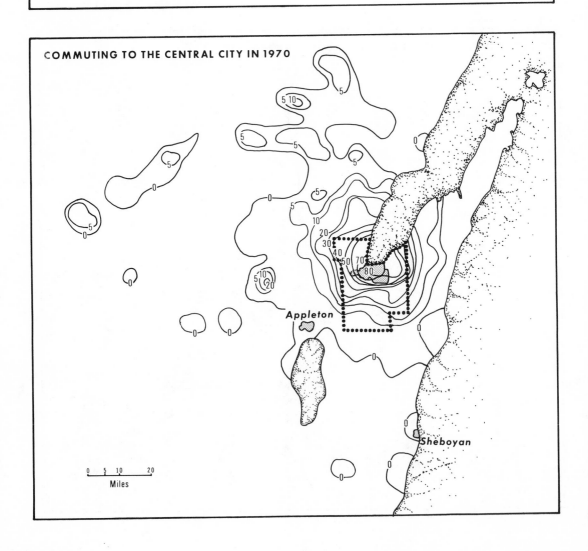

COMMUTING TO THE CENTRAL CITY IN 1970

Appleton

Sheboyan

0 5 10   20
Miles

305

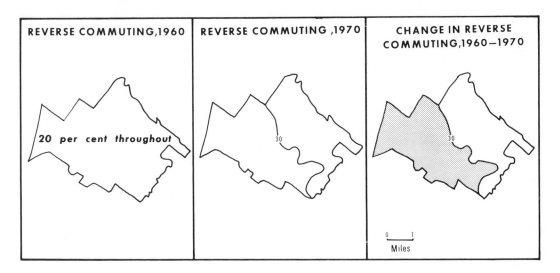

GREEN BAY, WI.

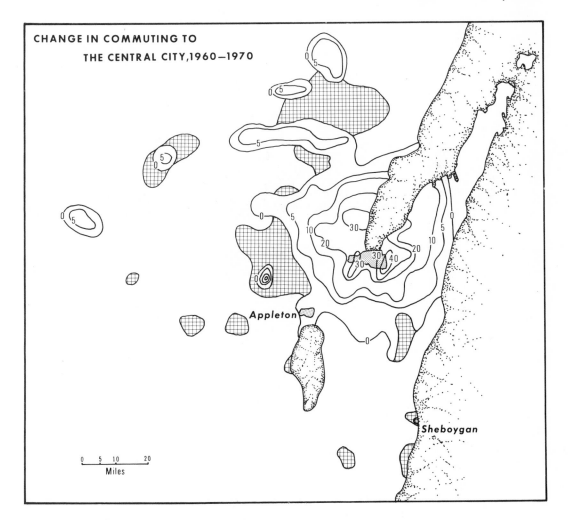

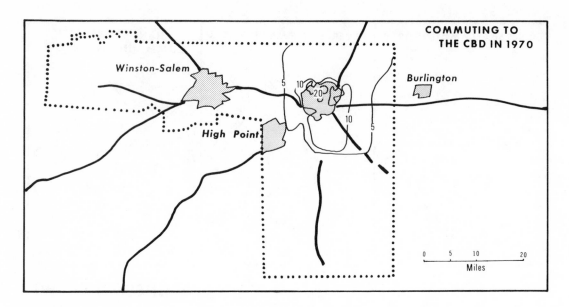

COMMUTING TO
THE CBD IN 1970

Winston-Salem

Burlington

High Point

5
10
20
10
5

0 5 10 20
Miles

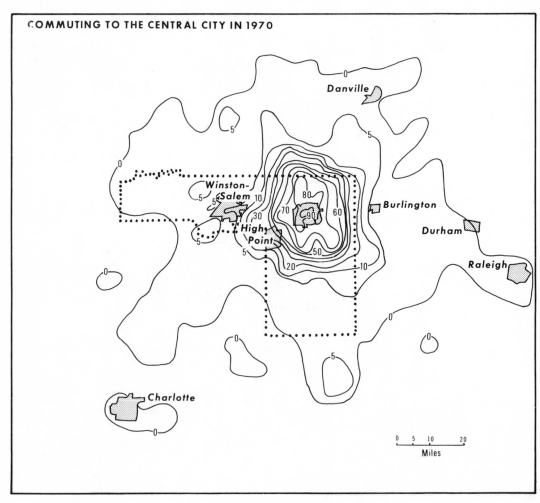

COMMUTING TO THE CENTRAL CITY IN 1970

Danville

5

5

0

Winston-Salem

5

5

10

80

70

90

60

Burlington

Durham

Raleigh

30

High Point

5

50

20

10

5

0

0

0

Charlotte

0

5

0 5 10 20
Miles

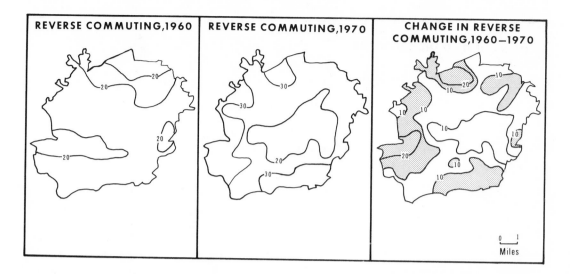

REVERSE COMMUTING, 1960

REVERSE COMMUTING, 1970

CHANGE IN REVERSE COMMUTING, 1960—1970

GREENSBORO, N.C.

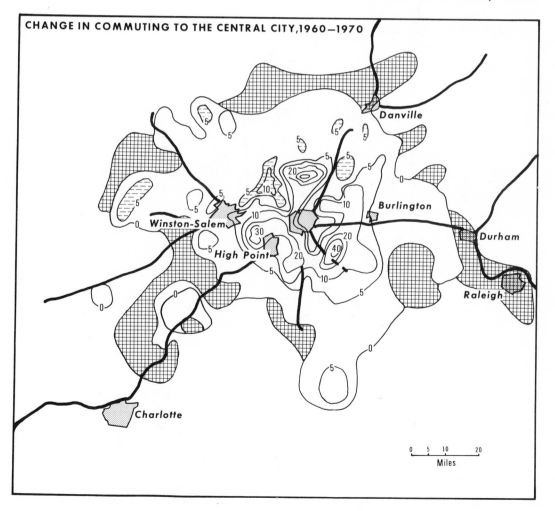

CHANGE IN COMMUTING TO THE CENTRAL CITY, 1960—1970

COMMUTING TO THE CBD IN 1970

NO DATA COLLECTED

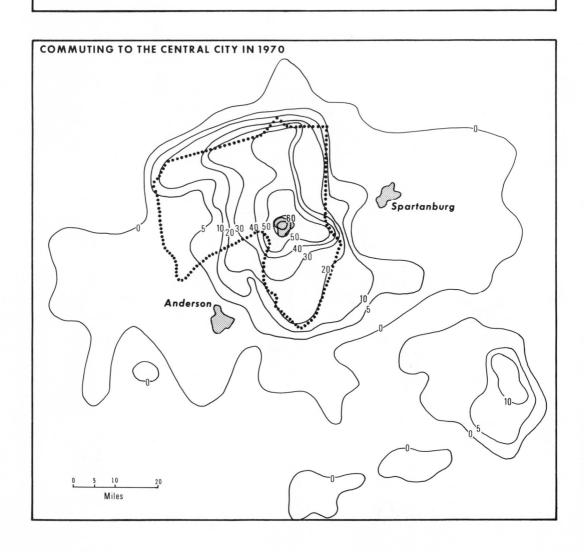

COMMUTING TO THE CENTRAL CITY IN 1970

309

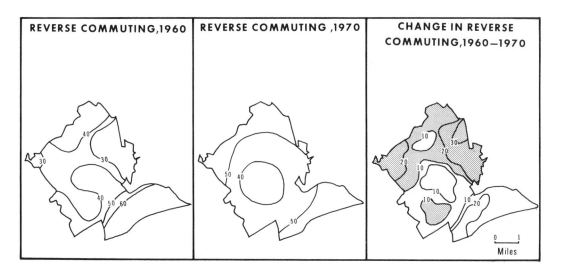

GREENVILLE, S.C.

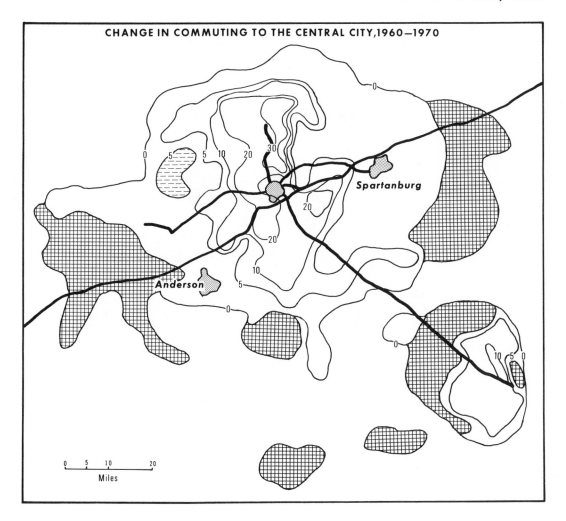

COMMUTING TO THE CBD IN 1970

NO DATA COLLECTED

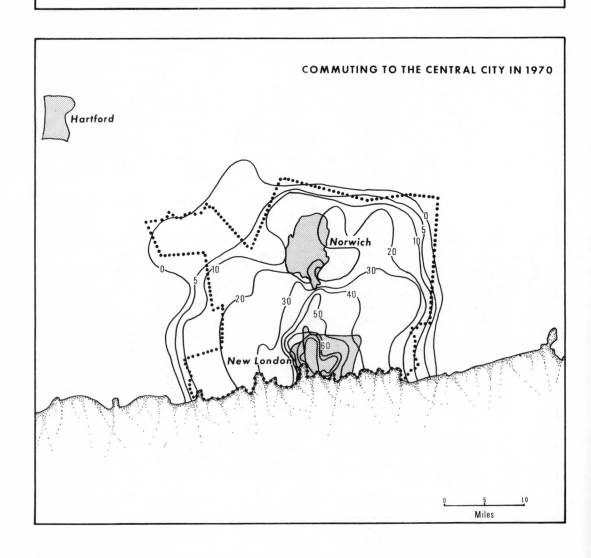

COMMUTING TO THE CENTRAL CITY IN 1970

REVERSE COMMUTING,1960	REVERSE COMMUTING,1970	CHANGE IN REVERSE COMMUTING,1960—1970
NO DATA COLLECTED		NO DATA COLLECTED

30

40

0 ___ 1
Miles

GROTON, CT.

CHANGE IN COMMUTING TO THE CENTRAL CITY,1960—1970

NO DATA COLLECTED

COMMUTING TO THE CBD IN 1970

NO DATA COLLECTED

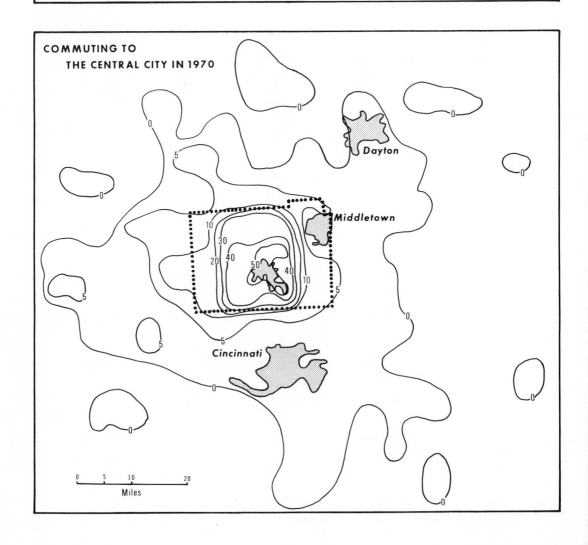

COMMUTING TO THE CENTRAL CITY IN 1970

Dayton

Middletown

Cincinnati

0   5   10   20
Miles

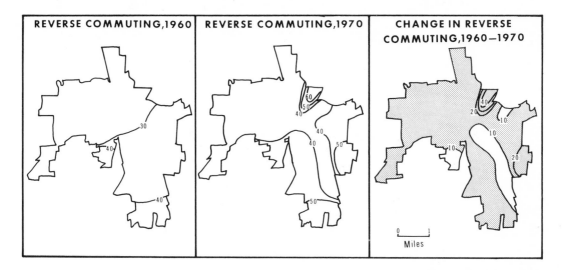

REVERSE COMMUTING, 1960

REVERSE COMMUTING, 1970

CHANGE IN REVERSE
COMMUTING, 1960—1970

HAMILTON, OH.

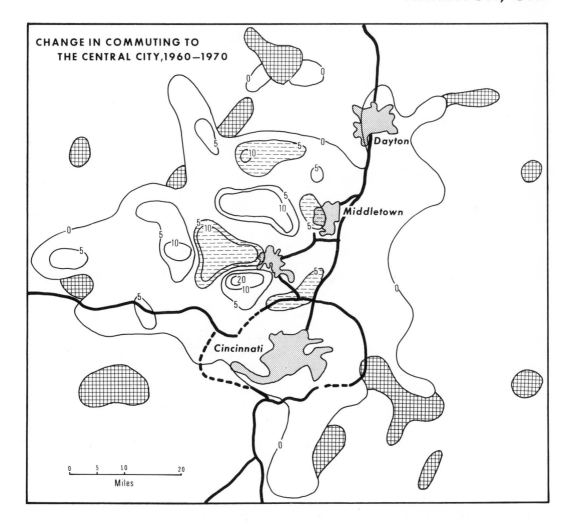

CHANGE IN COMMUTING TO
THE CENTRAL CITY, 1960—1970

Dayton

Middletown

Cincinnati

COMMUTING TO THE CBD IN 1970

NO DATA COLLECTED

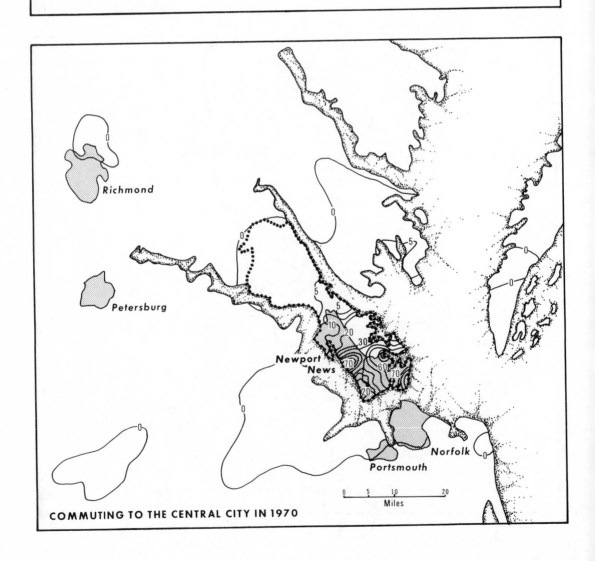

COMMUTING TO THE CENTRAL CITY IN 1970

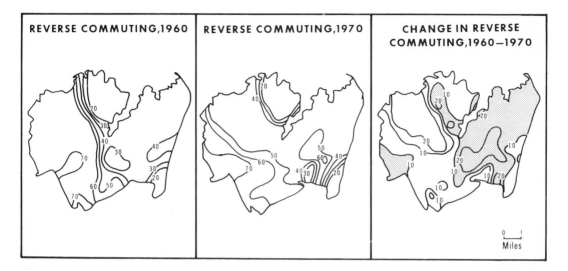

| REVERSE COMMUTING,1960 | REVERSE COMMUTING,1970 | CHANGE IN REVERSE COMMUTING,1960—1970 |

HAMPTON, VA.

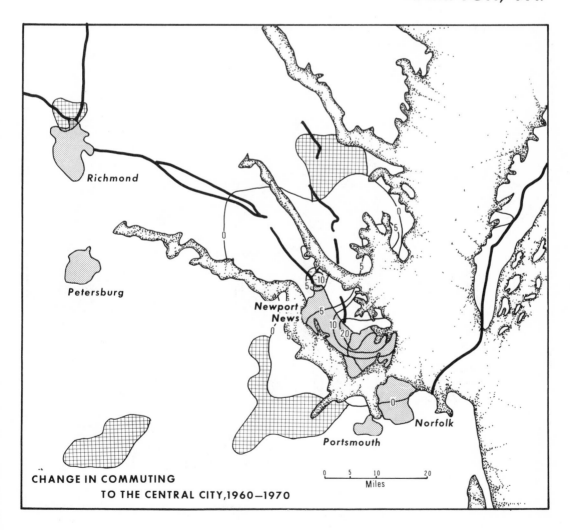

CHANGE IN COMMUTING TO THE CENTRAL CITY,1960—1970

COMMUTING TO THE CBD IN 1970

NO DATA COLLECTED

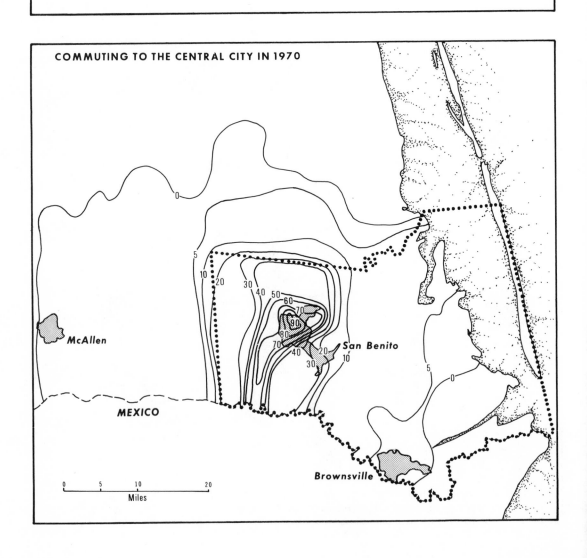

COMMUTING TO THE CENTRAL CITY IN 1970

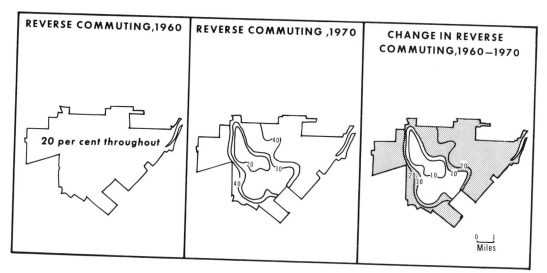

REVERSE COMMUTING, 1960

20 per cent throughout

REVERSE COMMUTING, 1970

CHANGE IN REVERSE
COMMUTING, 1960—1970

0   1
Miles

HARLINGEN, TX.

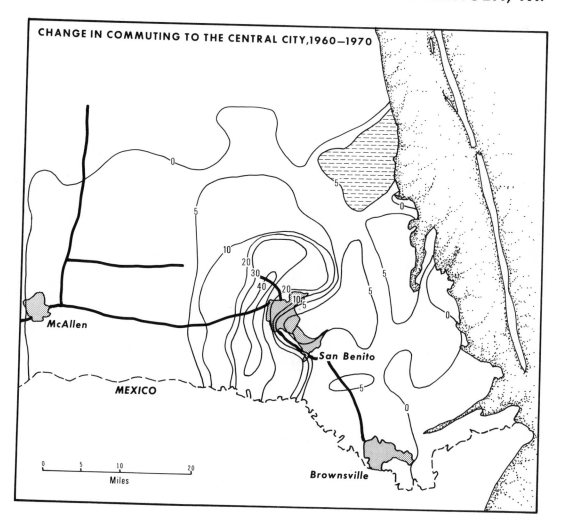

CHANGE IN COMMUTING TO THE CENTRAL CITY, 1960—1970

McAllen

San Benito

MEXICO

Brownsville

0   5   10   20
Miles

COMMUTING TO THE CBD IN 1970

NO DATA COLLECTED

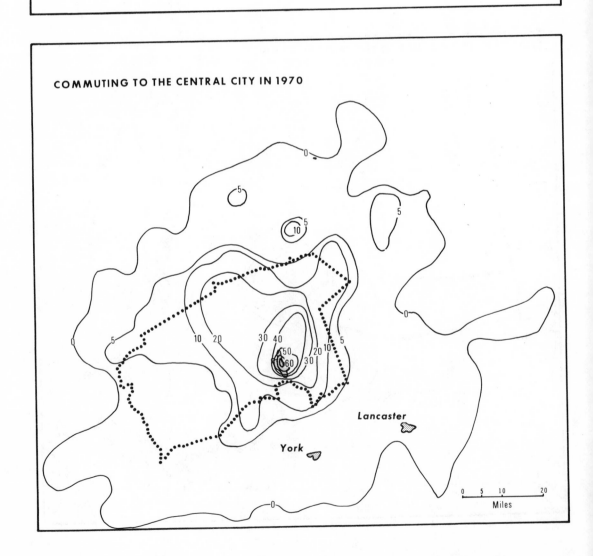

COMMUTING TO THE CENTRAL CITY IN 1970

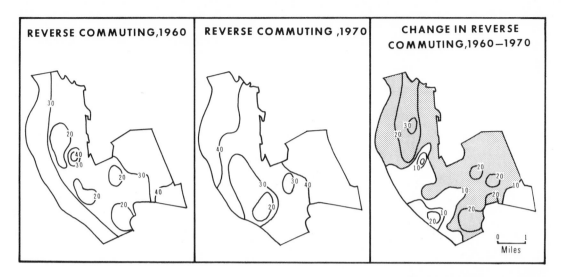

REVERSE COMMUTING, 1960

REVERSE COMMUTING, 1970

CHANGE IN REVERSE COMMUTING, 1960–1970

HARRISBURG, PA.

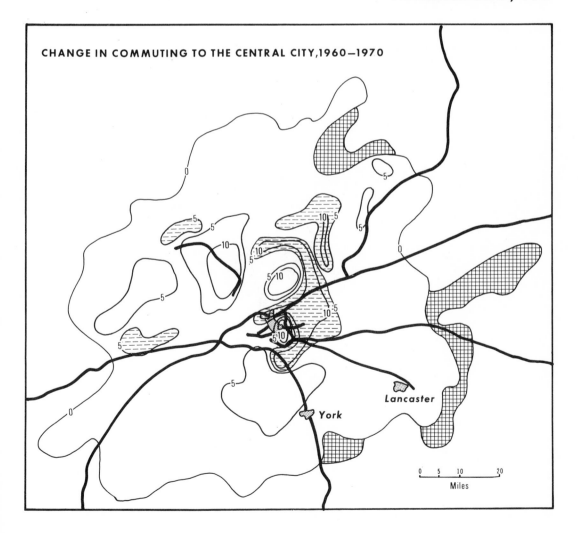

CHANGE IN COMMUTING TO THE CENTRAL CITY, 1960–1970

Lancaster

York

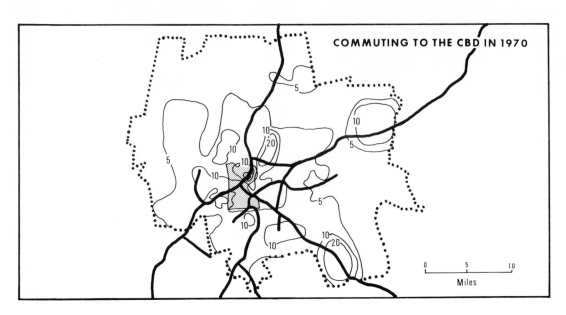

COMMUTING TO THE CBD IN 1970

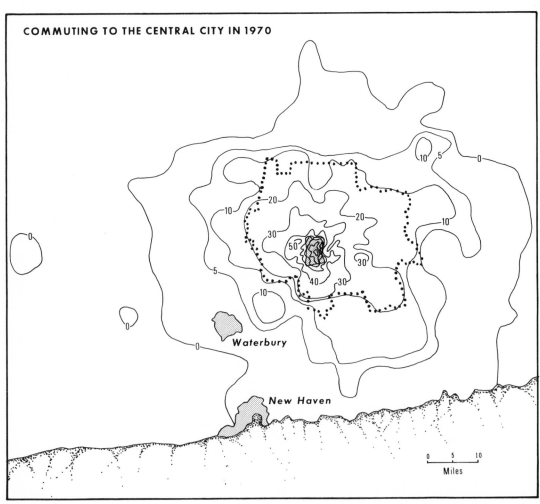

COMMUTING TO THE CENTRAL CITY IN 1970

Waterbury

New Haven

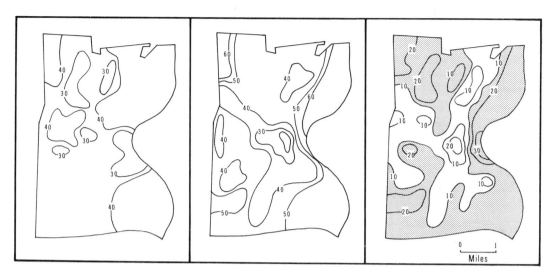

HARTFORD, CT.

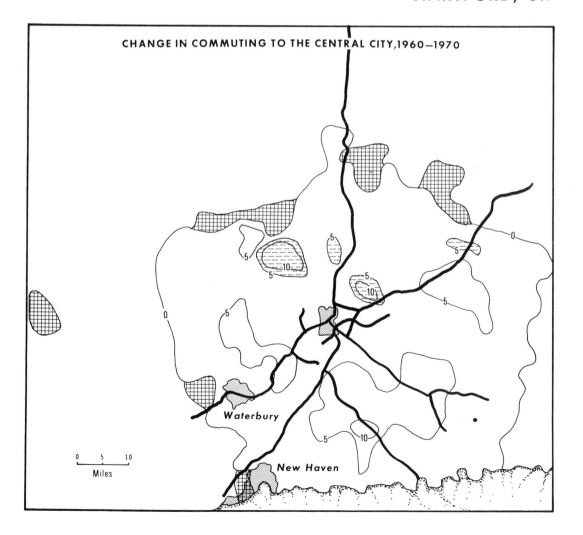

CHANGE IN COMMUTING TO THE CENTRAL CITY, 1960–1970

COMMUTING TO THE CBD IN 1970

NO DATA COLLECTED

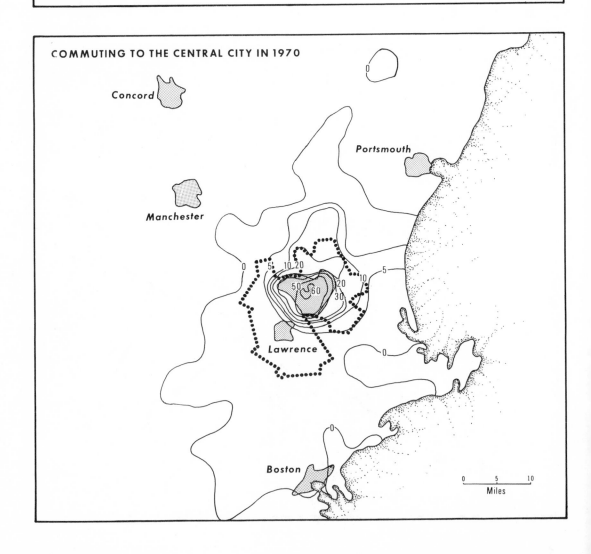

COMMUTING TO THE CENTRAL CITY IN 1970

Concord

Portsmouth

Manchester

Lawrence

Boston

0   5   10
Miles

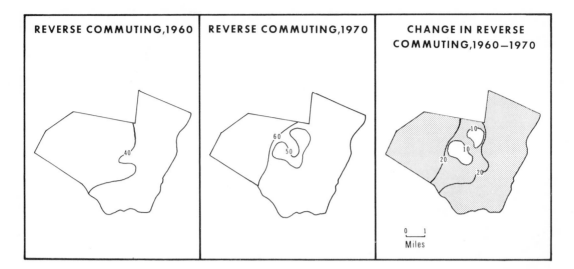

REVERSE COMMUTING,1960

REVERSE COMMUTING,1970

CHANGE IN REVERSE COMMUTING,1960—1970

HAVERHILL, MA.

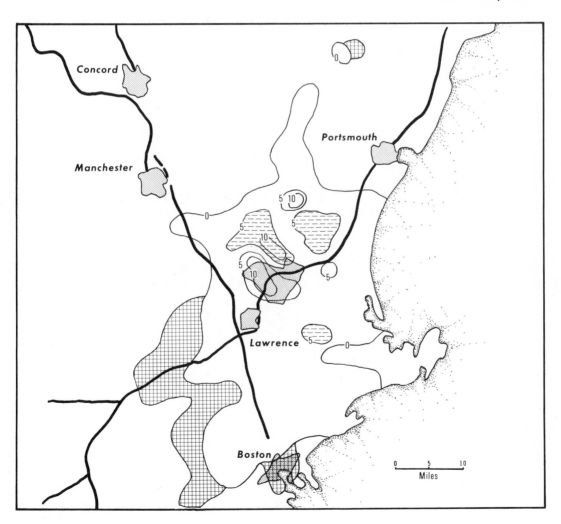

324

COMMUTING TO THE CBD IN 1970

NO DATA COLLECTED

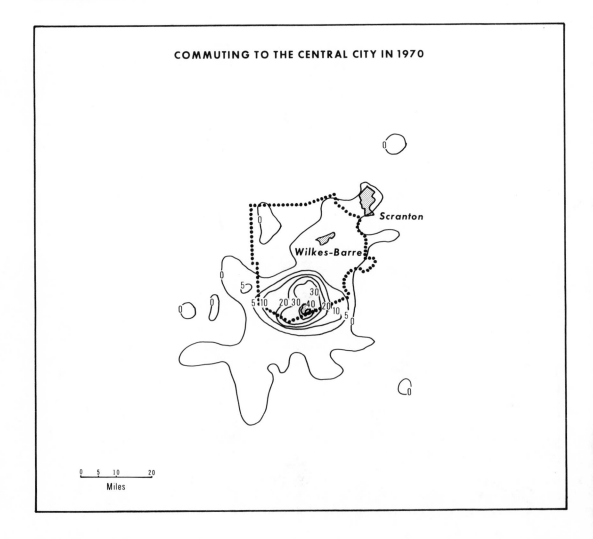

COMMUTING TO THE CENTRAL CITY IN 1970

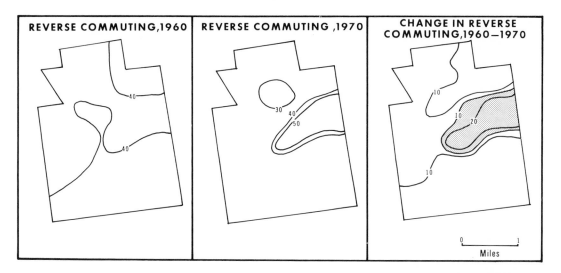

| REVERSE COMMUTING,1960 | REVERSE COMMUTING ,1970 | CHANGE IN REVERSE COMMUTING,1960—1970 |

HAZLETON, PA.

CHANGE IN COMMUTING TO THE CENTRAL CITY,1960—1970

NO DATA COLLECTED

COMMUTING TO THE CBD IN 1970

NO DATA COLLECTED

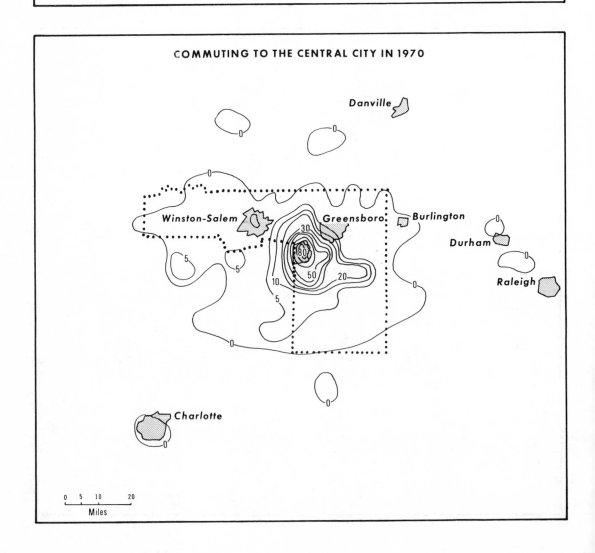

COMMUTING TO THE CENTRAL CITY IN 1970

Danville

Winston-Salem   Greensboro   Burlington

Durham

Raleigh

Charlotte

0   5   10   20
Miles

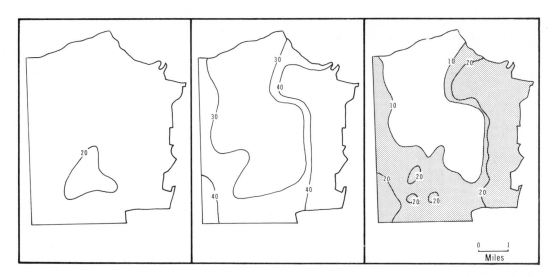

HIGH POINT, N.C.

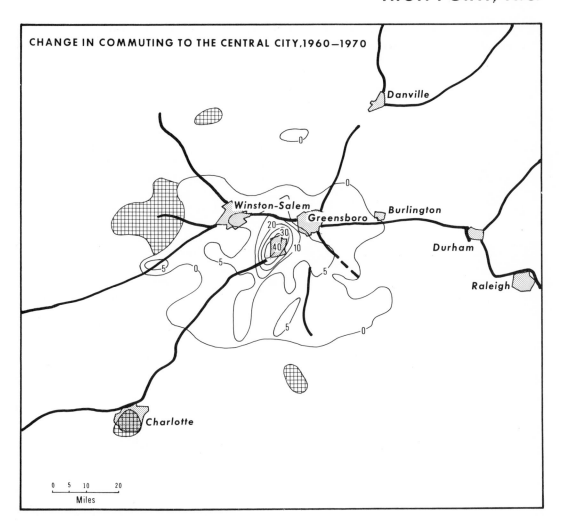

CHANGE IN COMMUTING TO THE CENTRAL CITY, 1960–1970

COMMUTING TO THE CBD IN 1970

NO DATA COLLECTED

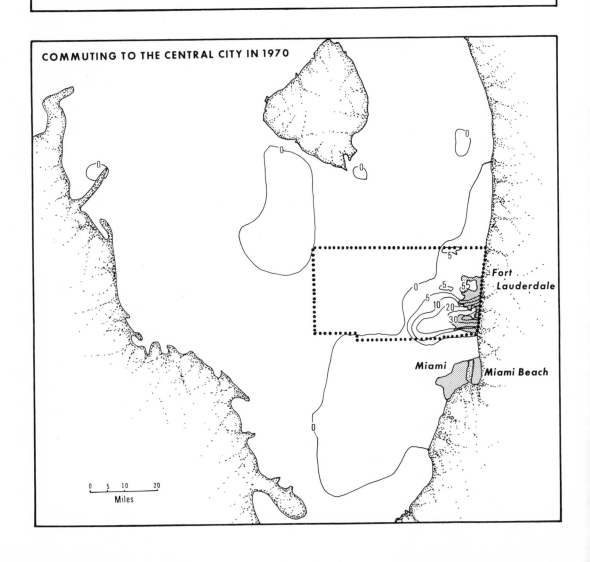

COMMUTING TO THE CENTRAL CITY IN 1970

Fort Lauderdale

Miami

Miami Beach

0 5 10 20
Miles

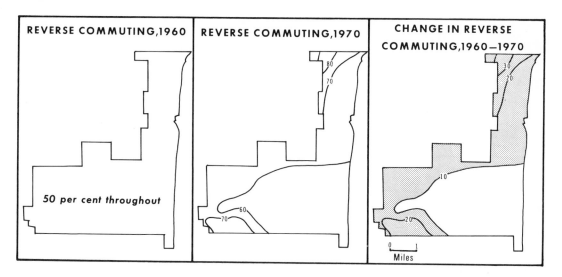

REVERSE COMMUTING, 1960

REVERSE COMMUTING, 1970

CHANGE IN REVERSE COMMUTING, 1960–1970

50 per cent throughout

HOLLYWOOD, FL.

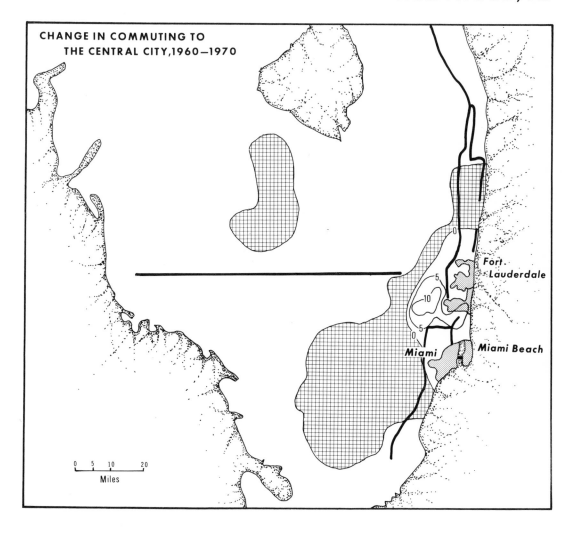

CHANGE IN COMMUTING TO THE CENTRAL CITY, 1960–1970

Fort Lauderdale

Miami

Miami Beach

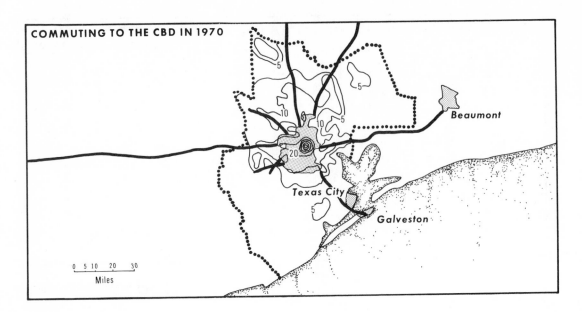

COMMUTING TO THE CBD IN 1970

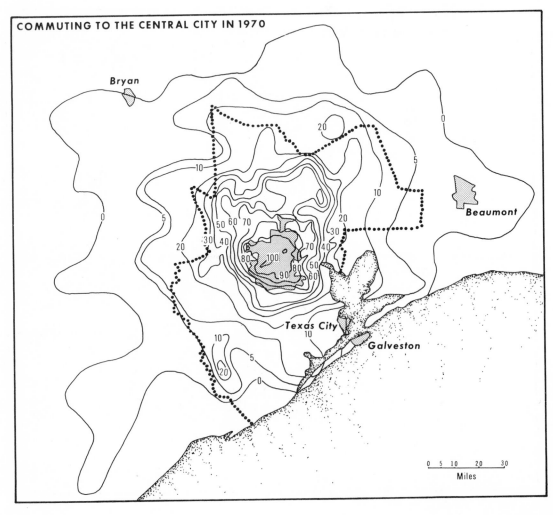

COMMUTING TO THE CENTRAL CITY IN 1970

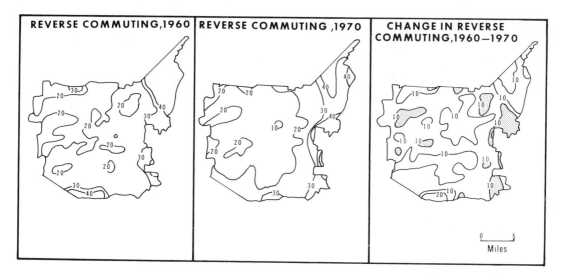

REVERSE COMMUTING, 1960

REVERSE COMMUTING, 1970

CHANGE IN REVERSE COMMUTING, 1960—1970

HOUSTON, TX.

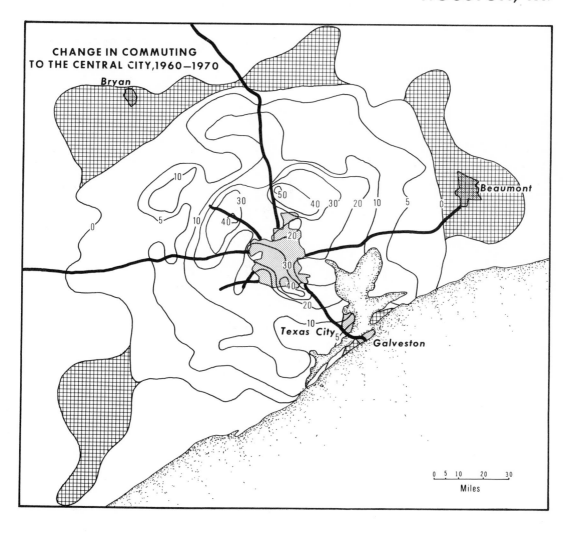

CHANGE IN COMMUTING
TO THE CENTRAL CITY, 1960—1970

Bryan

Beaumont

Texas City

Galveston

COMMUTING TO THE CBD IN 1970

NO DATA COLLECTED

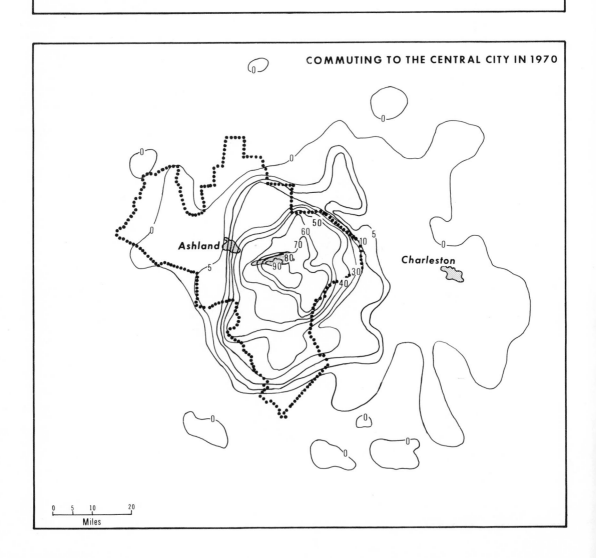

COMMUTING TO THE CENTRAL CITY IN 1970

Ashland

Charleston

0   5   10   20
Miles

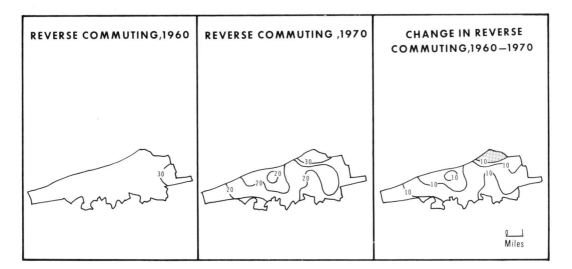

| REVERSE COMMUTING,1960 | REVERSE COMMUTING ,1970 | CHANGE IN REVERSE COMMUTING,1960—1970 |

HUNTINGTON, WV.

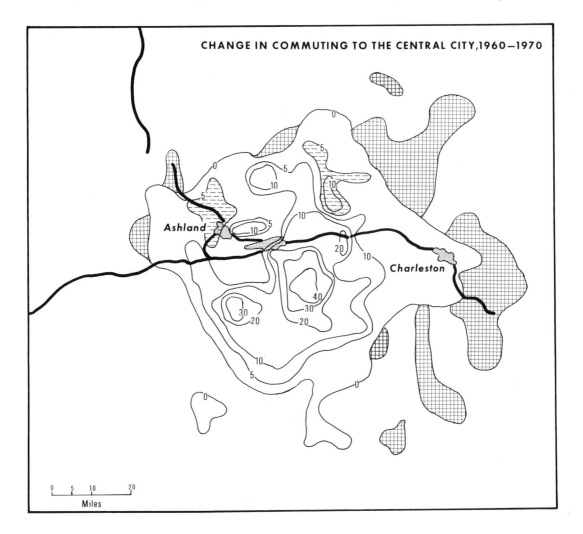

CHANGE IN COMMUTING TO THE CENTRAL CITY,1960—1970

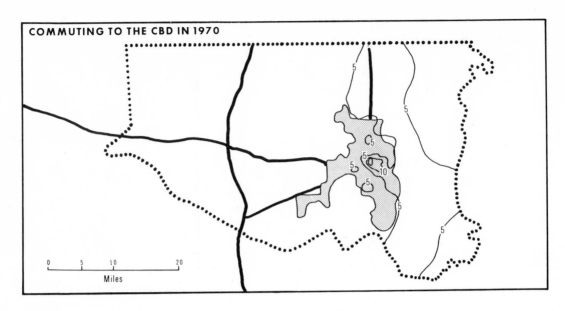

COMMUTING TO THE CBD IN 1970

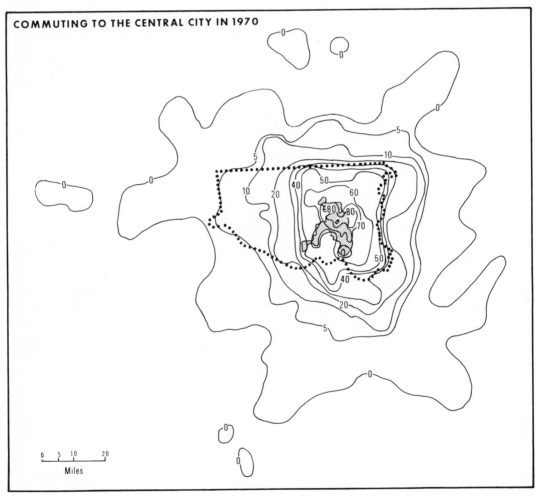

COMMUTING TO THE CENTRAL CITY IN 1970

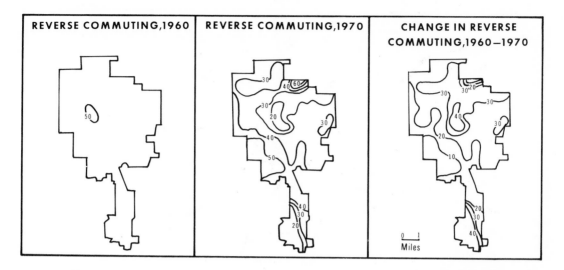

| REVERSE COMMUTING,1960 | REVERSE COMMUTING,1970 | CHANGE IN REVERSE COMMUTING,1960−1970 |

HUNTSVILLE, AL.

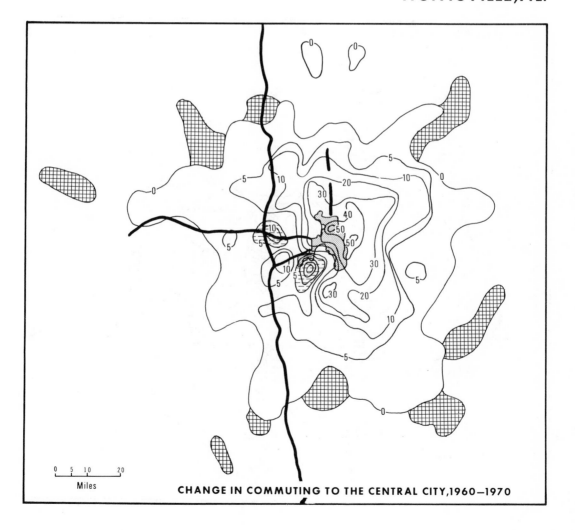

CHANGE IN COMMUTING TO THE CENTRAL CITY,1960−1970

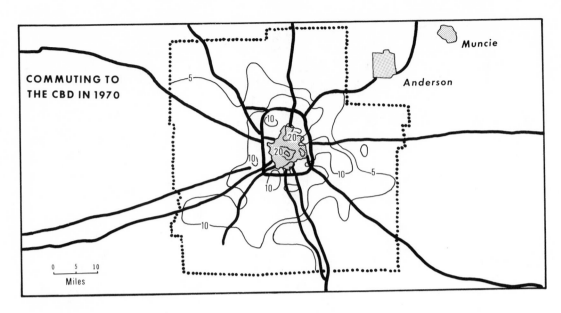

COMMUTING TO
THE CBD IN 1970

Muncie

Anderson

0   5   10
Miles

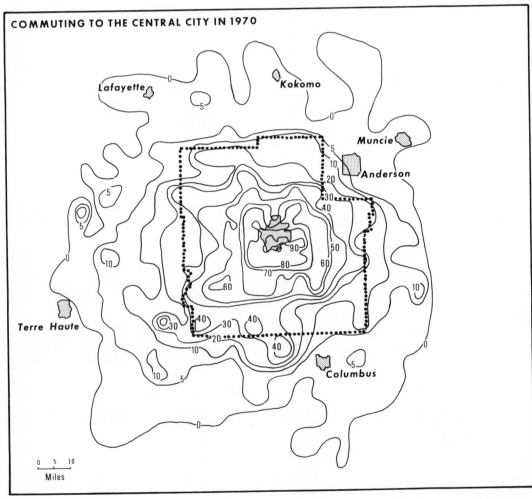

COMMUTING TO THE CENTRAL CITY IN 1970

Lafayette

Kokomo

Muncie

Anderson

Terre Haute

Columbus

0   5   10
Miles

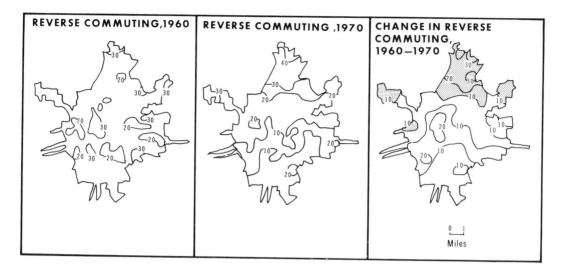

REVERSE COMMUTING, 1960

REVERSE COMMUTING, 1970

CHANGE IN REVERSE COMMUTING, 1960–1970

Miles

INDIANAPOLIS, IN.

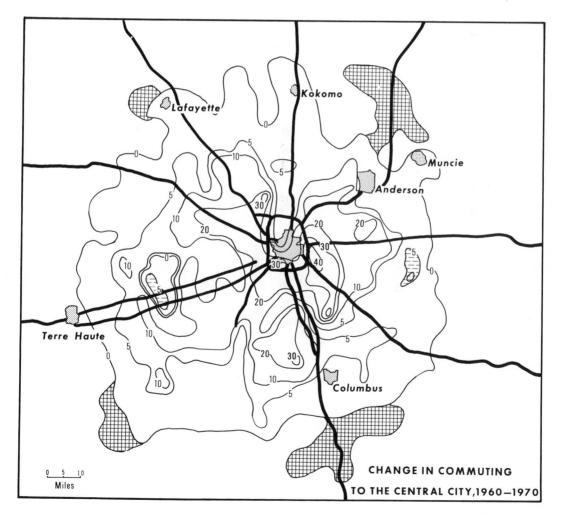

Lafayette

Kokomo

Muncie

Anderson

Terre Haute

Columbus

CHANGE IN COMMUTING

TO THE CENTRAL CITY, 1960–1970

Miles

338

COMMUTING TO THE CBD IN 1970

NO DATA COLLECTED

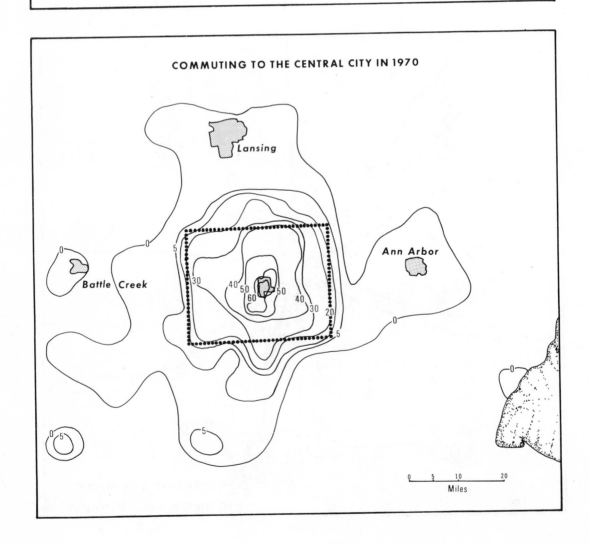

COMMUTING TO THE CENTRAL CITY IN 1970

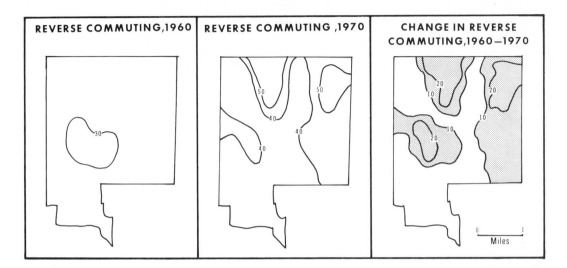

REVERSE COMMUTING,1960

REVERSE COMMUTING ,1970

CHANGE IN REVERSE COMMUTING,1960—1970

JACKSON, MI.

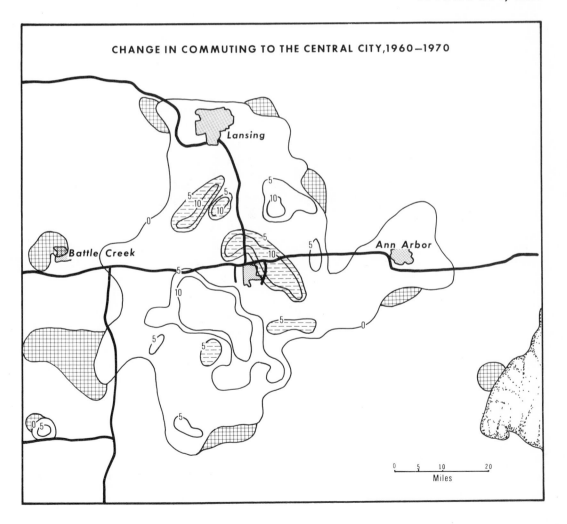

CHANGE IN COMMUTING TO THE CENTRAL CITY,1960—1970

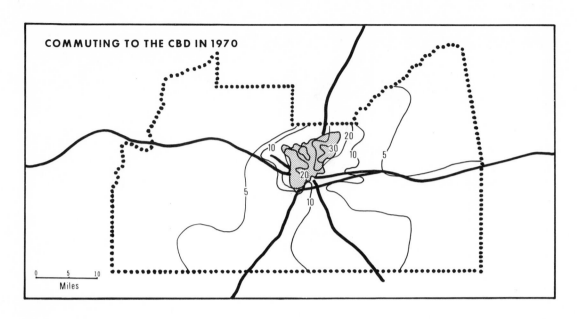

COMMUTING TO THE CBD IN 1970

0   5   10
Miles

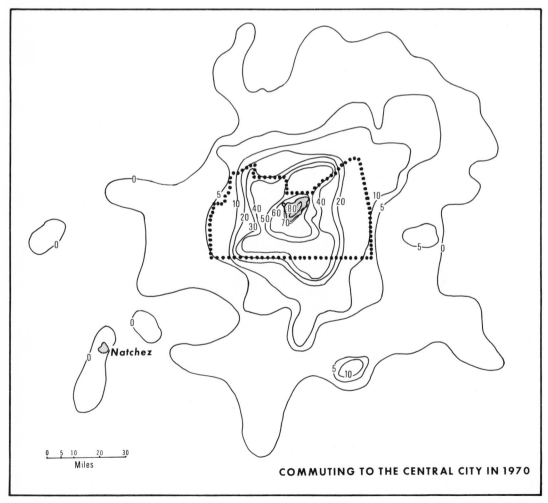

Natchez

0 5 10   20   30
Miles

COMMUTING TO THE CENTRAL CITY IN 1970

341

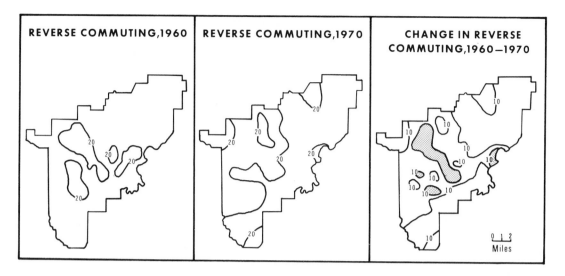

JACKSON, MS.

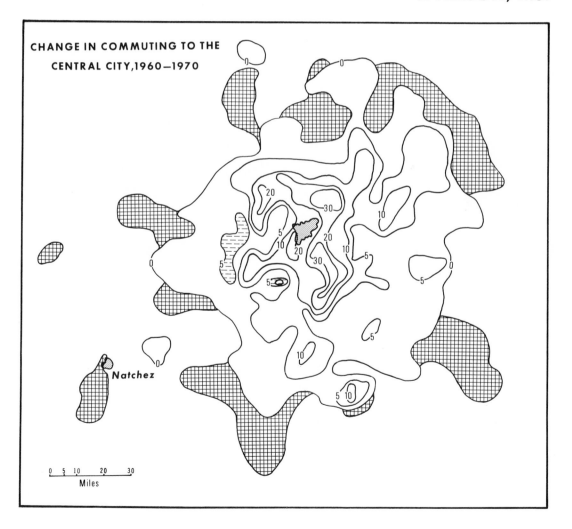

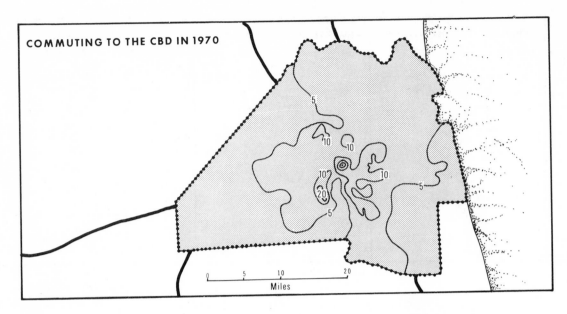

COMMUTING TO THE CBD IN 1970

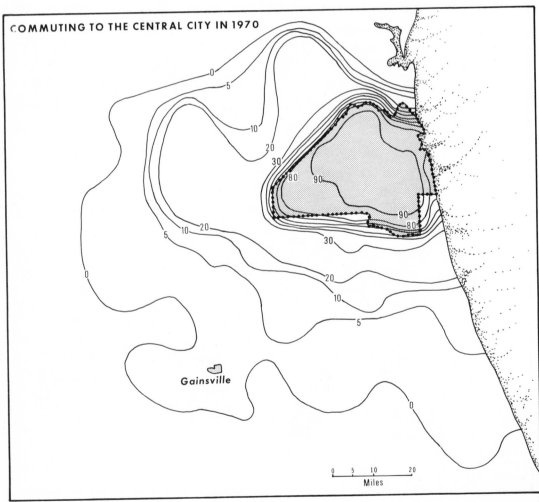

COMMUTING TO THE CENTRAL CITY IN 1970

Gainsville

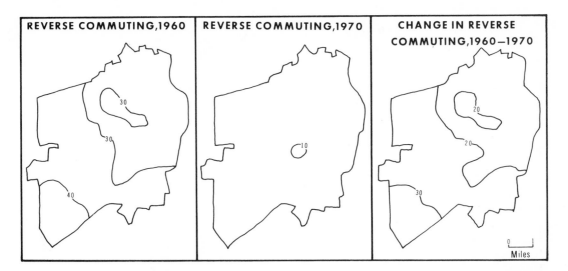

REVERSE COMMUTING, 1960

REVERSE COMMUTING, 1970

CHANGE IN REVERSE COMMUTING, 1960—1970

Miles

JACKSONVILLE, FL.

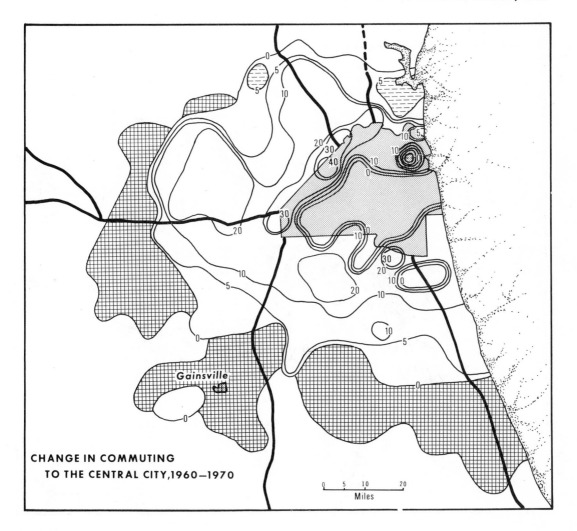

CHANGE IN COMMUTING
TO THE CENTRAL CITY, 1960—1970

Gainsville

Miles

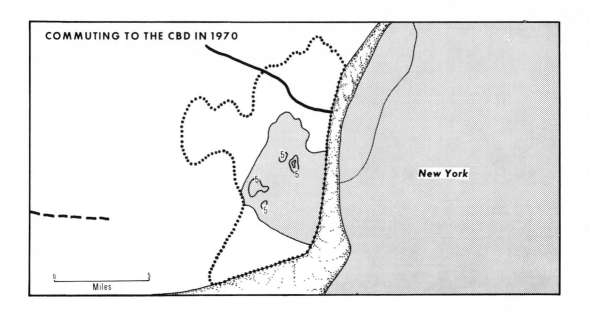

COMMUTING TO THE CBD IN 1970

New York

Miles
0   5

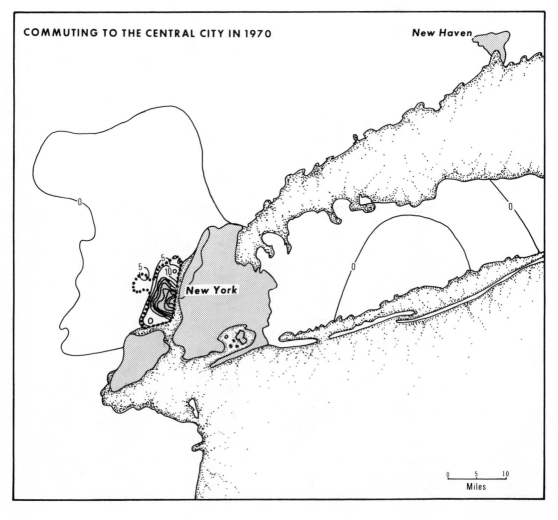

COMMUTING TO THE CENTRAL CITY IN 1970

New Haven

New York

Miles
0   5   10

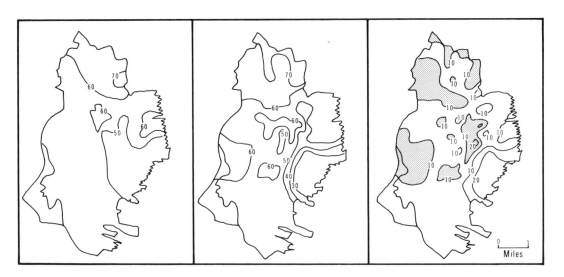

JERSEY CITY, N.J.

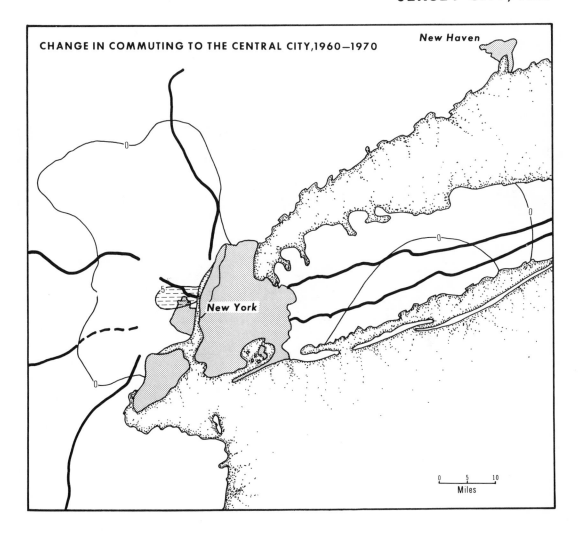

CHANGE IN COMMUTING TO THE CENTRAL CITY, 1960—1970

New Haven

New York

346

COMMUTING TO THE CBD IN 1970

NO DATA COLLECTED

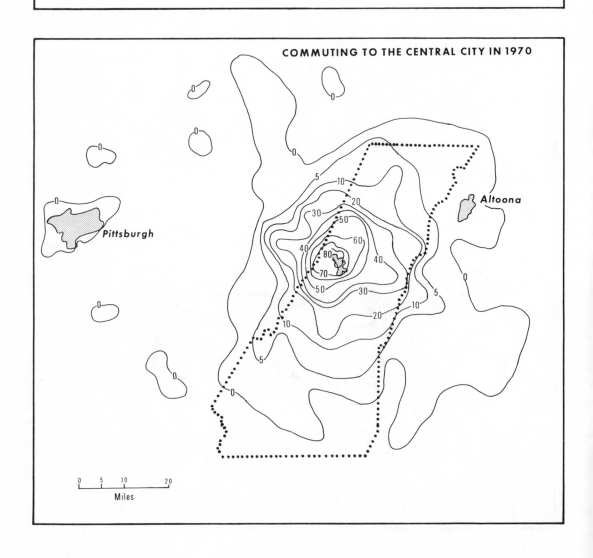
COMMUTING TO THE CENTRAL CITY IN 1970

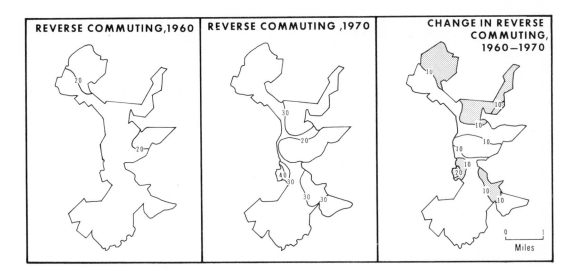

JOHNSTOWN, PA.

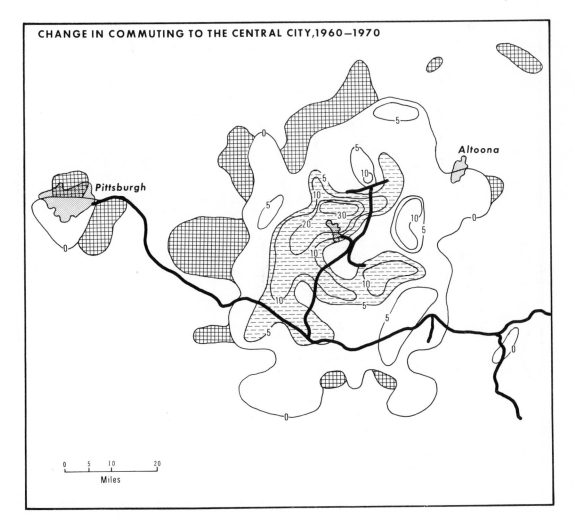

COMMUTING TO THE CBD IN 1970

NO DATA COLLECTED

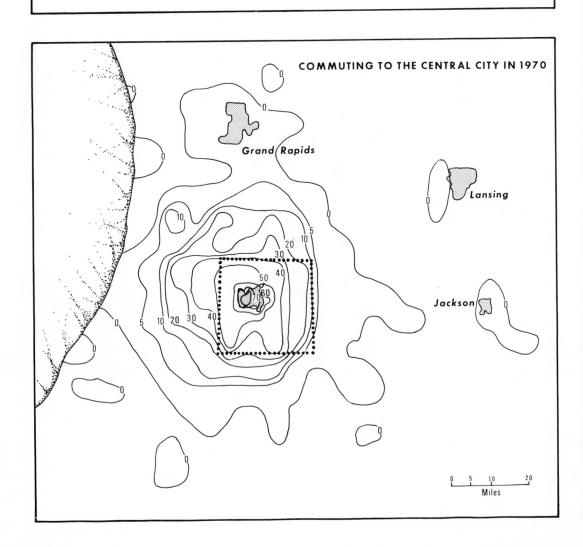

COMMUTING TO THE CENTRAL CITY IN 1970

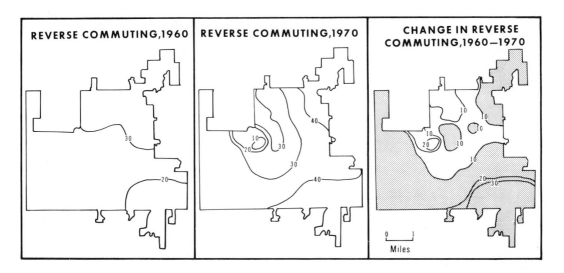

REVERSE COMMUTING, 1960

REVERSE COMMUTING, 1970

CHANGE IN REVERSE COMMUTING, 1960—1970

KALAMAZOO, MI.

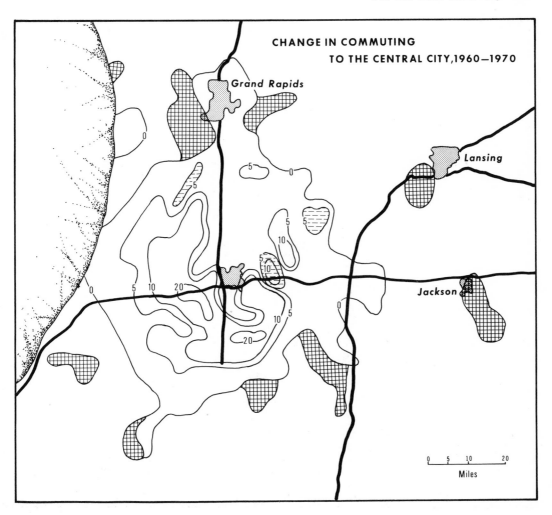

CHANGE IN COMMUTING
TO THE CENTRAL CITY, 1960—1970

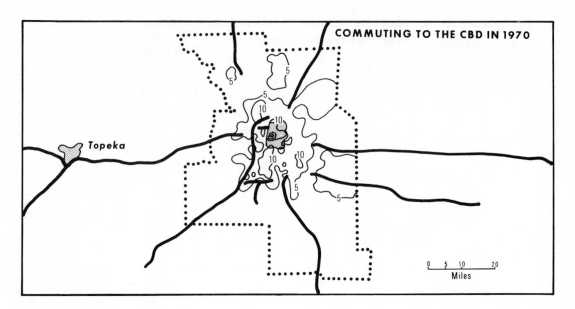

COMMUTING TO THE CBD IN 1970

Topeka

0 5 10 20
Miles

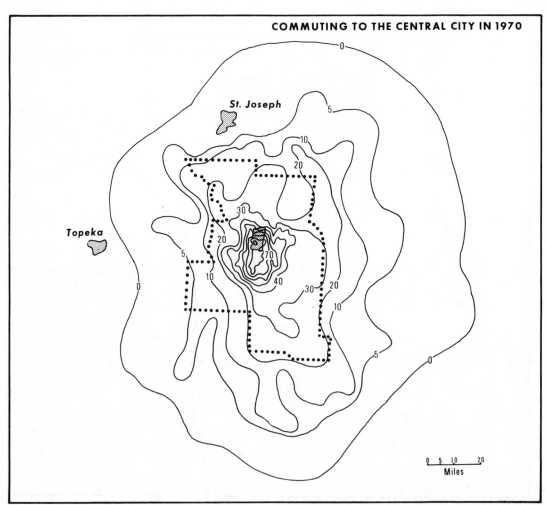

COMMUTING TO THE CENTRAL CITY IN 1970

St. Joseph

Topeka

0 5 10 20
Miles

KANSAS CITY, MO.

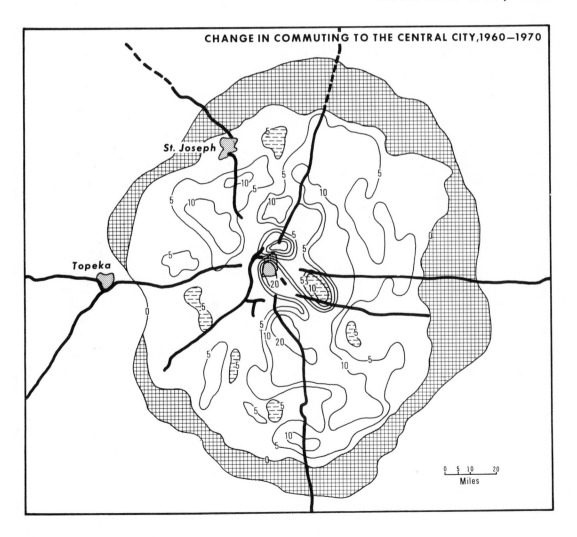

CHANGE IN COMMUTING TO THE CENTRAL CITY,1960—1970

COMMUTING TO THE CBD IN 1970

NO DATA COLLECTED

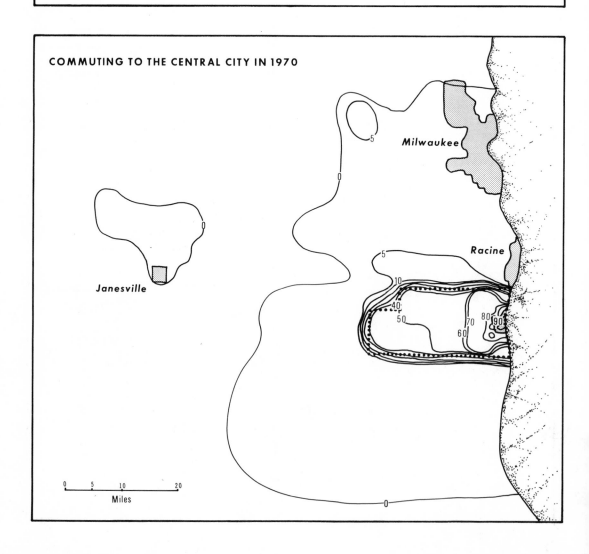

COMMUTING TO THE CENTRAL CITY IN 1970

Milwaukee

Racine

Janesville

0   5   10   20

Miles

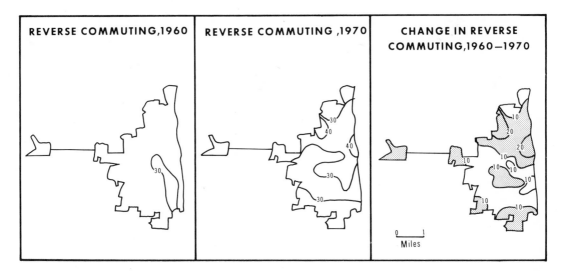

REVERSE COMMUTING, 1960

REVERSE COMMUTING, 1970

CHANGE IN REVERSE
COMMUTING, 1960—1970

KENOSHA, WI.

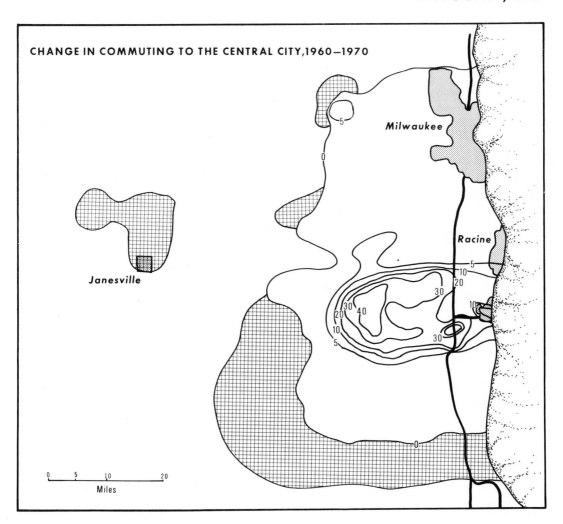

CHANGE IN COMMUTING TO THE CENTRAL CITY, 1960—1970

Milwaukee

Racine

Janesville

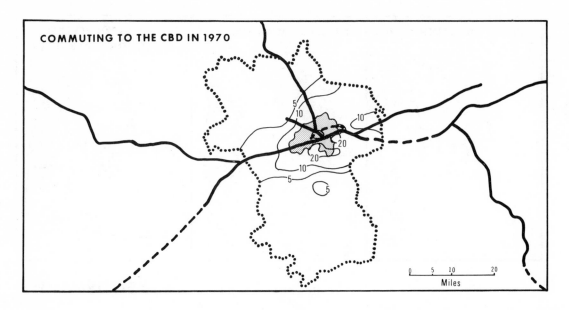

COMMUTING TO THE CBD IN 1970

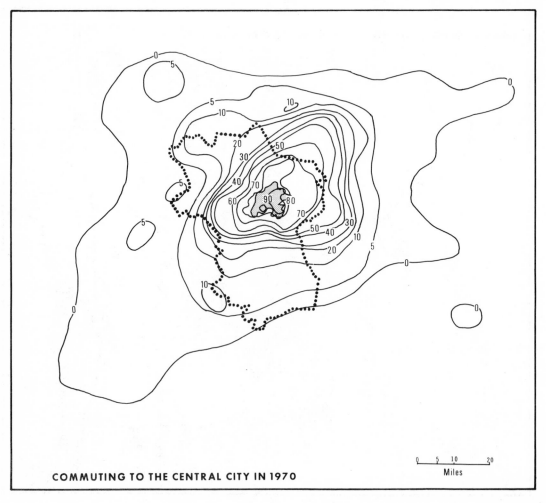

COMMUTING TO THE CENTRAL CITY IN 1970

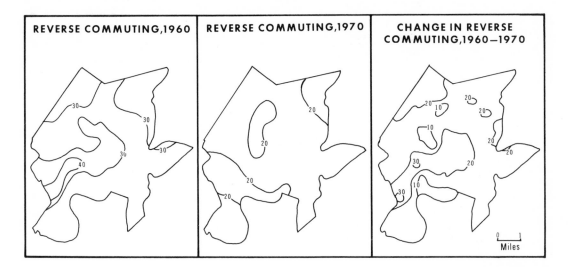

REVERSE COMMUTING, 1960

REVERSE COMMUTING, 1970

CHANGE IN REVERSE COMMUTING, 1960–1970

KNOXVILLE, TN.

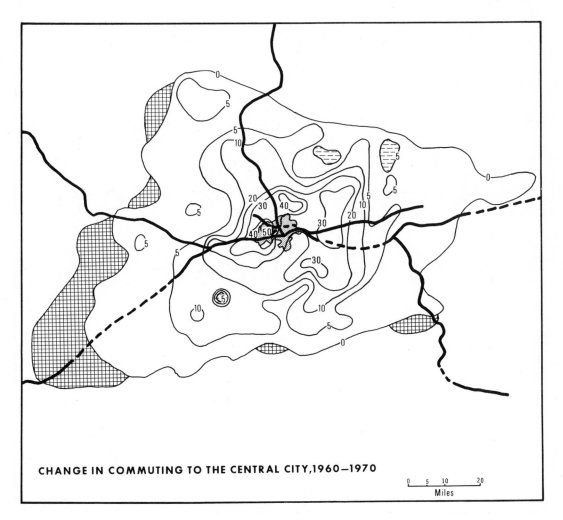

CHANGE IN COMMUTING TO THE CENTRAL CITY, 1960–1970

COMMUTING TO THE CBD IN 1970

NO DATA COLLECTED

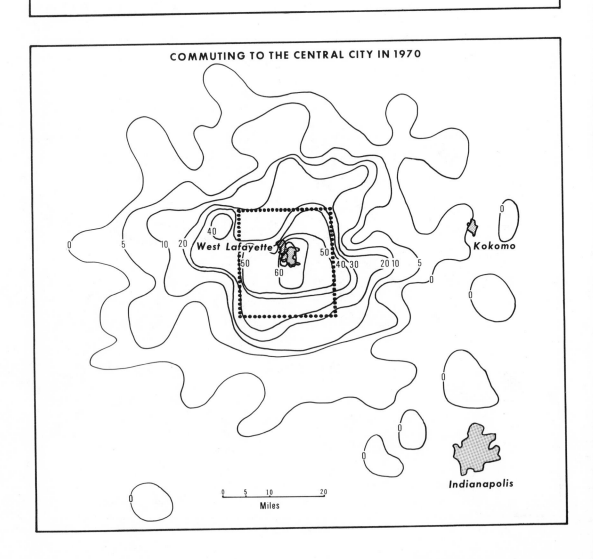

COMMUTING TO THE CENTRAL CITY IN 1970

REVERSE COMMUTING,1960	REVERSE COMMUTING ,1970	CHANGE IN REVERSE COMMUTING,1960—1970
NO DATA COLLECTED		NO DATA COLLECTED

REVERSE COMMUTING,1960

REVERSE COMMUTING ,1970

CHANGE IN REVERSE COMMUTING,1960—1970

NO DATA COLLECTED

30 30 30

30

40

0   1
Miles

NO DATA COLLECTED

LAFAYETTE, IN.

CHANGE IN COMMUTING TO THE CENTRAL CITY,1960—1970

NO DATA COLLECTED

COMMUTING TO THE CBD IN 1970

NO DATA COLLECTED

COMMUTING TO THE CENTRAL CITY IN 1970

Baton Rouge

0 5 10 20
Miles

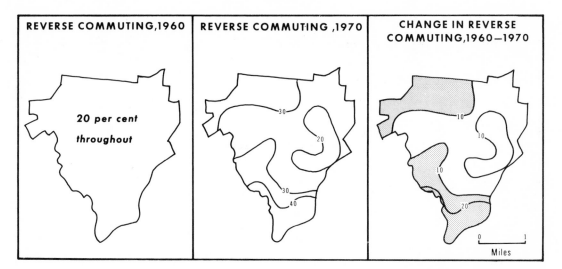

| REVERSE COMMUTING,1960 | REVERSE COMMUTING ,1970 | CHANGE IN REVERSE COMMUTING,1960—1970 |

20 per cent throughout

LAFAYETTE, LA.

CHANGE IN COMMUTING TO THE CENTRAL CITY,1960—1970

NO DATA COLLECTED

360

COMMUTING TO THE CBD IN 1970

NO DATA COLLECTED

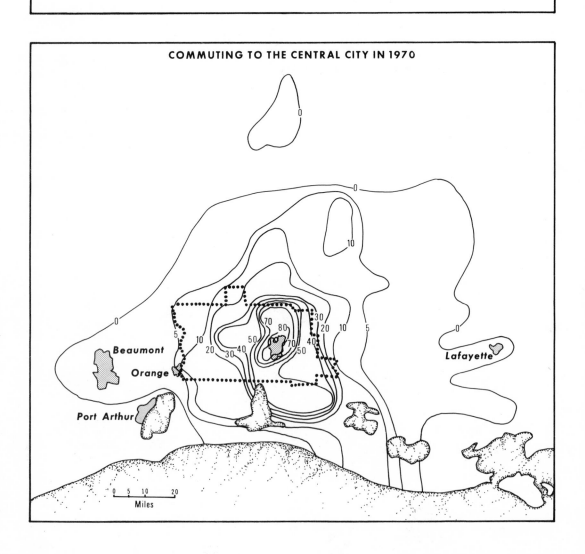

COMMUTING TO THE CENTRAL CITY IN 1970

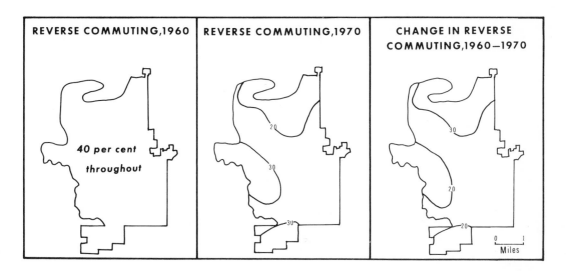

REVERSE COMMUTING, 1960

REVERSE COMMUTING, 1970

CHANGE IN REVERSE COMMUTING, 1960–1970

40 per cent throughout

LAKE CHARLES, LA.

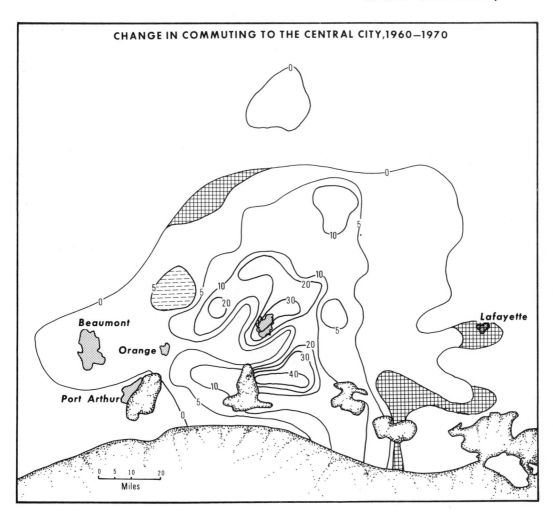

CHANGE IN COMMUTING TO THE CENTRAL CITY, 1960–1970

Beaumont

Orange

Port Arthur

Lafayette

COMMUTING TO THE CBD IN 1970

NO DATA COLLECTED

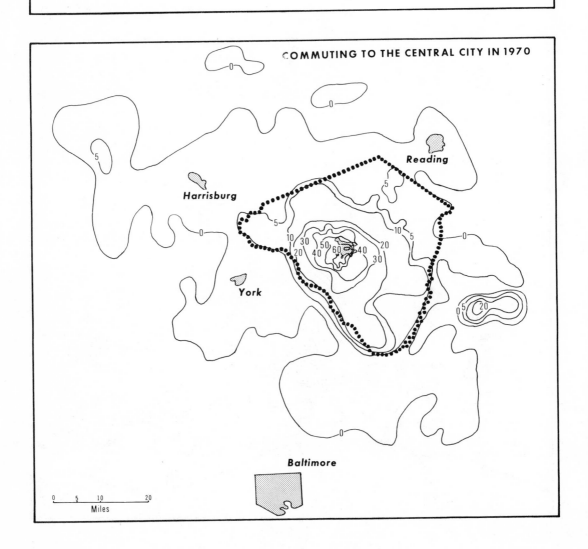

COMMUTING TO THE CENTRAL CITY IN 1970

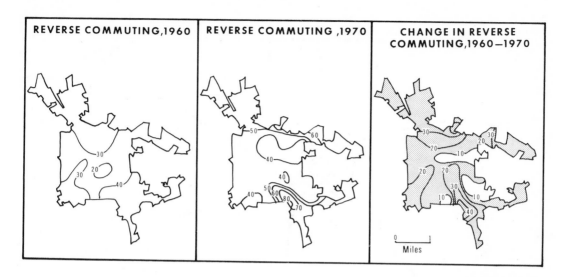

| REVERSE COMMUTING, 1960 | REVERSE COMMUTING, 1970 | CHANGE IN REVERSE COMMUTING, 1960—1970 |

LANCASTER, PA.

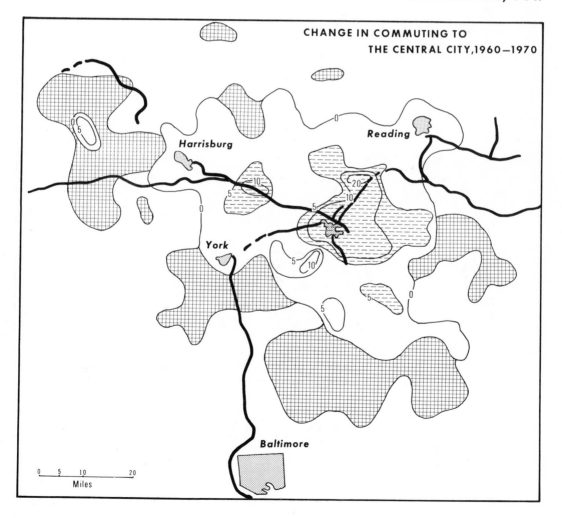

CHANGE IN COMMUTING TO
THE CENTRAL CITY, 1960—1970

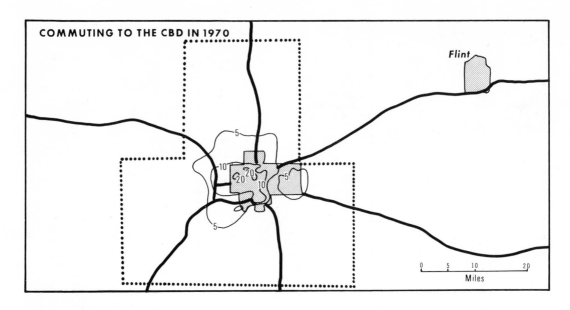

COMMUTING TO THE CBD IN 1970

Flint

0 5 10 20
Miles

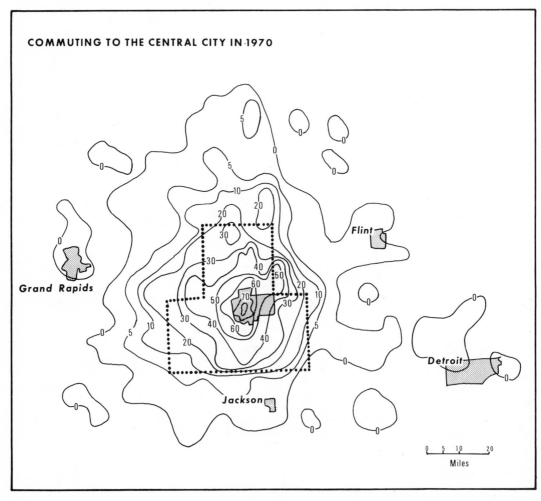

COMMUTING TO THE CENTRAL CITY IN 1970

Grand Rapids

Flint

Detroit

Jackson

0 5 10 20
Miles

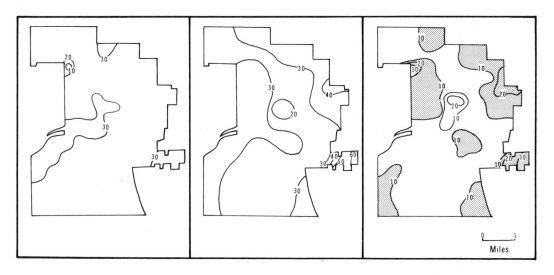

LANSING, MI.

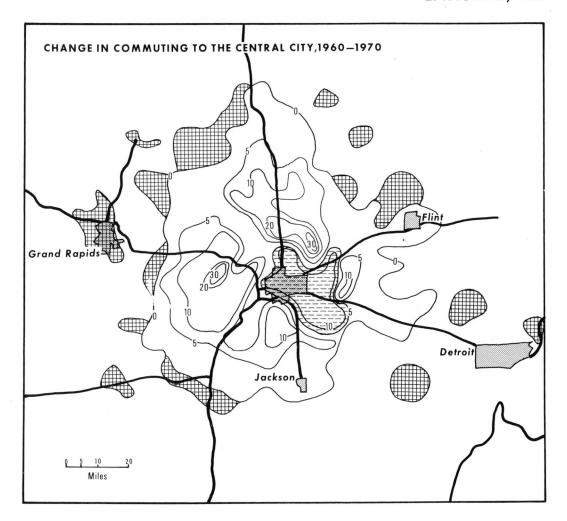

CHANGE IN COMMUTING TO THE CENTRAL CITY,1960—1970

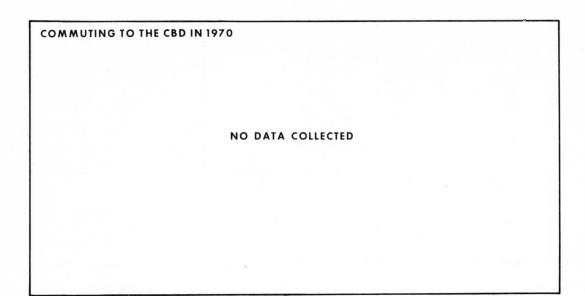

COMMUTING TO THE CBD IN 1970

NO DATA COLLECTED

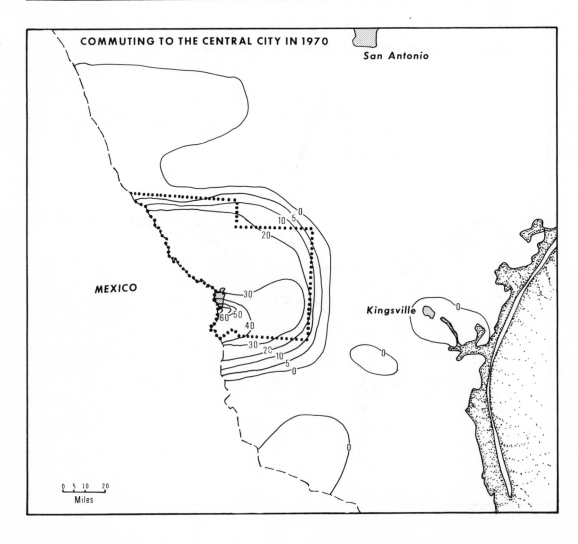

COMMUTING TO THE CENTRAL CITY IN 1970

San Antonio

MEXICO

Kingsville

0 5 10 20
Miles

367

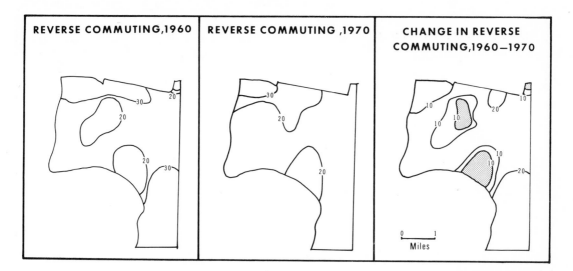

LAREDO, TX.

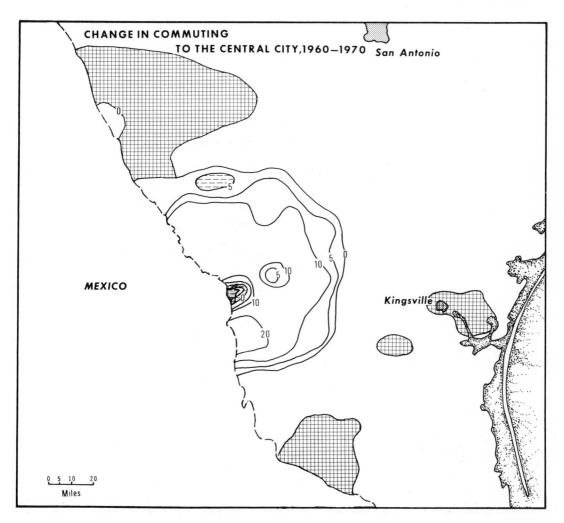

COMMUTING TO THE CBD IN 1970

NO DATA COLLECTED

COMMUTING TO THE CENTRAL CITY IN 1970

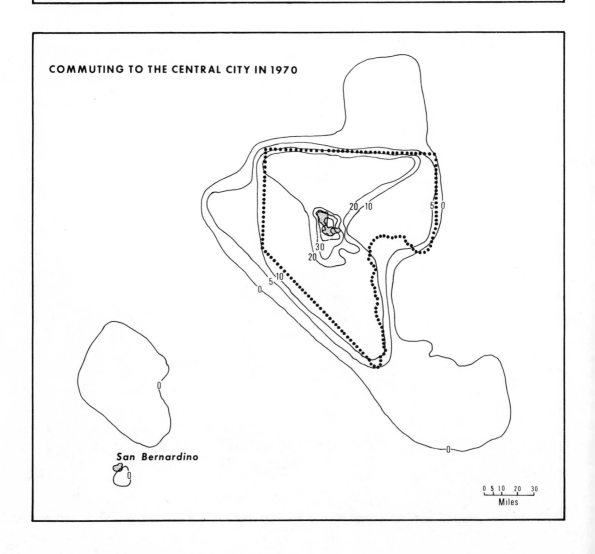

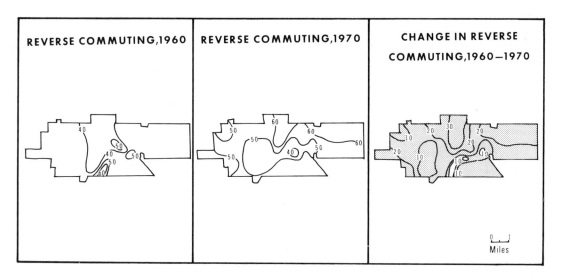

REVERSE COMMUTING, 1960   REVERSE COMMUTING, 1970   CHANGE IN REVERSE COMMUTING, 1960—1970

LAS VEGAS, NV.

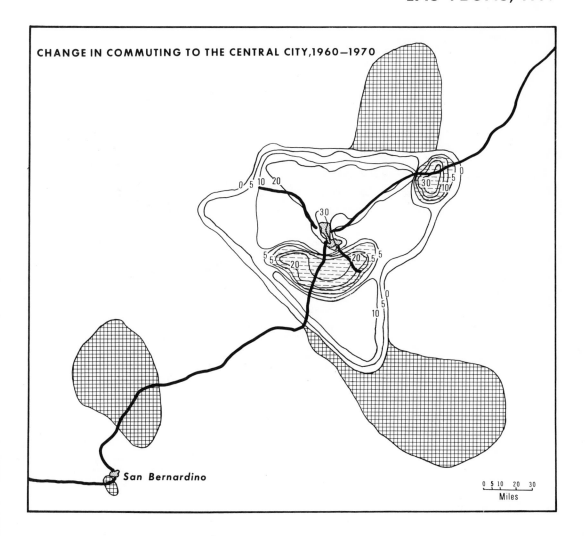

CHANGE IN COMMUTING TO THE CENTRAL CITY, 1960—1970

San Bernardino

COMMUTING TO THE CBD IN 1970

NO DATA COLLECTED

COMMUTING TO THE CENTRAL CITY IN 1970

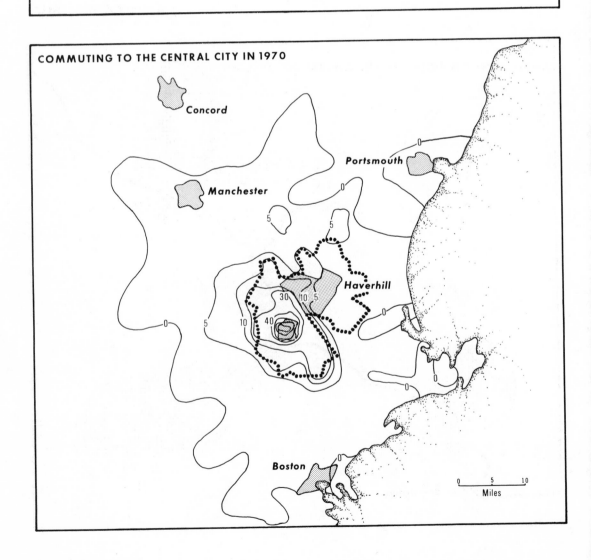

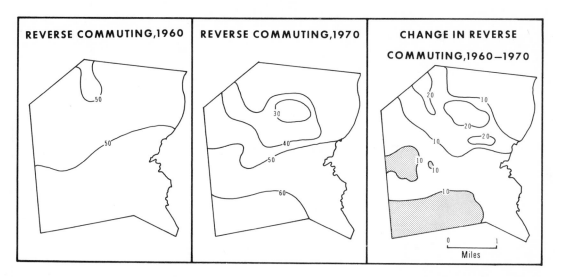

| REVERSE COMMUTING,1960 | REVERSE COMMUTING,1970 | CHANGE IN REVERSE COMMUTING,1960—1970 |

LAWRENCE, MA.

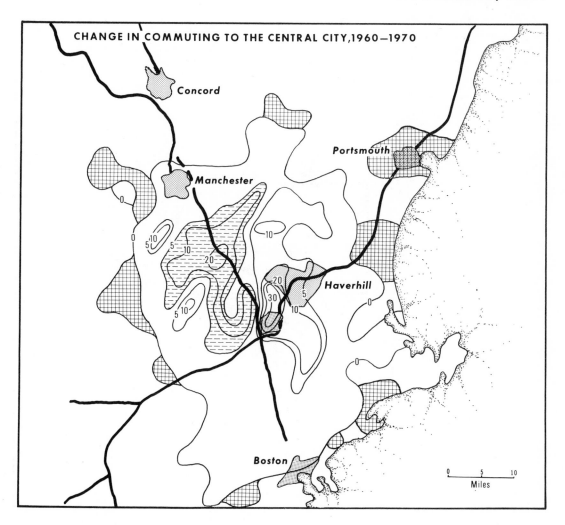

CHANGE IN COMMUTING TO THE CENTRAL CITY,1960—1970

COMMUTING TO THE CBD IN 1970

NO DATA COLLECTED

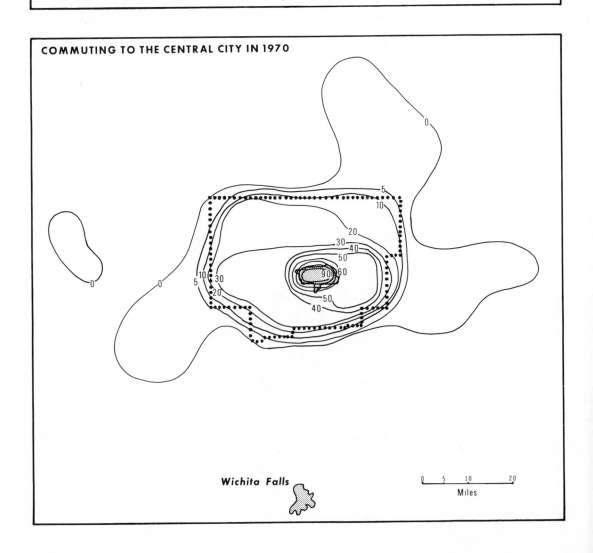

COMMUTING TO THE CENTRAL CITY IN 1970

Wichita Falls

Miles

373

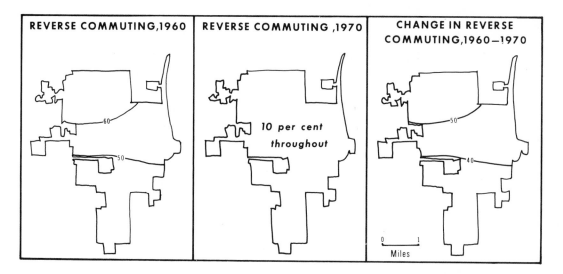

REVERSE COMMUTING,1960 | REVERSE COMMUTING ,1970 | CHANGE IN REVERSE COMMUTING,1960–1970

10 per cent throughout

LAWTON, OK.

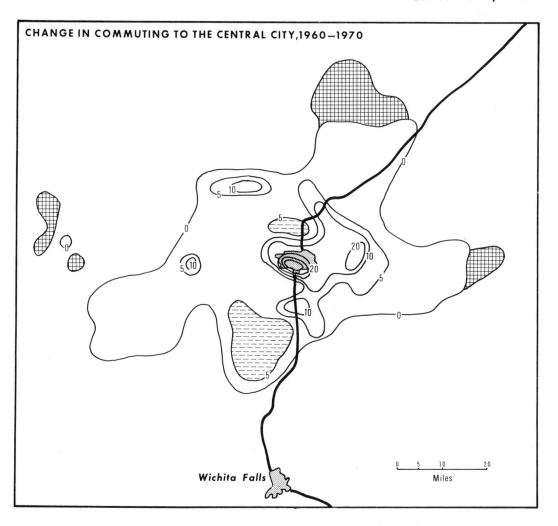

CHANGE IN COMMUTING TO THE CENTRAL CITY,1960–1970

Wichita Falls

COMMUTING TO THE CBD IN 1970

NO DATA COLLECTED

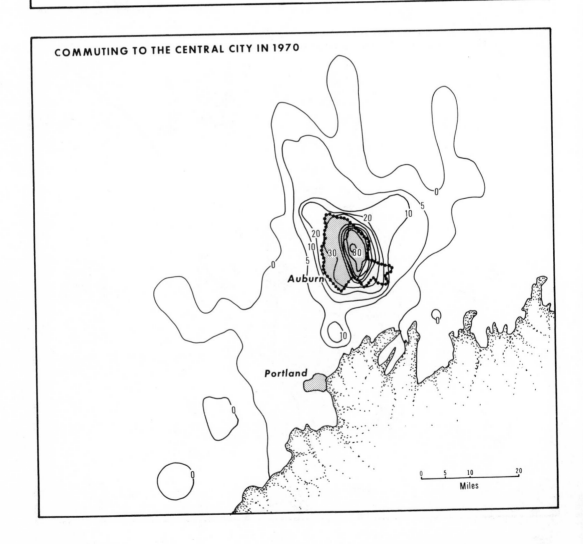

COMMUTING TO THE CENTRAL CITY IN 1970

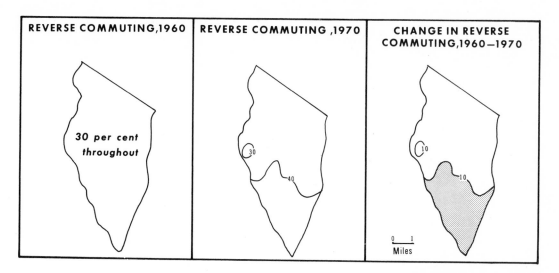

REVERSE COMMUTING, 1960

30 per cent throughout

REVERSE COMMUTING, 1970

CHANGE IN REVERSE
COMMUTING, 1960—1970

0   1
Miles

LEWISTON, ME.

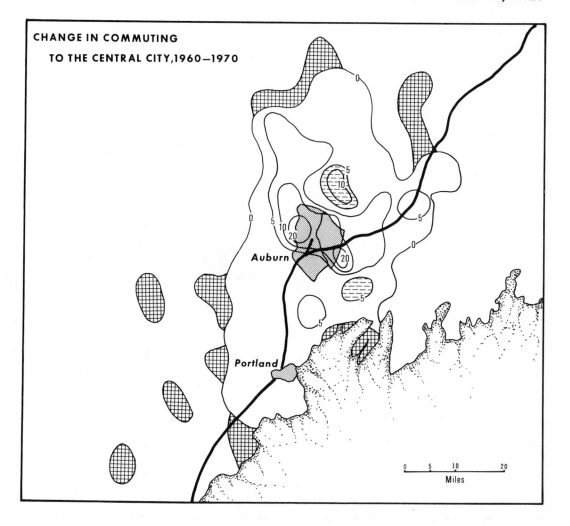

CHANGE IN COMMUTING
TO THE CENTRAL CITY, 1960—1970

Auburn

Portland

0   5   10   20
Miles

COMMUTING TO THE CBD IN 1970

NO DATA COLLECTED

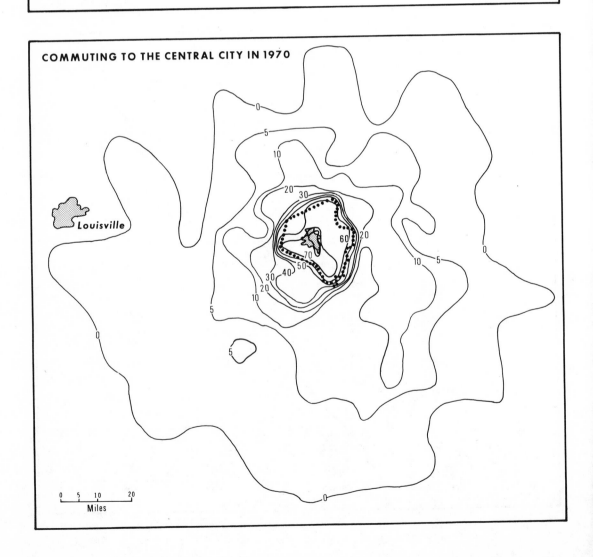

COMMUTING TO THE CENTRAL CITY IN 1970

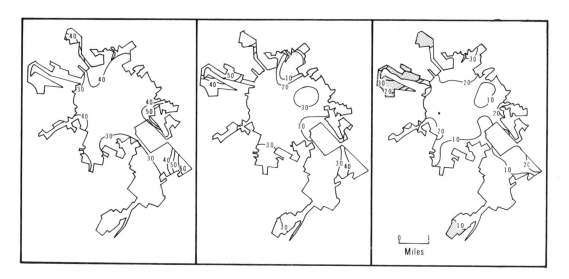

LEXINGTON, KY.

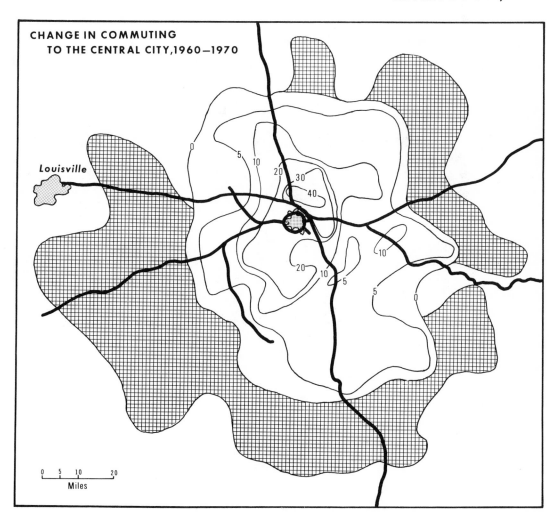

CHANGE IN COMMUTING
TO THE CENTRAL CITY, 1960–1970

COMMUTING TO THE CBD IN 1970

NO DATA COLLECTED

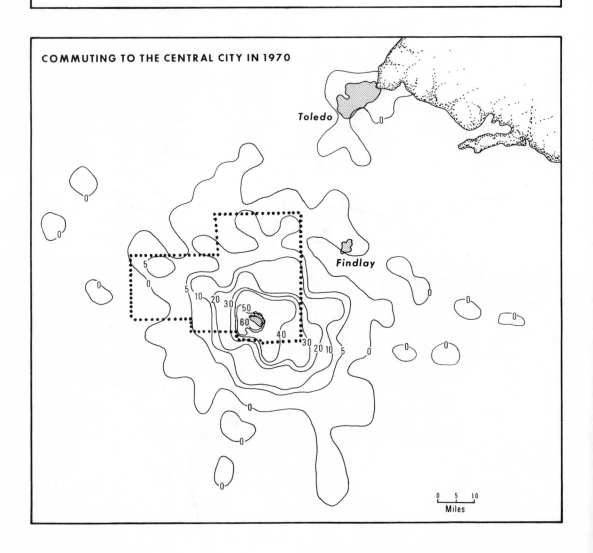

COMMUTING TO THE CENTRAL CITY IN 1970

Toledo

Findlay

0   5   10
Miles

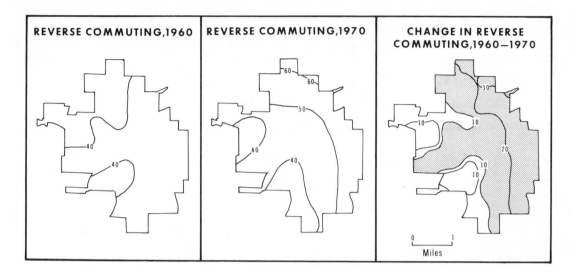

REVERSE COMMUTING, 1960

REVERSE COMMUTING, 1970

CHANGE IN REVERSE COMMUTING, 1960–1970

LIMA, OH.

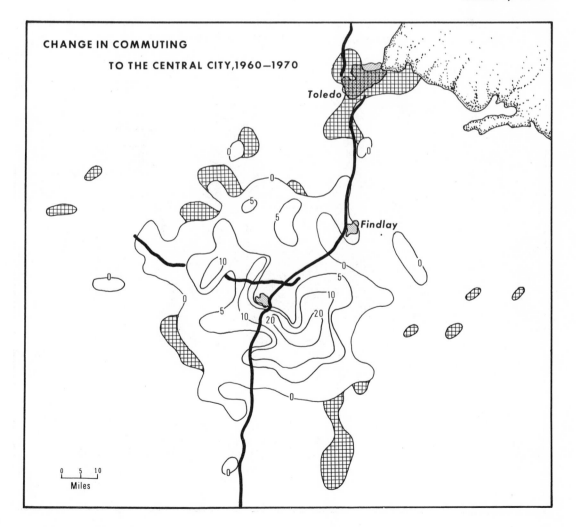

CHANGE IN COMMUTING

TO THE CENTRAL CITY, 1960–1970

Toledo

Findlay

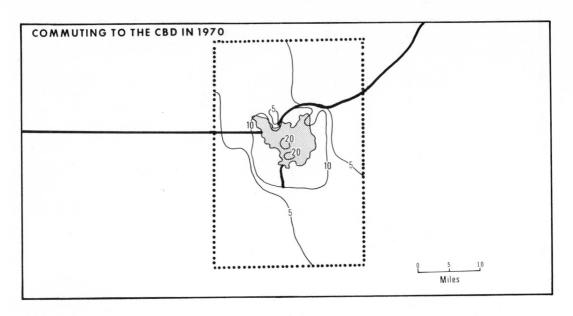

COMMUTING TO THE CBD IN 1970

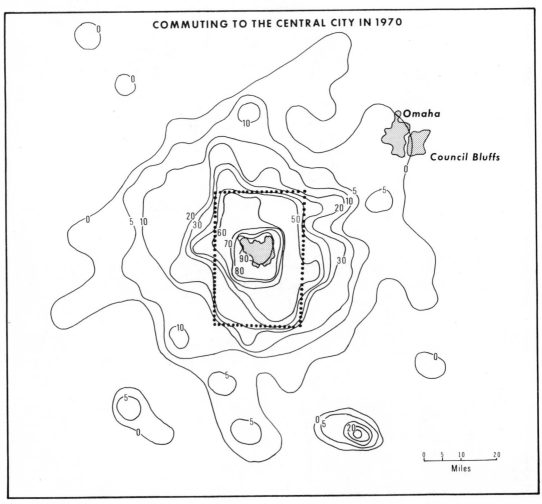

COMMUTING TO THE CENTRAL CITY IN 1970

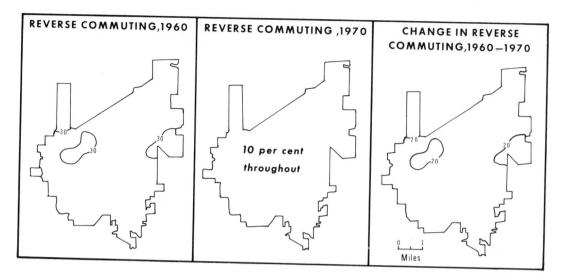

LINCOLN, NE.

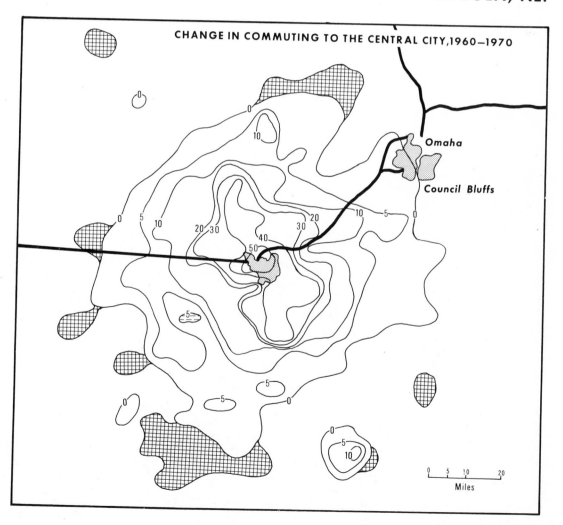

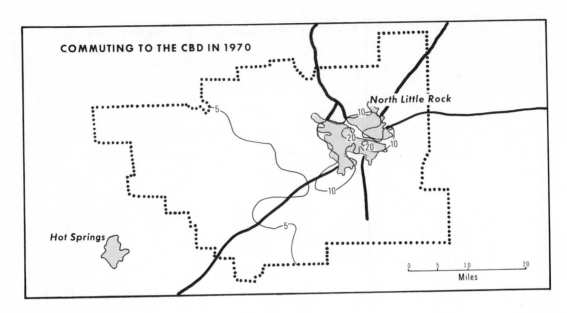

COMMUTING TO THE CBD IN 1970

North Little Rock

Hot Springs

0   5   10   20
Miles

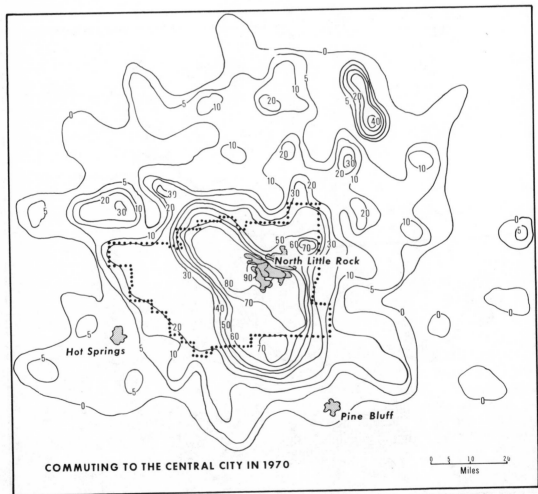

North Little Rock

Hot Springs

Pine Bluff

COMMUTING TO THE CENTRAL CITY IN 1970

0   5   10   20
Miles

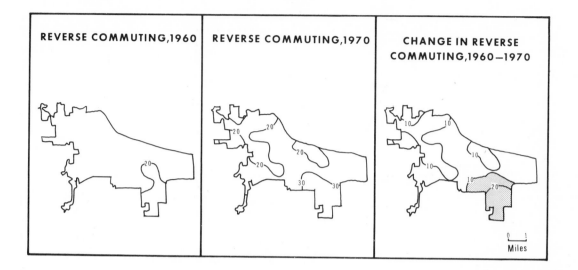

REVERSE COMMUTING,1960   REVERSE COMMUTING,1970   CHANGE IN REVERSE COMMUTING,1960—1970

LITTLE ROCK, AR.

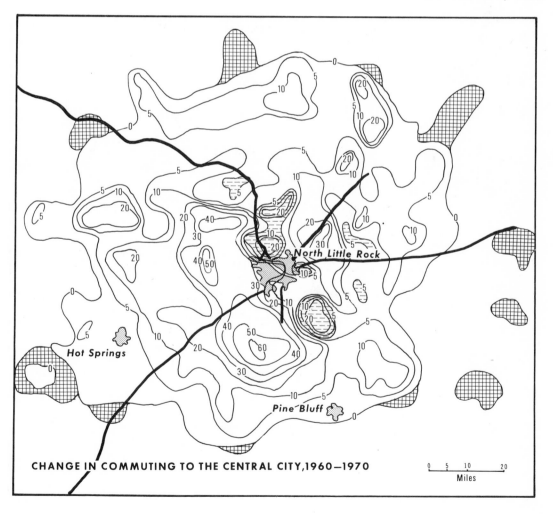

CHANGE IN COMMUTING TO THE CENTRAL CITY,1960—1970

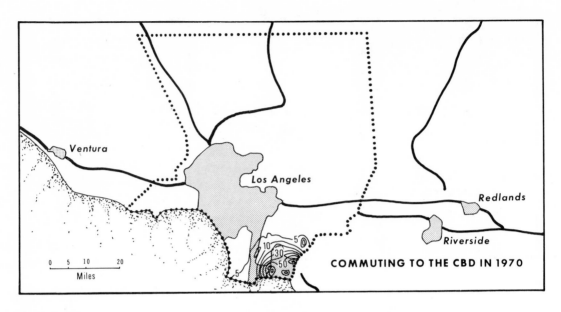

COMMUTING TO THE CBD IN 1970

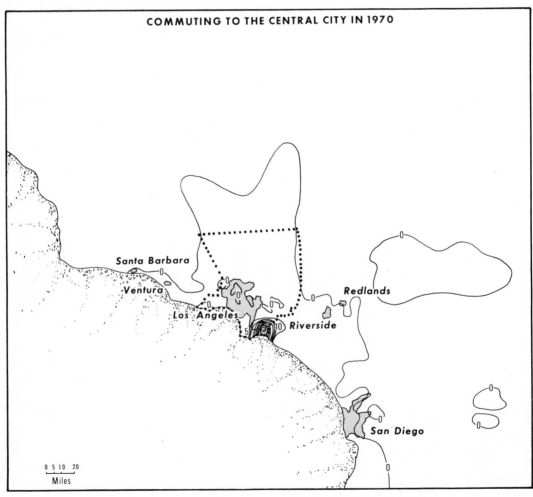

COMMUTING TO THE CENTRAL CITY IN 1970

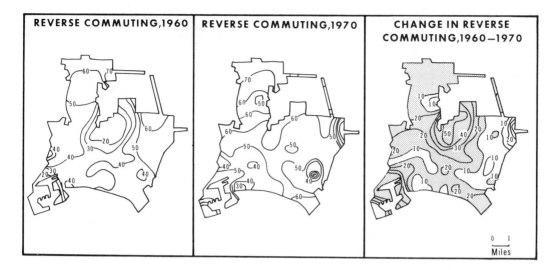

| REVERSE COMMUTING,1960 | REVERSE COMMUTING,1970 | CHANGE IN REVERSE COMMUTING,1960–1970 |

LONG BEACH, CA.

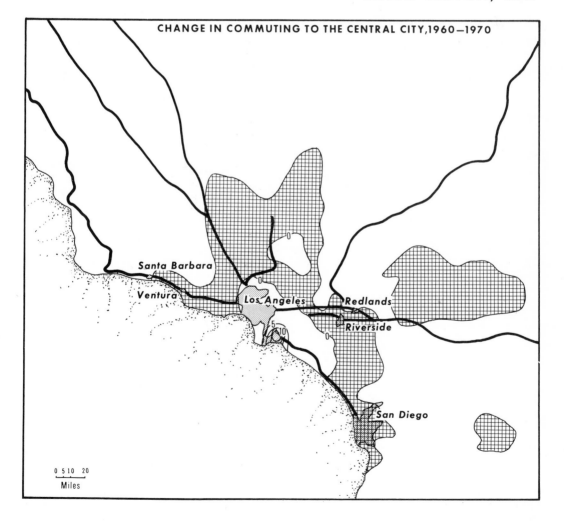

CHANGE IN COMMUTING TO THE CENTRAL CITY,1960–1970

Santa Barbara

Ventura

Los Angeles

Redlands

Riverside

San Diego

0 5 10 20
Miles

COMMUTING TO THE CBD IN 1970

NO DATA COLLECTED

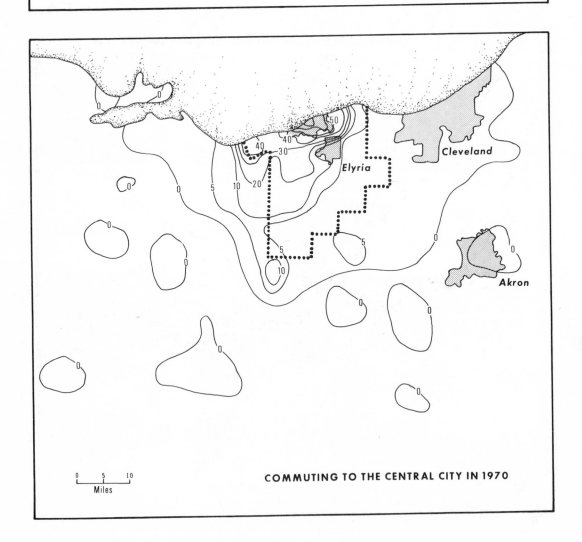

COMMUTING TO THE CENTRAL CITY IN 1970

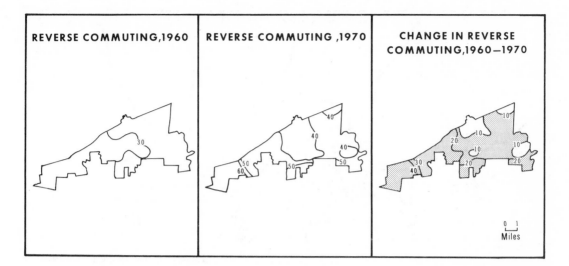

| REVERSE COMMUTING,1960 | REVERSE COMMUTING ,1970 | CHANGE IN REVERSE COMMUTING,1960—1970 |

LORAIN, OH.

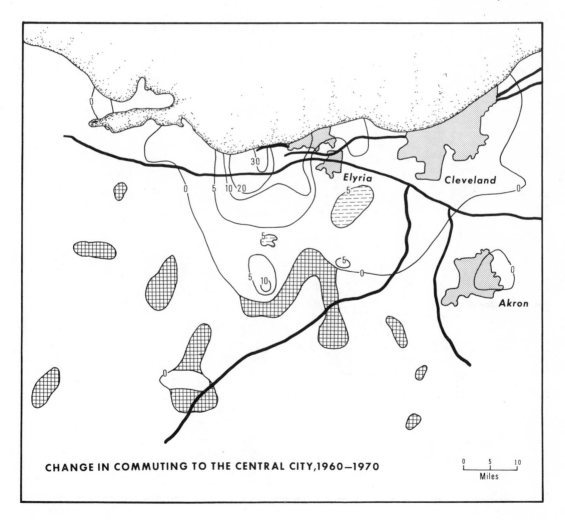

CHANGE IN COMMUTING TO THE CENTRAL CITY,1960—1970

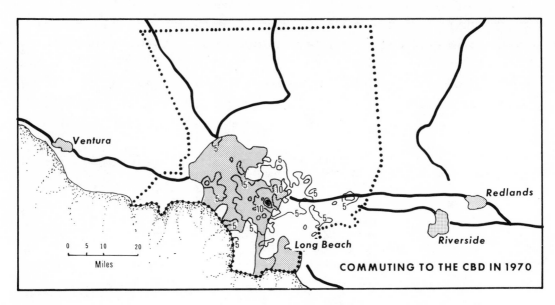

Ventura

Redlands

Riverside

Long Beach

0   5   10   20

Miles

COMMUTING TO THE CBD IN 1970

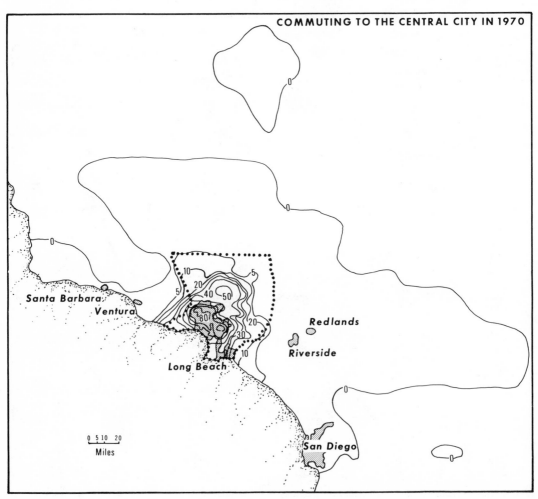

COMMUTING TO THE CENTRAL CITY IN 1970

Santa Barbara

Ventura

Redlands

Riverside

Long Beach

San Diego

0 5 10   20

Miles

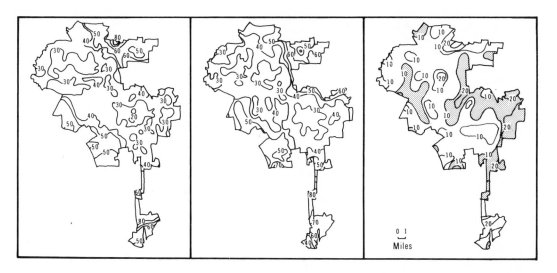

LOS ANGELES, CA.

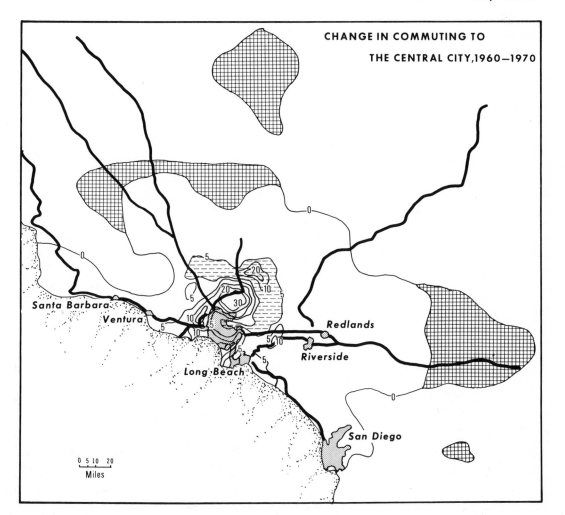

CHANGE IN COMMUTING TO
THE CENTRAL CITY, 1960–1970

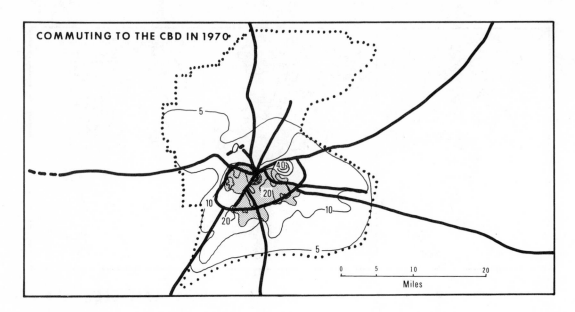

COMMUTING TO THE CBD IN 1970

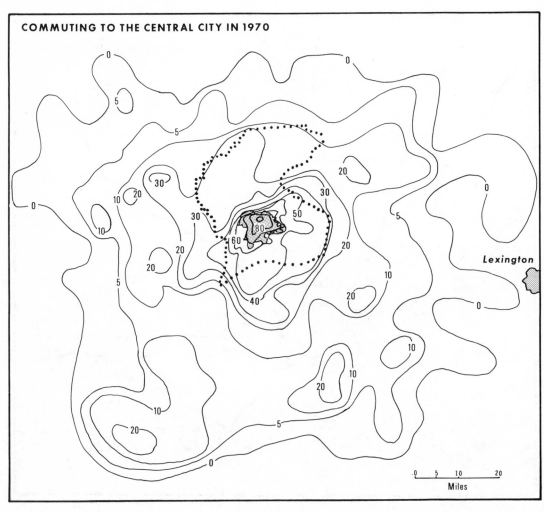

COMMUTING TO THE CENTRAL CITY IN 1970

Lexington

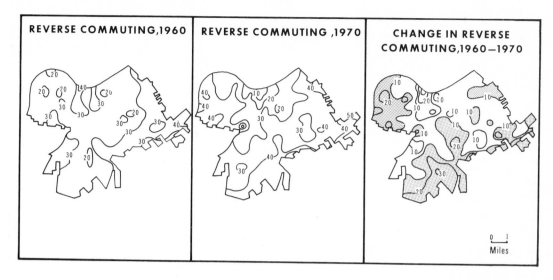

REVERSE COMMUTING, 1960

REVERSE COMMUTING, 1970

CHANGE IN REVERSE COMMUTING, 1960—1970

LOUISVILLE, KY.

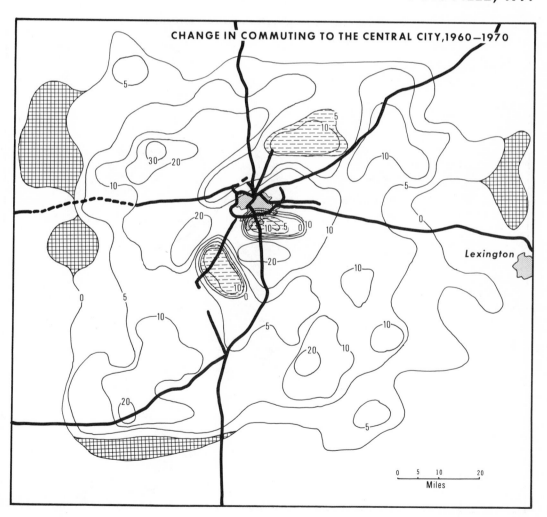

CHANGE IN COMMUTING TO THE CENTRAL CITY, 1960—1970

Lexington

COMMUTING TO THE CBD IN 1970

NO DATA COLLECTED

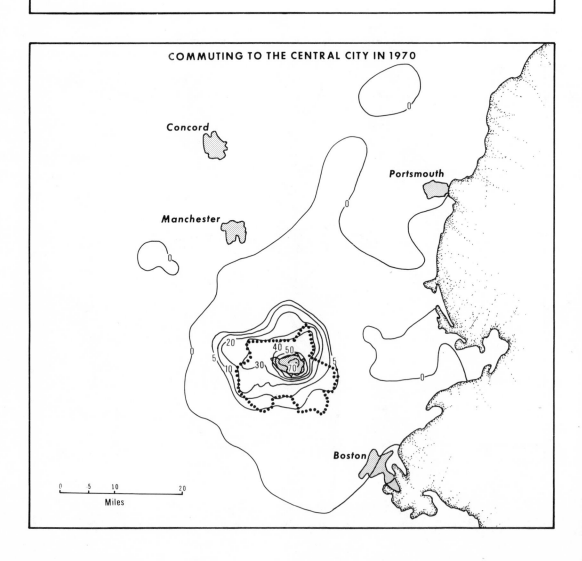

COMMUTING TO THE CENTRAL CITY IN 1970

393

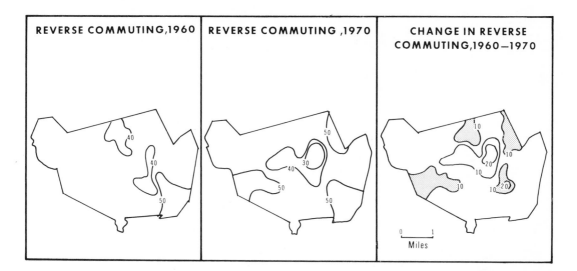

REVERSE COMMUTING, 1960

REVERSE COMMUTING, 1970

CHANGE IN REVERSE COMMUTING, 1960—1970

LOWELL, MA.

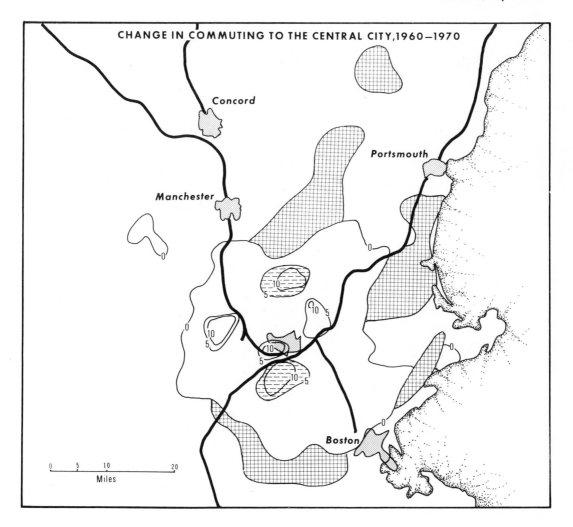

CHANGE IN COMMUTING TO THE CENTRAL CITY, 1960—1970

COMMUTING TO THE CBD IN 1970

NO DATA COLLECTED

COMMUTING TO THE
CENTRAL CITY IN 1970

Amarillo

0 5 10   20
Miles

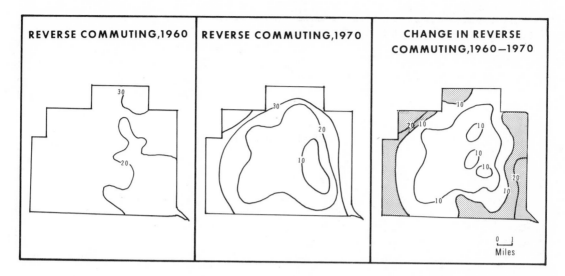

REVERSE COMMUTING, 1960

REVERSE COMMUTING, 1970

CHANGE IN REVERSE COMMUTING, 1960—1970

LUBBOCK, TX.

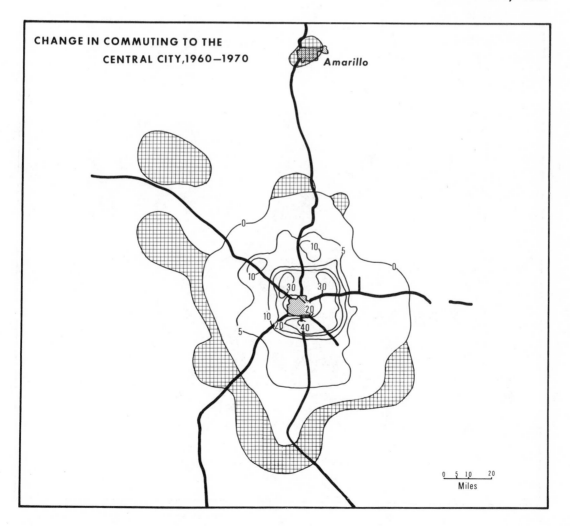

CHANGE IN COMMUTING TO THE CENTRAL CITY, 1960—1970

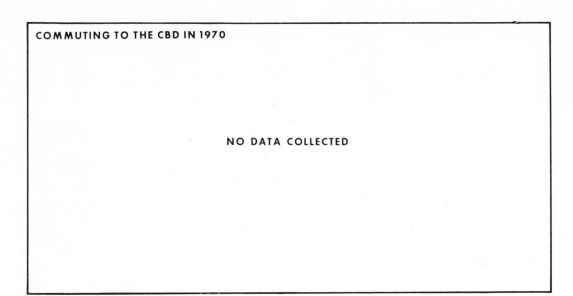

COMMUTING TO THE CBD IN 1970

NO DATA COLLECTED

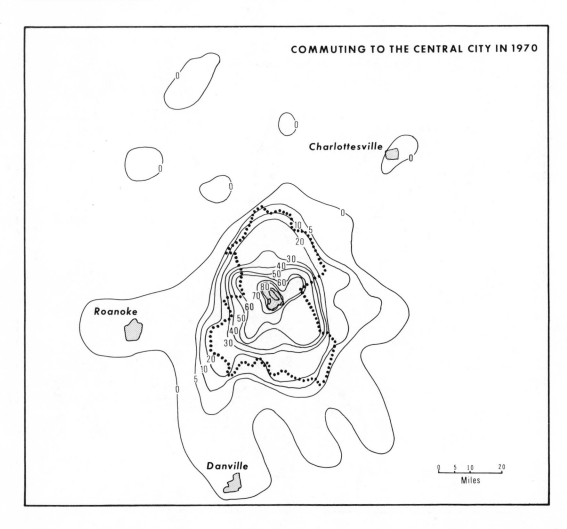

COMMUTING TO THE CENTRAL CITY IN 1970

Charlottesville

Roanoke

Danville

0 5 10   20
Miles

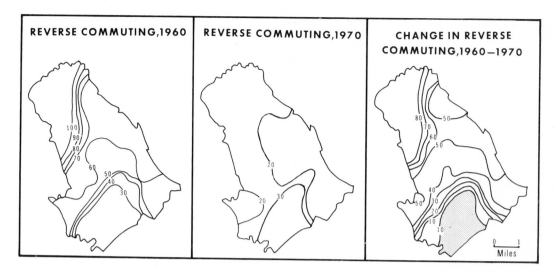

REVERSE COMMUTING, 1960

REVERSE COMMUTING, 1970

CHANGE IN REVERSE COMMUTING, 1960—1970

LYNCHBURG, VA.

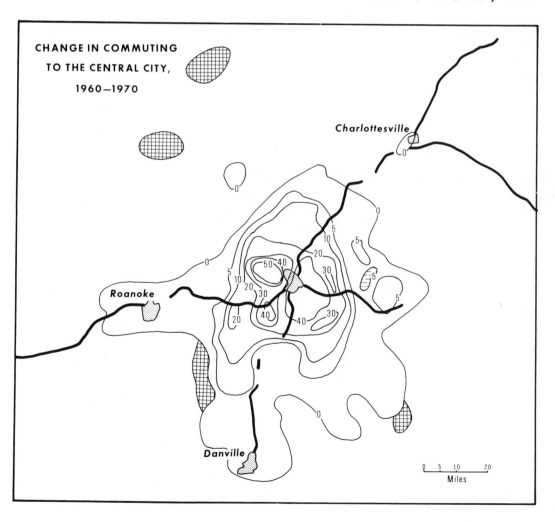

CHANGE IN COMMUTING TO THE CENTRAL CITY, 1960—1970

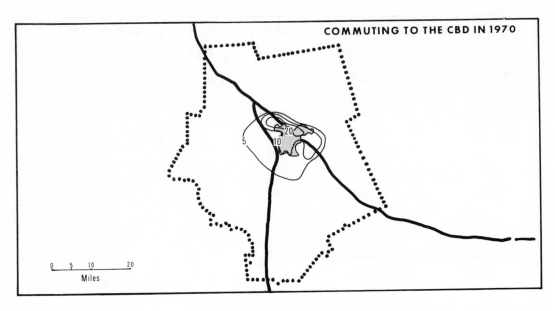

COMMUTING TO THE CBD IN 1970

0 5 10   20
Miles

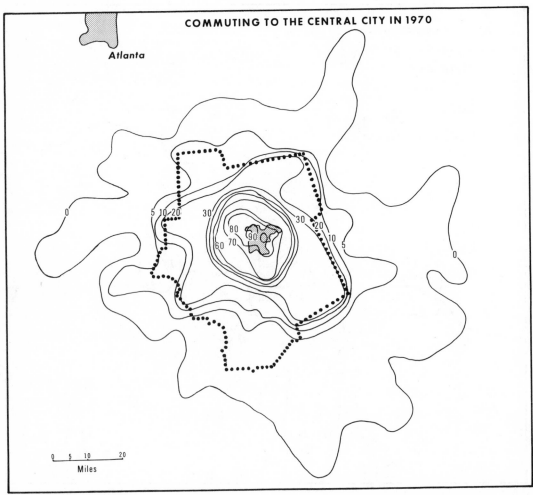

COMMUTING TO THE CENTRAL CITY IN 1970

Atlanta

0 5 10   20
Miles

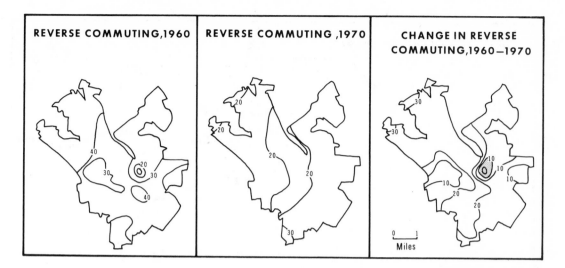

MACON, GA.

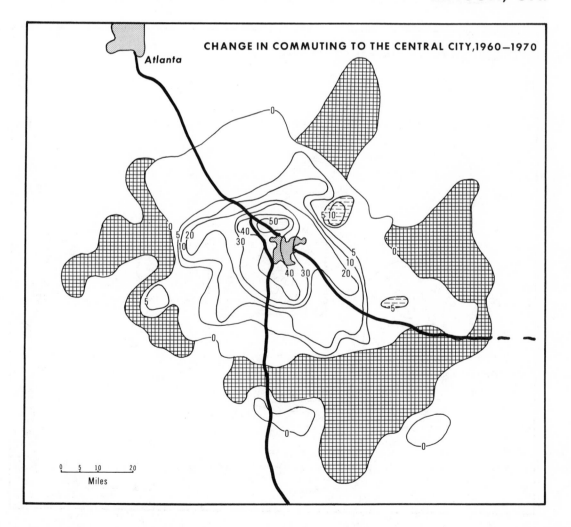

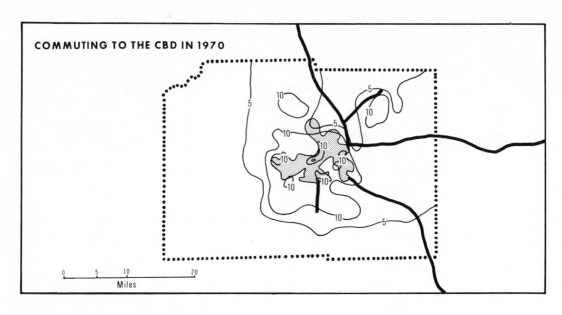

COMMUTING TO THE CBD IN 1970

0 5 10   20
Miles

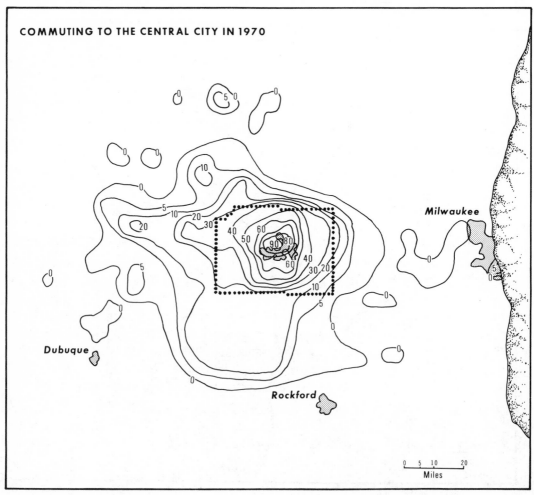

COMMUTING TO THE CENTRAL CITY IN 1970

Milwaukee

Dubuque

Rockford

0 5 10   20
Miles

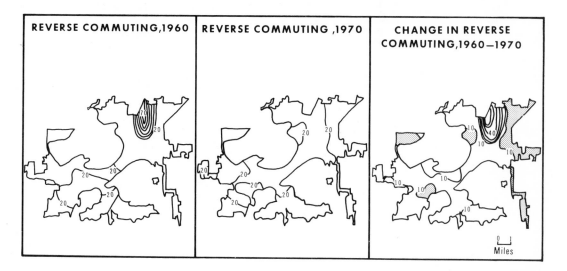

REVERSE COMMUTING,1960 REVERSE COMMUTING ,1970 CHANGE IN REVERSE COMMUTING,1960—1970

MADISON, WI.

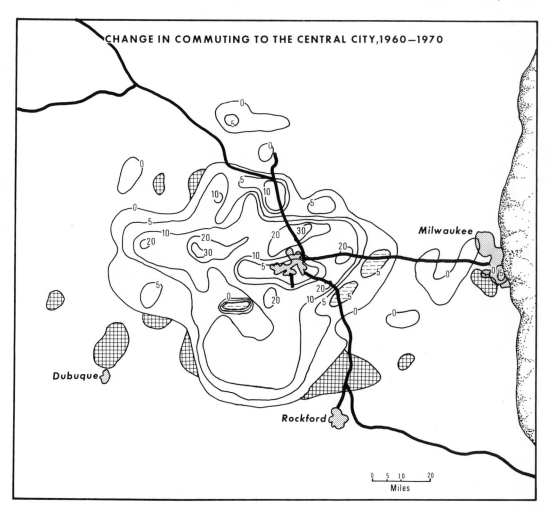

CHANGE IN COMMUTING TO THE CENTRAL CITY,1960—1970

COMMUTING TO THE CBD IN 1970

NO DATA COLLECTED

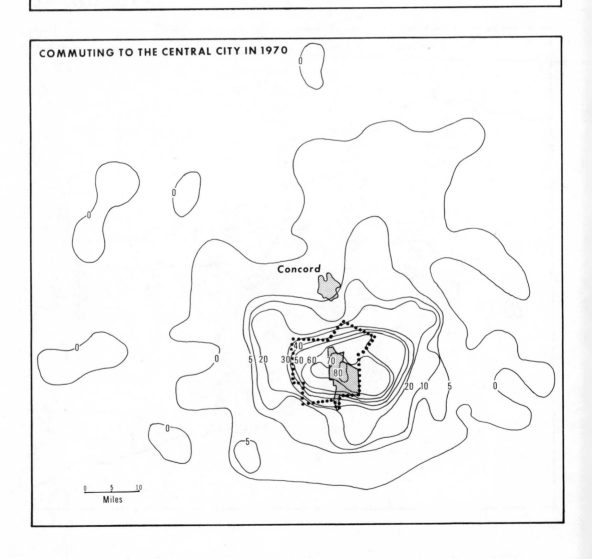

COMMUTING TO THE CENTRAL CITY IN 1970

Concord

0 5 10
Miles

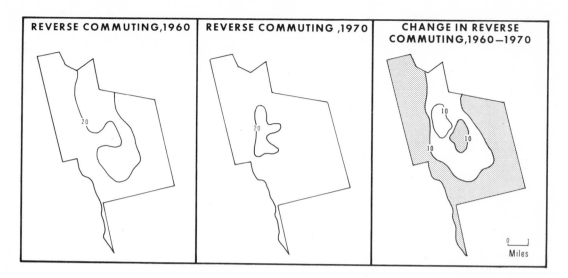

REVERSE COMMUTING, 1960

REVERSE COMMUTING, 1970

CHANGE IN REVERSE COMMUTING, 1960—1970

MANCHESTER, N.H.

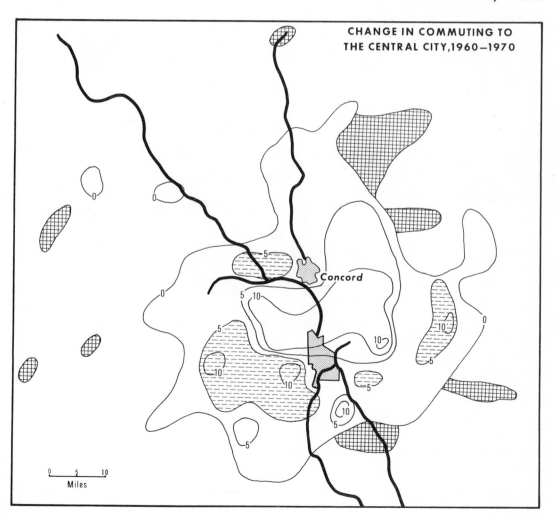

CHANGE IN COMMUTING TO THE CENTRAL CITY, 1960—1970

Concord

COMMUTING TO THE CBD IN 1970

NO DATA COLLECTED

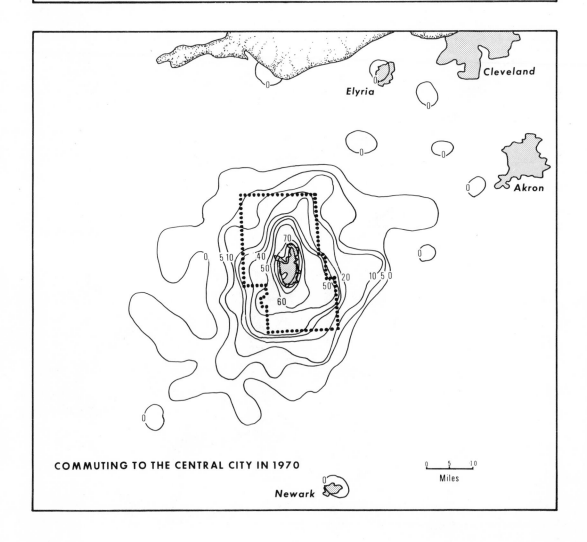

COMMUTING TO THE CENTRAL CITY IN 1970

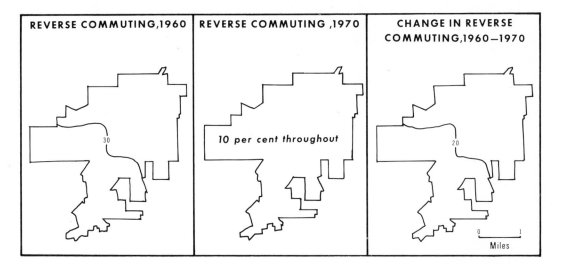

| REVERSE COMMUTING,1960 | REVERSE COMMUTING ,1970 | CHANGE IN REVERSE COMMUTING,1960—1970 |

10 per cent throughout

30

20

0   1
Miles

MANSFIELD, OH.

CHANGE IN COMMUTING TO THE CENTRAL CITY,1960—1970

NO DATA COLLECTED

COMMUTING TO THE CBD IN 1970

NO DATA COLLECTED

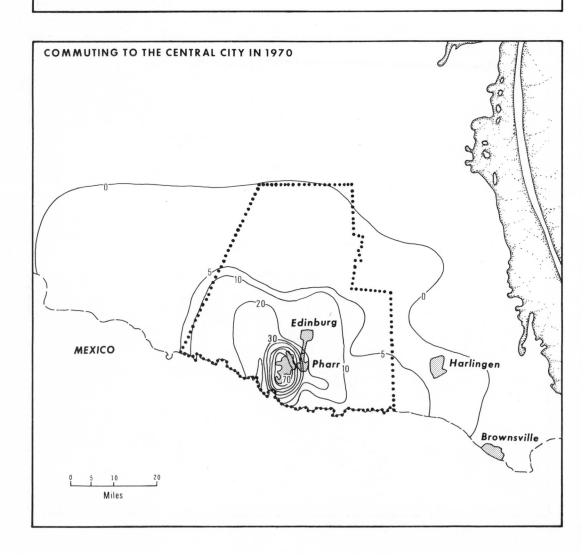

COMMUTING TO THE CENTRAL CITY IN 1970

MEXICO

Edinburg

Pharr

Harlingen

Brownsville

0   5   10   20
Miles

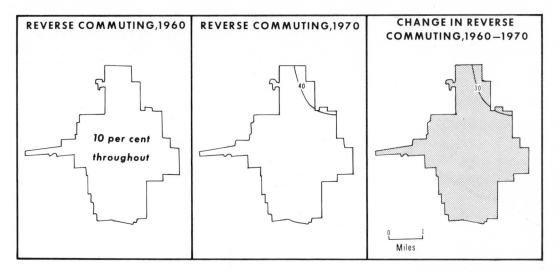

| REVERSE COMMUTING,1960 | REVERSE COMMUTING,1970 | CHANGE IN REVERSE COMMUTING,1960—1970 |

10 per cent throughout

40

30

0   1
Miles

MC ALLEN, TX.

CHANGE IN COMMUTING TO THE CENTRAL CITY,1960—1970

NO DATA COLLECTED

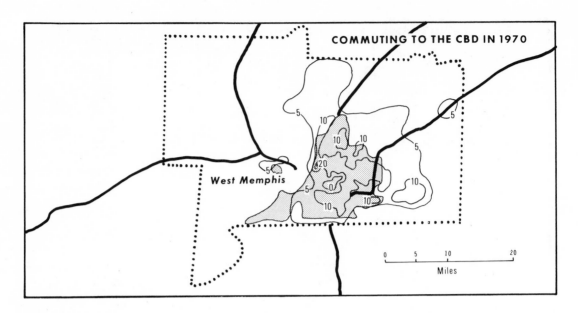

COMMUTING TO THE CBD IN 1970

West Memphis

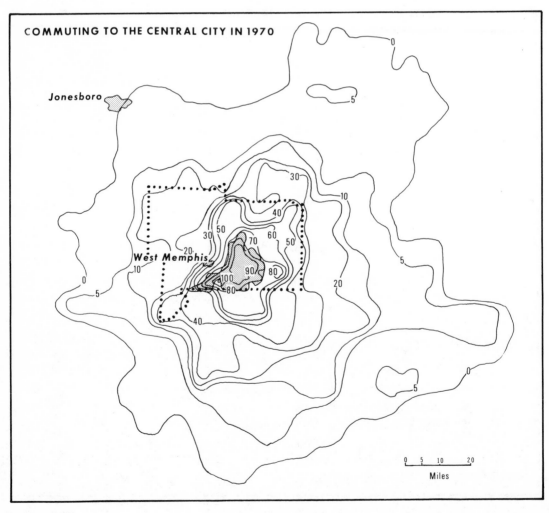

COMMUTING TO THE CENTRAL CITY IN 1970

Jonesboro

West Memphis

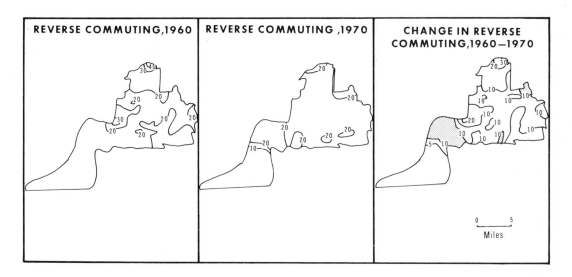

REVERSE COMMUTING, 1960

REVERSE COMMUTING, 1970

CHANGE IN REVERSE COMMUTING, 1960–1970

0 5
Miles

MEMPHIS, TN.

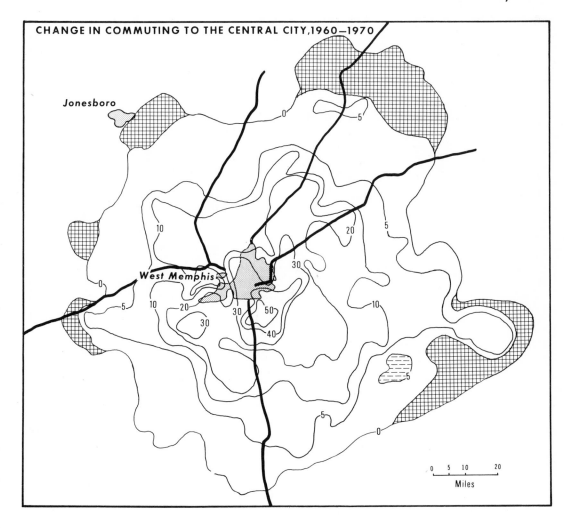

CHANGE IN COMMUTING TO THE CENTRAL CITY, 1960–1970

Jonesboro

West Memphis

0 5 10 20
Miles

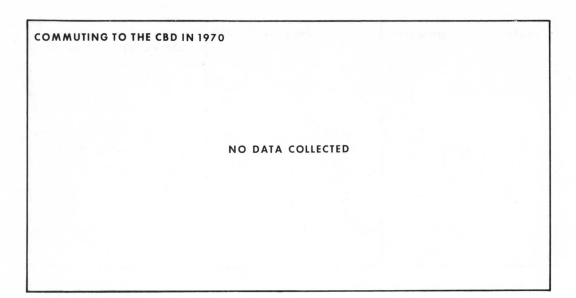

COMMUTING TO THE CBD IN 1970

NO DATA COLLECTED

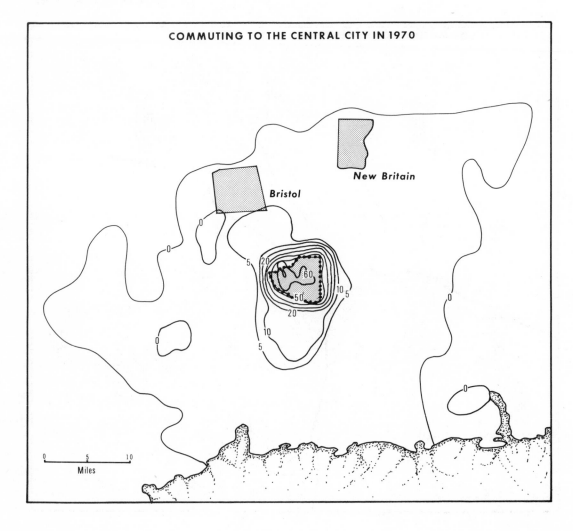

COMMUTING TO THE CENTRAL CITY IN 1970

Bristol

New Britain

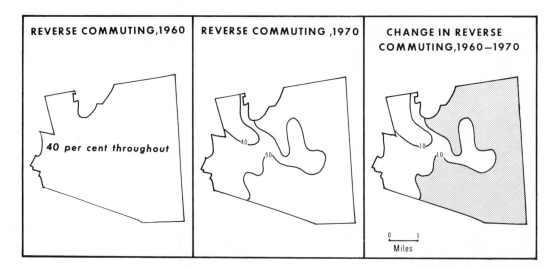

REVERSE COMMUTING,1960	REVERSE COMMUTING ,1970	CHANGE IN REVERSE COMMUTING,1960—1970
40 per cent throughout		

MERIDEN, CT.

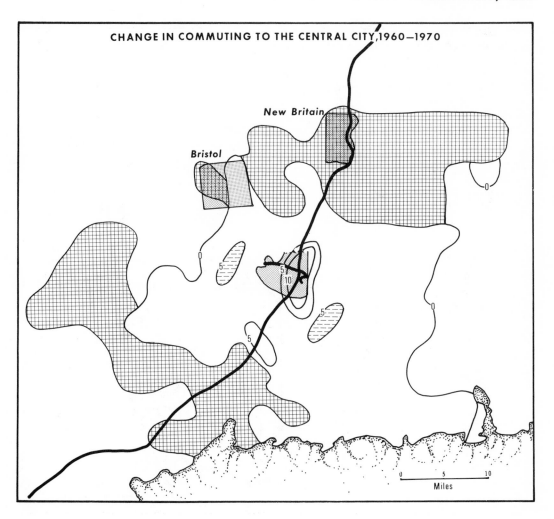

CHANGE IN COMMUTING TO THE CENTRAL CITY,1960—1970

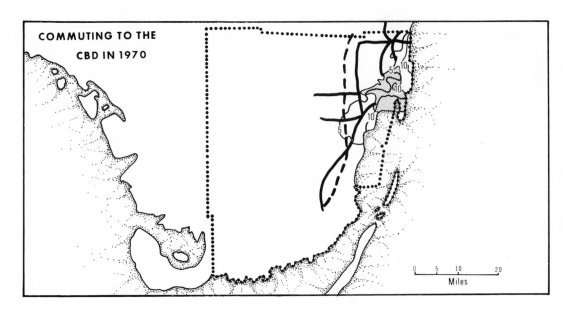

COMMUTING TO THE
CBD IN 1970

5 10

10

10

5 10

5

0 5 10 20
Miles

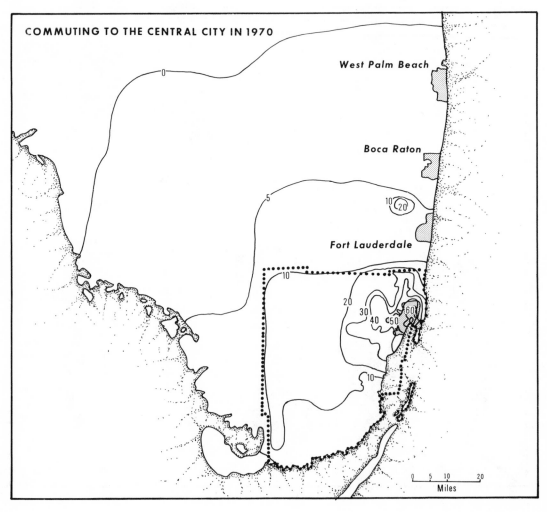

COMMUTING TO THE CENTRAL CITY IN 1970

West Palm Beach

Boca Raton

Fort Lauderdale

0

5

10 20

10

10

20

30 40 50 60

10

0 5 10 20
Miles

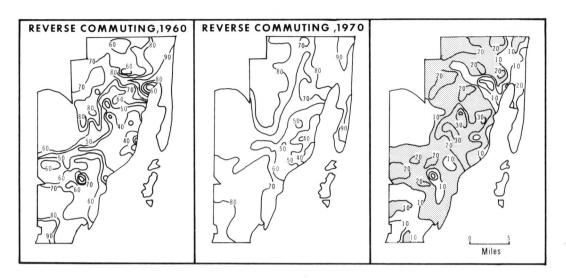

REVERSE COMMUTING,1960

REVERSE COMMUTING ,1970

MIAMI, FL.

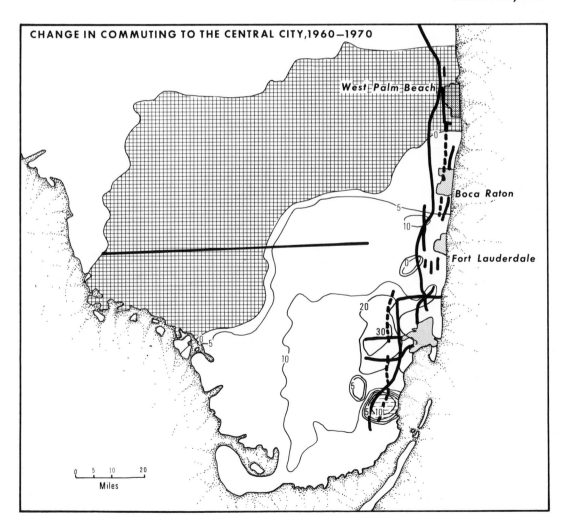

CHANGE IN COMMUTING TO THE CENTRAL CITY,1960—1970

West Palm Beach

Boca Raton

Fort Lauderdale

0 5 10 20
Miles

COMMUTING TO THE CBD IN 1970

NO DATA COLLECTED

COMMUTING TO THE CENTRAL CITY IN 1970

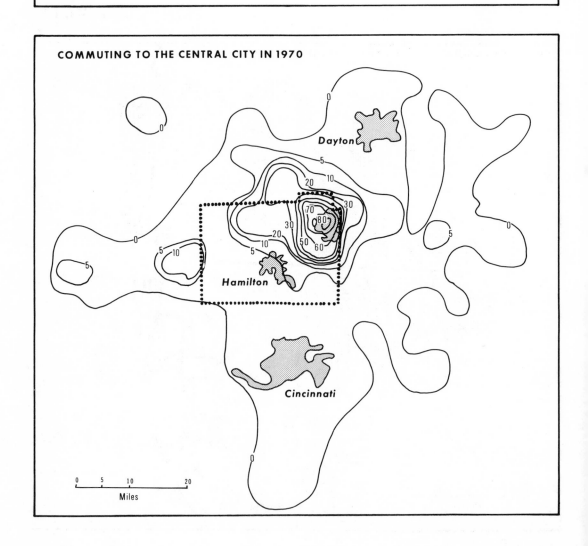

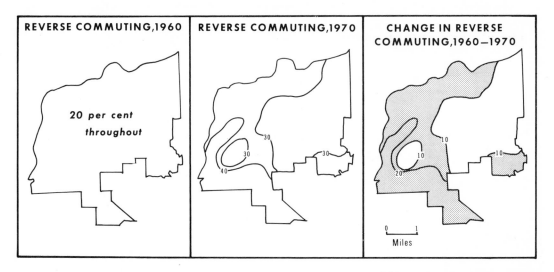

REVERSE COMMUTING, 1960

20 per cent throughout

REVERSE COMMUTING, 1970

CHANGE IN REVERSE COMMUTING, 1960–1970

MIDDLETOWN, OH.

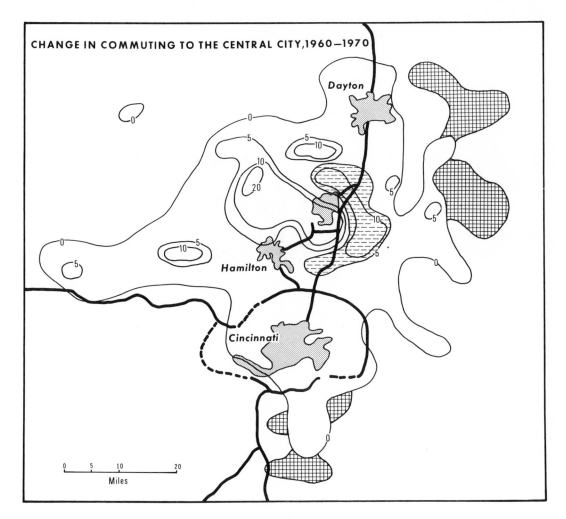

CHANGE IN COMMUTING TO THE CENTRAL CITY, 1960–1970

Dayton

Hamilton

Cincinnati

COMMUTING TO THE CBD IN 1970

NO DATA COLLECTED

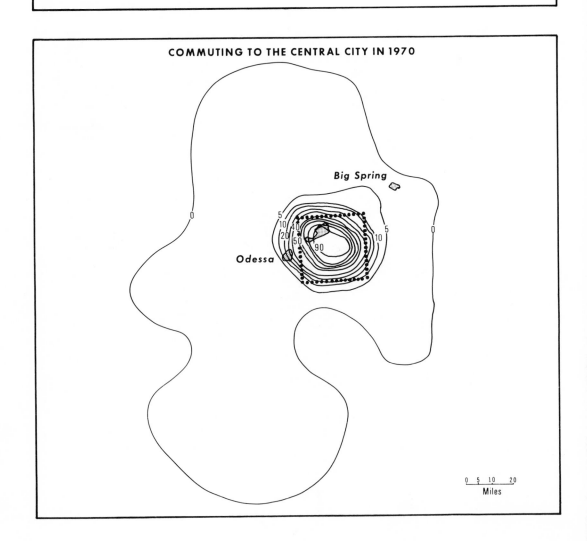

COMMUTING TO THE CENTRAL CITY IN 1970

Big Spring

Odessa

0   5   10   20
Miles

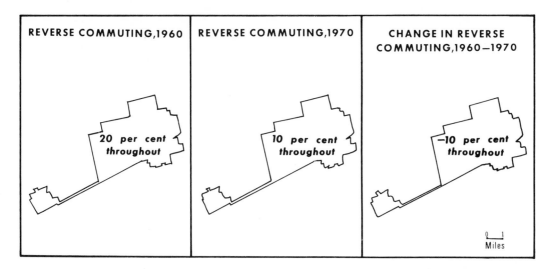

MIDLAND, TX.

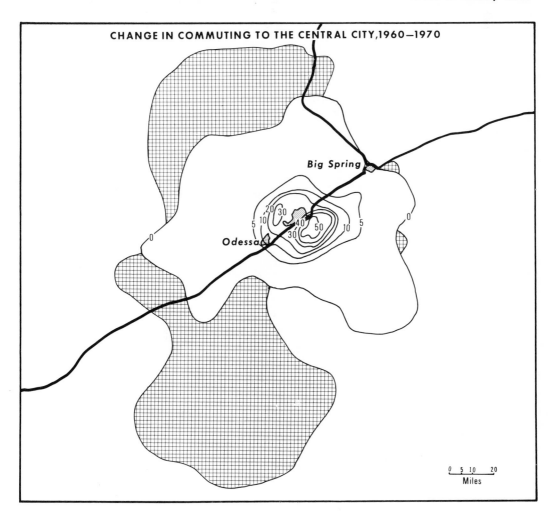

COMMUTING TO THE CBD IN 1970

NO DATA COLLECTED

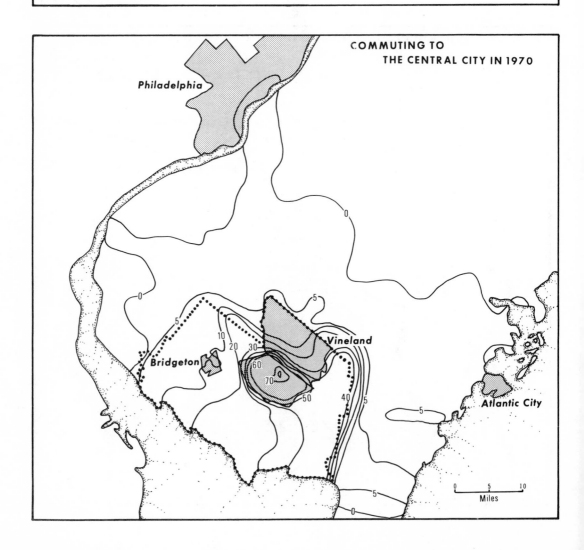

COMMUTING TO
THE CENTRAL CITY IN 1970

Philadelphia

Vineland

Bridgeton

Atlantic City

0

5

10
20
30
60
70
50
40
5

5

5

5

0

0

0

5

10
Miles

419

REVERSE COMMUTING, 1960	REVERSE COMMUTING, 1970	CHANGE IN REVERSE COMMUTING, 1960—1970
NO DATA COLLECTED		NO DATA COLLECTED

0   1
Miles

MILLVILLE, N.J.

CHANGE IN COMMUTING TO THE CENTRAL CITY, 1960—1970

NO DATA COLLECTED

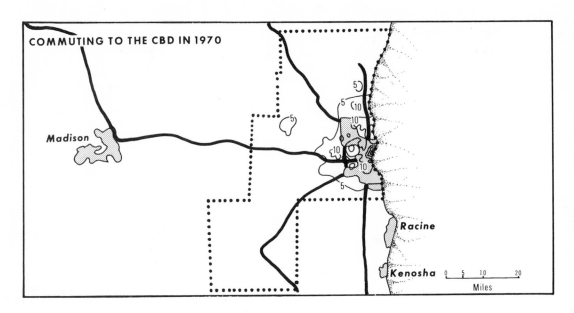

COMMUTING TO THE CBD IN 1970

Madison

Racine

Kenosha

0   5   10   20
        Miles

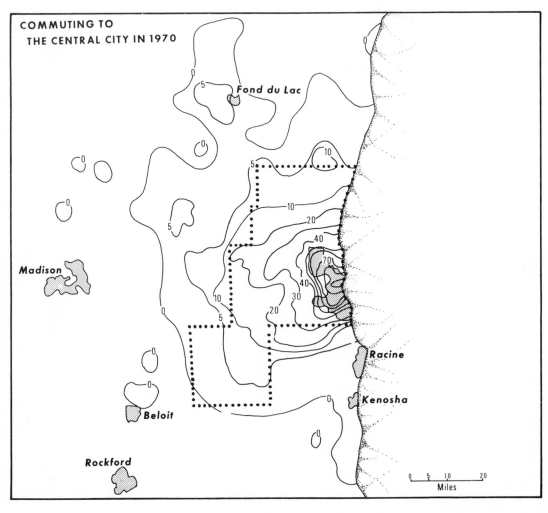

COMMUTING TO
THE CENTRAL CITY IN 1970

Fond du Lac

Madison

Racine

Kenosha

Beloit

Rockford

0   5   10   20
        Miles

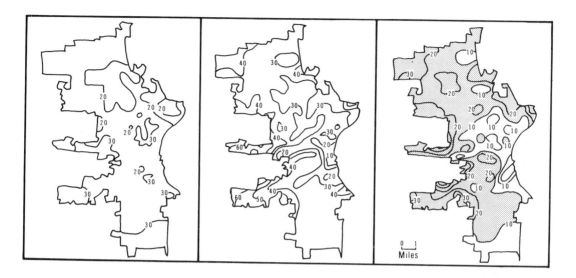

MILWAUKEE, WI.

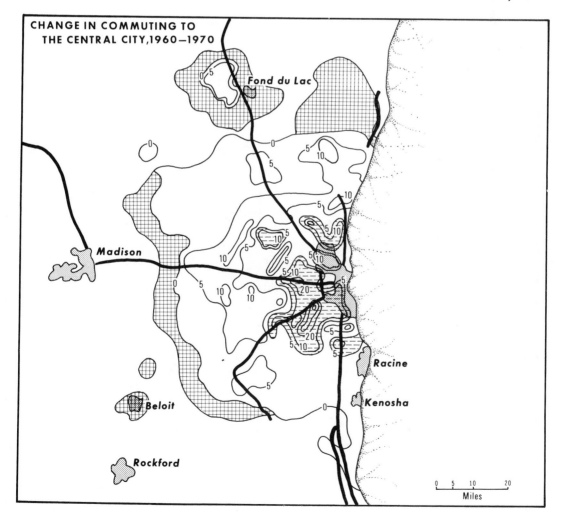

CHANGE IN COMMUTING TO
THE CENTRAL CITY, 1960—1970

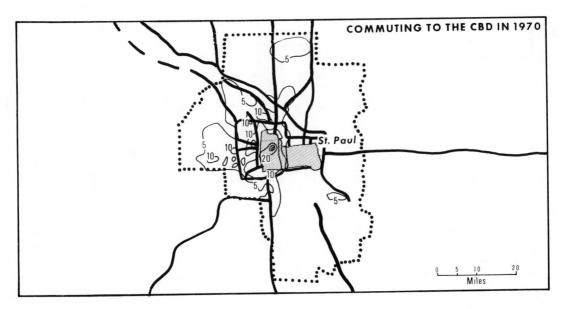

COMMUTING TO THE CBD IN 1970

St. Paul

0 5 10   20
Miles

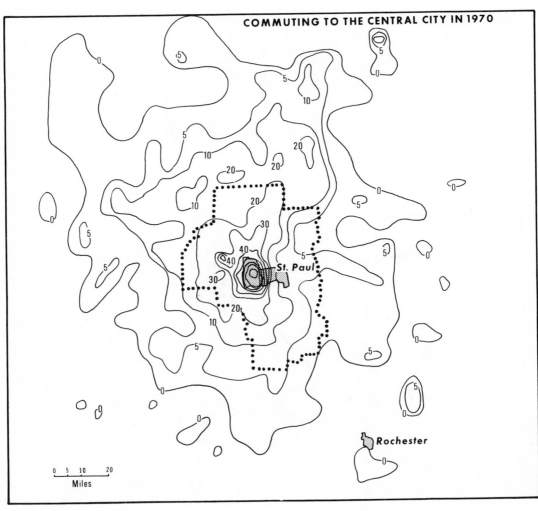

COMMUTING TO THE CENTRAL CITY IN 1970

St. Paul

Rochester

0 5 10   20
Miles

MINNEAPOLIS, MN.

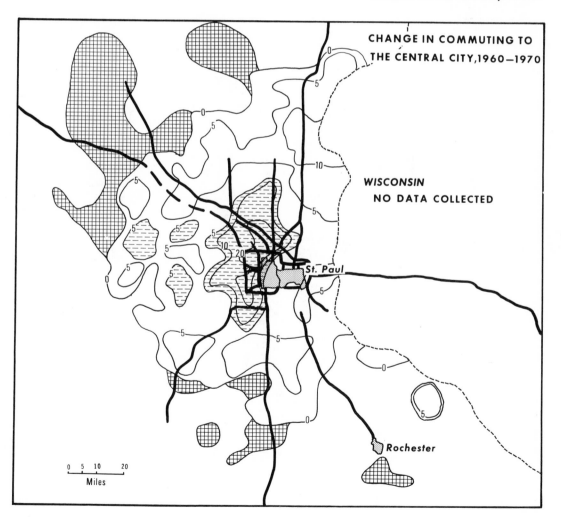

CHANGE IN COMMUTING TO
THE CENTRAL CITY, 1960—1970

WISCONSIN
NO DATA COLLECTED

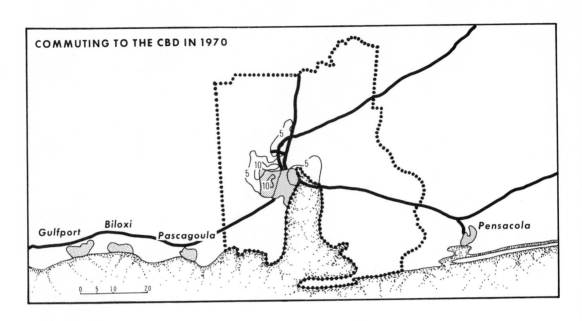

COMMUTING TO THE CBD IN 1970

Gulfport   Biloxi   Pascagoula   Pensacola

0   5   10   20

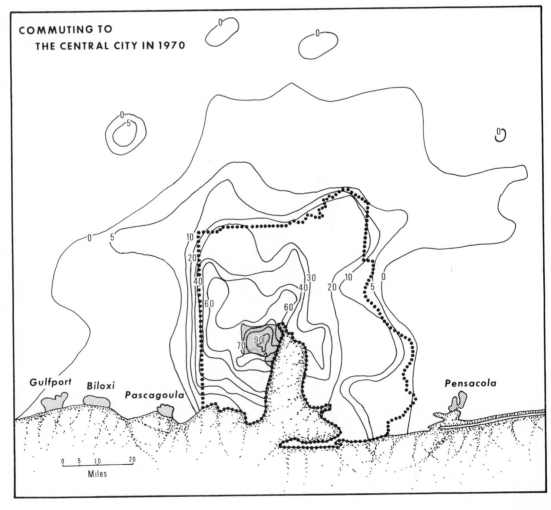

COMMUTING TO
THE CENTRAL CITY IN 1970

Gulfport   Biloxi   Pascagoula   Pensacola

0   5   10   20
Miles

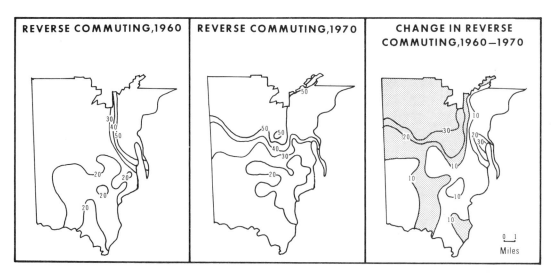

REVERSE COMMUTING, 1960

REVERSE COMMUTING, 1970

CHANGE IN REVERSE COMMUTING, 1960—1970

MOBILE, AL.

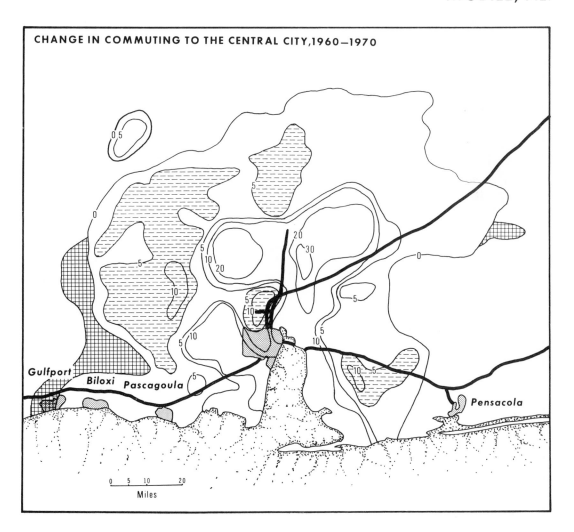

CHANGE IN COMMUTING TO THE CENTRAL CITY, 1960—1970

Gulfport

Biloxi Pascagoula

Pensacola

0 5 10   20
Miles

COMMUTING TO THE CBD IN 1970

NO DATA COLLECTED

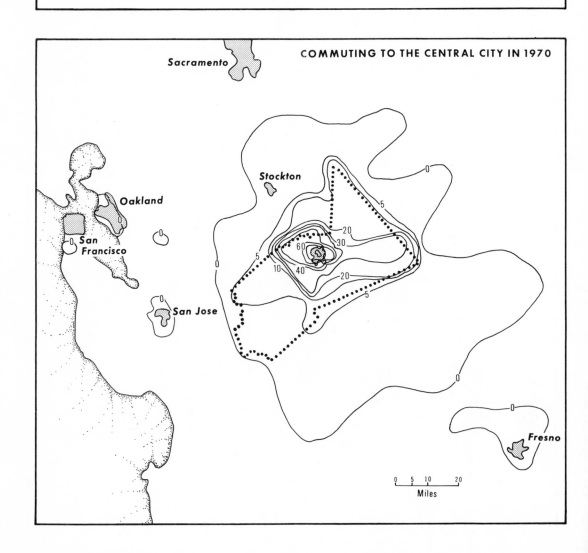

COMMUTING TO THE CENTRAL CITY IN 1970

REVERSE COMMUTING, 1960	REVERSE COMMUTING, 1970	CHANGE IN REVERSE COMMUTING, 1960—1970
NO DATA COLLECTED		NO DATA COLLECTED

30

40

50

0 _____ 1
Miles

MODESTO, CA.

CHANGE IN COMMUTING TO THE CENTRAL CITY, 1960—1970

NO DATA COLLECTED

COMMUTING TO THE CBD IN 1970

NO DATA COLLECTED

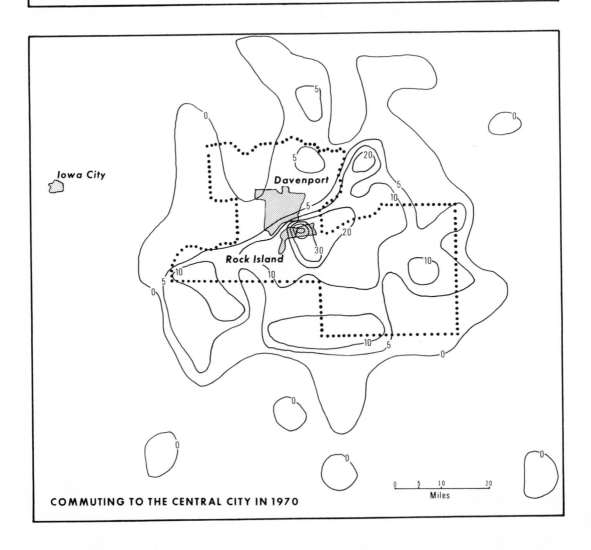

COMMUTING TO THE CENTRAL CITY IN 1970

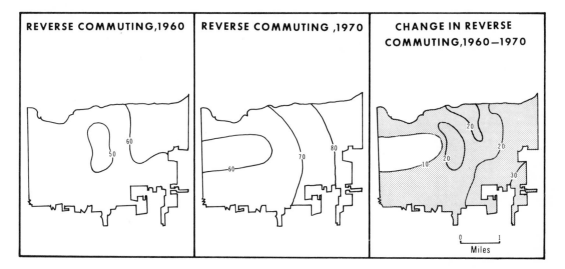

REVERSE COMMUTING,1960

REVERSE COMMUTING ,1970

CHANGE IN REVERSE
COMMUTING,1960—1970

MOLINE, IL.

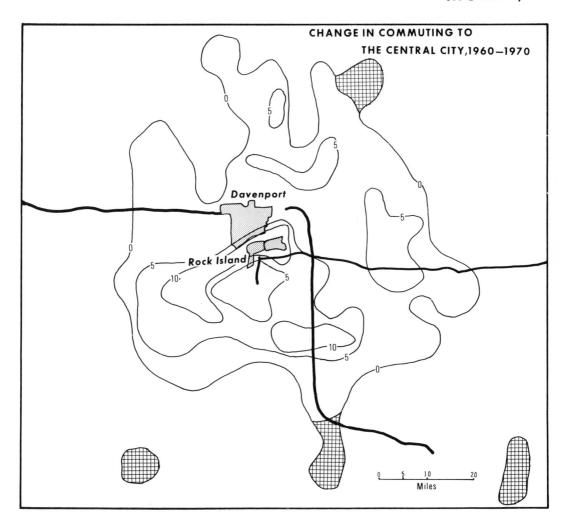

CHANGE IN COMMUTING TO
THE CENTRAL CITY,1960—1970

COMMUTING TO THE CBD IN 1970

NO DATA COLLECTED

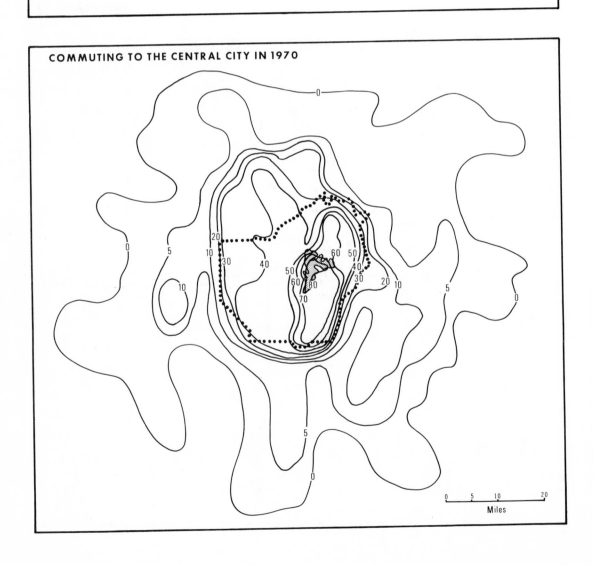

COMMUTING TO THE CENTRAL CITY IN 1970

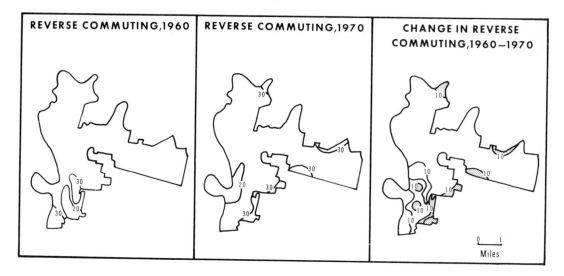

REVERSE COMMUTING, 1960

REVERSE COMMUTING, 1970

CHANGE IN REVERSE COMMUTING, 1960—1970

MONROE, LA.

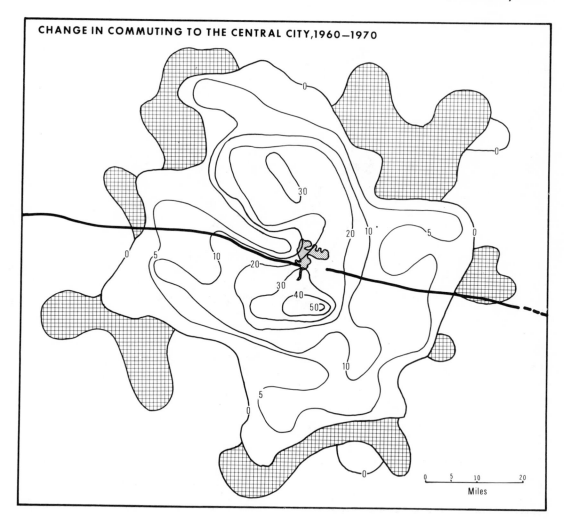

CHANGE IN COMMUTING TO THE CENTRAL CITY, 1960—1970

COMMUTING TO THE CBD IN 1970

NO DATA COLLECTED

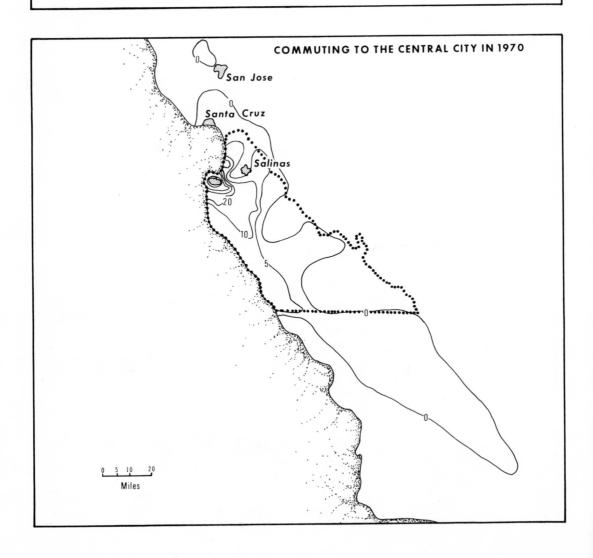

COMMUTING TO THE CENTRAL CITY IN 1970

San Jose

Santa Cruz

Salinas

20

10

5

0

0

0

0 5 10 20
Miles

REVERSE COMMUTING,1960	REVERSE COMMUTING,1970	CHANGE IN REVERSE COMMUTING,1960—1970
NO DATA COLLECTED		NO DATA COLLECTED

Miles

MONTEREY, CA.

CHANGE IN COMMUTING TO THE CENTRAL CITY,1960—1970

NO DATA COLLECTED

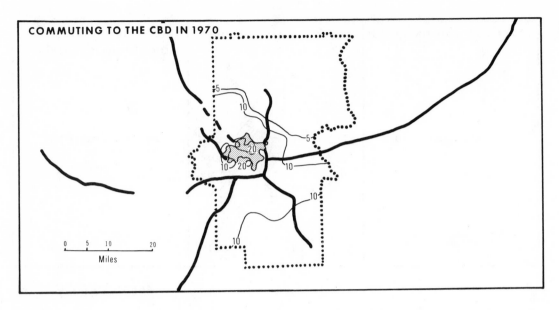

COMMUTING TO THE CBD IN 1970

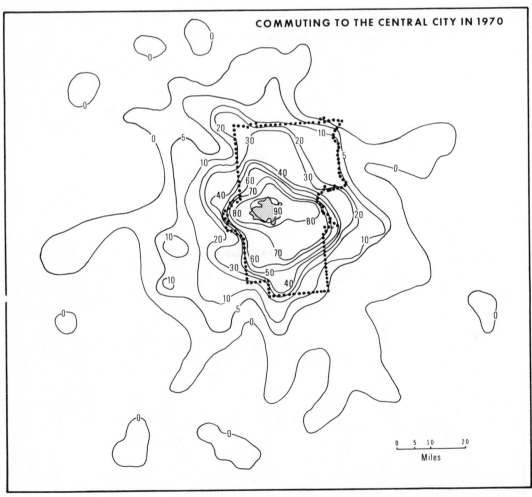

COMMUTING TO THE CENTRAL CITY IN 1970

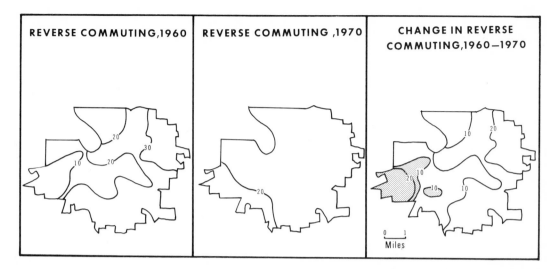

REVERSE COMMUTING,1960   REVERSE COMMUTING ,1970   CHANGE IN REVERSE
COMMUTING,1960—1970

MONTGOMERY, AL.

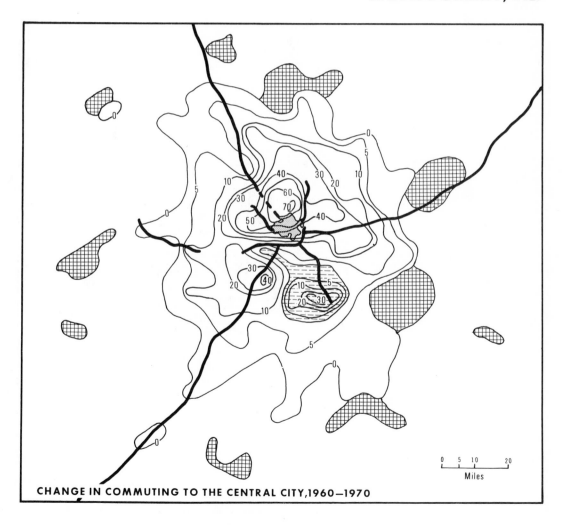

CHANGE IN COMMUTING TO THE CENTRAL CITY,1960—1970

COMMUTING TO THE CBD IN 1970

NO DATA COLLECTED

COMMUTING TO THE CENTRAL CITY IN 1970

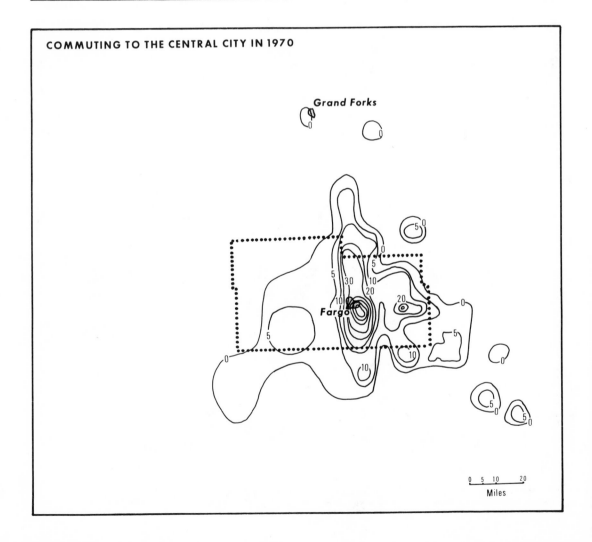

REVERSE COMMUTING,1960	REVERSE COMMUTING ,1970	CHANGE IN REVERSE COMMUTING,1960—1970
NO DATA COLLECTED		NO DATA COLLECTED

Miles

MOORHEAD, N.D.

CHANGE IN COMMUTING TO THE CENTRAL CITY,1960—1970

NO DATA COLLECTED

438

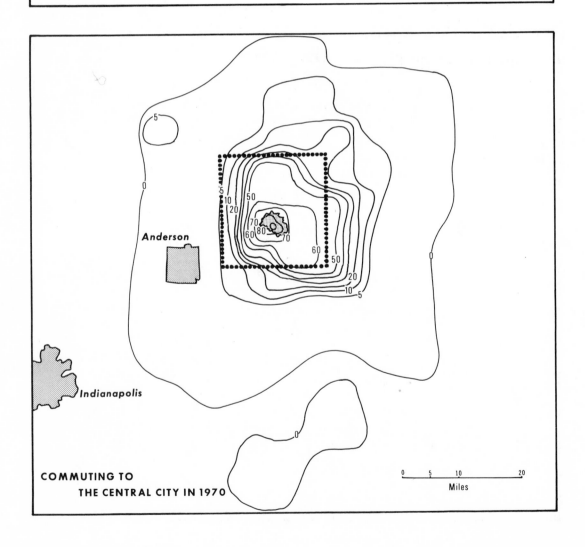

COMMUTING TO THE CBD IN 1970

NO DATA COLLECTED

COMMUTING TO
THE CENTRAL CITY IN 1970

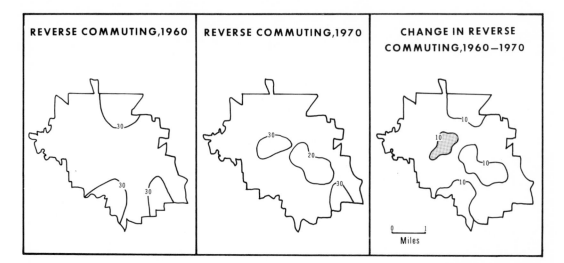

REVERSE COMMUTING, 1960

REVERSE COMMUTING, 1970

CHANGE IN REVERSE COMMUTING, 1960—1970

MUNCIE, IN.

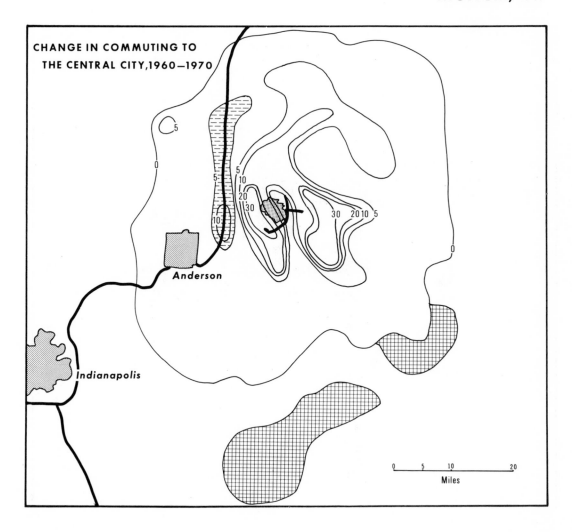

CHANGE IN COMMUTING TO THE CENTRAL CITY, 1960—1970

Anderson

Indianapolis

COMMUTING TO THE CBD IN 1970

NO DATA COLLECTED

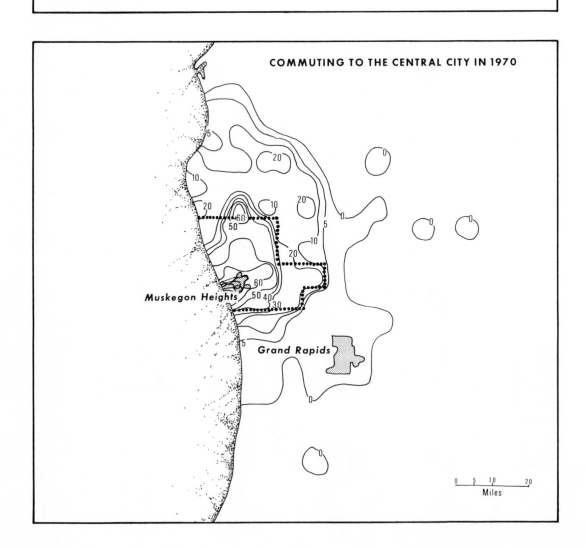

COMMUTING TO THE CENTRAL CITY IN 1970

Muskegon Heights

Grand Rapids

0 5 10   20
      Miles

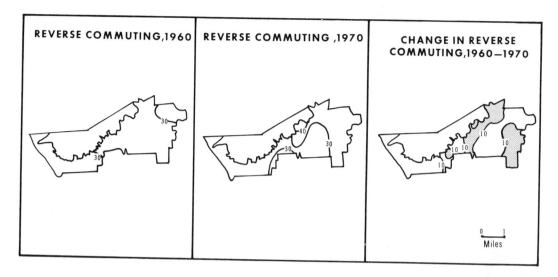

| REVERSE COMMUTING,1960 | REVERSE COMMUTING ,1970 | CHANGE IN REVERSE COMMUTING,1960—1970 |

MUSKEGON, MI.

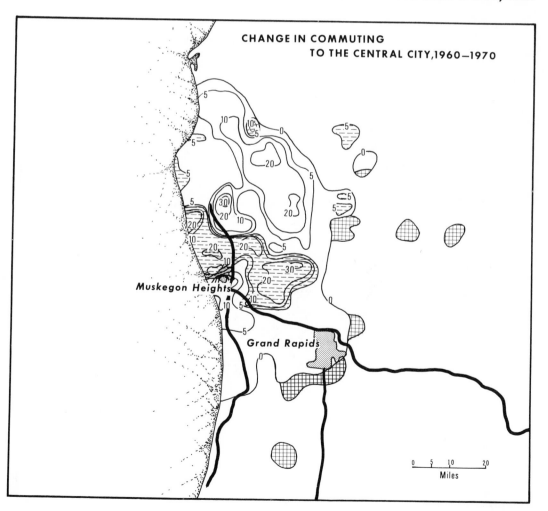

CHANGE IN COMMUTING TO THE CENTRAL CITY,1960—1970

Muskegon Heights

Grand Rapids

COMMUTING TO THE CBD IN 1970

NO DATA COLLECTED

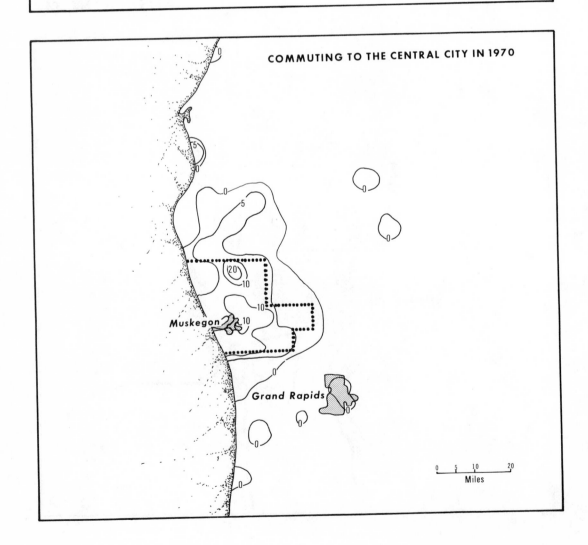

COMMUTING TO THE CENTRAL CITY IN 1970

Muskegon

Grand Rapids

0 5 10 20
Miles

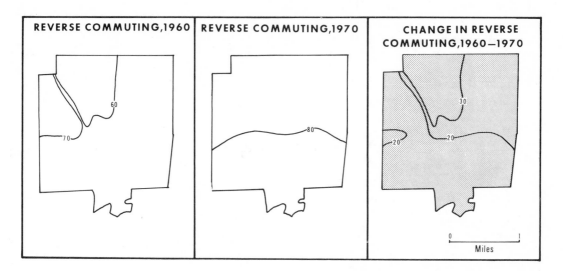

REVERSE COMMUTING, 1960

REVERSE COMMUTING, 1970

CHANGE IN REVERSE COMMUTING, 1960—1970

MUSKEGON HEIGHTS, MI.

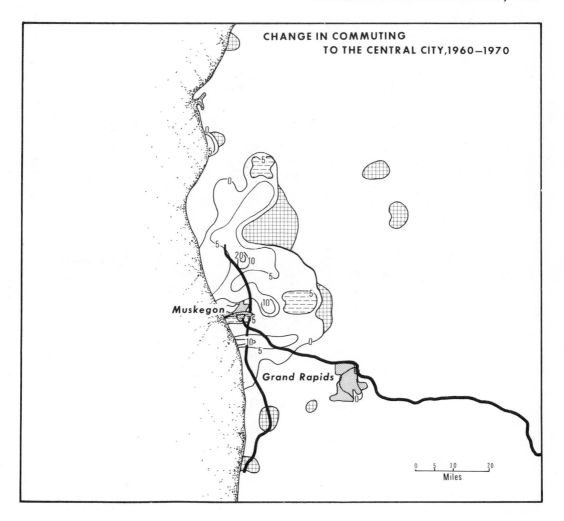

CHANGE IN COMMUTING TO THE CENTRAL CITY, 1960—1970

Muskegon

Grand Rapids

COMMUTING TO THE CBD IN 1970

NO DATA COLLECTED

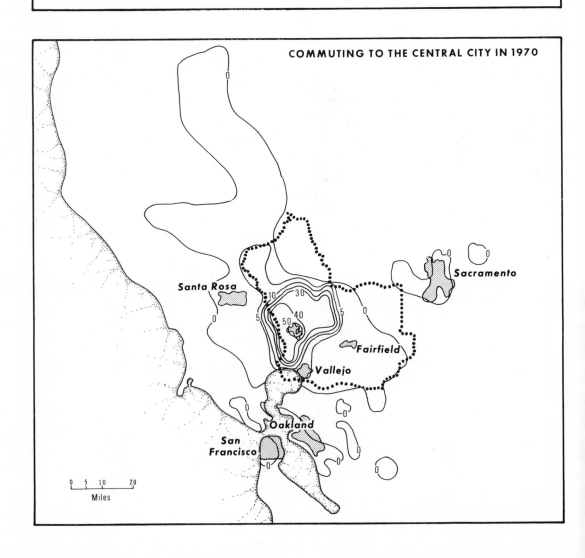

COMMUTING TO THE CENTRAL CITY IN 1970

Sacramento

Santa Rosa

Fairfield

Vallejo

Oakland

San
Francisco

0   5   10   20
Miles

REVERSE COMMUTING,1960	REVERSE COMMUTING,1970	CHANGE IN REVERSE COMMUTING,1960—1970
NO DATA COLLECTED	50 60 70 80 0 1 Miles	NO DATA COLLECTED

NAPA, CA.

CHANGE IN COMMUTING TO THE CENTRAL CITY,1960—1970

NO DATA COLLECTED

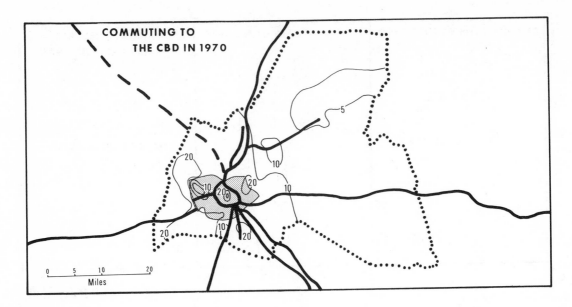

COMMUTING TO
THE CBD IN 1970

0 5 10   20
Miles

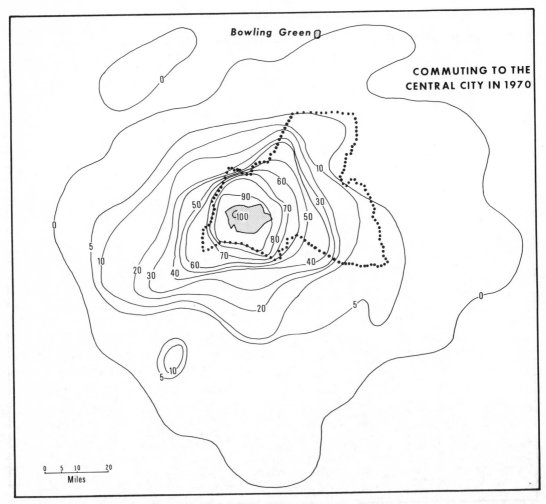

Bowling Green

COMMUTING TO THE
CENTRAL CITY IN 1970

0 5 10 20
Miles

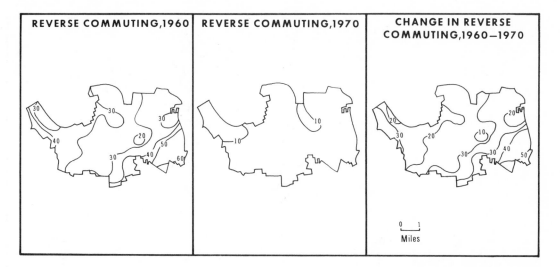

| REVERSE COMMUTING,1960 | REVERSE COMMUTING,1970 | CHANGE IN REVERSE COMMUTING,1960–1970 |

NASHVILLE, TN.

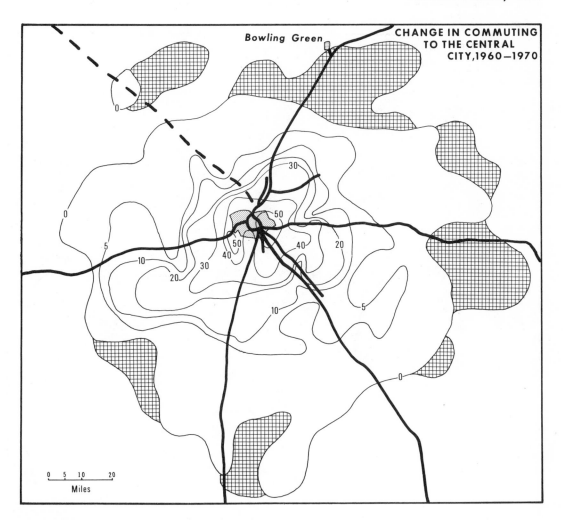

CHANGE IN COMMUTING TO THE CENTRAL CITY,1960–1970

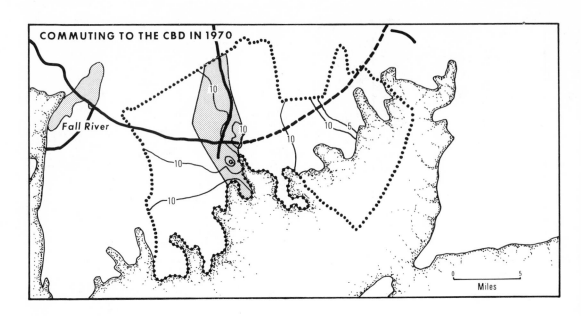

COMMUTING TO THE CBD IN 1970

Fall River

10

10

10

10

10

10

10

5

Miles

0   5

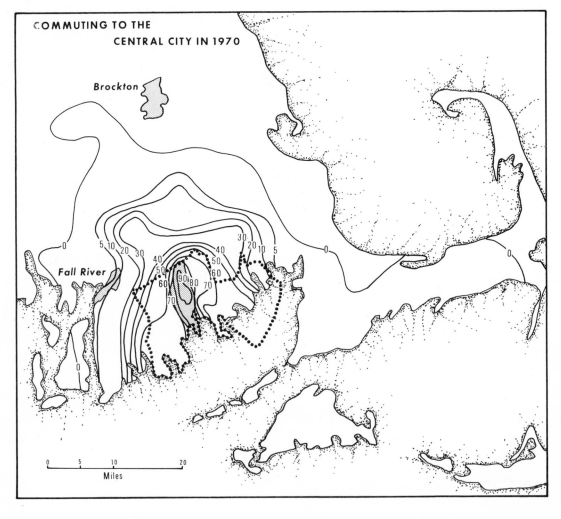

COMMUTING TO THE
CENTRAL CITY IN 1970

Brockton

Fall River

0   5 10 20 30   40   50 60   90 80 70   60   30 20 10 5   0   0

40
50
60

70

0

Miles

0   5   10   20

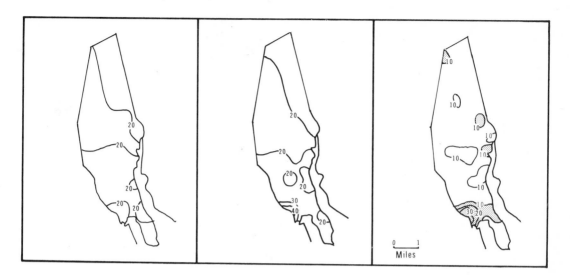

NEW BEDFORD, MA.

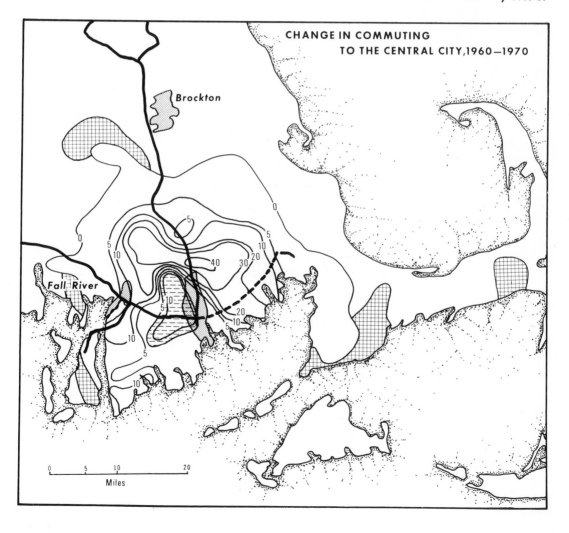

CHANGE IN COMMUTING
TO THE CENTRAL CITY, 1960–1970

COMMUTING TO THE CBD IN 1970

NO DATA COLLECTED

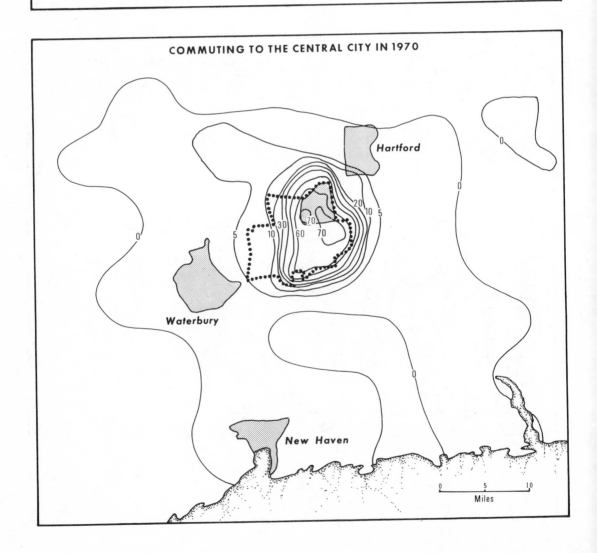

COMMUTING TO THE CENTRAL CITY IN 1970

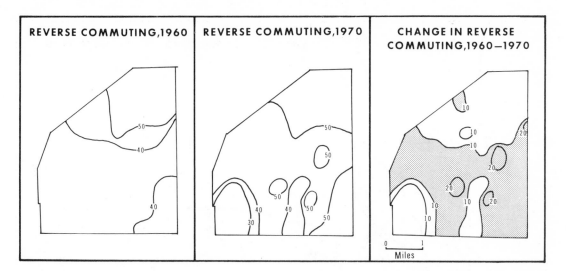

REVERSE COMMUTING, 1960

REVERSE COMMUTING, 1970

CHANGE IN REVERSE COMMUTING, 1960—1970

NEW BRITAIN, CT.

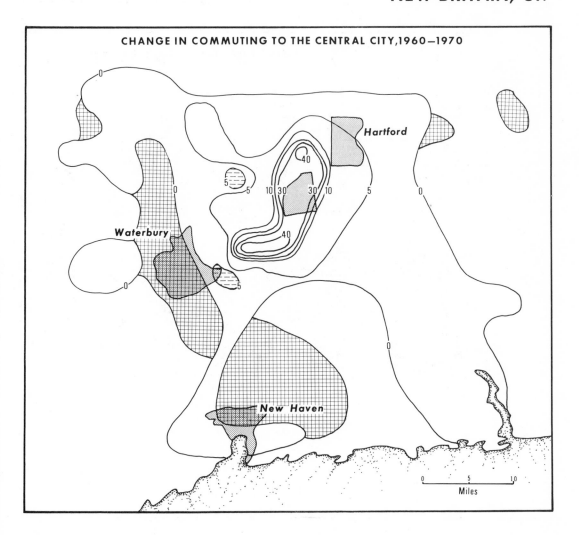

CHANGE IN COMMUTING TO THE CENTRAL CITY, 1960—1970

Hartford

Waterbury

New Haven

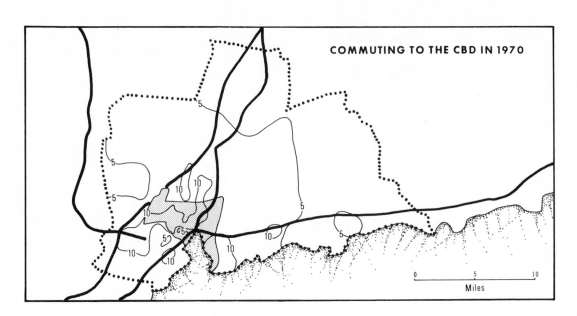

COMMUTING TO THE CBD IN 1970

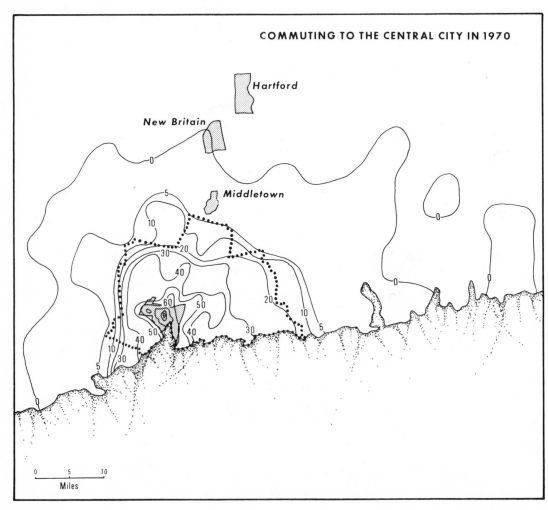

COMMUTING TO THE CENTRAL CITY IN 1970

Hartford

New Britain

Middletown

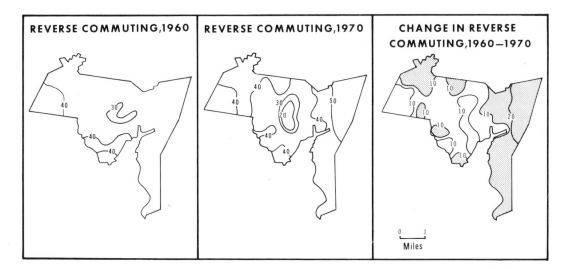

REVERSE COMMUTING, 1960

REVERSE COMMUTING, 1970

CHANGE IN REVERSE COMMUTING, 1960—1970

NEW HAVEN, CT.

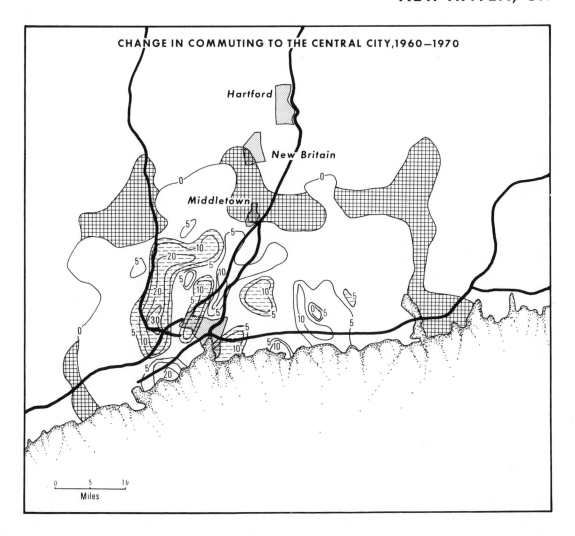

CHANGE IN COMMUTING TO THE CENTRAL CITY, 1960—1970

COMMUTING TO THE CBD IN 1970

NO DATA COLLECTED

COMMUTING TO THE CENTRAL CITY IN 1970

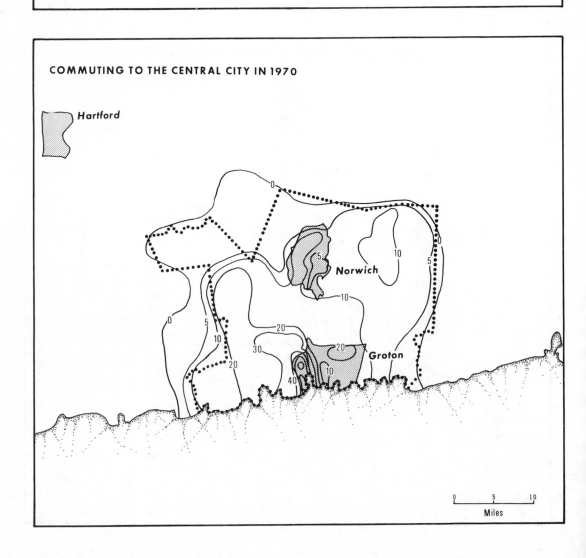

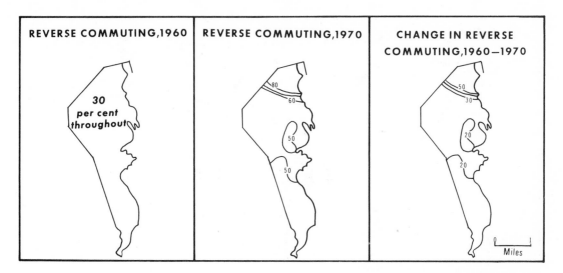

| REVERSE COMMUTING, 1960 | REVERSE COMMUTING, 1970 | CHANGE IN REVERSE COMMUTING, 1960—1970 |

NEW LONDON, CT.

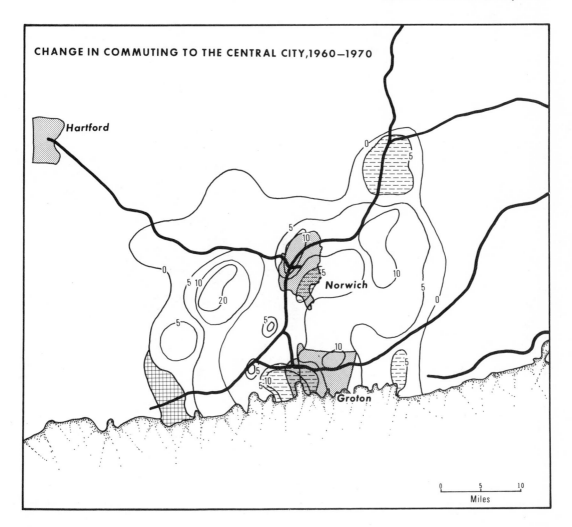

CHANGE IN COMMUTING TO THE CENTRAL CITY, 1960—1970

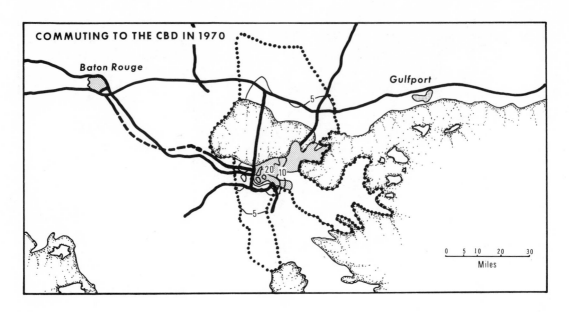

COMMUTING TO THE CBD IN 1970

Baton Rouge

Gulfport

5

20
10

5

0 5 10   20   30
Miles

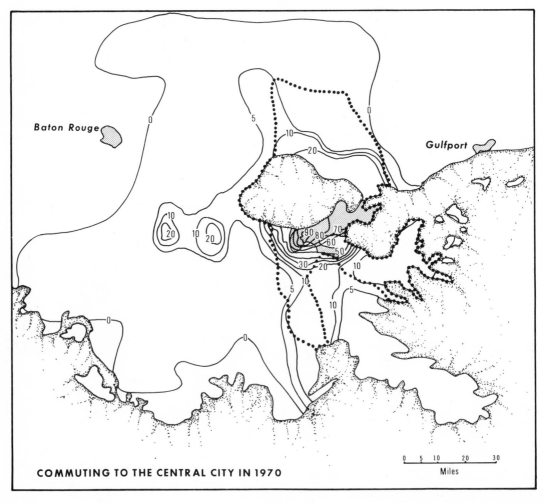

Baton Rouge

Gulfport

0

5

10

20

10
20

10

20

90
80
70
60
50
30
20
10

10

5

10

5

0

0

0 5 10   20   30
Miles

COMMUTING TO THE CENTRAL CITY IN 1970

457

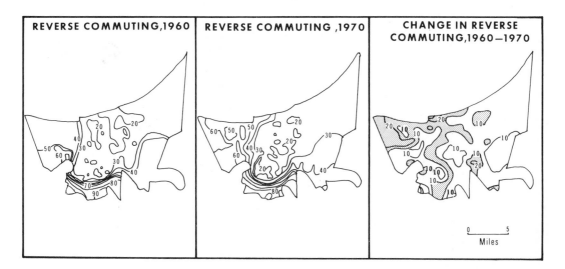

REVERSE COMMUTING, 1960   REVERSE COMMUTING, 1970   CHANGE IN REVERSE COMMUTING, 1960–1970

NEW ORLEANS, LA.

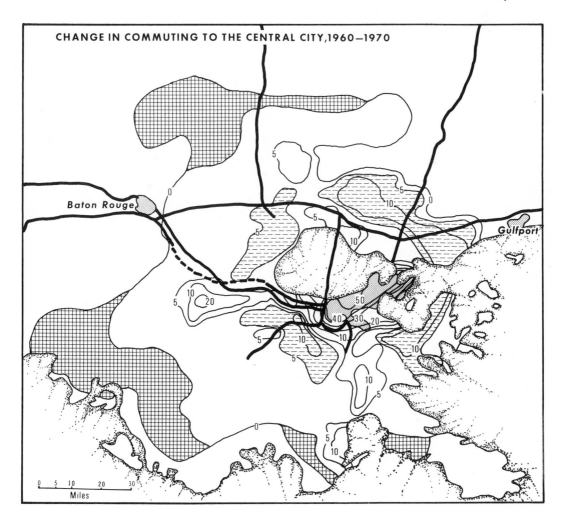

CHANGE IN COMMUTING TO THE CENTRAL CITY, 1960–1970

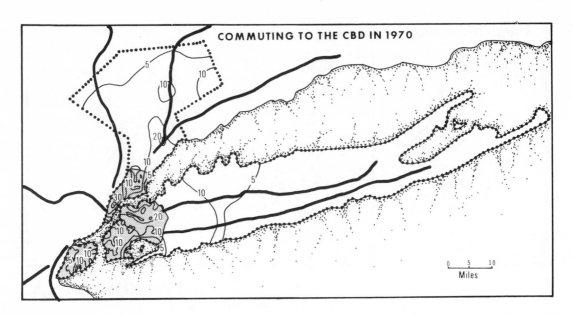

COMMUTING TO THE CBD IN 1970

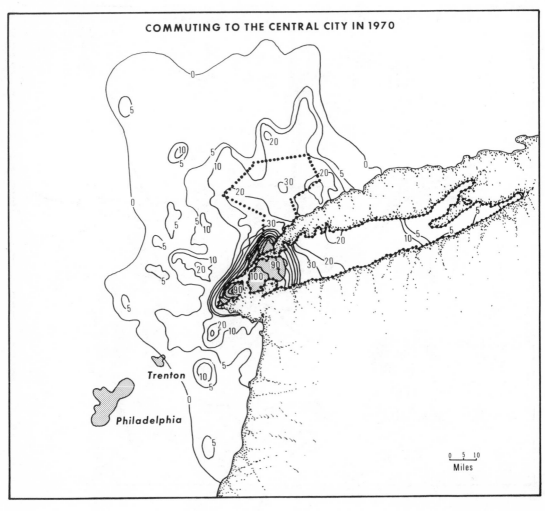

COMMUTING TO THE CENTRAL CITY IN 1970

Trenton

Philadelphia

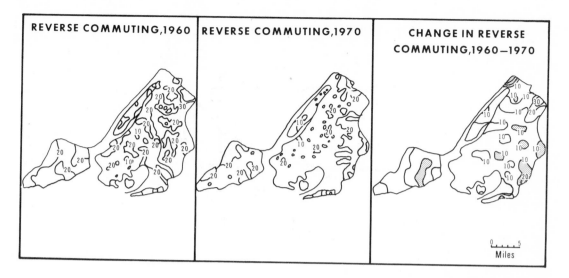

NEW YORK, N.Y.

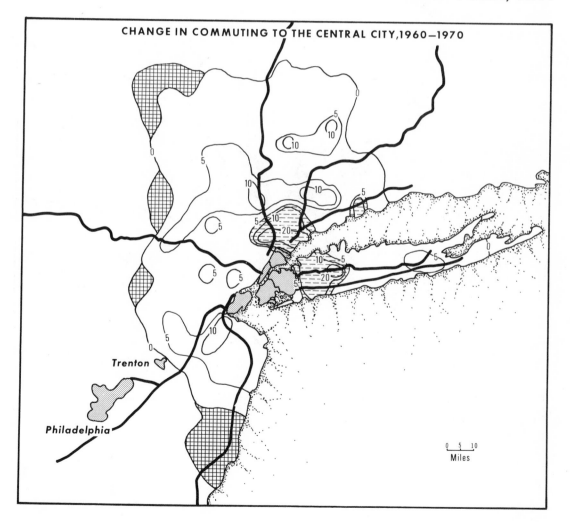

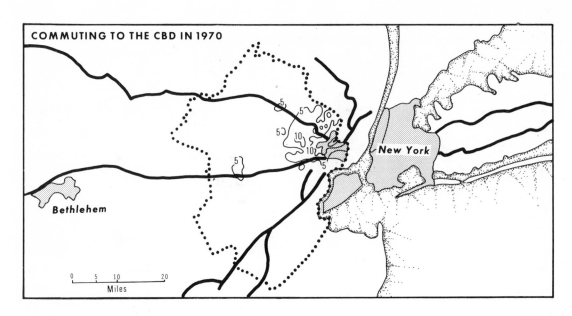

COMMUTING TO THE CBD IN 1970

Bethlehem

New York

0 5 10   20
Miles

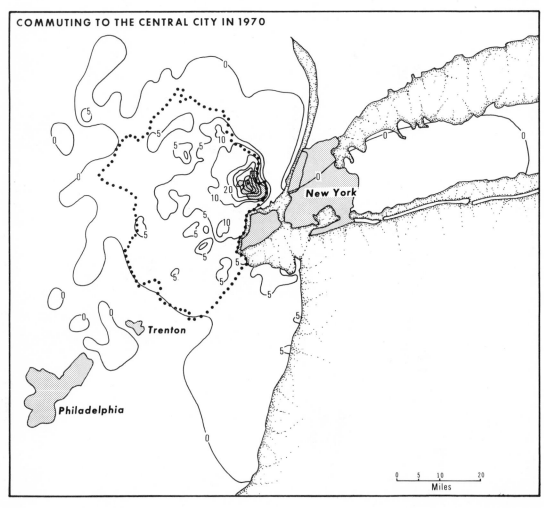

COMMUTING TO THE CENTRAL CITY IN 1970

New York

Trenton

Philadelphia

0 5 10   20
Miles

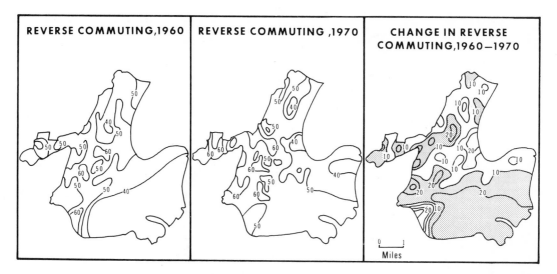

REVERSE COMMUTING,1960   REVERSE COMMUTING ,1970   CHANGE IN REVERSE COMMUTING,1960−1970

NEWARK, N.J.

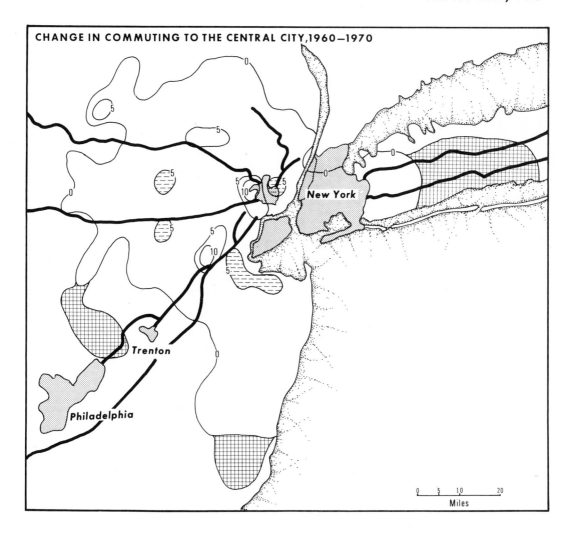

CHANGE IN COMMUTING TO THE CENTRAL CITY,1960−1970

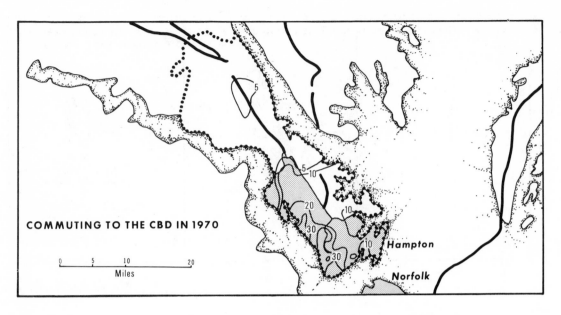

COMMUTING TO THE CBD IN 1970

0   5   10   20
Miles

Hampton

Norfolk

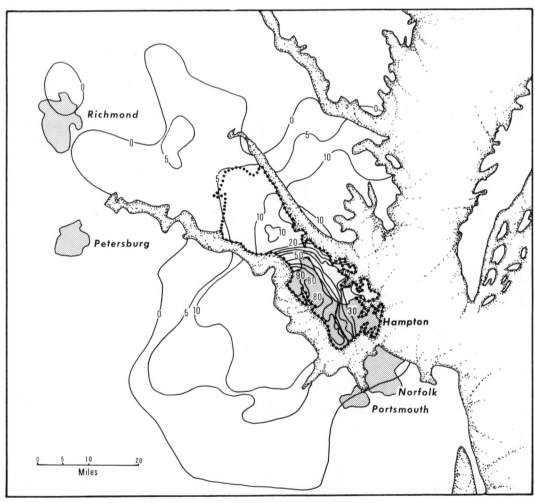

Richmond

Petersburg

Hampton

Norfolk

Portsmouth

0   5   10   20
Miles

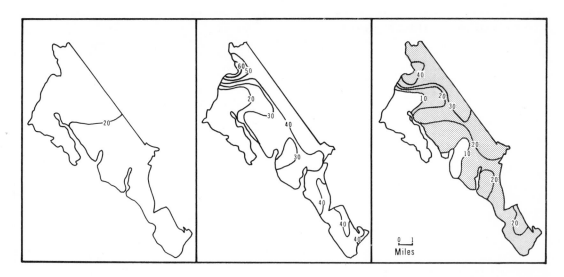

NEWPORT NEWS, VA.

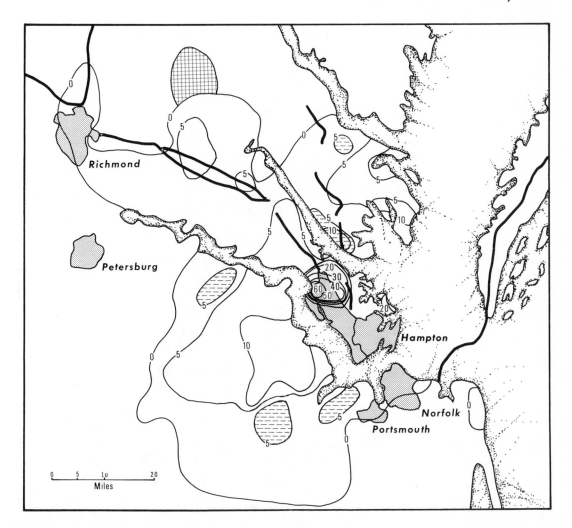

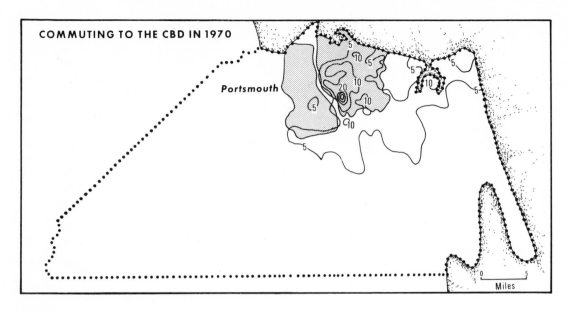

COMMUTING TO THE CBD IN 1970

Portsmouth

Miles

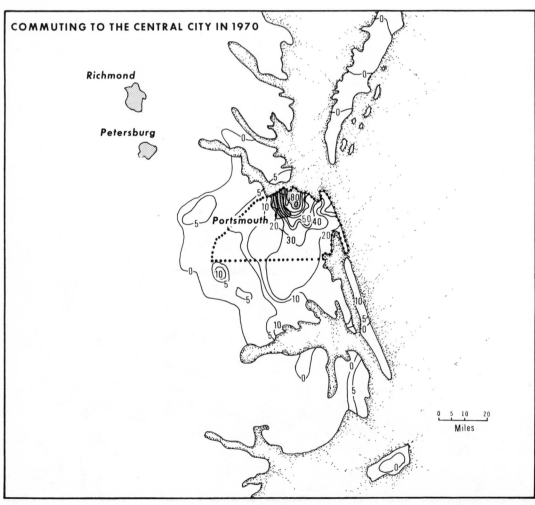

COMMUTING TO THE CENTRAL CITY IN 1970

Richmond

Petersburg

Portsmouth

Miles

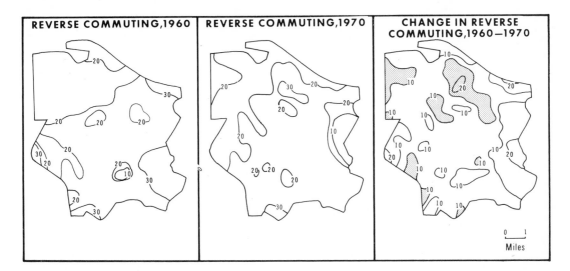

REVERSE COMMUTING, 1960

REVERSE COMMUTING, 1970

CHANGE IN REVERSE COMMUTING, 1960–1970

NORFOLK, VA.

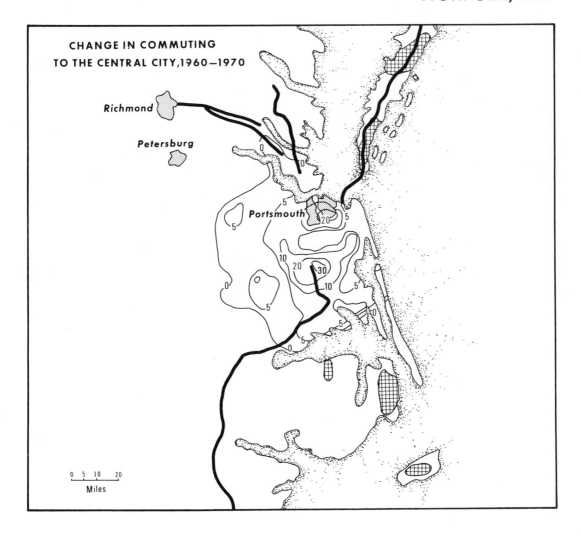

CHANGE IN COMMUTING
TO THE CENTRAL CITY, 1960–1970

Richmond

Petersburg

Portsmouth

COMMUTING TO THE CBD IN 1970

NO DATA COLLECTED

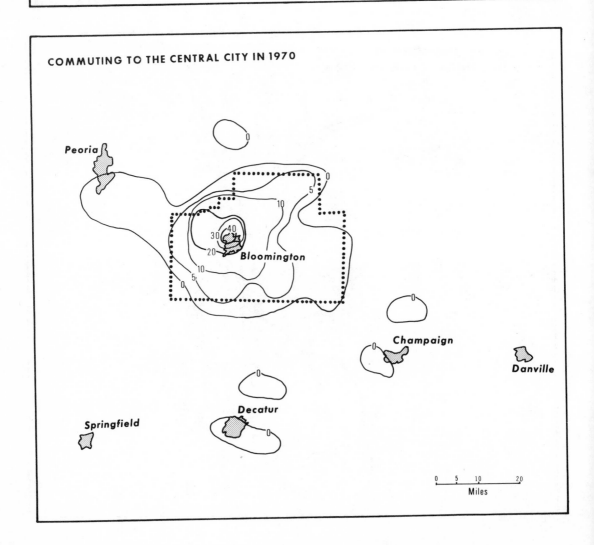

COMMUTING TO THE CENTRAL CITY IN 1970

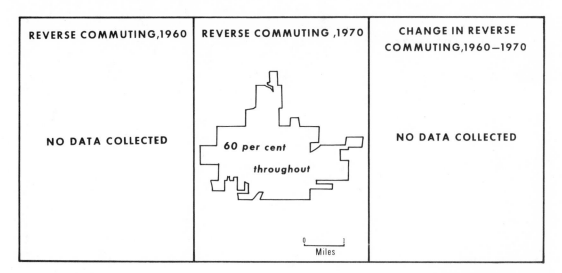

REVERSE COMMUTING, 1960	REVERSE COMMUTING, 1970	CHANGE IN REVERSE COMMUTING, 1960–1970
NO DATA COLLECTED	60 per cent throughout	NO DATA COLLECTED

0 1 Miles

NORMAL, IL.

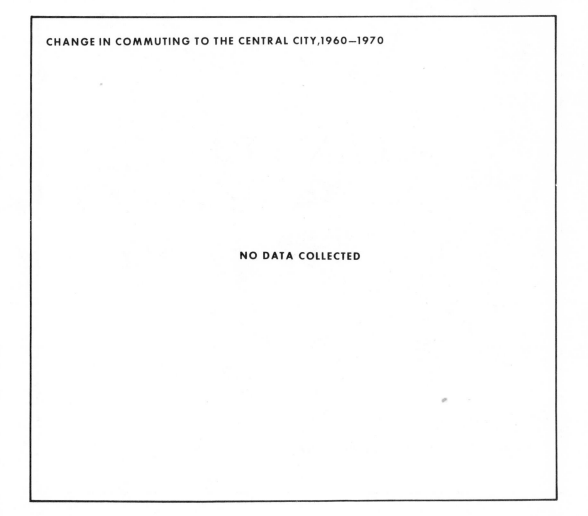

CHANGE IN COMMUTING TO THE CENTRAL CITY, 1960–1970

NO DATA COLLECTED

COMMUTING TO THE CBD IN 1970

NO DATA COLLECTED

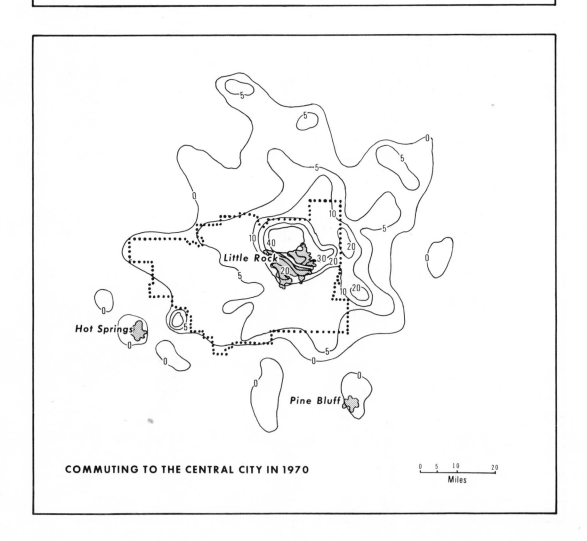

COMMUTING TO THE CENTRAL CITY IN 1970

0 5 10   20
Miles

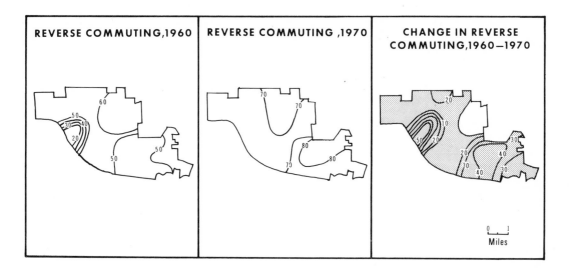

REVERSE COMMUTING,1960

REVERSE COMMUTING ,1970

CHANGE IN REVERSE COMMUTING,1960—1970

0   1
Miles

NORTH LITTLE ROCK, AR.

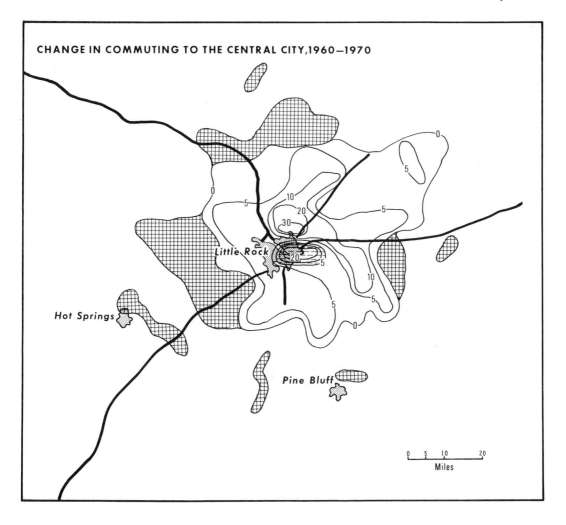

CHANGE IN COMMUTING TO THE CENTRAL CITY,1960—1970

Little Rock

Hot Springs

Pine Bluff

0   5   10   20
Miles

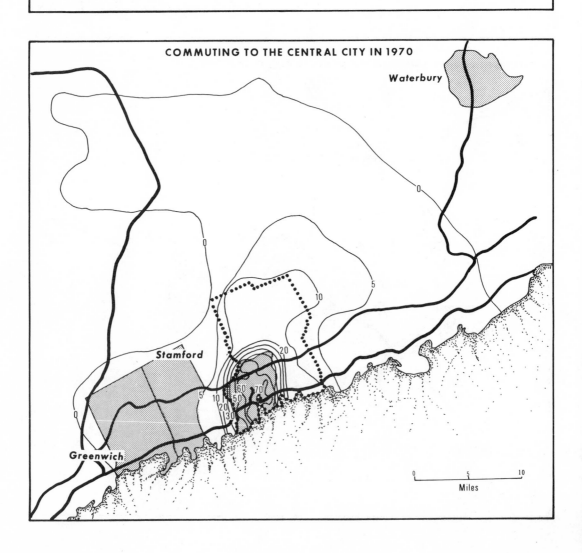

COMMUTING TO THE CBD IN 1970

NO DATA COLLECTED

COMMUTING TO THE CENTRAL CITY IN 1970

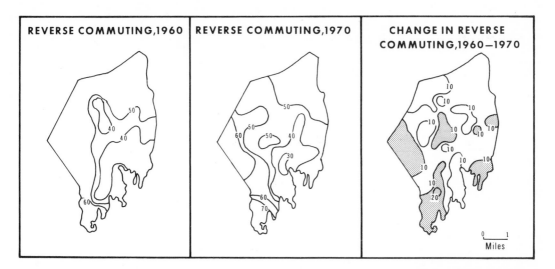

REVERSE COMMUTING, 1960

REVERSE COMMUTING, 1970

CHANGE IN REVERSE COMMUTING, 1960—1970

NORWALK, CT.

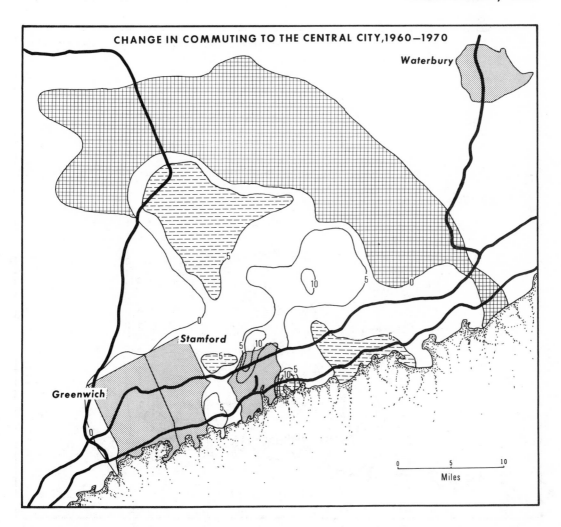

CHANGE IN COMMUTING TO THE CENTRAL CITY, 1960—1970

COMMUTING TO THE CBD IN 1970

NO DATA COLLECTED

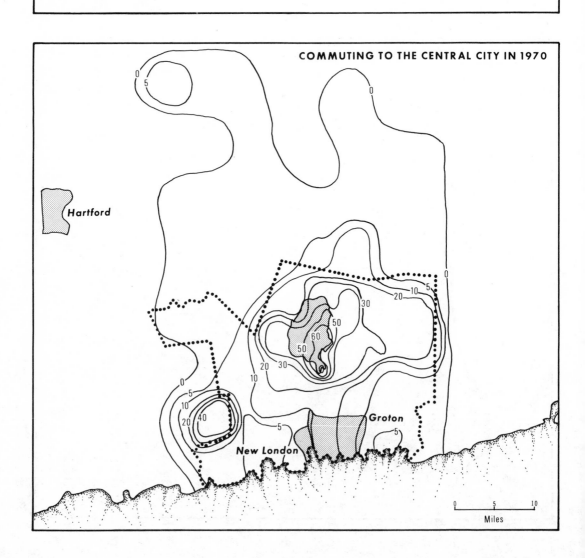

COMMUTING TO THE CENTRAL CITY IN 1970

Hartford

Groton

New London

0   5   10
Miles

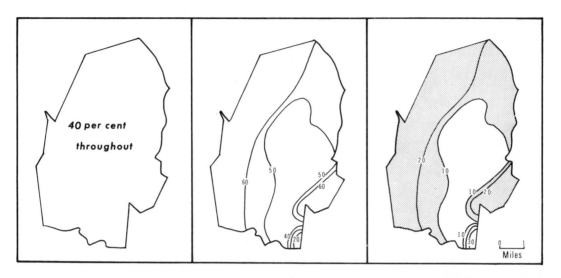

NORWICH, CT.

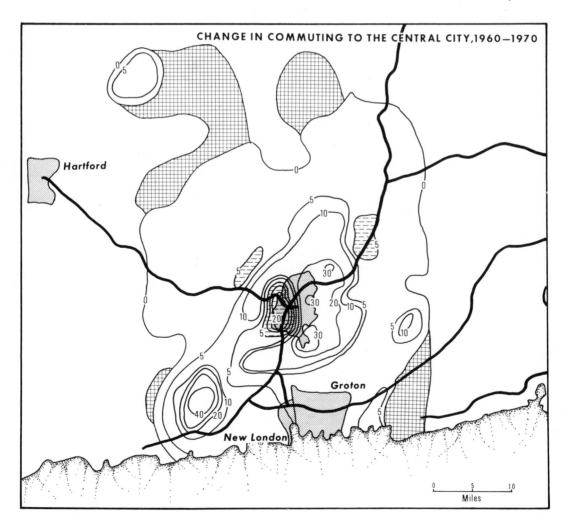

CHANGE IN COMMUTING TO THE CENTRAL CITY, 1960–1970

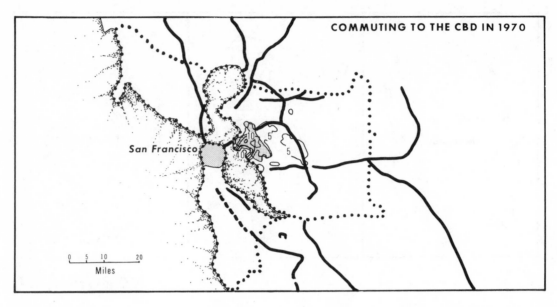

COMMUTING TO THE CBD IN 1970

San Francisco

0 5 10 20
Miles

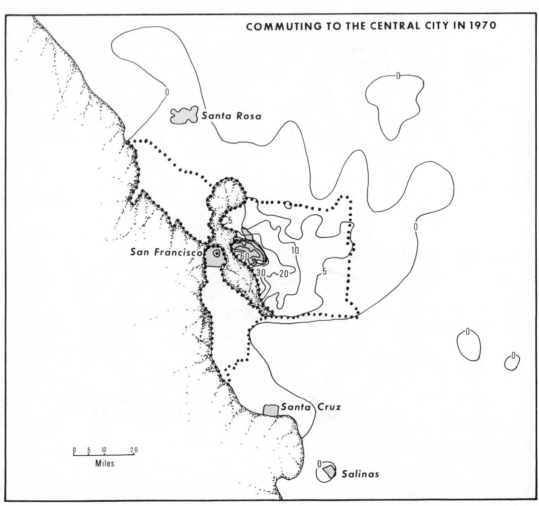

COMMUTING TO THE CENTRAL CITY IN 1970

Santa Rosa

San Francisco

Santa Cruz

Salinas

0 5 10 20
Miles

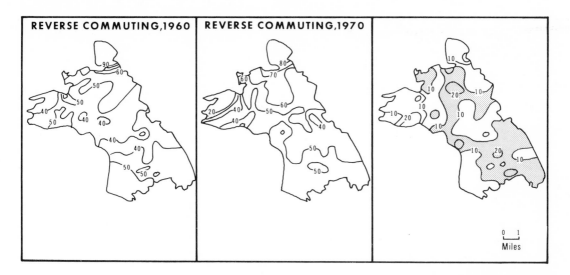

REVERSE COMMUTING,1960

REVERSE COMMUTING,1970

OAKLAND, CA.

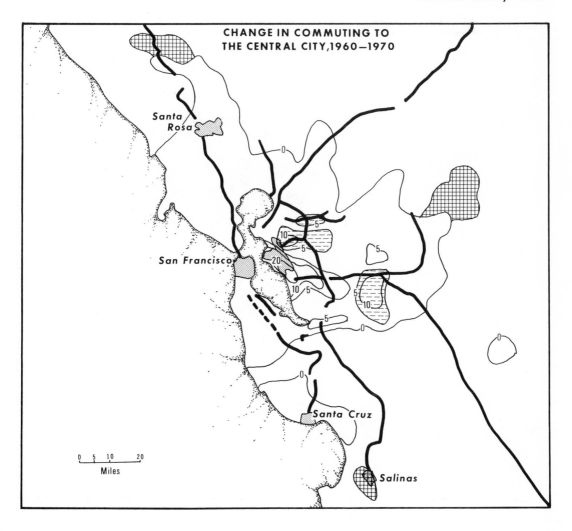

CHANGE IN COMMUTING TO
THE CENTRAL CITY,1960—1970

COMMUTING TO THE CBD IN 1970

NO DATA COLLECTED

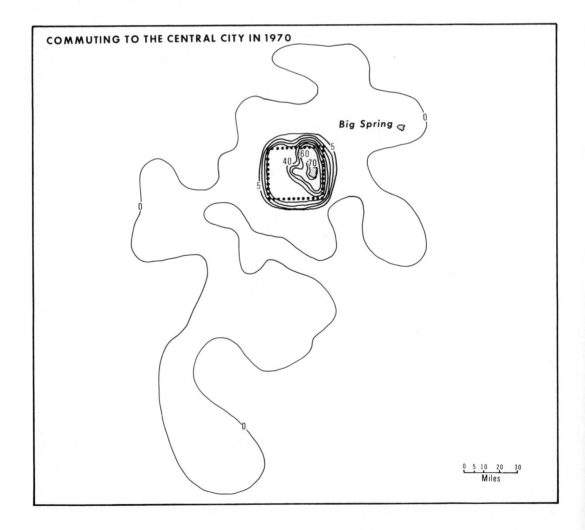

COMMUTING TO THE CENTRAL CITY IN 1970

Big Spring

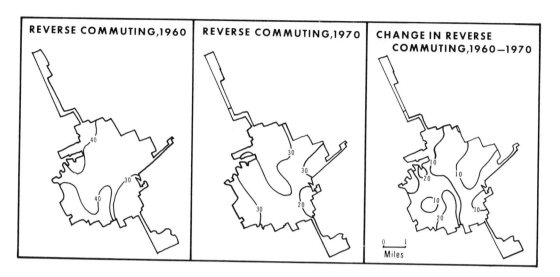

REVERSE COMMUTING, 1960

REVERSE COMMUTING, 1970

CHANGE IN REVERSE COMMUTING, 1960–1970

ODESSA, TX.

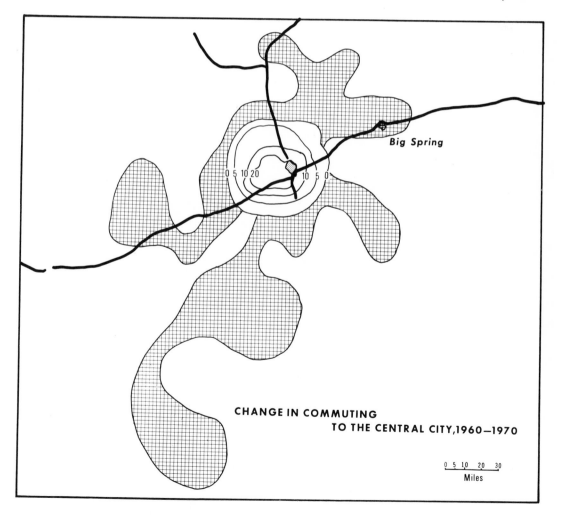

Big Spring

CHANGE IN COMMUTING TO THE CENTRAL CITY, 1960–1970

COMMUTING TO THE CBD IN 1970

NO DATA COLLECTED

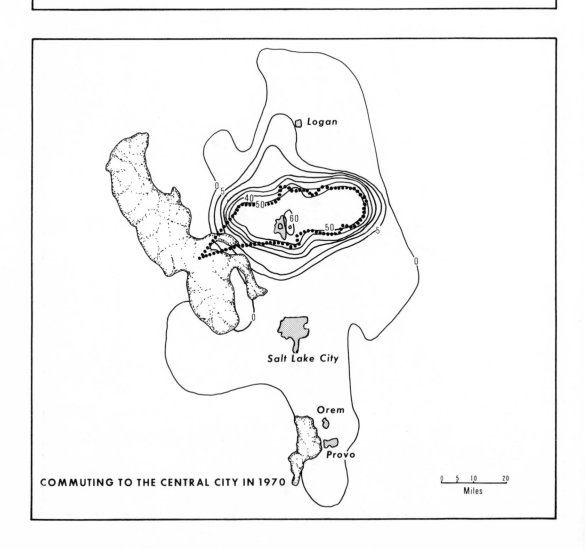

COMMUTING TO THE CENTRAL CITY IN 1970

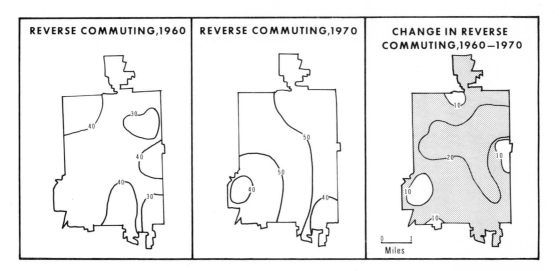

| REVERSE COMMUTING,1960 | REVERSE COMMUTING,1970 | CHANGE IN REVERSE COMMUTING,1960—1970 |

OGDEN, UT.

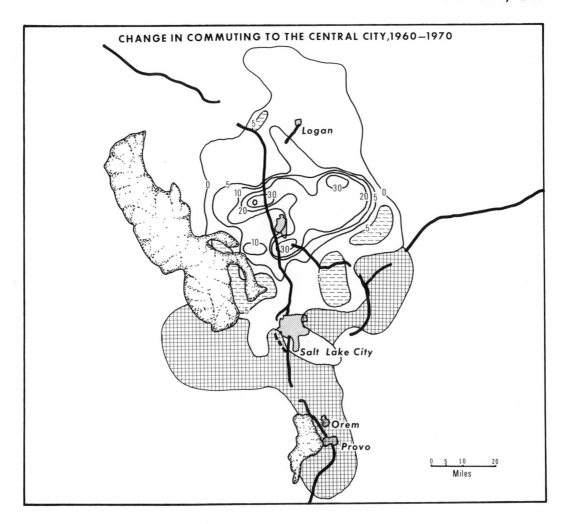

CHANGE IN COMMUTING TO THE CENTRAL CITY,1960—1970

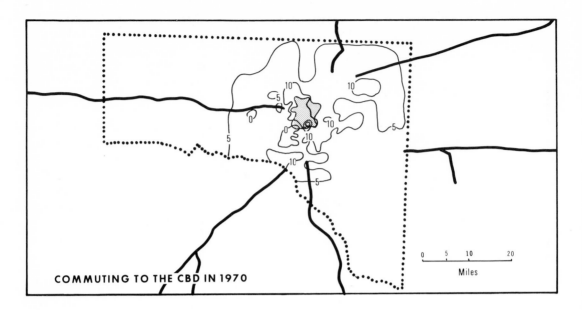

COMMUTING TO THE CBD IN 1970

0 5 10 20
Miles

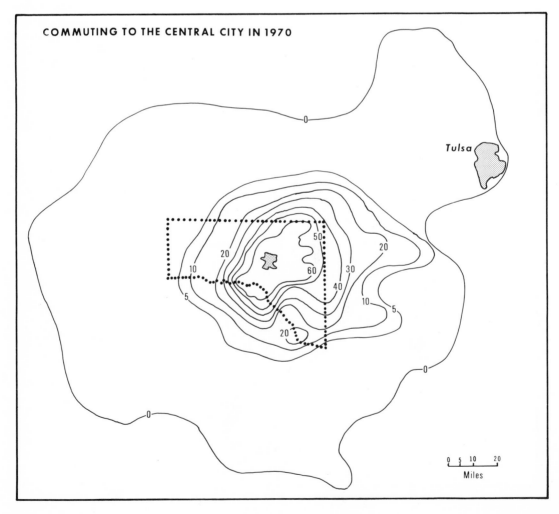

COMMUTING TO THE CENTRAL CITY IN 1970

Tulsa

0 5 10 20
Miles

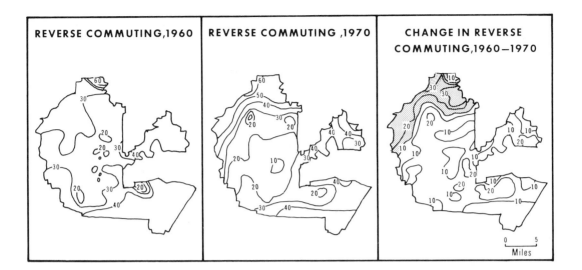

REVERSE COMMUTING, 1960 | REVERSE COMMUTING, 1970 | CHANGE IN REVERSE COMMUTING, 1960–1970

OKLAHOMA CITY, OK.

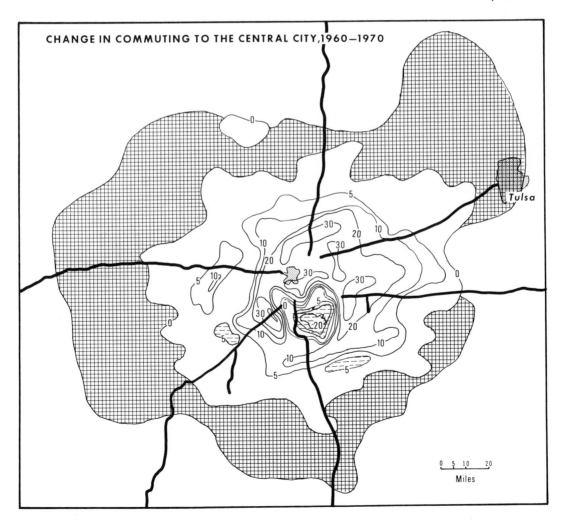

CHANGE IN COMMUTING TO THE CENTRAL CITY, 1960–1970

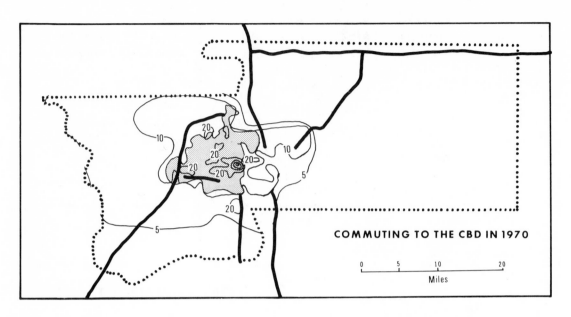

COMMUTING TO THE CBD IN 1970

0   5   10   20
Miles

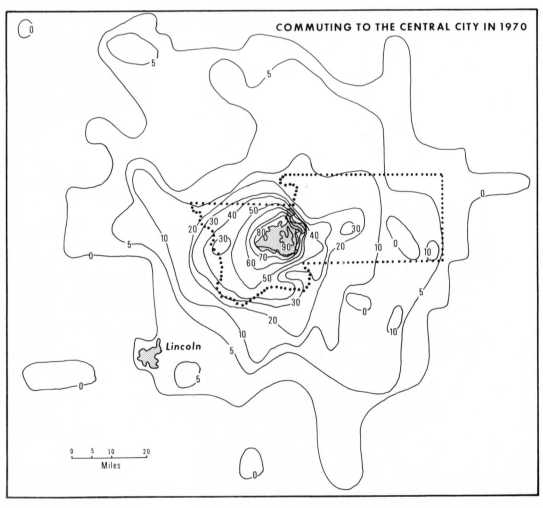

COMMUTING TO THE CENTRAL CITY IN 1970

Lincoln

0   5 10   20
Miles

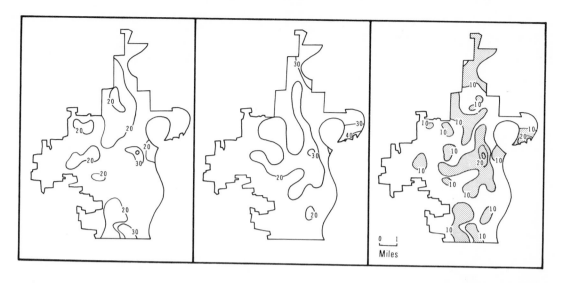

OMAHA, NE.

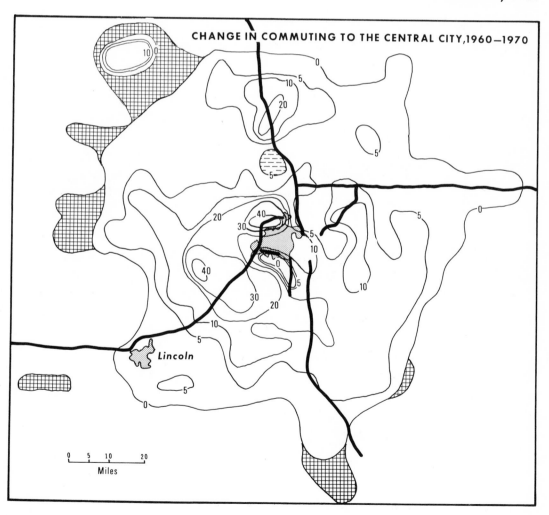

CHANGE IN COMMUTING TO THE CENTRAL CITY, 1960—1970

COMMUTING TO THE CBD IN 1970

NO DATA COLLECTED

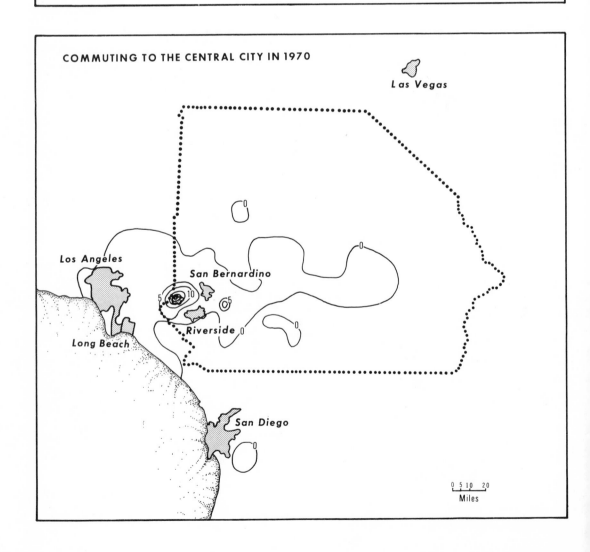

COMMUTING TO THE CENTRAL CITY IN 1970

Las Vegas

Los Angeles

San Bernardino

5 10

05

Riverside 0

Long Beach

San Diego

0 5 10 20
Miles

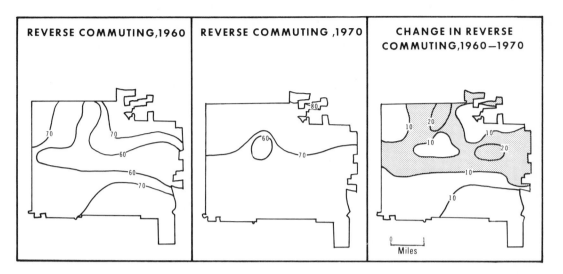

ONTARIO, CA.

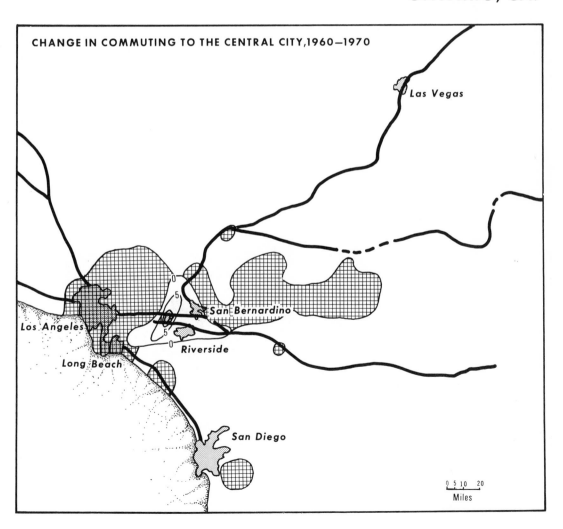

COMMUTING TO THE CBD IN 1970

NO DATA COLLECTED

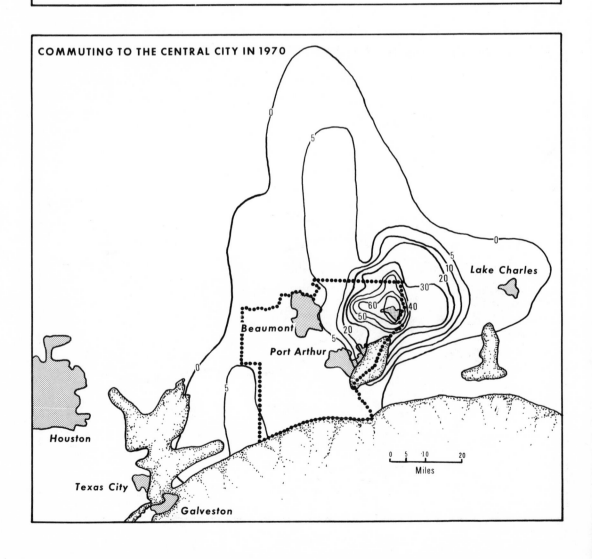

COMMUTING TO THE CENTRAL CITY IN 1970

REVERSE COMMUTING,1960	REVERSE COMMUTING ,1970	CHANGE IN REVERSE COMMUTING,1960—1970
NO DATA COLLECTED		NO DATA COLLECTED

50
40
50
60
40

0   1
Miles

ORANGE, TX.

CHANGE IN COMMUTING TO THE CENTRAL CITY,1960—1970

NO DATA COLLECTED

COMMUTING TO THE CBD IN 1970

NO DATA COLLECTED

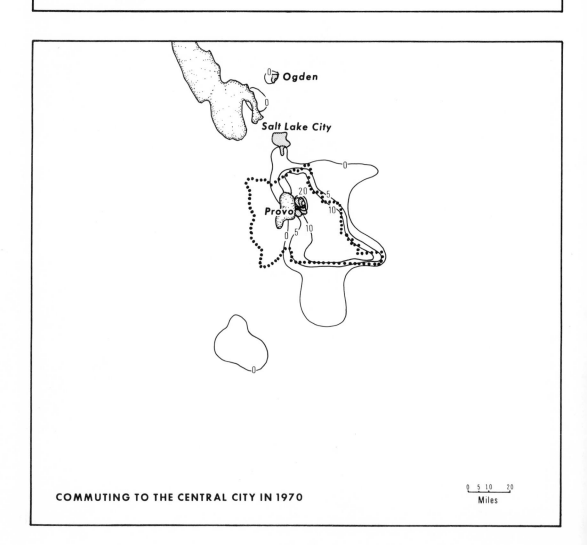

COMMUTING TO THE CENTRAL CITY IN 1970

0 5 10 20
Miles

REVERSE COMMUTING, 1960	REVERSE COMMUTING, 1970	CHANGE IN REVERSE COMMUTING, 1960–1970
NO DATA COLLECTED	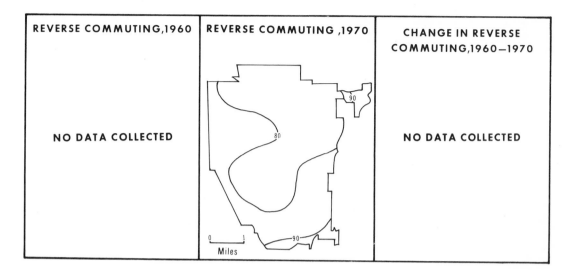	NO DATA COLLECTED

OREM, UT.

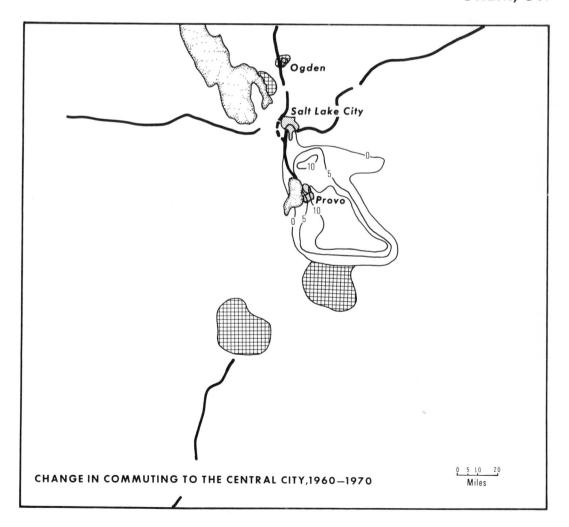

CHANGE IN COMMUTING TO THE CENTRAL CITY, 1960–1970

COMMUTING TO THE CBD IN 1970

NO DATA COLLECTED

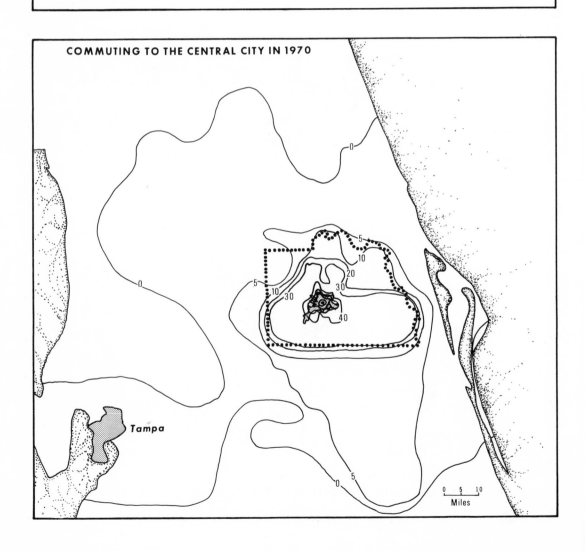

COMMUTING TO THE CENTRAL CITY IN 1970

Tampa

0   5   10
Miles

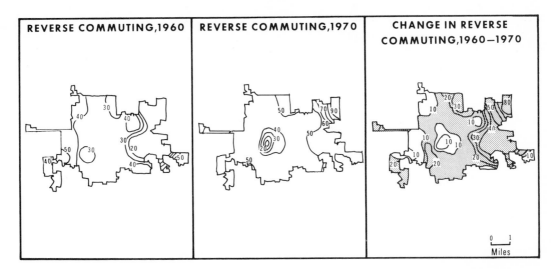

REVERSE COMMUTING,1960　　REVERSE COMMUTING,1970　　CHANGE IN REVERSE COMMUTING,1960—1970

ORLANDO, FL.

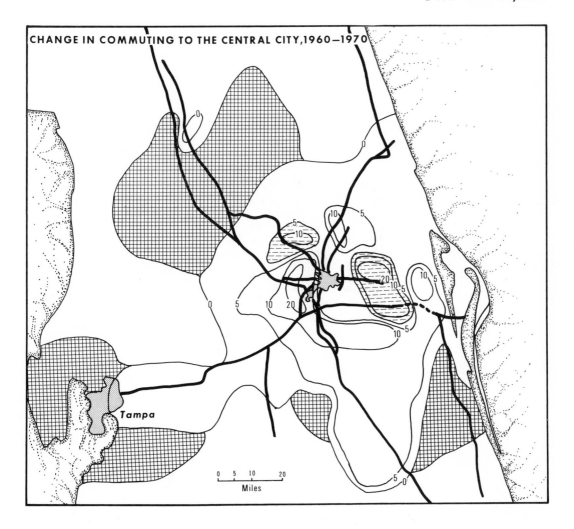

CHANGE IN COMMUTING TO THE CENTRAL CITY,1960—1970

Tampa

COMMUTING TO THE CBD IN 1970

NO DATA COLLECTED

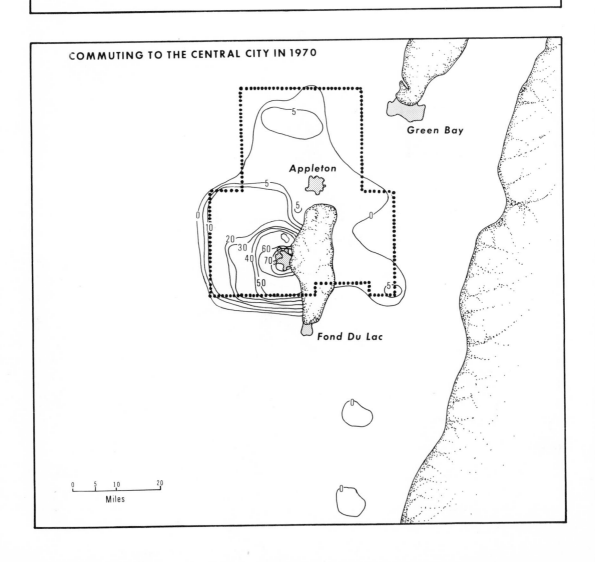

COMMUTING TO THE CENTRAL CITY IN 1970

Green Bay

Appleton

Fond Du Lac

0 5 10   20
Miles

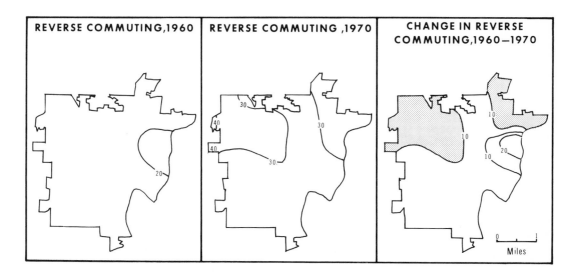

REVERSE COMMUTING,1960

REVERSE COMMUTING ,1970

CHANGE IN REVERSE COMMUTING,1960—1970

OSHKOSH, WI.

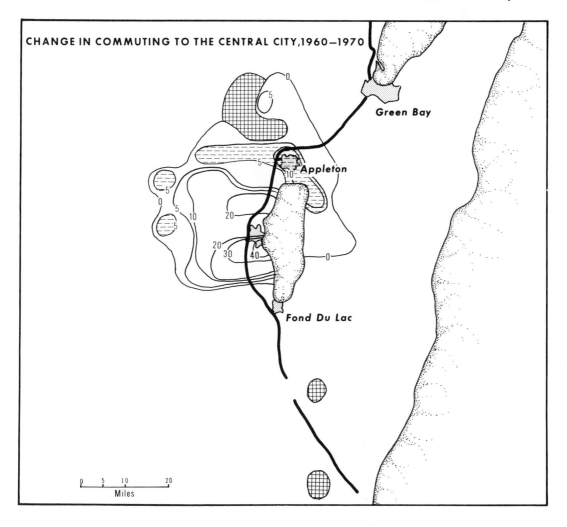

CHANGE IN COMMUTING TO THE CENTRAL CITY,1960—1970

Green Bay

Appleton

Fond Du Lac

COMMUTING TO THE CBD IN 1970

NO DATA COLLECTED

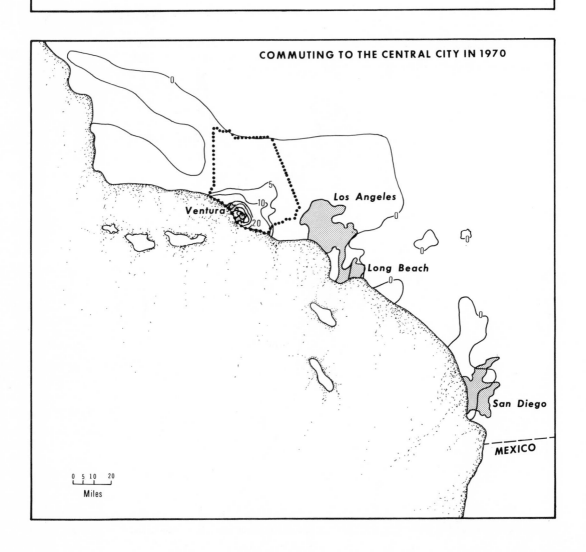

COMMUTING TO THE CENTRAL CITY IN 1970

REVERSE COMMUTING,1960	REVERSE COMMUTING ,1970	CHANGE IN REVERSE COMMUTING,1960—1970
NO DATA COLLECTED	50 60 70 80 0 1 Miles	NO DATA COLLECTED

OXNARD, CA.

CHANGE IN COMMUTING TO THE CENTRAL CITY,1960—1970

NO DATA COLLECTED

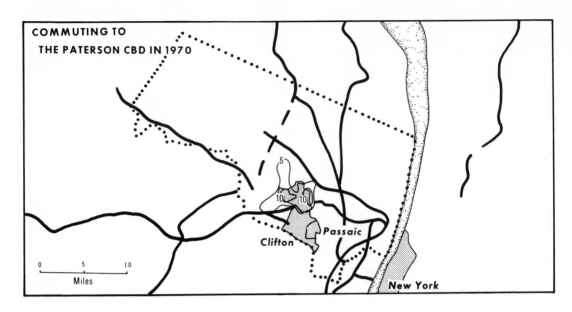

COMMUTING TO
THE PATERSON CBD IN 1970

5

10 10

Passaic

Clifton

New York

0 5 10
Miles

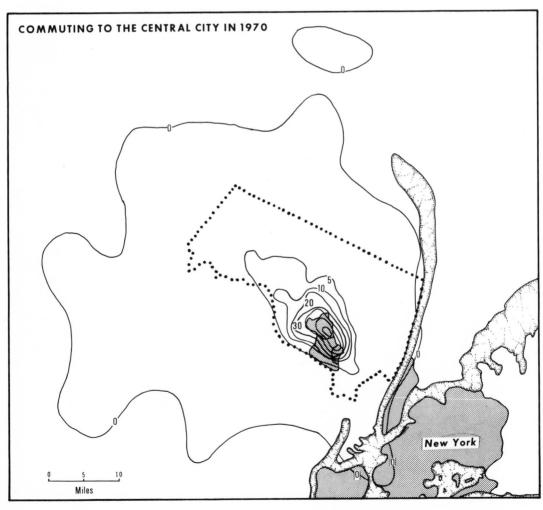

COMMUTING TO THE CENTRAL CITY IN 1970

0

0

5
10
20
30

0

New York

0

10

0

0 5 10
Miles

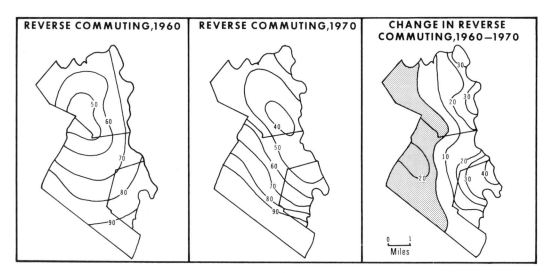

PATERSON - CLIFTON - PASSAIC, N.J.

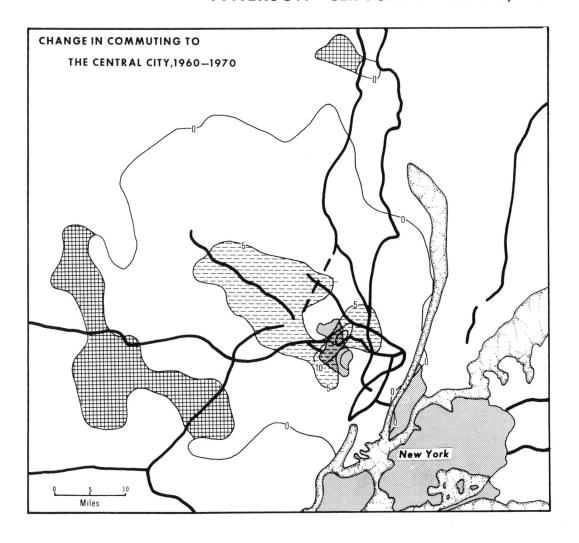

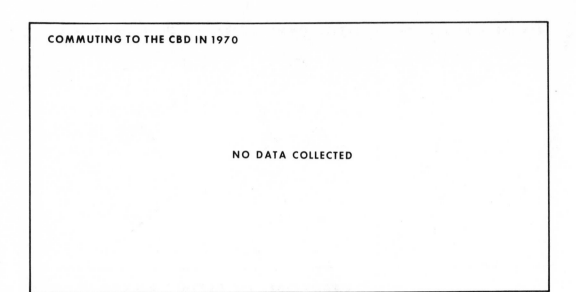

COMMUTING TO THE CBD IN 1970

NO DATA COLLECTED

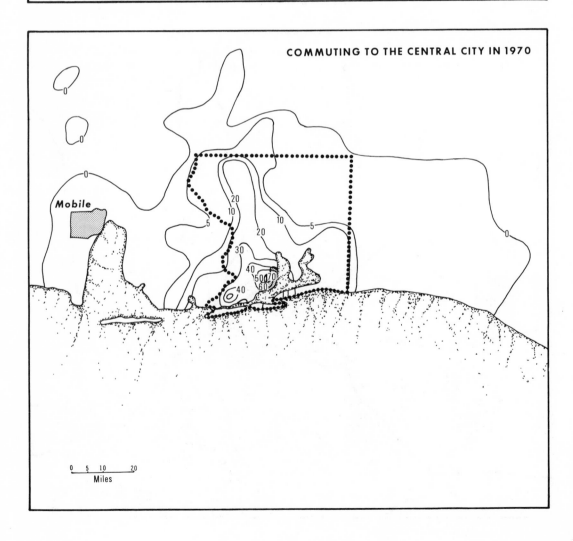

COMMUTING TO THE CENTRAL CITY IN 1970

Mobile

0   5   10   20
Miles

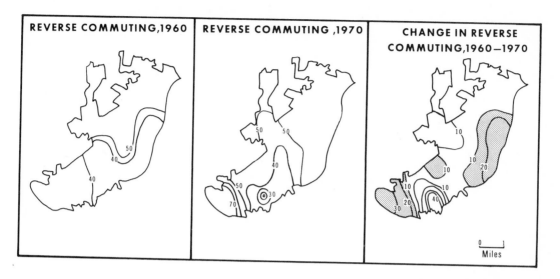

REVERSE COMMUTING, 1960

REVERSE COMMUTING, 1970

CHANGE IN REVERSE COMMUTING, 1960-1970

PENSACOLA, FL.

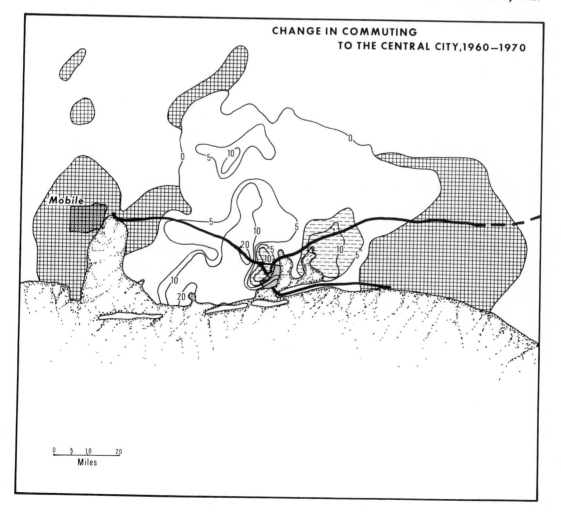

CHANGE IN COMMUTING TO THE CENTRAL CITY, 1960-1970

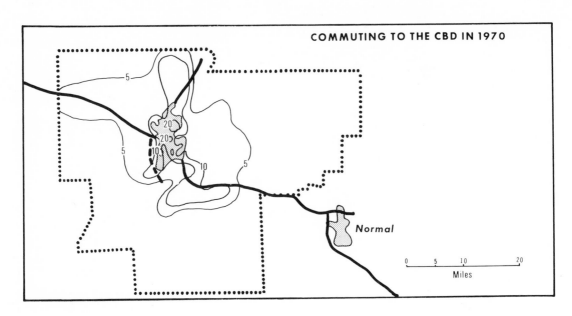

COMMUTING TO THE CBD IN 1970

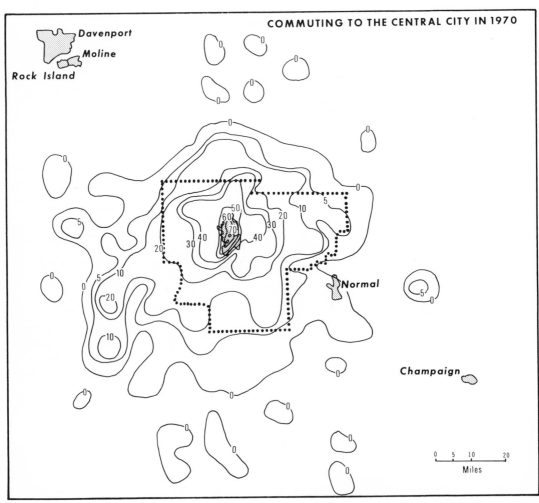

COMMUTING TO THE CENTRAL CITY IN 1970

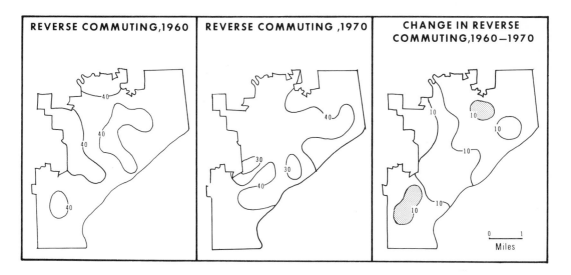

REVERSE COMMUTING, 1960

REVERSE COMMUTING, 1970

CHANGE IN REVERSE COMMUTING, 1960—1970

PEORIA, IL.

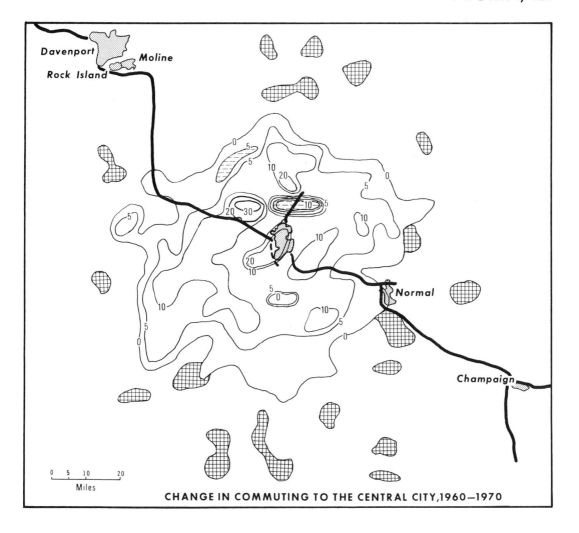

CHANGE IN COMMUTING TO THE CENTRAL CITY, 1960—1970

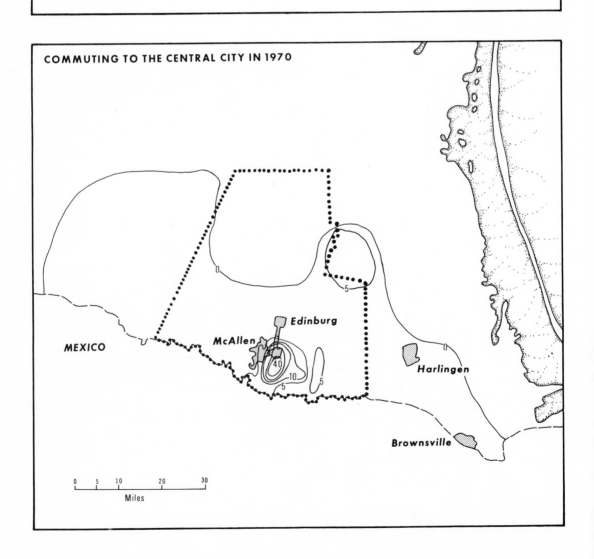

COMMUTING TO THE CBD IN 1970

NO DATA COLLECTED

COMMUTING TO THE CENTRAL CITY IN 1970

MEXICO

Edinburg

McAllen

Harlingen

Brownsville

0 5 10 20 30
Miles

REVERSE COMMUTING,1960	REVERSE COMMUTING ,1970	CHANGE IN REVERSE COMMUTING,1960—1970
NO DATA COLLECTED		NO DATA COLLECTED

0 ___ 1
Miles

PHARR, TX.

CHANGE IN COMMUTING TO THE CENTRAL CITY,1960—1970

NO DATA COLLECTED

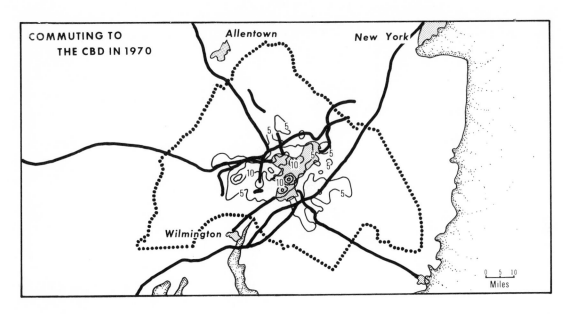

COMMUTING TO
THE CBD IN 1970

Allentown

New York

Wilmington

0 5 10
Miles

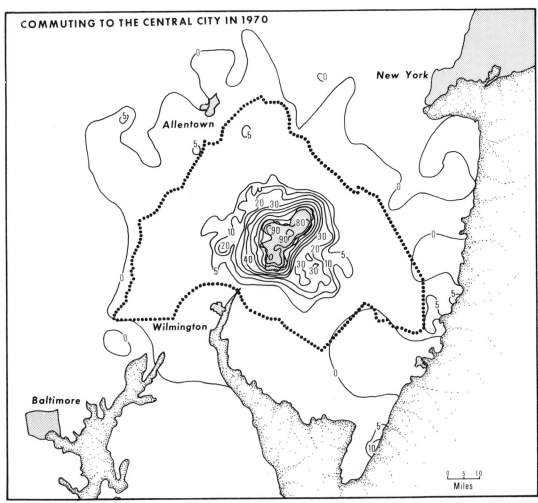

COMMUTING TO THE CENTRAL CITY IN 1970

New York

Allentown

Wilmington

Baltimore

0 5 10
Miles

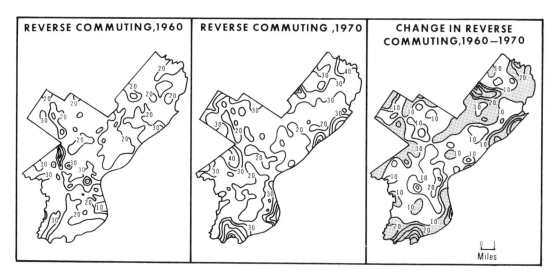

PHILADELPHIA, PA.

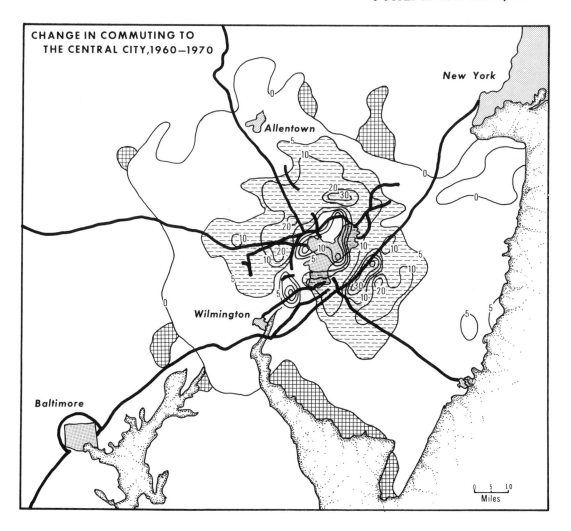

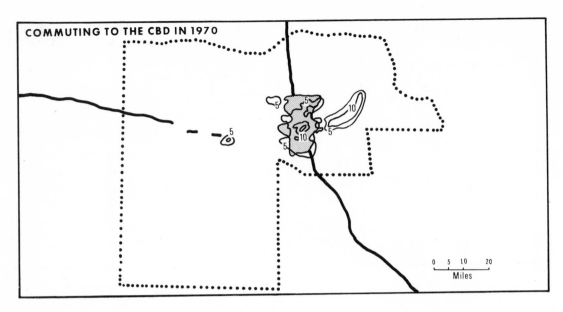

COMMUTING TO THE CBD IN 1970

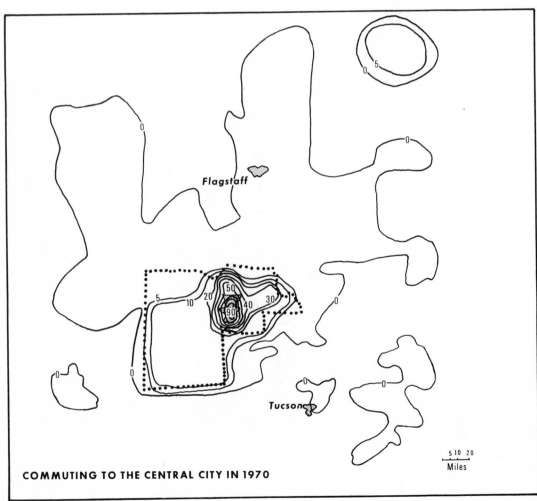

COMMUTING TO THE CENTRAL CITY IN 1970

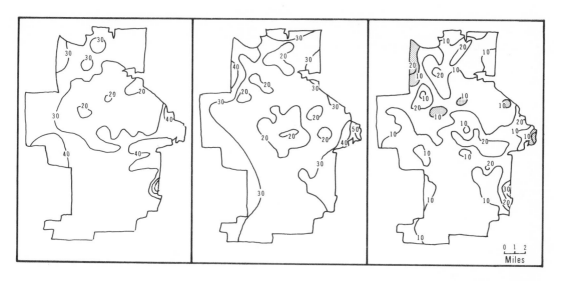

PHOENIX, AZ.

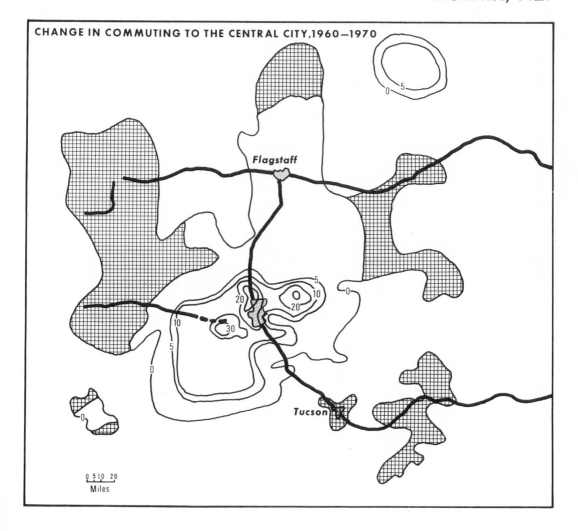

CHANGE IN COMMUTING TO THE CENTRAL CITY,1960—1970

COMMUTING TO THE CBD IN 1970

NO DATA COLLECTED

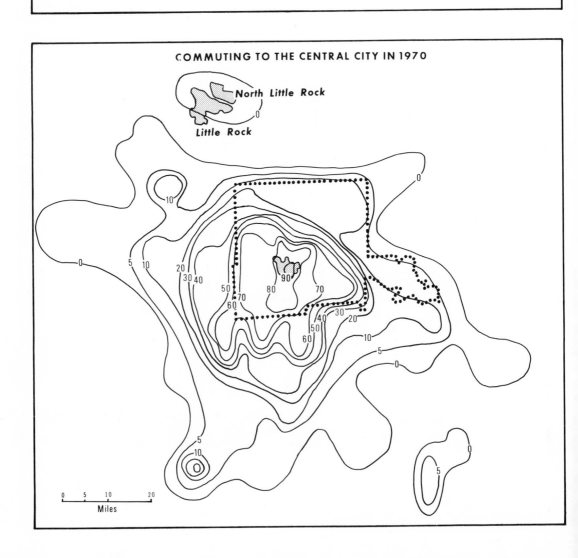

COMMUTING TO THE CENTRAL CITY IN 1970

REVERSE COMMUTING,1960	REVERSE COMMUTING,1970	CHANGE IN REVERSE COMMUTING,1960—1970
NO DATA COLLECTED		NO DATA COLLECTED

20

30

20

0   1
Miles

PINE BLUFF, AR.

CHANGE IN COMMUTING TO THE CENTRAL CITY,1960—1970

NO DATA COLLECTED

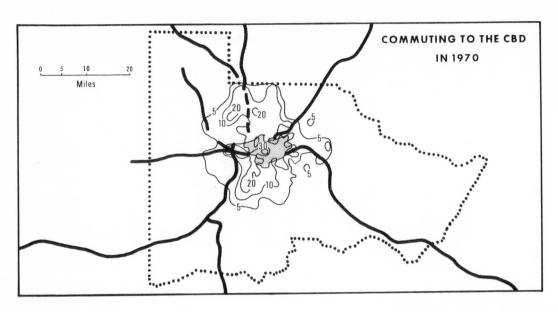

COMMUTING TO THE CBD
IN 1970

0   5   10   20
Miles

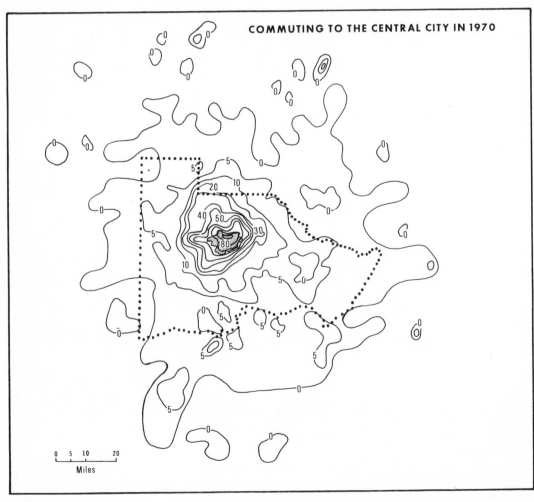

COMMUTING TO THE CENTRAL CITY IN 1970

0 5 10   20
Miles

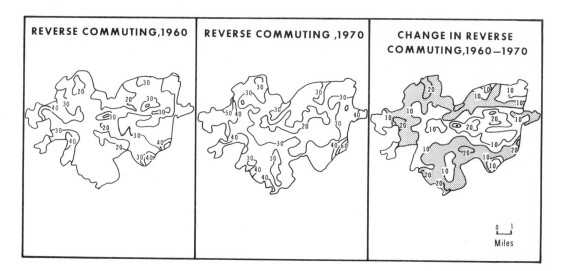

PITTSBURGH, PA.

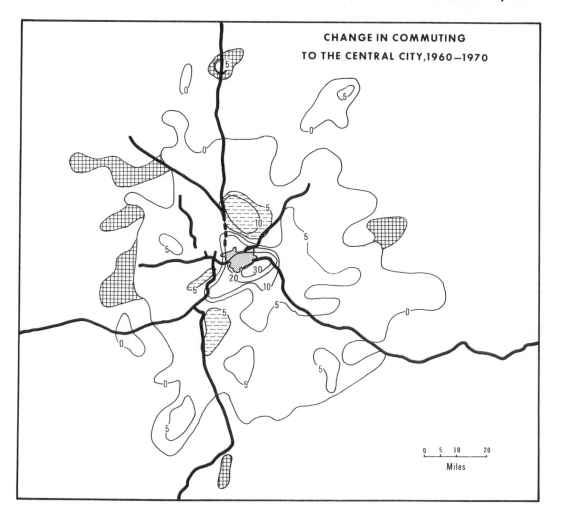

COMMUTING TO THE CBD IN 1970

NO DATA COLLECTED

COMMUTING TO THE CENTRAL CITY IN 1970

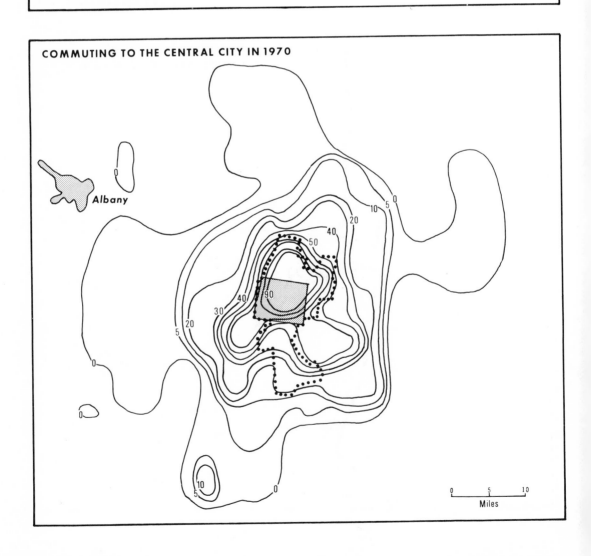

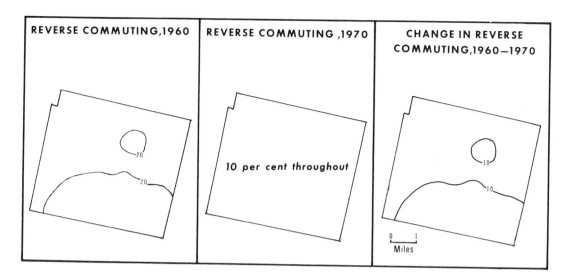

| REVERSE COMMUTING, 1960 | REVERSE COMMUTING, 1970 | CHANGE IN REVERSE COMMUTING, 1960–1970 |

PITTSFIELD, MA.

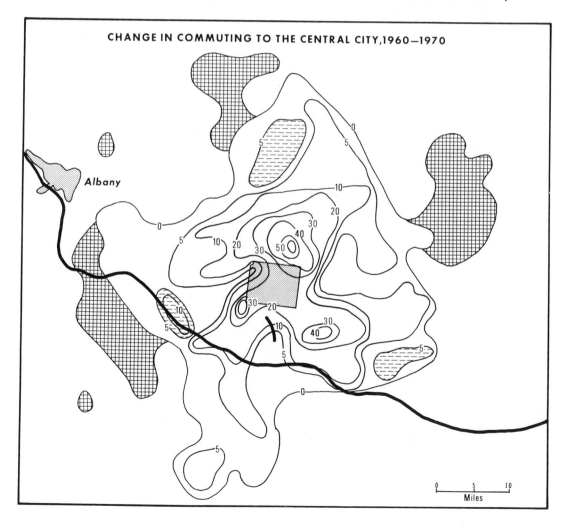

CHANGE IN COMMUTING TO THE CENTRAL CITY, 1960–1970

514

COMMUTING TO THE CBD IN 1970

NO DATA COLLECTED

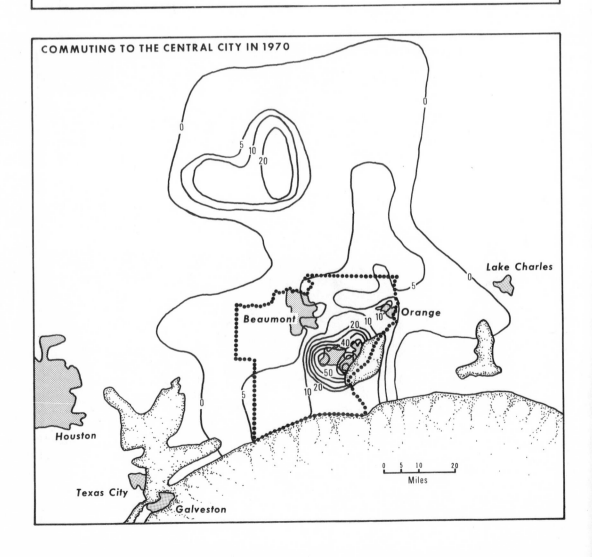

COMMUTING TO THE CENTRAL CITY IN 1970

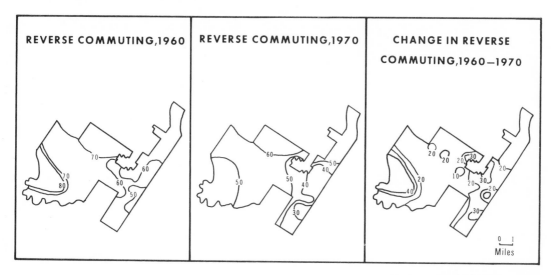

REVERSE COMMUTING,1960

REVERSE COMMUTING,1970

CHANGE IN REVERSE COMMUTING,1960—1970

PORT ARTHUR, TX.

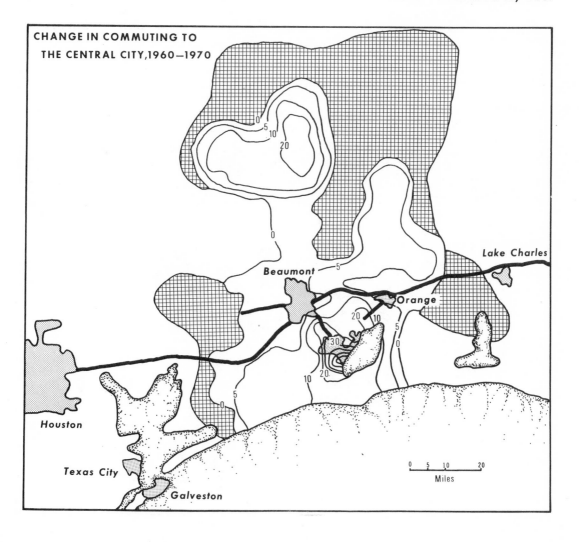

CHANGE IN COMMUTING TO THE CENTRAL CITY,1960—1970

COMMUTING TO THE CBD IN 1970

NO DATA COLLECTED

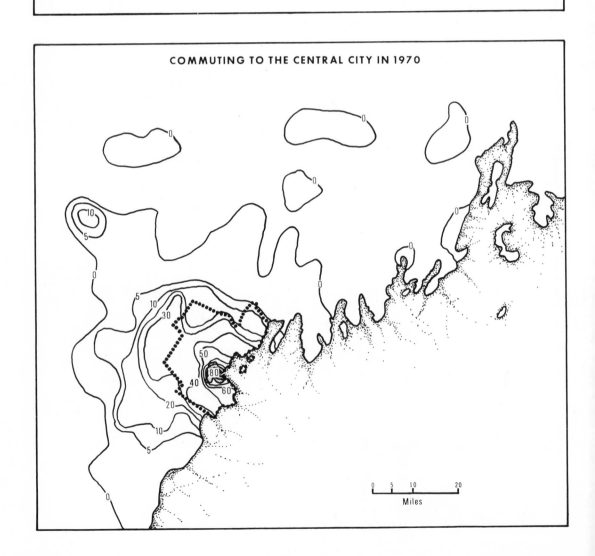

COMMUTING TO THE CENTRAL CITY IN 1970

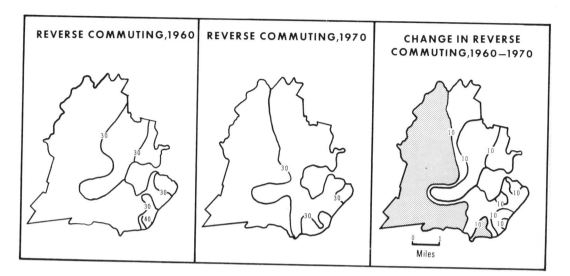

REVERSE COMMUTING, 1960

REVERSE COMMUTING, 1970

CHANGE IN REVERSE
COMMUTING, 1960—1970

Miles

PORTLAND, ME.

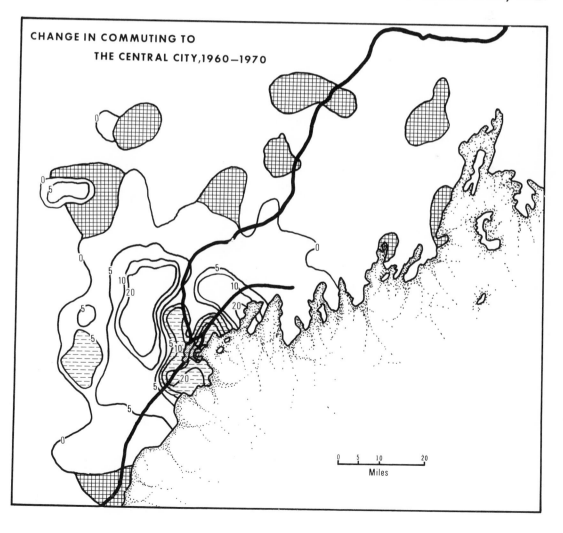

CHANGE IN COMMUTING TO
THE CENTRAL CITY, 1960—1970

Miles

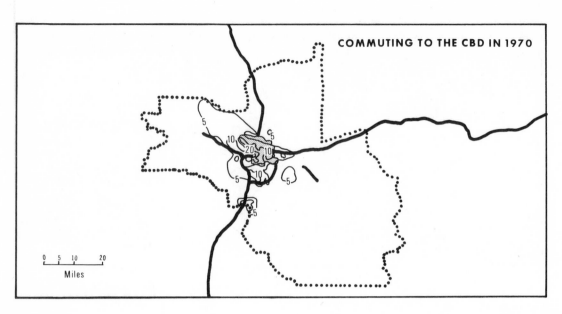

COMMUTING TO THE CBD IN 1970

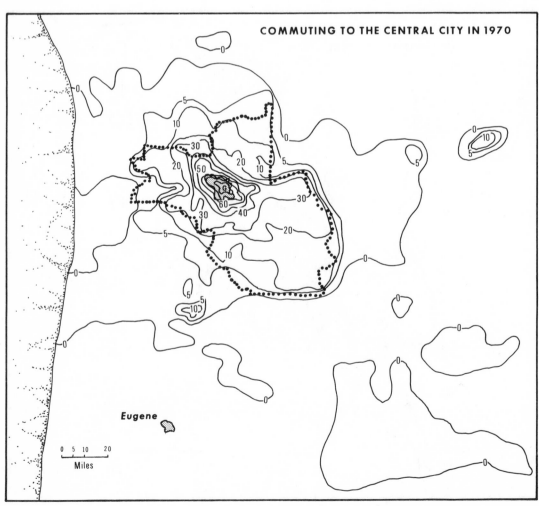

COMMUTING TO THE CENTRAL CITY IN 1970

Eugene

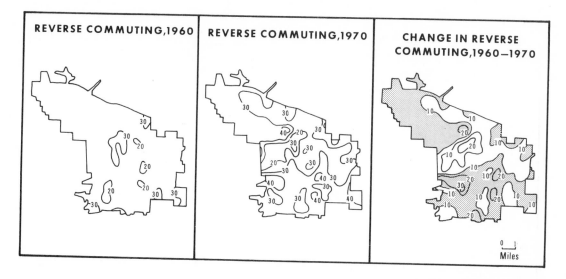

REVERSE COMMUTING, 1960

REVERSE COMMUTING, 1970

CHANGE IN REVERSE
COMMUTING, 1960–1970

PORTLAND, OR.

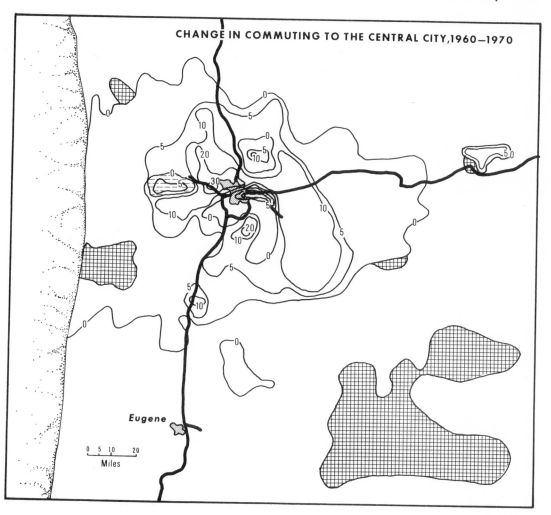

CHANGE IN COMMUTING TO THE CENTRAL CITY, 1960–1970

Eugene

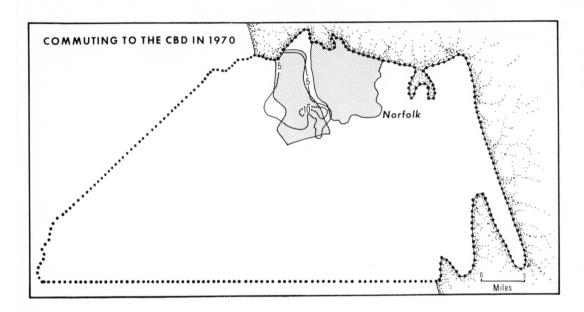

COMMUTING TO THE CBD IN 1970

Norfolk

Miles

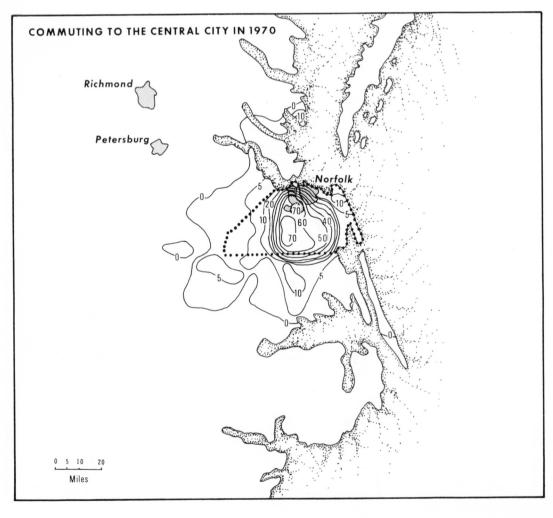

COMMUTING TO THE CENTRAL CITY IN 1970

Richmond

Petersburg

Norfolk

Miles

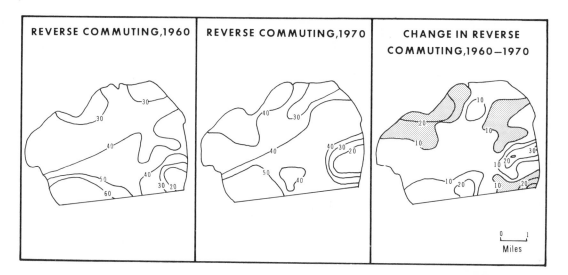

REVERSE COMMUTING, 1960   REVERSE COMMUTING, 1970   CHANGE IN REVERSE COMMUTING, 1960—1970

0   1
Miles

PORTSMOUTH, VA.

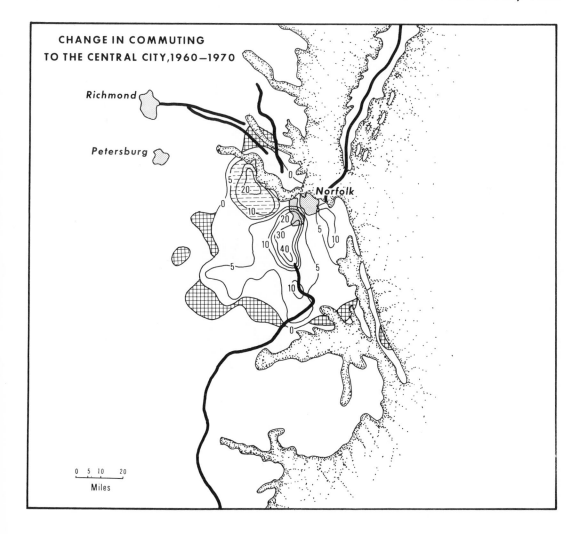

CHANGE IN COMMUTING
TO THE CENTRAL CITY, 1960—1970

Richmond

Petersburg

Norfolk

0 5 10   20
Miles

521

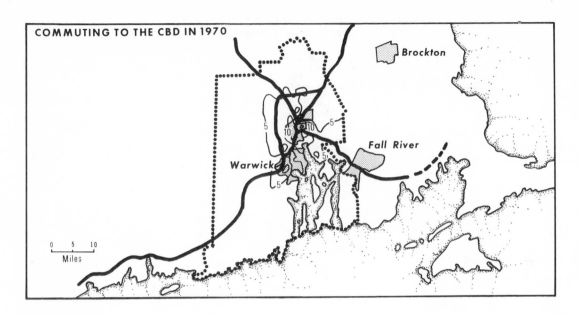

COMMUTING TO THE CBD IN 1970

Brockton

Fall River

Warwick

0 5 10
Miles

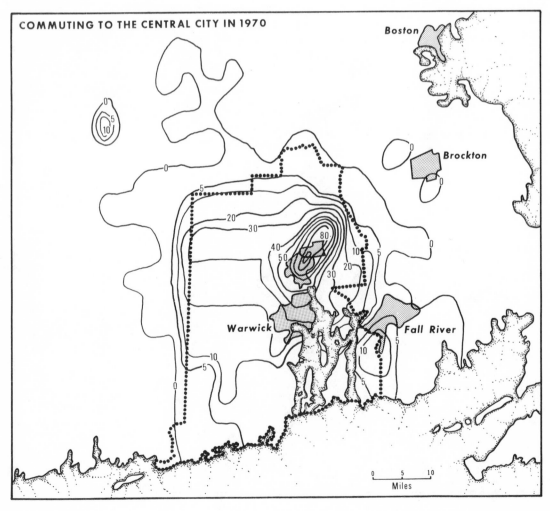

COMMUTING TO THE CENTRAL CITY IN 1970

Boston

Brockton

Warwick

Fall River

0 5 10
Miles

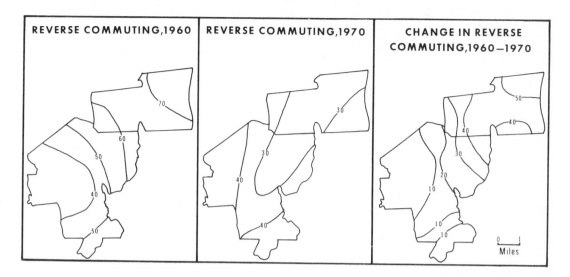

PROVIDENCE - PAWTUCKET, R.I.

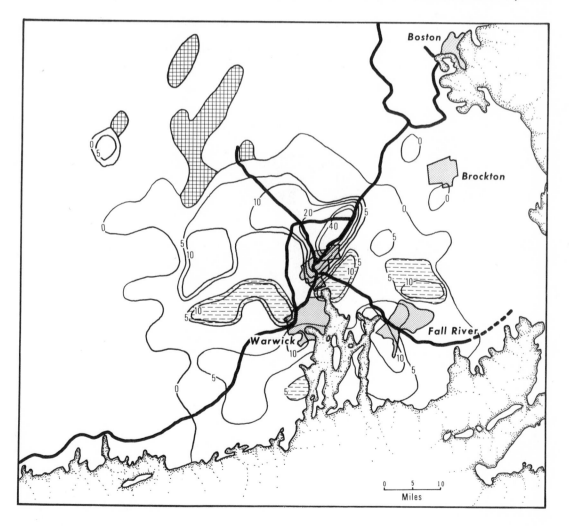

COMMUTING TO THE CBD IN 1970

NO DATA COLLECTED

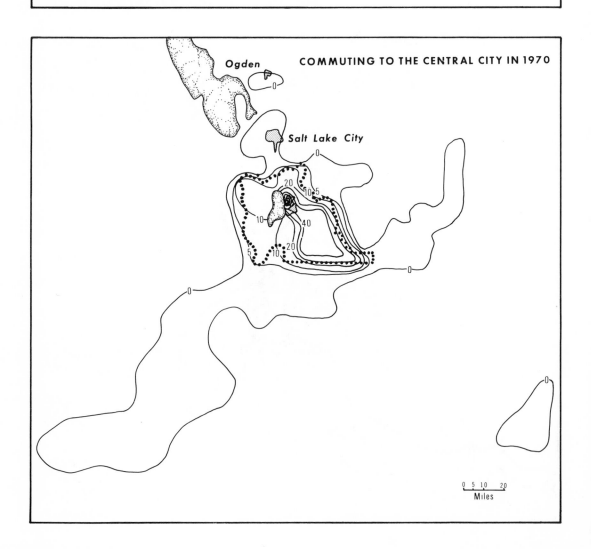

COMMUTING TO THE CENTRAL CITY IN 1970

Ogden

Salt Lake City

0   5 10   20
Miles

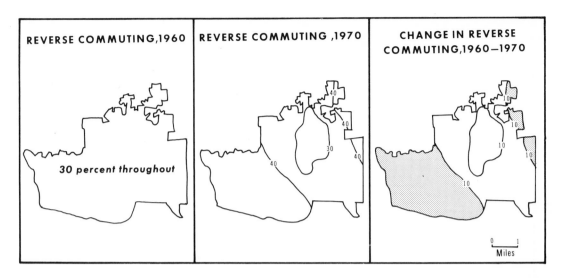

PROVO, UT.

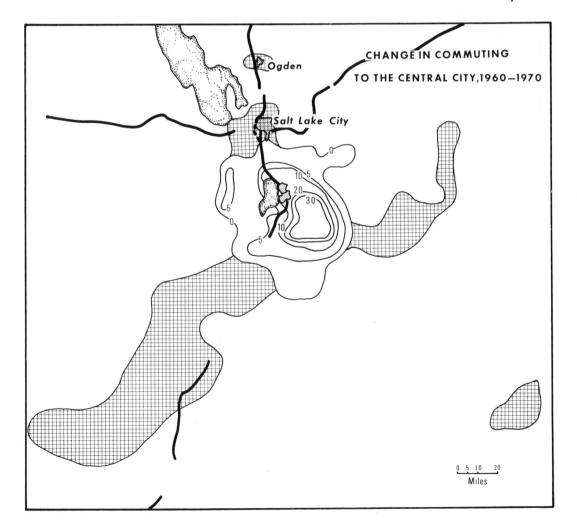

COMMUTING TO THE CBD IN 1970

NO DATA COLLECTED

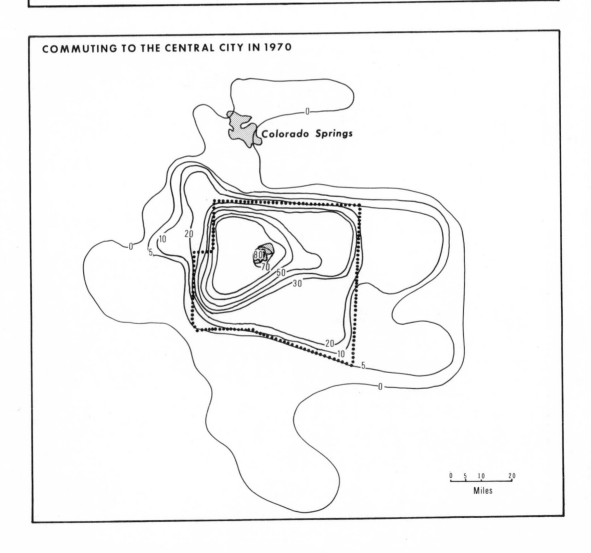

COMMUTING TO THE CENTRAL CITY IN 1970

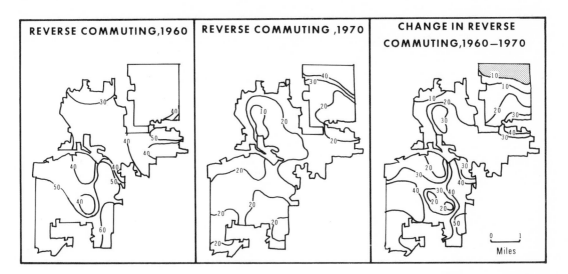

REVERSE COMMUTING,1960   REVERSE COMMUTING ,1970   CHANGE IN REVERSE COMMUTING,1960–1970

PUEBLO, CO.

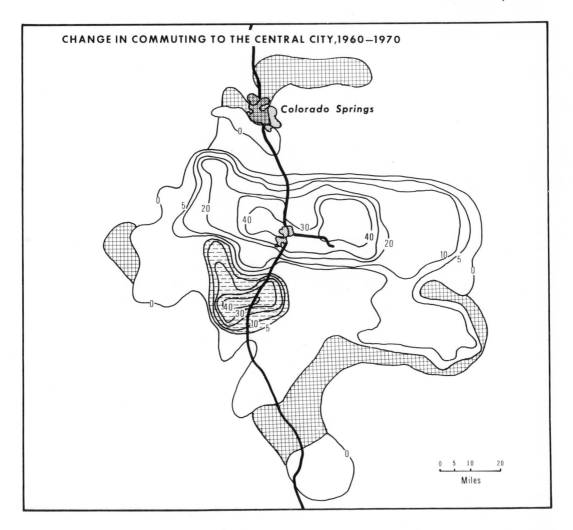

CHANGE IN COMMUTING TO THE CENTRAL CITY,1960–1970

Colorado Springs

COMMUTING TO THE CBD IN 1970

NO DATA COLLECTED

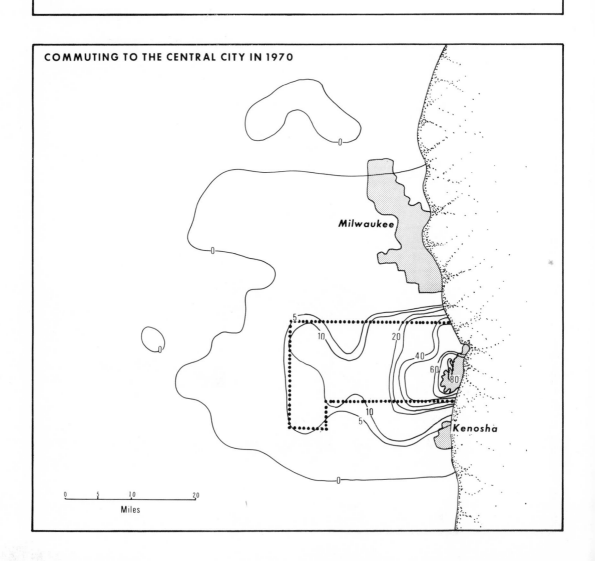

COMMUTING TO THE CENTRAL CITY IN 1970

Milwaukee

Kenosha

0   5   10   20
Miles

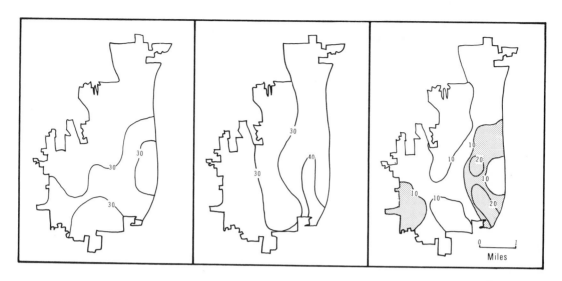

RACINE, WI.

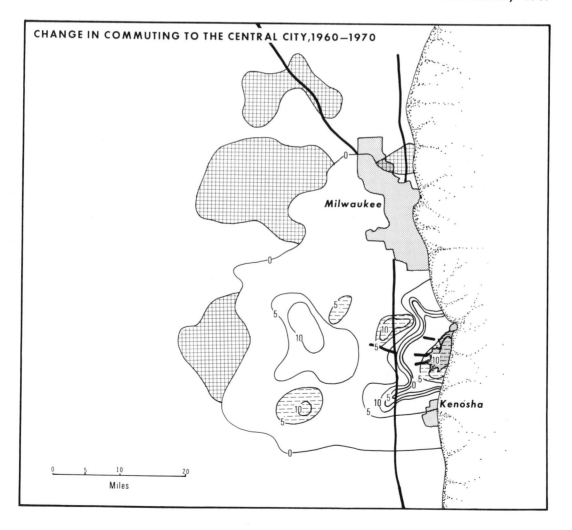

CHANGE IN COMMUTING TO THE CENTRAL CITY, 1960–1970

Milwaukee

Kenosha

530

COMMUTING TO THE CBD IN 1970

NO DATA COLLECTED

COMMUTING TO THE CENTRAL CITY IN 1970

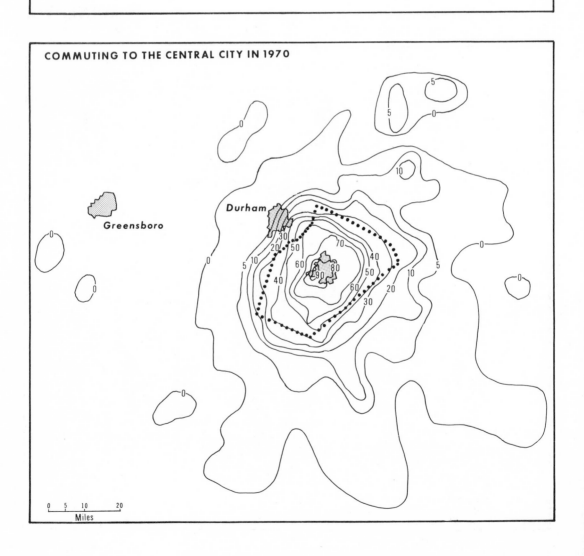

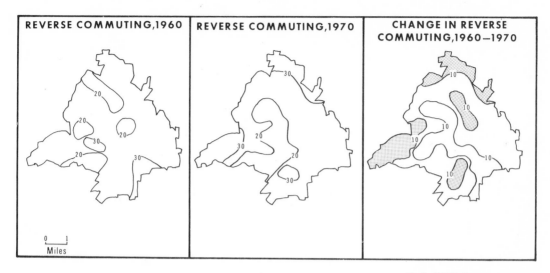

REVERSE COMMUTING, 1960

REVERSE COMMUTING, 1970

CHANGE IN REVERSE
COMMUTING, 1960—1970

RALEIGH, N.C.

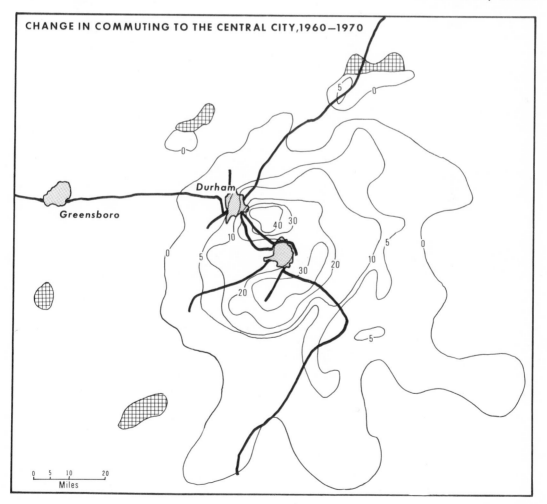

CHANGE IN COMMUTING TO THE CENTRAL CITY, 1960—1970

Durham

Greensboro

COMMUTING TO THE CBD IN 1970

NO DATA COLLECTED

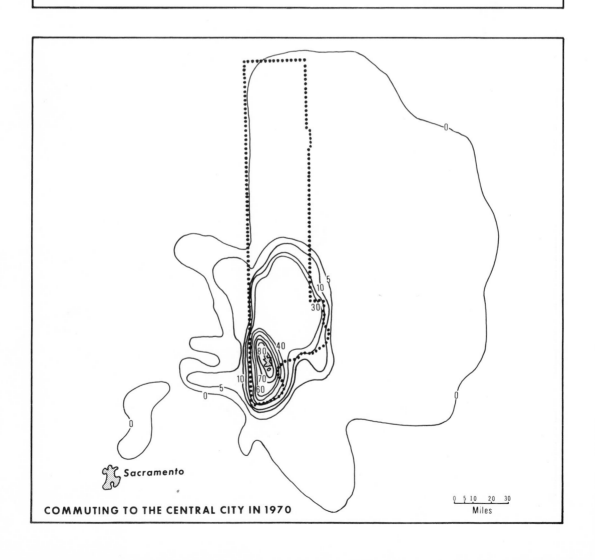

COMMUTING TO THE CENTRAL CITY IN 1970

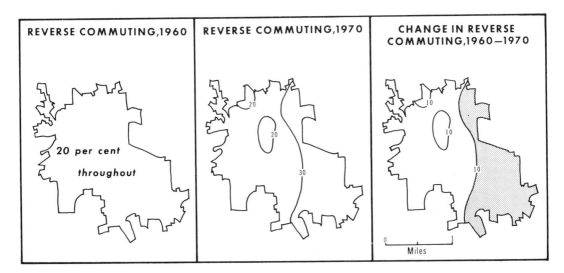

| REVERSE COMMUTING,1960 | REVERSE COMMUTING,1970 | CHANGE IN REVERSE COMMUTING,1960—1970 |

20 per cent throughout

RENO, NV.

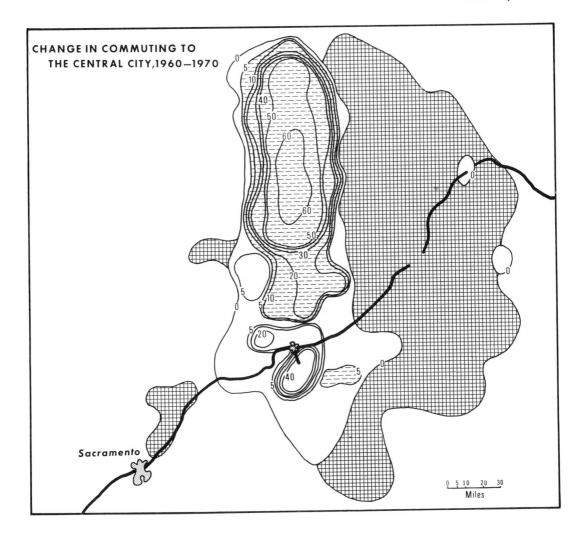

CHANGE IN COMMUTING TO THE CENTRAL CITY,1960—1970

Sacramento

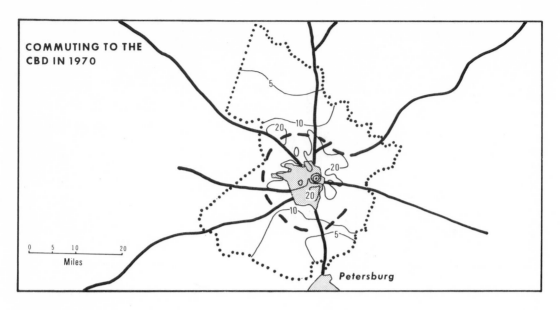

COMMUTING TO THE
CBD IN 1970

5

10

20

20

20

10

5

0   5   10   20
Miles

Petersburg

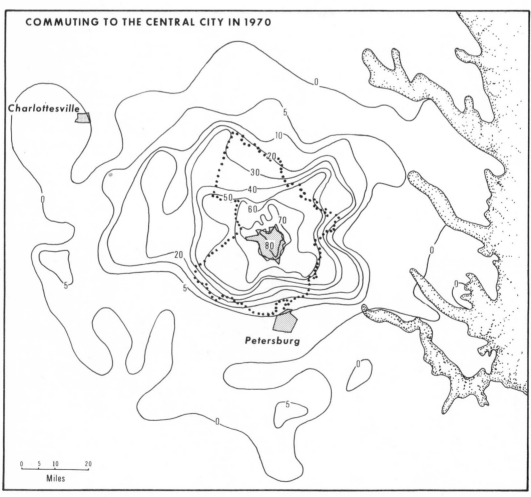

COMMUTING TO THE CENTRAL CITY IN 1970

Charlottesville

0

5

10

20

30

40

50

60

70

80

20

5

0

0

0

0

0

20

5

5

0

5

Petersburg

0   5   10   20
Miles

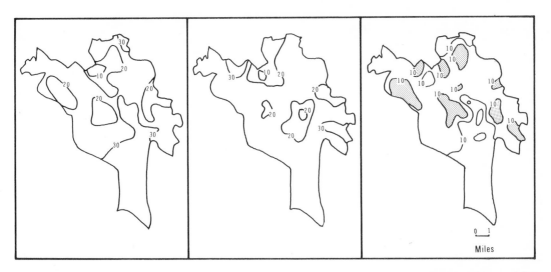

RICHMOND, VA.

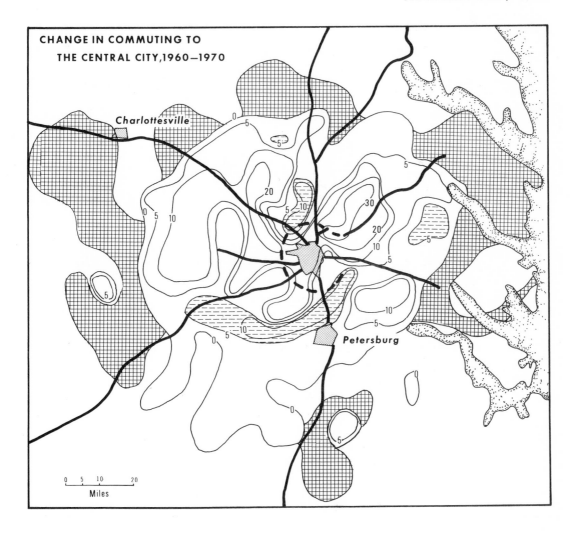

COMMUTING TO THE CBD IN 1970

NO DATA COLLECTED

COMMUTING TO THE CENTRAL CITY IN 1970

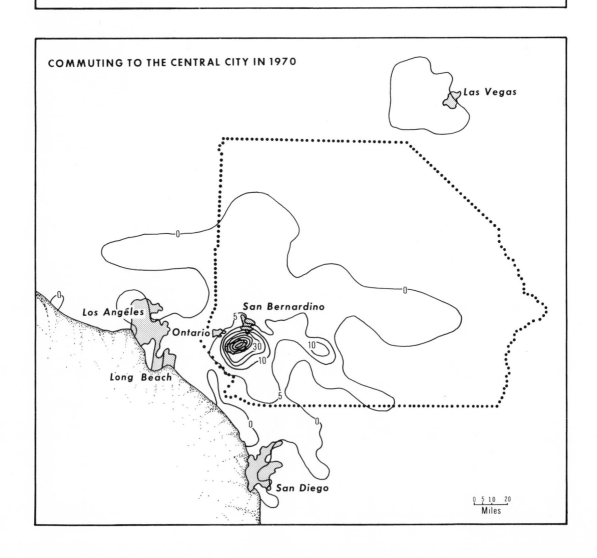

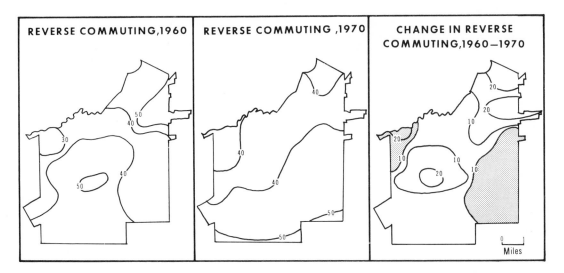

RIVERSIDE, CA.

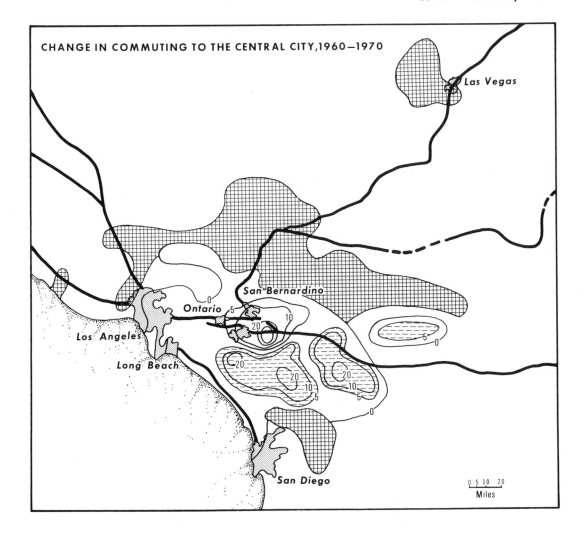

COMMUTING TO THE CBD IN 1970

NO DATA COLLECTED

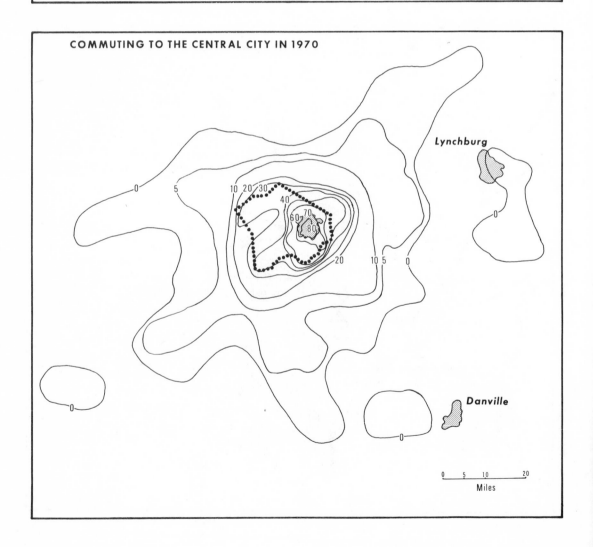

COMMUTING TO THE CENTRAL CITY IN 1970

Lynchburg

Danville

0   5   10   20
Miles

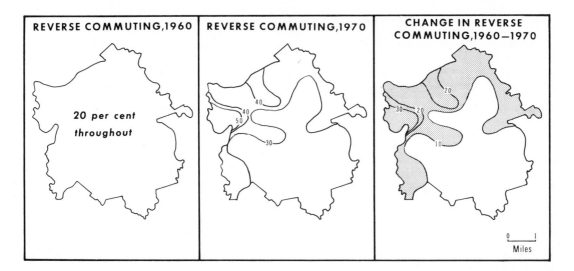

| REVERSE COMMUTING, 1960 | REVERSE COMMUTING, 1970 | CHANGE IN REVERSE COMMUTING, 1960—1970 |

20 per cent throughout

ROANOKE, VA.

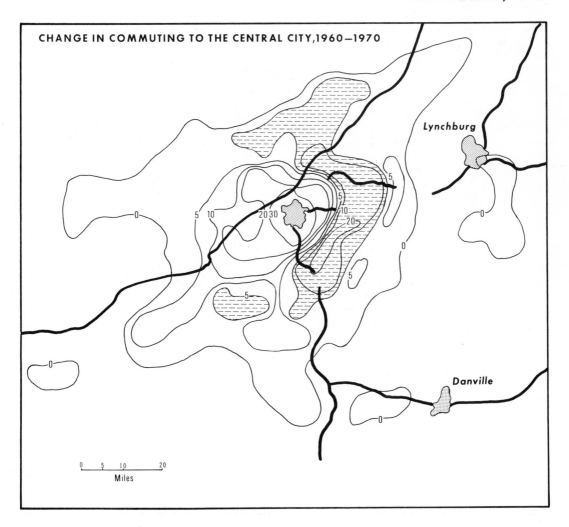

CHANGE IN COMMUTING TO THE CENTRAL CITY, 1960—1970

COMMUTING TO THE CBD IN 1970

NO DATA COLLECTED

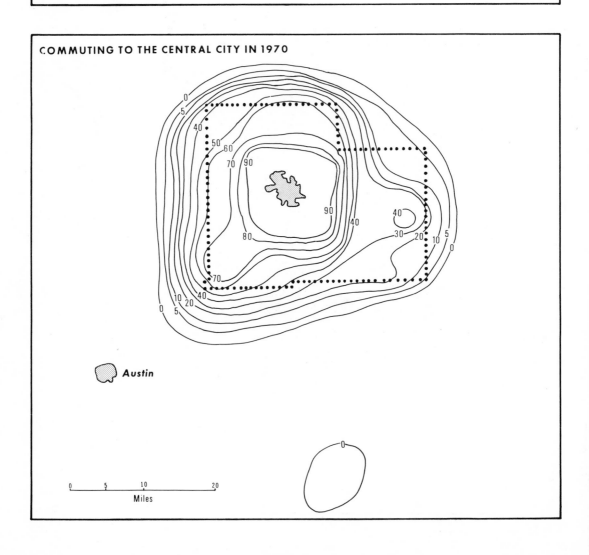

COMMUTING TO THE CENTRAL CITY IN 1970

Austin

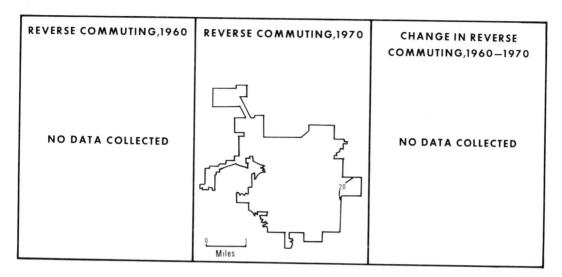

REVERSE COMMUTING,1960	REVERSE COMMUTING,1970	CHANGE IN REVERSE COMMUTING,1960—1970
NO DATA COLLECTED		NO DATA COLLECTED

0   1
Miles

20

ROCHESTER, MN.

CHANGE IN COMMUTING TO THE CENTRAL CITY,1960—1970

NO DATA COLLECTED

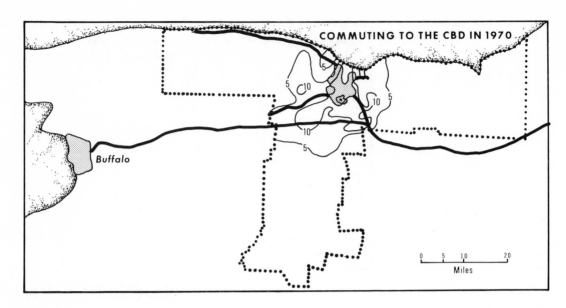

COMMUTING TO THE CBD IN 1970

Buffalo

0   5   10   20
Miles

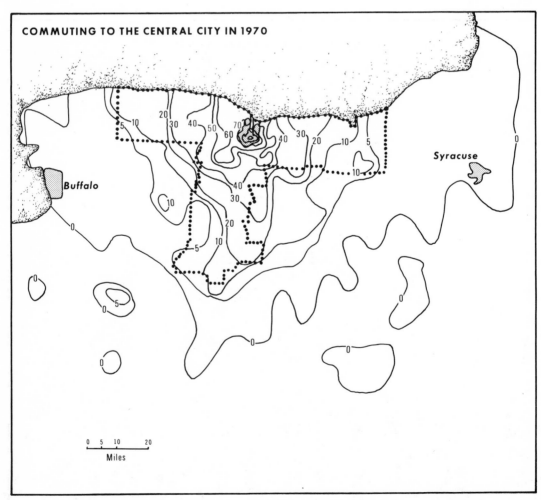

COMMUTING TO THE CENTRAL CITY IN 1970

Buffalo

Syracuse

0 5 10   20
Miles

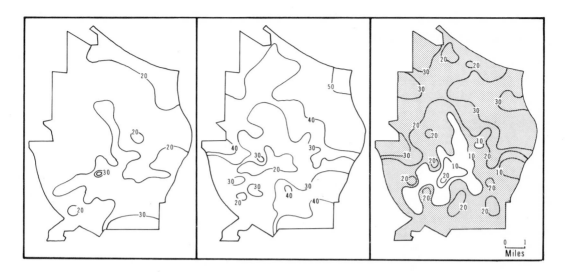

ROCHESTER, N.Y.

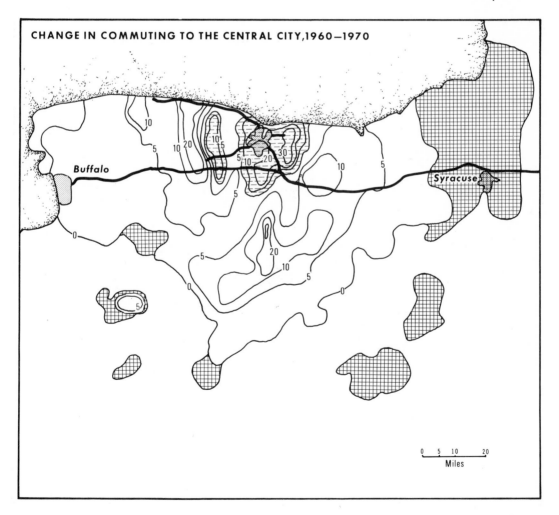

CHANGE IN COMMUTING TO THE CENTRAL CITY, 1960–1970

544

COMMUTING TO THE CBD IN 1970

NO DATA COLLECTED

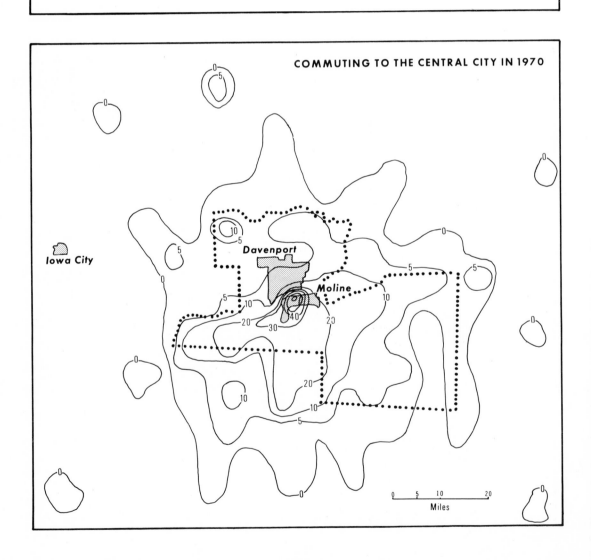

COMMUTING TO THE CENTRAL CITY IN 1970

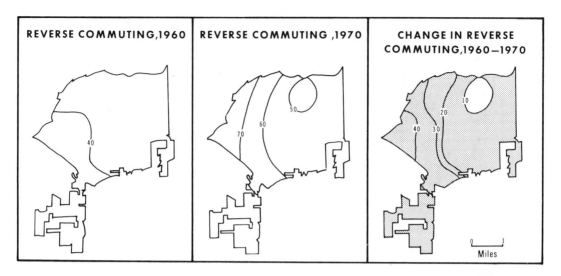

ROCK ISLAND, IL.

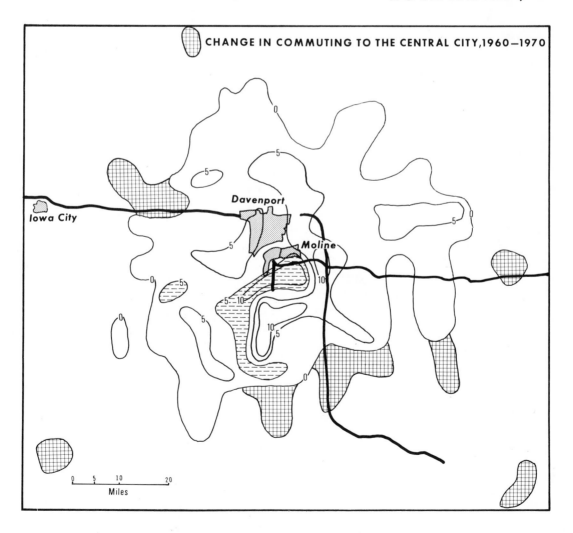

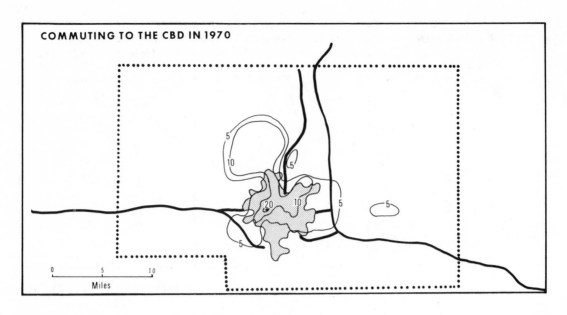

COMMUTING TO THE CBD IN 1970

COMMUTING TO THE CENTRAL CITY IN 1970

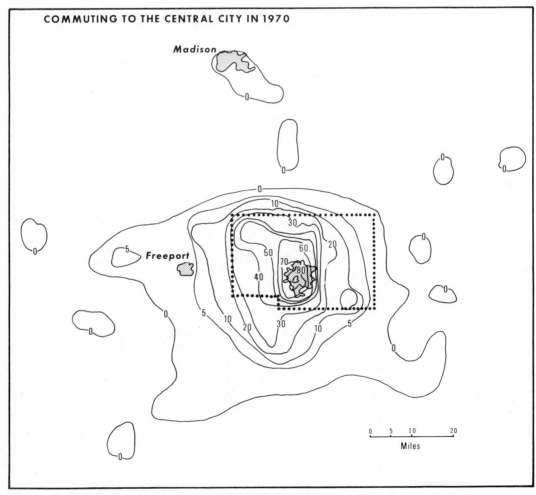

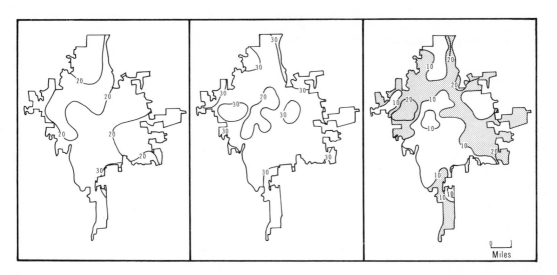

ROCKFORD, IL.

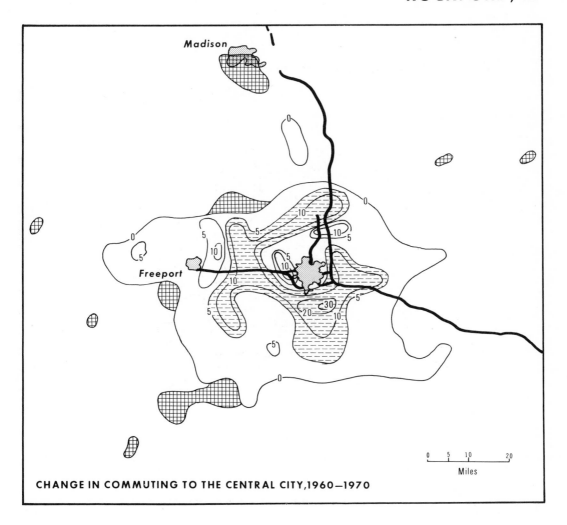

CHANGE IN COMMUTING TO THE CENTRAL CITY, 1960—1970

COMMUTING TO THE CBD IN 1970

NO DATA COLLECTED

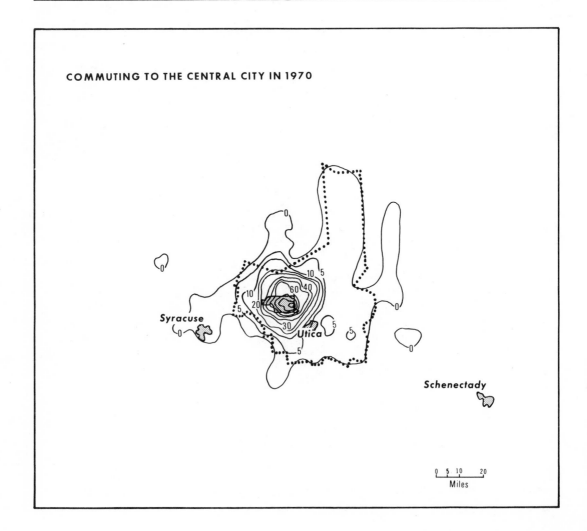

COMMUTING TO THE CENTRAL CITY IN 1970

Syracuse

Utica

Schenectady

0 5 10   20
Miles

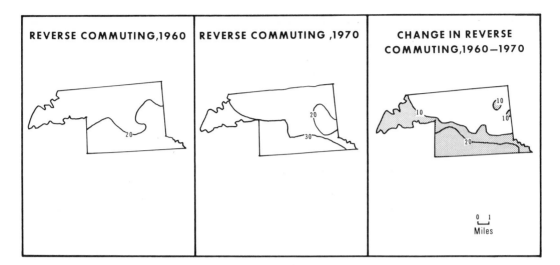

| REVERSE COMMUTING,1960 | REVERSE COMMUTING ,1970 | CHANGE IN REVERSE COMMUTING,1960—1970 |

ROME, N.Y.

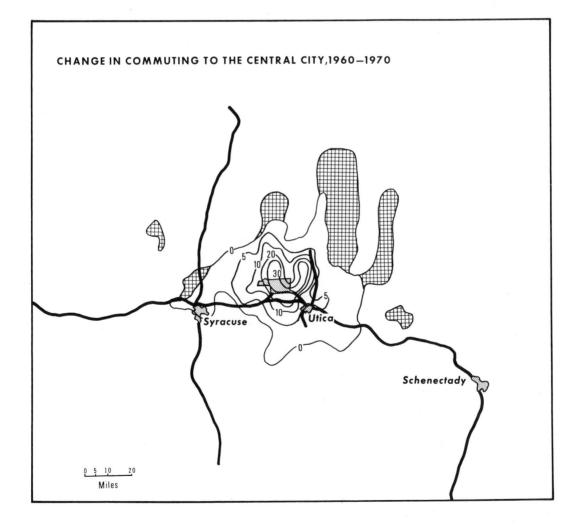

CHANGE IN COMMUTING TO THE CENTRAL CITY,1960—1970

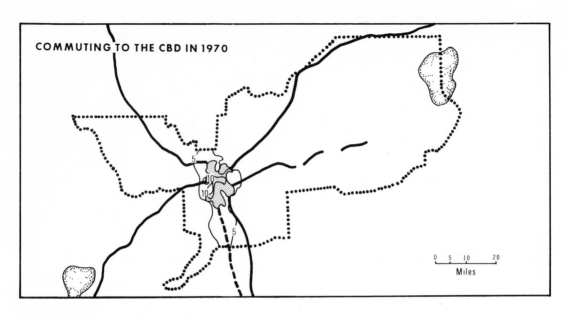

COMMUTING TO THE CBD IN 1970

0 5 10   20
Miles

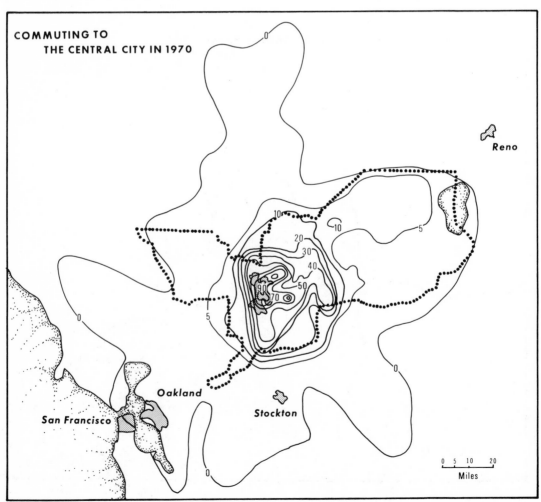

COMMUTING TO
THE CENTRAL CITY IN 1970

Reno

Oakland

San Francisco

Stockton

0 5 10   20
Miles

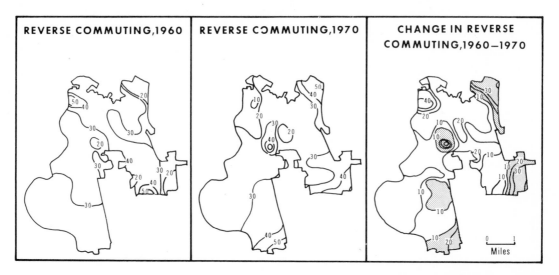

REVERSE COMMUTING, 1960

REVERSE COMMUTING, 1970

CHANGE IN REVERSE COMMUTING, 1960—1970

SACRAMENTO, CA.

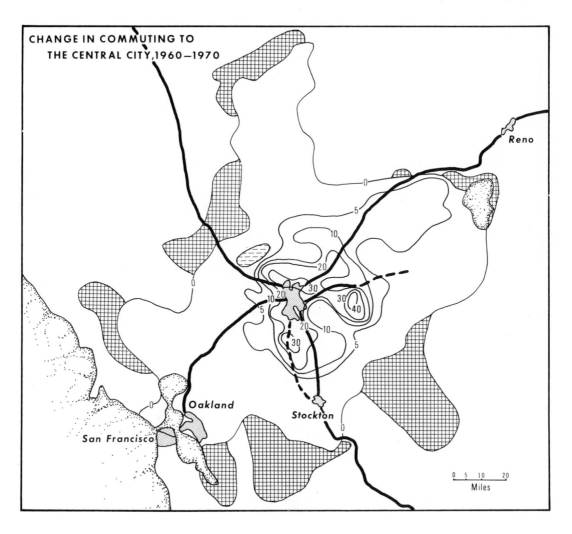

CHANGE IN COMMUTING TO THE CENTRAL CITY, 1960—1970

Reno

Oakland

Stockton

San Francisco

COMMUTING TO THE CBD IN 1970

NO DATA COLLECTED

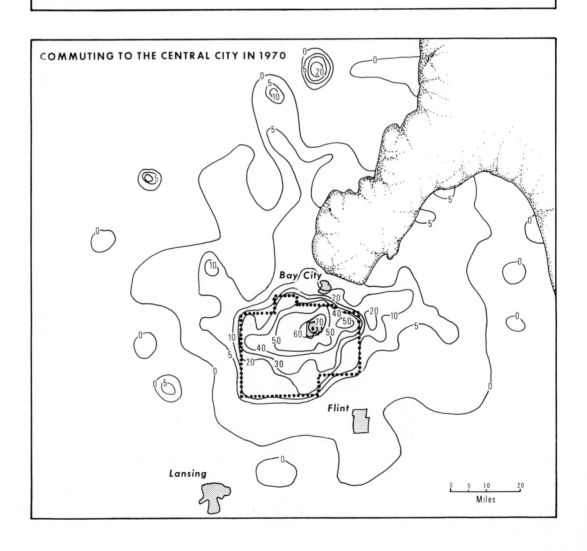

COMMUTING TO THE CENTRAL CITY IN 1970

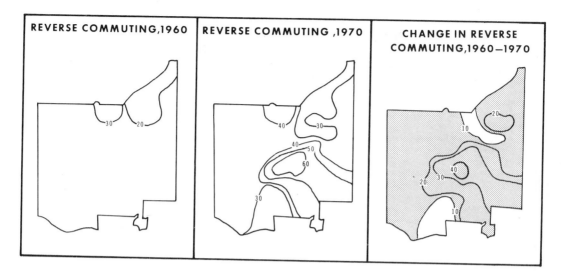

REVERSE COMMUTING, 1960

REVERSE COMMUTING, 1970

CHANGE IN REVERSE
COMMUTING, 1960—1970

SAGINAW, MI.

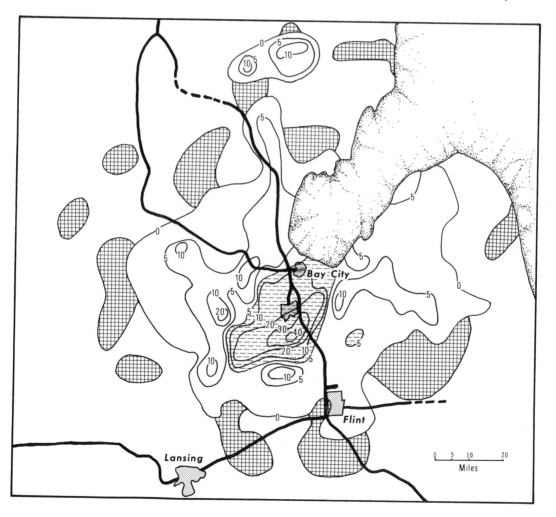

COMMUTING TO THE CBD IN 1970

NO DATA COLLECTED

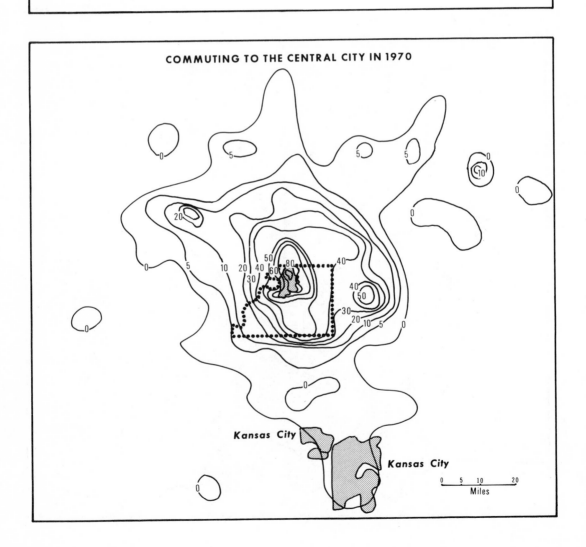

COMMUTING TO THE CENTRAL CITY IN 1970

Kansas City

Kansas City

0 5 10   20
        Miles

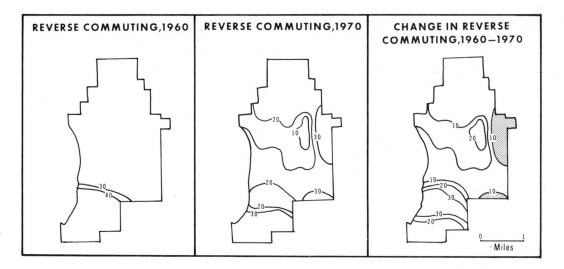

| REVERSE COMMUTING,1960 | REVERSE COMMUTING,1970 | CHANGE IN REVERSE COMMUTING,1960—1970 |

ST. JOSEPH, MO.

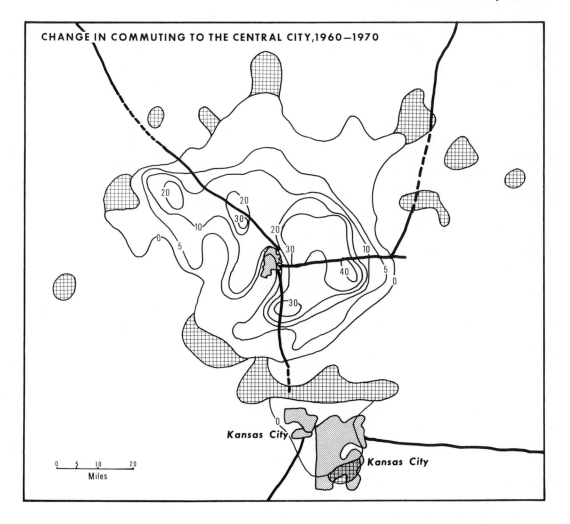

CHANGE IN COMMUTING TO THE CENTRAL CITY,1960—1970

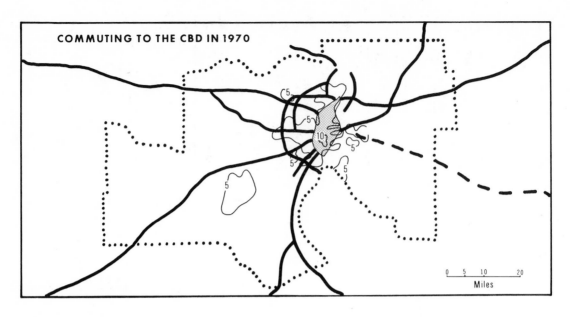

COMMUTING TO THE CBD IN 1970

0 5 10   20
Miles

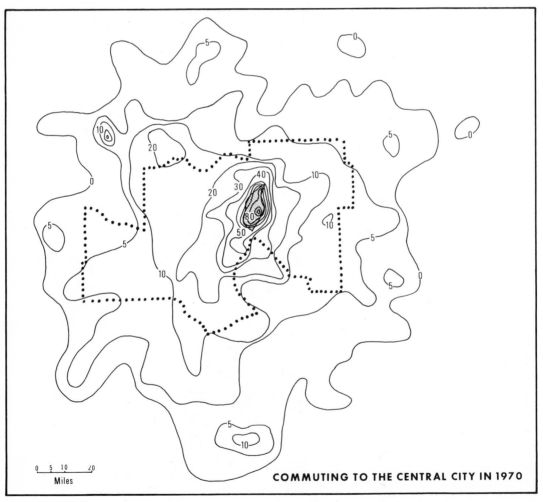

0 5 10   20
Miles

COMMUTING TO THE CENTRAL CITY IN 1970

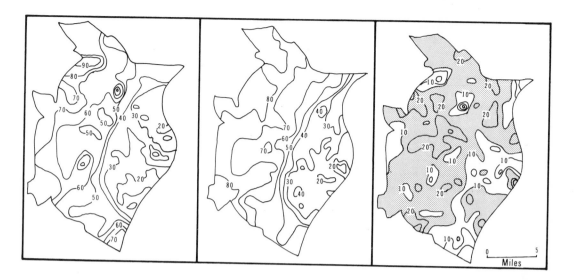

ST. LOUIS, MO.

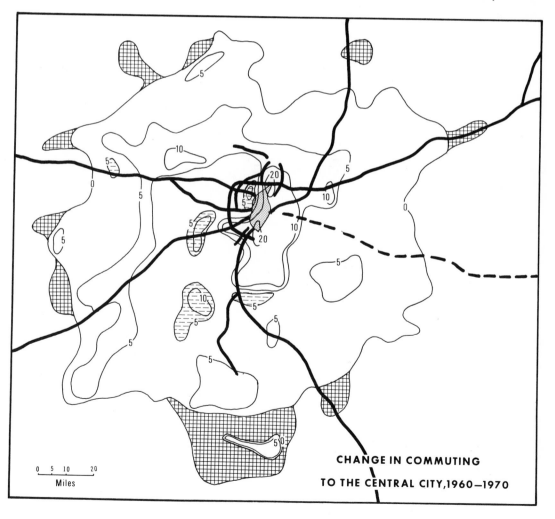

CHANGE IN COMMUTING
TO THE CENTRAL CITY, 1960–1970

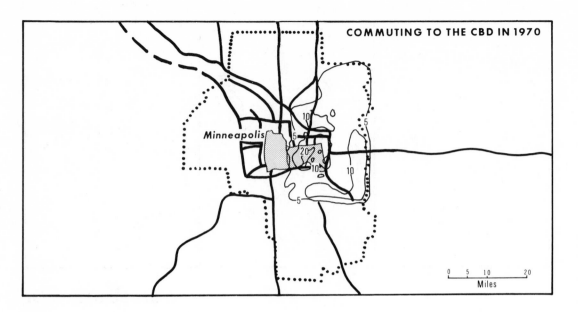

COMMUTING TO THE CBD IN 1970

Minneapolis

0 5 10 20
Miles

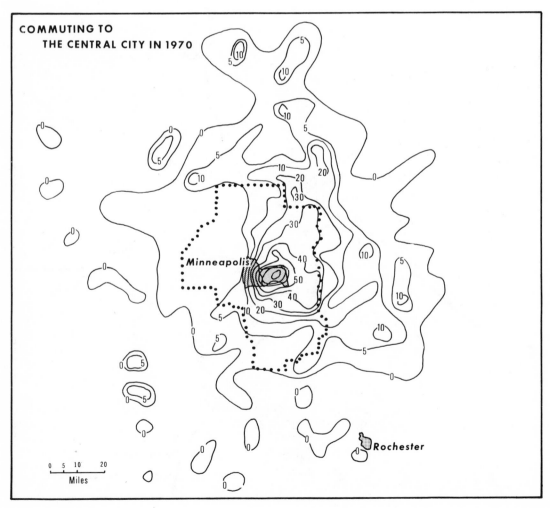

COMMUTING TO
THE CENTRAL CITY IN 1970

Minneapolis

Rochester

0 5 10 20
Miles

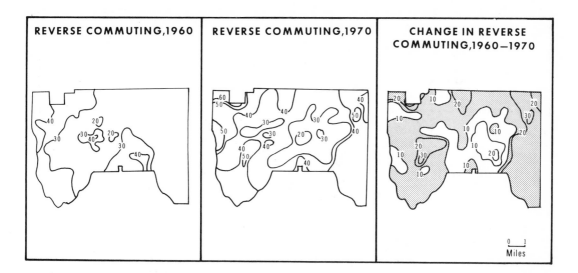

| REVERSE COMMUTING,1960 | REVERSE COMMUTING,1970 | CHANGE IN REVERSE COMMUTING,1960—1970 |

ST. PAUL, MN.

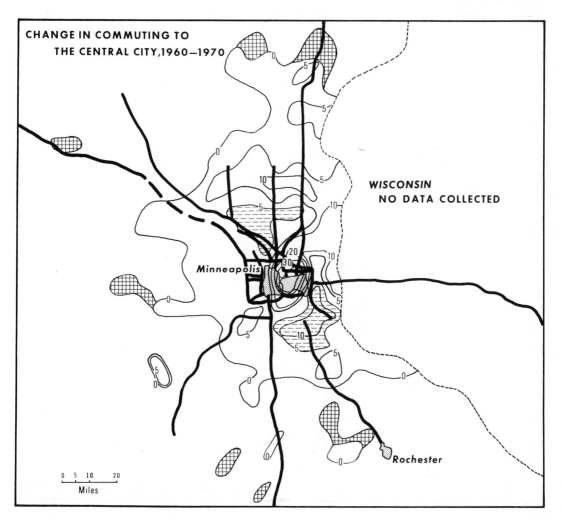

CHANGE IN COMMUTING TO
THE CENTRAL CITY,1960—1970

WISCONSIN
NO DATA COLLECTED

Minneapolis

Rochester

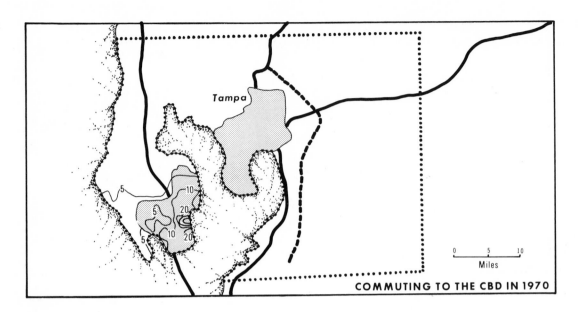

0   5   10
Miles

COMMUTING TO THE CBD IN 1970

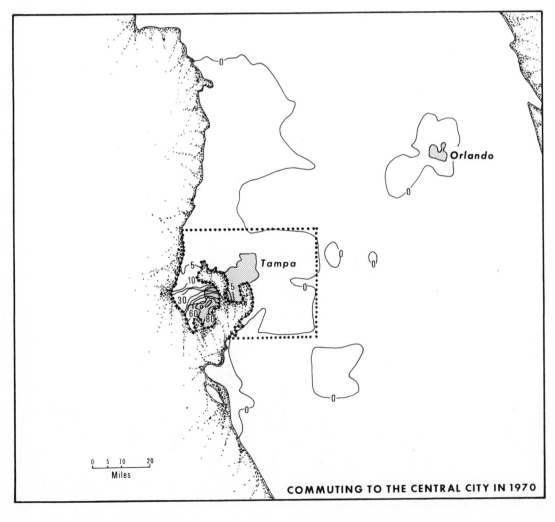

0 5 10   20
Miles

COMMUTING TO THE CENTRAL CITY IN 1970

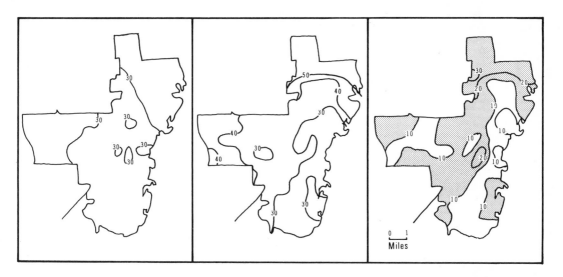

ST. PETERSBURG, FL.

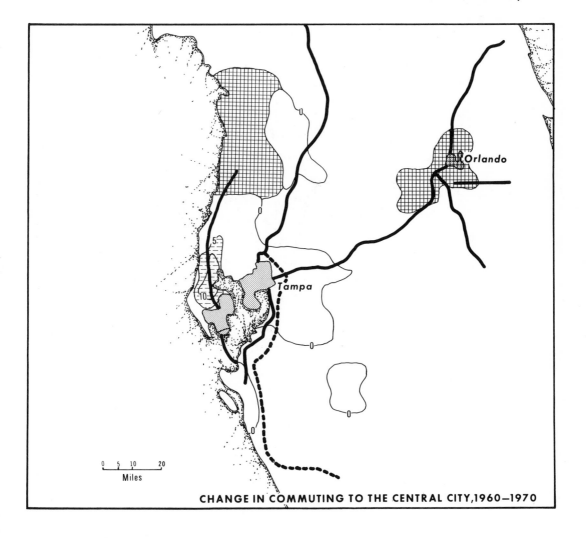

CHANGE IN COMMUTING TO THE CENTRAL CITY, 1960–1970

COMMUTING TO THE CBD IN 1970

NO DATA COLLECTED

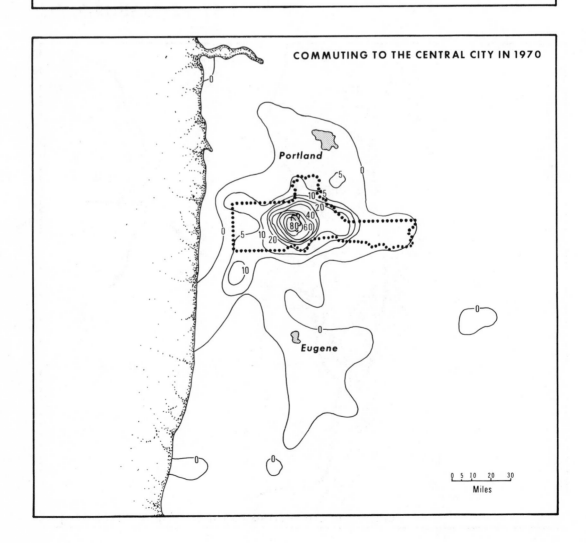

COMMUTING TO THE CENTRAL CITY IN 1970

563

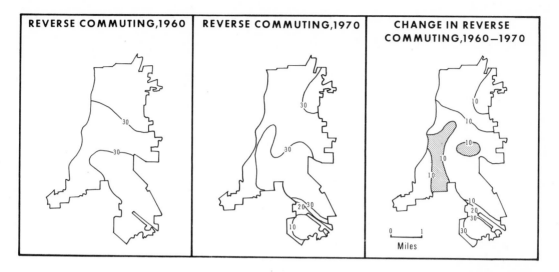

| REVERSE COMMUTING,1960 | REVERSE COMMUTING,1970 | CHANGE IN REVERSE COMMUTING,1960-1970 |

SALEM, OR.

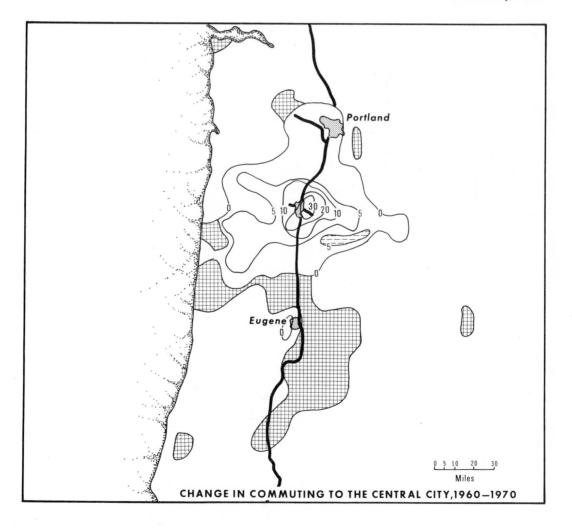

CHANGE IN COMMUTING TO THE CENTRAL CITY,1960-1970

COMMUTING TO THE CBD IN 1970

NO DATA COLLECTED

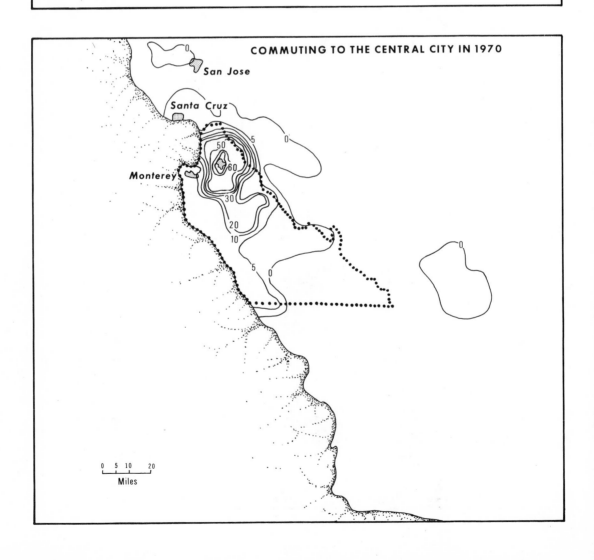

COMMUTING TO THE CENTRAL CITY IN 1970

San Jose

Santa Cruz

Monterey

0 5 10 20

Miles

REVERSE COMMUTING,1960	REVERSE COMMUTING,1970	CHANGE IN REVERSE COMMUTING,1960—1970
NO DATA COLLECTED		NO DATA COLLECTED

0 ___ 1
Miles

SALINAS, CA.

CHANGE IN COMMUTING TO THE CENTRAL CITY,1960—1970

NO DATA COLLECTED

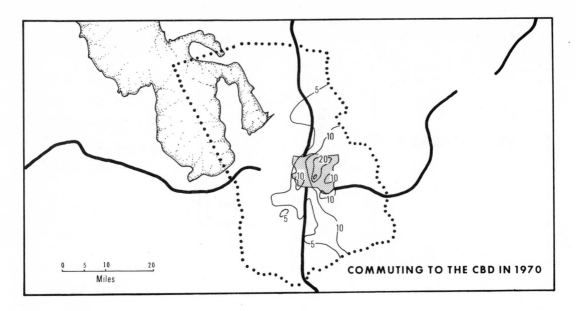

COMMUTING TO THE CBD IN 1970

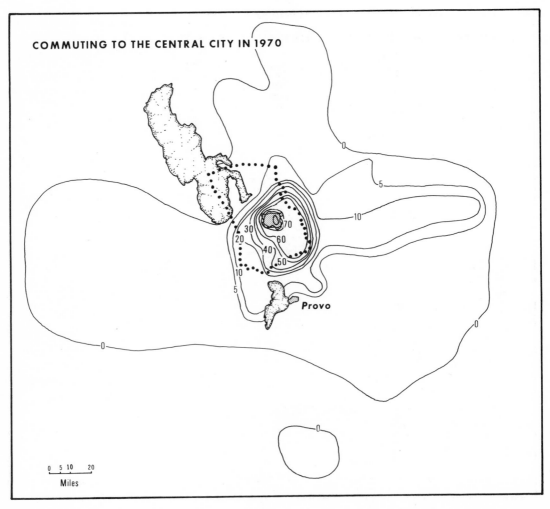

COMMUTING TO THE CENTRAL CITY IN 1970

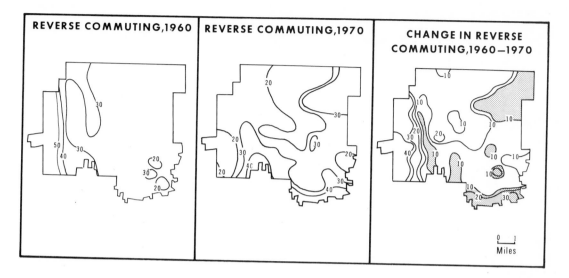

REVERSE COMMUTING, 1960

REVERSE COMMUTING, 1970

CHANGE IN REVERSE COMMUTING, 1960–1970

SALT LAKE CITY, UT.

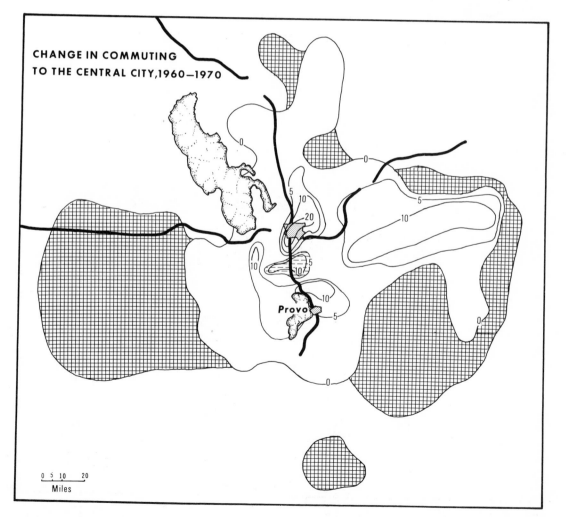

CHANGE IN COMMUTING TO THE CENTRAL CITY, 1960–1970

Provo

COMMUTING TO THE CBD IN 1970

NO DATA COLLECTED

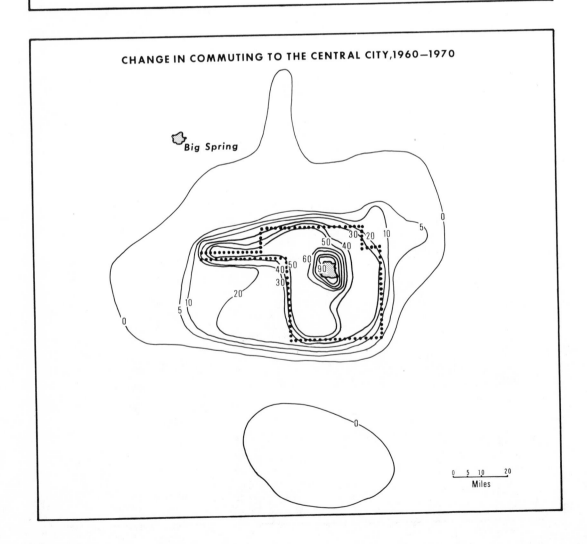

CHANGE IN COMMUTING TO THE CENTRAL CITY, 1960—1970

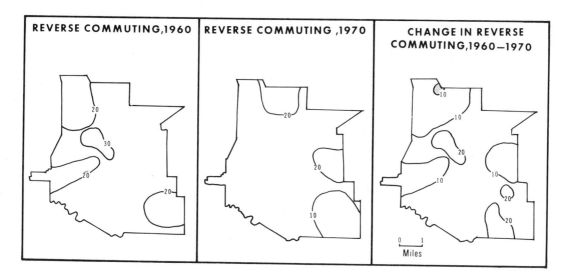

SAN ANGELO, TX.

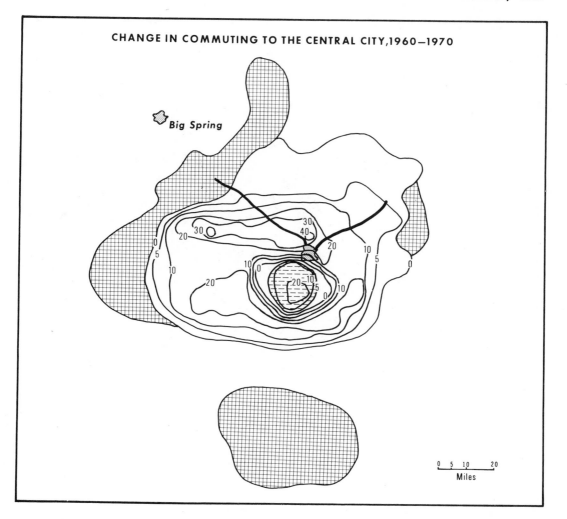

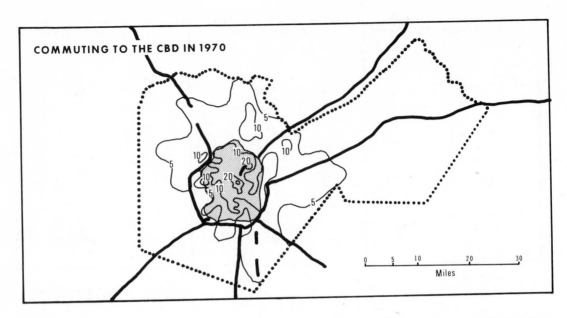

COMMUTING TO THE CBD IN 1970

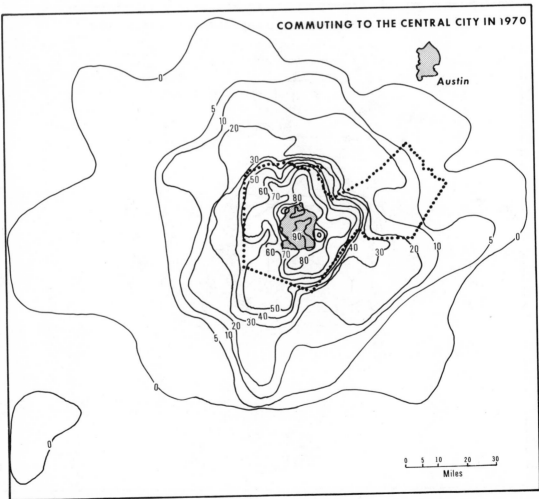

COMMUTING TO THE CENTRAL CITY IN 1970

Austin

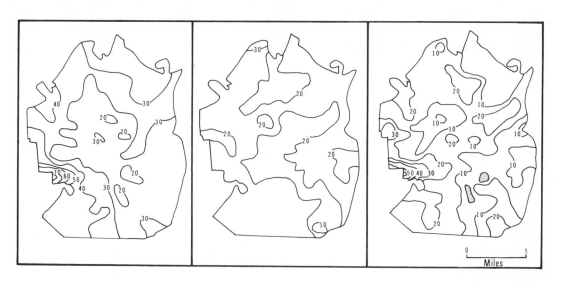

SAN ANTONIO, TX.

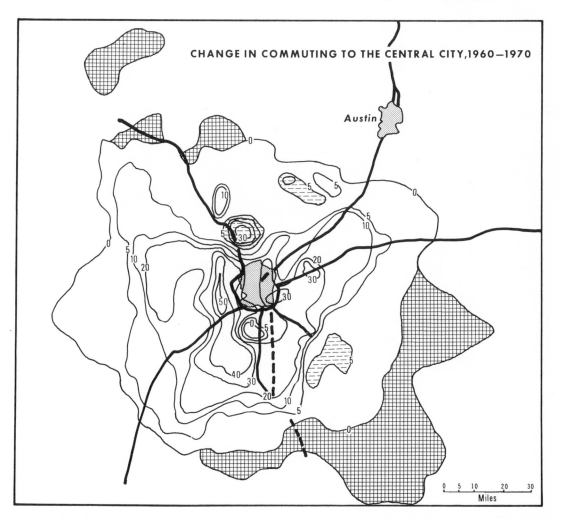

CHANGE IN COMMUTING TO THE CENTRAL CITY, 1960–1970

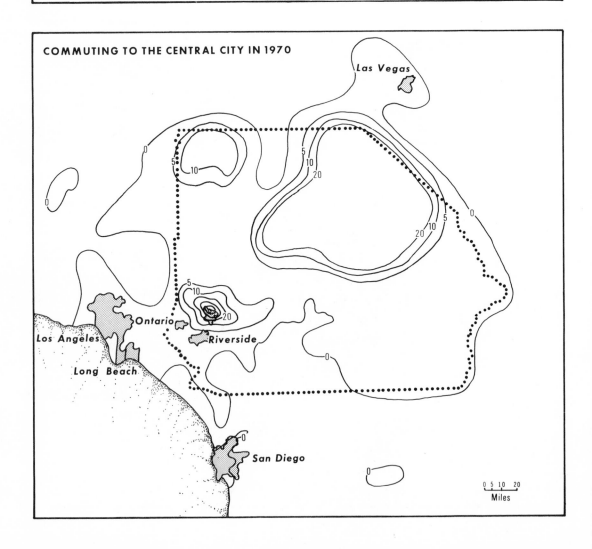

COMMUTING TO THE CBD IN 1970

NO DATA COLLECTED

COMMUTING TO THE CENTRAL CITY IN 1970

Las Vegas

Los Angeles

Long Beach

Ontario

Riverside

San Diego

0 5 10 20
Miles

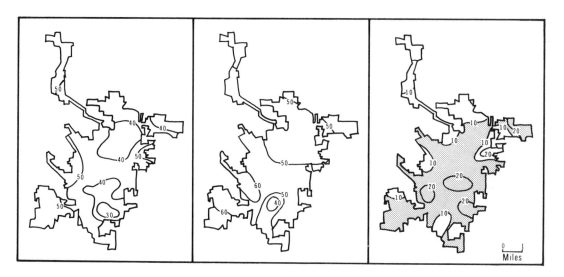

SAN BERNARDINO, CA.

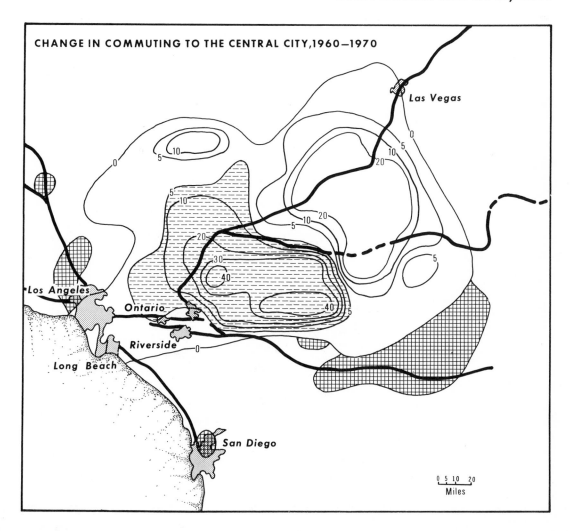

CHANGE IN COMMUTING TO THE CENTRAL CITY, 1960–1970

COMMUTING TO THE CBD IN 1970

NO DATA COLLECTED

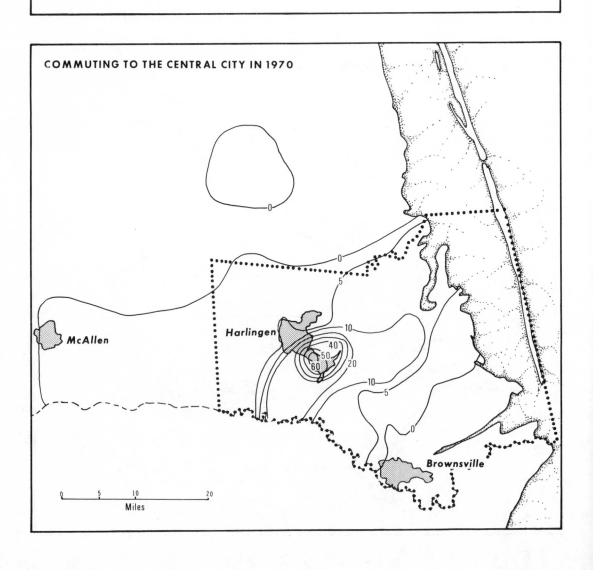

COMMUTING TO THE CENTRAL CITY IN 1970

McAllen

Harlingen

Brownsville

0

5 10 20

Miles

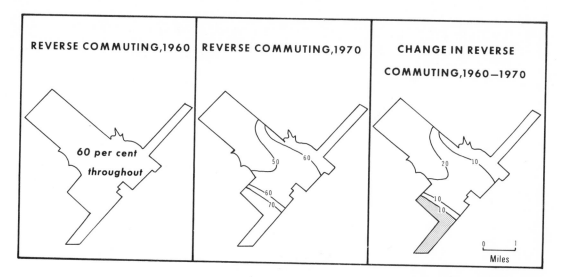

| REVERSE COMMUTING,1960 | REVERSE COMMUTING,1970 | CHANGE IN REVERSE COMMUTING,1960–1970 |

60 per cent throughout

SAN BENITO, TX.

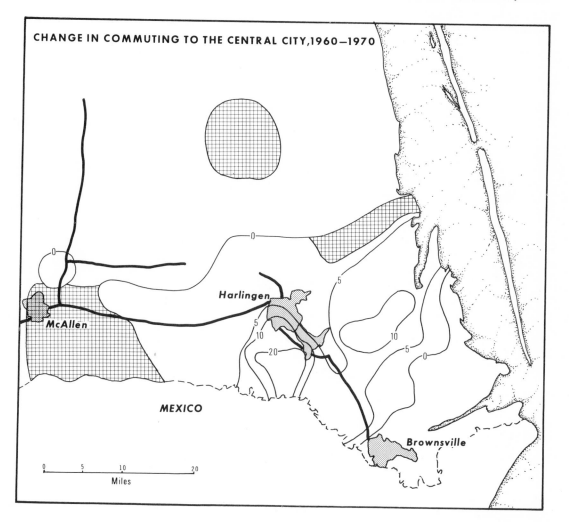

CHANGE IN COMMUTING TO THE CENTRAL CITY,1960–1970

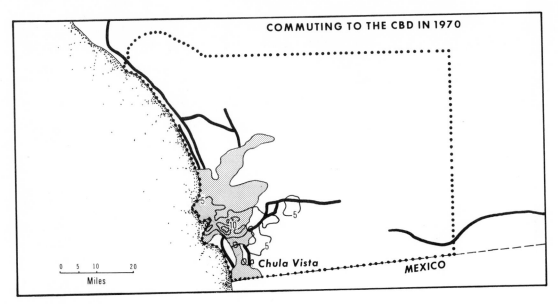

COMMUTING TO THE CBD IN 1970

5

10

5

5

0 5 10 20
Miles

Chula Vista

MEXICO

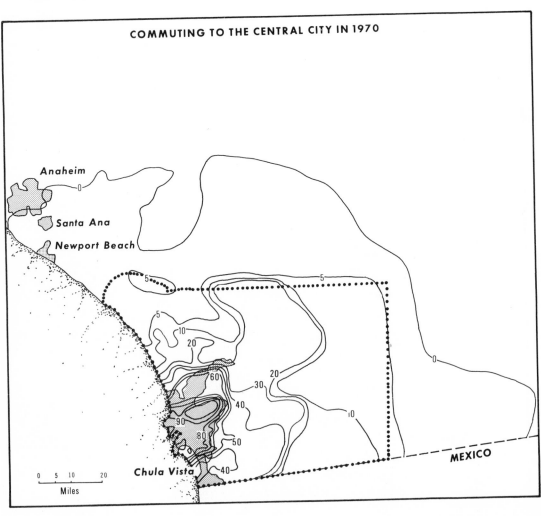

COMMUTING TO THE CENTRAL CITY IN 1970

Anaheim

0

Santa Ana

Newport Beach

5

5

5

10

20

0

60

20

30

40

10

90

80

50

Chula Vista

40

0 5 10 20
Miles

MEXICO

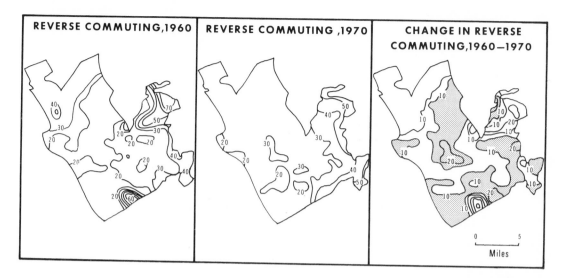

REVERSE COMMUTING, 1960

REVERSE COMMUTING, 1970

CHANGE IN REVERSE COMMUTING, 1960–1970

SAN DIEGO, CA.

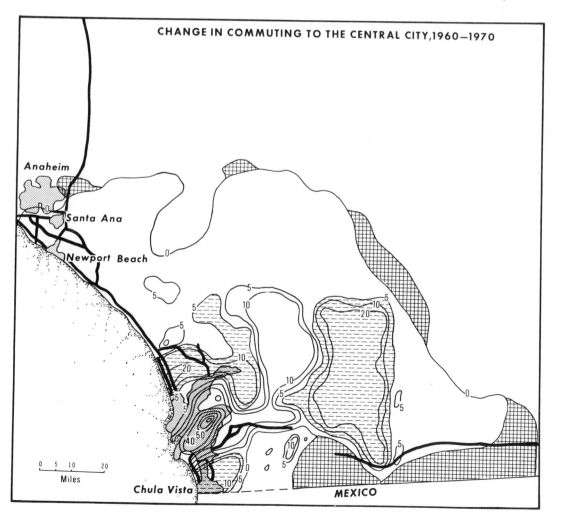

CHANGE IN COMMUTING TO THE CENTRAL CITY, 1960–1970

Anaheim

Santa Ana

Newport Beach

Chula Vista

MEXICO

578

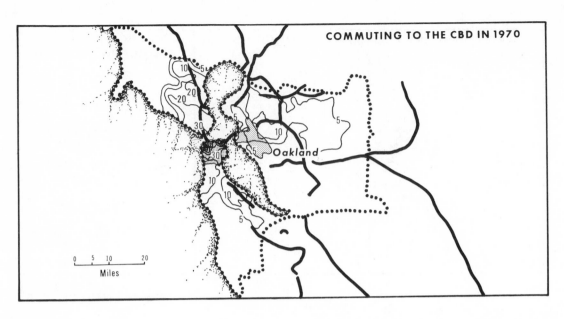

COMMUTING TO THE CBD IN 1970

Oakland

0 5 10 20
Miles

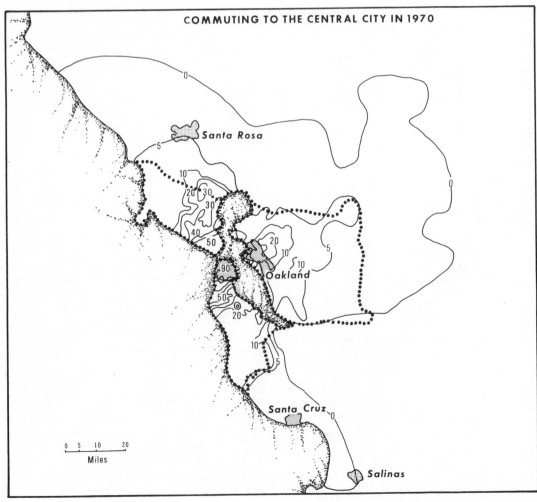

COMMUTING TO THE CENTRAL CITY IN 1970

Santa Rosa

Oakland

Santa Cruz

Salinas

0 5 10 20
Miles

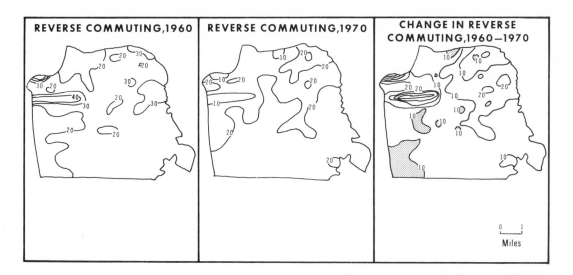

REVERSE COMMUTING,1960

REVERSE COMMUTING,1970

CHANGE IN REVERSE
COMMUTING,1960—1970

0   1
Miles

SAN FRANCISCO, CA.

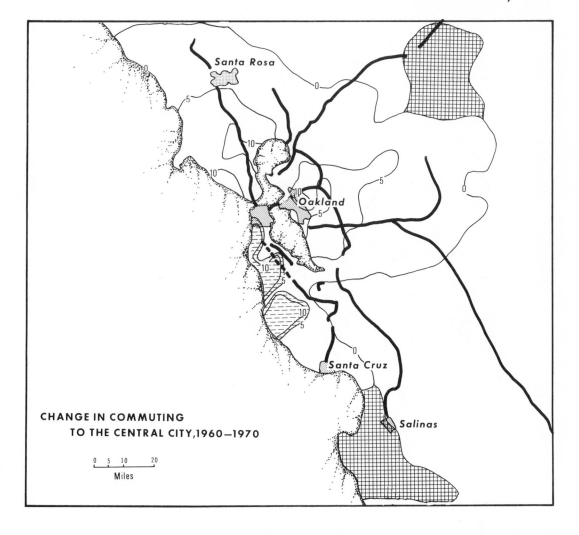

CHANGE IN COMMUTING
TO THE CENTRAL CITY,1960—1970

0 5 10   20
Miles

Santa Rosa

Oakland

Santa Cruz

Salinas

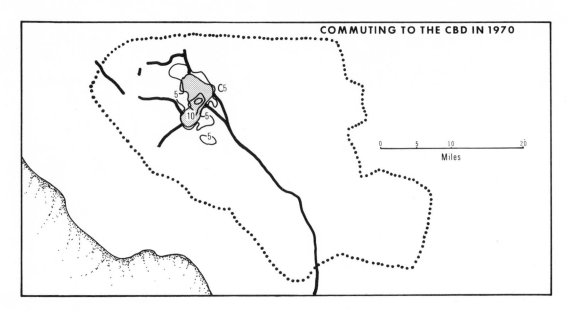

COMMUTING TO THE CBD IN 1970

0 5 10 20
Miles

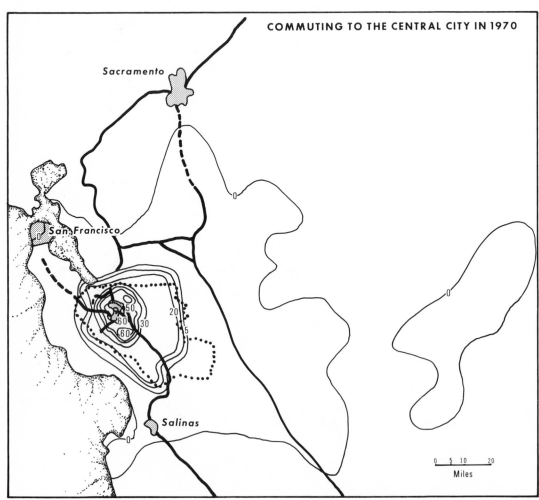

COMMUTING TO THE CENTRAL CITY IN 1970

Sacramento

San Francisco

Salinas

0 5 10 20
Miles

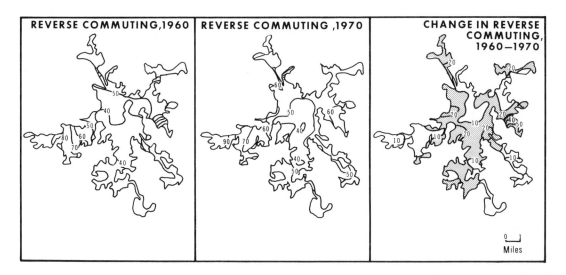

REVERSE COMMUTING, 1960

REVERSE COMMUTING, 1970

CHANGE IN REVERSE COMMUTING, 1960–1970

SAN JOSE, CA.

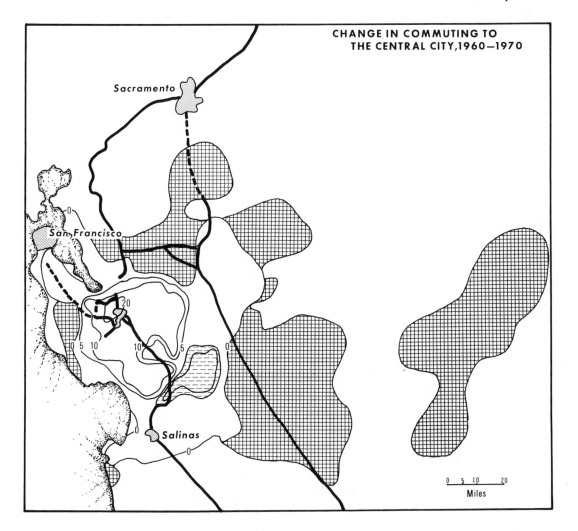

CHANGE IN COMMUTING TO THE CENTRAL CITY, 1960–1970

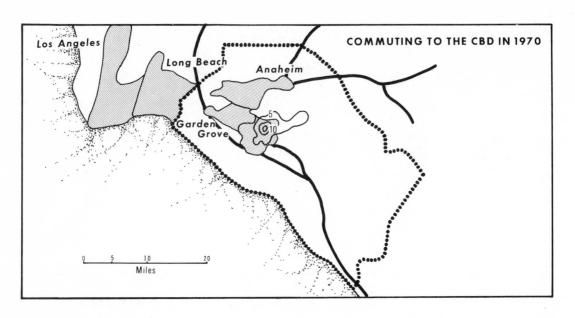

COMMUTING TO THE CBD IN 1970

Los Angeles

Long Beach

Anaheim

Garden
Grove

5

10

0   5   10   20
Miles

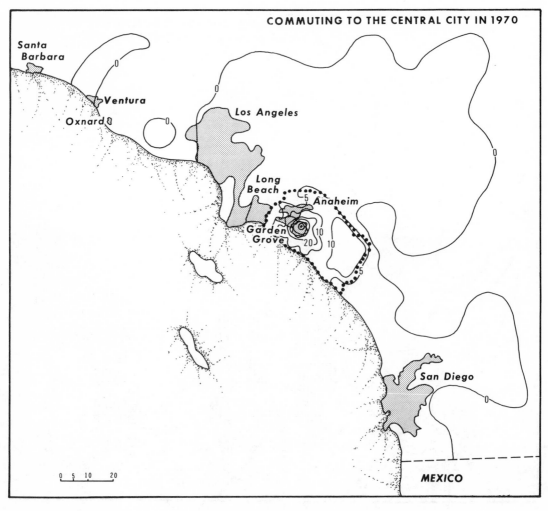

COMMUTING TO THE CENTRAL CITY IN 1970

Santa
Barbara

0

Ventura

0

Oxnard

0

Los Angeles

0

0

Long
Beach

5

Anaheim

Garden
Grove

10

20

10

5

0

San Diego

0

0   5   10   20

MEXICO

REVERSE COMMUTING,1960	REVERSE COMMUTING,1970	CHANGE IN REVERSE COMMUTING,1960–1970
NO DATA COLLECTED		NO DATA COLLECTED

90
80
70 60
80
70
70
70
80
70

0 1
Miles

SANTA ANA, CA.

CHANGE IN COMMUTING TO THE CENTRAL CITY,1960–1970

NO DATA COLLECTED

COMMUTING TO THE CBD IN 1970

NO DATA COLLECTED

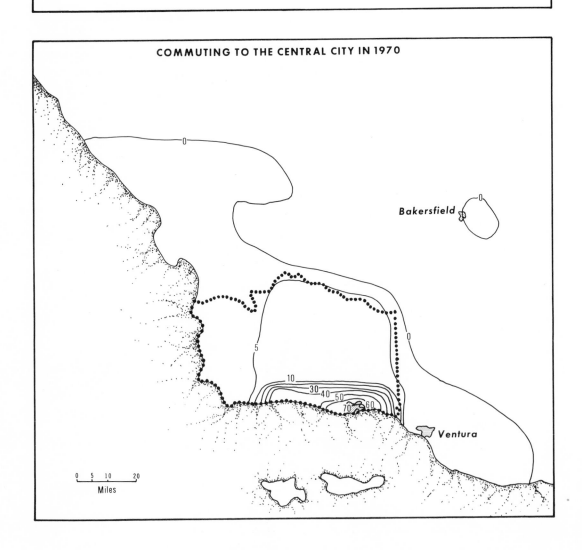

COMMUTING TO THE CENTRAL CITY IN 1970

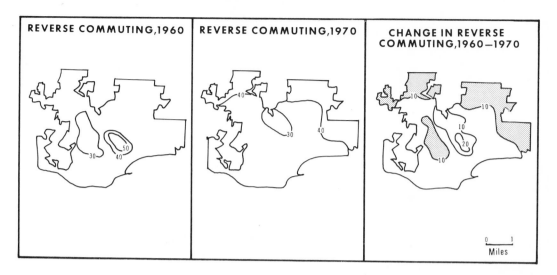

REVERSE COMMUTING, 1960

REVERSE COMMUTING, 1970

CHANGE IN REVERSE COMMUTING, 1960–1970

SANTA BARBARA, CA.

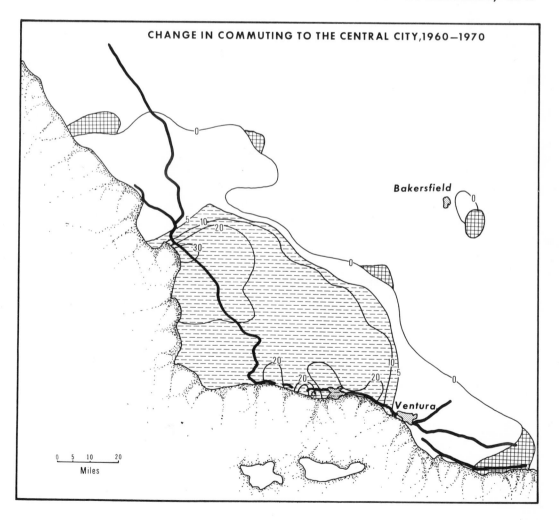

CHANGE IN COMMUTING TO THE CENTRAL CITY, 1960–1970

Bakersfield

Ventura

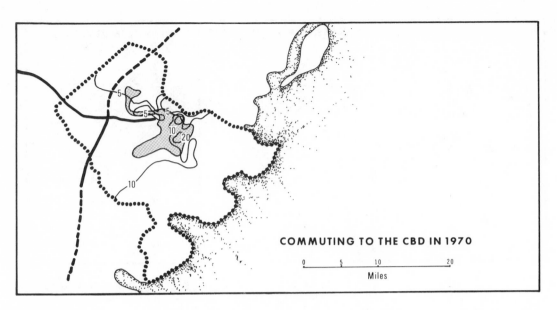

COMMUTING TO THE CBD IN 1970

0 5 10 20
Miles

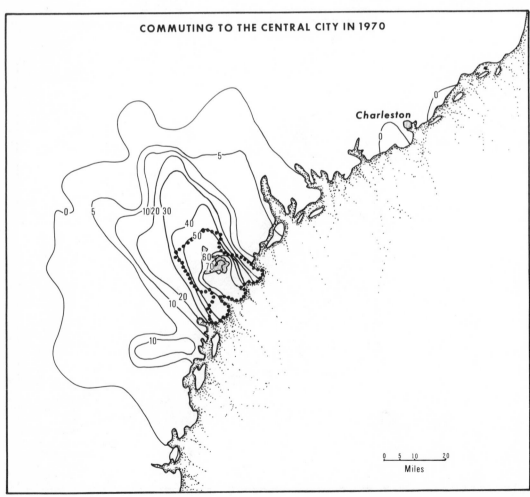

COMMUTING TO THE CENTRAL CITY IN 1970

Charleston

0 5 10 20
Miles

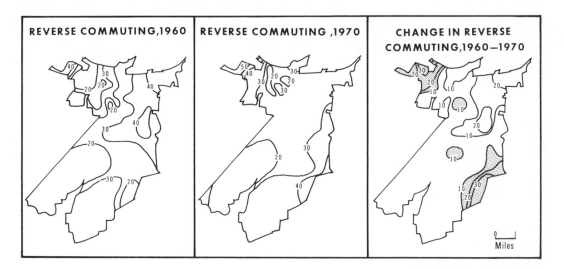

| REVERSE COMMUTING,1960 | REVERSE COMMUTING ,1970 | CHANGE IN REVERSE COMMUTING,1960—1970 |

SAVANNAH, GA.

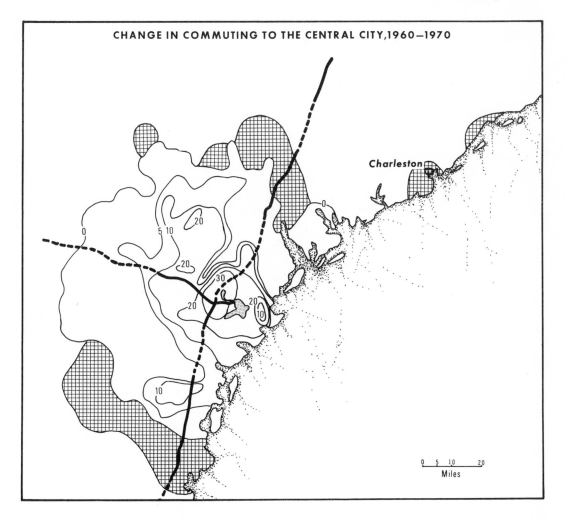

CHANGE IN COMMUTING TO THE CENTRAL CITY,1960—1970

Charleston

COMMUTING TO THE CBD IN 1970

NO DATA COLLECTED

COMMUTING TO THE CENTRAL CITY IN 1970

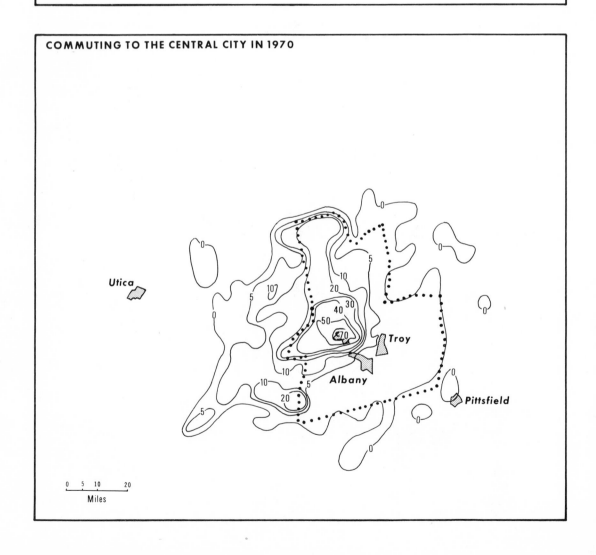

Utica

0

10

5

0

10

20

30

40

50

70

Troy

10

Albany

10

5

20

5

Pittsfield

0

0

0

0

5

0

0   5   10   20
Miles

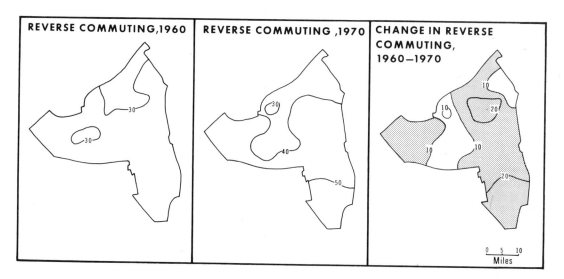

REVERSE COMMUTING,1960

REVERSE COMMUTING ,1970

CHANGE IN REVERSE COMMUTING, 1960—1970

0 5 10
Miles

SCHENECTADY, N.Y.

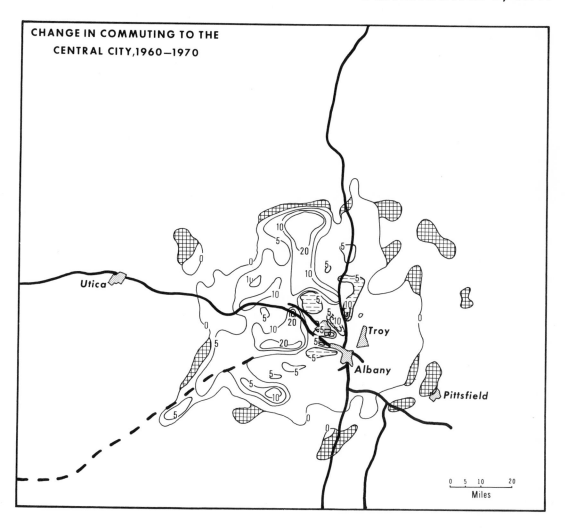

CHANGE IN COMMUTING TO THE CENTRAL CITY,1960—1970

Utica

Troy

Albany

Pittsfield

0 5 10   20
Miles

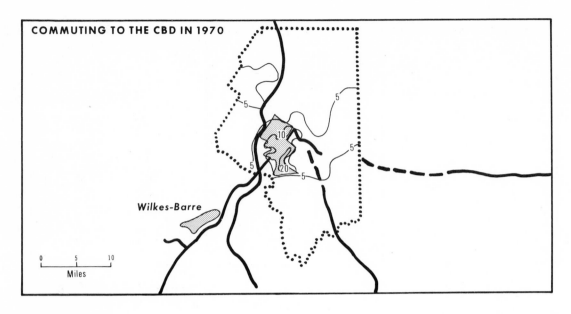

COMMUTING TO THE CBD IN 1970

Wilkes-Barre

0 5 10
Miles

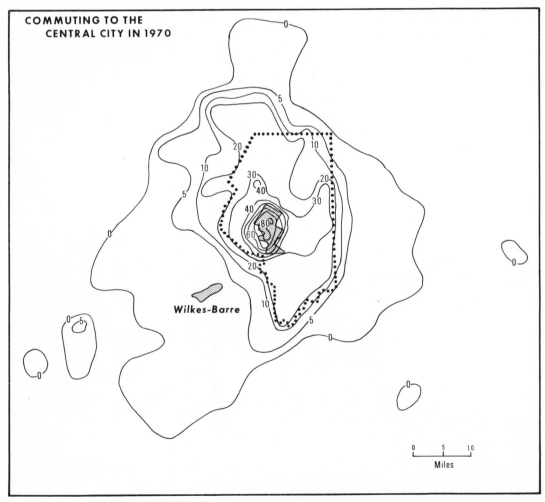

COMMUTING TO THE
CENTRAL CITY IN 1970

Wilkes-Barre

0 5 10
Miles

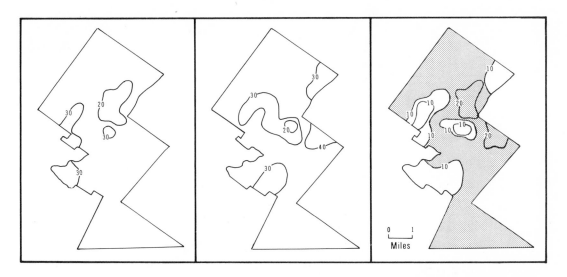

SCRANTON, PA.

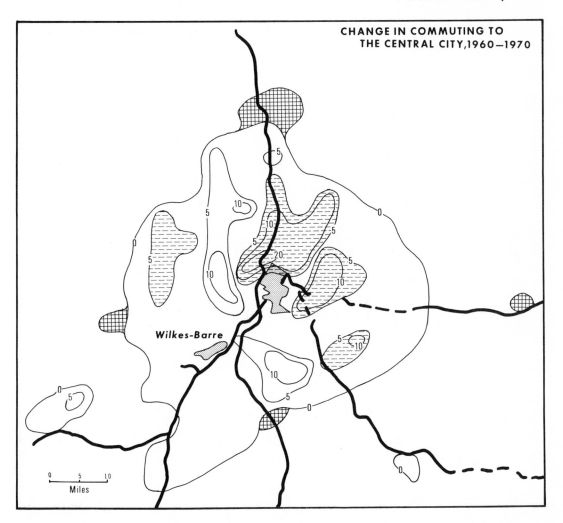

CHANGE IN COMMUTING TO THE CENTRAL CITY, 1960—1970

Wilkes-Barre

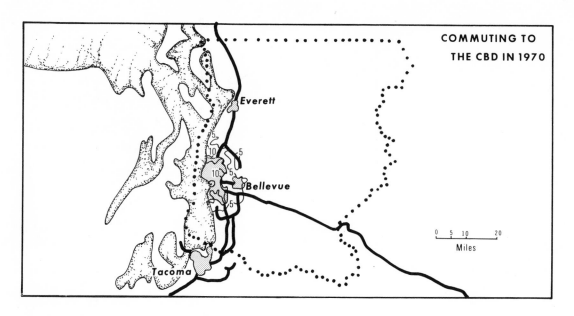

COMMUTING TO
THE CBD IN 1970

Everett

Bellevue

Tacoma

0 5 10 20
Miles

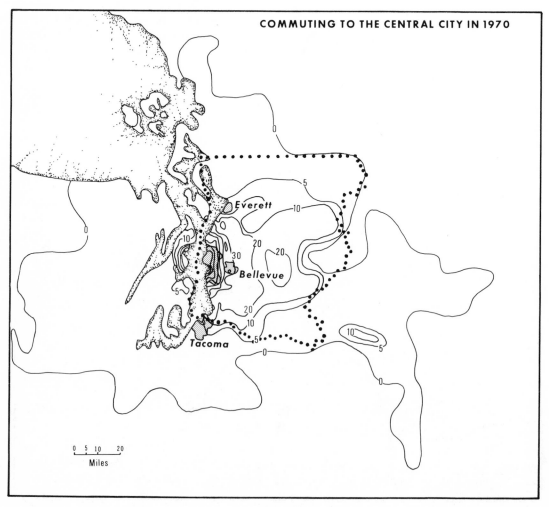

COMMUTING TO THE CENTRAL CITY IN 1970

Everett

Bellevue

Tacoma

0 5 10 20
Miles

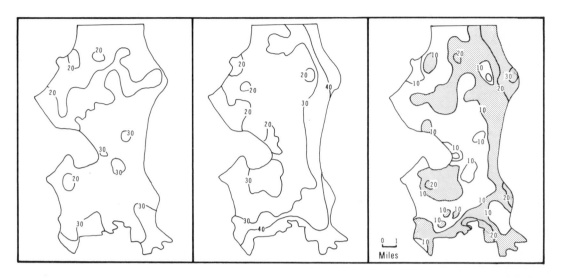

SEATTLE, WA.

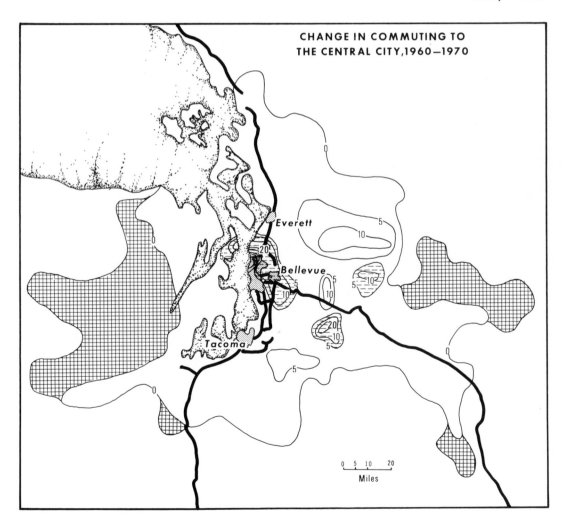

CHANGE IN COMMUTING TO
THE CENTRAL CITY, 1960—1970

594

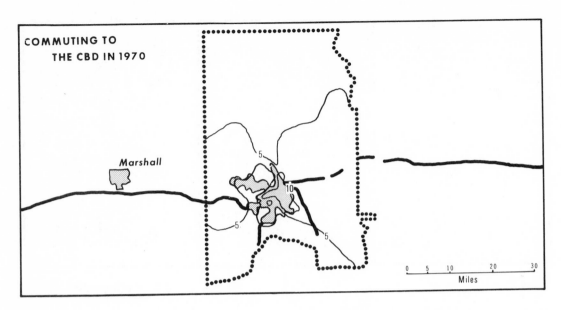

COMMUTING TO
THE CBD IN 1970

Marshall

0 5 10 20 30
Miles

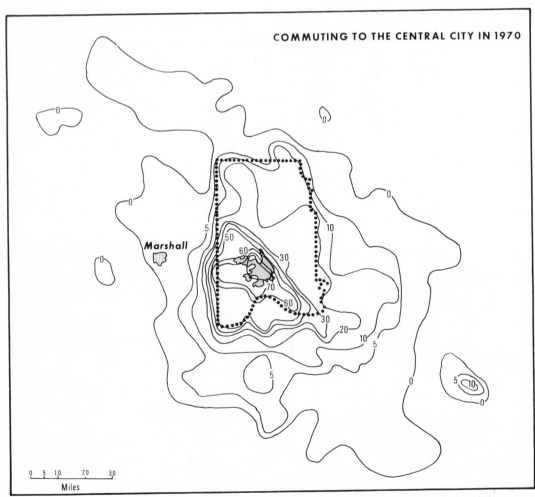

COMMUTING TO THE CENTRAL CITY IN 1970

Marshall

0 5 10 20 30
Miles

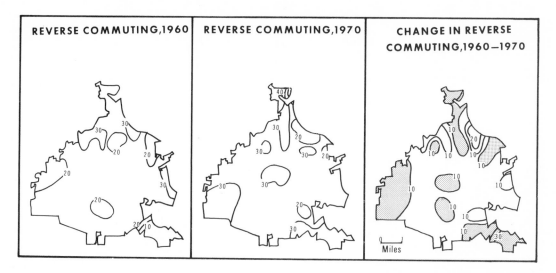

| REVERSE COMMUTING,1960 | REVERSE COMMUTING,1970 | CHANGE IN REVERSE COMMUTING,1960—1970 |

SHREVEPORT, LA.

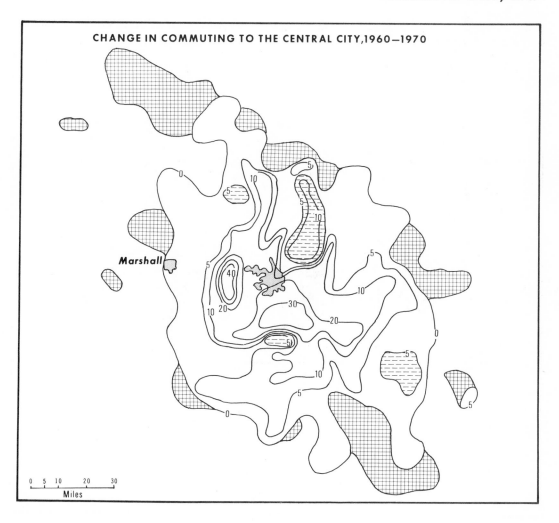

CHANGE IN COMMUTING TO THE CENTRAL CITY,1960—1970

Marshall

COMMUTING TO THE CBD IN 1970

NO DATA COLLECTED

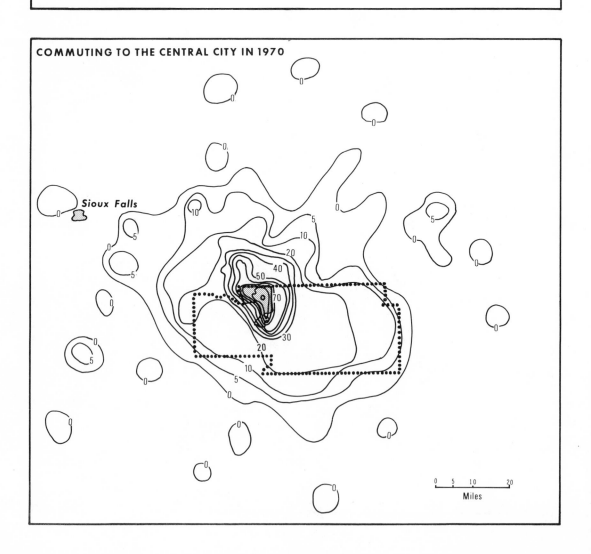

COMMUTING TO THE CENTRAL CITY IN 1970

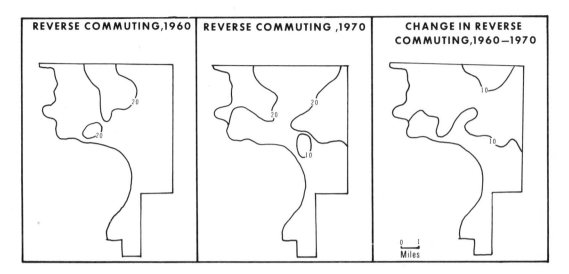

REVERSE COMMUTING, 1960

REVERSE COMMUTING, 1970

CHANGE IN REVERSE
COMMUTING, 1960—1970

SIOUX CITY, IA.

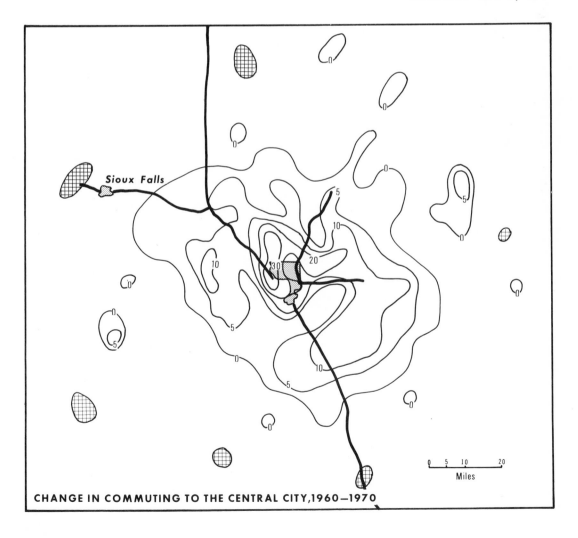

Sioux Falls

CHANGE IN COMMUTING TO THE CENTRAL CITY, 1960—1970

COMMUTING TO THE CBD IN 1970

NO DATA COLLECTED

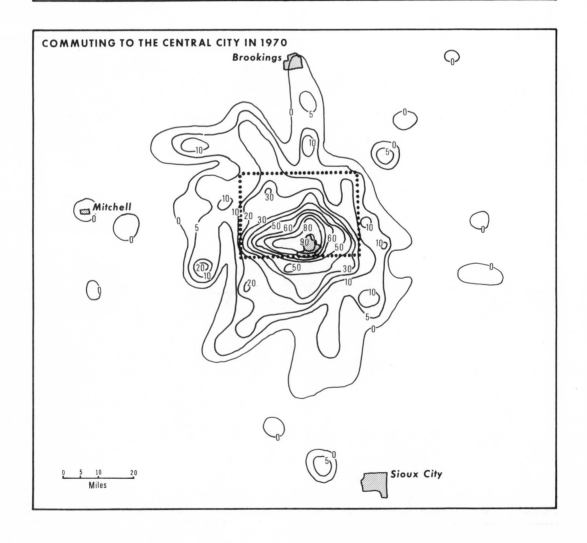

COMMUTING TO THE CENTRAL CITY IN 1970

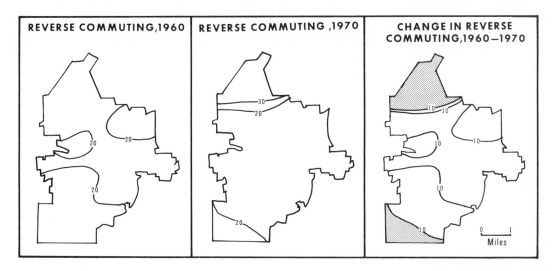

REVERSE COMMUTING,1960

REVERSE COMMUTING ,1970

CHANGE IN REVERSE
COMMUTING,1960—1970

SIOUX FALLS, S.D.

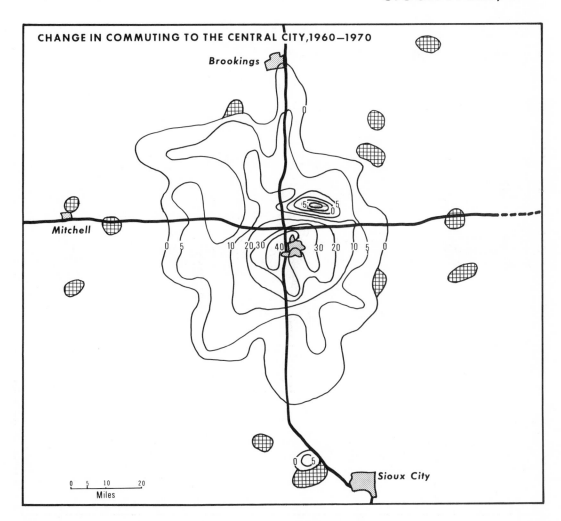

CHANGE IN COMMUTING TO THE CENTRAL CITY,1960—1970

Brookings

Mitchell

Sioux City

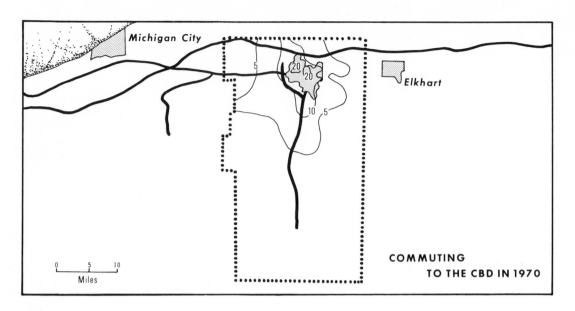

Michigan City

Elkhart

COMMUTING
TO THE CBD IN 1970

0   5   10
Miles

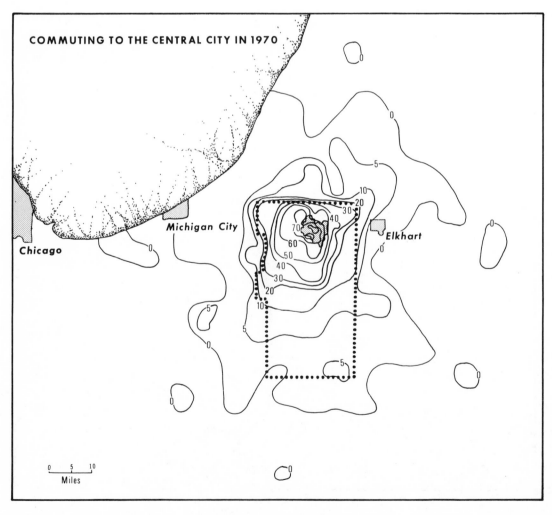

COMMUTING TO THE CENTRAL CITY IN 1970

Chicago

Michigan City

Elkhart

0   5   10
Miles

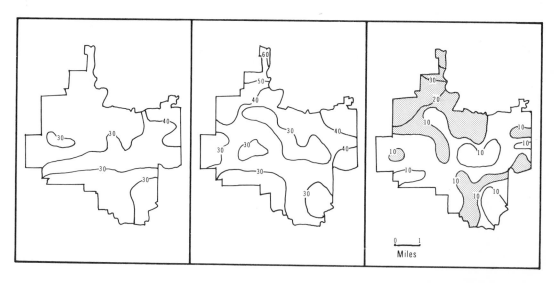

SOUTH BEND, IN.

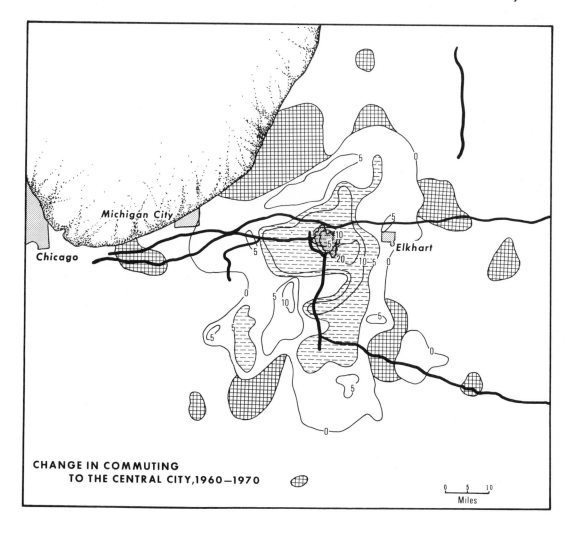

CHANGE IN COMMUTING TO THE CENTRAL CITY, 1960–1970

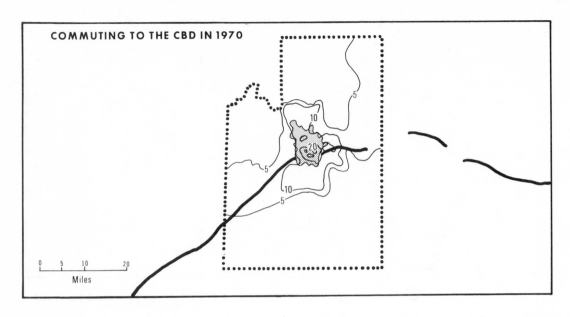

COMMUTING TO THE CBD IN 1970

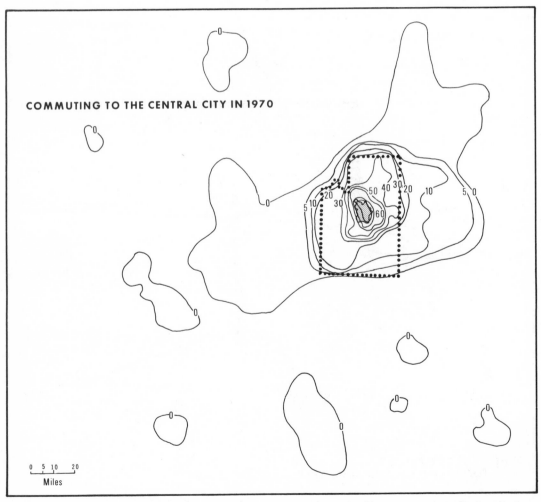

COMMUTING TO THE CENTRAL CITY IN 1970

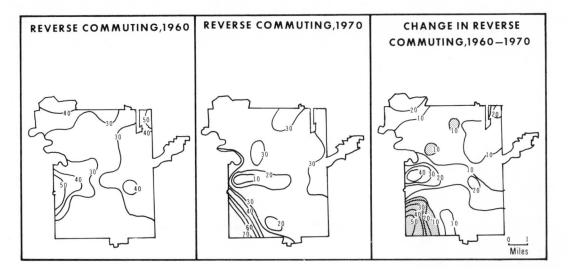

REVERSE COMMUTING, 1960

REVERSE COMMUTING, 1970

CHANGE IN REVERSE COMMUTING, 1960—1970

SPOKANE, WA.

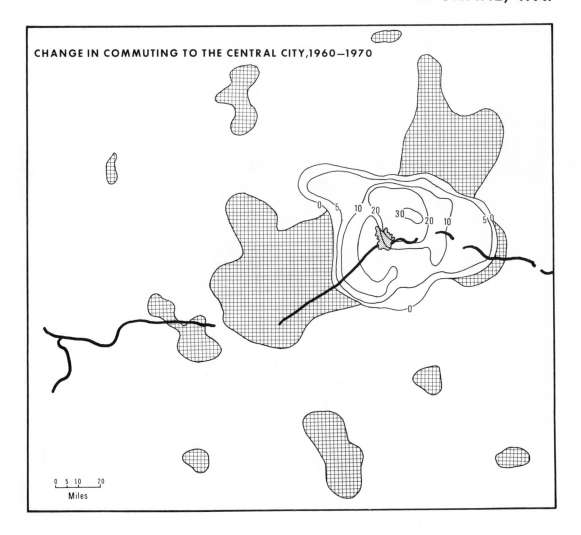

CHANGE IN COMMUTING TO THE CENTRAL CITY, 1960—1970

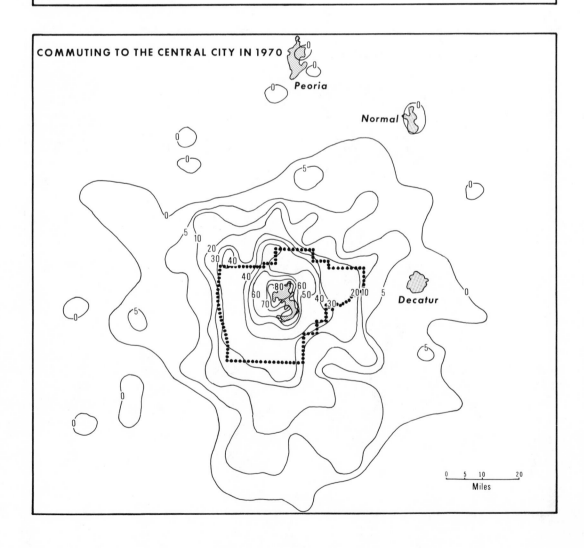

COMMUTING TO THE CBD IN 1970

NO DATA COLLECTED

COMMUTING TO THE CENTRAL CITY IN 1970

Peoria

Normal

Decatur

0 5 10   20
Miles

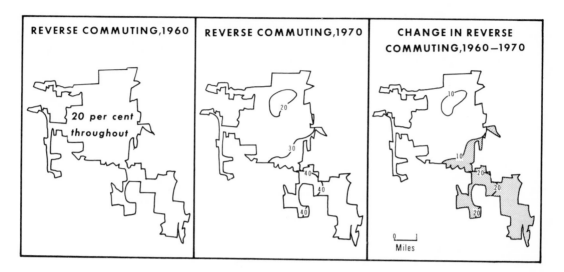

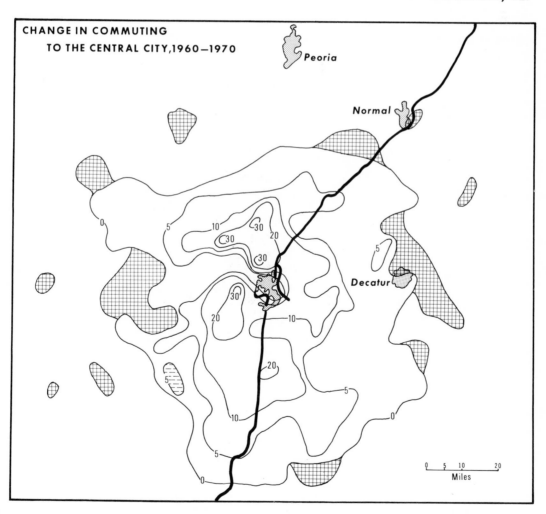

SPRINGFIELD, IL.

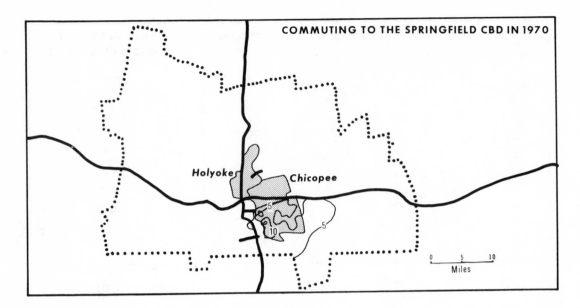

COMMUTING TO THE SPRINGFIELD CBD IN 1970

Holyoke   Chicopee

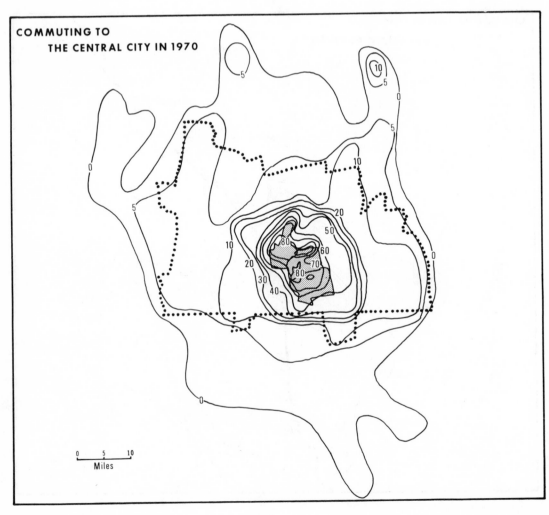

COMMUTING TO
THE CENTRAL CITY IN 1970

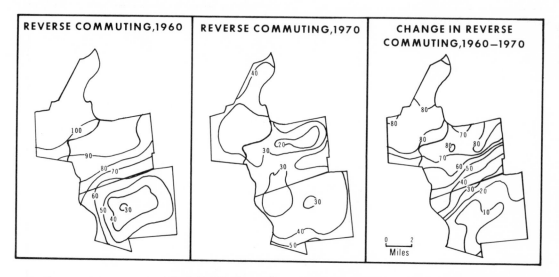

REVERSE COMMUTING, 1960

REVERSE COMMUTING, 1970

CHANGE IN REVERSE COMMUTING, 1960–1970

SPRINGFIELD - CHICOPEE - HOLYOKE, MA.

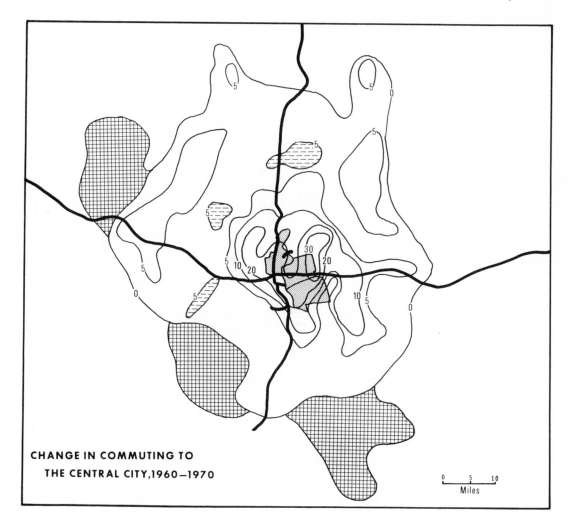

CHANGE IN COMMUTING TO THE CENTRAL CITY, 1960–1970

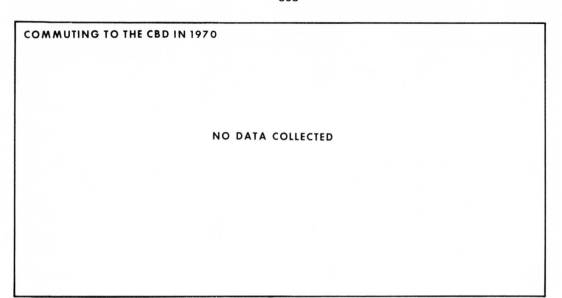

COMMUTING TO THE CBD IN 1970

NO DATA COLLECTED

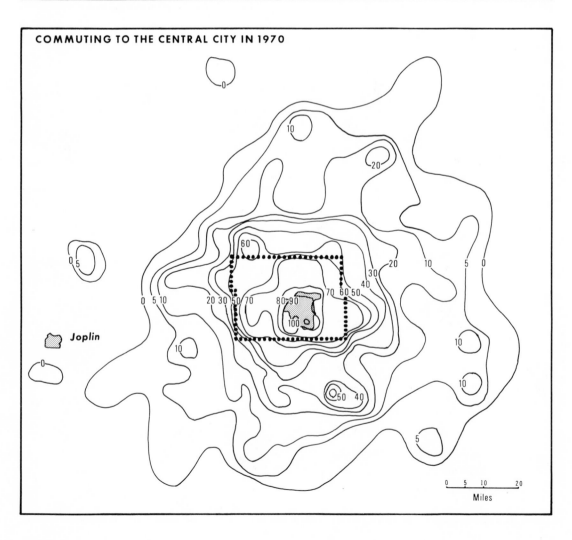

COMMUTING TO THE CENTRAL CITY IN 1970

Joplin

0   5   10   20
Miles

609

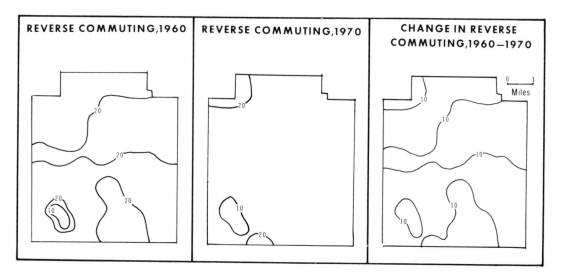

SPRINGFIELD, MO.

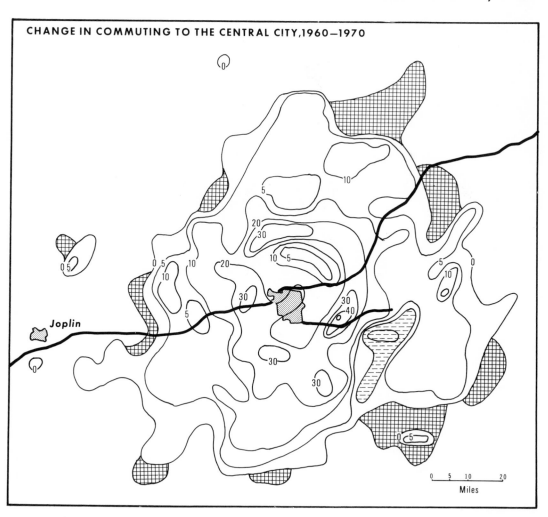

COMMUTING TO THE CBD IN 1970

NO DATA COLLECTED

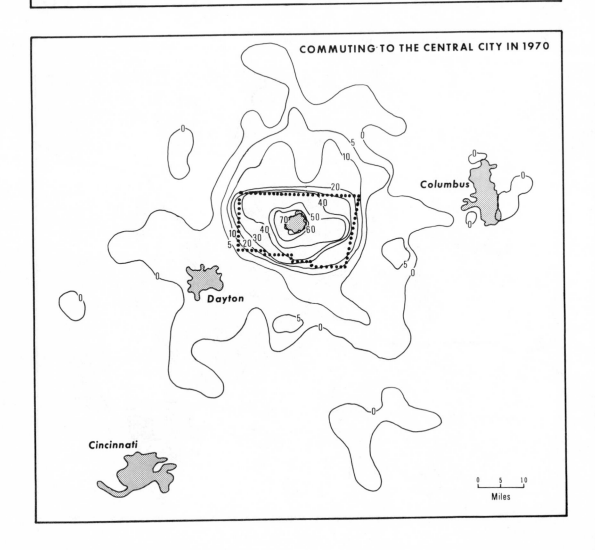

COMMUTING TO THE CENTRAL CITY IN 1970

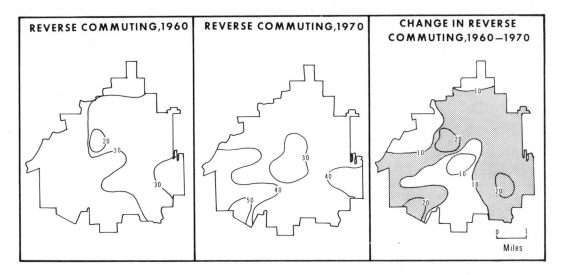

| REVERSE COMMUTING, 1960 | REVERSE COMMUTING, 1970 | CHANGE IN REVERSE COMMUTING, 1960–1970 |

SPRINGFIELD, OH.

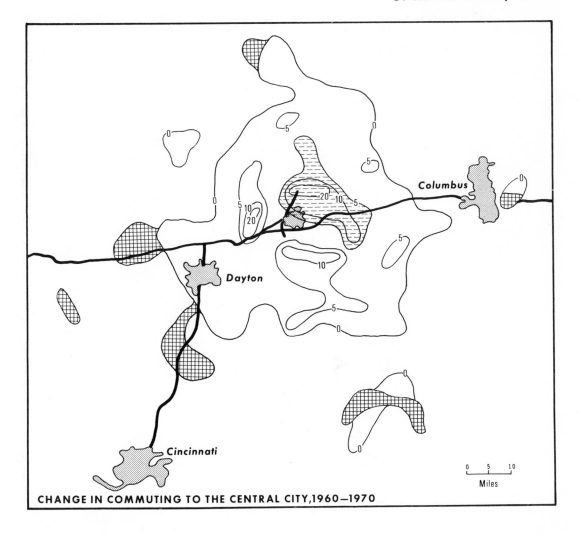

CHANGE IN COMMUTING TO THE CENTRAL CITY, 1960–1970

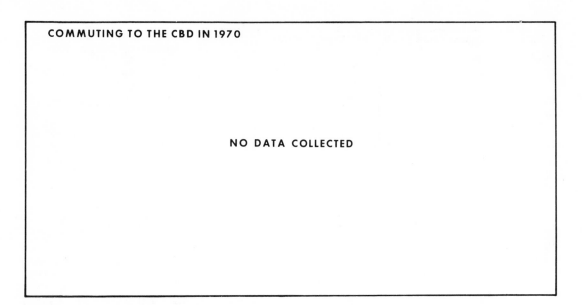

COMMUTING TO THE CBD IN 1970

NO DATA COLLECTED

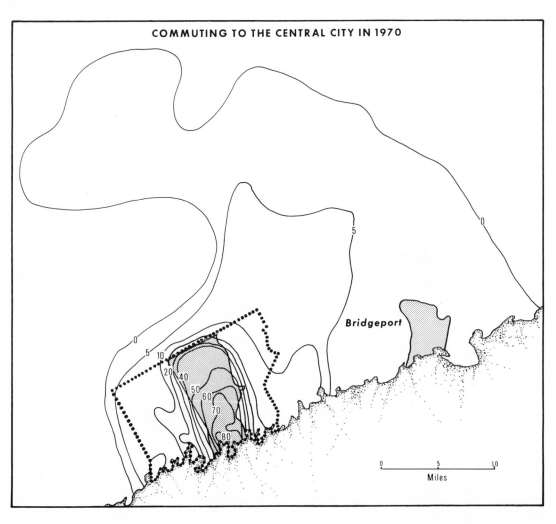

COMMUTING TO THE CENTRAL CITY IN 1970

Bridgeport

0
5
10
20
40
50
60
70
80

0   5   10
Miles

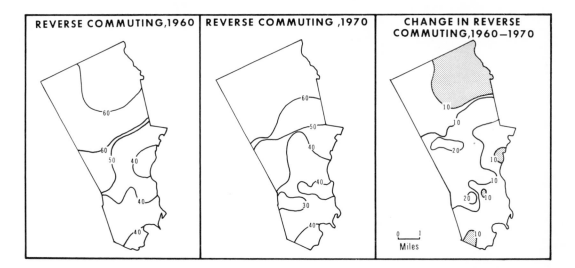

REVERSE COMMUTING,1960

REVERSE COMMUTING ,1970

CHANGE IN REVERSE COMMUTING,1960—1970

Miles

STAMFORD, CT.

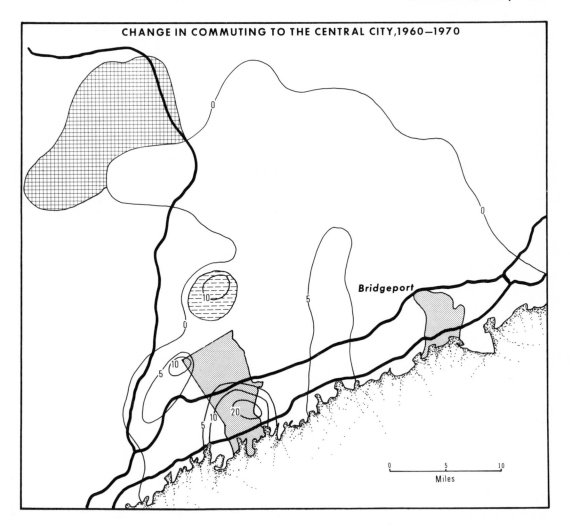

CHANGE IN COMMUTING TO THE CENTRAL CITY,1960—1970

Bridgeport

Miles

COMMUTING TO THE CBD IN 1970

NO DATA COLLECTED

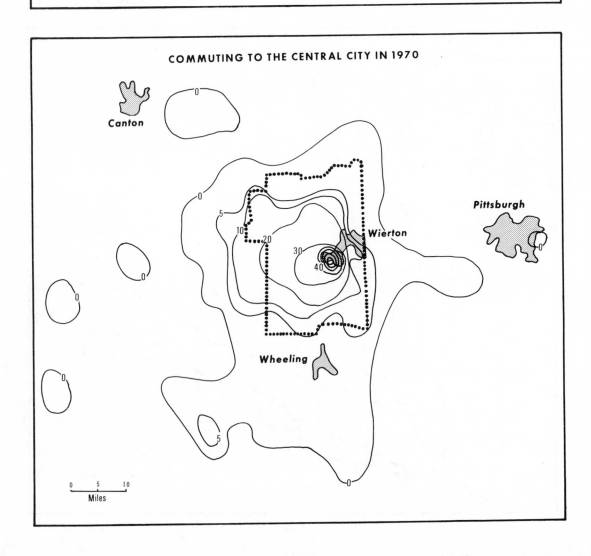

COMMUTING TO THE CENTRAL CITY IN 1970

Canton

Pittsburgh

Wierton

Wheeling

0 5 10
Miles

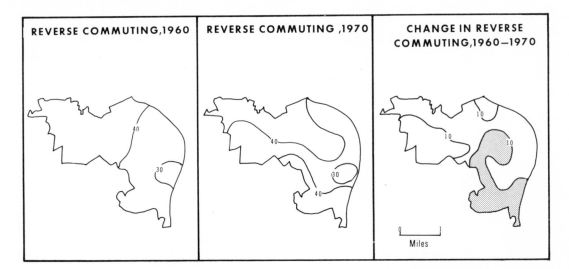

| REVERSE COMMUTING,1960 | REVERSE COMMUTING ,1970 | CHANGE IN REVERSE COMMUTING,1960–1970 |

STEUBENVILLE, OH.

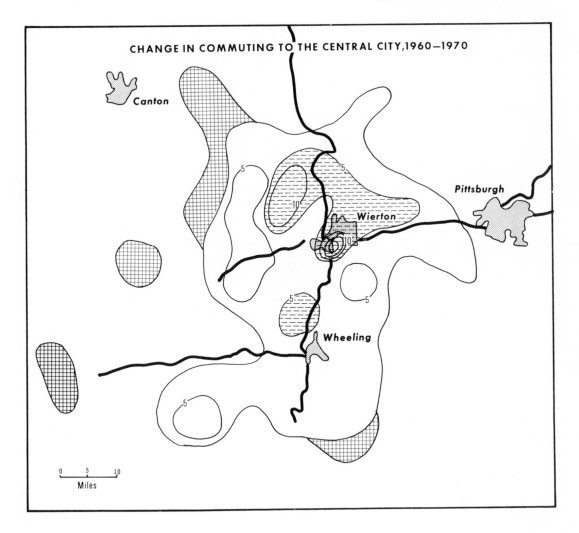

CHANGE IN COMMUTING TO THE CENTRAL CITY,1960–1970

Canton

Pittsburgh

Wierton

Wheeling

COMMUTING TO THE CBD IN 1970

NO DATA COLLECTED

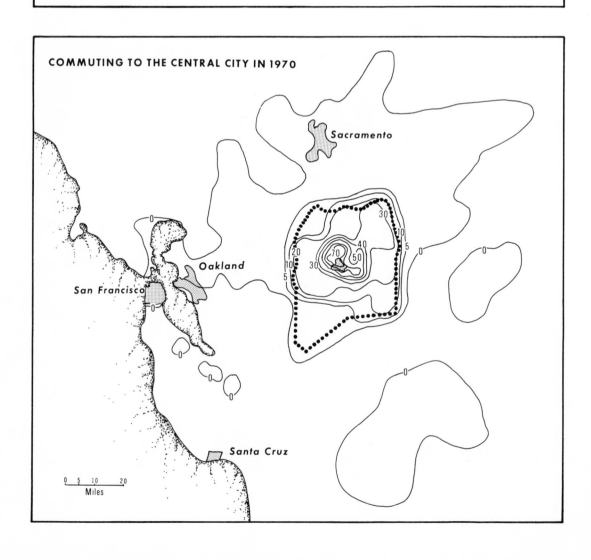

COMMUTING TO THE CENTRAL CITY IN 1970

Sacramento

Oakland

San Francisco

Santa Cruz

0 5 10   20
Miles

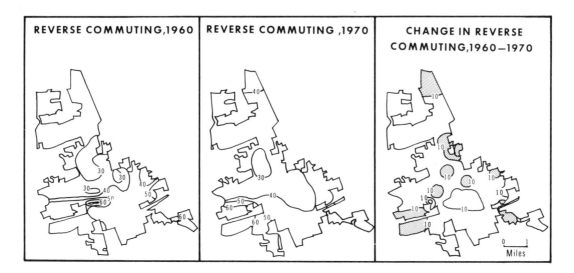

REVERSE COMMUTING,1960

REVERSE COMMUTING ,1970

CHANGE IN REVERSE
COMMUTING,1960—1970

STOCKTON, CA.

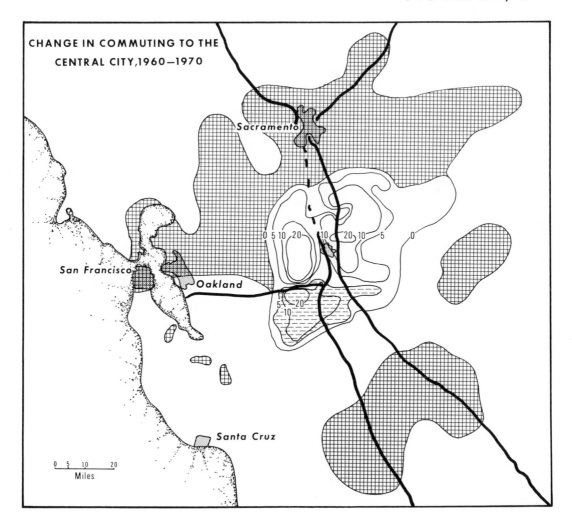

CHANGE IN COMMUTING TO THE
CENTRAL CITY,1960—1970

COMMUTING TO THE CBD IN 1970

NO DATA COLLECTED

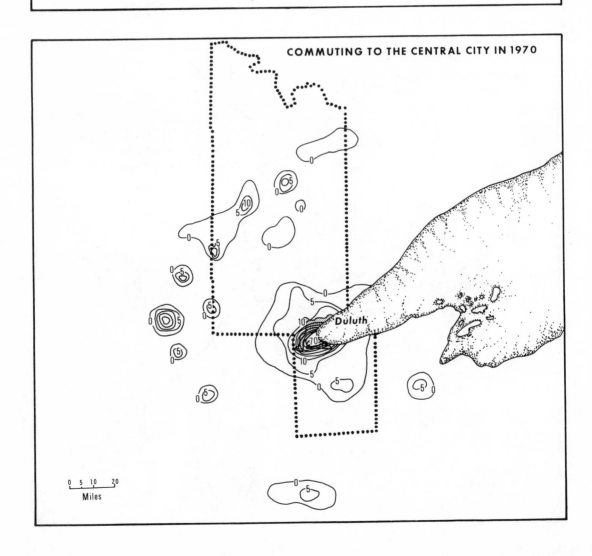

COMMUTING TO THE CENTRAL CITY IN 1970

Duluth

0 5 10   20
Miles

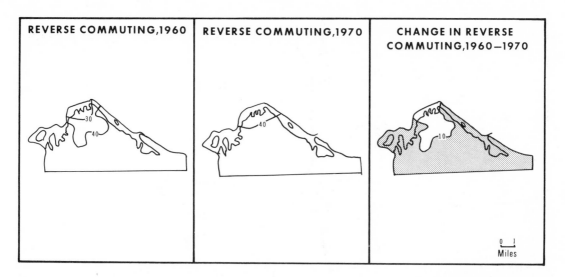

| REVERSE COMMUTING,1960 | REVERSE COMMUTING,1970 | CHANGE IN REVERSE COMMUTING,1960—1970 |

SUPERIOR, WI.

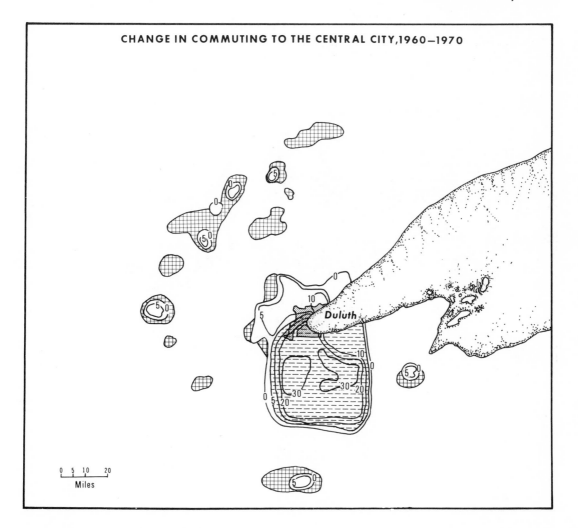

CHANGE IN COMMUTING TO THE CENTRAL CITY,1960—1970

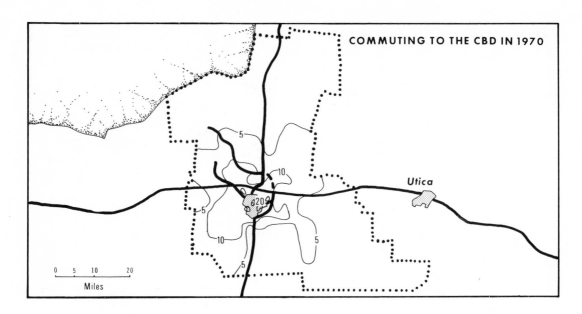

COMMUTING TO THE CBD IN 1970

Utica

5

10

20

5

10

5

5

0   5 10   20
Miles

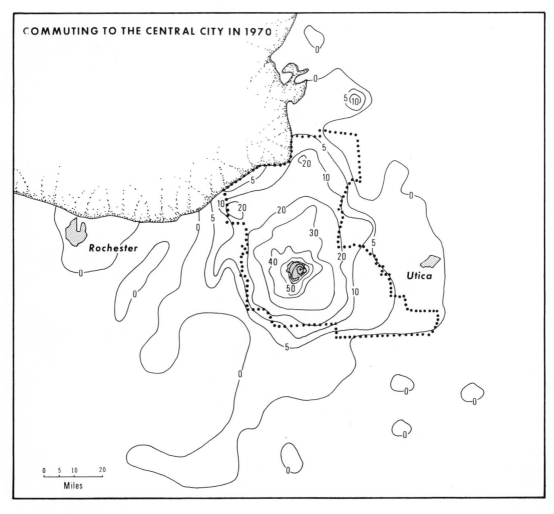

COMMUTING TO THE CENTRAL CITY IN 1970

0

5 10

0

5

20

10

0

5

10

20

5

0

5

20

20

30

20

0

40

Rochester

Utica

0

50

10

0

5

0

0

0

0

0

0   5 10   20
Miles

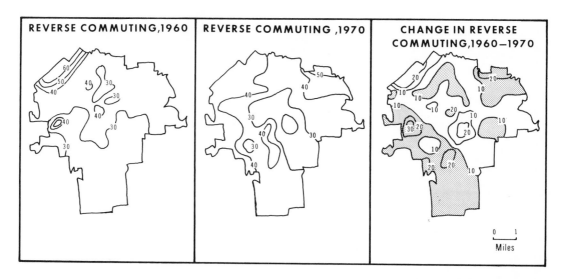

SYRACUSE, N.Y.

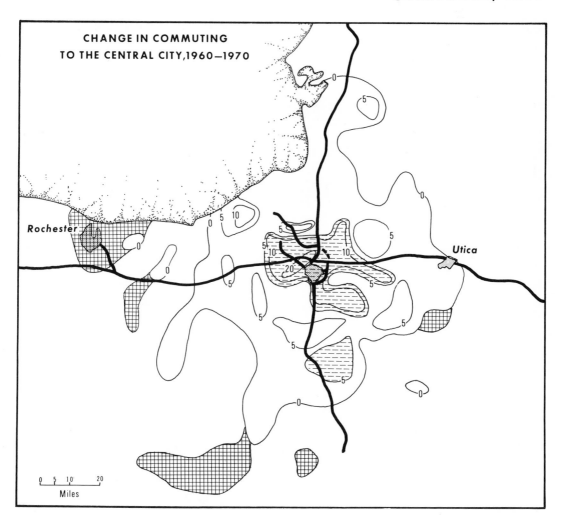

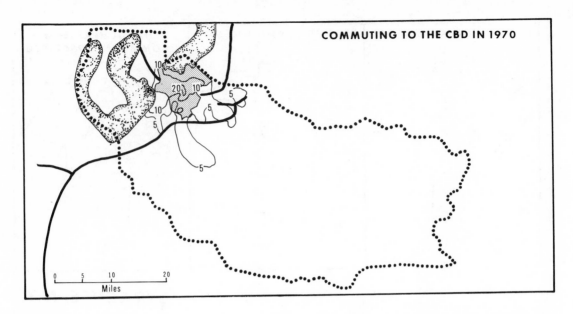

COMMUTING TO THE CBD IN 1970

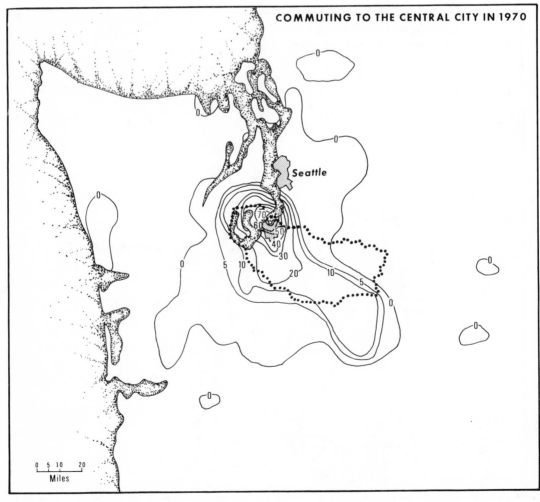

COMMUTING TO THE CENTRAL CITY IN 1970

Seattle

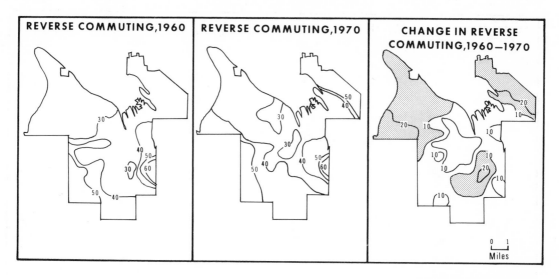

REVERSE COMMUTING, 1960

REVERSE COMMUTING, 1970

CHANGE IN REVERSE
COMMUTING, 1960—1970

TACOMA, WA.

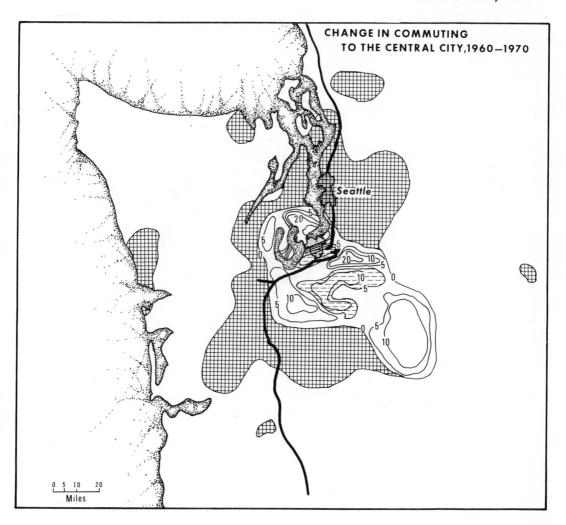

CHANGE IN COMMUTING
TO THE CENTRAL CITY, 1960—1970

Seattle

COMMUTING TO THE CBD IN 1970

NO DATA COLLECTED

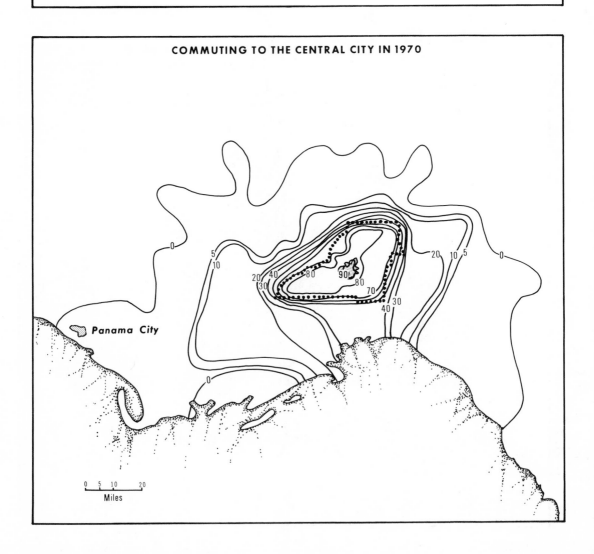

COMMUTING TO THE CENTRAL CITY IN 1970

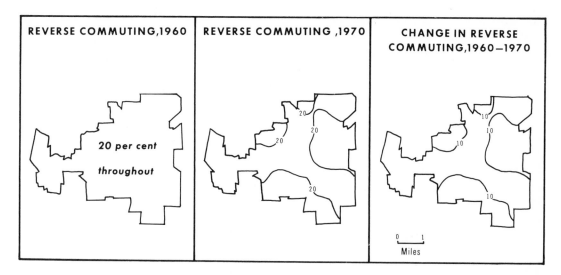

REVERSE COMMUTING, 1960

REVERSE COMMUTING, 1970

CHANGE IN REVERSE COMMUTING, 1960–1970

20 per cent throughout

TALLAHASSEE, FL.

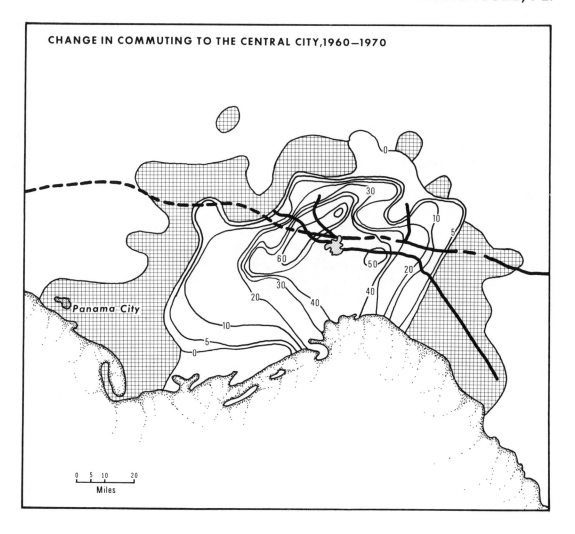

CHANGE IN COMMUTING TO THE CENTRAL CITY, 1960–1970

Panama City

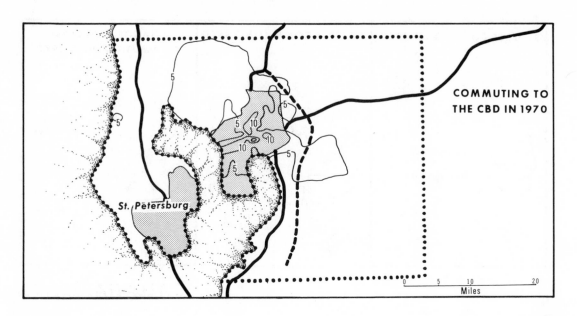

COMMUTING TO
THE CBD IN 1970

St. Petersburg

0   5   10   20
Miles

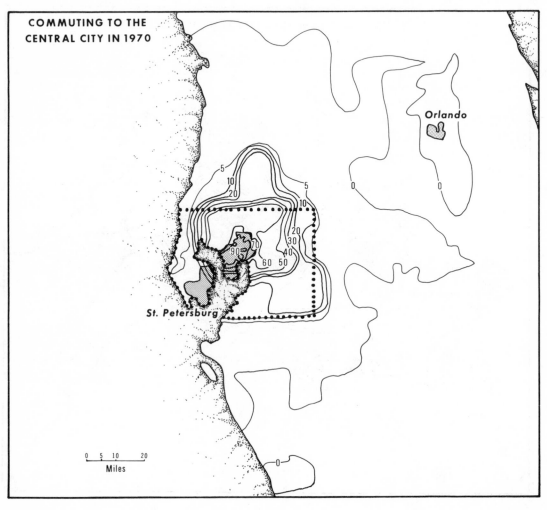

COMMUTING TO THE
CENTRAL CITY IN 1970

Orlando

St. Petersburg

0   5 10   20
Miles

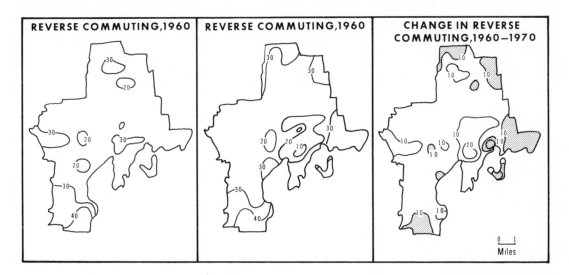

REVERSE COMMUTING,1960   REVERSE COMMUTING,1960   CHANGE IN REVERSE
COMMUTING,1960—1970

0   1
Miles

TAMPA, FL.

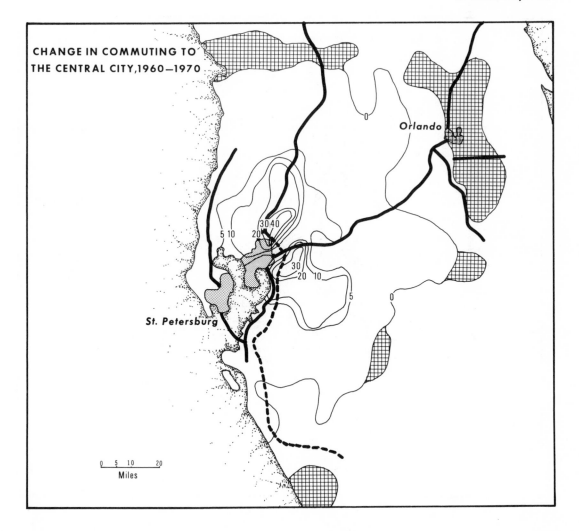

CHANGE IN COMMUTING TO
THE CENTRAL CITY,1960—1970

Orlando

St. Petersburg

0   5   10   20
Miles

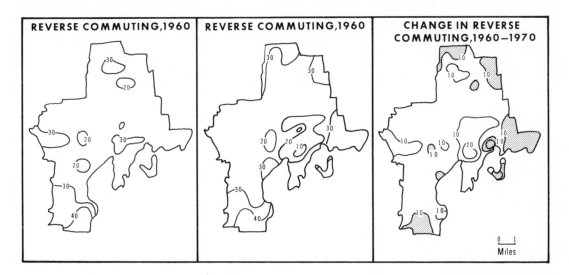

REVERSE COMMUTING,1960   REVERSE COMMUTING,1960   CHANGE IN REVERSE COMMUTING,1960—1970

0   1
Miles

TAMPA, FL.

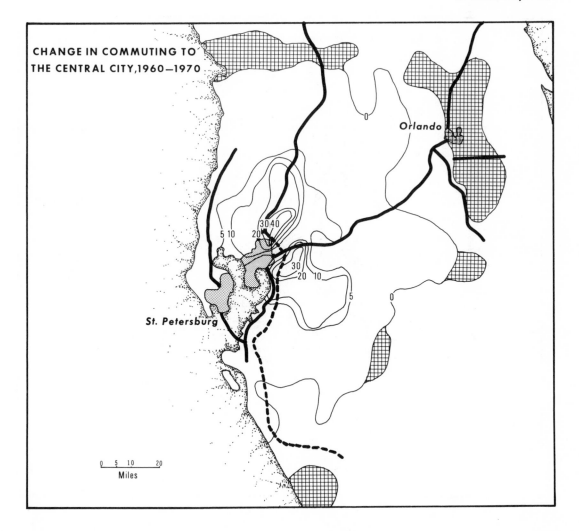

CHANGE IN COMMUTING TO
THE CENTRAL CITY,1960—1970

Orlando

St. Petersburg

0   5   10   20
Miles

COMMUTING TO THE CBD IN 1970

NO DATA COLLECTED

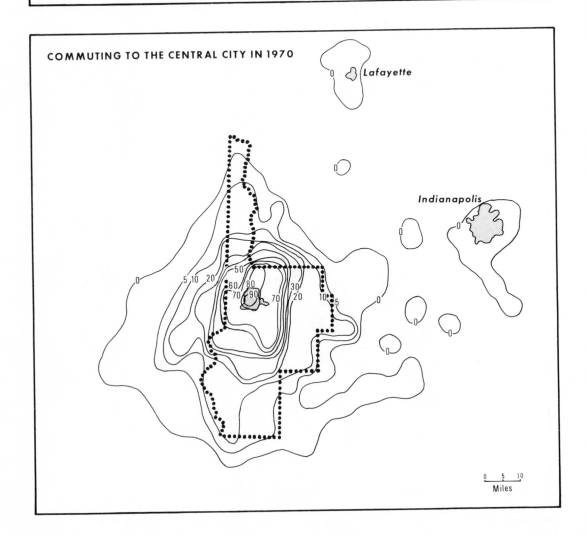

COMMUTING TO THE CENTRAL CITY IN 1970

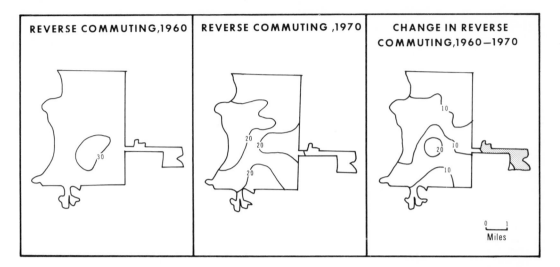

| REVERSE COMMUTING,1960 | REVERSE COMMUTING ,1970 | CHANGE IN REVERSE COMMUTING,1960—1970 |

TERRE HAUTE, IN.

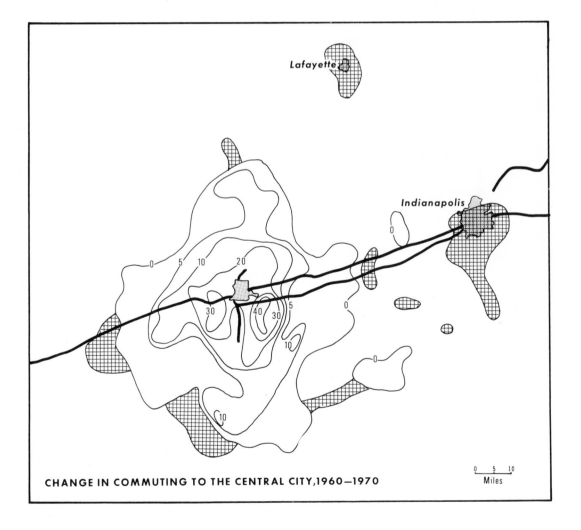

CHANGE IN COMMUTING TO THE CENTRAL CITY,1960—1970

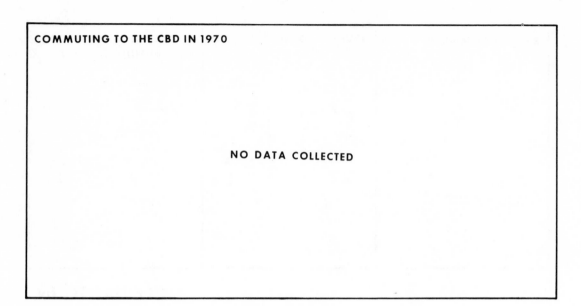

COMMUTING TO THE CBD IN 1970

NO DATA COLLECTED

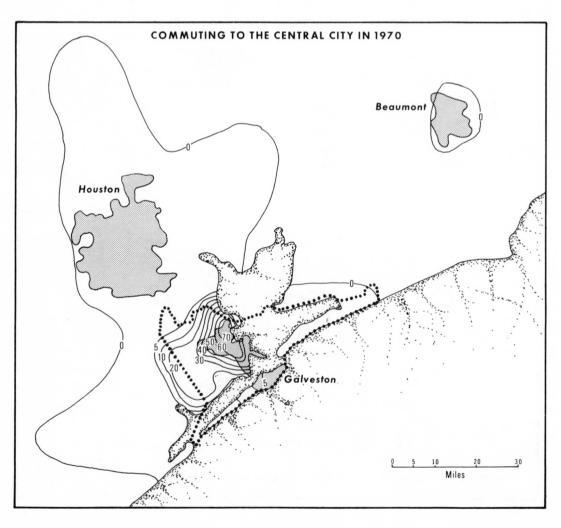

COMMUTING TO THE CENTRAL CITY IN 1970

Beaumont

Houston

Galveston

5   10   20   30
Miles

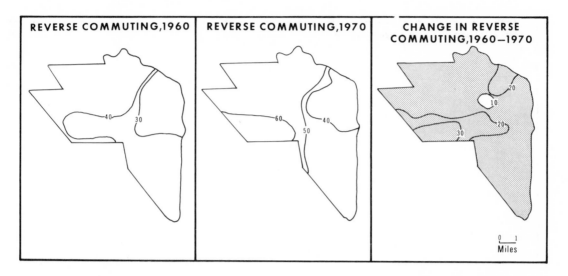

REVERSE COMMUTING,1960

REVERSE COMMUTING,1970

CHANGE IN REVERSE
COMMUTING,1960—1970

0   1
Miles

TEXAS CITY, TX.

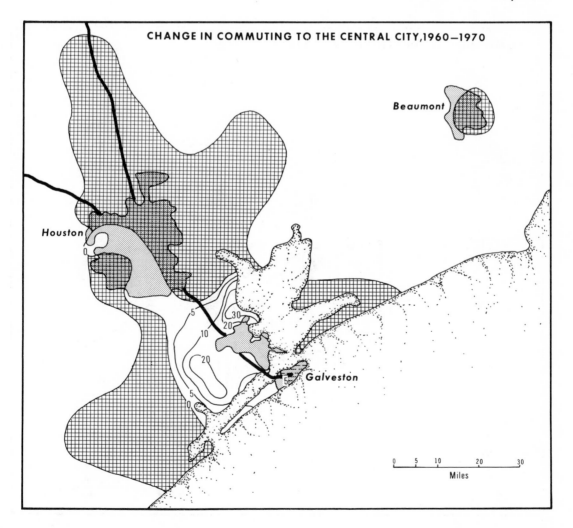

CHANGE IN COMMUTING TO THE CENTRAL CITY,1960—1970

Beaumont

Houston

Galveston

0   5   10   20   30
Miles

COMMUTING TO THE CBD IN 1970

NO DATA COLLECTED

COMMUTING TO THE CENTRAL CITY IN 1970

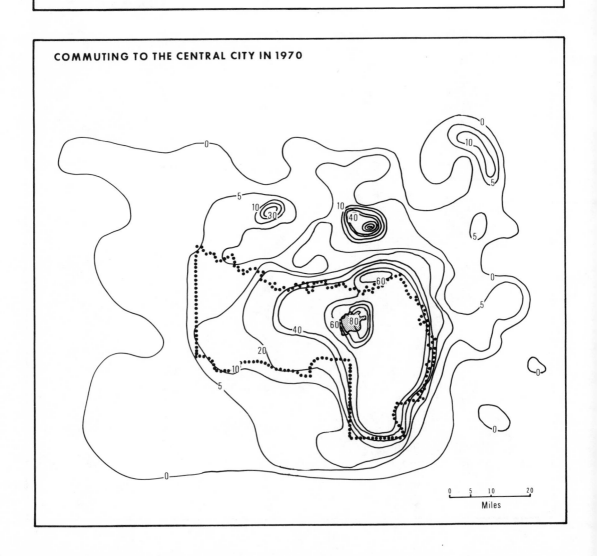

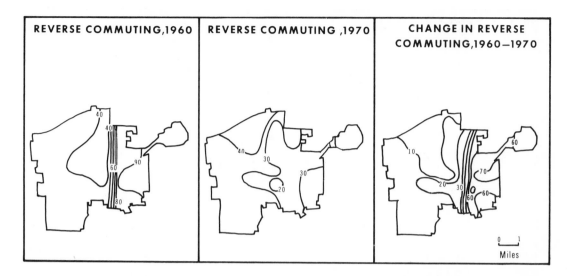

REVERSE COMMUTING,1960   REVERSE COMMUTING ,1970   CHANGE IN REVERSE COMMUTING,1960—1970

TEXARKANA, AR.

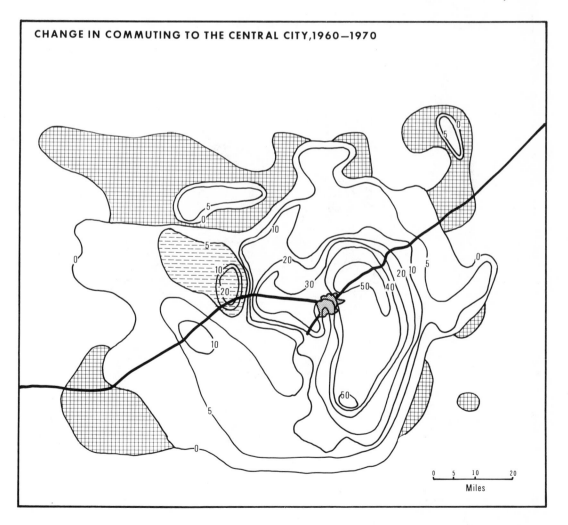

CHANGE IN COMMUTING TO THE CENTRAL CITY,1960—1970

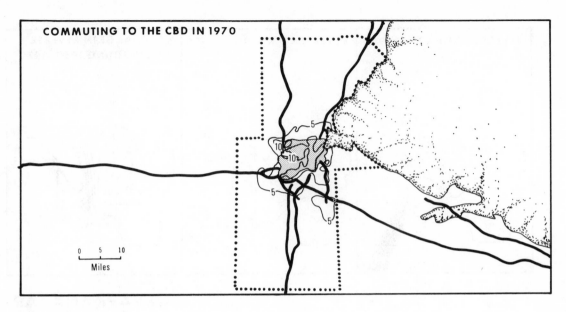

COMMUTING TO THE CBD IN 1970

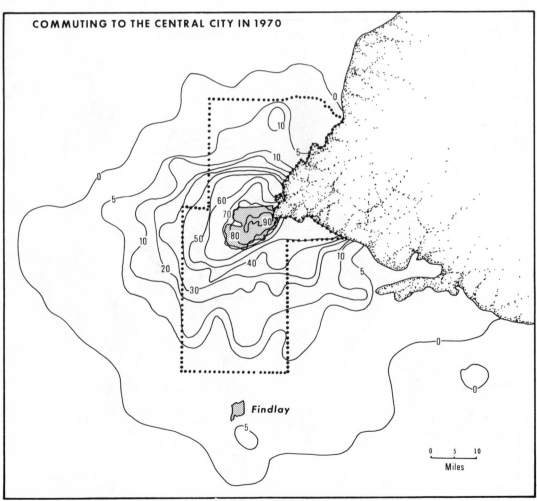

COMMUTING TO THE CENTRAL CITY IN 1970

Findlay

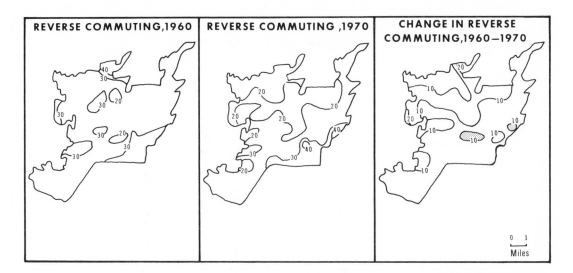

| REVERSE COMMUTING,1960 | REVERSE COMMUTING ,1970 | CHANGE IN REVERSE COMMUTING,1960—1970 |

TOLEDO, OH.

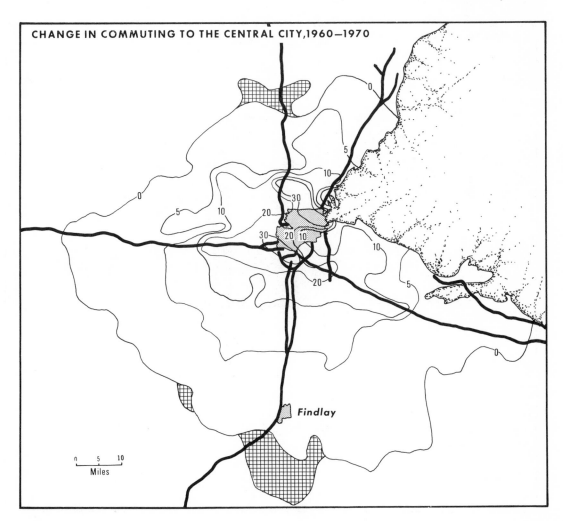

CHANGE IN COMMUTING TO THE CENTRAL CITY,1960—1970

Findlay

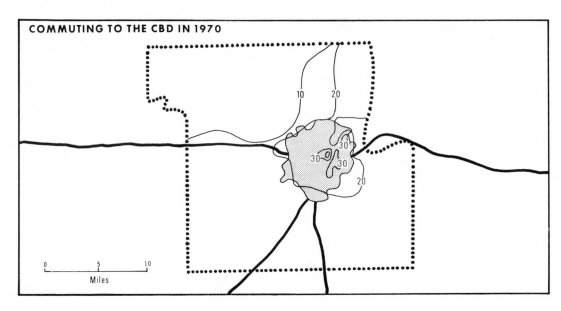

COMMUTING TO THE CBD IN 1970

10   20

30

30   30

20

0   5   10
Miles

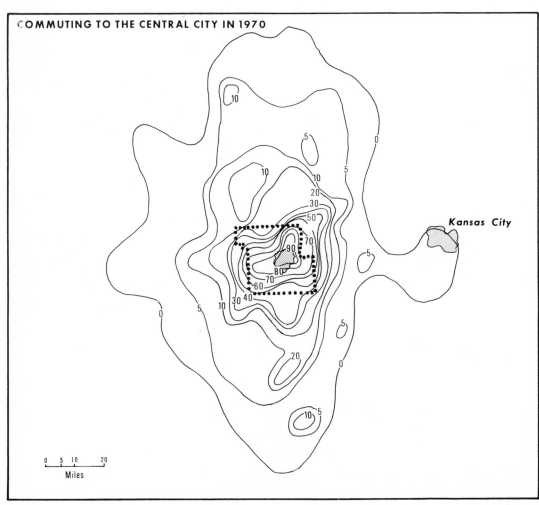

COMMUTING TO THE CENTRAL CITY IN 1970

10

5

0

10

10

20

30

50

70

90

80

70

60

40

30

10   30

5

0

20

0

5

10   5

Kansas City

5

0   5   10   20
Miles

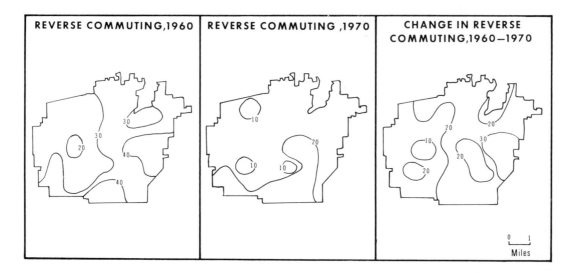

REVERSE COMMUTING,1960

REVERSE COMMUTING ,1970

CHANGE IN REVERSE
COMMUTING,1960—1970

TOPEKA, KS.

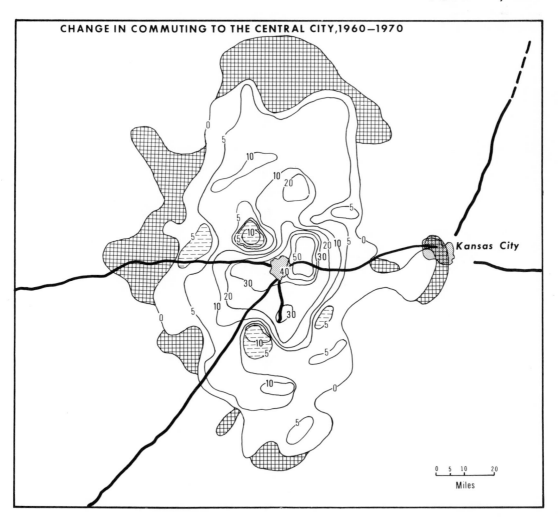

CHANGE IN COMMUTING TO THE CENTRAL CITY,1960—1970

Kansas City

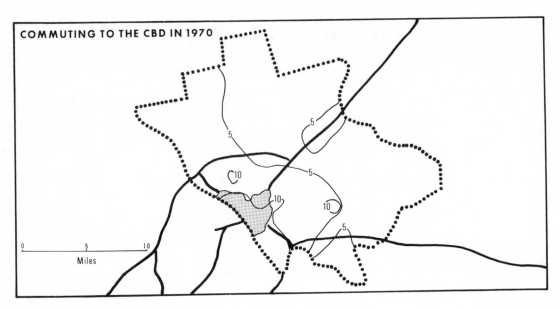

COMMUTING TO THE CBD IN 1970

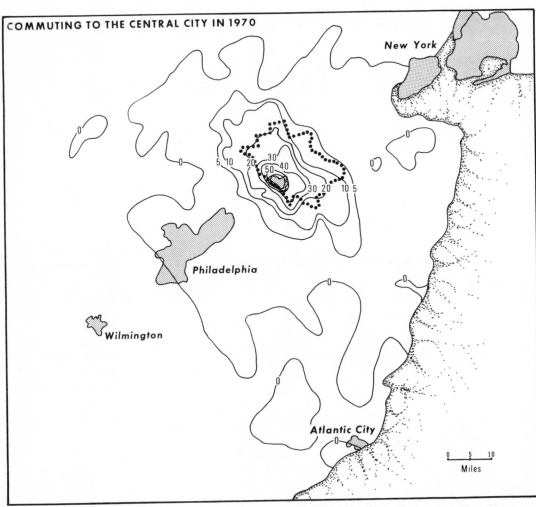

COMMUTING TO THE CENTRAL CITY IN 1970

New York

Philadelphia

Wilmington

Atlantic City

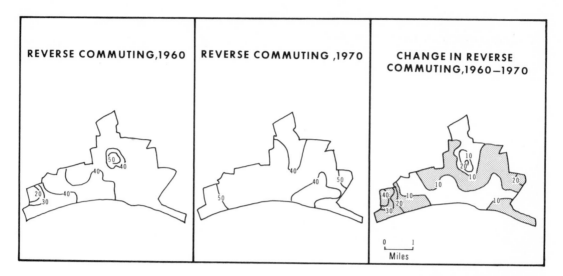

TRENTON, N.J.

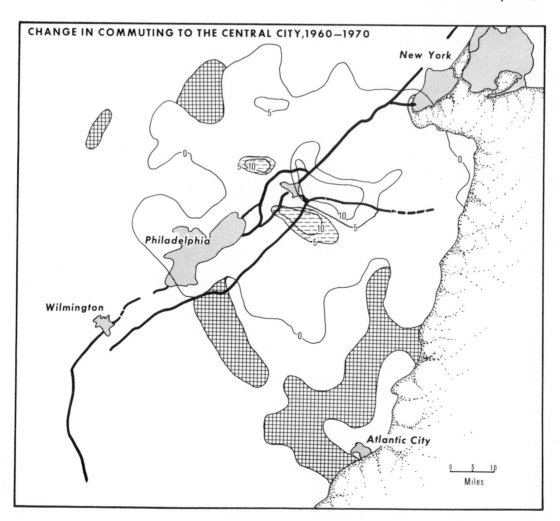

COMMUTING TO THE CBD IN 1970

NO DATA COLLECTED

COMMUTING TO THE CENTRAL CITY IN 1970

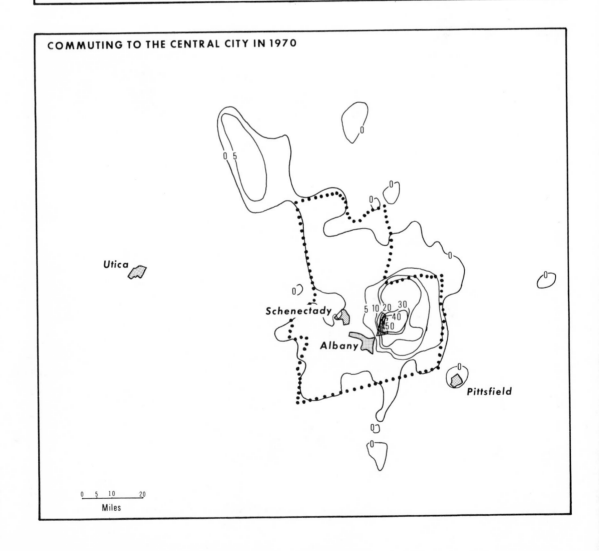

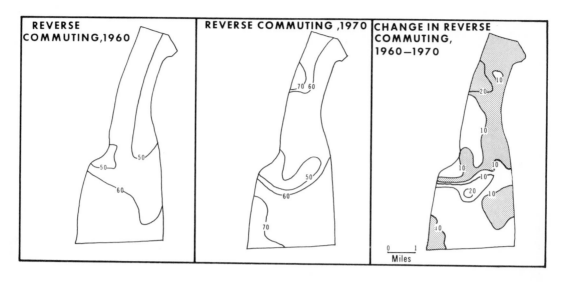

REVERSE COMMUTING, 1960

REVERSE COMMUTING, 1970

CHANGE IN REVERSE COMMUTING, 1960–1970

TROY, N.Y.

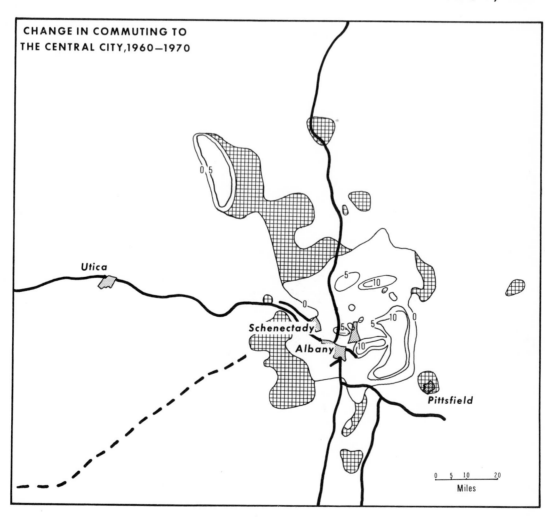

CHANGE IN COMMUTING TO THE CENTRAL CITY, 1960–1970

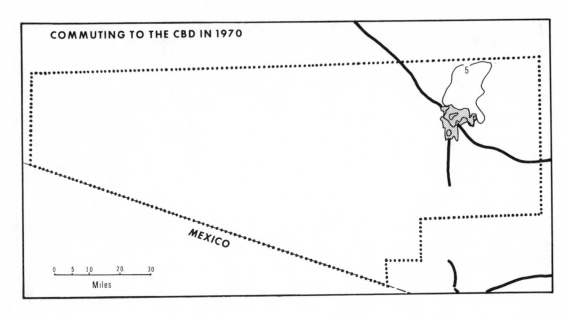

COMMUTING TO THE CBD IN 1970

MEXICO

0 5 10   20   30
Miles

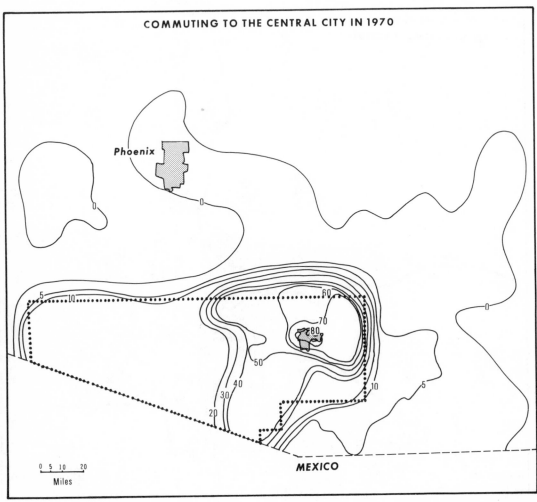

COMMUTING TO THE CENTRAL CITY IN 1970

Phoenix

MEXICO

0 5 10   20
Miles

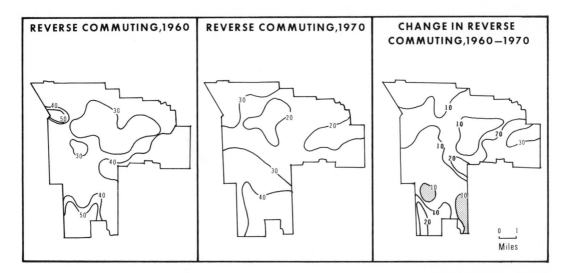

| REVERSE COMMUTING,1960 | REVERSE COMMUTING,1970 | CHANGE IN REVERSE COMMUTING,1960—1970 |

TUCSON, AZ.

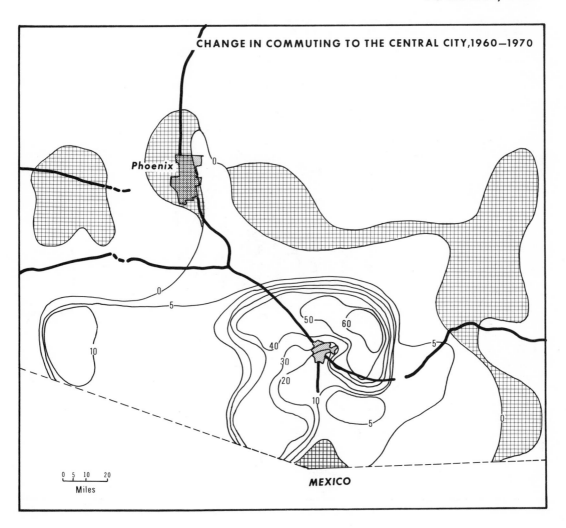

CHANGE IN COMMUTING TO THE CENTRAL CITY,1960—1970

Phoenix

MEXICO

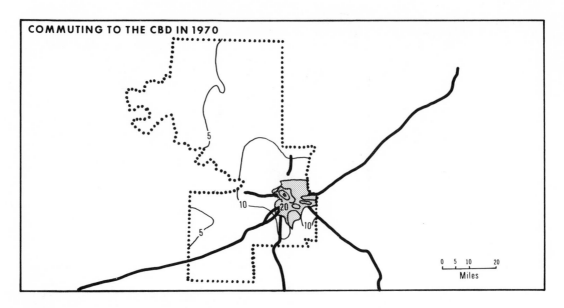

COMMUTING TO THE CBD IN 1970

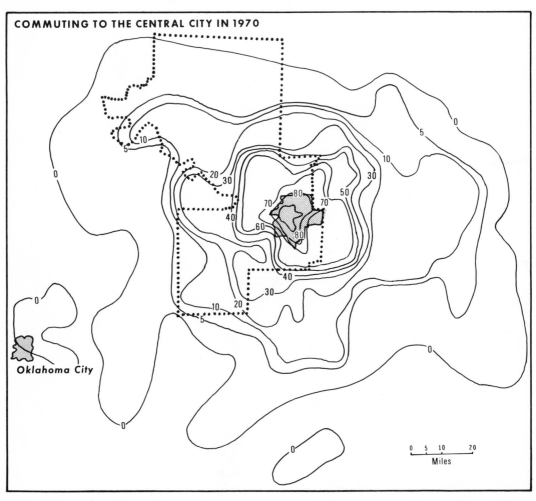

COMMUTING TO THE CENTRAL CITY IN 1970

Oklahoma City

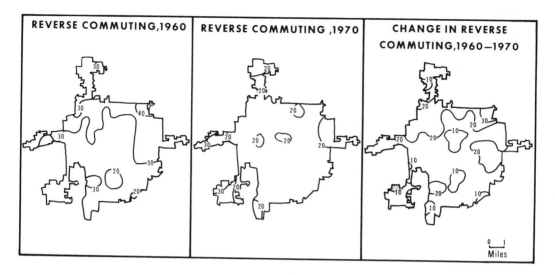

| REVERSE COMMUTING,1960 | REVERSE COMMUTING ,1970 | CHANGE IN REVERSE COMMUTING,1960—1970 |

TULSA, OK.

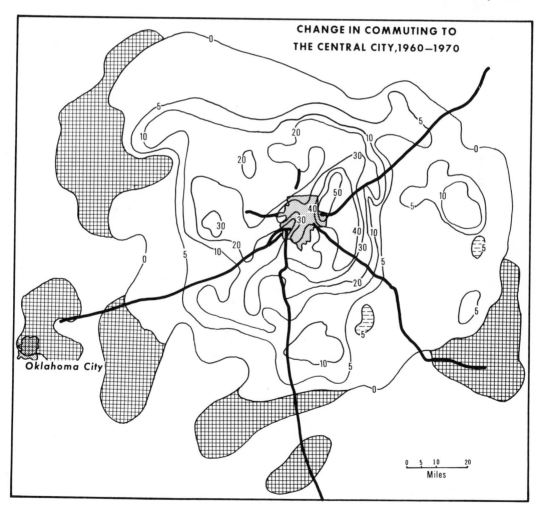

CHANGE IN COMMUTING TO THE CENTRAL CITY,1960—1970

Oklahoma City

COMMUTING TO THE CBD IN 1970

NO DATA COLLECTED

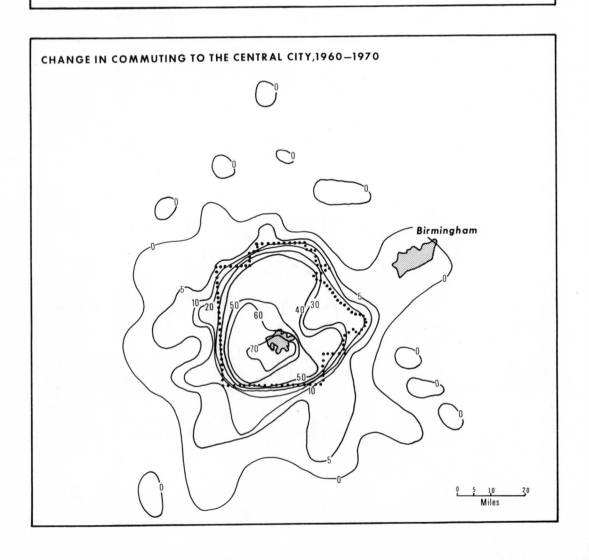

CHANGE IN COMMUTING TO THE CENTRAL CITY,1960—1970

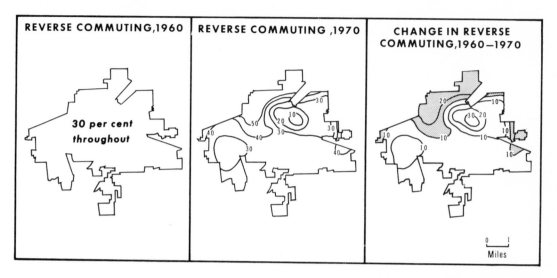

TUSCALOOSA, AL.

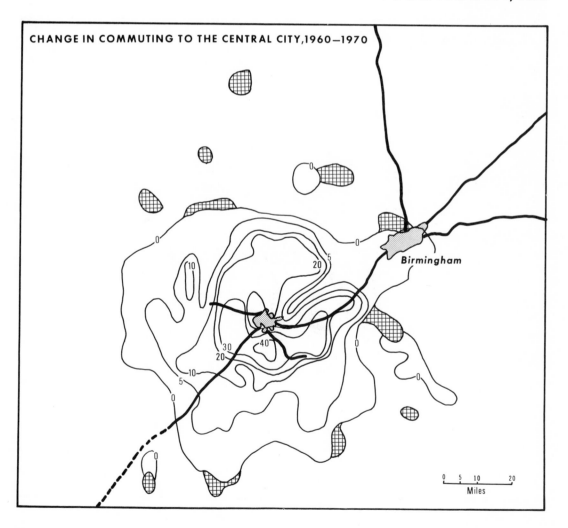

COMMUTING TO THE CBD IN 1970

NO DATA COLLECTED

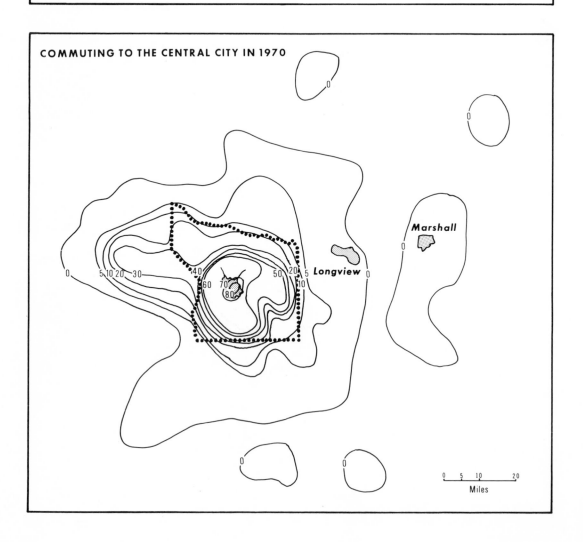

COMMUTING TO THE CENTRAL CITY IN 1970

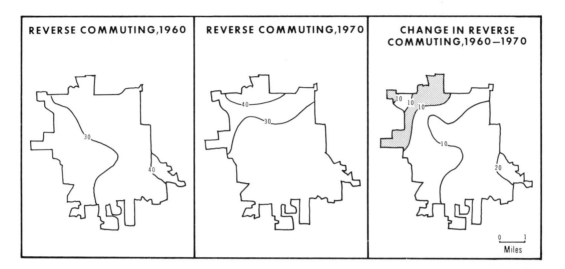

TYLER, TX.

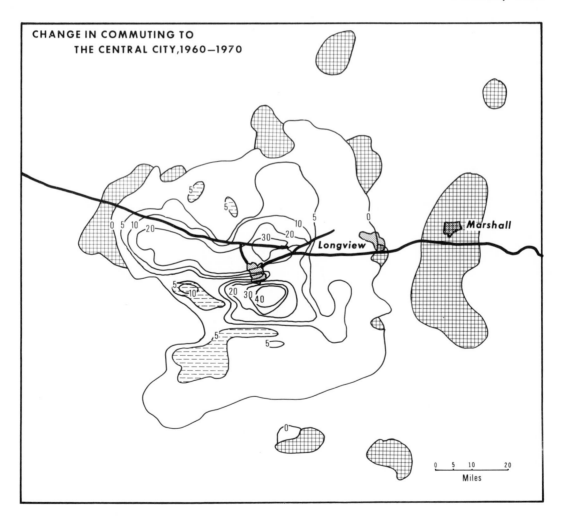

COMMUTING TO THE CBD IN 1970

NO DATA COLLECTED

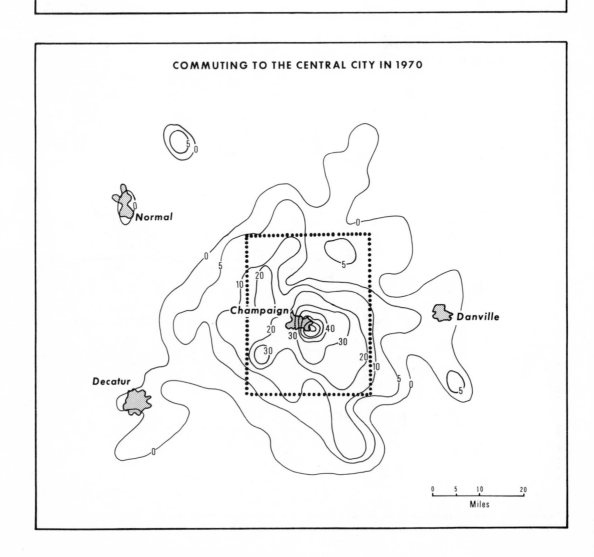

COMMUTING TO THE CENTRAL CITY IN 1970

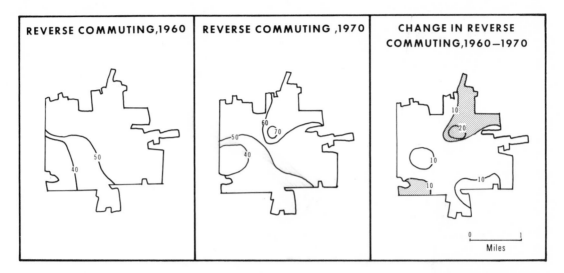

REVERSE COMMUTING, 1960

REVERSE COMMUTING, 1970

CHANGE IN REVERSE COMMUTING, 1960–1970

URBANA, IL.

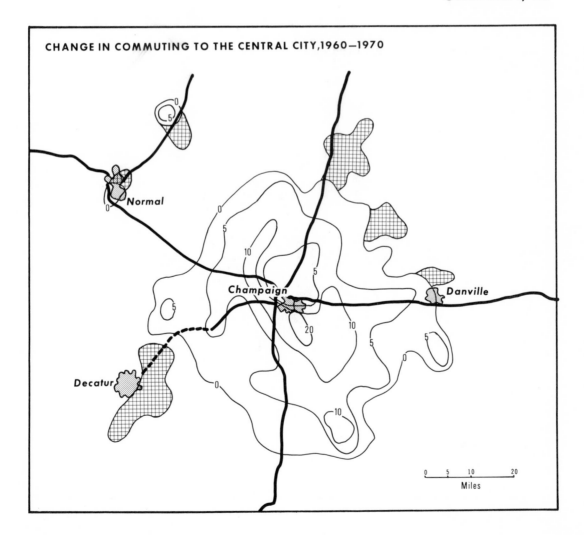

CHANGE IN COMMUTING TO THE CENTRAL CITY, 1960–1970

Normal

Champaign

Danville

Decatur

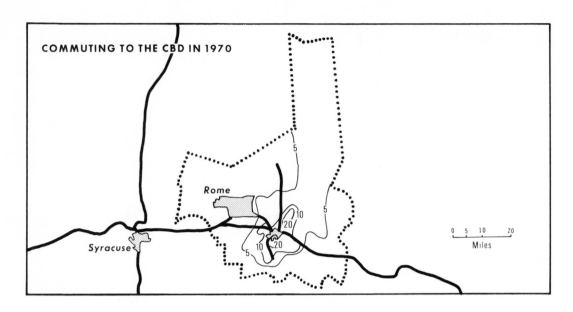

COMMUTING TO THE CBD IN 1970

Rome

Syracuse

0 5 10   20
Miles

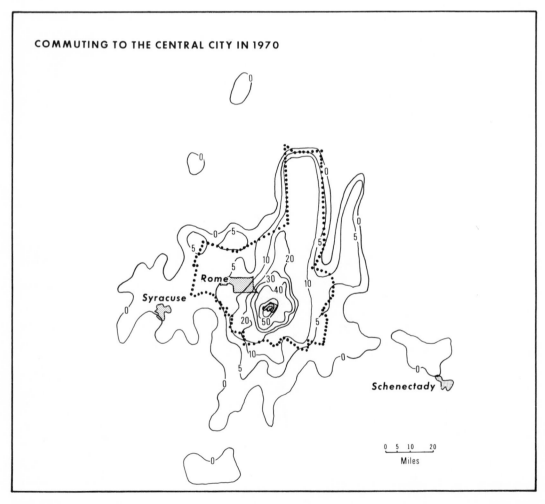

COMMUTING TO THE CENTRAL CITY IN 1970

0

0

0

0

5

0

5

5

0

5

5

10

20

5

Rome

30

10

40

Syracuse

0

0

20

50

5

10

0

0

Schenectady

5

0

0

0 5 10   20
Miles

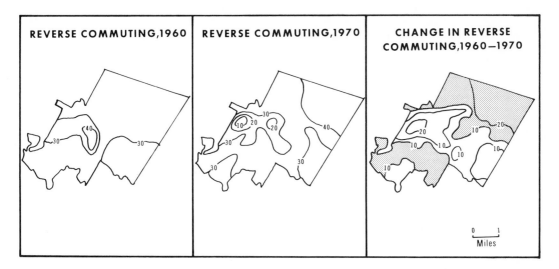

REVERSE COMMUTING, 1960

REVERSE COMMUTING, 1970

CHANGE IN REVERSE COMMUTING, 1960–1970

UTICA, N.Y.

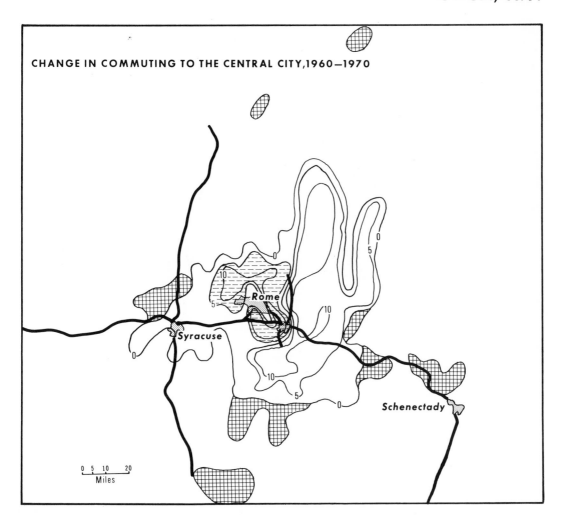

CHANGE IN COMMUTING TO THE CENTRAL CITY, 1960–1970

COMMUTING TO THE CBD IN 1970

NO DATA COLLECTED

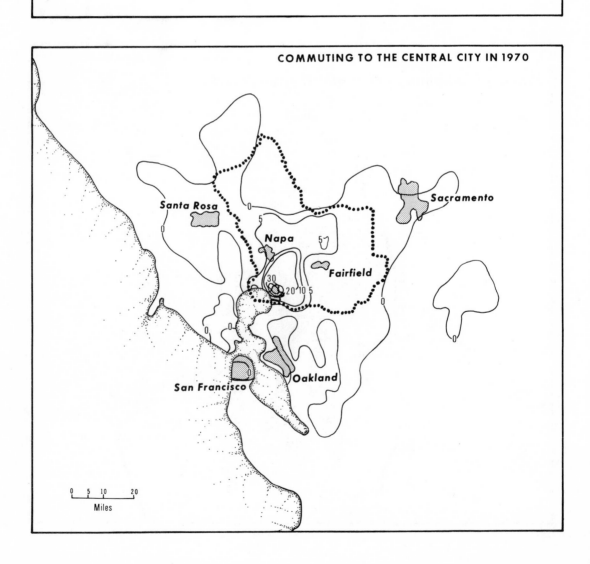

COMMUTING TO THE CENTRAL CITY IN 1970

Santa Rosa

Sacramento

Napa

Fairfield

San Francisco

Oakland

0   5   10   20
Miles

655

REVERSE COMMUTING,1960	REVERSE COMMUTING ,1970	CHANGE IN REVERSE COMMUTING,1960—1970
NO DATA COLLECTED		NO DATA COLLECTED

Miles

VALLEJO, CA.

CHANGE IN COMMUTING TO THE CENTRAL CITY,1960—1970

NO DATA COLLECTED

COMMUTING TO THE CBD IN 1970

NO DATA COLLECTED

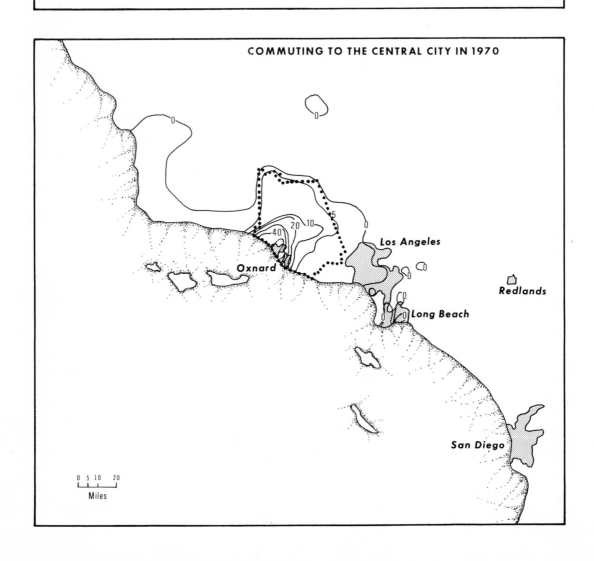

COMMUTING TO THE CENTRAL CITY IN 1970

0

0

40 20 10 5 0

Oxnard

Los Angeles

Redlands

Long Beach

San Diego

0 5 10   20
Miles

REVERSE COMMUTING,1960	REVERSE COMMUTING,1970	CHANGE IN REVERSE COMMUTING,1960—1970
NO DATA COLLECTED		NO DATA COLLECTED

5 0

0 1
Miles

VENTURA, CA.

CHANGE IN COMMUTING TO THE CENTRAL CITY,1960—1970

NO DATA COLLECTED

COMMUTING TO THE CBD IN 1970

NO DATA COLLECTED

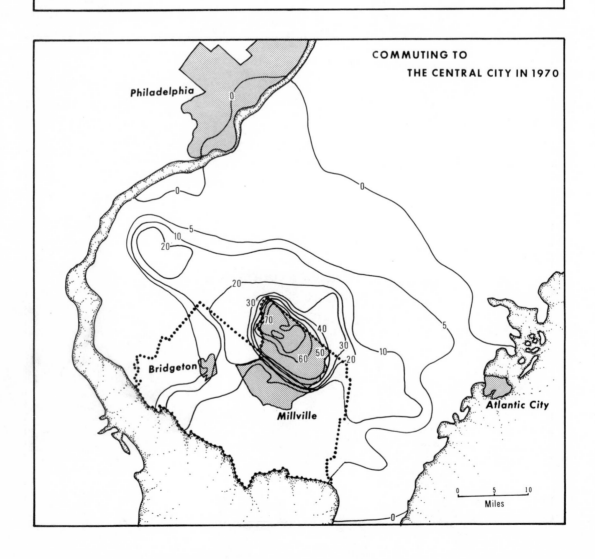

COMMUTING TO
THE CENTRAL CITY IN 1970

Philadelphia

Bridgeton

Millville

Atlantic City

0 5 10
Miles

REVERSE COMMUTING,1960	REVERSE COMMUTING ,1970	CHANGE IN REVERSE COMMUTING,1960—1970
NO DATA COLLECTED		NO DATA COLLECTED

0   1
Miles

VINELAND, N.J.

CHANGE IN COMMUTING TO THE CENTRAL CITY,1960—1970

NO DATA COLLECTED

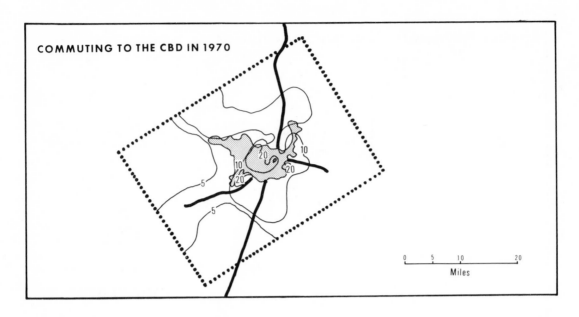

COMMUTING TO THE CBD IN 1970

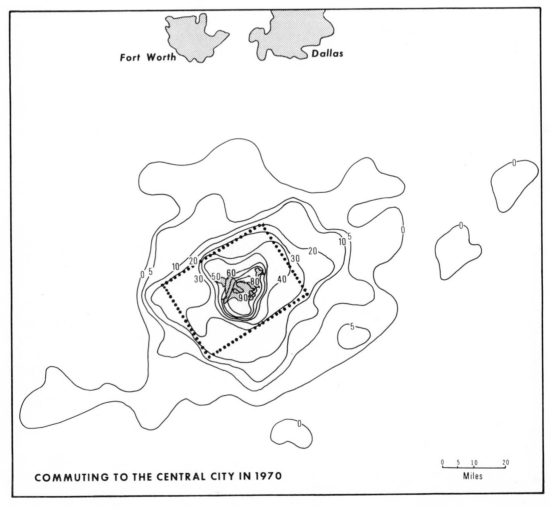

Fort Worth Dallas

COMMUTING TO THE CENTRAL CITY IN 1970

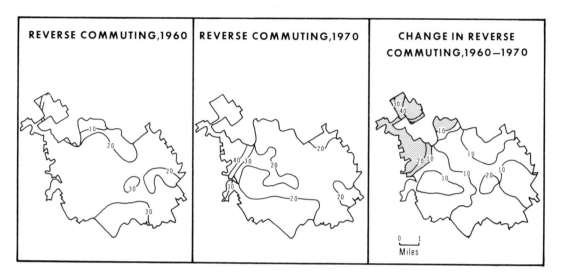

| REVERSE COMMUTING,1960 | REVERSE COMMUTING,1970 | CHANGE IN REVERSE COMMUTING,1960—1970 |

WACO, TX.

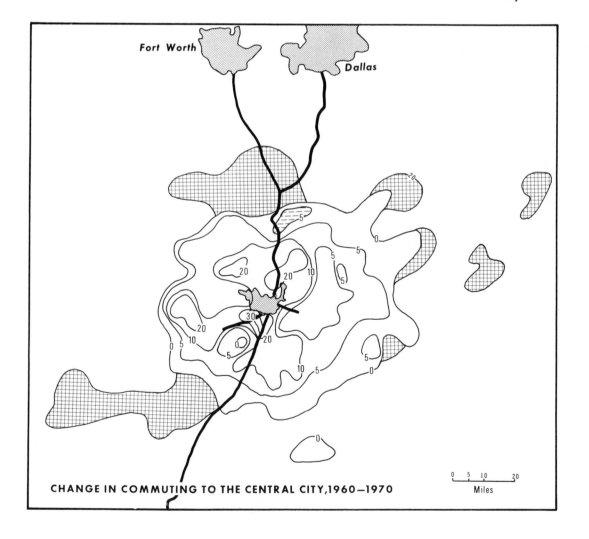

CHANGE IN COMMUTING TO THE CENTRAL CITY,1960—1970

COMMUTING TO THE CBD IN 1970

NO DATA COLLECTED

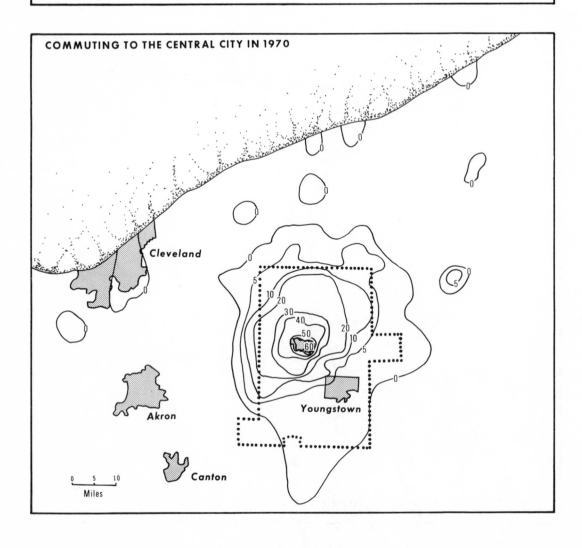

COMMUTING TO THE CENTRAL CITY IN 1970

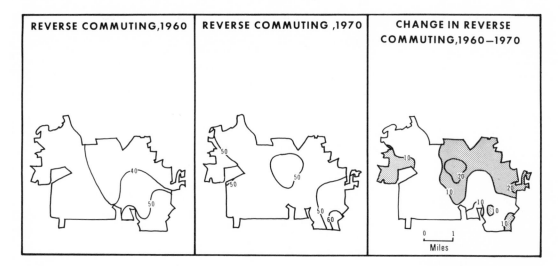

WARREN, OH.

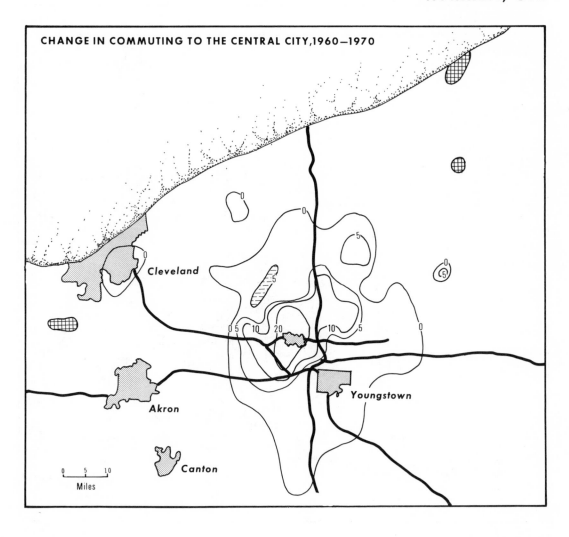

COMMUTING TO THE CBD IN 1970

NO DATA COLLECTED

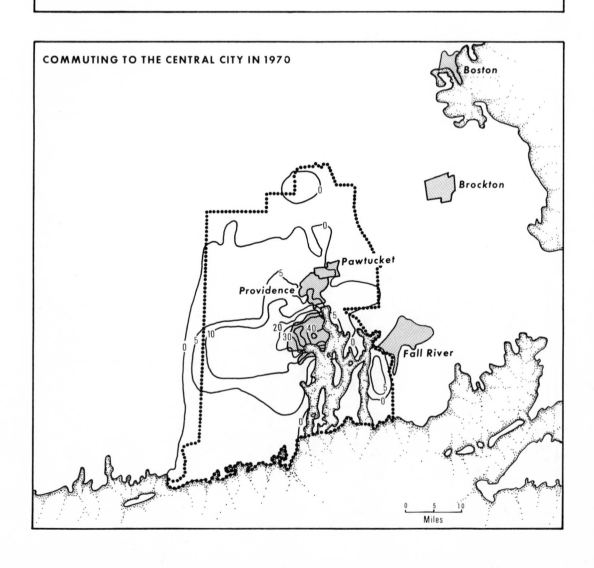

COMMUTING TO THE CENTRAL CITY IN 1970

Boston

Brockton

Pawtucket

Providence

Fall River

Miles

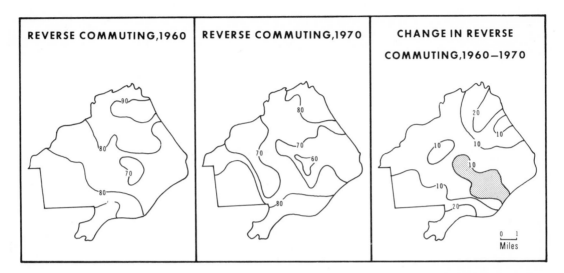

WARWICK, R.I.

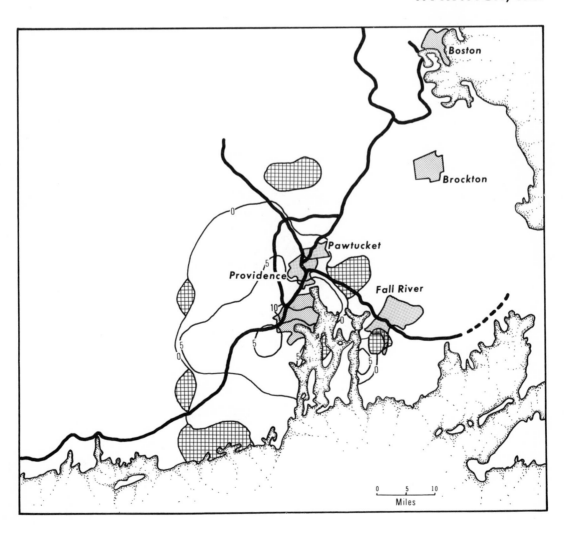

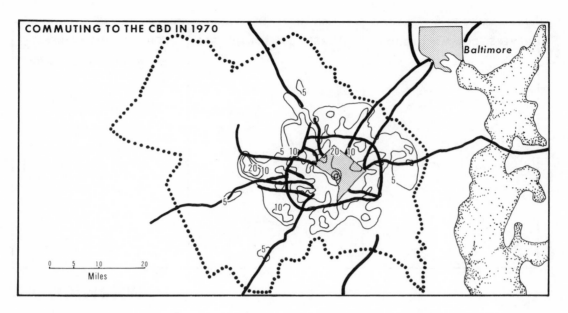

COMMUTING TO THE CBD IN 1970

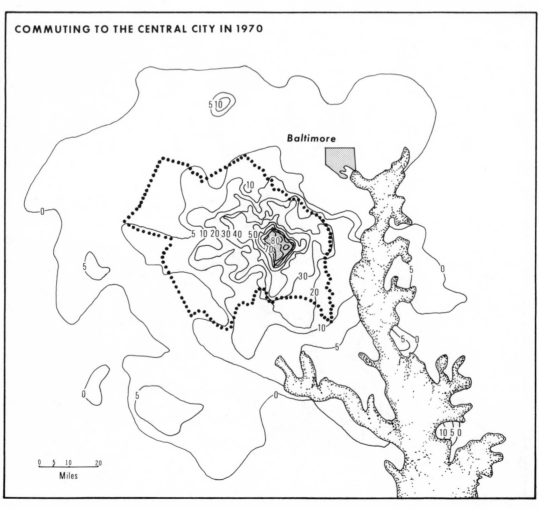

COMMUTING TO THE CENTRAL CITY IN 1970

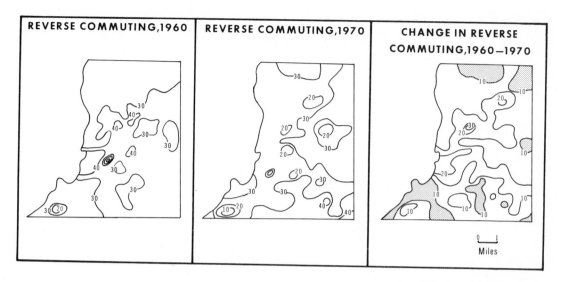

REVERSE COMMUTING,1960

REVERSE COMMUTING,1970

CHANGE IN REVERSE
COMMUTING,1960—1970

WASHINGTON, D.C.

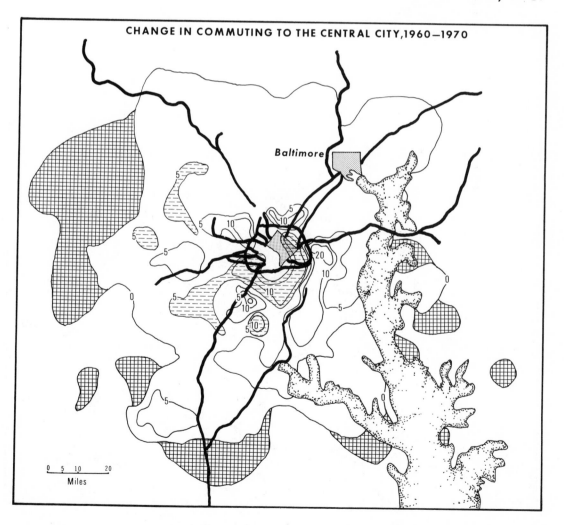

CHANGE IN COMMUTING TO THE CENTRAL CITY,1960—1970

Baltimore

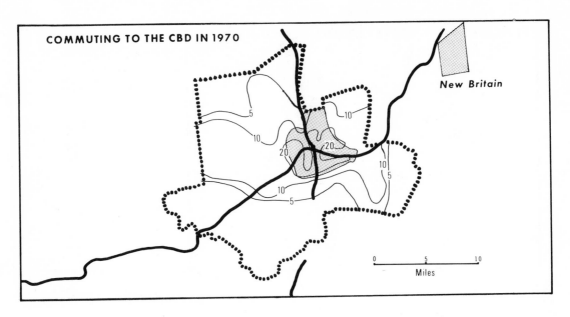

COMMUTING TO THE CBD IN 1970

New Britain

0   5   10
Miles

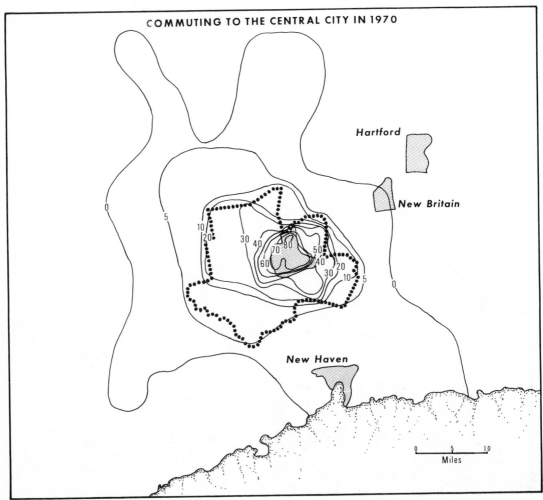

COMMUTING TO THE CENTRAL CITY IN 1970

Hartford

New Britain

New Haven

0   5   10
Miles

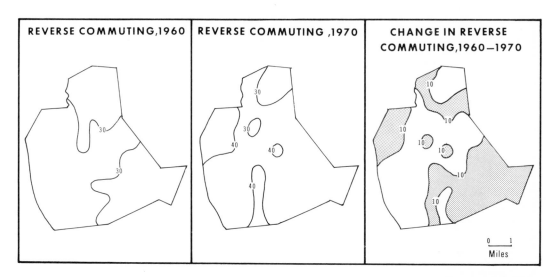

REVERSE COMMUTING, 1960

REVERSE COMMUTING, 1970

CHANGE IN REVERSE COMMUTING, 1960—1970

WATERBURY, CT.

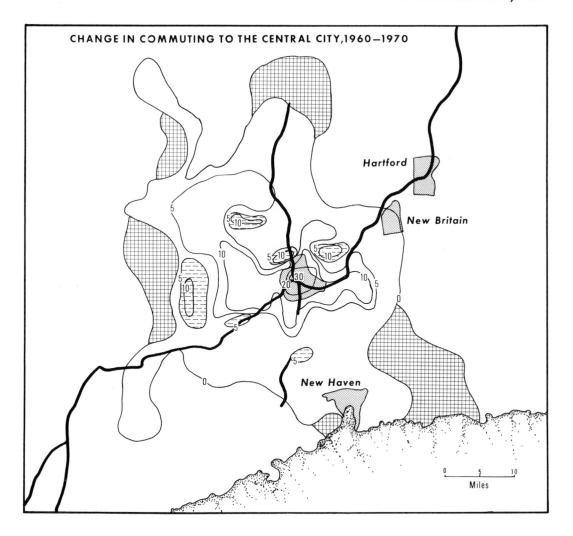

CHANGE IN COMMUTING TO THE CENTRAL CITY, 1960—1970

COMMUTING TO THE CBD IN 1970

NO DATA COLLECTED

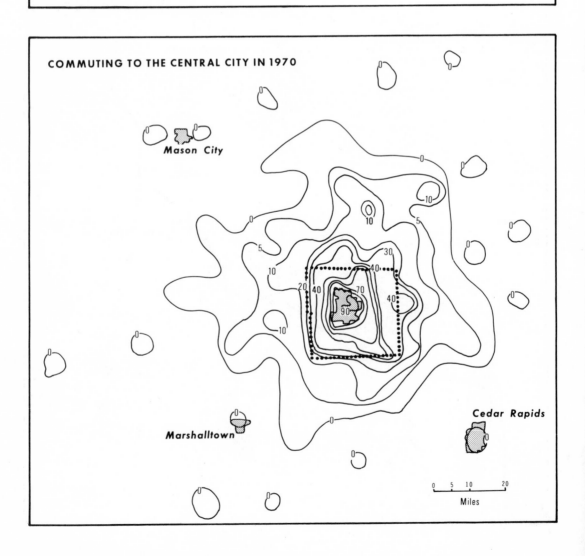

COMMUTING TO THE CENTRAL CITY IN 1970

Mason City

Marshalltown

Cedar Rapids

0 5 10   20
Miles

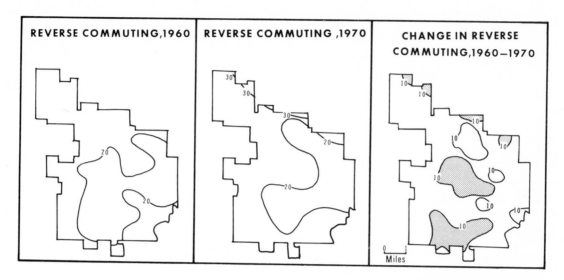

WATERLOO, IA.

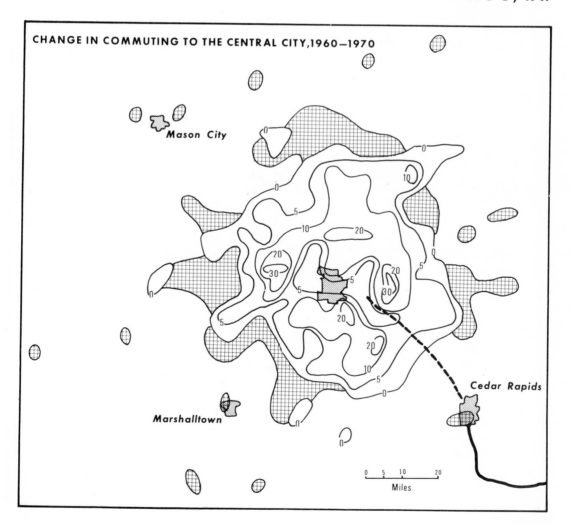

672

COMMUTING TO THE CBD IN 1970

NO DATA COLLECTED

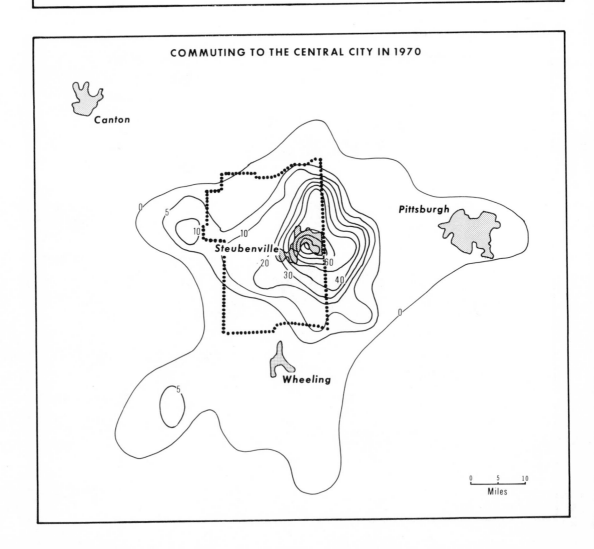

COMMUTING TO THE CENTRAL CITY IN 1970

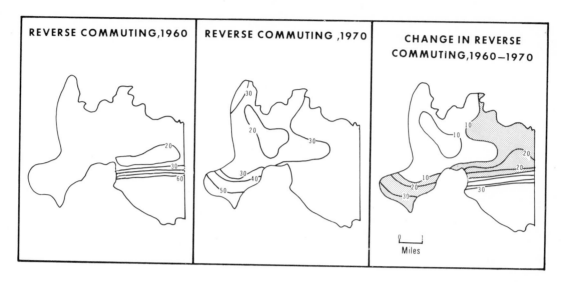

REVERSE COMMUTING, 1960

REVERSE COMMUTING, 1970

CHANGE IN REVERSE COMMUTING, 1960–1970

WEIRTON, W.V.

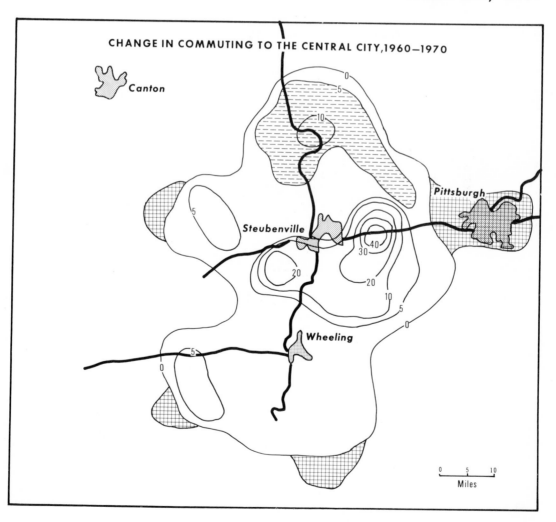

CHANGE IN COMMUTING TO THE CENTRAL CITY, 1960–1970

Canton

Pittsburgh

Steubenville

Wheeling

COMMUTING TO THE CBD IN 1970

NO DATA COLLECTED

COMMUTING TO THE CENTRAL CITY IN 1970

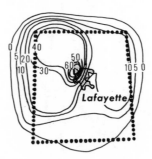

Lafayette

Kokomo

Indianapolis

0   5   10   20
Miles

REVERSE COMMUTING,1960	REVERSE COMMUTING,1970	CHANGE IN REVERSE COMMUTING,1960—1970
NO DATA COLLECTED		NO DATA COLLECTED

50

40

50

0   1
Miles

WEST LAFAYETTE, IN.

CHANGE IN COMMUTING TO THE CENTRAL CITY,1960—1970

NO DATA COLLECTED

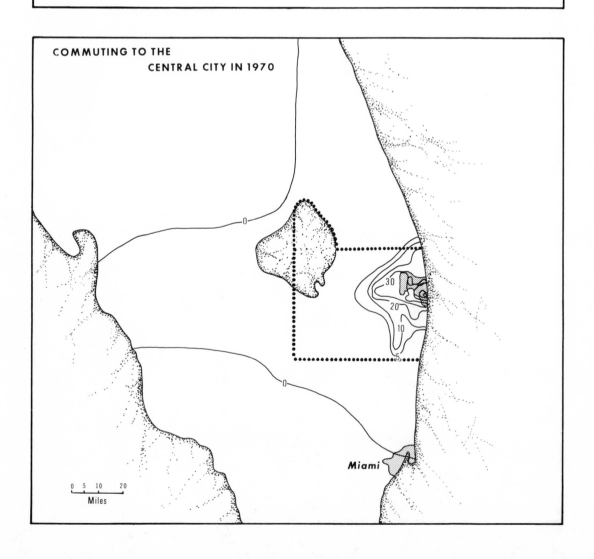

COMMUTING TO THE CBD IN 1970

NO DATA COLLECTED

COMMUTING TO THE
CENTRAL CITY IN 1970

30

20

10

5

0

0

Miami

0 5 10   20
Miles

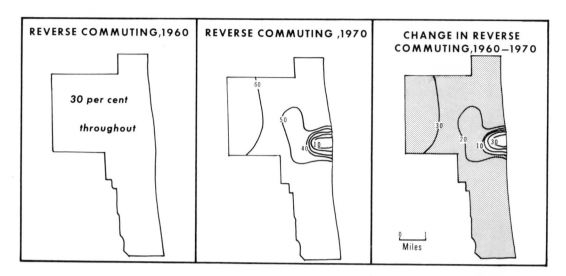

REVERSE COMMUTING, 1960

30 per cent
throughout

REVERSE COMMUTING, 1970

CHANGE IN REVERSE
COMMUTING, 1960–1970

0 1
Miles

WEST PALM BEACH, FL.

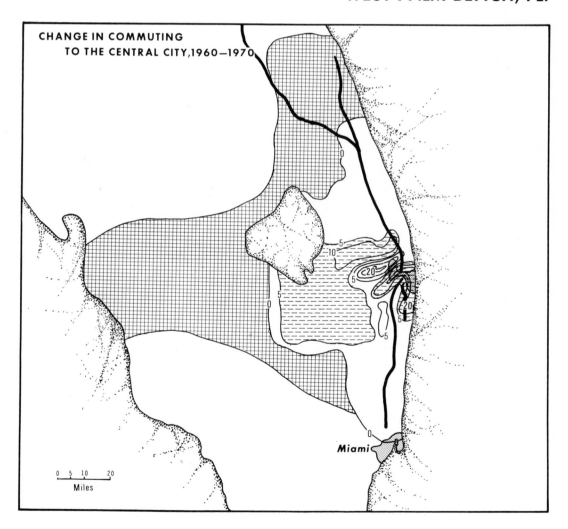

CHANGE IN COMMUTING
TO THE CENTRAL CITY, 1960–1970

Miami

0 5 10 20
Miles

COMMUTING TO THE CBD IN 1970

NO DATA COLLECTED

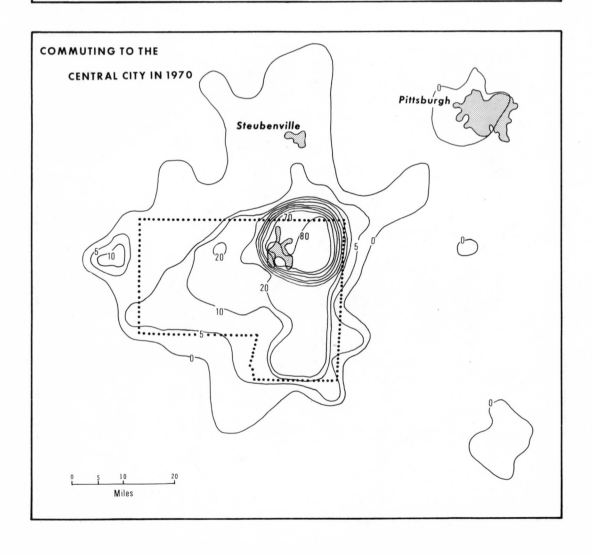

COMMUTING TO THE

CENTRAL CITY IN 1970

Pittsburgh

Steubenville

0   5   10   20
Miles

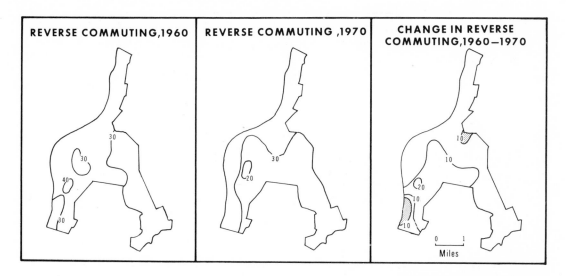

REVERSE COMMUTING, 1960

REVERSE COMMUTING, 1970

CHANGE IN REVERSE COMMUTING, 1960—1970

WHEELING, W.V.

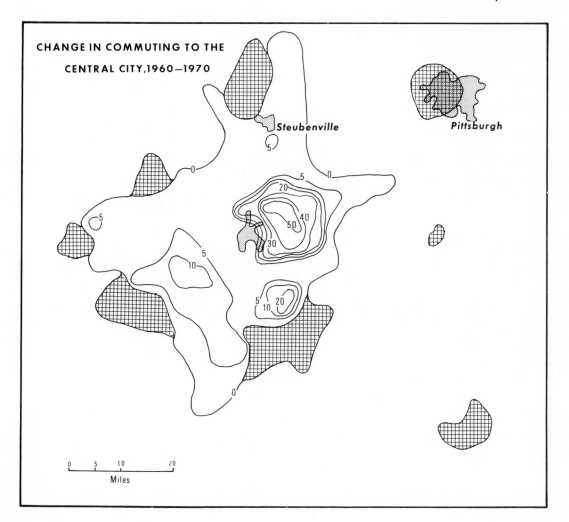

CHANGE IN COMMUTING TO THE CENTRAL CITY, 1960—1970

Steubenville

Pittsburgh

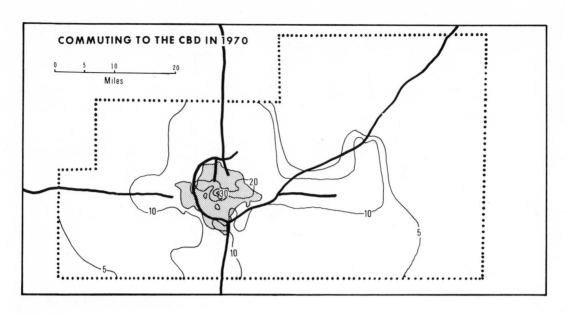

COMMUTING TO THE CBD IN 1970

0   5   10   20
Miles

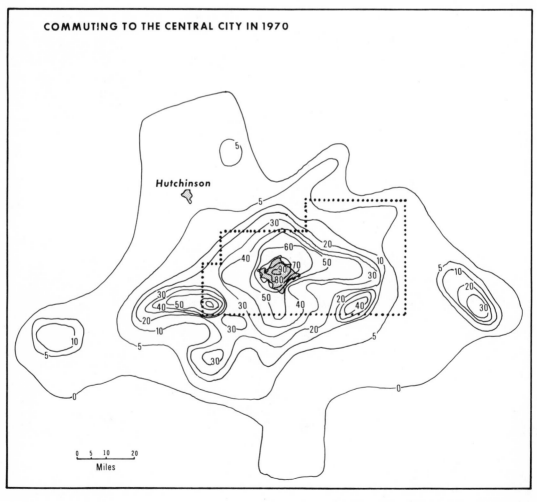

COMMUTING TO THE CENTRAL CITY IN 1970

Hutchinson

0 5 10   20
Miles

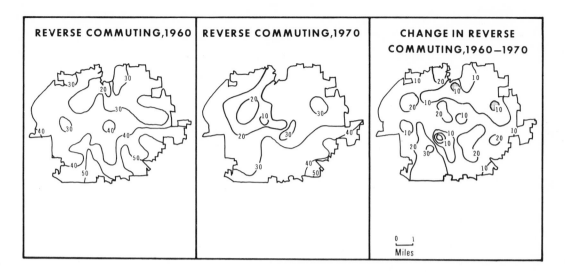

REVERSE COMMUTING, 1960

REVERSE COMMUTING, 1970

CHANGE IN REVERSE COMMUTING, 1960—1970

WICHITA, KS.

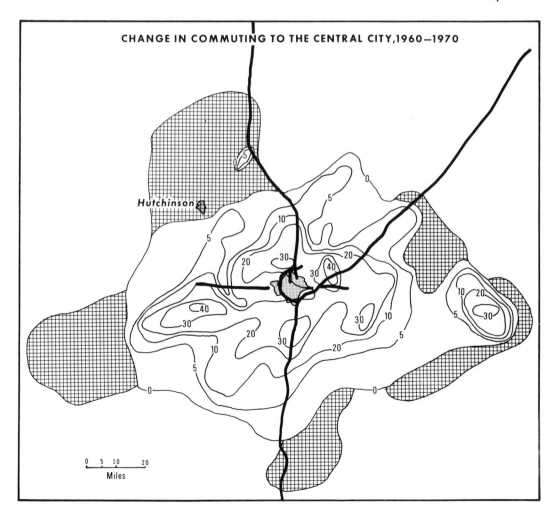

CHANGE IN COMMUTING TO THE CENTRAL CITY, 1960—1970

Hutchinson

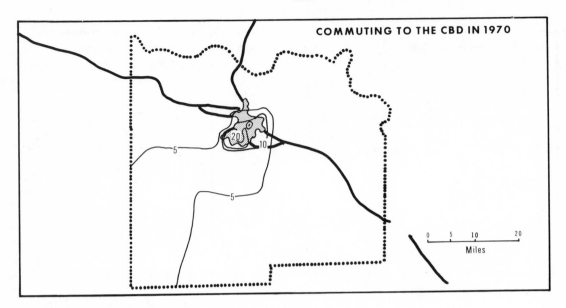

COMMUTING TO THE CBD IN 1970

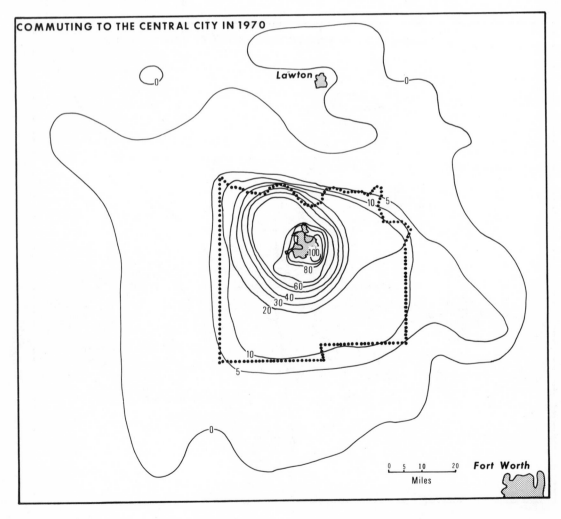

COMMUTING TO THE CENTRAL CITY IN 1970

Lawton

Fort Worth

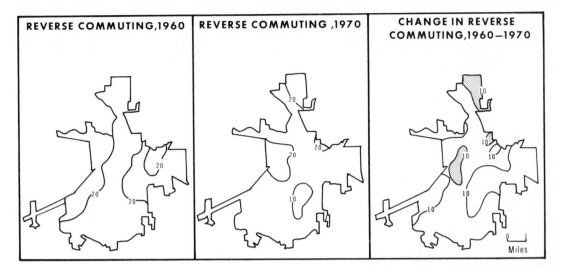

REVERSE COMMUTING, 1960

REVERSE COMMUTING, 1970

CHANGE IN REVERSE COMMUTING, 1960–1970

WICHITA FALLS, TX.

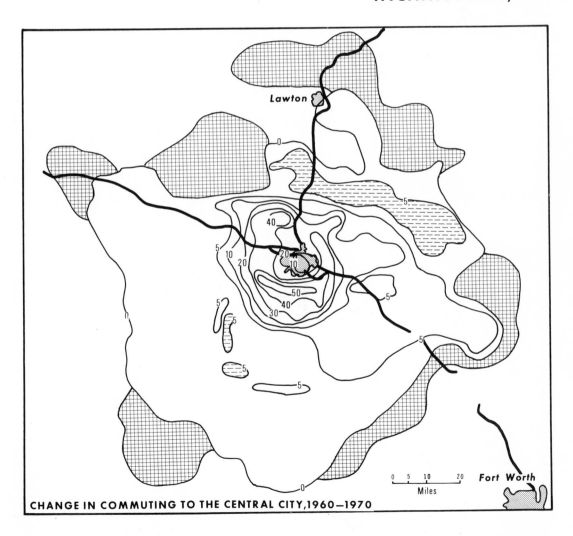

CHANGE IN COMMUTING TO THE CENTRAL CITY, 1960–1970

684

COMMUTING TO THE CBD IN 1970

NO DATA COLLECTED

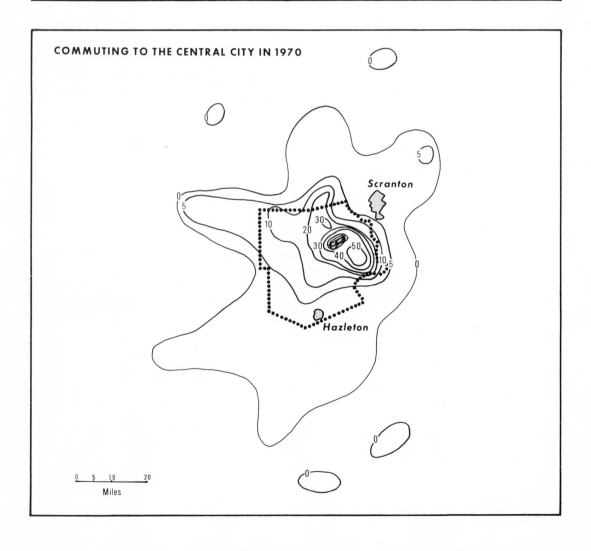

COMMUTING TO THE CENTRAL CITY IN 1970

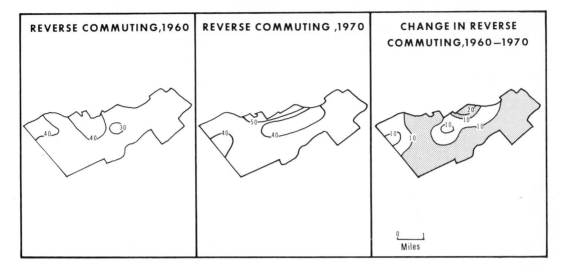

WILKES-BARRE, PA.

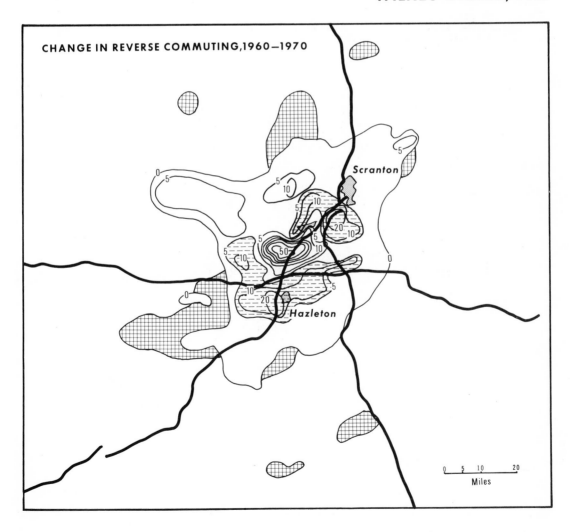

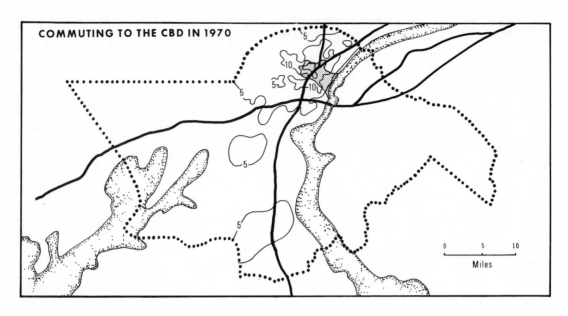

COMMUTING TO THE CBD IN 1970

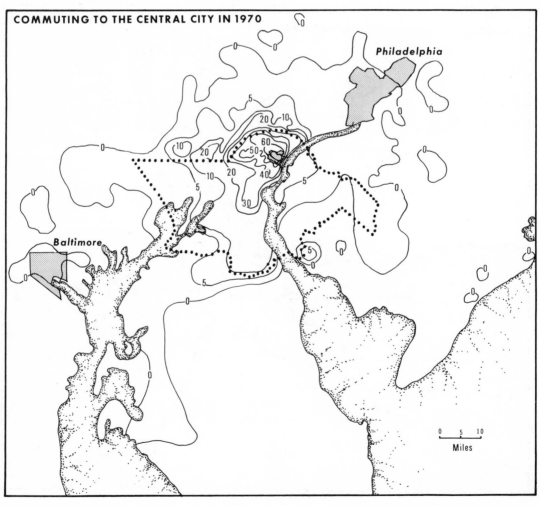

COMMUTING TO THE CENTRAL CITY IN 1970

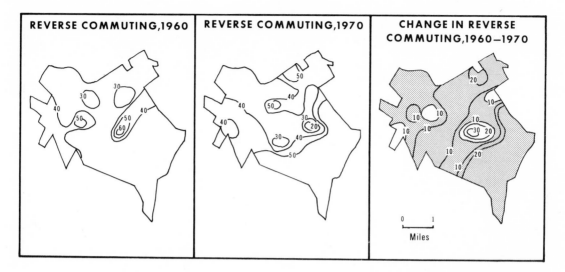

REVERSE COMMUTING, 1960

REVERSE COMMUTING, 1970

CHANGE IN REVERSE COMMUTING, 1960—1970

Miles

WILMINGTON, DE.

CHANGE IN COMMUTING TO THE CENTRAL CITY, 1960—1970

NO DATA COLLECTED

COMMUTING TO THE CBD IN 1970

NO DATA COLLECTED

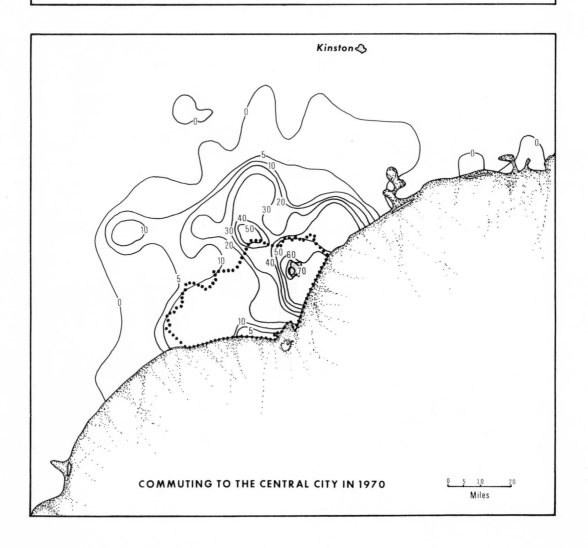

Kinston

COMMUTING TO THE CENTRAL CITY IN 1970

0 5 10   20
Miles

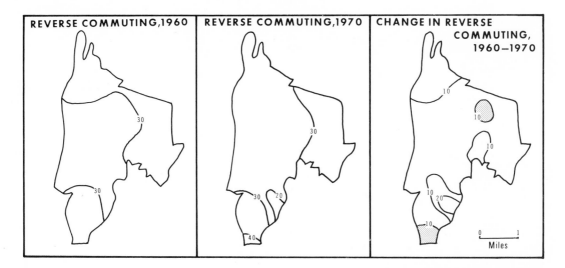

| REVERSE COMMUTING,1960 | REVERSE COMMUTING,1970 | CHANGE IN REVERSE COMMUTING, 1960–1970 |

WILMINGTON, N.C.

CHANGE IN COMMUTING TO THE CENTRAL CITY,1960–1970

NO DATA COLLECTED

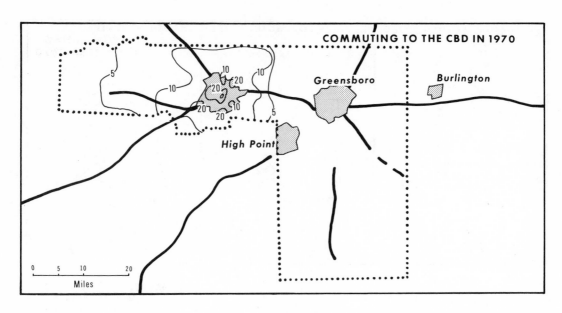

COMMUTING TO THE CBD IN 1970

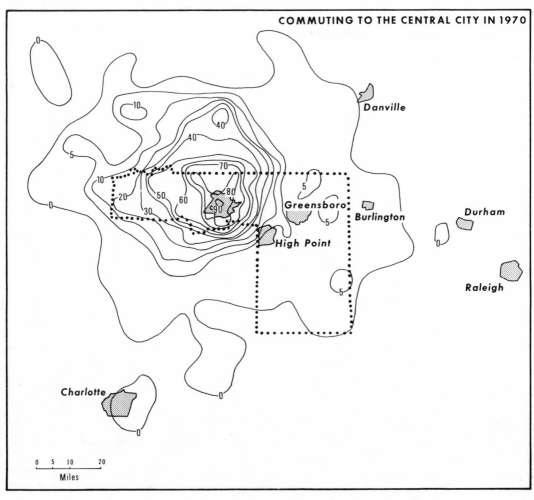

COMMUTING TO THE CENTRAL CITY IN 1970

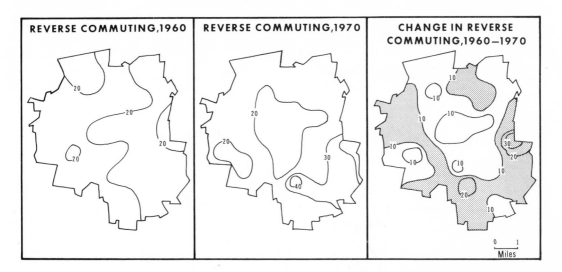

| REVERSE COMMUTING, 1960 | REVERSE COMMUTING, 1970 | CHANGE IN REVERSE COMMUTING, 1960–1970 |

WINSTON-SALEM, N.C.

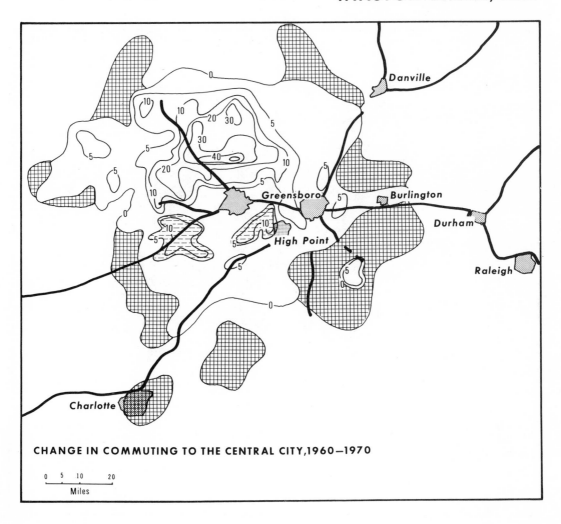

CHANGE IN COMMUTING TO THE CENTRAL CITY, 1960–1970

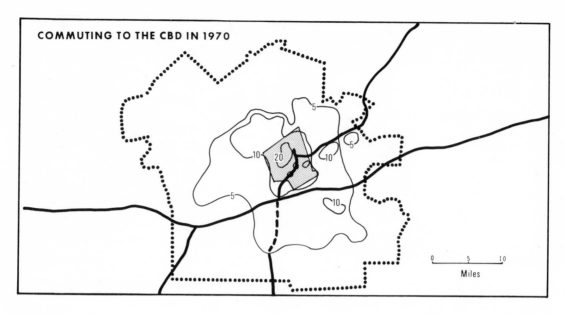

COMMUTING TO THE CBD IN 1970

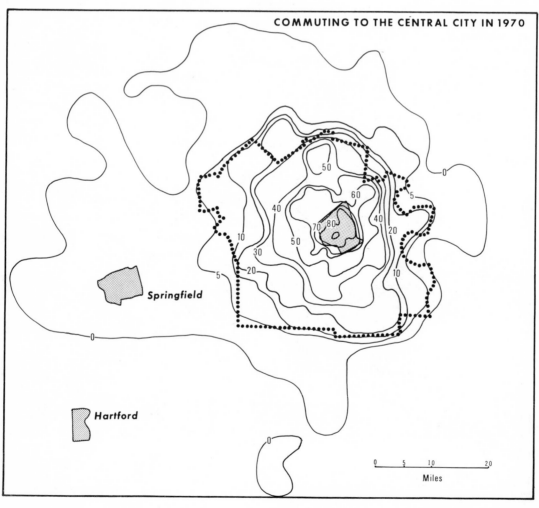

COMMUTING TO THE CENTRAL CITY IN 1970

Springfield

Hartford

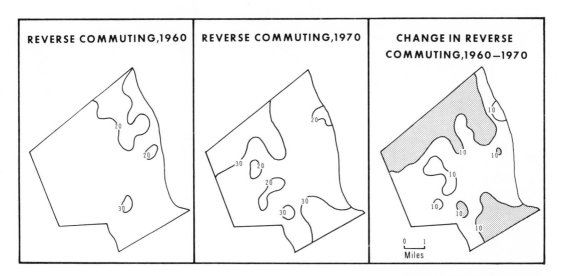

WORCESTER, MA.

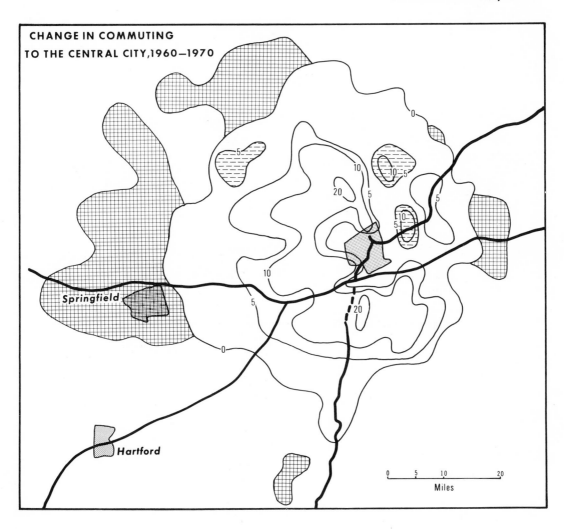

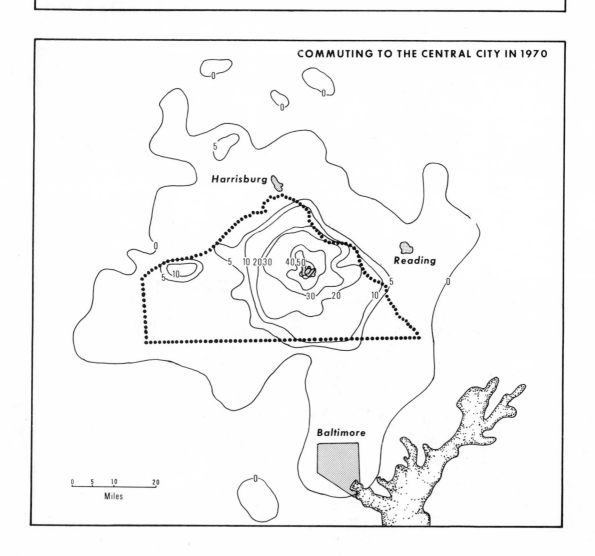

COMMUTING TO THE CBD IN 1970

NO DATA COLLECTED

COMMUTING TO THE CENTRAL CITY IN 1970

Harrisburg

Reading

Baltimore

0 5 10   20
Miles

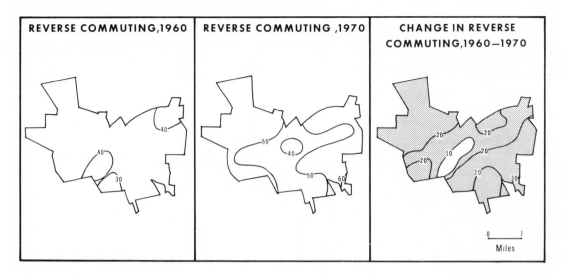

YORK, PA.

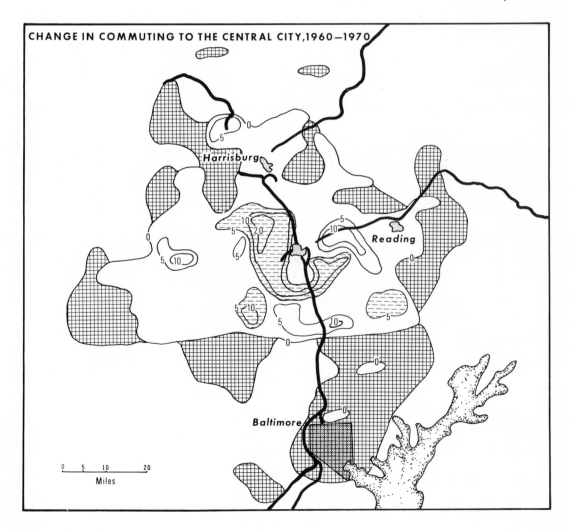

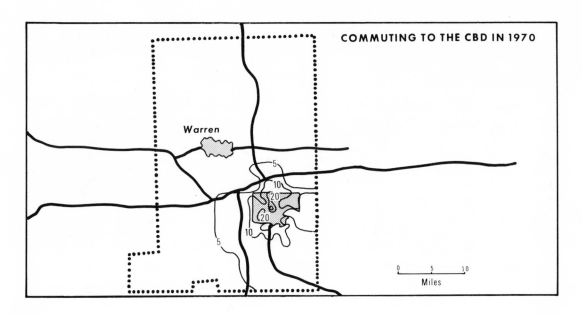

COMMUTING TO THE CBD IN 1970

Warren

0   5   10
Miles

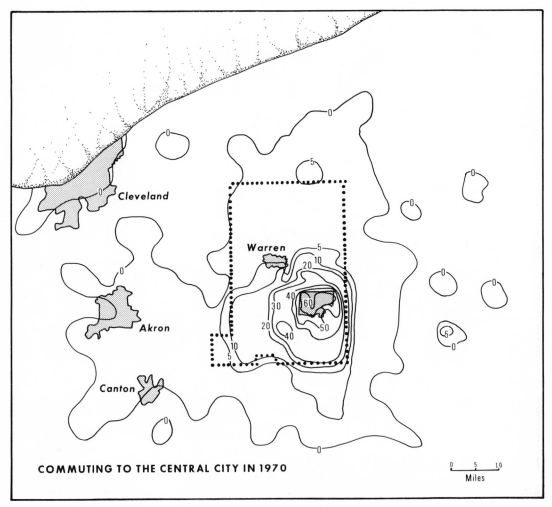

Cleveland

Warren

Akron

Canton

COMMUTING TO THE CENTRAL CITY IN 1970

0   5   10
Miles

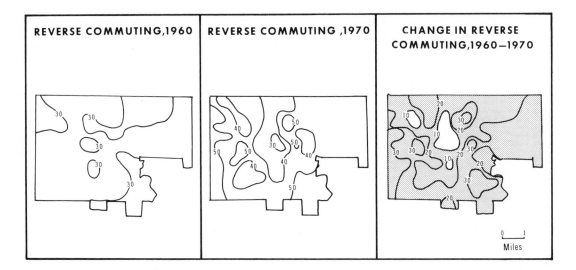

REVERSE COMMUTING, 1960

REVERSE COMMUTING, 1970

CHANGE IN REVERSE COMMUTING, 1960–1970

YOUNGSTOWN, OH.

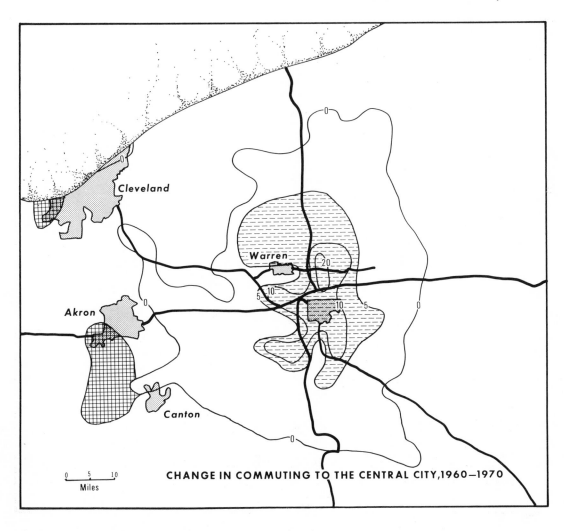

CHANGE IN COMMUTING TO THE CENTRAL CITY, 1960–1970